Study Guide to Accompany

■ Introduction to ■

PSYCHOLOGY

Exploration and Application

SIXTH EDITION

Dennis Coon
Santa Barbara City College, California

Prepared by:
Faren Akins

With crossword puzzles prepared by:
David E. Cunningham
IECC-Olney Central College, Illinois

West Publishing Company
St. Paul   New York   Los Angeles   San Francisco

WEST'S COMMITMENT TO THE ENVIRONMENT

In 1906, West Publishing Company began recycling materials left over from the production of books. This began a tradition of efficient and responsible use of resources. Today, up to 95% of our legal books and 70% of our college texts are printed on recycled, acid-free stock. West also recycles nearly 22 million pounds of scrap paper annually—the equivalent of 181,717 trees. Since the 1960s, West has devised ways to capture and recycle waste inks, solvents, oils, and vapors created in the printing process. We also recycle plastics of all kinds, wood, glass, corrugated cardboard, and batteries, and have eliminated the use of styrofoam book packaging. We at West are proud of the longevity and the scope of our commitment to our environment.

Production, Prepress, Printing and Binding by West Publishing Company.

COPYRIGHT © 1992 by   WEST PUBLISHING CO.
610 Opperman Drive
P.O. Box 64526
St. Paul, MN 55164–0526

∞

ISBN 0–314–00693–1

 CONTENTS

ACKNOWLEDGEMENTS

The author wishes to thank Dr. Dennis L. Coon for his help in the evaluation and criticism of the Study Guide. Thanks also go to Dr. and Mrs. Coon for their friendship and encouragement throughout each phase of this project.

Appreciation is also extended to my West editor for his assistance and positive guidance. The excellent staff at West also deserves praise for their efficiency and reliability.

Finally,

TO HER
Hand In Hand We Come
    Christopher Robin and I
To Lay This Book In Your Lap.
    Say You're Surprised?
    Say You Like It?
    Say It's Just What You Wanted?
        Because It's Yours—
        Because We Love You.

                Faren R. Akins, Ph.D.

■ PREFACE ■

Welcome to the world of psychology, and to the *Study Guide* which accompanies *Introduction to Psychology: Exploration and Application*. It is hoped that this manual will help you in mastering the principles presented in the text and stimulate your interest in the field of psychology.

If you have read the preface to the text you know that each chapter is designed to help you use the SQ3R method. As discussed in Chapter One's Applications, Dr. Francis Robinson designed the SQ3R approach to help you

1) select what is important;
2) understand these ideas quickly;
3) remember what you have read; and
4) review effectively for tests.

The *Study Guide* has also been designed to help you use this learning technique.

Each chapter of the *Study Guide* is divided into seven sections. The first section (Contents) provides you with an overview of the main topics discussed in the text. Use these headings as a foundation for outlining your own notes and organizing your thoughts. Remember that effective note-taking is an extremely important way for you to learn and remember. When reviewing for tests use the headings as a starting point to quiz yourself about the material in those sections. Remember that self-testing is an excellent way to catch your errors before actually taking in-class tests. As you review each topic, ask yourself, "What could I be asked about this?" Ask as many questions as you can and be sure you can answer them.

The next two sections of the *Study Guide* (Terms and Concepts, Important Individuals) provide you with a listing of key items from the text. These sections are designed to help you *select what is important*. They are listed in the same order as presented in the text and, like "Contents," can also help you check the thoroughness of your notes. When using your flaschcards, remember that study beyond "bare mastery" of a topic improves performance on class exams.

The Programmed Review section of each chapter is designed to give you immediate *feedback* on your knowledge of the material in the text. After thoroughly reading the chapter, work through the Programmed Review by writing words or phrases in the blank spaces provided. Then check the Answer Section at the end of each chapter to evaluate your accuracy. It's a good idea to put a check by any items you missed and be sure to give yourself extra practice on those items and the material they discuss. The Programmed Review section provides you with a handy study guide to help you do this. In the parentheses to the left of each question, you'll find the page of the text on which the correct answer to that question appears. You can then easily find pages of the text pertinent to each question in the *Study Guide*.

While the Programmed Review is designed to help you *review effectively for tests*, remember that this is only a study guide. Not every detail, example, or question in the text is covered in the Programmed Review. Rather, this section of the *Study Guide* is designed to help you *select what is important* by reviewing the main ideas of each text chapter. As with the other *Study Guide* sections use it as a foundation for notes, evaluation of your understanding, and review of important principles.

The best way to prepare for in-class exams is to test yourself using questions similar to those you might expect to face on actual exams. That is the purpose of the Self-Test section of the *Study Guide*. These questions are written in multiple-choice and true-false format since that is what the majority of college instructors use for introductory classes. (If your instructor uses essay questions you'll want to give special attention to the Survey Questions at the beginning of each main text chapter and to the Questions for Discussion section at the end of each main text chapter.) When you work on the Self-Test items, remember these guidelines for taking tests:

1) Read each statement or question carefully.
2) In the case of multiple-choice items, read each alternative answer carefully.
3) Eliminate certain alternatives.
4) Feel free to change your answers, especially if you feel *very* uncertain of your first answer. When you have strong doubts, your second answer is more likely to be correct.

After you complete the Self-Test items, check your answers with those in the Answer Section at the end of each chapter. Make special note of any items you missed; reread and study the main text pages and the Programmed Review items that relate to that topic. The number of the main text page which answers each Self-Test question appears in the parentheses at the beginning of each question.

To get the most out of your study experiences and your introductory psychology text, work on the special projects suggested in the sections labelled "Applying Your Knowledge." These exercises are designed to help you relate basic principles of psychology to "real world" situations and to expand your understanding of concepts you learn about through the main text.

An enjoyable feature in this *Study Guide* is a set of crossword puzzles, one for each chapter prepared by David E. Cunningham of IECC-Olney Central College. The puzzles test your knowledge of terminology and emphasize key concepts from the chapters. Answer keys for all the puzzles are found at the end of the *Study Guide*.

While the *Study Guide* and the main text are designed to help you learn, remember that motivation, time management, consistency, and practice are all important. If you need help in any of these areas make use of the Suggestions for Further Reading presented at the end of the text's introduction. Good luck!

■ How to Use Your Study Guide ■ More Effectively

Dear Student:

Many college students read the text with the study guide open—filling in the answers to the study guide items by shifting back and forth between the open text and the open study guide. This is *not* an effective way to use a study guide. Very little information is being stored in the long term memory, due to the lack of rehearsal.

The following method is highly recommended as a way of possible improving your test performance. The method is initially somewhat time-consuming, but with continued practice, it becomes easier and easier to use. Using Chapter One of your book, do the following:

1. Chunk chapter one based upon what makes sense to you (about four to six pages to a chunk).
2. Read only the first chunk in the text.
3. Close the text.
4. Open the study guide to the beginning of the section which relates to this chunk.
5. Fill in as many blanks as you can without re-opening the text. Most students fill in from five to twenty percent of the blanks.
6. Close the study guide—open the text.
7. Re-read chunk one in the text—close the text.
8. Open the study guide—fill in as many more blanks as you can.
9. Continue repeating steps six through eight above until 80% of the blanks are completed. Then as a reinforcement check your answers against those supplied at the end of the study guide chapter.
10. Try to determine why you were not able to complete the empty blanks, and re-read the parts of the text relating to these empty blanks.
11. Now repeat steps one through ten for chunks two, three, four, etc. Take a break each time you complete these steps.
12. When you have completed the chapter, then take the Self-Test at the end of the study guide chapter. Your results on the Self-Test will usually be a good indicator of how you will perform on an in-class, multiple-choice test given by your instructor at this point in time. If a test is given at a later time, you will need to review the material in chapter one, so that it is "fresh" in your memory.

If you follow the procedures outlined above, you will not only be engaging in spaced practice studying, but you will also be constantly rehearsing the material, so that it may more easily become part of your long term memory.

Try this method with four or five chapters. Students report that this method helps them read more carefully for main ideas and cause-and-effect relationships.

—With Special Thanks to
Charles Croll
Broome Community College

Psychology and Psychologists

CONTENTS

TERMS AND CONCEPTS

psychology
empirical evidence
data
scientific observation
scientific method
comparative psychology
anthropomorphic fallacy
models
psychometrics
introspection
experimental self-observation
structuralism
functionalism
natural selection
educational psychology
behaviorism
stimulus-response psychology
conditioned response
Skinner Box
cognitive behaviorism
behavior modification
Gestalt psychology
psychoanalytic psychology
unconscious
psychoanalysis

neo-Freudians
humanistic psychology
determinism
free will
self-image
self-evaluation
frame of reference
self-actualization
psychobiology
cognitive psychology
basic research
applied research
American Psychological Association (APA)
SQ3R
LISAN
mnemonic
overlearning
critical thinking
pseudo-psychologies
palmistry
phrenology
graphology
astrology
fallacy of positive instances

IMPORTANT INDIVIDUALS

Douglas Kenrick
Steven MacFarlane
Wilhelm Wundt
Edward B. Titchener

William James
Charles Darwin
John B. Watson
Ivan Pavlov

B. F. Skinner
Max Washburn
Christine Ladd-Franklin
Margaret Wertheimer

1

Sigmund Freud   Jane Burka   Franz Gall
Francis Robinson   Lenora Yuen

PROGRAMMED REVIEW

1. (p. 2)   Psychology is the scientific study of human and animal _behavior_ .

2. (p. 2)   Behavior is defined as anything you do. Behavior can refer to _____ (private, internal)
             activities as well as _____ (visible) actions.

3. (p. 2)   Much of our overt behavior can be studied by direct _____. However,
             it usually takes skillful detective work to deduce what is happening internally.

4. (p. 2)   For example, most people find it easier to answer whether a horse is bigger than a mouse, than
             whether a collie is bigger than a German shepherd. This is because it is more difficult to
             compare mental images that are _____ in size.

5. (p. 2)   Information gained through direct observation and measurement is called _____
             evidence.

6. (p. 2)   Whenever possible, psychologists settle differences by collecting _____ (observed facts)
             that can be verified by two or more observers. Psychologists are keenly aware that opinions,
             or claims made by an "authority," may be wrong.

7. (p. 3)   An example of collecting data to answer questions is provided by psychologists Douglas
             Kenrick and Steven MacFarlane. They recorded the number of times drivers honked at a stalled
             car when temperatures ranged from 88 degrees to 116 degrees. They found that the higher
             temperatures were linked with an _____ in the amount of time spent honking.

8. (p. 4)   Empiricism alone is not enough to make a science. True scientific observation must also be
             _____. That is, it has to be structured so that observations reveal something
             about the underlying nature of behavior. They must be carefully planned and recorded.

9. (p. 4)   Many fields are interested in human behavior. What sets psychology apart is that it applies the
             _____ _____ to questions about behavior. This is also what
             separates scientific psychology from "pop" psychology.

10. (p. 4)   While psychology is definitely a science, it is a "young" science. Sometimes, psychologists are
             unable to answer questions because of ethical or practical concerns. More frequently,
             psychological questions remain unanswered because a suitable _____
             _____ does not yet exist. For example, only since the development of the
             electroencephalograph have researchers been able to objectively determine when a person is
             dreaming.

11. (p. 5)   As a group, psychologists are interested in the natural laws governing the behavior of any living
             creature. Indeed, specialists known as _____ psychologists may spend their
             entire careers comparing the behavior of different species to learn about their similarities and
             differences.

12. (p. 5)   Attributing human thoughts, feelings, and motives to animals constitutes the
             _____ _____ and should be avoided because it can lead to false
             conclusions and cloud our understanding of animal behavior.

13. (p. 6) Research psychologists use animals in experiments to discover principles that help solve human problems. In fact, animals serving as _____ may sometimes provide the only information available on a subject.

14. (p. 6) Psychological knowledge also benefits animals. Behavioral research has provided ways to avoid killing animals that destroy crops or livestock. Also the successful care of endangered species in _____ relies on behavioral research.

15. (p. 6) Animals are very much a part of psychology. In fact, a _____ panel concluded that in psychology there is often no substitute for ethically done animal research.

16. (p. 6) In general, the goals of psychology are to _____, _____, _____, and _____. Beyond this, psychology's ultimate goal is to gather knowledge to benefit humanity.

17. (p. 6) Useful knowledge begins with accurate _____, or naming and classifying. But understanding behavior is met when we can _____ why an event occurs.

18. (p. 6) Psychology's third goal, _____, is the ability to accurately forecast behavior. Behavioral predictions are often quite useful. For example, psychological research predicts that you will suffer less jet lag if you fly _____ early in the day and _____ late in the day.

19. (p. 6) Prediction is especially important in _____, a specialty that focuses on mental measurement. Experts in this area use various tests to predict such things as success in school, work, or career.

20. (p. 6) To most psychologists the fourth goal, _____, simply means altering conditions that influence behavior in predictable ways. For example, a psychologist might suggest changes in a classroom that help children learn better.

21. (p. 6) Control is also present if behavioral research is used to design an aircraft instrument panel that reduces pilot errors. Clearly, there is value in such work since the U.S. Federal Aviation Administration estimates that _____ percent of all aircraft accidents are due to human error.

22. (p. 7) Psychology's past is centuries old because it includes _____ the study of knowledge, reality, and human nature. But, modern psychology's history began only about _____ years ago.

23. (p. 7) Psychology's history as a separate science began in 1879 at Leipzig, Germany where the "father" of psychology, Wilhelm _____, created the first psychological laboratory to study conscious experience.

24. (p. 7) Wundt wondered how sensations, images, and feelings are formed. To find out, he observed and carefully measured _____ of various kinds (lights, sounds, weights).

25. (p. 6) Wundt combined this objective measurement with _____ (or "looking inward") and called this approach _____ _____ _____.

26. (p. 7) Experimental self-observation was a highly developed skill, much like that needed to be a professional wine taster. Wundt's subjects had to make at least _____ practice observations before they were allowed to take part in a real experiment.

27. (p. 7) Wundt's ideas were carried to the United States by one of his students, Edward
_____, who helped launch a school of thought called _____
because they dealt with the structure of mental life.

28. (p. 7) The structuralists hoped to develop a sort of "mental chemistry" by analyzing experience into
basic _____ or building blocks. They relied greatly upon introspection.

29. (p. 8) Introspection was a poor way to answer many questions because the structuralists were studying
the contents of their own minds, something no one else could observe. As a result, they
frequently _____ and there was no way of settling differences. Still, "looking
inward" is a useful part of today's psychology in the study of hypnosis, meditation, drug
effects, problem-solving, etc.

30. (p. 8) William _____, an American psychologist, broadened the scope of psychology to include
animal behavior, religious experience, and abnormal behavior.

31. (p. 8) James' first book, _____ of Psychology (1890), is still in print today. It helped
establish psychology as a serious discipline in colleges and universities.

32. (p. 8) James was interested in how the mind _____ to adapt us to a changing
environment, hence the term _____ describing James' school of thought.

33. (p. 8) The functionalists were strongly influenced by Charles _____ and his theory of
evolution.

34. (p. 8) According to Darwin, creatures evolve through _____ _____ in
ways that favor their survival. That is, features which help animals adapt to their environment
are retained in evolution.

35. (p. 8) The functionalists, then, sought to understand how thought, perceptions, habits, and emotions
aid human _____. They wanted to study the mind in use.

36. (p. 8) Functionalism brought the study of animals into psychology by linking human and animal
_____.

37. (p. 8) Functionalists emphasized that learning makes us more adaptable, and urged psychologists to
help improve education. Thus, they helped to foster the development of
_____ psychology.

38. (p. 8) Functionalism also spurred the rise of _____ psychology, a specialty
involving the application of psychology to work, especially to personnel selection, human
relations, and machine design.

39. (p. 8) Functionalism was soon challenged by a new viewpoint called _____ or
_____-_____ psychology, led in part by John B. Watson.

40. (p. 9) Watson objected to introspection and rejected the functionalists' use of mentalistic concepts.
Instead, he observed the relationship between _____ (events in the
environment) and an animal's _____ (any muscular action, glandular activity,
or other identifiable behavior) to them.

41. (p. 9) Watson adopted the _____ _____ (a learned reaction to a particular stimulus) as an explanation for most behavior. This concept was originally introduced by Russian physiologist Ivan Pavlov.

42. (p. 9) One of the best-known and most influential modern behaviorists is B. F. _____ who maintains that behavior is shaped and maintained by its _____.

43. (p. 9) Skinner was one of the most fascinating and controversial psychologists of the 20th Century. He believed that our behavior is primarily controlled by the _____, especially by rewards, or positive reinforcers.

44. (p. 9) Skinner created the "_____ _____" to observe laboratory animals in a controlled environment. The apparatus allowed him to control what stimuli an animal was exposed to and to focus on changes in a single response.

45. (p. 10) In his most controversial book, *Beyond Freedom and Dignity*, Skinner claimed that society can no longer afford to rely on the human conceit we call "free will." Instead, he said, we need a "designed culture" in which behavior is guided into desirable patterns by _____ _____.

46. (p. 10) Among the general public, Skinner was perhaps best known as the man who taught pigeons to play table tennis, as the inventor of teaching machines, and as the creator of a mechanical "_____ _____" (a crib-sized chamber) that he used with his own daughter for $2^{1}/_{2}$ years.

47. (p. 10) Skinner's emphasis on stimulus-response relationships, and his tendency to ignore thought and subjective experience has led some observers to charge that Skinnerian psychology has "lost consciousness." However, most psychologists would still agree that human behavior is greatly influenced by _____.

48. (p. 10) A broader behavioral view, called _____ behaviorism, has answered many of the criticisms lodged against Skinner by combining thinking and environmental control to explain behavior.

49. (p. 10) The behavioristic approach is responsible for much of what we know today about learning, conditioning, and the proper use of reward and punishment. A direct product of behavioristic thought is _____ _____, a system which uses conditioning principles to treat problems such as overeating, phobias, or temper tantrums.

50. (p. 10) The _____ (meaning form, pattern, or whole) school of thought was founded by Max Wertheimer.

51. (p. 10) The Gestaltists thought it was a mistake to analyze psychological events into pieces or "elements." Instead, they tried to study experiences as _____.

52. (p. 10) They emphasized the _____ between elements, such as the notes in a musical melody. Their slogan was, "The whole is greater than the sum of its parts."

53. (p. 10) Many experiences resist analysis into parts or pieces. For this reason, the Gestalt viewpoint remains influential in the study of _____ and _____. It has also given rise to a type of psychotherapy.

54. (p. 11)   Histories of psychology seldom mention women because men dominated academic life in the late 1800s. Even so, by 1906 in America about one psychologist in every _____ was a woman.

55. (p. 11)   Christine _____ was the first American woman to complete requirements for the doctorate in psychology, in 1882. However, her degree was not awarded due to a university policy that denied women the doctorate.

56. (p. 11)   The first woman to be awarded a Ph.D. in psychology was Margaret _____, in 1894.

57. (p. 11)   Today the number of males and females receiving doctoral degrees in psychology is roughly _____. And, in recent years, the number of female psychology graduates at the bachelor's level has far _____ the number of male psychology graduates.

58. (p. 11)   As the mainstream of psychology was becoming more objective and scientific, Sigmund _____, an Austrian physician, was developing a theory of personality known today as _____ psychology.

59. (p. 11)   Freud felt that mental experience was like an iceberg, only part is exposed to view. There are vast areas of _____ thoughts, impulses, and desires, which cannot be experienced directly.

60. (p. 12)   Because these thoughts are usually of a threatening, sexual, or aggressive nature they _____ (actively held out of consciousness).

61. (p. 12)   Sometimes these thoughts are revealed in dreams, emotions, or _____ _____ (slips of the tongue).

62. (p. 12)   Freud made many contributions to the field of psychology. One of these was his insistence that all thoughts, emotions, and actions are _____ (nothing is an accident).

63. (p. 12)   Another contribution was his emphasis on the importance of _____ in later personality development. Thus the phrase, "the child is father to the man."

64. (p. 12)   Also, Freud developed a method of psychotherapy called _____, which is used to explore the unconscious roots of emotional problems.

65. (p. 12)   Not long after Freud's rise, some of his students, such as Carl Jung, began to break away from him. These psychologists, known as _____-_____, accepted the broad features of Freud's theory, but revised it to fit their own concepts.

66. (p. 12)   Today, Freud's ideas have been altered, revised, and adapted to the point that few strictly psychoanalytic psychologists are left. However, Freud's legacy is still evident in various _____ approaches to psychology, which focus on the internal motives, conflicts, and unconscious forces that influence our behavior.

67. (p. 12)   The "third force" in psychology is _____, a relatively recent development. The other two forces are _____ psychology and _____.

68. (p. 12)   Psychologists Carl Rogers, Abraham Maslow, and others developed the humanistic approach to counter the negativity they saw in other views. They are uncomfortable with determinism and in contrast stress _____ _____, the human ability to make choices.

69. (p. 12) Humanists do admit that past experiences affect personality. However, they also believe that people can freely _____ to live more creative, meaningful, and satisfying lives.

70. (p. 12) Humanists helped stimulate interest in psychological _____ for love, self-esteem, belonging, self-expression, creativity, and spirituality. As an example of how important these factors are, they point out that newborn infants who are deprived of human love and emotional warmth may die just as surely as they would if deprived of food.

71. (p. 12) While humanists collect data and seek evidence to support their ideas, they tend to be less interested in treating psychology as an objective, behavioral science. Instead, they stress the importance of _____ factors.

72. (p. 12) As examples of such subjective factors, they focus on _____-_____, which refers to your total perception of yourself, including images of your body, personality, and abilities.

73. (p. 12) Another important subjective factor is your _____-_____, which consists of positive and negative feelings you hold toward yourself.

74. (p. 12) The humanists also stress the concept of your _____ of _____. That is, the mental and emotional perspective you use to judge events.

75. (p. 12) A unique feature of the humanistic approach is Maslow's description of _____-_____, the need to develop one's potential fully, to lead a rich and meaningful life, and to become the best person one can become.

76. (p. 13) Today, several of the traditional schools of thought have given way to a blending of ideas and perspectives. Many psychologists can be described as _____ (drawing from many sources) in their approach.

77. (p. 13) In addition to the more traditional views within the field, other approaches have recently become increasingly valuable. Based on new knowledge about how the brain works and its relation to thought, feelings, perception, and abnormal behavior, _____ approaches for understanding behavior have become a major emphasis.

78. (p. 13) A similar trend has occurred for _____ psychology. This approach studies thoughts, expectations, language, perception, problem solving, consciousness, creativity, and other mental processes.

79. (p. 13) Some of the topics now studied by cognitive psychologists were neglected for so many years that psychology can be said to have recently "regained consciousness." _____ models of human thinking have been especially important in spurring recent advances in cognitive psychology.

80. (p. 14) Psychologists usually have a _____ degree or a _____ in psychology; that is, from 3 to 8 years of specialized postgraduate training in psychological theory and research methods.

81. (p. 14) Psychologists interested in human emotional problems and their treatment specialize in _____ or _____ psychology.

82. (p. 14) The practice of counseling was once limited to problems not involving serious _____ _____, such as adjustment at work or school. Recently, however, differences between counseling and clinical psychology are beginning to fade as more counseling psychologists have shifted to doing psychotherapy primarily.

83. (p. 14) To enter the profession of psychology today, you would probably find it necessary to have a doctorate in order to be licensed or to qualify for employment. Most clinical psychologists now have a Ph.D. or a Psy.D.(Doctor of Psychology). The latter is a new degree that emphasizes practical _____ skills rather than research.

84. (p. 14) Psychiatrists are physicians who specialize in abnormal behavior and psychotherapy. They are trained to treat the _____ causes of psychological problems and in the vast majority of cases, they do so by prescribing _____.

85. (p. 15) This latter distinction between psychologists and psychiatrists may disappear, however. A 1991 poll found that _____ percent of the psychologists surveyed believe that they should be granted prescription privileges after receiving additional training.

86. (p. 15) To be a _____, you must have an M.D. or Ph.D. degree plus further specialized training in the theory and practice of Freudian psychoanalysis.

87. (p. 15) Today, few psychiatrists and almost no psychologists become analysts. Traditional psychoanalysis is _____ and _____ consuming and fewer clients are seeking this form of treatment. In practice, many psychotherapists find that a flexible and eclectic approach is most effective.

88. (p. 15) In many states counselors (such as marriage and family counselors, _____ counselors or _____ counselors) also do mental health work. To be a licensed counselor typically requires a master's degree plus one or two years of full-time supervised counseling experience. There is little emphasis on research.

89. (p. 15) To be legally called a _____, a person must now meet a rigorous set of educational requirements. To work as a clinical or counseling psychologist, an individual must have a _____ issued by a state examining board.

90. (p. 15) Most psychologists take pride in following a professional code established by the American Psychological Association (APA) that stresses: (1) high levels of _____ and responsibility; (2) high moral and _____ standards; (3) _____ handling of personal information in teaching, practice, or research; and (4) protection of the client's _____.

91. (p. 15) The APA also encourages psychologists to make their services available to anyone who seeks them regardless of social considerations. Many psychologists do provide some of their work for _____ or do _____ work in their communities.

92. (p. 15) Only about _____ percent of psychologists are clinical or counseling psychologists. The rest divide into _____ specialties currently recognized by the APA.

93. (p. 15) Roughly one psychologist out of every _____ is employed full-time at a college or university where he/she teaches and may also do research, consulting, or therapy.

94. (p. 15) Psychologists engaged in research may do _____ research, seeking knowledge for the sake of knowledge, or _____ research, in which immediate practical uses are planned for the information gained.

95. (p. 16) Be familiar with the wide range of interests and specialties within the field of psychology described in Table 1-3 and in the main body of the text. As one example, a _____ psychologist carries out research on child development, adult developmental trends and aging; and may do clinical work with disturbed children or act as a consultant to preschools or programs for the aged.

96. (p. 18) Over 40 years ago, educator Francis _____ developed a method of combining studying with reading. The technique was called the _____ method.

97. (p. 18) The symbols S-Q-R-R-R stand for five steps that can help you understand ideas quickly, remember more, and review effectively for tests. The letters represent _____, _____, _____, _____, and _____.

98. (p. 19) Experiments show that using the SQ3R method improves both reading _____ and _____.

99. (p. 19) While the SQ3R method is good for reading, it is also important to understand and practice how to be an effective note taker. This skill requires _____ listening—the ability to control one's attention to avoid classroom daydreaming.

100. (p. 20) LISAN is a listening/note-taking plan that involves five steps, each represented by a letter in the word. The five steps are _____, _____. _____, _____, _____ _____ and _____-_____.

101. (p. 20) A recent study found that most students do take reasonably good notes and then don't use them. This practice may help explain why students do poorly on test items based on _____.

102. (p. 20) Instead of waiting until just before exams to review notes, it pays to review them on a _____ basis—daily is not too often.

103. (p. 20) Making a course interesting means both students and teachers must do their part. As a student, interest has much to do with your _____. Students who believe that success is due to effort and motivation do better in the long run.

104. (p. 20) To make the most of your study time, work in a quiet, well-lighted area free of distractions. If possible, you should also have at least one place where you _____ _____. In this way, studying will become strongly linked with a specific place and make it easier to get work done.

105. (p. 20) Using a large number of relatively short study sessions has been shown to be a more efficient way to study than to use one or two long periods. Cramming places a tremendous burden on memory. Therefore, use _____ practice rather than _____ practice when learning information for the first time.

106. (p. 21) To help in memorizing material for classes, it can be helpful to use a _____— that is, a memory aid. Most link new information to ideas or images that are easy to remember.

107. (p. 21) A good way to improve test scores is to arrange to take several "practice tests" before the real one in class. Studying should include _____-_____ by use of flashcards, Learning Checks, a study guide, or questions you ask yourself.

108. (p. 21) In order to avoid underpreparing for exams, make sure to _____—that is, continue studying beyond "bare mastery" of a topic.

109. (p. 21) It is probably best to approach all tests as if they were _____. Research shows that students who expect multiple-choice questions actually score lower.

110. (p. 21) A tendency to _____ is almost universal among college students. This can lead to putting off work until the last possible moment, working only under pressure, skipping classes, giving false reasons for late work, and feeling ashamed of last-minute efforts.

111. (p. 21) Psychologists Jane Burka and Lenora Yuen observe that many students seem to equate performance in school with their _____ _____. By procrastinating, students can blame poor work on a late start, rather than a lack of ability.

112. (p. 21) _____ is a related problem. If you have high expectations for yourself, you may find it hard to start an assignment and end up with all-or-nothing work habits.

113. (p. 21) A formal _____ _____ can do much to prevent procrastination and maintain motivation in school. Start by making a chart showing all of the hours in each day of the week. Then fill in committed times, times when you will study for various classes, and add the remaining hours as open or free times.

114. (p. 22) Many students also find it helpful to set _____ _____ for themselves. If you have trouble staying motivated, it's a good idea to set goals for the semester, the week, the day, and even for single study sessions.

115. (p. 22) Objective tests evaluate your ability to recognize a correct statement among wrong answers. When taking multiple-choice and true-false items, remember these points: (1) Read the _____ carefully—they may give you good advice or clues for the test. (2) Read _____ of the choices for each question before you make a decision. (3) Read rapidly and _____ items you are uncertain about. (4) Eliminate certain alternatives. (5) Unless there is a penalty for guessing, be sure to answer every question. (6) When you have strong doubts, your _____ answer is more likely to be correct.

116. (p. 22) When taking essay exams remember these points: (1) Read the question carefully and make sure that you note _____ words. (2) Think about your answer before _____; make a brief list of the points you want to make. (3) Don't pad your answer. Be direct. Make a point and support it. (4) Check your essay for spelling errors, sentence errors, and grammatical errors.

117. (p. 24) _____ thinking refers to an ability to evaluate, compare, analyze, critique, and synthesize information. It involves a willingness to take an active role in evaluating ideas.

118. (p. 24) Critical thinking is built upon four basic principles: (1) Few "truths" transcend the need for _____ testing. (2) Evidence varies in _____. (3) _____ or claimed expertise does not automatically make an idea true. (4) Critical thinking requires an _____ mind.

119. (p. 25)   A _____-_____ is any dubious and unfounded system that resembles psychology. Many offer elaborate systems that give the appearance of science, but are actually false.

120. (p. 25)   As one example of pseudo-psychologies, _____ claims that lines in the hand are indicators of personality and a person's future.

121. (p. 25)   Franz _____ popularized _____, the notion that personality is revealed by the shape of the skull.

122. (p. 26)   However, modern research has shown that bumps on the head have nothing to do with talents or abilities. In fact, the area of the brain that controls _____ was listed on phrenology charts as the center for "combativeness" and "destructiveness."

123. (p. 26)   _____ postulates that personality traits are revealed by handwriting. This technique is moderately popular in the United States where at least _____ companies use handwriting analysis to evaluate job applicants.

124. (p. 26)   These uses are distressing to psychologists because studies show that graphologists score close to _____ on careful tests of accuracy in rating personality.

125. (p. 26)   One study has found that graphologists do _____ _____ than untrained college students in rating personality and job performance.

126. (p. 26)   _____, probably the most popular pseudo-psychology, is based on the assumption that the position of the stars and planets at the time of a person's birth determines personality characteristics and affects behavior.

127. (p. 26)   _____ percent of the American public believes in astrology and another _____ percent say they are not sure if the stars and planets can or cannot affect people's lives.

128. (p. 26)   The problems with astrology are numerous and devastating. For one, the zodiac has shifted by one full _____ since astrology was first set up. Most astrologers simply ignore this shift. You should be familiar with other objections. Also, review the arguments and counter-arguments summarized by psychologist Richard Crowe.

129. (p. 27)   Astrology seems to work for several reasons. For one, it tends to describe personality in _____ terms, showing mostly flattering traits.

130. (p. 27)   All pseudo-psychologies are subject to the _____ of _____ _____ in which persons remember or notice things that confirm their expectations and forget the rest.

131. (p. 27)   This illusion was demonstrated in an experiment in which a psychologist read a "personality profile" containing both sides of several personality dimensions to 79 college students who had taken a personality test. Only _____ students felt that the description failed to adequately capture their personality.

132. (p. 27)   Another study found that people rated this "personality profile" as more _____ than their actual horoscopes.

133. (p. 27)   Finally, pseudo-psychologies are stated in such _____ terms that they always have "a little something for everybody." We can call this the P. T. Barnum Effect.

134. (p. 27) One experiment showed that among people given the same personality description, those who had initially provided more detailed information considered their horoscopes to be more _____. Thus, the more "hocus-pocus" to the pseudo-psychology, the more believable the results.

SELF-TEST

1. (p. 2) Psychology is the scientific study of human and animal _____.
   a. psyche
   b. behavior
   c. physiology
   d. social organization

2. (p. 2) Psychologists try to be objective in their observations and place special importance on information obtained through:
   a. empirical evidence
   b. open communication
   c. professional opinion
   d. reliance on authority

3. (p. 4) Scientific study of some topics in psychology is not yet possible. Which of the following best explains why?
   a. ethical and practical limitations exist or there is a lack of suitable research methods
   b. in some areas, humans have not yet evolved to the point where behavior can be properly observed and measured
   c. we have everything we need to scientifically study all behavior, but the social climate does not always permit this
   d. most psychologists feel that behavior should not be studied scientifically

4. (p. 5) Which of the following is an example of an anthropomorphic statement?
   a. Johnny hoped the dog would come to him.
   b. The dog hoped Johnny would come to him.
   c. Johnny looked at the dog.
   d. The dog looked at Johnny.

5. (p. 6) Which of the following is *not* a goal of psychology?
   a. description of behavior
   b. prediction of behavior
   c. depiction of behavior
   d. understanding behavior

6. (p. 6) Control is an important goal of psychology. For most psychologists, control means:
   a. heavy reliance upon rewards rather than punishments
   b. manipulation of behavior by government, educators, scientists, or authorities
   c. altering conditions that influence behavior in predictable ways
   d. explaining why a phenomenon occurs or exists under structured conditions

7. (p. 7) The goal of Wilhelm Wundt, the "father" of psychology, was:
   a. to understand how humans perceive thoughts
   b. to understand how sensations, images, and feelings are formed
   c. to compare animal and human behaviors in functional ways
   d. to explore behavior in an "armchair" fashion using the principles of philosophy

8. (p. 7) Wundt combined scientific measurement with careful introspection to create an approach he called:
   a. experimental structuralism
   b. psychoanalysis
   c. scientific self-actualization
   d. experimental self-observation

9. (p. 7)   Wundt's student, Edward B. Titchener, helped launch a school of psychology called _____ that sought to analyze conscious experience into basic "elements."
            a. structuralism   c. functionalism
            b. chemical psychology   d. humanism

10. (p. 8)   The functionalist school of thought developed from William James' interest in:
            a. how basic elements of behavior function in the mind
            b. how the mind functions to adapt us to a changing environment
            c. how functional relationships exist such that the whole exceeds the sum of its parts
            d. how responses are a function of stimuli

11. (p. 8)   Which of the following is *not* a contribution to psychology made by the functionalists?
            a. introducing the study of animals into psychology
            b. contributing to the development of educational psychology
            c. developing an important form of psychotherapy
            d. spurring the development of industrial psychology

12. (p. 9)   John B. Watson, who helped define the behavioristic viewpoint, relied heavily upon which concept in explaining behavior?
            a. consciousness   c. conditioned response
            b. behavior modification   d. functional relationships

13. (p. 9)   "In order to understand human behavior we must take into account what the environment does to an organism before and after it responds." This quote defines the position of which of the following?
            a. William James   c. B. F. Skinner
            b. Sigmund Freud   d. Wilhelm Wundt

14. (p. 10) The slogan, "The whole is greater than the sum of its parts," is associated with which school of thought?
            a. functionalism   c. behaviorism
            b. structuralism   d. Gestalt

15. (p. 11) The first American woman to be awarded a Ph.D. in psychology in 1894 was:
            a. Mary Calkins   c. Lillien Martin
            b. Christine Ladd-Franklin   d. Margaret Washburn

16. (p. 12) Which of the following is *not* a contribution to psychology made by Sigmund Freud and the psychoanalytic school of thought?
            a. insistence that all thoughts, emotions, and actions are determined
            b. introducing the study of animals into psychology
            c. emphasis on the importance of childhood in later personality development
            d. developing a method of psychotherapy

17. (p. 12) True-False. Humanism is a science interested in humane research with animals.

18. (p. 12) The humanistic viewpoint emphasizes the importance of:
            a. free will   c. unconscious processes
            b. biological needs   d. behavior determined by the environment

19. (p. 13) The _____ approach in psychology has provided a new and increasingly important perspective. Here, the emphasis is on the study of thoughts, expectations, language, perception, problem solving, etc.
    a. biological
    b. cognitive
    c. humanistic
    d. psychoanalytic

20. (p. 14) A _____ is trained to treat physical causes of psychological difficulties and can prescribe drugs.
    a. psychoanalyst
    b. psychiatrist
    c. school or child counselor
    d. clinical or counseling psychologist

21. (p. 15) True-False. The majority of psychologists today still practice the theories of Sigmund Freud.

22. (p. 15) True-False. To practice as a clinical or counseling psychologist, an individual must have a master's degree, two years of full-time supervised experience, and sometimes a license issued by a state examining board.

23. (p. 15) Psychologists adhere to a professional code established by the APA. Which of the following is *not* a part of the code?
    a. protection of the client's welfare
    b. high levels of competence and responsibility
    c. ensuring availability of services to everyone by charging the same rates regardless of the client's financial or social status
    d. confidentiality in handling personal information in teaching, practice, or research

24. (p. 15) Roughly one-third of psychologists are employed full-time in:
    a. private practices
    b. government projects
    c. research facilities
    d. educational institutions

25. (p. 16) Who among the following would be most likely to do clinical work with disturbed children, explore aging and adult trends, or act as consultants to preschools or programs for the aged?
    a. social psychologists
    b. clinical psychologists
    c. comparative psychologists
    d. developmental psychologists

26. (p. 17) True-False. Social psychologists are primarily interested in studying people in a group setting, or under any circumstance in which social factors play a part.

27. (p. 18) Which of the following is a method developed by Francis Robinson for learning new information that combines studying with reading?
    a. LISAN
    b. SQ3R
    c. APA
    d. structuralism

28. (p. 20) True-False. Massed practice is a better way to learn new material than spaced practice because it allows for more continuous study and therefore less problems with forgetting.

29. (p. 21) A memory aid that links new information to ideas or images that are easy to remember is called a:
    a. learning basic
    b. massing practice
    c. recitation
    d. mnemonic

30. (p. 21) Working under pressure, skipping classes, giving false reasons for late work, and feeling ashamed of last-minute efforts may be signs that a student has significant problems with:
    a. procrastination
    b. perfectionism
    c. overlearning
    d. impossibly high self-standards

31. (p. 25) True-False. Pseudo-psychologies are legitimate subdisciplines within psychology.

32. (p. 25) The theory that personality is revealed by the shape of the skull was popularized by Franz Gall during the 19th century and is known as:
    a. astrology
    b. palmistry
    c. phenomenology
    d. phrenology

33. (p. 27) Which of the following is *not* a reason why astrology, phrenology, graphology, and palmistry tend to be dubious, unfounded systems?
    a. They are popular and are practiced by significant numbers of people.
    b. They are subject to the fallacy of positive instances.
    c. Their predictions or descriptions are often stated in such desirable terms which encourage uncritical acceptance.
    d. Their predictions or descriptions are often stated in such general terms that they can hardly miss being vaguely accurate.

APPLYING YOUR KNOWLEDGE

1. Histories of psychology abound in "forefathers" but seldom mention women. Do a research paper focusing on a female figure important to the history of psychology.

2. Animal research is an important part of psychology in many different fields. Choose three different specialty areas from Table 1-3 of the text and research some examples of how animal research contributes to our knowledge within these specialties.

3. To help you better understand what psychologists from different specialties actually do as a part of their profession, contact psychologists from three different sub-disciplines and interview them about their training, experience, and current efforts.

4. Pick a psychology topic of interest to you. How would each of the five major perspectives evident in modern psychology approach the topic? See if you can write a brief summary of the direction and techniques each of the views might pursue in addressing the topic.

ANSWERS—PROGRAMMED REVIEW

1. behavior
2. covert; overt
3. observation
4. similar
5. empirical
6. data
7. increase
8. systematic
9. scientific method
10. research method
11. comparative
12. anthropomorphic fallacy
13. models
14. zoos
15. government
16. describe, understand, predict, control
17. description; explain
18. prediction; east; west
19. psychometries
20. control
21. 65
22. philosophy; 100
23. Wilhelm Wundt
24. stimuli
25. instrospection; experimental self-observation
26. 10,000
27. Edward B. Titchener; structuralism
28. elements
29. disagreed
30. William James
31. Principles
32. functions; functionalism
33. Charles Darwin
34. natural selection
35. adaptation
36. adaptation
37. educational
38. industrial
39. behaviorism; stimulus-response
40. stimuli; responses
41. conditioned response
42. B. F. Skinner; consequences
43. environment
44. Skinner Box
45. positive reinforcement
46. baby tender
47. learning
48. cognitive

49. behavior modification
40. Gestalt
51. wholes
52. relationship
53. perception; personality
54. 10
55. Christine Ladd-Franklin
56. Margaret Washburn
57. equal; exceeded
58. Sigmund Freud; psychoanalytic
59. unconscious
60. repressed
61. Freudian slips
62. determined
63. childhood
64. psychoanalysis
65. neo-Freudians
66. psychodynamic
67. humanism; psychodynamic; behaviorism
68. free will
69. choose
70. needs
71. subjective
72. self-image
73. self-evaluation
74. frame of reference
75. self-actualization
76. eclectic
77. psychobiological

78. cognitive
79. Computer
80. master's; doctorate
81. clinical; counseling
82. mental disorder
83. clinical
84. physical; drugs
85. 68
86. psychoanalyst
87. expensive; time
88. child; school
89. psychologist; license
90. competence; ethical; confidential; welfare
91. free; volunteer
92. 50; 46
93. 3
94. basic; applied
95. developmental
96. Francis Robinson; SQ3R
97. Survey; Question, Read; Recite; Review
98. comprehension; grades
99. active
100. Lead; Ideas; Signal words; Actively listen; Note-taking
101. lecture
102. regular
103. attitude
104. only study
105. spaced; massed

106. mnemonic
107. self-testing
108. overlearn
109. essays
110. procrastinate
111. personal worth
112. Perfectionism
113. time schedule
114. specific goals
115. directions; all; skip; second
116. key; writing
117. Critical
118. empirical; quality; Authority; open
119. Pseudo-psychologies
120. palmistry
121. Gall; phrenology
122. hearing
123. Graphology; 3000
124. zero
125. no better; chance
126. Astrology
127. Twenty-five; 22
128. constellation
129. desirable
130. fallacy of positive instances
131. five
132. accurate
133. general
134. accurate

ANSWERS—SELF-TEST

1. b
2. a
3. a
4. b
5. c
6. c
7. b
8. d
9. a
10. b
11. c
12. c
13. c
14. d
15. d
16. b
17. False
18. a
19. b
20. b
21. False
22. False
23. c
24. d
25. d
26. True
27. b
28. False
29. d
30. a
31. False
32. d
33. a

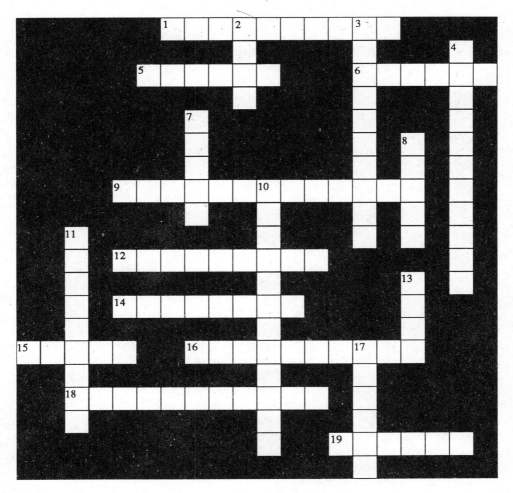

ACROSS

1. science studying organisms' behavior and mental processes
5. he considered introspection unscientific
6. psychologists concerned about learning disabilities of students
9. "looking inward"
12. evidence gained via observation and measurement
14. psychologists who study crime prevention
15. bearded psychoanalyst watched for slips of the tongue
16. he advanced gestaltism
18. psychologist concerned with design of machinery, autos and airplanes
19. psychologist studying attitudes and groups

DOWN

2. authored your *Introduction to Psychology* text
3. school of thought professing "whole exceeds sum of parts"
4. psychologist that "compares" behavior of different animals
7. visible, observable behavior
8. father of first psychology lab
10. M.D. specializing in abnormal behavior or psychotherapy
11. he is associated with structuralism
13. super technique to study and read by
14. self-actualization is his concept

CHAPTER 2

Research Methods in Psychology

CONTENTS

Scientific Method—Can a Horse Add?
Naturalistic Observation—Psychology Steps Out!
Correlational Studies—In Search of the Perfect Relationship
The Psychology Experiment—Where Cause Meets Effect
Placebo Effects—Sugar Pills and Salt Water
The Clinical Method—Data by the Case
Survey Method—Here, Have a Sample
Psychology in the News—Notes on Reading the Popular Press
Smile, You're on Candid Camera!—The Ethics of Psychological Research

TERMS AND CONCEPTS

scientific method
hypothesis
operational definition
naturalist observation
observer effect
observer bias
correlational studies
coefficient of correlation
positive correlation
negative correlation
linear relationship
curvilinear relationship
experiment
subjects
experimental group
control group
independent variable
dependent variable
extraneous variable

random assignment
laboratory experiments
field experiments
replication
parascience
placebo
placebo effect
endorphins
single-blind procedure
double-blind procedure
experimenter effect
self-fulfilling prophecy
clinical method
case study
survey method
representative sample
Gallup poll
Harris poll
courtesy bias

IMPORTANT INDIVIDUALS

Jane Goodall
James Bryan
Mary Test
Cleve Backster
Robert Rosenthal

J. M. Harlow
Edward Tolman
Barbara Gutek
Martin Gardner
Phillip Zimbardo

Bernard Leikind
Jeanne Dixon
Eric Knowles
Stanley Milgram

PROGRAMMED REVIEW

1.   (p. 31)   To avoid the trap of faulty observation, psychologists use the _____ _____, defined in its ideal form by five steps:
     1) Observation
     2) Defining a problem
     3) Proposing a hypothesis
     4) Experimentation
     5) Theory formulation

2.   (p. 31)   A _____ is a tentative explanation of an event or observation, clearly stated and testable.

3.   (p. 32)   In testing a hypothesis you must specify the exact procedures used to represent the concepts within the hypothesis. You must define the relevant terms using _____ definitions.

4.   (p. 32)   Operational definitions are important because they allow _____ concepts to be tested in real-world terms. In general, concepts become more useful when they have been tested with a variety of operational definitions.

5.   (p. 32)   A good example of how to apply the five steps of the scientific method is seen in the story of _____ _____, the mathematical wonder horse.

6.   (p. 32)   A _____ interrelates concepts and facts in a way that summarizes the results of a large number of observations. It should account for existing data, predict new observations, and guide further research.

7.   (p. 32)   A good scientific theory is stated in terms that make it _____—its concepts are defined in ways that allow them to be put to a test.

8.   (p. 33)   When we actively observe subjects in their natural setting, we are making _____ _____.

9.   (p. 33)   Jane Goodall has conducted naturalistic observations of chimpanzees and discovered that they, like humans, use _____ to obtain some goals.

10. (p. 33)   Naturalistic observation only provides _____ of behavior. To explain what has been observed often requires more information from other research methods.

11. (p. 33)   An advantage of naturalistic observation is that the behavior under study has not been tampered with by outside influences. However, a major problem is the _____ effect—changes in a subject's behavior brought about by an awareness of being observed. This problem is minimized by concealing the observer.

12. (p. 33)   A closely related problem is _____ _____, in which observers see what they expect to see, or record only selected details. For example, one study showed that the ratings teachers gave children differed markedly, depending upon the label (learning-disabled, normal, etc.) applied to the child.

13. (p. 33)   Psychologists doing naturalistic studies make a special effort to minimize observer bias by keeping careful _____ _____.

14. (p. 34) A _____ study is one that determines the degree to which two factors of interest (traits, behaviors, events, etc.) are co-related (linked together in an orderly way). Such studies can be done either in the lab or in a natural environment.

15. (p. 34) Correlations can be expressed as a _____ of correlation, which is a number that falls between _____ and _____.

16. (p. 34) If the coefficient of correlation is _____ or close to it, this indicates a weak or non-existent relationship (such as between shoe size and intelligence).

17. (p. 34) If the correlation is +1.00 a perfect _____ correlation exists; if it is -1.00 a perfect _____ correlation has been discovered.

18. (p. 34) Perfect correlations rarely exist in psychology, most fall between zero and plus or minus one. The closer the correlation coefficient is to +1.00 or -1.00, the _____ the relationship.

19. (p. 34) In a positive correlation, increases in one measure are matched by _____ in another (or decreases in the first factor correspond with _____ in the second). An example is the positive correlation between high school grades and college grades.

20. (p. 34) In a negative correlation, increases in the first measure are associated with _____ in the second. For example, we might observe such a relationship between air temperature and the activity levels of zoo animals.

21. (p. 34) Correlational studies help us discover relationships and make useful predictions, but correlation does not demonstrate _____.

22. (p. 35) When using correlational studies, psychologists sometimes draw graphs to help clarify the relationship between the measures. Some graphs reveal a _____ (or straight-line) relationship. Other graphs are _____ consisting of a curved line.

23. (p. 36) To identify cause-effect relationships, psychologists use a powerful research tool, the _____—a formal trial to confirm or disconfirm a fact or principle.

24. (p. 36) To perform a psychological experiment, you would:
     1) directly _____ a condition you think might cause changes in a behavior.
     2) create two or more groups of _____ who are treated alike in all ways except the condition you are varying.
     3) _____ whether varying the condition had any effect on behavior.

25. (p. 37) The simplest psychological experiment is based on two groups of _____ either animals or people. The two groups used are called the _____ group and the _____ group.

26. (p. 37) Both groups are treated exactly alike except for one condition, the independent _____ (anything that can change or vary, and which might affect the outcome or the experiment).

27. (p. 37) There are three essential elements contained in an experiment:
    1) _____ variables, which are conditions altered or varied by the experimenter. They are suspected causes in the experiment.
    2) _____ variables, which measure the outcome of the experiment. They are the results of the experiment.
    3) _____ variables, which are conditions the researcher wishes to prevent from affecting the experiment.

28. (p. 37) The group exposed to the independent variable is called the _____ group; the group not exposed to the independent variable is called the _____ group.

29. (p. 37) The control group is needed in an experiment to allow us to compare differences between the experimental group, which is exposed to the independent variable, with subjects not exposed to this factor. Thus, the control group serves as a _____ of _____.

30. (p. 37) The _____ _____ is what is measured in an experiment. This measure will be different between the two groups if the independent variable does have an affect on the experimental group's performance.

31. (p. 37) Differences in personal characteristics of subjects that might influence the outcome of an experiment can be controlled by _____ assigning subjects to the two groups.

32. (p. 37) Random assignment means that a subject has an _____ chance of being a member of either the experimental group or the control group. Random assignment helps ensure that subject differences are evenly balanced across the two groups.

33. (p. 37) Any variables, such as sex of the subject, temperature of the testing situation, time of day, etc. that could influence the behavior of subjects (besides the independent variable) are called _____, or outside, variables. Such influences can be prevented from affecting the outcome of an experiment by making all conditions exactly the same for both groups.

34. (p. 37) Thus, if we have controlled all _____ variables and the experimental and control groups differ in the value of the _____ variable, changes in the _____ variable can be the only possible cause.

35. (p. 38) An alternative to the laboratory experiment is the _____ experiment which uses the "real world" as a laboratory. This is illustrated by the work of James Bryan and Mary Test who tested whether people are more likely to help a person in distress when they have recently seen someone else being helpful.

36. (p. 38) The problem of deciding whether or not an independent variable really made enough difference in the outcome of an experiment to call it meaningful is handled _____.

37. (p. 38) When results are said to be statistically _____, this means that the obtained results in a particular experiment would occur very rarely by chance alone.

38. (p. 39) For a difference to be considered significant, it usually must be sufficiently large so that it would occur by chance in less than _____ experiments out of 100.

39. (p. 39) A key element in any science is the ability to _____ (repeat) observations or experiments. This is necessary to ensure the scientific believability of obtained results.

40. (p. 39) The failure to replicate observations is a major failing of _____ (that which resembles science, but is not truly scientific).

41. (p. 39) A good example of the failure of replication is Cleve Backster's "experiments" claiming that plants wired to a polygraph respond to music, threats, and other stimuli. When scientists tried to repeat his experiments, using either identical or improved methods, the results were completely _____.

42. (p. 39) In drug experiments, an accurate test cannot be achieved if the experimental group is given the drug and the control group gets nothing. Without using _____ a (fake pill or injection) it is impossible to tell if the drug actually affected the dependent variable or if just swallowing a pill did.

43. (p. 40) As an example of the placebo effect, one study showed that injections of saline solution had _____ percent of the effectiveness of morphine in reducing pain for hospital patients.

44. (p. 40) Although this effect is not entirely understood, experiments suggest that expectations trigger the release of brain chemicals called _____, which are similar to opiate drugs such as morphine.

45. (p. 40) To control for placebo effects, a psychologist doing drug research could use a _____-_____ arrangement where all subjects get a pill or injection (the experimental group gets the real drug, the control group receives a placebo).

46. (p. 40) Using this procedure, subjects are blind as to whether or not they receive the drug, but the experimenter is not. For added control, researchers use the _____-_____ arrangement where the experimenter also lacks knowledge of who does and does not receive the real drug.

47. (p. 40) Human subjects are very sensitive to hints from an experimenter about what is expected from them. This may produce the _____ _____, which causes a powerful impact on a subject's behavior.

48. (p. 40) Robert Rosenthal demonstrated this phenomenon in an experiment where airmen were randomly assigned to one of five math classes and their teachers were told that class members were selected for _____ or _____ levels of ability.

49. (p. 40) Students in the supposed "high-ability" classes showed substantially more improvement despite the fact that initially the classes were of equal ability. Apparently, the teacher's expectations created a _____-_____ prophecy.

50. (p. 41) The clinical method employs _____ _____, which are in-depth studies on all aspects of a single subject.

51. (p. 41) Case may sometimes be thought of as natural clinical tests of the effect of unusual variables. For example, in the remarkable case reported by J. M. Harlow, Phineas Gage suffered an accidental _____ _____, the destruction of frontal brain matter. This resulted in profound personality change.

52. (p. 41) When Michael Melnick suffered a similar freakish accident over 120 years after Gage, Melnick recovered completely with no sign of lasting ill-effects. These very different reactions to a similar injury show why psychologists prefer controlled _____ and often use lab _____ for studies of the brain.

53. (p. 42)   Another classic psychology case study is *The Three Faces of Eve*. Eve demonstrated
              _____ _____ in the form of Eve White, Eve
              Black, and Jane.

54. (p. 42)   Multiple personality disorders are quite rare. Eve's case was particularly interesting in that over
              the years, she manifested _____ different personalities.

55. (p. 42)   In the _____ method, people in a representative sample are asked a carefully
              worded series of questions. This technique can provide an accurate picture of how large
              segments of the general population feel about current issues, even though only a small
              percentage of people are polled.

56. (p. 42)   A representative sample means that the same _____ of men, women,
              Republicans, Democrats, whites, blacks, and so on, are included in the sample as are found in
              the population as a whole. Such samples are often obtained by randomly selecting who will be
              included.

57. (p. 42)   Survey quesitons must be carefully phrased because wording can greatly affect how people
              answer. For example, when polled if people were concerned about "collateral damage" caused
              by allied bombing in Iraq, _____ percent said yes, while _____ percentage agreed when
              "civilian casualties" was used.

58. (p. 42)   Edward Tolman has noted that much of American psychology is based on rats and college
              sophomores as subjects. Indeed, _____ percent of human subjects in psychology experiments
              are recruited from introductory psychology courses.

59. (p. 43)   Modern surveys like the Gallup and Harris polls are quite accurate. The Gallup poll has erred
              in its election predictions by only _____ percent since 1954.

60. (p. 43)   Some polls have at times made major blunders. The Literary Digest predicted that Alfred
              Landon would defeat Franklin Roosevelt by a landslide, but Roosevelt won overwhelmingly.
              The sample for the poll was _____ (slanted or distorted) rather than representative, a
              critical problem for the survey method.

61. (p. 43)   Replies to survey questions are not always accurate or truthful. Many people show a
              _____ _____, or tendency to give answers that are agreeable and
              socially acceptable. For example, pollsters found that black persons talking to white
              interviewers were less likely to admit support for an African American candidate. White
              persons talking to black interviewers were more likely to claim support for the African
              American candidate.

62. (p. 43)   Barbara Gutek's assessment of sexual harassment on the job is another example of the use of
              the survey method. Gutek found that _____ percent of women, but only _____ percent of men
              had experienced this problem.

63. (p. 44)   When reading psychological claims in the popular press, there are several steps to use in
              evaluating their truthfulness. One is to be _____. Since psychological
              reports often have a definite bias, you must be a critical thinker.

64. (p. 44)   This point is illustrated by the critical thinking of Martin Gardner in exploring _____-
              _____ perception, the supposed ability of people to identify colors and read
              print while blindfolded.

65. (p. 44) Another example is provided by psychologist Philip _____. After making a casual statement to a reporter that women patients in two mental hospitals seemed to use more obscenities than male patients, he was later quoted as an authority claiming that all women have become uninhibitied in using obscene language.

66. (p. 45) Another helpful suggestion is to consider the _____ of information. Claims made by an individual or company intent on selling a product often reflect the profit motive more than objective truth.

67. (p. 45) One factor that should always be considered is, "Was there a _____ group?" It is not always possible to determine if an event or situation really does have a meaningful impact unless there is a frame of reference for comparison.

68. (p. 45) The need for a control group is evident in the study conducted by physicist Bernard Leikind. He investigated whether people really need to learn "_____ programming" in order to walk barefoot on hot coals. He found that student volunteers without special training could do so, because the coals of such beds are light fluffy carbon that transmit little heat when touched.

69. (p. 45) Looking for errors in distinguishing between _____ and _____ is also important. As we know, it is dangerous to assume that because two factors correlate, one factor caused the other. Such was the mistake made by the nutritionist quoted as saying that drinking excessive amounts of milk may cause "juvenile delinquency."

70. (p. 46) Another example of mistaking correlation for causation is provided by Jeanne Dixon, a popular astrologer who believes that the moon affects human behavior. She points out that the rate of _____ _____ rises and falls with lunar cycles. However, direct studies of the alleged "lunar effect" have show that it doesn't occur.

71. (p. 46) A fifth suggestion is to be sure to distinguish between _____ and _____. What we see does not always support what we think this must mean. Assuming this someone is sad because he or she is crying is an example.

72. (p. 47) Beware of _____ _____, especially those motivated by monetary gains. Courses, programs, or products that claim rapid or immediate gains or success should be suspect.

73. (p. 47) A final tip is to remember that "_____" is no proof. The fact that something appears to be beneficial for one individual does not necessarily mean it will be equally helpful for everyone.

74. (p. 48) Experiments such as those conducted by Phillip Zimbardo to investigate the effects of imprisonment have raised new questions about the _____ of psychological research.

75. (p. 48) One area of ethical concern involves experiments where the true interests of a researcher are concealed by _____. For example, a researcher interested in guilt once falsely led subjects to believe they had broken an expensive piece of machinery. Subjects later asked to sign a petition (almost universally refused by control subjects) signed because of their guilt.

76. (p. 48) A second area of debate concerns the extent to which invasions of _____ should be allowed. For example, Eric Knowles, interested in stress caused by "personal space" invasions, secretly monitored activity in public restrooms.

77. (p. 48) Perhaps the most serious ethical problem is whether experiments may cause _____ _____ as in Stanley Milgram's study of obedience to authority.

78. (p. 49) To ensure appropriate ethics in psychological research, the American Psychological Association has adopted guidelines emphasizing the dignity and welfare of subjects. Also, most college psychology departments have _____ _____ that oversee proposed research.

79. (p. 49) If you become a subject you have a right to expect that your reactions will remain _____; that you will be debriefed about the _____ of the research; that you will receive an _____ of your responses or test results; and that the results of the research project will be made available to you.

80. (p. 49) Research with animals can raise difficult ethical questions. The animal _____ _____ opposes animal research of all kinds. At the other extreme are scientists who believe human welfare always takes precedence over animal welfare. Animal research, therefore, is inescapable.

81. (p. 49) The majority of scientists, _____ percent of the general public, and many animal welfare advocates, take a more moderate position. A middle ground seems to be to ensure humane treatment of animals and to minimize their use where possible.

SELF-TEST

1. (p. 31) Which of the following is not a step in the ideal use of the scientific method?
   a. observation
   b. defining a problem
   c. incubation of ideas
   d. theory formulation

2. (p. 32) True-False. Clever Hans was a horse who seemed to solve difficult math problems.

3. (p. 33) Research psychologists sometimes actively observe subjects in their native habitats. Such work involves primarily:
   a. casual observations
   b. common sense
   c. experimental manipulations
   d. naturalistic observations

4. (p. 33) True-False. Jane Goodall used naturalistic observations to study tool-using behavior among chimpanzees in Tanzania.

5. (p. 33) Which of the following is not a disadvantage or limitation to the use of naturalistic observations?
   a. Unless careful, observers may show bias in what they see or record.
   b. The presence of an observer may change the behavior of the observed.
   c. Naturalistic observations only provide descriptions, not explanations.
   d. Behavior being studied has not been altered by outside influences.

6. (p. 34) True-False. A negative coefficient of correlation means that two events or observations do not systematically vary together since there is no positive relationship.

7. (p. 34) Which of the following correlations might you expect to obtain if you studied the relationship between shoe size and intelligence?
   a. -1.00
   b. 0
   c. +.50
   d. + 1.00

8.   (p. 34)   True-False. The important value of correlational studies is that correlation demonstrates causation.

9.   (p. 37)   The two subject groups in an experiment are called the:
     a.   experimental and control groups
     b.   dependent and independent
          groups
     c.   extraneous and random groups
     d.   scientific and placebo groups

10. (p. 37)   In an experiment, the variable to which only the experimental group is exposed is called the _____ variable.
     a.   dependent   c.   independent
     b.   extraneous   d.   experimental

11. (p. 37)   The _____ variable is what is measured in an experiment to determine the effects of the _____ variable.
     a.   dependent, extraneous   c.   dependent, independent
     b.   independent, dependent   d.   independent, extraneous

12. (p. 37)   True-False. Differences in the personal characteristics of subjects that are extraneous to and might influence the outcome of the experiment can be controlled by randomly assigning subjects to the experimental and control groups.

13. (p. 37)   Conditions which vary across experimental and control groups such as sex, intelligence, etc., but which are not of interest in the experiment, are called _____ variables.
     a.   independent   c.   extraneous
     b.   dependent   d.   personal

14. (p. 38)   True-False. Field experiments usually do not provide objective, empirical data because they cannot be done in an actual laboratory under highly controlled conditions.

15. (p. 39)   The results of an experiment are said to be statistically significant when statistical procedures show that:
     a.   differences between the experimental and control groups would occur due to the independent variable at least 50% of the time
     b.   differences between the experimental and control groups were very unlikely to have occurred by chance alone
     c.   correlations between events are very strong and graphically linear
     d.   all extraneous variables have been controlled for, yet measures of the experimental and control group performance are still quite similar

16. (p. 40)   A _____ is a fake pill or injection.
     a.   sham   c.   neo
     b.   pseudo   d.   placebo

17. (p. 40)   Placebos can have a tremendous psychological impact, as in the reduction of pain. Recent experiments suggest this effect may be due to the release of brain chemicals called:
     a.   metamorphins   c.   saline
     b.   endorphins   d.   opiates

18.   (p. 40)   What is the procedure used most effectively to control for placebo effects?
      a.   randomization   c.   controlled subject selection
      b.   extraneous analysis   d.   double-blind testing

19.   (p. 41)   A _____ _____ is an in-depth focus on all aspects of a single subject.
      a.   naturalistic observation   c.   case study
      b.   controlled experiment   d.   casual observation

20.   (p. 41)   J. M. Harlow offered a classic example of a natural clinical test. He reported the case of
                Phineas Gage, a victim of an accidental _____.
      a.   frontal lobotomy   c.   cerebral contusion
      b.   cortical ablation   d.   anatomical diffusion

21.   (p. 42)   The case study of Eve White involved detailed observations regarding:
      a.   frontal lobotomy   c.   sexual conduct
      b.   multiple personalities   d.   brain functioning

22.   (p. 42)   The _____ _____ involves asking a representative sample of people a carefully worded series
                of questions.
      a.   experimental method   c.   observational method
      b.   clinical method   d.   survey method

23.   (p. 43)   True-False. Modern surveys, like the Gallup and Harris polls, are frequently inaccurate as in
                the Landon-Roosevelt election prediction.

24.   (p. 43)   True-False. Using the survey method, Barbara Gutek found that women are about twice as
                likely as men to be the target of sexual comments, gestures, or touching on the job.

25.   (p. 44)   Which of the following is *not* a useful suggestion in evaluating coverage of psychological
                research and theories in popular magazines and daily newspapers?
      a.   Be skeptical.   c.   Consider the source of information.
      b.   Use creative imagination.   d.   Beware of oversimplification.

26.   (p. 44)   True-False. Individuals who can identify colors and read print while blindfolded are said to
                have dermo-optical perception. Carefully designed psychological experiments suggest that such
                abilities exist in a large segment of the population.

27.   (p. 46)   True-False. The rate of violent crimes rises and falls with lunar cycles meaning that the moon
                affects human behavior. This statement fails to distinguish correlation and causation.

28.   (p. 48)   Which of the following is not an issue involved in the ethics of psychological research?
      a.   invasion of privacy   c.   lasting harm
      b.   deception   d.   student recruitment for research

29.   (p. 48)   True-False. Stanley Milgram's research on obedience to authority, in which subjects believed
                they inflicted shocks on another person, raises the ethical issue of whether psychological
                experiments can do lasting harm.

30.   (p. 49)   True-False. Ethical guidelines for psychological research have been adopted by the American
                Psychological Association; most college psychology departments have ethics committees that
                oversee proposed research.

APPLYING YOUR KNOWLEDGE

1. Pick a psychology topic of interest to you and develop a specific question about that topic. How might you use each of the research methods in psychology to explore your question?

2. The Applications section of the text (Notes on Reading the Popular Press) discusses six different suggestions for how to be a critical, selective, and informed consumer of information. See if you can find some good examples where each of the suggestions applies.

3. In order to better understand how research in psychology is done, volunteer to be a student in a psychology study. After your experiences summarize what you did, what research method(s) the investigator used, your debriefing if any, the findings of the study, and whether there were any ethical guidelines the investigator had to consider and follow.

ANSWERS—PROGRAMMED REVIEW

1. scientific method
2. hypothesis
3. operational
4. abstract
5. Clever Hans
6. theory
7. falsifiable
8. naturalistic observations
9. tools
10. descriptions
11. observer
12. observer bias
13. observational records
14. correlational
15. coefficient; +1.00, -1.00
16. zero
17. positive; negative
18. stronger
19. increases; decreases
20. decreases
21. causation
22. linear; curvilinear
23. experiment
24. vary; subjects; record
25. subjects; experimental; control
26. variable
27. Independent; Dependent; Extraneous
28. experimental; control
29. point of reference
30. dependent variable
31. randomly
32. equal
33. extraneous
34. extraneous; dependent; independent
35. field
36. statistically
37. significant
38. 5
39. replicate
40. parascience
41. negative
42. placebo
43. 70
44. endorphins
45. single-blind
46. double-blind
47. experimenter effect
48. high, low
49. self-fulfilling prophecy
50. case studies
51. frontal lobotomy
52. experiments; animals
53. multiple personalities
54. 21
55. survey
56. proportion
57. 55; 82
58. 93
59. 1.5
60. biased
61. courtesy bias
62. 53; 37
63. skeptical
64. dermo-optical
65. Zimbardo
66. source
67. control
68. neurolinguistic
69. correlation, causation
70. violent crime
71. observation, inference
72. over-simplification
73. for example
74. ethics
75. deception
76. privacy
77. lasting harm
78. ethics committees
79. confidential; purpose; interpretation
80. liberation movement
81. 80

ANSWERS—SELF-TEST

1.	c	6.	False	11.	c	16.	d	21.	b	26.	False
2.	True	7.	b	12.	True	17.	b	22.	d	27.	True
3.	d	8.	False	13.	c	18.	d	23.	False	28.	d
4.	True	9.	a	14.	False	19.	c	24.	True	29.	True
5.	d	10.	c	15.	b	20.	a	25.	b	30.	True

ACROSS

2. relation between two events
6. repeat
7. observer sees what he expects to see
8. summarizes existing data and predicts future observation
10. educated guess
12. method polling large groups of people
14. this group provides a basis for comparison
15. _____ assignment places subjects to control and experimental groups
16. fake pill

DOWN

1. a clever mathematical horse
3. outside variables
4. variables altered by the experimenter
5. the _____ Method has five steps and follows in a logical fashion
9. used to identify cause-effect relationship
11. participants in an experiment
13. researcher carried out "shocking" experiment

The Brain, Biology, and Behavior

CONTENTS

Neurons—Building a "Biocomputer"
A Brief Tour of the Nervous System—Wired for Action
The Cerebral Cortex—My, What a Big Brain You Have!
The Subcortex—At the Core of the (Brain) Matter
The Brain in Perspective—Beyond the Biocomputer
The Endocrine System—Slow but Sure Messenger Service
Handedness—If Your Brain is Right, What's Left?
Charting the Brain's Inner Realms

TERMS AND CONCEPTS

neuron
biopsychology
dendrites
soma
axon
axon terminals
ions
cell membrane
resting potential
threshold
action potential
ion channels
all-or-nothing event
negative after-potential
myelin
neurotransmitter
synapse
receptor sites
acetylcholine
curare
noradrenaline
neuropeptides
enkephalins
endorphins
nerves
neurilemma
central nervous system (CNS)
peripheral nervous system
somatic system
autonomic system
sympathetic branch

parasympathetic branch
white matter
spinal nerves
cranial nerves
reflex arc
sensory neuron
connector neuron (interneuron)
motor neuron
effector cells
brain-body ratio
cerebrum
cerebral cortex
grey matter
corticalization
positron emission tomography (PET)
hemispheres
corpus callosum
"split brain"
electrode
occipital lobes
tumors
parietal lobes
somatosensory area
temporal lobes
primary auditory area
frontal lobes
olfaction
motor cortex
association cortex
neglect
Broca's area

Wernicke's area
aphasia
agnosia (mindblindness)
subcortex
brainstem (hindbrain)
midbrain
forebrain
medulla
cerebellum
reticular formation (RF)
reticular activating system (RAS)
thalamus
hypothalamus
limbic system
electrical stimulation of the brain (ESB)
electrode
amygdala
hippocampus
pleasure centers
aversive centers
redundancy
plasticity
endocrine system
hormone
pituitary gland
growth hormone
giantism
acromegaly

hypopituitary dwarf
thyroid gland
metabolism
hyperthyroidism
hypothyroidism
adrenaline
noradrenaline
adrenal gland
adrenal medulla
adrenal cortex
corticoids
anabolic steroids
virilism
premature puberty
handedness
lateralization
dissection
tissue staining
ablation
deep lesioning
micro-electrode recordings
computed tomography (CT)
magnetic resonance imaging (MRI)
electroencephalography (EEG)
electroencephalograph
mental activity network scanner (MANSCAN)
magnetoencephalography (MEG)

IMPORTANT INDIVIDUALS

Richard J. Haier   Robert Sperry   Alan Gevins

PROGRAMMED REVIEW

1.   (p. 53)   The human brain is about the size of a large grapefruit and weighs a little over three pounds.
              It is composed of some 100 billion nerve cells called _____.

2.   (p. 53)   Neurons specialize in carrying and processing information. They also activate muscles and
              glands. Each neuron is linked to as many as _____ others.

3.   (p. 54)   _____ is the study of how the brain and nervous system
              relate to behavior.

4.   (p. 54)   The nervous system is made up of long "chains" of neurons. No two neurons are exactly alike
              in size and shape, but most have four basic parts. One of these, the _____,
              look like the roots of a tree and serve as a receiving area for information from other neurons.

5.   (p. 54)   The _____, or cell body, also accepts incoming information, which it collects and
              combines.

6.   (p. 54)   Periodically, the soma sends nerve impulses down a long thin fiber called an _____.

7.   (p. 54) Most axons branch at their ends to form an array of _____ _____ which connect the neuron to the dendrites and somas of other nerve cells.

8.   (p. 54) Some axons are only about _____ millimeter long. Others stretch up to a _____ through the adult nervous system. They carry messages from the sensory organs to the brain, from the brain to muscles or glands, or from one neuron to the next.

9.   (p. 54) Electrically charged molecules called _____ are found in differing numbers inside and outside each nerve cell. As a result, a tiny difference in electrical charge exists across the cell membrane (or "skin").

10. (p. 54) In humans, this electrical charge, called a _____ _____, is about 70 millivolts.

11. (p. 54) Messages arriving from other neurons alter the resting potential until it reaches a _____, or trigger point, for firing of about 50 millivolts.

12. (p. 54) Reaching the threshold triggers an _____ _____, or nerve impulse, which then sweeps down the axon.

13. (p. 54) The action potential occurs because tiny tunnels, called _____ _____, pierce the axon membrane.

14. (p. 54) These channels are normally closed by molecular "gates." During an action potential, the gates pop open and allow sodium ions to rush into the axon. This happens first near the _____. Then, as the axon potential moves along, the gates open in sequence down the length of the axon.

15. (p. 54) The existence of a threshold for firing makes the action potential an _____-_____- _____ event: it occurs completely or not at all.

16. (p. 55) After an action potential occurs, the cell's voltage briefly drops below its resting level. This drop is called a negative _____-_____ and is due to an outward flow of potassium ions (K+) that occurs while the gates are open.

17. (p. 55) After each nerve impulse, the neuron must recharge. It does this by shifting _____ back across the cell membrane until the resting potential is restored.

18. (p. 55) It takes about one-thousandth of a second for a neuron to fire an impulse and return to its resting level. Thus, a maximum of about 1,000 nerve impulses per second is possible. However, firing rates of one per second to _____ or _____ per second are more typical.

19. (p. 55) The speed of an action potential depends on many factors, including axon size. In small, thin axons, impulses travel at about _____ meters (roughly, eight feet) per second and up to _____ meters per second (about 225 miles per hour) in large axons.

20. (p. 55) The speed of nerve impulses is also higher with the presence of _____ which forms a fatty layer covering some axons. This material typically has small gaps every millimeter or so which allow nerve impulses to move faster by jumping from gap to gap.

21. (p. 56) The nerve impulse is primarily an electrical event. That is why electrically stimulating the brain affects behavior. In contrast, communication between neurons is _____.

22. (p. 56) When a nerve impulse reaches the tips of the axon terminals it causes a release of
_____.

23. (p. 56) These potent chemicals cross the _____, the tiny space between two neurons.

24. (p. 56) Transmitter molecules then attach to special _____ _____ on the
dendrites and soma of the next neuron that are sensitive to neurotransmitters. This process is
also how muscles and glands are activated.

25. (p. 56) Neurotransmitters may _____ the next neuron (move it closer to firing) or
_____ it (make it less likely to discharge).

26. (p. 57) If several "exciting" messages arrive close in time, and they are not canceled by "inhibiting"
messages, the neuron reaches its threshold for firing. This means that chemical messages are
_____ before a neuron "decides" to send on its all-or-nothing message.

27. (p. 57) There are now some _____ known or suspected neurotransmitters in the brain including
acetylcholine, adrenaline, noradrenaline, serotonin, dopamine, histamine, and various amino
acids.

28. (p. 57) Thousands of drugs may affect mood and behavior by imitating, duplicating, or blocking the
actions of neurotransmitters. For example, the drug _____ attaches to receptor sites
on muscles, which prevents acetylcholine (a transmitter that normally activates muscles) from
reaching the sites. Paralysis occurs as a result.

29. (p. 57) Recently a new class of brain transmitters called _____, or simply brain
peptides, has been discovered. These chemicals seem to regulate the activity of other neurons
and in so doing affect memory, pain, emotion, pleasure, mood, hunger, sexual behavior, and
other basic processes.

30. (p. 57) The fact that some neurons have specific receptor sites for opiate drugs such as morphine led
scientists to search for natural opiatelike peptides in the brain. Scientists found that the brain
produces opiate-like neural regulators called _____ to relieve pain and
stress.

31. (p. 57) Related chemicals called _____ are released by the pituitary gland.
These chemicals, along with enkephalins, may help explain phenomena as diverse as "runner's
high," the placebo effect, and acupuncture.

32. (p. 58) When you touch something hot, you jerk your hand away. The neural messages for this action
are carried by _____. At the same time, pain may
cause the brain to release enkephalins and endorphins. These chemical regulators reduce the
pain so that it is not too disabling.

33. (p. 58) _____ are bundles of axons and dendrites often whitish in color due to a coating
of myelin.

34. (p. 58) Nerve fibers outside the brain and spinal cord usually have a thin layer of cells called
_____, which provide a tunnel through which damaged nerve fibers can grow
when repairing themselves.

35. (p. 58) If damage occurs to neurons within the _____ or _____ _____ generally no
regeneration is possible. Damage to these areas may cause permanent loss of function.

36. (p. 58) Also, if the cell body of a neuron is destroyed, the damage cannot be reversed. For example, this type of damage is the cause of _____, a crippling disease in which the cell bodies of neurons controlling muscles are destroyed.

37. (p. 58) Damage to brain cells can sometimes be repaired with grafts of healthy brain cells. In one experiment, the brains of rats were damaged in an area that affects learning. Rats that received implants of healthy brain tissue did significantly _____ on a later maze-learning test than untreated controls.

38. (p. 58) Implants may also provide a cure for some brain-centered diseases. For instance, some human patients with severe _____ disease (caused by a loss of brain cells that release dopamine) have improved greatly when dopamine-producing cells have been grafted into their brains.

39. (p. 58) A problem with brain grafts is that they are unlikely to be accepted by the body unless immature _____ cells are used. However, researchers recently succeeded in growing normal, mature brain cells in the laboratory which may eventually be available to help repair brain injuries and to treat Parkinson's disease.

40. (p. 59) Progress is also being made in coaxing regrowth of damaged neurons in the brain and spinal cord. Swiss scientists recently found a way to trigger regrowth of up to a _____ inch in the severed spinal cords of rats.

41. (p. 59) The _____ nervous system consists of the brain and spinal cord. The _____ nervous system consists of nerves which carry information to and from the CNS.

42. (p. 59) The peripheral system is divided into two subparts: the _____ system which conveys information from the sense organs and the skeletal muscles; and the _____ system which conveys information to and from the internal organs and glands.

43. (p. 59) In general, the somatic system controls _____ behavior and the autonomic system controls _____ activities.

44. (p. 49) The _____ branch of the autonomic nervous system responds during times of danger or emotion to prepare the body for "fight or flight." It arouses the body for action.

45. (p. 59) The _____ or "sustaining" branch is most active immediately after a stressful or emotional event. Its role is to return the body to a lower level of arousal and to maintain certain vital functions at moderate levels.

46. (p. 60) If you were to cut through the spinal cord, you would see columns of _____ _____, nervous tissue made up of axons which leave the spinal cord at various points to form peripheral nerves.

47. (p. 60) There are 30 pairs of _____ _____ leaving the spinal cord and one pair leaving the bottom tip.

48. (p. 60) These nerves, together with an additional _____ nerves which leave the brain directly (the cranial nerves), place the body in contact with the brain.

49. (p. 60) Within the spinal cord, the simplest behavior pattern, a _____ _____, can be carried out without any help from the brain.

50. (p. 60) The reflex arc begins when sensory information is detected by a _____ _____ and a message in the form of an action potential is carried to the spinal cord.

51. (p. 60) Next, the sensory neuron synapses with an _____, or connector neuron, inside the spinal cord, which in turn activates another connector cell, in this case a _____ _____ that leads back to muscle fibers.

52. (p. 61) The muscle fibers are made up of _____ cells which contract and move the muscle.

53. (p. 62) Relative to body size, humans have very large brains. The proportion of brain weight to body weight for humans is _____ to _____ compared, for example, with the 1 to 1000 ratio of elephants or the 1 to 10,000 ratio of sperm whales.

54. (p. 62) The only creatures that compare well with humans in both brain size and brain-body ratio are dolphins and _____. It is possible that these animals may be as intelligent (or more so) as humans. We already know that dolphins communicate with sounds as complex as our own. However, they may use larger portions of their brains for swimming and "lower" sensory-motor functions.

55. (p. 63) As we move from lower to higher animals, an ever-increasing proportion of the brain is devoted to the _____.

56. (p. 63) The outer layer of the cerebrum, known as the cerebral cortex, contains no less than _____ percent of the neurons in the central nervous system.

57. (p. 63) The cerebral cortex covers most of the visible portions of the brain with a mantle of _____ _____ (spongy tissue made up mostly of cell bodies).

58. (p. 63) Human intellectual superiority appears to be related to _____, an increase in the size and wrinkling of the cortex.

59. (p. 63) According to folklore, a person with a large head and a high forehead is likely to be intelligent. But psychologist Richard J. Haier has found that brain _____ probably has more to do with intelligence. He and his colleagues found that people who perform well on mental tests consume less energy than the brains of poor performers.

60. (p. 63) Haier measured brain activity with a technique called _____ _____ tomography or PET, a scan that records the amount of glucose (sugar) used by brain cells.

61. (p. 63) The cortex is composed of two sides, or _____. They are connected by a thick band of fibers called the _____ _____.

62. (p. 63) The two hemispheres control _____ sides of the body and perform differently on tests of language, perception, music, and other capabilities.

63. (p. 64) Roger Sperry has studied people who have had a radical form of brain surgery that disconnects the hemispheres—"_____-_____" operations. The result is a person with essentially two brains in one body.

64. (p. 64) On occasion, having two "brains" creates dilmmas like those described by Gazzaniga. However, most split-brain individuals act normally because both halves of the brain have about the same experience at the same time. Also, if any conflict arises, one hemisphere tends to _____ the other.

65. (p. 64) However, if a dollar sign is flashed to the right brain and a question mark to the left, when "split-brain" patients are asked to draw what they saw using the left hand, they draw a _____ _____. If asked to point with the right hand to a picture of what the left hand drew, they will point to a _____ _____.

66. (p. 65) The brain divides its work between the two hemispheres. For example, roughly 95 percent of all adults use the _____ brain for speaking, writing, and understanding language.

67. (p. 65) Also, the left hemisphere is better at _____, judging time and rhythm, and at coordinating complex movements (especially those needed for _____).

68. (p. 65) The right hemisphere is superior at _____ skills such as recognizing visual patterns, faces, and melodies and is also involved in detecting and expressing _____.

69. (p. 65) The right brain is also better at tasks requiring _____, and "manipulo-spatial" skills such as drawing a picture or putting together a puzzle.

70. (p. 66) It is possible to prefer right- or left-brain modes of thought. A recent study found that students who prefer _____-brain thinking tend to major in subjects such as music, journalism, art, oral communication, and architecture. A _____-brain preference was associated with majors in such subjects as management, computer science, mathematics, nursing, criminal justice, and education.

71. (p. 66) Direct studies of brain activity show that _____ hemispheres are activated for virtually all tasks. People do not rely on only one hemisphere or the other for thinking as some popularized courses seem to claim.

72. (p. 66) In general, the left hemisphere is mainly involved with _____ (breaking information into parts). It also processes information sequentially. The right hemisphere appears to process information simultaneously and _____ (all at once).

73. (p. 66) In addition to hemispheres, the cerebral cortex can be divided into several smaller areas called _____.

74. (p. 66) To determine the function of each lobe, the cortex can be activated by a small electrified needle or wire called an _____.

75. (p. 66) The functions of the cortex have also been identified by _____ _____ of changes in personality, behavior, or sensory capacity caused by diseases or injury of the brain.

76. (p. 66) The _____ lobes, located at the back of the brain, are the primary visual area of the cortex.

77. (p. 66) Patients with _____ (a growth of cells which interferes with brain activity) in the occipital lobes experience blind spots in areas of the visual field.

78. (p. 66) Visual images are mapped onto the cortex, but the map is greatly stretched and _____. It does not create a TV-like image.

79. (p. 66) The _____ lobes are located just above the occipital lobes.

80. (p. 66) Touch, temperature, pressure and other somatic, or bodily sensations are channeled to the _____ area on the parietal lobes.

81. (p. 66) The correspondence between areas of the parietal lobes and parts of the body is not a perfect one. As a map of the sensations, the cortex reflects the _____ of areas, not their size.

82. (p. 66) The _____ lobes are located on each side of the brain. They are the site where hearing registers.

83. (p. 66) If we were to stimulate the _____ _____ area of a temporal lobe, our subject would "hear" a series of sounds.

84. (p. 67) Sound qualities are clearly mapped on the surface of the cortex. Sounds from top to bottom vary in _____, while stimulation in another direction affects _____.

85. (p. 67) For most people, the _____ temporal lobe also contains a language "center." Damage to this area can severely limit ability to use language.

86. (p. 67) The _____ lobes perform a mixture of functions. For one thing, _____ (smell) information registers on the underside of these lobes.

87. (p. 67) The _____ _____, an arch of tissue running over the top of the brain, directs the body's muscles. Like the somatosensory area, it corresponds to the importance of bodily areas, not to their size.

88. (p. 67) Damage to the frontal lobes in humans tends to alter personality and _____. Doing intellectual tasks based on reasoning or planning also seems to rely on the frontal lobes. Patients with frontal lobe damage often get "stuck" on such tasks and repeat the same wrong answers.

89. (p. 68) Frontal lboe damage in childhood leads to a lowered adult _____ and significant social impairment.

90. (p. 68) All other areas of the cerebral cortex besides the primary sensory and motor areas, are called the _____ cortex. The size and relative amount of these areas increase strikingly as one ascends the evolutionary scale.

91. (p. 68) The association cortex seems to process and combine information from the various senses. It is probably also related to higher mental abilities. The _____ lobes' link with thinking skills is a good example of such abilities.

92. (p. 68) Damage to the right brain often results in paralysis on the _____ side of the body; this situation is reversed for damage to the left brain.

93. (p. 68) Damage to the right hemisphere may also cause a curious problem called _____. Affected patients pay no attention to the left side of visual space. Often, the patient will not eat food on the left side of a plate and may refuse to acknowledge a paralyzed left arm as his or her own.

94. (p. 68) Brain injuries may also impair the special abilities of the hemispheres. A person with damage in the _____ brain may lose the ability to speak, read, write, or spell. Yet the same person may remain able to draw or hum with skill.

95. (p. 68) Persons with right brain damage may get _____ while driving, or they may have difficulty understanding _____ and pictures. Yet they can speak and read as before.

96. (p. 68) A person with _____ brain damage may not understand what you say, but he or she will pick up your emotional tone. With _____ hemisphere damage, the person can understand what is said but fails to recognize if it is spoken in an angry or humorous way.

97. (p. 68) Generally, damage to the left hemisphere is more serious. However, if you are an artist, right brain dysfunction may be more problematic. For instance, painters with right brain damage may neglect the left side of the canvas, distort outlines, or portray _____ and _____ subject matter.

98. (p. 68) Injury to cortical areas related to language can cause _____, meaning an impaired ability to use language.

99. (p. 68) Persons with damage in _____ area can read and understand the speech of others, but have great difficulty speaking or writing. Typically, their grammar and pronunciation is poor and their speech is slow and labored.

100. (p. 69) In Wernicke's aphasia, grammar is normal and pronunciation is correct, but the person has problems with the _____ of words. People with such injuries often speak in incredibly roundabout ways to avoid using certain nouns.

101. (p. 69) Brain injury which involves an inability to identify seen objects is called _____ and sometimes referred to as _____.

102. (p. 69) Someone with agnosia might describe or draw a viewed object correctly, yet be unable to name it. This condition is not limited to objects however, for some patients demonstrate _____ _____, the inability to identify familiar persons.

103. (p. 69) Study of facial agnosias shows that a brain area devoted to recognizing others is located on the underside of the _____ _____.

104. (p. 70) Structures below the cerebral cortex are collectively termed the subcortex. They can be divided into three general areas called the _____ or _____, the _____, and the _____.

105. (p. 70) One part of the brainstem, the _____, contains centers important for the reflex control of vital life functions such as heart rate, breathing, and swallowing.

106. (p. 70) Various drugs, diseases, or injuries can interrupt the vital functions of the medulla enough to end or endanger life. That's why a karate chop to the back of the _____, like those depicted in movies, can be extremely dangerous.

107. (p. 70) The other component of the brainstem, the _____, lies at the base of the brain and is closely connected to many areas in the brain and spinal cord.

108. (p. 70) The cerebellum primarily regulates posture, muscle tone, and muscular coordination. It may also play a role in some types of _____.

109. (p. 71) The importance of the cerebellum is indicated by the effects of a crippling disease called _____ _____. This disease first produces tremor, dizziness, and muscular weakness. Eventually, victims have difficulty standing, walking, or even feeding themselves.

110. (p. 71) In a cavity within the medulla, brainstem, and pons is a network of fibers and cell bodies called the _____ _____ (RF). It acts as a kind of central clearinghouse for most of the information coming to and from the brain. It gives priority to some incoming messages while excluding others, basically what we mean by _____, and appears to be responsible for alertness and wakefulness.

111. (p. 71) Incoming impulses from the sense organs branch into the reticular formation where they form a _____ _____ _____ which bombards the cortex with stimulation, keeping it active and alert.

112. (p. 71) Destroying the RAS causes animals to enter a _____ resembling sleep. Electrical stimulation of the same area instantly _____ sleeping animals.

113. (p. 71) The _____ of the forebrain is a football-shaped structure that acts as a final "switching station" for sensory information on its way to the cortex.

114. (p. 71) Injury to even small areas of the thalamus could cause deafness, blindness, or loss of any of the other senses, except _____.

115. (p. 71) The _____ of the forebrain is about the size of a thumbnail (in humans) and is a kind of master control center for emotion and many basic motives. It's a sort of "crossroads" that connects with many other areas of the cortex and subcortex.

116. (p. 71) The hypothalamus acts as a "final path" for many kinds of behavior leaving the brain. It has been implicated in the control of behaviors as diverse as _____, rage, _____ control, _____ release, eating and drinking, sleep, waking, and emotion.

117. (p. 71) The hypothalamus, parts of the thalamus, and several structures buried within the cortex form the _____ _____. As a group they share a role in the production of _____ and _____ behavior.

118. (p. 71) _____ _____ of the brain is used to explore brain-behavior connections. This technique allows an animal (or person) to function normally while the experimenter turns various brain areas on and off.

119. (p. 71) ESB begins with the implantation of thin metal _____ deep within the brain. They can be used to electrically activate a specific brain area.

120. (p. 71) Electrical activation of parts of the limbic system often produces emotional responses. During medical testing one woman reacted with a sudden outburst of anger when the _____ was stimulated.

121. (p. 72) When the _____ lobe was activated, another patient giggled, became flirtatious, said she enjoyed the stimulation very much, and expressed a desire to marry the therapist. When ESB ceased, she again became quiet, reserved, and proper.

122. (p. 72) The details of emotions and behaviors elicited by ESB are usually modified by the individual's _____ and by the situation. It would be impossible for anyone to enslave people by "radio controlling" their brains.

123. (p. 72) During evolution, the limbic system was the _____ layer of the forebrain to develop. In lower, relatively primitive animals, the limbic system helps organize the appropriate response to stimuli: feeding, fleeing, fighting, or reproduction.

124. (p. 72) In humans, the link to emotion remains. However, some parts of the limbic system have taken on additional, higher-level functions. For example, the _____, found at the core of the temporal lobes, appears to be linked to memory.

125. (p. 73) Several reward or "_____" pathways have been found in the limbic system, and many in the hypothalamus where they overlap with areas associated with drives such as thirst, sex, and hunger. Rats can be trained to press a bar to receive stimulation of these areas.

126. (p. 73) Commonly abused drugs, such as _____, amphetamine, heroin, _____, _____, and alcohol activate many of the same pleasure pathways. This appears to explain, in part, the rewarding properties of such drugs.

127. (p. 73) In addition, punishment or "_____" areas have been found. When these areas are stimulated, animals show discomfort and will work to turn off the stimulation.

128. (p. 73) One reason for the brain's great complexity is the fact that it shows tremendous _____, or duplication. This phenomenon yields an impressive capacity for reorganization and recovery after injury.

129. (p. 73) Children show greater _____ (or flexibility) of brain organization than adults. As examples, children under the age of two can usually shift language processing to the right brain.

130. (p. 73) If left hemispheric damage occurs between ages two and _____, language areas remain in the left brain but shift to new locations.

131. (p. 73) As adults, people born without a _____ _____ can answer questions from both hemispheres, and can write, draw, and solve block-design puzzles with both hands.

132. (p. 73) In general, brain plasticity appears to be based on increased branching of dendrites. After age _____, such plasticity becomes rare.

133. (p. 73) The brain is both highly vulnerable and amazingly resilient. Brain damage before age _____ almost always lowers adult IQ.

134. (p. 73) In an astounding case, an adult who had the entire _____ hemisphere of his brain removed at age five was able to speak, read, write, and comprehend so well that he maintained a double major in college and has an above average IQ despite being paralyzed on the right side and blind in his right visual field.

135. (p. 73)   The nervous system is not the only communication network in the body. The _____ _____ is made up of a number of glands which pour chemicals directly into the bloodstream.

136. (p. 73)   These chemicals, called _____, are carried throughout the body where they affect internal activities and behavior.

137. (p. 73)   Hormones are chemically related to neurotransmitters. Like transmitters, hormones activate cells in the body. To respond, the cells must have _____ _____ for the hormone.

138. (p. 73)   The _____ is a small grape-sized structure hanging from the base of the brain. It is important in the regulation of bodily growth.

139. (p. 74)   The pituitary secretes _____ hormone that speeds bodily development. If too little is released, a person may remain far smaller than average. Too much of this hormone produces _____.

140. (p. 74)   Secretion of too much growth hormone late in the growth period causes enlargement of the arms, hands, feet, and facial bones. This condition is known as _____.

141. (p. 74)   Insufficient production of growth hormone can cause children to fall _____ to _____ inches behind agemates in height. As adults, some will be _____ _____ who are perfectly proportioned, but tiny.

142. (p. 75)   Dwarfism used to be treated with injections of human growth hormone extracted from the pituitary glands of human cadavers. Now, a _____ growth hormone has become available. Its use should be weighed against various medical and ethical issues.

143. (p. 75)   The pituitary also regulates the thyroid, adrenal glands, ovaries, and testes, which in turn regulate reproduction, metabolism, and responses to stress. Because of its many effects, the pituitary is often called the "_____ _____."

144. (p. 75)   The _____, which lies directly above the pituitary in the brain directs the activity of the pituitary and provides the major link between the brain and the glandular system.

145. (p. 75)   The _____ gland is found in the neck, on each side of the windpipe. It regulates _____ (the rate of energy production and expenditure in the body).

146. (p. 75)   The thyroid can have a sizeable effect on personality. A person with an overactive thyroid, termed _____, tends to be thin, tense, excitable, and nervous.

147. (p. 75)   An underactive thyroid, termed _____, in an adult can cause inactivity, sleepiness, slowness, and overweight. In infancy this condition limits development of the nervous system and can cause severe mental retardation.

148. (p. 75)   When you are frightened or angry, important changes take place in your body that are brought about by the ANS. The sympathetic branch of the ANS causes the hormones _____ and _____ to be released by the adrenal glands, which are located just under the back of the rib cage, atop the kidneys.

149. (p. 75)   The _____ _____ or inner core of the adrenal glands is the source of adrenaline and noradrenaline.

150. (p. 75) The _____ _____, or outer "bark" of the adrenal glands, produces a second set of important hormones called _____ which regulate salt balance in the body, help the body resist stress, and are a secondary source of sex hormones.

151. (p. 75) Athletes sometimes use _____ _____, a synthetic version of male corticoids, in efforts to promote muscle growth. However, there is no evidence that they improve performance and they may cause voice deepening or baldness in women, and shrinkage of the testicles or breast development in men. For some users they may cause emotional disturbances and near-psychotic reactions.

152. (p. 75) An over-secretion of the adrenal sex hormones can cause _____, in which a woman grows a beard or a man's voice becomes so low it is difficult to understand.

153. (p. 75) Over-secretion of sex hormones in children may cause _____ _____, resulting in full sexual development. Such was the remarkable case of a 5-year-old Peruvian girl who gave birth to a son.

154. (p. 77) There is no real difference in the strength or dexterity of the hands themselves. The agility of the dominant hand is an outward expression of superior motor control on one side of the _____.

155. (p. 77) It is not necessarily true that the right rain is dominant in left-handed people. About _____ percent of left-handers produce speech from the left hemisphere, just as 97 percent of right-handed people do. About a quarter of all lefties use their right brain for language, while approximately _____ percent of left-handers use both sides of the brain for language processing.

156. (p. 77) The way a person writes can be a clue to which hemisphere is dominant. Right-handed individuals who write with a straight hand, and lefties who write with a hooked hand, are usually _____-brain dominant for language. Left-handed people who write with their hand below the line, and righties who use a hooked position, are usually _____-brain dominant.

157. (p. 77) Writing position is not a foolproof sign of brain organization. The only sure way to determine brain dominance is to do a medical test that involves briefly _____ one cerebral hemisphere at a time.

158. (p. 78) Animals such as monkeys show definite hand preferences, split about 50-50 between right and left. Among humans the split is about _____-_____ in favor of right-handedness. This probably reflects the left brain's specialization for language production.

159. (p. 78) A recent study of ultrasound images made before birth showed that even during fetal development clear hand preferences are apparent. This suggests that handedness is _____.

160. (p. 78) However, left handedness can also be caused by elevated levels of _____ hormones in the womb and by various birth _____.

161. (p. 78) Early preference for handedness underscores the fact that parents should never try to force a left-handed child to use the right hand. To do so invites _____ or _____ problems.

162. (p. 78) Lefties living in a right-handed world run a greater risk of suffering accidental _____ and _____.

163. (p. 78)   The subgroup of people who are left-handed because of birth traumas have a higher incidence of _____, _____ disorders, and other problems. But genetic left-handedness, which accounts for most lefties, shows no correlation to general _____.

164. (p. 78)   A notable number of _____ have been lefties. Conceivably, since the right hemisphere is superior at imagery and visual abilities, there is some advantage to using the left hand for drawing or painting.

165. (p. 78)   The left-handed do seem better at putting together verbal and pictorial symbols or ideas. This may be why there are more left-handed _____ and _____ than would be expected.

166. (p. 78)   Left-handed individuals are generally less _____, that is, they show less specialization in the two sides of the brain.

167. (p. 78)   The physical _____ and _____ of the cerebral hemispheres are more alike among left-handers. Generally, left-handers are more symmetrical on almost everything, including eye dominance, fingerprints, foot size, etc.

168. (p. 78)   In some situations, less lateralization may be an advantage. Individuals who are moderately left-handed or ambidextrous seem to have better than average _____ _____, a basic music skill.

169. (p. 78)   More musicians are _____ than would normally be expected. It's not clear, however, if those who are musically gifted were initially _____ lateralized or if playing music develops both hands, or possibly both sides of the brain.

170. (p. 78)   Math abilities may also benefit from fuller use of the _____ hemisphere. Extremely mathematically gifted students are much more likely to be left handed or ambidextrous than other students are.

171. (p. 78)   The clearest advantage to being left-handed and mildly lateralized comes up when brain injury occurs. Lefties typically experience less _____ loss after damage to either hemisphere and recover more easily.

172. (p. 79)   Researchers use _____, separation into parts, to identify major brain structures and pathways. This is often aided by chemically staining thin slices of brain tissue so smaller details become visible.

173. (p. 79)   Many studies in biopsychology are based on _____, surgical removal, of parts of the brain. When this is followed by a change in behavior or capacity, we gain insight into the purpose of the missing structure.

174. (p. 80)   In _____ _____, a thin wire electrode, insulated except at the tip, is lowered into a selected target area inside the brain. An electric current is then used to destroy a small amount of brain tissue and the observed changes then noted.

175. (p. 80)   It is also possible to activate target areas, rather than removing them, by using a weaker current. This is called _____ _____ of the brain (abbreviated _____).

176. (p. 80)   The _____ signals of the brain can also be directly measured. By using wire probes and special measuring devices, you record activity in various circuits of the brain to assess functioning.

177. (p. 80)   Researchers use electrodes to record the firing of large populations of neurons within the brain. Even more revealing, are _____-_____ recordings. Here a tiny glass tube filled with a salty, electrically conducting fluid is used to measure the activity of a single neuron.

178. (p. 80)   Computerized scanning equipment has virtually revolutionized the study of brain diseases and injuries. For instance, _____ _____ scanning is a specialized type of X-ray that does a much better job of making the interior of the brain visible than conventional X-rays.

179. (p. 80)   In a CT scan, the head is placed inside a large doughnut-shaped metal ring and very thin X-ray beams are passed through from all points. The X-ray information is collected by a computer and formed into an image of the brain. The scan can reveal the effects of _____, _____, tumors, and other brain disorders.

180. (p. 80)   _____ _____ imaging uses a very strong magnetic field, rather than X-rays, to produce an image of the body's interior.

181. (p. 80)   During an MRI scan, the body is placed inside a magnetic field. A detector measures how each hydrogen atom in the body responds to the magnetism. Processing by a computer then creates a composite, _____-_____ representation of the brain or body.

182. (p. 80)   _____ measures the waves of electrical activity produced by the brain.

183. (p. 80)   EEG involves placing small disk-shaped metal electrodes at various locations on a person's scalp. Electrical impulses from the brain are detected by the electrodes and sent to an _____ which amplifies these very weak signals and records them on a moving sheet of paper.

184. (p. 80)   Various brain-wave patterns can help identify the presence of _____, _____ and other diseases. The EEG also reveals changes in brain activity during sleep, daydreaming, hypnosis, and other mental states.

185. (p. 81)   Neuroscientist Alan Gevins has developed a new technique called the _____ _____ _____ scanner. It consists of a soft helmet that records EEG data from 124 points. A computer tracks brain wave activity and maps it onto a three-dimensional MRI scan of the brain.

186. (p. 81)   MANSCAN takes 250 "snapshots" of brain waves per second. After processing and analysis, the computer creates a diagram of brain activity. This is providing new information on _____, mental _____, coordination, and _____ use.

187. (p. 82)   _____ _____ _____ scans detect sub-atomic particles emitted by weakly radioactive glucose as it is consumed by the brain. It shows which brain areas are using more energy. A computer is used to create a moving, color picture of changes in brain activity.

188. (p. 82) In a further refinement of the PET scan, tiny amounts of a radioactive _____ compound are injected into a person's bloodstream. It remains active for only a few minutes, while glucose is active for several hours.

189. (p. 82) Each dose of oxygen allows a brief PET scan to be made and compared with others in a way that isolates a fleeting moment of brain activity. This procedure has revealed that very specific brain areas are active when you are reading, hearing, saying, or thinking about the meaning of a _____.

190. (p. 82) PET images of this type can also be superimposed on an MRI scan. The _____ scan shows the brain in detail and the _____ scan tells which areas are linked with various abilities.

191. (p. 82) Newer techniques are being developed to make full use of computerized imaging techniques. One is called _____. It uses exotic electronic devices to detect the exceedingly weak magnetic fields created when neurons fire.

SELF-TEST

1.   (p. 54) Which of the following is not part of a neuron?
     a. axon   c. soma
     b. effector cells   d. dendrites

2.   (p. 54) The long, thin neural fiber along which nerve impulses travel is the:
     a. axon   c. dendrite
     b. soma   d. synapse

3.   (p. 54) The firing of a nerve impulse down the axon is called a(n):
     a. resting potential   c. moving potential
     b. action threshold   d. action potential

4.   (p. 54) Which of the following is not associated with the firing of a neuron?
     a. all-or-nothing event   c. exceeding threshold
     b. negative after-potential   d. reticular potential

5.   (p. 56) When a nerve impulse reaches the tips of the axon terminals, it causes a release of _____ across the _____.
     a. myelin, dendrites   c. neurotransmitters, synapse
     b. sodium ions, soma   d. adrenaline, arc

6.   (p. 56) True-False. Neurotransmitters may either excite or inhibit an adjoining neuron when they attach to the receptor sites on the dendrites or soma.

7.   (p. 57) True-False. Many drugs imitate or duplicate the effects of neurotransmitters, while other drugs like curare block the action of certain neurotransmitters.

8.   (p. 57) Natural relief from pain and stress, the placebo effect, acupuncture, and "runnner's high" have all been linked with:
     a. enkephalins and endorphins   c. corticalization
     b. myelin and neurilemma   d. corticoids and steroids

9. (p. 58) Nerve fibers outside the brain and spinal cord usually have a thin layer of cells called:
    a. myelin   c. neurilemma
    b. nuclei   d. soma

10. (p. 58) True-False. Implants of healthy dopamine-producing tissue into diseased brain areas has recently been shown to be helpful in the treatment of Parkinson's disease.

11. (p. 59) True-False. The central nervous system is composed of two subparts, the somatic and autonomic systems.

12. (p. 59) The _____ branch of the autonomic nervous system responds during times of arousal or emotional upheaval to prepare the body for "fight or flight."
    a. sympathetic   c. parasympathetic
    b. peripheral   d. somatic

13. (p. 60) Which of the following represents the sequence of neuronal travel in a spinal cord reflex arc?
    a. sensory neuron, interneuron, motor neuron, effector cells
    b. effector cells, connector neuron, motor neuron, sensory neuron
    c. motor neuron, effector cells, sensory neuron, connector neuron
    d. sensory neuron, effector cells, interneuron, motor neuron

14. (p. 63) True-False. In most people, the left side of the brain controls the left side of the body.

15. (p. 64) When the corpus callosum is severed, the resulting condition is referred to as:
    a. "split-brain"   c. spinocerebellar degeneration
    b. hypothyroidism   d. hyperthyroidism

16. (p. 66) Usually, the left hemisphere is superior to the right for which of the following functions?
    a. spatial tasks
    b. perceptual skills
    c. recognition of patterns, faces, and melodies
    d. language

17. (p. 66) The visual area of the brain is the:
    a. temporal lobes   c. occipital lobes
    b. frontal lobes   d. parietal lobes

18. (p. 66) Touch, temperature, pressure, and other somatic functions are channeled to which area of the brain?
    a. temporal lobes   c. occipital lobes
    b. frontal lobes   d. parietal lobes

19. (p. 66) The brain sites in which hearing is registered are the:
    a. parietal lobes   c. temporal lobes
    b. occipital lobes   d. frontal lobes

20. (p. 67) Which of the following is not associated with the temporal lobes?
    a. hearing   c. dream-like experiences when stimulated
    b. storage of long-term memories   d. olfaction

21. (p. 67) Olfaction, muscle action, and time judgments are among the functions performed by the:
    a. temporal lobes   c. frontal lobes
    b. hypothalamus   d. brainstem

22. (p. 68)   True-False. All areas of the brain not specifically sensory or motor in function are collectively called the association cortex.

23. (p. 68)   A brain-injured individual who has normal grammar and correct pronunciation, but has problems with the meaning of words is most likely suffering from which of the following?
   a.   Broca's aphasia   c.   Wernicke's aphasia
   b.   spinocerebellar degeneration   d.   agnosia

24. (p. 69)   True-False. Persons with damage in Broca's area can read and understand the speech of others, but may speak in incredibly roundabout ways to avoid using certain nouns.

25. (p. 69)   The condition in which an individual is unable to identify seen objects or even familiar faces is known as:
   a.   Wernicke's aphasia   c.   Broca's aphasia
   b.   agnosticism   d.   agnosia

26. (p. 69)   True-False. Persons suffering from facial agnosia can recognize familiar faces they see, but not the voices of the same individuals when heard.

27. (p. 70)   The _____ contains centers important for the reflex control of vital life functions, including heart rate, swallowing and breathing.
   a.   reticular formation   c.   medulla
   b.   cerebellum   d.   forebrain

28. (p. 70)   The _____, a part of the hindbrain located at the base of the brain, functions primarily to regulate posture, muscle tone, and muscular coordination.
   a.   cerebellum   c.   medulla
   b.   reticular formation   d.   corpus callosum

29. (p. 71)   Which of the following is not a function of the reticular formation?
   a.   acts as a clearinghouse directing information to and from the brain
   b.   responsible for alertness and wakefulness by bombarding the cortex with stimulation
   c.   responsible for attention: gives priority to some incoming messages while excluding others
   d.   regulates basic drives such as hunger, thirst, and sex

30. (p. 71)   The _____ acts as a final "switching station" by relaying visual, auditory, taste, and touch information to the cortex after undergoing preliminary processing and analysis.
   a.   medulla   c.   hypothalamus
   b.   reticular formation   d.   thalamus

31. (p. 71)   The _____ acts as a "final path" for many kinds of behavior leaving the brain and is involved in the control of sex, eating, drinking, sleeping and emotion.
   a.   medulla   c.   hypothalamus
   b.   reticular formation   d.   thalamus

32. (p. 71)   The _____ is important in the production of emotion and motivated behavior, including rage, fear, sexual response, and other intense arousal.
   a.   limbic system   c.   corpus callosum
   b.   reticular formation   d.   frontal lobe

33. (p. 72)   True-False. Animals can be trained to press a lever in order to deliver electrical stimulation to "pleasure" centers of the brain or to turn off stimulation directed at "aversive" areas of the brain.

34. (p. 73) True-False. One of the reasons why the brain demonstrates an impressive capacity for reorganization and recovery after injury is that there is so little redundancy in the functions of the brain.

35. (p. 73) True-False. Plasticity refers to changes in brain functions which result from corticalization.

36. (p. 73) Which of the following is not a function of the pituitary gland?
    a. regulation of emotion and motivated behavior
    b. regulation of bodily growth
    c. regulation of other important glands
    d. regulation of milk production during pregnancy

37. (p. 74) Which of the following is not a condition which can result from inadequate hormonal regulation by the pituitary gland?
    a. giantism   c. amygdalism
    b. acromegaly   d. dwarfism

38. (p. 75) Which of the following conditions would NOT be expected to result from inadequate functioning of the thyroid gland?
    a. thinness, tenseness, excitability, nervousness
    b. hearing loss combined with impaired vision and an inability to spatially locate objects
    c. underactivity, sleepiness, slowness, and overweight
    d. limited development of the nervous system and severe mental retardation

39. (p. 75) The source of adrenaline and noradrenaline, important when you are frightened or angry, is the:
    a. thyroid gland   c. adrenal cortex
    b. adrenal medulla   d. hypothalamus

40. (p. 75) The functions of corticoids include which of the following?
    a. salt regulation, adjustment to stress, secondary source of sex hormones
    b. regulates metabolism and has important implications for personality
    c. regulates bodily growth, directs connecting glands, produces milk during pregnancy
    d. builds muscles, increases strength, improves performance

41. (p. 75) Virilism, premature puberty, and powerful cravings for salt are all conditions associated with inadequate functioning of the:
    a. thyroid gland   c. pituitary gland
    b. thalamus   d. adrenal glands

42. (p. 77) True-False. About a quarter of left-handed people produce speech from the right brain, compared with three percent for right-handed individuals.

43. (p. 77) A clue to determine hemisphere dominance is to observe:
    a. eye movements   c. agility
    b. how a person writes   d. handedness

44. (p. 78) Which of the following is not true of handedness?
    a. About 10 percent of humans are left-handed.
    b. Handedness is an hereditary characteristic.
    c. Parents should insist that left-handed children become right hand dominant.
    d. About 15 percent of lefties use both sides of the brain for language processing.

45. (p. 78) Which of the following professionals have a higher percentage of left-handers than would be expected?
    a.   architects and engineers   c.   athletes and coaches
    b.   teachers and scholars   d.   nurses and doctors

46. (p. 78) Left-handers are generally less brain lateralized than right-handers, meaning that:
    a.   there is less distinct specialization in the two sides of the brain
    b.   there is less dependency upon the lateral part of the brain
    c.   there is less specialization, and thus less plasticity
    d.   there is more asymmetry in the size and shape of the two hemispheres

47. (p. 79) Which of the following is not a procedure used by researchers to study the brain?
    a.   dissection   c.   axon terminal grafting
    b.   ablation   d.   deep lesioning

48. (p. 80) True-False. It is now possible to detect the activity of a single neuron through the use of micro-electrode recordings.

49. (p. 80) Which of the following uses X-ray information collected by a computer to form an image of the brain?
    a.   MEG   c.   CT
    b.   MRI   d.   PET

50. (p. 80) Which of the following can produce a three-dimensional representation of the brain based on how hydrogen atoms in the body react to magnetism?
    a.   MEG   c.   CT
    b.   MRI   d.   PET

51. (p. 81) MANSCAN is a technique
    a.   used to create a diagram of brain activity based on 124 EEG points taking 250 "snapshots" of brain waves each second.
    b.   used to assess changes in brain activity based on changes in brain glucose composition.
    c.   that uses exotic electronic devices to detect the exceedingly weak magnetic fields created when neurons fire.
    d.   whereby very thin X-rays are passed through the head and a computer collects the information and creates an image of the brain.

ANSWERS—PROGRAMMED REVIEW

1.	neurons	15.	all-or-nothing	29.	neuropeptides
2.	15,000	16.	negative after-potential	30.	enkephalins
3.	Biopsychology	17.	ions	31.	endorphins
4.	dendrites	18.	300; 400	32.	neurotransmitters
5.	soma	19.	2.5; 100	33.	Nerves
6.	axon	20.	myelin	34.	neurilemma
7.	axon terminals	21.	molecular	35.	brain; spinal cord
8.	0.1, meter	22.	neurotransmitters	36.	polio
9.	ions	23.	synapse	37.	better
10.	resting potential	24.	receptor sites	38.	Parkison's
11.	threshold	25.	excite; inhibit	39.	fetal
12.	action potential	26.	combined	40.	half
13.	ion channels	27.	30	41.	central; peripheral
14.	soma	28.	curare	42.	somatic; autonomic

43. voluntary; involuntary
44. sympathetic
45. parasympathetic
46. white matter
47. spinal nerves
48. 12
49. reflex arc
50. sensory neuron
51. interneuron; motor neuron
52. effector
53. 1 to 60
54. porpoises
55. cerebrum
56. 70
57. gray matter
58. corticalization
59. efficiency
60. positron emission
61. hemispheres; corpus callosum
62. opposite
63. split-brain
64. override
65. dollar sign; question mark
66. left
67. math; speech
68. perceptual; emotion
69. visualization
70. right; left
71. both
72. analysis; holistically
73. lobes
74. electrode
75. clinical studies
76. occipital
77. tumors
78. distorted
79. parietal
80. somatosensory
81. sensitivity
82. temporal
83. primary auditory
84. pitch; loudness
85. left
86. frontal; olfactory
87. motor cortex
88. emotionality
89. IQ
90. association
91. frontal
92. left

93. neglect
94. left
95. lost; diagrams
96. left; right
97. bizarre, repulsive
98. aphasia
99. Broca's
100. meaning
101. agnosia; mindblindness
102. facial agnosia
103. occipital lobes
104. brainstem, hindbrain; midbrain, forebrain
105. medulla
106. neck
107. medulla
108. memory
109. spinocerebellar degeneration
110. reticular formation; attention
111. reticular activating system
112. coma; awakens
113. thalamus
114. smell
115. hypothalamus
116. sex; temperature; hormone
117. limbic system; emotion; motivated
118. Electrical stimulation
119. electrodes
120. amygdala
121. temporal
122. personality
123. earliest
124. hippocampus
125. pleasure
126. cocaine; nicotine; marijuana
127. aversive
128. redundancy
129. plasticity
130. five
131. corpus callosum
132. 10
133. five
134. left
135. endocrine system
136. hormones
137. receptor sites
138. pituitary

139. growth; giantism
140. acromegaly
141. 6; 12; hypopituitary dwarfs
142. synthetic
143. master gland
144. hypothalamus
145. thyroid; metabolism
146. hyperthyroidism
147. hypothyroidism
148. adrenaline, noradrenaline
149. adrenal medulla
150. adrenal cortex; corticoids
151. anabolic steroids
152. virilism
153. premature puberty
154. brain
155. 60; 15
156. left; right
157. anesthetizing
158. 90-10
159. genetic
160. male; traumas
161. speech, reading
162. injury; death
163. allergies; learning; intelligence
164. artists
165. architects, engineers
166. lateralized
167. size, shape
168. pitch memory
169. ambidextrous; less
170. right
171. language
172. dissection
173. ablation
174. deep lesioning
175. electrical stimulation; ESB
176. electrical
177. micro-electrical
178. computed tomography
179. strokes, injuries
180. Magnetic resonance
181. three-dimensional
182. Electroencephalography
183. electroencephalograph
184. tumors, epilepsy
185. mental activity network
186. memory; fatigue; language

187. Positron emission   188. oxygen   190. MRI; PET
     tomography   189. word   191. magnetoencephalography

ANSWERS—SELF-TEST

1.	b	10.	True	19.	c	28.	a	37.	c	46.	a
2.	a	11.	False	20.	d	29.	d	38.	b	47.	c
3.	d	12.	a	21.	c	30.	d	39.	b	48.	True
4.	d	13.	a	22.	True	31.	c	40.	a	49.	c
5.	c	14.	False	23.	c	32.	a	41.	d	50.	b
6.	True	15.	a	24.	False	33.	True	42.	True	51.	a
7.	True	16.	d	25.	d	34.	False	43.	b		
8.	a	17.	c	26.	False	35.	False	44.	c		
9.	c	18.	d	27.	c	36.	a	45.	a		

ACROSS

4. chemicals crossing synapse
6. usually carries messages away from soma
9. drug used as arrow poison by S. American Indians
11. lobe associated with touch, temperature and pressure
13. this branch prepares you for "fight or flight"
16. relay station to cortex for sensory information
17. damage to this area causes difficulty in speaking and writing

DOWN

1. lobe associated with hearing and language
2. damage to this lobe decreases ability to think, reason and plan
3. this branch calms the body to a lower level of arousal
5. tiny gap between neurons
7. "tunnel" by which damaged nerve fibers can repair themselves
8. corpus _____ connects the two brain hemispheres
10. tumors found in this lobe may cause visual problems.
12. "mindblindness"
14. cell body of neuron
15. electrical stimulation of the brain (abbr.)

■ Chapter 4 ■

Sensation and Reality

Contents

Terms and Concepts

data reduction system
electromagnetic spectrum
transducer
perceptual features
feature detectors
phosphenes
localization of function
sensations
psychophysics
absolute threshold
photon
hertz
perceptual defense
limen
subliminal perception
difference threshold
just noticeable difference (JND)
Weber's law
visible spectrum
hue
saturation
brightness
lens
photoreceptors
retina
cornea
accommodation
hyperopia
myopia

astigmatism
presbyopia
iris
pupil
dilation
constriction
rods
cones
blind spot
fovea
visual acuity
peripheral vision
tunnel vision
trichromatic theory
opponent-process theory
afterimage
visual pigments
color blindness
color weakness
Ishihara test
dark adaptation
rhodopsin
retinal
night blindness
compression
rarefaction
sound waves
frequency
pitch

amplitude
loudness
pinna
eardrum
auditory ossicles
malleus
incus
stapes
oval widow
cochlea
hair cells
organ of Corti
frequency theory
place theory
hunter's notch
conduction deafness
somesthetic senses
skin senses
kinesthetic senses
vestibular senses
visceral pain
referred pain
somatic pain
sensory adaptation

physiological nystagmus
selective attention
sensory gates
gate control theory
acupuncture
beta-endorphin
prepared childbirth training
counterirritation
space adaptation syndrome
otolith organs
semicircular canals
ampulla
sensory conflict theory
nerve deafness
cochlear implants
stimulation deafness
temporary threshold shift
tinnitus
chemical senses
olfaction
gustation
anosmia
lock and key theory
taste bud

IMPORTANT INDIVIDUALS

Jerome Lettvin	David Hubel	Ronald Melzack
John Vokey	Torsten Wiesel	Patrick Wall
Don Read		

PROGRAMMED REVIEW

1. (p. 87) Our sensory organs can detect only a limited range of physical energies. They act as a _____ _____ system in boiling down floods of information into a select stream of useful data.

2. (p. 87) Using vision as an example, "light" is only a small slice of the _____ _____ which also includes infrared and ultraviolet light, radio frequencies, television broadcasts, gamma rays, and other energies.

3. (p. 87) Selection of information reduces confusion that would be overwhelming if we were sensitive to all energies. One way our sensory system facilitates selection is the fact that sensory receptors act as biological _____, converting one kind of energy into another.

4. (p. 87) Each sensory receptor is most sensitive to a select range of energy, which it most easily translates into nerve impulses. Also, many sensory systems _____ the environment into important features before sending nerve impulses to the brain.

5. (p. 87) _____ _____ are basic elements of a stimulus pattern, such as line, shapes, edges, spots, or colors. The neural circuits of many sensory systems act as feature detectors. In other words, they are highly attuned to specific stimulus patterns.

6. (p. 87) For example, a frog's eye seems to be especially sensitive to small, dark, moving spots. It seems that the frog's eyes are "wired" to detect bugs flying nearby. Jerome Lettvin has called such sensitivity a "_____-_____."

7. (p. 87) Sensory systems also _____ important features into messages understood by the brain. For example, the eye is only prepared to _____ stimulation, including pressure, into visual features.

8. (p. 87) The concept of sensory coding for the visual system can be demonstrated when you press firmly on your eyelids covering the eye itself. This produces flashes of "light" called _____, even though nothing has really been "seen."

9. (p. 88) The sensations you experience often depend on the area of the brain activated. This is known as _____ of _____.

10. (p. 88) One practical implication of this phenomenon is that it may be possible someday to artificially route visual information to the brain. Another implication is that "seeing" does not take place in the eyes, but rather involves the entire eye-brain system. It is this flow of information from the senses to the brain that we call _____.

11. (p. 88) _____ is the approach whereby changes in physical stimuli are measured and related to psychological sensations, such as loudness, brightness, or taste.

12. (p. 88) If we seek the absolute minimum amount of stimulation necessary for a sensation to occur, we are looking for the _____ _____.

13. (p. 88) Testing for absolute thresholds is a good indication of just how sensitive we are. For example, it takes only _____ photons (the smallest possible particle of light) striking the retina to produce a visual sensation.

14. (p. 88) Humans can hear sounds ranging in pitch from about _____ hertz (vibrations) per second to about _____ hertz.

15. (p. 89) The "silent" dog whistle may produce sounds as high as _____ or _____ thousand hertz, well beyond the range of humans, but still within a dog's range.

16. (p. 89) Absolute thresholds not only vary from person to person, they also vary from time to time for a single person. The type of _____, the state of one's _____ system, and the costs of false "detections" are also factors.

17. (p. 89) Emotional factors are also important. Unpleasant stimuli may raise the threshold for recognition. This effect is called _____ _____ and was first demonstrated in experiments on the recognition of "dirty" and "clean" words.

18. (p. 89) Anytime information is processed below the _____ (threshold or limit) for awareness it is referred to as _____.

19. (p. 89) Subliminal perception was demonstrated by a recent study in which college students saw a cartoon character rapidly flashed on a screen along with photographs of faces expressing joy or disgust. Later, the students chose more _____ terms to describe the cartoon character that had been paired with a "disgusted" face.

20. (p. 89)   Advertising using subliminal stimuli has caused much furor. However, controlled laboratory experiments show that subliminal stimuli are basically weak stimuli and that this approach is largely _____.

21. (p. 90)   Subliminal perception critics have heatedly charged that spoken messages recorded backward (called "_____") in rock music are perceived unconsciously by listeners.

22. (p. 90)   However, psychologists John Vokey and Don Read found no evidence of conscious or unconscious _____ of meaning when subjects were exposed to a variety of backward sentences. They were also unable to influence subjects' _____ with backward messages.

23. (p. 90)   When we seek the amount of stimulus change necessary to be perceived as different, we are looking for the _____ _____.

24. (p. 90)   This process involves determining how much stimulus change (increase or decrease) must occur to be _____ _____ _____, abbreviated _____.

25. (p. 90)   _____ _____ states that the amount of change in a stimulus needed to produce a JND is a constant proportion of the original stimulus intensity.

26. (p. 90)   Proportions for some common judgments determined by Weber's law include: pitch 1/333; weight _____; loudness _____; and taste _____.

27. (p. 90)   Weber's law is really just an approximation because it applies mainly to stimuli in the _____ rather than at the extremities. For other than pure sensory judgments, it is even more approximate.

28. (p. 91)   You are constantly surrounded by electromagnetic radiation which includes light and other energies. The _____ _____ is composed of light with various wavelengths.

29. (p. 91)   The spectrum starts at wavelengths of _____ nanometers (one-billionth of a meter) which produce sensations of purple or violet.

30. (p. 91)   Longer and longer wavelengths of light produce sensations of blue, green, yellow, and orange, until _____, with a wavelength of 700 nm, is reached.

31. (p. 91)   As a physical property of light, wavelength corresponds to the psychological experience of _____, or the specific color of a stimulus.

32. (p. 91)   Colors produced by a very narrow band of wavelengths are said to be very _____, or "pure."

33. (p. 91)   A third dimension of vision, _____, corresponds roughly to the amplitude (or height) of light waves.

34. (p. 92)   Several of the basic elements of a camera and the eye are similar. Both have a _____ that focuses an image on a light-sensitive layer at the back of a closed space.

35. (p. 92)   In a camera this layer is the film; in the eye it is a layer of _____ (light-sensitive cells) about the size and thickness of a postage stamp, called the _____.

36. (p. 92) The eye focuses using multiple processes. For one, the front of the eye has a curved, clear covering called the _____, that bends light rays inward.

37. (p. 92) Next, the lens, which is elastic, is stretched or thickened by a series of muscles, so that more or less additional bending of light occurs. This process is called _____.

38. (p. 92) The shape of the eye also affects focusing. If the eye is too short, objects close to the eye cannot be focused and farsightedness or _____ results.

39. (p. 92) If the eyeball is too long, the image falls short of the retina and objects in the distance cannot be focused, resulting in nearsightedness or _____.

40. (p. 92) When the cornea or the lens is misshapen, some of the visual field will be focused and some will be fuzzy, a problem called _____.

41. (p. 92) _____ or "old vision" occurs when the lens becomes less resilient and less able to accommodate, often due to aging. The result is farsightedness.

42. (p. 92) In front of the lens in both a camera and the eye, there is a mechanism to control the amount of light entering. It is the diaphragm in a camera; in the eye it is the _____.

43. (p. 92) The iris is a colored circular muscle that expands and contracts to control the size of the _____, or dark opening at the center of the eye.

44. (p. 93) The retina can adapt to changing light conditions only very slowly, while the iris can do so very quickly. In dim light the pupils _____ (enlarge) and in bright light they _____ (narrow).

45. (p. 93) The eye is equipped with two types of receptor cells. One type, called _____, number about 6.5 million in each eye, function in bright light, produce color sensations, and pick up fine details.

46. (p. 93) In contrast, _____ numbering about 100 million, function in dim light, and are capable of producing only sensations of black or white.

47. (p. 93) However, the rods are much more _____ to light than cones and therefore mainly responsible for our ability to see in very dim light.

48. (p. 93) Nobel Prize-winning psychobiologists David Hubel and Torsten Wiesel have shown that vision acts more like a computer than a camera. They shone lights of various sizes and shapes on the retina and a recorded reactions from _____ _____ in the visual cortex.

49. (p. 94) They found that many brain cells respond only to lines of a certain width or orientation. Other cells respond to lines at certain _____, or lines of certain _____, or to lines moving in a particular _____.

50. (p. 94) Cells in the brain act as feature detectors. It's little wonder that as much as _____ percent of the human brain may be involved with vision.

51. (p. 94) At this point the comparison between the eye and the camera breaks down. The rods and cones points toward the _____ of the eye, away from incoming light.

52. (p. 94)   Also, each eye has a _____ _____ because there are no receptors where the optic nerve leaves the eye.

53. (p. 94)   And last, the eye is constantly in _____, a factor essential for normal vision but which would obviously be disasterous for a camera.

54. (p. 94)   The cup-shaped depression in the middle of the retina, packed with about 50,000 cones, is called the _____.

55. (p. 94)   The large number of cones in the fovea produce great visual _____, or sharpness. Thus, vision is sharpest when an image falls on the fovea and steadily decreases as images are moved to the edge of the retina.

56. (p. 94)   Normal acuity is designated as 20/20 vision: at 20 feet in distance you can distinguish what the average person can see at 20 feet. If vision can be corrected to no better than _____ acuity, a person is considered "legally blind."

57. (p. 94)   Areas outside the fovea also get light. This situation creates a large region of _____ (side) vision.

58. (p. 94)   The rods reach their greatest density about _____ degrees to each side of the fovea and are particularly sensitive to _____.

59. (p. 94)   Those who have lost peripheral vision are said to have _____ vision, a condition much like wearing blinders.

60. (p. 94)   Although the rods give poor acuity, they are many times more responsive to light than are cones. Thus, rods are most important for _____ vision which is best when looking to one side or the other of an object.

61. (p. 96)   In determining the brightest color, we must consider that rods and cones differ. Since cones show maximal color sensitivity to wavelengths in the _____-_____ region of the spectrum, this color range will appear brightest when all colors are tested in the daylight.

62. (p. 96)   Although rods do not produce color, they are most sensitive to _____-_____ lights. Thus, if all colors are tested at night or under other conditions of dim light, this color range will appear brightest.

63. (p. 96)   The _____, or three-color theory of color, holds that there are three types of cones, each with a heightened sensitivity to a specific color: _____, _____, or _____. Other colors are assumed to result from a combination of these three.

64. (p. 96)   However, there appear to be four colors psychologically primary, the original three and _____.

65. (p. 96)   The _____-_____ theory was developed to explain why you can't have a reddish-green or a yellowish-blue.

66. (p. 96)   According to this theory, the visual system analyzes information into "_____-_____" messages for red/green, yellow/blue, black/white. Coding one color in a pair seems to block the opposite message.

67. (p. 97) According to this theory, fatigue caused by making one response causes an _____ of the opposite color as the system recovers.

68. (p. 97) The three-color theory applies to the retina, where three types of light-sensitive _____ _____ have been found. Three types of cones fire nerve impulses at different rates when various colors are viewed.

69. (p. 97) In further support of the three-color theory, researchers recently confirmed that each cone contains only one pigment and that each pigment is controlled by its own _____.

70. (p. 97) The opponent-process theory seems to explain events recorded in the optic pathways _____ information leaves the eye. So both theories appear to be correct at a particular level in the visual system.

71. (p. 98) A person who is completely _____-_____ sees the world only in black and white. This has been shown by the few cases where people can see color in one eye, but not the other.

72. (p. 98) For the color-blind individual, two colors of equal _____ look exactly alike. These individuals either lack cones or have cones that do not function normally. This condition is rare.

73. (p. 98) _____ _____, or partial color blindness, is more common. Approximately 8 percent of the male population, but less than 1 percent of women, are red-green color blind.

74. (p. 98) Red-green color blindness is a recessive, _____-_____ trait, meaning it is carried on the X, or female chromosome.

75. (p. 98) Women are rarely red-green color blind because they have two X chromosomes, both of which must be defective for the condition to occur. Color-blind men, however, only have one X chromosome, so they can inherit the defect from their _____ (who are usually not color blind themselves).

76. (p. 98) The red-green color-blind individual perceives both reds and greens as the same color, usually a _____ _____.

77. (p. 98) Red-green color-blind individuals have normal vision for yellow and blue. They can judge traffic lights by the position of the lights. Also, "red" traffic signals usually have a background of _____ light mixed in, while the "green" light is really _____-_____.

78. (p. 98) A common test for color blindness is the _____ test, consisting of test numbers and other designs composed of dots. Color-blind individuals cannot detect the patterns in the designs.

79. (p. 98) _____ _____ is the increase in sensitivity to light that occurs after entering the dark.

80. (p. 100) Studies of this phenomenon indicate it takes about _____ to _____ minutes of complete darkness to reach maximum visual sensitivity. When complete, the eye can detect lights 10,000 times weaker than those to which it was originally sensitive.

81. (p. 100) Dark adaptation results from the bleaching, or chemical breakdown, or light-sensitive chemicals in both the rods and cones known as _____ _____.

82. (p. 100) To restore light sensitivity, the visual pigments must _____, which takes time.

83. (p. 100) Night vision is due mainly to an increase of the rod pigment _____.

84. (p. 100) Dark adaptation can be completely wiped out by a few seconds exposure to bright light. Glare recovery normally takes about 20 seconds, but after a few drinks may take _____ to _____ percent longer because alcohol dilates the pupils.

85. (p. 100) Submarines and airplane cockpits are illuminated with _____ light, since the _____ are insensitive to this color. This provision allows people to perform their duties while dark-adapting.

86. (p. 101) One of the components of rhodopsin is _____, which the body makes from vitamin A. When too little vitamin A is available, rhodopsin production declines.

87. (p. 101) A person suffering from vitamin A deficiency may develop _____ _____, where they see normally in bright light (using the cones), but become blind when the rods must function.

88. (p. 101) Sound travels as a series of invisible waves composed of _____ (peaks) and _____ (valleys).

89. (p. 101) Any vibrating object will produce _____ _____ by setting air molecules in motion. Other materials, such as fluids or solids, will also carry sound, but sound does not travel in a vacuum.

90. (p. 101) The frequency of sound waves (the number of waves per second) corresponds to the _____ of a sound. The _____ or height of a sound wave tells how much energy it contains and corresponds to loudness.

91. (p. 101) What we call the "ear" is only the _____, or visible external portion of the ear that helps funnel and concentrate sounds.

92. (p. 102) As sound waves are funneled into the ear, they collide with the _____, which is like a tight drumhead within the ear canal.

93. (p. 102) These sound waves move the eardrum, which in turn causes the vibration of three small bones called the _____ _____.

94. (p. 102) The ossicles are the _____, _____, and _____. Their common names are the hammer, anvil, and stirrup.

95. (p. 102) The third ossicle is attached to a second membrane, or drumhead, called the _____ _____.

96. (p. 102) As the oval window moves back and forth, it sets up waves in a fluid within the _____, which is really the organ of hearing.

97. (p. 102) Waves in the cochlear fluid are detected by tiny _____ _____ which generate nerve impulses to be sent to the brain.

98. (p. 102) The hair cells are part of a structure called the _____ of _____ which runs down the middle of the cochlea.

99. (p. 103) The _____ theory of hearing states that as pitch rises, nerve impulses of the same frequency are fed into the auditory nerve. This explains how sounds up to about 4000 hertz reach the brain.

100. (p. 103) The _____ theory of hearing applies to higher tones and states that high tones register most strongly at the base of the cochlea (near the oval window).

101. (p. 103) According to the place theory, lower tones mostly move hair cells near the _____ _____ of the cochlea. Pitch is therefore signaled by the area of the cochlea most strongly activated.

102. (p. 103) Place theory explains "_____ _____" so called because hunters sometimes lose hearing in a narrow pitch range. This phenomenon occurs when hair cells are damaged in the area activated by the pitch of gunfire.

103. (p. 103) There are three types of deafness. _____ _____ occurs when the auditory ossicles are damaged or immobilized by disease or injury.

104. (p. 103) Conduction deafness reduces the _____ of vibrations to the inner ear and can often be overcome through the use of a _____ _____, a device that makes sounds louder and clearer.

105. (p. 103) _____ _____ is a hearing loss resulting from damage to the hair cells or auditory nerve. Hearing aids are of no help to a person with this condition because messages cannot reach the brain.

106. (p. 103) Researchers have recently found that in many cases of "nerve" deafness, the nerve is actually intact. This finding has spurred development of _____ _____ that bypass hair cells and stimulate the auditory nerves directly.

107. (p. 103) Early implants allowed recipients to hear only _____-_____ sounds. But, newer multi-channel models make use of place theory to separate higher and lower tones. This has allowed some formerly deaf persons to hear human voices and other higher frequency sounds.

108. (p. 103) Artificial hearing remains crude and not always very effective. In fact, _____ percent of adults who have tried implants have given up on them. However, improvements are sure to come.

109. (p. 104) _____ _____ results from exposure to very loud noise that can damage fragile hair cells in the cochlea.

110. (p. 104) As examples, daily exposure to _____ decibels or more may cause permanent hearing loss, short periods of exposure to _____ decibels (as at rock concerts) may cause temporary deafness, and even brief exposure to _____ decibels (jet airplane nearby) can cause permanent deafness.

111. (p. 104) To prevent permanent hearing loss, you should be particularly wary of any activity that causes a _____ _____ _____ or temporary loss of hearing.

112. (p. 104) Be aware that decibels are plotted on a _____ scale. This means that every 20 decibels increase the amount of energy in a sound by a factor of 10. Therefore, a rock concert at 120 decibels is not just twice as powerful as normal voice at 60 decibels. It is actually 1,000 times stronger.

113. (p. 105) If a ringing sensation known as _____ follows exposure to loud sounds, chances are that hair cells have been damaged.

114. (p. 105) _____, or smell, is a chemical sense, responding primarily to gaseous substances carried in the air.

115. (p. 105) _____, or taste, is also a chemical sense. We could survive without taste and smell, but occasionally they do prevent poisonings and they add pleasure to our lives.

116. (p. 105) As air enters the nose, it passes over roughly _____ million nerve fibers embedded in the lining of the upper nasal passages. Airborne molecules passing over the exposed fibers trigger nerve signals that are sent to the brain.

117. (p. 105) It is still somewhat of a mystery as to how different odors are produced. One hint comes from the condition known as _____ where a short of "smell blindness" develops for only one odor. This suggests that there are specific receptors for different odors.

118. (p. 105) It seems that molecules having a particular odor are quite similar in shape. Specific shapes have been identified for _____ (flower-like), _____ (camphor-like), musky, minty, and _____.

119. (p. 105) This does not mean, however, that there are different olfactory _____ comparable to the three types of cones in vision. Each receptor in the nose is probably sensitive to many molecules or combinations of molecules.

120. (p. 105) It is currently believed that there are different shaped "holes," or depressions, on the odor receptors. When a molecule matches up with a hole, it produces an odor. This is the essence of the concept known as the _____ and _____ theory.

121. (p. 105) A recent large-scale test found that _____ of the population cannot smell at all. This can be a significant problem since many anosmics are unable to cook and they may be poisoned by spoiled food.

122. (p. 106) Factors that can cause anosmia include _____, _____, and blows to the head (which may tear the olfactory nerves). Exposure to chemicals such as _____, photo-developing chemicals, and hair-dressing potions can also produce olfactory loss.

123. (p. 106) There are at least four basic taste sensations. We are most sensitive to _____, next to _____, less sensitive to _____, and least sensitive to _____.

124. (p. 106) Flavors are actually more varied and complex than implied by the four taste qualities because we tend to include the sensations of _____, _____, _____, and even pain along with taste.

125. (p. 106) The primary receptors for taste are the _____ _____, located mainly on the top of the tongue, but also at other points in the mouth.

126. (p. 106) Like the skin senses, taste receptors are not _____ distributed. Also, like smell, taste appears to be based on a _____-and-_____ match between molecules and intricately shaped receptors.

127. (p. 106) Part of the reason people seem to have very different tastes is _____. For example, the chemical PTC tastes bitter to about 70 percent of those tested, and has no taste for the other 30 percent.

128. (p. 106) Another reason is that taste cells have a life of only several _____. With age, cell replacement rate slows down so the sense of taste diminishes. This is why many foods you disliked in childhood may be more acceptable now.

129. (p. 107) An additional reason for individual differences in taste is the fact that most taste preferences are _____. What you are exposed to and accustomed to will have much to do with your likes and dislikes in foods.

130. (p. 107) Gymnasts launching themselves through a complex routine on the uneven bars rely heavily on the _____ _____, of which there are three.

131. (p. 107) The somesthetic senses include the _____ senses which produce light touch, pressure, pain, cold, and warmth.

132. (p. 107) _____ _____, receptors in the muscles and joints that detect body position and movement, are another type of somesthetic sense.

133. (p. 107) Another type of somesthetic sense, the _____ _____, involves receptors in the inner ear that signal balance and are involved in motion sickness.

134. (p. 107) Receptors specialize somewhat in various sensations. However, the surface of the eye, which has only free nerve endings, produces all five sensations. Altogether the skin has about 200,000 nerve endings for _____, 500,000 for touch and pressure, and three million for _____.

135. (p. 108) A _____-_____ touch test can be used to show that sensitivity roughly corresponds to the number of skin receptors in a given area. Generally speaking, important body areas have higher concentrations of receptors and are thus more sensitive.

136. (p. 108) _____ receptors are heavily represented, but do vary in their distribution, averaging about 232 points per square centimeter behind the knee, 184 per centimeter on the buttocks, 60 on the pad of the thumb, and 44 on the tip of the nose.

137. (p. 108) Pain fibers are also found in the internal organs of the body. Stimulation of these fibers causes _____ pain.

138. (p. 108) Visceral pain is often felt on the surface of body, at a site some distance from the point of origin. Experiences of this type are called _____ pain.

139. (p. 108) Pain from the skin, muscles, joints, and tendons is known as _____ pain. Carried by large nerve fibers, it is sharp, bright, fast, and seems to come from specific body areas. This is the body's warning system.

140. (p. 108) The second type of pain, representing the body's reminding system, is carried by _____ nerve fibers, is slower, nagging, aching, widespread, and very unpleasant. It gets worse if the stimulus is repeated.

141. (p. 109) The decrease in sensory response that accompanies a constant or unchanging stimulus is called _____ _____.

142. (p. 109) _____ receptors are among the most quickly adapting. When exposed to a constant odor, they send fewer and fewer nerve impulses to the brain until the odor is no longer noticed.

143. (p. 109) Vision does not usually undergo sensory adaptation because the eye normally makes thousands of tiny movements every minute. These movements are caused by tremors in the eye muscles known as _____ _____. It is these movements which shift visual images from one another and prevent adaptation.

144. (p. 109) This phenomenon has been demonstrated by using special equipment designed to follow the exact movements of the eye. When projected geometric designs are stabilized on the _____ they fade within a few seconds.

145. (p. 109) The ability to select, by "tuning in on" any of the many sensory messages bombarding us while excluding others, is called _____ _____.

146. (p. 110) Selective attention appears to be based on the ability of various brain structures to select and divert incoming sensory messages. Recent evidence suggests that there are _____ _____ that control the flow of incoming nerve impulses to the brain.

147. (p. 110) For example, researchers Ronald Melzack and Patrick Wall have studied "_____ _____" in the spinal cord, and suggest that if the gate is closed by one pain message other messages may not be able to pass through.

148. (p. 110) Pain clinics use this effect by applying a mild _____ _____ to the skin. Such stimulation, at or just below the threshold of pain, can greatly reduce more agonizing skin.

149. (p. 110) This gate control theory is an explanation for the effectiveness of the ancient Chinese art of _____. The needles activate small fibers which relay through the biasing system to close the gates to intense or chronic pain.

150. (p. 110) Controlled studies have shown that acupuncture produces short-term pain relief for _____ to _____ percent of patients tested.

151. (p. 110) People undergoing acupuncture often report feelings of light-headedness, relaxation, or euphoria. This effect seems to be due to the body's ability to produce opiate-like chemicals. To combat pain, the brain causes the pituitary gland to release a chemical called _____- _____, which is similar to morphine.

152. (p. 110) Receptor sites for endorphins are found in large numbers in the _____ system and other brain areas associated with pleasure, pain, and emotion.

153. (p. 111) The nervous system makes its own "drugs" to block pain. This relates to the idea of pain gates in that the central biasing system, which closes pain gates in the spinal cord, is highly _____ to morphine and other opiate painkillers.

154. (p. 111) The discovery of endorphins helps explain many puzzling phenomena. A release of endorphins may underlie the pain-killing effect of _____ (fake pills or injections), as well as the euphoria of runner's "high," _____, acupuncture, _____, and painful initiation rites in primitive cultures.

155. (p. 111) The "high" often felt by long-distance runners is an example of endorphin's effect. One study showed that after running a mile (a stress which causes the brain to release endorphins), subjects could tolerate pain about _____ percent longer than before.

156. (p. 111) When _____, a drug that blocks the effects of endorphines, was administered to subjects before running a mile, subjects lost their protection from pain.

157. (p. 112) Fear or high levels of _____ increases pain. That fact explains why the relief of being excused from combat sometimes leaves soldiers insensitive to wounds.

158. (p. 112) Loss of _____ over pain seems to increase pain by increasing anxiety and emotional distress. People who are allowed to regulate, avoid, or _____ a painful stimulus suffer less.

159. (p. 112) _____ can radically reduce pain. Pain can be "tuned out" just like any other sensation. This fact was illustrated in experiments where subjects experienced pain relief when they were required to read letters aloud and to name their high school courses and teachers.

160. (p. 113) The meaning or _____ given a painful stimulus also affects pain. For example, in one experiment it was found that thinking of pain as pleasurable (denying the pain) greatly increased pain tolerance.

161. (p. 113) _____ _____ _____, which emphasizes birth with a minimum of drugs or painkillers, utilizes all four of the factors involved in pain.

162. (p. 113) Natural childbirth techniques reduce pain by an average of about _____ percent. Even so, many women who have had prepared childbirth training still end up asking for an epidural block because of the very severe pain.

163. (p. 113) In any situation where pain can be anticipated, lowered anxiety may be achieved by making sure that you are fully _____. Be sure you know what will happen or could happen.

164. (p. 113) In other situations, shifting attention away from pain can be aided by focusing on some _____ object. Prior practice in meditation can be a tremendous aid to such attention shifts.

165. (p. 113) Research suggests that distraction through attention shifts works best for mild or brief pain. For chronic or strong pain, _____ is more effective.

166. (p. 113) Physicians have found that intense surface stimulation of the skin can control pain from other parts of the body, and that a brief, mildly painful stimulus can relieve more severe pain. Such procedures, known as _____ are evident when applying ice packs, hot-water bottles, or mustard packs.

167. (p. 114) At least one-half of all astronauts have suffered from _____ _____ _____ or "space sickness"—a type of motion sickness.

168. (p. 114) Like sea sickness, car sickness, and air sickness, its initial signs are _____ and mild _____. However, it usually does not produce the pallor, "cold sweating," and nausea so common on earth.

169. (p. 114) In most types of motion sickness, these signs warn that vomiting is about to occur. But in space, vomiting is usually _____ and _____.

170. (p. 115) The _____ organs are fluid-filled sacs which contain tiny crystals in a soft, gelatin-like mass. The tug of gravity or rapid head movements can cause the mass to shift, which stimulates hair-like receptor cells, allowing us to sense gravity and movement.

171. (p. 115) Another part of the vestibular system are three fluid-filled tubes called the _____ _____.

172. (p. 115) Head movements cause the fluid in the canals to swirl about, which bends a small "flap" called an _____. This bending stimulates hair cells that signal head rotation.

173. (p. 115) The most widely accepted explanation of motion sickness is the _____ _____ theory. It states that dizziness and nausea occur when sensory information from the vestibular system fails to match information received from tne eyes and body.

174. (p. 116) The reason why sensory conflict causes nausea may be rooted in evolution. Many _____ disturb the coordination of messages from the vestibular system, vision, and the body. It may be that we react to sensory conflict by vomiting to expel _____.

175. (p. 116) During _____, the otolith organs send unexpected signals to the brain and head movements are no longer confirmed by the semicircular canals. This can produce sensory conflict.

176. (p. 116) A further problem in space is that few of the messages the brain receives from the vestibular system and kinesthetic receptors agree with a lifetime of past _____.

177. (p. 116) Space sickness usually disappears in two or three days. This adaptation seems to occur because astronauts shift to using _____ cues instead of vestibular information.

178. (p. 116) This same shift can cause "earth sickness." Immediately after returning to earth some astronauts have experienced _____ and _____. All had considerable difficulty in standing with their eyes closed for the first day or two.

179. (p. 116) The most successful medication for motion sickness is _____ Nonprescription "sea sickness" pills also offer some protection. Alcohol and other intoxicating drugs usually make symptoms worse.

180. (p. 116) Soviet cosmonauts have had some success with a system that limits _____ _____ for the first two days in space.

181. (p. 116) To minimize sensory conflict, stay out of the cabin on boats. In cars and airplanes, try closing your eyes. It can help to fixate your eyes on an _____ _____ or look above the horizon at the unmoving sky.

182. (p. 116) If possible, you should _____ _____. The otoliths are less sensitive to vertical movements when you are horizontal, and your head will move less.

183. (p. 116) _____ seems to intensify motion sickness. Try to breathe slowly and deeply since this can be a good focus for attention.

SELF-TEST

1. (p. 87) Which of the following is not a factor in the data reduction system of the senses?
   a. transduction of energy into nerve impulses
   b. analysis of environment into important features prior to neural transmission
   c. coding of important environmental features into messages understood by the brain
   d. activation of sensory receptors by the brain to prepare them for transmission

2. (p. 87) True-False. Pressure to the eye produces visual perceptions of stars, checkerboards, and flashes of color called phosphates.

3. (p. 88) The principle that the sensations you experience depend on the area of the brain stimulated is called:
   a. Weber's Law
   b. localization of function
   c. nerve impulse transduction
   d. selective attention

4. (p. 88) True-False. Study of sensory systems shows that seeing takes place in the eyes.

5. (p. 88) True-False. Psychophysics is the study of how changes in psychological functioning affect stimuli in the brain.

6. (p. 88) The minimum amount of stimulation necessary for a sensation to occur is called the:
   a. difference threshold
   b. absolute threshold
   c. stimulation threshold
   d. minimum threshold

7. (p. 88) Humans can hear sounds ranging from ____ hertz to ____ hertz.
   a. 200 - 2,000
   b. 20 - 20,000
   c. 20 - 200,000
   d. 20 - 200

8. (p. 89) True-False. Absolute thresholds are absolutely the same from person to person.

9. (p. 89) The fact that subjects take longer to recognize "dirty" rather than "clean" words illustrates which of the following?
   a. perceptual vigilance
   b. perceptual adaptation
   c. perceptual defense
   d. subliminal perception

10. (p. 89) True-False. Subliminal stimuli are unusually effective in commercial advertisements designed to increase product sales.

11. (p. 90) The principle that the amount of change in a stimulus needed to produce a JND is a constant proportion of the original stimulus intensity is called:
  a. sensory adaptation   c. opponent-process theory
  b. absolute threshold   d. Weber's Law

12. (p. 91) True-False. The visible spectrum of electromagnetic radiation is made up of light producing a range of color sensations from purple or violet, through blue, green, yellow, and orange, until red is reached.

13. (p. 91) Which of the following is NOT a dimension of vision?
  a. hue   c. saturation
  b. brightness   d. pitch

14. (p. 92) One part of the eye that focuses an image on the retina is the:
  a. pupil   c. rod
  b. cone   d. lens

15. (p. 92) The process whereby the lens of the eye stretches or thickens due to a series of muscle and ligament adjustments is called _____.
  a. facilitation   c. adaptation
  b. accommodation   d. acuity

16. (p. 92) Which of the following is improperly associated?
  a. hyperopia, farsightedness   c. myopia, nearsightedness
  b. astigmatism, "old vision"   d. presbyopia, farsightedness due to aging

17. (p. 92) The mechanism of the eye that controls the amount of light entering is the _____.
  a. lens   c. diaphragm
  b. cornea   d. iris

18. (p. 93) The receptors of the eye primarily responsible for color vision and seeing fine details are the _____.
  a. rods   c. foveas
  b. retinas   d. cones

19. (p. 94) True-False. Visual acuity is best when an image falls on the fovea because of the large number of cones in that part of the retina.

20. (p. 94) Which of the following is not associated with the functioning of the rods of the eye?
  a. sensitive to movement   c. less responsive to light than cones
  b. essential for night vision   d. facilitate peripheral vision

21. (p. 96) True-False. Rods and cones have different maximal color sensitivities. Rods are most sensitive to blue-green lights, while yellowish-green colors appear brightest when cones are tested.

22. (p. 96) The theory that the visual system analyzes information into "either-or" color messages is known as:
  a. the trichromatic theory   c. the gating theory
  b. the opponent-process theory   d. Weber's theory

23. (p. 96) True-False. The trichromatic theory of color vision seems to work at the level of the retina, while the opponent-process theory seems to apply to events recorded in the optic pathways, after information leaves the retina.

24. (p. 98) Which of the following is not true of red-green color blindness?
    a. It occurs in about 1 percent of women and 8 percent of men.
    b. It is a recessive, sex-linked trait.
    c. Red-green color-blind individuals perceive both colors as a yellowish brown.
    d. It is less common than blue-yellow color blindness.

25. (p. 98) True-False. A common test for measuring farsightedness is the Ishihara test.

26. (p. 98) The increase in sensitivity to light that occurs when you stay in the dark for some time is called:
    a. light enhancement   c. dark facilitation
    b. dark adaptation   d. light adaptation

27. (p. 100) Rhodopsin is:
    a. a light-sensitive pigment in the rods important in night vision
    b. an ingredient of vitamin A important in color vision
    c. a visual pigment in the cones sensitive to artificial illumination
    d. an important chemical missing in the eyes of red-green colorblind individuals

28. (p. 100) True-False. Complete dark adaptation takes about 30 to 35 minutes, but can be completely wiped out by just a few seconds exposure to bright lights, such as the head lights of an approaching car during night driving.

29. (p. 101) One of the components of rhodopsin is retinal, which the body makes from _____.
    a. vitamin A   c. vitamin C
    b. vitamin B   d. vitamin D

30. (p. 101) Where hearing is concerned, wave frequency corresponds to pitch, while wave amplitude corresponds to:
    a. sound   c. tone
    b. loudness   d. depth

31. (p. 101) True-False. What we usually call the ear is really only the pinna or visible external part of the ear.

32. (p. 102) Sound waves travel through the ear and affect the process of hearing through which sequence?
    a. eardrum, auditory ossicles, oval window, cochlea, hair cells
    b. cochlea, eardrum, oval window, auditory ossicles, hair cells
    c. auditory ossicles, oval window, cochlea, eardrum, hair cells
    d. eardrum, oval window, auditory ossicles, cochlea, hair cells

33. (p. 102) True-False. The eardrum is the ultimate receptor for hearing.

34. (p. 103) When the eardrums or ossicles are damaged or immobilized by disease or injury, deafness results.
    a. stimulation   c. impulse
    b. nerve   d. conduction

35. (p. 103) True-False. Hearing aids are of no help to a person with nerve deafness because auditory messages cannot reach the brain due to damage to the hair cells or auditory nerve.

36. (p. 104) Which of the following is not a warning signal of stimulation deafness?
      a.   temporary threshold shift
      b.   perceived temporary reduction in hearing
      c.   tinnitus
      d.   anosmia

37. (p. 105) Which of the following are chemical senses?
      a.   vision, audition   c.   gustation, olfaction
      b.   skin, vestibular   d.   somesthetic, kinesthetic

38. (p. 105) Anosmia refers to:
      a.   smell blindness for one type of odor
      b.   heavily saturated colors
      c.   one ingredient of rhodopsin
      d.   a distortion of the eye lens

39. (p. 105) The lock and key theory generally appears to explain the process of:
      a.   gustation   c.   olfaction
      b.   pain gating   d.   psychologically perceived colors

40. (p. 106) The principle organ of taste is the:
      a.   pinna   c.   cochlea
      b.   taste bud   d.   cornea

41. (p. 106) True-False. You may find as an adult that there are foods you now like which were not preferred as a child. This phenomenon is because of sensory adaptation.

42. (p. 107) Which of the following is NOT a somesthetic sense?
      a.   skin senses   c.   kinesthetic senses
      b.   vestibular senses   d.   gustation senses

43. (p. 107) True-False. Skin receptors are about equally sensitive to each of the five different sensations, although they are found in varying concentrations all over the body surface.

44. (p. 108) True-False. The body's warning system for pain involves sharp, bright pain carried by large nerve fibers associated with specific body areas.

45. (p. 109) The fact that you do not notice the smell of cooking fish after you have been in a room for a few minutes, illustrates the phenomenon of:
      a.   selective functioning   c.   function localization
      b.   sensory adaptation   d.   sensory deprivation

46. (p. 109) True-False. The rods and cones would undergo sensory adaptation were it not for physiological nystagmus, which shifts visual images from one receptor to another.

47. (p. 109) Our ability to tune in on any one of the many sensory messages while excluding others defines the process of:
      a.   selective attention   c.   sensory adaptation
      b.   sensory selection   d.   selective sensation

48. (p. 110) The presence of sensory gates possibly explains all of the following *except*:
    a.   selective attention
    b.   the effectiveness of acupuncture
    c.   sensory adaptation
    d.   how one type of pain can cancel another

49. (p. 110) True-False. The study of endorphins suggests that pain and stress may be counteracted by the release of morphine-like substances in the body.

50. (p. 112) Which of the following is not a factor that can be used to influence the amount of pain produced by a particular stimulus?
    a.   diffusion   c.   control
    b.   attention   d.   interpretation

51. (p. 113) Which of the following would not be expected to reduce pain?
    a.   counterirritation   c.   denying pain
    b.   fear of pain   d.   meditation

52. (p. 114) A type of motion sickness called _____ has affected at least one-half of all astronauts, producing sudden and unexpected vomiting.
    a.   vestibular conflict sickness   c.   sensory conflict syndrome
    b.   space adaptation syndrome   d.   ampulla illness

53. (p. 115) Which of the following is not true of sensory conflict theory?
    a.   It postulates that space sickness vomiting may be due to an evolutionary link whereby poisons are expelled from the body.
    b.   It postulates that during weightlessness conflict between messages sent by the otolith organs and the semicircular canals produces illness.
    c.   It postulates that as biological systems adapt to the unusual conditions of space that space sickness should disappear within two or three hours.
    d.   All of the above

54. (p. 116) Immediately after returning from space, astronauts have experienced dizziness, nausea, and an inability to stand with eyes closed. This pattern has become known as:
    a.   space sickness   c.   air sickness
    b.   space rebound sickness   d.   earth sickness

55. (p. 116) True-False. Becoming intoxicated can diminish motion sickness symptoms because alcohol acts as a depressant to numb the effects of sensory conflict.

APPLYING YOUR KNOWLEDGE

1.   Ask around your classmates and friends to locate someone who has color weakness. Give them the Ishihara Test replicated in your text. What kind of color weakness do they have? Find out how this genetic trait affects their life—does it cause them any problems or inconveniences? How does the person deal with these difficulties?

2.   Sensory adaptation for various kinds of odors occurs at different rates. Pick some foods with strong odors and conduct an experiment to see how quickly you adapt to each of the odors.

ANSWERS—PROGRAMMED REVIEW

1. data reduction
2. electromagnetic spectrum
3. transducers
4. analyze
5. Perceptual features
6. bug detector
7. code; code
8. phosphenes
9. localization of function
10. sensation
11. Psychophysics
12. absolute threshold
13. three
14. 20; 20,000
15. 40; 50
16. stimulus; nervous
17. perceptual defense
18. limen; subliminal
19. negative
20. ineffective
21. backmasking
22. recognition; behavior
23. difference threshold
24. just noticeably different; JND
25. Weber's law
26. 1/50; 1/10; 1/5
27. midrange
28. visible spectrum
29. 400
30. red
31. hue
32. saturated
33. brightness
34. lens
35. photoreceptors; retina
36. cornea
37. accommodation
38. hyperopia
39. myopia
40. astigmatism
41. Presbyopia
42. iris
43. pupil
44. dilate; constrict
45. cones
46. rods
47. sensitive
48. single cells

49. angles; lengths; direction
50. 30
51. back
52. blind spot
53. motion
54. fovea
55. acuity
56. 20/200
57. peripheral
58. 20; movement
59. tunnel
60. night
61. yellowish-green
62. blue-green
63. trichromatic; red, green, blue
64. yellow
65. opponent-process
66. either-or
67. afterimage
68. visual pigments
69. gene
70. after
71. color-blind
72. brightness
73. Color weakness
74. sex-linked
75. mothers
76. yellowish brown
77. yellow, blue-green
78. Ishihara
79. Dark adaptation
80. 30; 35
81. visual pigments
82. recombine
83. rhodopsin
84. 30; 50
85. red; rods
86. retinal
87. night blindness
88. compression; rarefaction
89. sound waves
90. pitch; amplitude
91. pinna
92. eardrum
93. auditory ossicles
94. malleus, incus, stapes
95. oval window

96. cochlea
97. hair cells
98. organ of Corti
99. frequency
100. place
101. outer tip
102. hunter's notch
103. Conduction deafness
104. transfer; hearing aid
105. Nerve deafness
106. cochlear implants
107. low-frequency
108. 30
109. Stimulation deafness
110. 85; 120; 150
111. temporary threshold shift
112. logarithmic
113. tinnitus
114. Olfaction
115. Gustation
116. 20
117. anosmia
118. floral; camphor; etherish
119. receptors
120. lock and key
121. 1.2
122. infections, allergies; ammonia
123. bitter; sour; salt; sweet
124. texture, temperature, smell
125. taste buds
126. equally; lock-and-key
127. genetic
128. days
129. acquired
130. somesthetic senses
131. skin
132. Kinesthetic senses
133. vestibular senses
134. temperature; pain
135. two-point
136. Pain
137. visceral
138. referred
139. somatic
140. small
141. sensory adaptation

142. Olfactory
143. physiological nystagmus
144. retina
145. selective attention
146. sensory gates
147. pain gates
148. electrical current
149. acupuncture
150. 50; 80
151. beta-endorphin
152. limbic
153. sensitive
154. placebos; masochism; childbirth
155. 70

156. naloxone
157. anxiety
158. control; control
159. Distraction
160. interpretation
161. Prepared childbirth training
162. 30
163. informed
164. external
165. reinterpretation
166. counterirritation
167. space adaptation syndrome
168. dizziness; disorientation
169. sudden; unexpected

170. otolith
171. semicircular canals
172. ampulla
173. sensory conflict
174. poisons, poison
175. weightlessness
176. experience
177. visual
178. dizziness; nausea
179. scopolamine
180. head movements
181. unmoving point
182. lie down
183. Anxiety

ANSWERS—SELF-TEST

1.	d	11.	d	21.	True	31.	True	41.	False	51.	b
2.	False	12.	True	22.	b	32.	a	42.	d	52.	b
3.	b	13.	d	23.	True	33.	False	43.	False	53.	c
4.	False	14.	d	24.	d	34.	d	44.	True	54.	d
5.	False	15.	b	25.	False	35.	True	45.	b	55.	False
6.	b	16.	b	26.	b	36.	d	46.	True		
7.	b	17.	d	27.	a	37.	c	47.	a		
8.	False	18.	d	28.	True	38.	a	48.	c		
9.	c	19.	True	29.	a	39.	c	49.	True		
10.	False	20.	c	30.	b	40.	b	50.	a		

ACROSS

1. misshapen cornea or lens causes this condition
4. below the limen (limit or threshold)
5. receptor cells producing color sensations
8. farsightedness
9. sharpness of vision
11. receptor cells allow us to see at night
13. the sense of taste
15. _____ nerve fibers carry sharp pain very quickly
17. a color with a narrow band of wavelength is "pure" or _____
18. brain releases this chemical to combat pain

DOWN

2. _____ (3-color) theory
3. nearsightedness
6. the study of thresholds and other related topics
7. specific "color" of a stimulus
10. three tiny bones of middle ear
12. drug used to treat space sickness
14. the sense of smell
16. contains only cones—about 50,000 of them

CHAPTER 5

Perceiving the World

CONTENTS

TERMS AND CONCEPTS

perception
size constancy
shape constancy
brightness constancy
figure-ground organization
reversible figures
nearness
similarity
continuation (continuity)
closure
contiguity
illusory figures
camouflage figures
perceptual hypothesis
ambiguous stimuli
impossible figures
depth perception
nativists
empiricists
visual cliff
depth perception
depth cues
monocular cues
binocular cues
accommodation
convergence
retinal disparity
stereoscopic vision
random dot stereograms
optical ray-tracing
pictorial depth cues

linear perspective
relative size
light and shadow
overlap (interposition)
texture gradients
aerial perspective
relative motion (motion parallax)
moon illusion
apparent distance hypothesis
perceptual habits
Ames Room
inverted vision
stimulus context
frame of reference
adaptation level
illusion
hallucination
stroboscopic movement
Müller-Lyer illusion
size-distance invariance
attention
selective attention
divided attention
habituation
orientation response (OR)
bottom-up processing
top-down processing
perceptual expectancy
tachistoscope
perceptual categories
weapon focus

reality testing   telepathy
extrasensory perception (ESP)   precognition
parapsychology   prophetic dreams
psi phenomenon   psychokinesis
clairvoyance   Zener cards

IMPORTANT INDIVIDUALS

Richard Gregory   William Hudson   Sidney Jourard
Colin Turnbull   Colin Blakemore   Abraham Maslow
Jane Gwiazada   Graham Cooper   J. B. Rhine
Bela Julesz   Norman Mackworth   Walter J. Levy
Jerry Waldvogel   Geoffrey Loftus   Uri Geller
Ping-Kang Hsiung   Jerome Bruner   Ray Hyman

PROGRAMMED REVIEW

1.   (p. 119) The process of assembling sensations into usable patterns that provide a "picture" or model of the world is called _____.

2.   (p. 120) Newly sighted persons do not immediately recognize their environment, but rather must _____ to identify objects, to read clocks, numbers and letters, and to judge sizes and distances. Such was the case for Mr. S. B. as described by Richard Gregory.

3.   (p. 120) The fact that the perceived size of an object remains the same even though the size of its retinal image changes is called _____ _____.

4.   (p. 120) Some perceptions, like seeing a line on a piece of paper, are so basic they seem to be _____ (inborn). In fact, newborn babies exhibit this phenomenon.

5.   (p. 120) Much perception is _____, or based on prior experience. For example, Colin Turnbull showed that a jungle-dwelling _____ had limited size constancy. Since he had no past experience with seeing objects far away, a buffalo in the distance looked like an insect.

6.   (p. 121) _____ _____ refers to the fact that objects are perceived as having the same form even though the retinal image of the object changes with the angle at which the object is viewed.

7.   (p. 121) In a movie theater, preserving shape constancy becomes difficult if you sit in the front row or near the front and to the side. Nevertheless, most people are able to tolerate a fair amount of shape distortion, as long as _____ objects on the screen are similarly distorted.

8.   (p. 121) On the highway, _____ _____ impairs size and shape constancy, adding to the accident rate among drunk drivers.

9.   (p. 121) _____ _____ refers to the fact that under changing lighting conditions the same object reflects different total amounts of light, and yet the psychological brightness of the object does not change.

10. (p. 121) This principle is true because the _____ of light reflected by an object is still the same, relative to other objects in the environment, under any lighting conditions.

11. (p. 122) The simplest organization is to group some sensations into an object or "thing" that stands out against some plainer background. This process is called _____ _____ organization.

12. (p. 122) It is probably _____ since it is the first perceptual ability to emerge when a cataract patient regains sight. Even 5-month-old babies respond to figure-ground patterns.

13. (p. 122) In normal figure-ground perception only one figure is seen. However, in _____ _____ figure and ground can be switched.

14. (p. 122) Gestalt psychologists have studied extensively what causes the formation of a "figure." According to their studies, the principles that bring order to your perceptions include:
     1) Stimuli that are _____ each other tend to be grouped together.
     2) Stimuli that are _____ in size, shape, color, or form tend to be grouped together.
     3) Perceptions tend toward simplicity and _____.
     4) The tendency to complete a figure so that it has a consistent overall form is known as _____.
     5) The principle of _____, or nearness in time and space, is often responsible for the perception that one thing has caused another.

15. (p. 122) The principle of closure is evidenced through the use of _____ figures. Even young children can identify the implied shapes seen in such forms.

16. (p. 122) Other factors which greatly affect perceptual organization include learning and past experience. While the normal person could easily solve _____ patterns (those that break up figure-ground organization), individuals like Mr. S. B. would be at a total loss.

17. (p. 123) A meaningful pattern represents a _____ hypothesis, or initial guess, about how to organize sensations. Pre-existing ideas and expectations actively guide our interpretation of sensations.

18. (p. 123) The active nature of perceptual organization is perhaps most apparent in the case of _____ _____ (patterns allowing more than one interpretation). For example, clouds can be perceptually organized to resemble many shapes and scenes.

19. (p. 123) In some instances, a stimulus may present such a conflict that perceptual organization becomes impossible. For example, the tendency to make a three-dimensional object out of a drawing is frustrated by the "three-pronged widget"—an _____ figure.

20. (p. 124) Humans almost always appear to understand lines that represent the _____ of surfaces. We also have no problem with a single line used to depict the _____ edges of a narrow object. However, we do not easily recognize lines that show color boundaries on the surface of an object. This was demonstrated in studies with the Songe tribe of New Guinea.

21. (p. 125) _____ _____ is the ability to see three-dimensional space and to accurately judge distances.

22. (p. 125) Some psychologists, called "_____," hold that depth perception is inborn. Others, called "_____," view it as learned. Most likely, it involves elements of both positions.

23. (p. 125) Some evidence regarding depth perception comes from work with the _____ _____, a table covered with glass. On one side, a checkered surface lies directly beneath the glass, while on the other side, the surface is four feet below the glass.

24. (p. 125) Using this device, 6- to 14-month-old infants were placed in the middle and given the choice of crawling to the "shallow" or the "deep" side. The majority chose the _____ side and most refused the _____ side even when their mothers tried to call them towards it.

25. (p. 126) Psychologist Jane Gwiazda has expanded this work by testing babies with goggles that make some designs stand out three-dimensionally, while others remain flat. Recognition of "3-D" designs emerges at about age _____ months.

26. (p. 126) As soon as infants become active crawlers, they refuse to cross the deep side of the visual cliff. When babies accidentally crawl off tables or beds, this is most likely due to a lack of _____ than to an inability to see depth.

27. (p. 126) _____ _____ are features of the environment, or messages from the body, that supply information about distance and space.

28. (p. 126) Depth cues that will function using only one eye are referred to as _____ cues; those requiring both eyes are called _____ cues.

29. (p. 126) Muscular cues come from within the body. One such cue is _____, which refers to the ability of the eye lens to bend more to focus objects close to the eye than those at a distance.

30. (p. 126) However, accommodation, a monocular depth cue, has a limited effect on depth perception beyond _____ feet.

31. (p. 126) A second bodily cue for depth is _____. This binocular depth cue stems from the fact that when you look at something 50 feet or less in distance, your eyes must turn in to focus the object.

32. (p. 126) Both accommodation and convergence provide depth cues based on the relationship between muscle sensations and distance. The former relies on muscles which support the _____, the latter on muscles attached to the _____.

33. (p. 126) The most basic source of depth perception is _____ _____, in which each eye receives a slightly different view of the world. It is also a binocular eye.

34. (p. 126) When the images seen by both eyes are _____ into one overall image, a powerful sensation of depth occurs. This is the principle behind _____ movies where two cameras film a scene from slightly different angles.

35. (p. 126) In such 3-D movies, the two separate films are then simultaneously projected on a screen while the audience wears glasses that filter out one of the images to each eye. This duplicates normal _____ _____ _____.

36. (p. 127) Three-dimensional space is woven from countless tiny differences between what the right and left eyes see. This effect is demonstrated by random dot stereograms created by Bela Julesz to show how sensitive the brain is to any _____ of information from the eyes.

37. (p. 127) Recent direct studies of the brain have shown that visual areas do, in fact, contain
_____ that detect disparities.

38. (p. 128) Scientist Jerry Waldvogel has found that many birds see the world in ways that would seem
strange to a human. For example, pigeons, ducks, and hummingbirds can see
_____ light.

39. (p. 128) Also, homing pigeons and many migrating birds can perceive the
_____ of light, which aids navigation by allowing the birds
to see geometric patterns in sunlight.

40. (p. 128) Many birds have an unusually wide field of view. An extreme case is the American woodcock
that can survey a _____ degree panorama without moving its eyes or head. However, the
trade-off is that they have very limited binocular vision.

41. (p. 128) Computer scientist Ping-Kang Hsiung has used a method known as _____
_____-tracing to simulate the woodcock's view.

42. (p. 128) Specialized adaptations resulting from evolution are found in the eyes of other animals as well.
Scientists theorize that human _____ perception is an evolutionary holdover from
life in the tree-tops.

43. (p. 128) _____ depth cues are features found in paintings, drawings, and
photographs that impart information about space, depth, and distance. They are all monocular
depth cues.

44. (p. 128) One such pictorial depth cue is _____ _____, which refers
to the apparent convergence of parallel lines in the environment.

45. (p. 129) If artists wish to depict two objects of the same size at different distances, they make the more
distant object smaller. Thus, they use _____ _____ to reproduce depth.

46. (p. 129) Most objects in the environment are lighted in such a way as to create definite patterns of
_____ and _____. Appropriate use of these qualities can give a two-
dimensional design a three-dimensional feeling.

47. (p. 129) _____, or interposition, describes a depth cue caused by one object partially
blocking the view of another.

48. (p. 129) If you are standing in the middle of a cobblestone street, the street looks coarse near your feet
but the _____ of the stones gets smaller and finer as you look off into the distance.
This gradual decrease in fine detail refers to a texture _____.

49. (p. 129) Smog, fog, dust and haze add to the apparent depth of an object. Objects seen at a distance tend
to be hazy, washed-out in color, and lacking in detail due to _____
_____.

50. (p. 130) Relative motion, also known as _____ _____, can be seen by looking out a
window and moving your head from side to side. Objects near to you seem to move more than
objects in the distance.

51.   (p. 130) Pictorial depth cues do appear to require learning. William Hudson has tested members of remote tribes who are unfamiliar with these cues. They see simplified drawings as _____-_____ designs.

52.   (p. 130) The moon illusion refers to the fact that the moon looks _____ when it is low in the sky than when it is overhead.

53.   (p. 130) This illusion occurs because the _____ _____ of the moon is greater when it is on the horizon and seen behind houses, trees, etc.

54.   (p. 131) The moon illusion is best explained by the _____ _____ hypothesis, which states that if two objects form identical images, but one is more distant, the more distant object must be larger.

55.   (p. 131) The moon illusion is directly related to changes in _____. Extra depth cues near the horizon cause the eyes to focus on a more distant point than they do when you look overhead. Such changes appear to provide the brain with a "yardstick" for judging the size of images, including the moon.

56.   (p. 131) Learning may affect perception through ingrained patterns of organization and attention, referred to as _____ _____.

57.   (p. 132) Perceptual habits may become so ingrained that they lead us to distort or misperceive a stimulus. For example, in the Ames Room, the left corner is further from the viewer than the right. This makes a person standing in the left corner look very _____, whereas one standing in the right corner looks very _____.

58.   (p. 132) The brain is especially sensitive to perceptual features such as lines, shapes, edges, spots, and colors. For example, Colin Blakemore and Graham Cooper found that kittens raised in rooms with _____ stripes could jump onto a chair, but bumped into chairs when walking on the floor. Likewise, "_____" cats easily avoided chair legs but missed when trying to jump onto chairs.

59.   (p. 132) Other experiments show that for such animals there is a decrease in _____ _____ tuned to the missing features.

60.   (p. 132) The question of whether an adult can adapt to a completely new perceptual world is addressed by experiments involving _____ _____, where, special glasses turn the world upside down and reverse objects from right to left.

61.   (p. 133) At first, even the simplest tasks are incredibly difficult. Eventually, human inverted vision subjects do adapt (unlike _____ who swim in circles and rarely adapt when their eyes are surgically turned upside down).

62.   (p. 133) Throughout the period that subjects wore their goggles, their visual images remained upside down. But, subjects learned to perform most routine activities and some were able to drive cars and fly airplanes. Such a high degree of adaptation is related to superior human _____ abilities.

63.   (p. 134) _____ _____ in a new visual world (as with inverted vision) seems to be a key in adaptation. Subjects who walked on their own adapted more quickly than subjects pushed around in a wheeled cart.

64. (p. 134) An important factor affecting perception is the external _____ in which a stimulus is judged. For example, a man six feet in height looks tall when surrounded by others of medium height and short among professional basketball players.

65. (p. 134) In addition to external contexts, we all have internal _____ of _____, or standards by which stimuli are judged.

66. (p. 134) Your own personal "medium point" is called your _____ _____. It determines how heavy you judge a particular weight to be when given no artificial standard with which to compare it.

67. (p. 134) Perceptual learning is responsible for a number of _____ in which length, position, motion, curvature, or direction is consistently misjudged.

68. (p. 134) While illusions distort stimuli that actually exist, people who are _____ perceive objects or events that have no external reality (like hearing "voices" that are not there).

69. (p. 134) The illusion of _____ _____ is responsible for putting the "motion" in motion pictures. Movies project a series of rapid "snapshots" on the screen giving the sense of normal motion.

70. (p. 135) The familiar _____-_____ illusion illustrates how perceptual habits and past experience combine to produce illusions. In this illusion, a horizontal line with "arrowheads" appears _____ than a horizontal line with "Vs" on each end.

71. (p. 135) Richard Gregory uses the concept of _____-_____ _____ to explain this illusion. The V-tipped line looks farther away than the arrowhead-tipped line, so you compensate by seeing the V-tipped line as larger.

72. (p. 136) The South African _____ who live in a "round" world typically do not experience the Müller-Lyer illusion because they have had little previous experience with straight lines. At most, he or she sees the V-shaped line as slightly longer than the other.

73. (p. 136) The first stage of perception is _____, the selection of incoming stimuli.

74. (p. 136) _____ attention refers to the fact that we give some messages priority and put others on hold. Think of this concept as a sort of bottleneck or narrowing in the information channel linking the senses to perception. When one message enters the bottleneck, it seems to prevent others from passing through.

75. (p. 136) _____ attention often arises from our limited capacity for processing information. Overload may occur because at any moment we must split our mental effort among tasks, each of which requires more or less attention.

76. (p. 137) Very _____ stimuli are attention getting. That is, stimuli that are brighter, louder, or larger tend to capture attention.

77. (p. 137) A dripping faucet at night makes little noise by normal standards, but because of _____ it may become as attention-getting as a single sound many times louder.

78. (p. 137) Attention is also frequently related to contrast or _____ in stimulation. For example, Norman Mackworth and Geoffrey Loftus found that people who look at commonplace drawings with unusual elements focus first and longest on the unexpected parts.

79. (p. 137) Change, contrast, and incongruity are perhaps the most basic sources of attention. We quickly _____ (respond less) to predictable and unchanging stimuli.

80. (p. 137) Messages arriving at the brain are selected by attention. Then the body makes an _____ _____ (OR) characterized by enlarged pupils, brain wave changes, a short pause in breathing, increased blood flow to the head, and turning toward the stimulus.

81. (p. 137) When a stimulus is repeated without change, the OR _____, or decreases. For example, when an album becomes "old," a whole side may play without your really hearing it.

82. (p. 137) Advertisers take advantage of two motives, _____ and _____, in gaining your attention.

83. (p. 137) Motives may alter what is perceived, as in the supposed study of "the dating practices of male college students." Subjects who read a more sexually-arousing passage rated potential female blind dates as _____ _____.

84. (p. 138) An emotional stimulus can shift attention away from other information. Jewish subjects shown quickly-flashed pictures did not recognize symbols at the edge of the figures as well when the central item was an emotional symbol like a _____.

85. (p. 138) Perception seems to proceed to two major ways. In _____-_____ processing, we analyze information starting at the "bottom" with small units (low-level features) and build upward into a complete perception.

86. (p. 138) A second major means by which perception proceeds is _____-_____ processing. In this case, preexisting knowledge is used to rapidly organize features into a meaningful whole.

87. (p. 138) In perception, past experiences, motives, context, or suggestion may create a _____ _____ that sets you to perceive in a certain way.

88. (p. 139) Many perceptual expectancies are created by _____. In one experiment, students perceived a guest lecturer as unhappy and irritable when previously given the suggestion that the lecturer was "cold." Those who got a "warm" description responded positively.

89. (p. 139) Psychologist Jerome Bruner believes that perceptual learning builds up a set of mental _____.

90. (p. 139) Bruner demonstrated this by using a _____ to flash pictures of cards on a screen. Subjects often misperceived the cards that did not fit their expectations.

91. (p. 139) Perceptual categories have a strong impact on our perception of others. For example, psychotherapists told that a man was a job applicant described him as "realistic," "sincere," and "pleasant." When told he was a _____ _____, others described him as "defensive," "dependent," and "impulsive."

92. (p. 140) Most perceptions, such as our impression that the sun "sets" rather than the earth revolving backwards, reflect our active and creative _____ of events. We see what we believe.

93. (p. 140) The highly subjective quality of perception can be a liability, particularly in eyewitness testimony. Recent experiments show that a person's confidence in his or her testimony has almost no bearing on its _____.

94. (p. 140) In addition, misleading questions about what a person saw can greatly _____ eyewitness accuracy.

95. (p. 140) In one court case, a police officer testified that he saw the black defendant shoot the victim as both stood in a doorway 120 feet away. Measurements made by a psychologist demonstrated that identification under such conditions was _____.

96. (p. 141) Perception rarely provides an "instant replay" of events. Of 84 pilots who saw a DC-10 airline crash, _____ said the landing gear was up and _____ said it was down.

97. (p. 141) The same type of inaccuracies were reported when "eyewitness" subjects were interviewed following a staged attack on a college professor. The total accuracy score for the group tested was _____ percent of the maximum possible.

98. (p. 141) A recent experiment found that eyewitness accuracy was virtually the _____ for witnessing a crime as it was for being a victim. Jurors who place more weight on the testimony of victims may be making a serious mistake.

99. (p. 141) In many crimes, victims fall prey to _____ _____. They fix their entire attention on the weapon and fail to perceive details of appearance, dress, or other clues to identify the attacker.

100. (p. 142) Psychologist Sidney Jourard offers a suggestion to help individuals increase the accuracy of their perceptions. By _____ _____, we can obtain additional information as a check on our perceptions. This may be as simple as asking what someone thinks or feels.

101. (p. 142) Abraham Maslow has studied people who are especially alive, open, aware, and mentally happy. He found their perceptual styles marked by 1) immersion in the _____; 2) a lack of _____-_____; 3) freedom from selecting, criticizing, or evaluating; and 4) a general "surrender" to the experience.

102. (p. 142) Zen masters fail to show _____ to repeated stimuli. They show dishabituation in that they perceive objects as vividly after seeing them 500 times as they did the first time.

103. (p. 143) _____ _____ (ESP) is the purported ability to perceive events in ways that cannot be explained by accepted perceptual principles.

104. (p. 143) _____ is the study of ESP and other _____ phenomena, or events that seem to defy accepted scientific laws.

105. (p. 143) Three areas of parapsychological investigation can be distinguished. One area deals with _____, the ability to perceive events or gain information in ways that appear unaffected by distance or normal physical barriers.

106. (p. 143) Another area entails the study of _____, the extra sensory perception of another person's thoughts.

107. (p. 144) A third area involves researching _____, the ability to perceive or accurately predict future events.

108. (p. 144) Precognition may take the form of _____ _____ which foretell the future.

109. (p. 144) A fourth area deals with _____, the ability to exert influence over inanimate objects by "will power."

110. (p. 144) American psychologists as a group are highly skeptical about psi abilities. But the general public remains split on the issue. A 1991 national poll found that _____ percent of all American adults believe in ESP.

111. (p. 144) The difficulty of excluding _____ makes natural ESP occurrences less conclusive than they might be.

112. (p. 144) If by coincidence a "hunch" proves to be correct, it may be reinterpreted as a _____, or case of clairvoyance. If it is not confirmed, it is simply forgotten.

113. (p. 144) The formal study of psi events owes much to the late _____ who established the first parapsychological laboratory at Duke University.

114. (p. 144) Rhine tried to study ESP objectively. Many of his early experiments made use of _____ cards.

115. (p. 144) For example, in a typical test of _____ subjects tried to guess the symbols on the cards as they were turned up from a shuffled deck.

116. (p. 144) Unfortunately, some of Rhine's most dramatic early experiments used badly printed Zener cards that allowed the symbols to show faintly on the back. It is also very easy to cheat, by marking with a _____, or by noting marks on the cards caused by normal use.

117. (p. 144) Also, there is evidence that the experimenter knew which card was correct and unconsciously gave subjects cues with their _____, _____ gestures, or _____ movements.

118. (p. 145) Modern parapsychologists are now well aware of the need for _____-_____ experiments, maximum security and accuracy in _____ _____, meticulous control, and _____ of experiments.

119. (p. 145) In the last 10 years, _____ of experiments have been reported in parapsychological journals. Many of them seem to support the existence of psi abilities.

120. (p. 145) Most psychologists remain skeptical about psi abilities. For one reason, _____ continues to plague the field. As one example, Walter J. Levy, who was former director of Rhine's laboratory, was caught faking records.

121. (p. 145) A major criticism of psi research focuses on the inconsistency of psi abilities. It is rare for a subject to maintain psi ability over any sustained period. ESP researchers consider this "_____ _____" an indication that parapsychological skills are very fragile and unpredictable.

122. (p. 145) Critics argue that subjects who only temporarily score above chance have just received credit for a _____ of _____ .

123. (p. 145) Many of the most spectacular findings in parapsychology simply cannot _____ be (repeated). More importantly, improvements in _____ _____ usually result in fewer positive results.

124. (p. 145) Believers in ESP such as ex-astronaut Edgar Mitchell feel that the scientist's own mental processes may influence the phenomenon he or she is observing. Scientists who are true skeptics may _____ _____ the psychic subject.

125. (p. 146) If psychic phenomena do occur, they cannot be controlled by entertainers such as Uri Geller. As Professor Ray Hyman has pointed out, tests conducted on Geller were fraught with "incredible sloppiness." As one example, original reports of Geller's ability to reproduce sealed drawings failed to mention that there was a _____ in the _____ between the two rooms which allowed him to hear discussions of the pictures being drawn.

126. (p. 146) Also unreported was the fact that Geller's friend _____ _____ was present at every test and frequently acted as Geller's accomplice in trickery.

127. (p. 146) After close to 130 years of investigation, it is still impossible to say conclusively whether psi events occur. A survey of leading parapsychologists and skeptics found that almost all in both groups said their belief in psi had _____.

128. (p. 146) What is needed to scientifically demonstrate the existence of ESP is a set of _____ that would allow any competent, unbiased observer to produce a psi event under standardized conditions.

SELF-TEST

1. (p. 119) _____ is the process of assembling sensations into a usable mental representation of the world.
   a. Learning
   b. Conditioning
   c. Perception
   d. Motivation

2. (p. 120) An airplane in the distance appears very small, yet we know it has not shrunk. This exemplifies _____ _____, the perceived size of an object remains the same even though the size of its retinal image changes.
   a. perceived equality
   b. size constancy
   c. retinal disparity
   d. distance invariance

3. (p. 121) Shape constancy is the principle whereby:
   a. an object appears to have the same shape from whichever eye it is viewed
   b. an object appears to have the same shape from any angle it is viewed
   c. an object appears to change shape constantly from any angle it is viewed
   d. an object appears to have the same shape no matter what the lighting conditions

4. (p. 121) The principle of brightness constancy reflects the fact that objects always:
    a. reflect the same relative proportion of light
    b. appear equally bright under all lighting conditions
    c. appear brighter when constantly illuminated
    d. appear darker when constantly illuminated

5. (p. 122) The simplest perceptual ability is _____. It is probably inborn since it is the first perceptual ability to appear when a cataract patient regains sight.
    a. closure   c. size constancy
    b. size-distance invariance   d. figure-ground organization

6. (p. 122) Which of the following is *not* a factor that facilitates the organization of sensations into a figure?
    a. nearness   c. similarity
    b. continuity   d. disparity

7. (p. 122) True-False. In addition to nearness, similarity, continuity, closure, and contiguity, learning and past experience greatly affect perceptual organization.

8. (p. 125) True-False. Infants and newborn animals do not show evidence of depth perception; it is an acquired trait.

9. (p. 125) The visual cliff is:
    a. a device used in measuring depth perception
    b. the point on the visible spectrum where our vision begins to decline
    c. a mechanism in the eyeball that facilitates depth perception
    d. a pictorial representation of how the angles of objects determine our perception of distance

10. (p. 126) All of the following are muscular cues that facilitate depth perception EXCEPT:
    a. interposition   c. retinal disparity
    b. convergence   d. accommodation

11. (p. 126) True-False. Convergence, the most important bodily cue for depth perception, is a binocular cue based on the fusion of images received by the eyes.

12. (p. 126) Which of the following is most closely associated with the concept of retinal disparity?
    a. inverted vision, synesthesia
    b. random dot stereograms, 3-D movies
    c. moon illusion, Müller-Lyer illusion
    d. stroboscope, motion parallax

13. (p. 129) Which pictorial depth cue refers to the apparent convergence of parallel lines in the environment?
    a. convergency   c. aerial perspective
    b. linear perspective   d. interposition

14. (p. 129) Which of the following is *not* a pictorial depth cue?
    a. interposition   c. accommodation
    b. texture gradients   d. aerial perspective

15. (p. 130) True-False. Movies, television, and cartoon animation rely heavily upon motion parallax to produce visual depth.

16. (p. 130) True-False. The moon illusion refers to the fact that the moon appears larger when viewed on the horizon despite the fact that it is actually farther away than when overhead.

17. (p. 130) If two objects form identical images, but one is more distant, the more distant object must be larger. This principle is known as _____ and is exemplified by the _____.
     a. shape constancy; Ames Room.
     b. size constancy; three-pronged widget impossible figure
     c. brightness constancy; Müller-Lyer illusion
     d. apparent distance hypothesis; moon illusion

18. (p. 131) Learning affects perception through established patterns of organization and attention referred to as:
     a. perceptual constancies   c. perceptual habits
     b. sensory reconstructions   d. sensory constancies

19. (p. 132) True-False. Perceptual learning seems to program the brain for sensitivity to important features of the environment.

20. (p. 133) Inverted vision experiments with humans have shown that:
     a. with time, humans can learn to function normally with completely different visual cues
     b. perceptual habits are so ingrained that humans never learn to adapt to different cues
     c. we are like most animals in that we do adapt to the differences almost immediately
     d. basic physiology can be modified so that when the goggles are removed, we do not recover

21. (p. 134) The fact that you appear shorter, when standing among professional basketball players, than when you are standing with classmates, demonstrates:
     a. perceptual expectancy   c. stimulus context
     b. adaptation level   d. relative size

22. (p. 134) Adaptation level refers to:
     a. how quickly a given individual can adapt to changing environmental conditions (such as inverted vision)
     b. your own personal "medium" point or frame of reference in judging size, weight, age, etc.
     c. how perceptual learning influences our perception of external contexts
     d. the perceptual plateau that is reached once an individual has habituated to a repetitive stimulus

23. (p. 134) Perceptual learning is responsible for a number of _____ in which length, position, motion, curvature, or direction is consistently misjudged.
     a. habits   c. hallucinations
     b. inversions   d. illusions

24. (p. 135) Which of the following is *not* an illusion?
     a. stroboscopic movement   c. moon illusion
     b. Müller-Lyer illusion   d. hearing voices that do not exist

25. (p. 136) True-False. While past experience is quite important in contributing to illusions, some illusions appear to be inborn. For example, African Zulus exposed to the Müller-Lyer illusion experience the illusion immediately, although never before exposed to it.

26. (p. 137) Which of the following is *not* a factor which captures attention?
     a. very intense stimuli   c. repetitious stimuli
     b. constant, unchanging stimuli   d. contrast or change in stimulation

27. (p. 137) A(n) _____ is characterized by enlarged pupils, brain wave changes, a short pause in breathing, and increased blood flow to the head.
    a. orientation response   c. perceptual expectancy
    b. habituated response   d. synesthesia

28. (p. 137) True-False. When a stimulus is repeated without change, the OR increases or dishabituates.

29. (p. 137) Motives play a role in attention and may affect perception. Which of the following is *not* a true statement exemplifying this principle?
    a. Advertisers take advantage of sex and anxiety to merchandise a wide range of products.
    b. One experiment showed that students reading a sexually arousing passage rated potential blind dates more attractive.
    c. Members of a Jewish organization showed increased recognition for symbols at the edge of a figure when the central item was an "emotional" stimulus.
    d. A person who once seemed highly attractive may look quite different when your feelings change.

30. (p. 138) Perception seems to proceed in two major ways. One of these organizations, involves using preexisting knowledge to rapidly organize features into a meaningful whole.
    a. bottom-up processing   c. perceptual expectancy
    b. selective attention   d. top-down processing

31. (p. 139) Jerome Bruner found in his research on perceptual expectancies that subjects misperceived cards that did not fit their expectations. He believes that perceptual learning builds up a set of mental _____.
    a. categories   c. constancies
    b. illusions   d. cues

32. (p. 141) Which of the following is *not* a true statement with regard to witness testimony?
    a. A person's confidence in his or her testimony has almost no bearing on its accuracy.
    b. Eyewitness accuracy is virtually the same for witnessing a crime as it is for being a victim.
    c. Psychologists are gradually convincing lawyers, judges, and police officers of the fallibility of eyewitness testimony.
    d. Victims of crimes are more likely to be accurate in their testimony of the crime than are on-looking eyewitnesses.

33. (p. 141) Weapon focus refers to the fact that:
    a. victims usually focus their attention more on the identities of people holding weapons than on those who do not
    b. victims often fix their entire attention on the weapon and fail to perceive clues to the identity of the assailant
    c. eyewitnesses are often so frightened that they focus more on their own feelings than on the details of the situation, such as the weapons involved
    d. victim perceptions are often distorted; when focused on weapons they are often uncertain whether it was a knife, gun, or other object

34. (p. 142) True-False. Frequent reality testing may be required to maintain personal objectivity.

35. (p. 142) Abraham Maslow felt that some people are unusually accurate in perceptions of themselves and others. Which of the following is *not* a characteristic of the perceptual style of such people?
    a. freedom from selecting, criticizing, or evaluating
    b. general "surrender" to experience
    c. lack of self-consciousness
    d. immersion in the future

36. (p. 142) True-False. Zen masters show greater levels of habituation than most individuals.

37. (p. 143) The study of psychic or psi phenomena is called:
    a. psichology   c. magic
    b. demonology   d. parapsychology

38. (p. 143) The ability to perceive events or gain information in ways that appear unaffected by distance or normal physical barriers is called:
    a. telepathy   c. precognition
    b. clairvoyance   d. psychokinesis

39. (p. 144) The ability to read someone else's mind is called:
    a. psychokinesis   c. clairvoyance
    b. telepathy   d. precognition

39. (p. 144) _____ refers to the ability to exert influence over inanimate objects by will power.
    a. Telepathy   c. Precognition
    b. clairvoyance   d. Psychokinesis

40. (p. 144) Factors such as coincidence, statistics and consistency must be considered when investigating extrasensory skills.

41. (p. 144) True-False. _____ established the first parapsychological laboratory and made use of Zener cards in an effort to make the study of psi phenomena more objective.
    a. Edgar Mitchell   c. Sidney Jourard
    b. J. B. Rhine   d. Abraham Maslow

42. (p. 145) True-False. Skeptics and serious researchers in ESP both agree that if psychic phenomena do occur, they cannot be controlled well enough to be used by entertainers such as Uri Geller.

APPLYING YOUR KNOWLEDGE

1. Select a painting with which you are familiar. Can you apply your understanding of how each of the pictorial depth cues operate to produce a sense of depth?

2. How does you adaptation level compare to other people's? Design and conduct a simple experiment using objects of different weights to assess individual frames of reference. Ask classmates and friends to lift the various weights and rate them as to their heaviness. What factors (gender, age, weight, height, occupation, vocational interests, etc.) seem to operate in determining individual responses?

3. Many factors work to elicit our attention. See how many good examples you can find in newspapers and magazines of how advertisers use various stimulus features, motives, expectations, etc., to capture attention.

4. Your text describes a dramatic demonstration of how witnesses often misperceive details of surprising or threatening events (a professor was "attacked" by an actor). Set up a staged "incident" at a group setting and then interview each of the witnesses. How accurate are their descriptions of the events and the people involved?

ANSWERS—PROGRAMMED REVIEW

1. perception
2. learn
3. size constancy
4. native
5. empirical; Pygmy
6. Shape constancy
7. all
8. alcohol intoxication
9. Brightness constancy
10. proportion
11. figure-ground
12. inborn
13. reversible figures
14. near; similar; continuity; closure; contiguity
15. illusory
16. camouflage
17. perceptual
18. ambiguous stimuli
19. impossible
20. edges; parallel
21. Depth perception
22. nativists; empiricists
23. visual cliff
24. shallow; deep
25. 4
26. coordination
27. Depth cues
28. monocular; binocular
29. accommodation
30. 4
31. convergence
32. lens; eyeball
33. retinal disparity
34. fused; 3-D
35. stereoscopic vision
36. mismatch
37. cells
38. ultraviolet
39. polarization
40. 360
41. optical ray
42. depth
43. Pictorial

44. linear perspective
45. relative size
46. light, shadow
47. Overlap
48. texture; gradient
49. aerial perspective
50. motion parallax
51. two-dimensional
52. larger
53. apparent distance
54. apparent distance
55. accommodation
56. perceptual habits
57. small; large
58. horizontal; vertical
59. brain cells
60. inverted vision
61. goldfish
62. learning
63. Active movement
64. context
65. frames of reference
66. adaptation level
67. illusions
68. hallucinating
69. stroboscopic movement
70. Müller-Lyer; shorter
71. size-distance invariance
72. Zulus
73. attention
74. Selective
75. Divided
76. intense
77. repetition
78. change
79. habituate
80. orientation response
81. habituates
82. anxiety, sex
83. more attractive
84. swastika
85. bottom-up
86. top-down
87. perceptual expectancy
88. suggestion

89. categories
90. tachistoscope
91. mental patient
92. reconstruction
93. accuracy
94. decrease
95. improbable
96. 42; 42
97. 25
98. same
99. weapon focus
100. reality testing
101. present; self-consciousness
102. habituation
103. Extrasensory perception
104. Parapsychology; psi
105. clairvoyance
106. telepathy
107. precognition
108. prophetic dreams
109. psychokinesis
110. 49
111. coincidence
112. premonition
113. J. B. Rhine
114. Zener
115. clairvoyance
116. fingernail
117. eyes; facial; lip
118. double-blind; record keeping; repeatability
119. hundreds
120. fraud
121. decline effect
122. run of luck
123. replicated; research methods
124. turn off
125. hole in the wall
126. Shipi Stang
127. declined
128. instructions

ANSWERS—SELF-TEST

1.	c	9.	a	17.	d	25.	False	33.	b
2.	b	10.	a	18.	c	26.	b	34.	True
3.	b	11.	False	19.	True	27.	a	35.	d
4.	a	12.	b	20.	a	28.	False	36.	False
5.	d	13.	b	21.	c	29.	c	37.	d
6.	d	14.	c	22.	b	30.	d	38.	b
7.	True	15.	True	23.	d	31.	a	39.	b
8.	False	16.	False	24.	d	32.	d	40.	d

41.	True
42.	b
43.	True

ACROSS

2. produces a powerful sensation of depth with vision
8. perceptions of stimuli that *do not* exist
12. how sensations are assembled into a meaningful "picture"
13. stimuli that allow more than one interpretation
14. information or events perceived by ESP

DOWN

1. ability to foretell future events
3. mindreading
4. Extrasensory Perception (abbr.)
5. distortions of stimuli that actually exist
6. _____ psychologists studied the "figure-ground" organization
7. this cliff was used to study depth perception
8. respond less to an unchanging stimulus
9. _____ perspective refers to apparent convergence of parallel lines in the environment
10. this "looks" larger when low in the sky
11. most important source of depth perception is _____ disparity

States of Consciousness

CONTENTS

TERMS AND CONCEPTS

consciousness
waking consciousness
altered states of consciousness (ASC)
innate biological rhythm
microsleep
sleep-deprivation psychosis
short sleepers
long sleepers
sleep patterns
stages of sleep
electroencephalograph (EEG)
beta brain waves
alpha brain waves
hypnic jerk
myoclonus (restless leg syndrome)
sleep spindles
delta brain waves
deep sleep
rapid eye movement
REM sleep
NREM sleep
REM behavior disorder
somnambulist
sleeptalking
nightmares

night terrors
narcolepsy
cataplexy
insomnia
sedatives
drug-dependency insomnia
tryptophan
sleep apnea
hypersomnia
Sudden Infant Death Syndrome (SIDS)
REM rebound effect
REM myth
wish fulfillment
dream symbols
activation-synthesis hypothesis
hypnosis
mesmerize
animal magnetism
hypnotic susceptibility
Stanford Hypnotic Susceptibility Scale
basic suggestion effect
dissociation
hidden observer
sensory deprivation
hypnogogic images

theta waves   depressants
REST   barbiturates
psychoactive drugs   sedatives
physical dependence (addiction)   drug interaction
withdrawal symptoms   Seconal
drug tolerance   Tuinal
psychological dependence   Methaqualone (Quaalude, Sopor, Parest)
patterns of drug abuse   alcohol
stimulants   alcohol myopia
amphetamines   detoxification
Dexedrine   marijuana
Methedrine   hashish
Benzedrine   Cannabis sativa
amphetamine psychosis   tetrahydrocannabinol (THC)
ice   hallucinogen
cocaine   dream processes
anhedonia   condensation
crack   displacement
caffeine   symbolization
caffeinism   secondary elaboration
nicotine   lucid dream
carcinogens

IMPORTANT INDIVIDUALS

Peter Tripp   Sigmund Freud   Stanley Schachter
John Lilly   Allan Hobson   Roger Vogler
Wilse Webb   Robert McCarley   Wayne Bartz
Randy Gardner   Franz Mesmer   Rosalind Cartwright
Nathaniel Kleitman   James Braid   Ann Faraday
Eugene Aserinsky   Ernest Hilgard   Fritz Perls
William Dement   T. X. Barber   Gordon Globus
Jonathan Winson   D. O. Hebb   Stephen La Berge
Carlyle Smith   Peter Suedfeld   Thomas Szasz
Calvin Hall

PROGRAMMED REVIEW

1.   (p. 149) After 100 hours without sleep, New York disc-jockey Peter Tripp began to
     _____. After 170 hours his brain waves looked like those of
     _____, his memory was poor, and he struggled with even simple thoughts and problems.
     By 200 hours, Tripp could not distinguish between waking nightmares, hallucination, and
     reality.

2.   (p. 149) In John Lilly's womb tank experiments, he created an unusual sensory deprivation environment.
     Subjects wore darkened goggles and floated naked in a tank of body-temperature water. Cut
     off from all sensations, subjects often lose track of _____ and find it hard to concentrate.
     Some subjects also experience strange alterations in consciousness.

3.   (p. 150) To be conscious means to be aware. _____ consists of all the
     sensations, perceptions, memories, and feelings that you are aware of at any given instant.

4. (p. 150) We spend most of our lives in ordinary _____ consciousness, which is organized, meaningful, and clear. It is perceived as real, and it is marked by a familiar sense of time and place.

5. (p. 150) Altered states of consciousness (ASCs) related to fatigue, delirium, hypnosis, drugs, and ecstasy differ significantly from what might be considered normal. They represent a distinct change in the _____ and _____ of mental activity.

6. (p. 150) ASCs typically differ from normal waking consciousness with regard to: perceptions, emotions, _____, time sense, thinking, feelings of self-control, and _____.

7. (p. 150) The causes of ASCs are nearly endless. Some include sensory _____ (like a Mardi Gras crowd), _____ stimulation ("highway hypnotism" is an example), unusual physical conditions (high fever, hyperventilation, etc.), and sensory deprivation.

8. (p. 150) ASCs may have important cultural significance as in the sweat lodge ritual of the _____ Indians.

9. (p. 151) Almost every known religion has accepted at least some altered states as a source of mystical experience. Avenues have ranged from _____, meditation, prayer, isolation, sleep _____, whirling, and chanting, to self-inflicted _____ and _____ substances.

10. (p. 151) The _____ given to various states of consciousness may vary from one culture to another. Thus, cultural conditioning greatly affects what altered states a person recognizes, seeks, considers normal, and attains.

11. (p. 151) Contrary to common belief, we are not totally unresponsive during sleep. Experiments show that you are more likely to awaken if your _____ is spoken, instead of another. Likewise, a sleeping mother may ignore a jet rumbling by overhead, but wake at the slightest whimper of her child.

12. (p. 151) Some people can do simple tasks while asleep. In one experiment, subjects learned to avoid an _____ _____ by touching a switch each time a tone sounded. Eventually, they could do it without waking.

13. (p. 151) Sleep does impose limitations. For instance, there is _____ _____ that a person can learn math, a foreign language, or other complex skills while asleep.

14. (p. 151) Sleep expert Wilse Webb considers sleep an innate biological rhythm. While flexible, it has limits. Animals surgically prevented from sleeping fall into a _____ and _____ after several days.

15. (p. 151) Webb tried vigorously to teach animals to eliminate sleep, but sleep won out. After periods of forced wakefulness, Webb's animals began to engage in _____, a brief shift in brain activity to patterns normally found in sleep.

16. (p. 152) The world record for continuous wakefulness is held by Randy Gardner who went _____ days without sleep. He needed only 14 hours of sleep to recover.

17. (p. 152) Most symptoms of sleep deprivation, as with Randy Gardner, are removed by a _____ night of sleep.

18. (p. 152) The costs of sleep loss are partly determined by _____ and _____. For example, Randy Gardner remained coherent to the end of his vigil, whereas Peter Tripp's behavior became quite bizarre.

19. (p. 152) Most persons show no impairment on _____ mental tasks after two days without sleep. But most grow _____, and their ability to pay attention, remain vigilant, and follow simple routine _____.

20. (p. 152) Sleep loss doesn't have to be total to take a toll. For example, marathon tennis players who averaged about 3 hours of sleep per night for a week showed score declines on tests of _____ and perceptual-motor coordination.

21. (p. 152) With mild to moderate sleep deprivation, what usually suffers most is low-level, boring, _____-_____ tasks.

22. (p. 152) From these results, Webb concluded that moderate sleep loss does not diminish thinking or memory, but rather the _____ to _____.

23. (p. 152) Longer periods without sleep occasionally produce a temporary _____-_____ _____ like that experienced by Peter Tripp.

24. (p. 152) Common elements of sleep-deprivation psychosis include confusion and _____, _____ (false or distorted beliefs), and hallucinations.

25. (p. 152) Hallucinations may be _____, like Tripp's "coat of furry worm," or _____, such as feeling cobwebs on the face.

26. (p. 152) "Crazy" behavior such as Tripp's is less common than once thought. Hallucinations and delusions, if they occur at all, are never evident before _____ hours without sleep.

27. (p. 152) The most common reactions to extended sleep loss are inattention, staring, trembling _____, drooping _____, and an increased sensitivity to _____.

28. (p. 152) Rhythms of sleep and waking are so steady that they continue for many days even when clocks and light-dark cycles are eliminated. Under such conditions, humans eventually shift to a rhythm that averages _____ hours, not 24.

29. (p. 153) Individuals who can sleep only a few hours each night are rare. Only _____ percent of the population are short sleepers, averaging 5 hours of sleep or less per night.

30. (p. 153) The majority of people sleep on a 7- to 8-hour-per-night schedule. Long sleepers tend to be people who _____ a lot during the day.

31. (p. 153) As people age they usually sleep less. People over the age of 50 average _____ hours of sleep a night.

32. (p. 153) In contrast, infants spend up to 20 hours a day sleeping, usually in _____ to _____ hour cycles.

33. (p. 153) Most children, and some adults, maintain an afternoon "nap." Experts now regard midafternoon sleepiness as a natural part of the sleep cycle. There is a strong _____ readiness to fall asleep during the afternoon.

34. (p. 153) Brief, well-timed, _____ may be the key to maintaining alertness in people like truck drivers and hospital interns who often must fight drowsiness.

35. (p. 153) Shortened sleep periods are not effective, because people often can't get to sleep when the cycle calls for it. A more promising possibility is to adapt to longer than normal days. Such days can be tailored to match natural sleep patterns, which show a ratio of _____ to _____ between time awake and time asleep.

36. (p. 153) One study showed that _____-hour "days" work for some people. Unfortunately, subjects did poorly on longer 36-hour cycles (24 awake and 12 asleep) because they couldn't use the entire 12 hour sleep period.

37. (p. 153) Early concepts of sleep hypothesized that some substance related to _____ accumulated in the bloodstream causing sleep. But studies of _____ _____(individuals whose bodies are joined at birth) show this is false.

38. (p. 153) During extended wakefulness, a sleep-promoting chemical collects in the brain and _____ _____, not in the blood.

39. (p. 153) If this substance is extracted from one animal and injected into another, the second animal will fall _____. Unfortunately, this does not explain many other aspects of sleep.

40. (p. 154) Sleep is actively produced by several important structures in the brain: the _____; _____ _____; and a "sleep center" in the _____.

41. (p. 154) Rather than "shutting down" during sleep, the brain changes the _____ of its activity, not the amount.

42. (p. 154) The changes that come with sleep can be measured through the use of the _____, abbreviated _____.

43. (p. 154) When a person is awake and alert, the EEG shows a pattern of small, fast waves called _____. Immediately before sleep and when one is relaxed a pattern of _____ and _____ waves called _____ is observed.

44. (p. 154) As you close your eyes and begin to fall asleep, your breathing becomes slow and regular, your pulse rate slows, and body temperature drops. As you lose consciousness and enter _____ sleep, your heart rate slows even more.

45. (p. 154) During Stage 1 sleep, breathing becomes more irregular and the muscles of your body relax. This sometimes triggers a reflex contraction called a _____ jerk, which is quite normal.

46. (p. 154) Muscle spasms in the legs that occur later, during sleep itself, are called _____. This problem, also know as restless legs syndrome, causes about _____ to _____ percent of all cases of insomnia.

47. (p. 154) In Stage 1 sleep, the EEG is made up mainly of _____, _____ waves with some alpha. Persons awakened at this time may or may not say they were asleep.

48. (p. 155) During Stage 2 sleep, the EEG begins to show short bursts of activity called _____ _____, and body temperature drops further.

49. (p. 155) Sleep spindles seem to mark the true boundary of sleep. Within _____ minutes after they appear, the majority of subjects who are awakened report that they were asleep.

50. (p. 155) Stage 3 sleep is characterized by the appearance of a new brain wave called _____, which is very _____ and _____.

51. (p. 155) The final stage, also called _____ _____, is reached about an hour after sleep begins and is characterized by almost completely pure _____ brain waves. The sleeper eventually returns to Stage 1 (through Stages 3 and 2). Further shifts between deeper and lighter sleep occur throughout the night.

52. (p. 155) _____ _____ _____ or REMs are strongly associated with dreaming. Roughly _____ percent of awakenings made when REMs are present produce reports of vivid dreams.

53. (p. 155) The two most basic states of sleep now appear to be _____ sleep with its associated dreaming and _____-_____ sleep, abbreviated _____ which occurs mainly during Stages 2, 3, and 4.

54. (p. 155) NREM sleep is dream-free about _____ percent of the time. Dreams do occur during NREM, but during REM sleep they are usually longer, clearer, more detailed, and more "dream-like."

55. (p. 155) Your first period of stage 1 sleep is usually free of _____ and _____. Stage 1 sleep during the rest of the night is usually accompanied by rapid eye movements.

56. (p. 155) NREM sleep seems to help us recover from _____. It increases with _____ or physical exertion.

57. (p. 155) REM sleep totals about _____ minutes per night, but may increase when stress or emotionally charged events occur during the day.

58. (p. 155) During REM sleep, the heart beats _____ and blood pressure and breathing _____.

59. (p. 155) Males usually have an _____, and _____ blood flow increases in females, even if the dream is not erotic. When an erotic dream does occur, evidence of sexual arousal _____.

60. (p. 156) During REM sleep the body normally becomes quite still, as if the person were paralyzed. When REM paralysis fails, some people thrash violently about, leap out of bed, and may even attack their bedpartners. This recently recognized problem is called _____ _____ _____.

61. (p. 156) Sleepwalkers, or _____, usually have their eyes open, can negotiate obstacles, descend stairways, and climb trees, but a blank face, lack of recognition, and shuffling feet show they are still asleep.

62. (p. 156) Children of sleeptalkers and sleepwalkers are likely to have the same problems, which suggests that these sleep disturbances are at least partially _____.

63. (p. 156) A parent who finds a child sleepwalking should gently guide the child back to bed. Awakening a sleepwalker does _____ _____, but it is not necessary.

64. (p. 156) It might seem that sleepwalkers are acting out dream events, but somnambulism actually occurs during NREM Stages _____ and _____.

65. (p. 156) Sleeptalking occurs mostly in _____ stages of sleep. A link with the deeper stages of sleep seems to explain why sleeptalking makes little sense and why sleepwalkers are confused and remember little when awakened.

66. (p. 156) A nightmare is simply a bad dream (usually brief and remembered in detail) that takes place during _____ sleep. Nightmares have little connection with daytime anxieties.

67. (p. 156) For most people, nightmares occur, on average, about _____ per month.

68. (p. 156) _____ _____ are severely frightening dreams where the sleeper experiences blind panic and may hallucinate. Such experiences occur during Stage _____ sleep.

69. (p. 156) Such attacks may last _____ or _____ minutes during which the victim may sit up, scream, get out of bed, or run around the room. When over, the person awakens drenched in perspiration, but has only a vague memory of the terror itself.

70. (p. 156) Night terrors are most common during _____, although they may occur at other ages as well.

71. (p. 157) _____ is the dramatic sleep problem characterized by sudden, repeated, and irresistible "sleep attacks," when the person falls asleep for a few minutes to a few hours while standing, talking, or even driving. Emotional excitement, especially laughter, commonly triggers this problem.

72. (p. 157) Most of these victims also suffer from _____, a sudden temporary paralysis of the muscles leading to complete body collapse.

73. (p. 157) The EEGs of narcoleptics indicate that during attacks, they fall directly into _____ sleep. During normal sleep the first REM period doesn't occur until about 90 minutes after sleep begins.

74. (p. 157) Direct recordings in the _____ have identified cells that are highly active during both cataplexy and REM sleep.

75. (p. 157) Narcolepsy is quite rare and appears to be _____ as confirmed by breeding narcoleptic dogs. For humans there is no cure, but _____ drugs may diminish the frequency of attacks.

76. (p. 157) About 32 percent of adult Americans suffer from _____, the inability to sleep, awakening too early, frequent nighttime awakenings, or some combination. Roughly 15 to 20 percent have a serious or chronic problem.

77. (p. 158) Non-prescription sleeping pills have little or no sleep-inducing effect. Even worse are prescription _____ (usually barbiturates) which decrease both Stage _____ and _____ sleep and thereby reduce sleep quality.

78. (p. 158) An additional problem with prescription sedatives is that a drug tolerance rapidly builds so that the initial dosage becomes ineffective leading to "sleeping pill junkies" and _____-_____ insomnia.

79. (p. 158) Withdrawal from sleeping medications may produce terrible _____ and rebound insomnia, which often drive the user back to dependency.

80. (p. 158) A new drug called _____ appears to be effective for some cases of insomnia. However, even this pharmaceutical has drawbacks, and it too can cause rebound insomnia on the first few nights after it is withdrawn.

81. (p. 158) Temporary insomnia usually involves a cycle of physical arousal from worry, stress, or excitement which interferes with sleep, causing _____ and anger which causes more arousal, and so on.

82. (p. 158) One way to beat temporary insomnia is to avoid _____ it. Get up and do something useful or satisfying.

83. (p. 158) Some insomniacs have been found to have a drop in _____ _____ during the night. This result can be avoided by having a small snack before sleeping.

84. (p. 158) Also, it has been discovered that the amino acid _____ helps put people to sleep. This substance can be found in a glass of milk and in certain other items.

85. (p. 158) _____ _____ is said to exist if sleeping problems last for more than three weeks.

86. (p. 158) Treatment for chronic insomnia usually begins with a careful analysis of a person's sleep _____. Possible sources of insomnia, such as depression, anxiety, medical problems, lifestyle, stress, and sleep habits are carefully assessed.

87. (p. 158) The first thing that anyone suffering from insomnia should do is to reduce consumption of _____, _____, and _____.

88. (p. 158) Some insomniacs benefit from _____ training to lower arousal before sleep.

89. (p. 158) _____ _____ strategies are also helpful. For example, patients are told to strictly avoid doing anything other than sleeping when they go to bed so that only sleeping becomes associated with retiring.

90. (p. 158) Many insomniacs have scattered sleep habits. For these people, adopting a _____ _____ (getting up and going to sleep at exactly the same time each day) helps establish a firm body rhythm and greatly improves sleep.

91. (p. 158) When you suffer from insomnia, there are several things you can do to help. Avoid _____ such as coffee or cigarettes. Remember too that alcohol impairs sleep quality.

92. (p. 158) Schedule time in the _____ _____ to write down worries or concerns and what you will do about them the next day.

93. (p. 158) Learn a physical or mental strategy for relaxing such as _____ muscle relaxation, _____, or blotting out worries with calming images. Very light evening exercise may be helpful.

94. (p. 159) To implement stimulus control principles in the treatment of insomnia, be sure to: (1) go to bed only when you are feeling _____; (2) avoid _____; (3) awaken at the same time each morning; (4) avoid _____ activities in bed; (5) always leave the bedroom if sleep has not occurred within _____ minutes; (6) do something else when you are upset about not being able to sleep.

95. (p. 159) To remove the pressure of trying to get to sleep, use _____ intention. That is, try to keep your eyes open (in the dark) and stay awake as long as possible. This will allow sleep to overtake you unexpectedly and lower performance anxiety.

96. (p. 159) A person who snores loudly, with short silences and loud gasps or snorts, may suffer from _____ _____.

97. (p. 159) In sleep apnea, breathing stops for periods of _____ seconds to _____ minutes until need for oxygen becomes intense and the person awakens slightly and gulps in air, then returns to sleep until breathing again stops.

98. (p. 159) This cycle is repeated hundreds of times a night and is associated with complaints of daytime sleepiness known as _____.

99. (p. 159) Some apnea occurs because the _____ stops sending signals to the diaphragm to maintain breathing. Another cause is blockage of the upper _____ _____.

100. (p. 159) Individuals with sleep apnea can breathe normally during the day, so they may be unaware of the problem. Since this condition seriously endangers _____, persons who suspect they are apneic should seek treatment at a _____ _____.

101. (p. 159) Sleep apnea is especially dangerous in infancy, when it is suspected as one cause of "crib death" or _____ _____ _____ _____, abbreviated _____.

102. (p. 159) SIDS is the most frequent cause of death for infants under _____ year of age, claiming 10,000 victims each year in the U.S. alone. In a typical SIDS death, the infant is slightly premature, with a mild cold or infection.

103. (p. 159) Doctors think that some cases of SIDS are caused by apnea due to immature breathing centers in the _____. Others suspect a defect that stalls the _____ during sleep.

104. (p. 159) Sometimes it appears that direct blockage of the nose is responsible. These cases may be linked to babies who remain _____ when breathing is blocked.

105. (p. 159) Babies at risk for SIDS must be carefully watched for the first _____ months of life. To aid parents in this task, a special monitor may be used which sounds an alarm when breathing or pulse becomes weak.

106. (p. 159) Some warning signs for SIDS include: (1) the mother is a _____ or _____; (2) the baby is premature, (3) the baby has an unusual _____-_____ cry; (4) the baby engages in "snoring," breathholding, or frequent awakening at night; (5) the baby breathes mainly through an _____ _____; (6) the baby remains passive when its face rolls into a pillow or blanket.

107. (p. 160) When researchers Nathaniel _____ and Eugene _____ discovered REM sleep in 1952, they ushered in a "Golden Era" of dream inquiry.

108. (p. 160) Most people dream _____ or _____ times a night, but not all people remember their dreams.

109. (p. 160) Dreams are usually spaced about _____ minutes apart. The first dream of the evening lasts about _____ minutes; the last averages _____ minutes and may last as long as _____ minutes (in real time).

110. (p. 160) William Dement has shown that when subjects are deprived of REM sleep, they show an _____ tendency to dream. To prevent dreaming, Dement found that he had to wake subjects _____ or _____ times by the fifth night.

111. (p. 160) When subjects were finally allowed to sleep without interruption, they dreamed extra amounts. This is called the REM _____ effect.

112. (p. 160) This effect explains why alcoholics often have horrible nightmares after they quit drinking. Alcohol _____ REM sleep and sets up a powerful rebound effect when it is withdrawn.

113. (p. 160) While deprived of dream sleep, Dement's volunteers complained of lapses in _____ and _____. Also, they felt more _____ during the day.

114. (p. 160) For a time these and similar results led to the belief that a person would go crazy if permanently kept from dreaming. This belief is now called the "_____ _____."

115. (p. 160) Recent experiments indicate that missing out on any particular sleep stage can cause a rebound for that stage. Also, daytime disturbances are generally related to the _____ _____ of sleep lost, not the type of sleep lost.

116. (p. 160) Dream sleep may provide stimulation necessary for brain development. Newborn babies spend about 50 percent of their sleeping time in REM sleep, while premature infants get up to _____ percent REM sleep.

117. (p. 160) In adulthood, REM sleep may serve other purposes. For one thing, REM sleep _____ after learning, so it may help restore brain chemicals needed for learning and memory.

118. (p. 160) REM sleep also seems to help sort and integrate _____ formed during the day.

119. (p. 160) Dreams may prevent sensory _____ during sleep and aid the processing of _____ events.

120. (p. 160) In animals, REM sleep seems to help the brain store daytime experiences that are important for survival. Specifically, REM sleep boosts activity in the _____, an area of the brain crucial for memory.

121. (p. 160) Sleep biologist Jonathan Winson believes it is no accident that our dreams center on _____, insecurities, strengths, _____, failures, _____ feelings, desires, hates, jealousies, and _____. Our dreams may help us sort out and retain everyday "survival" strategies related to such primal motives and emotions.

122. (p. 160) Dreaming may aid learning. Carlyle Smith found in one study that college students who lost REM sleep did much _____ on a difficult mental task than did various control subjects.

123. (p. 161) Calvin Hall, a noted authority on dreams, has collected and analyzed over 10,000 dreams. He found that most dreams reflect _____ _____.

124. (p. 161) The favorite dreaming setting is familiar rooms in a _____. Action usually takes place between the dreamer and two or three other _____ important people. Dream actions are mostly familiar. Dreams of flying, floating, and falling occur less frequently.

125. (p. 161) About _____ of the dreams Hall recorded had sexual elements.

126. (p. 161) Unpleasant emotions such as fear, anger, and sadness are _____ frequent in dreams than pleasant emotions.

127. (p. 161) Most theorists agree that dreams reflect our waking _____, _____, and _____. However, some theorists believe that dreams have deeply hidden meanings, while others regard dreams as meaningless.

128. (p. 161) Upon analyzing his own dreams, Freud felt that many represented _____ _____.However, there is evidence against this since volunteers experiencing prolonged starvation showed no particular increase in dreams about food and eating.

129. (p. 161) Freud's response to this result probably would have been that not all wish fulfillment is so direct. One of his key insights is that dreams represent thoughts expressed in _____ or pictures, rather than in words.

130. (p. 161) Freud believed that the conscience relaxes during sleep, allowing dreams to express unconscious desires and conflicts in disguised _____ _____. For instance, death might be symbolized by a journey, children by small animals, or sexual intercourse by horseback riding or dancing.

131. (p. 162) A radically different view of dreaming is offered by Allan Hobson and Robert McCarley. Their approach is called the _____-_____ _____.

132. (p. 162) The activation-synthesis hypothesis states that certain brain cells are activated during REM sleep. These cells control eye movements, balance, etc. Messages from these cells are blocked from reaching the body, but continue to reach higher brain areas which interpret the incoming information by searching stored _____ and manufacturing a dream.

133. (p. 162) This approach seems to explain dreams where chases, flying, or floating are central, but many psychologists continue to believe that dreams have _____ _____.

134. (p. 163) _____ is an altered state of consciousness, characterized by narrowed attention and an increased openness to suggestion.

135. (p. 163) Some psychologists regard hypnosis as no more than a blend of _____, _____, _____, obedience, suggestion, and role-playing.

136. (p. 163) Interest in hypnosis began in the 1700s with Franz _____, who believed he could cure disease by passing _____ over the body of an afflicted person.

137. (p. 163) While Mesmer (whose name is the basis for the term mesmerize) enjoyed quite a following for a short time, his theories of _____ _____ were soon rejected and he was branded a quack and a fraud.

138. (p. 163) The term hypnosis was coined later by _____ _____ to refer to the sleep-like trance. Today we know that hypnosis is not sleep, since _____ recordings made during hypnosis are similar to those obtained when a person is awake.

139. (p. 163) Approximately _____ out of ten people can be hypnotized, but only _____ out of ten will be good hypnotic subjects.

140. (p. 163) People who are _____ and prone to _____ are often highly responsive to hypnosis. But people who lack these traits may also be hypnotized.

141. (p. 163) Hypnotic suggestibility can be measured by making a series of suggestions to subjects and recording the number of suggestions to which they respond. A typical hypnotic test is the _____ _____ _____ Scale.

142. (p. 163) If you were to score high on this scale today, you probably would do the same years from now. Hypnotizability is very _____ over time.

143. (p. 163) There are many hypnotic routines. Common factors in all techniques are that they encourage a person to: (1) focus _____ on what is being said; (2) relax and feel _____; (3) "let go" and accept _____ easily; and (4) to use vivid _____.

144. (p. 164) In deeper stages of hypnosis, "reality testing" may be relaxed so that a partial suspension of normal "_____" is achieved. But at first, one must cooperate willingly in order to become hypnotized.

145. (p. 164) Many theorists believe that all hypnosis is really _____-_____ and that the hypnotist simply serves as a guide to help the person achieve a state that could be reached alone.

146. (p. 164) During hypnosis you might experience mild feelings of _____, sinking, anesthesia, or _____ from your body. However, in all but the deepest stages of hypnosis, people remain aware of what is going on.

147. (p. 164) A key element in hypnosis is the _____ _____ effect. Hypnotized persons feel that suggested actions or experience are automatic.

148. (p. 164) Hypnosis may cause a _____ or "split" in awareness. For example, Ernest Hilgard told hypnotized subjects to feel no pain when they plunged their hands into icewater. When asked if they felt pain, subjects reported none. When asked if any part of their minds felt pain, many wrote that they did.

149. (p. 164) Hilgard has referred to this later part as the _____ _____—it is aware of pain but remains in the background.

150. (p. 164) Hypnosis has no more effect on physical strength than instructions that encourage subjects to make their best effort. It does not produce _____ acts of strength.

151. (p. 164) There is some evidence that hypnosis can enhance memory. However, it also frequently increases the number of _____ _____. Because of this, many states now bar persons who have been hypnotized from testifying in court cases.

152. (p. 164) Hypnosis can relieve _____. Therefore, it can be especially useful in situations where chemical painkillers cannot be used, or are ineffective.

153. (p. 164) As an example of the usefulness of hypnosis in relieving pain, it can be successfully used to control _____ _____ pain where amputees sometimes experience recurring pains which feel as if they come from the missing limb.

154. (p. 164) Through hypnosis, subjects have been "_____" to childhood. Doubt is cast on this possibility by the fact that such persons continue to use knowledge they could only have learned as adults.

155. (p. 164) Hypnotic suggestions concerning _____ seem to be among the most effective. It is possible to alter color vision, hearing sensitivity, time sense, perception of illusions, etc.

156. (p. 166) Generally, hypnosis seems to have greatest value as a tool for inducing _____, as a means of controlling _____ (in dentistry and childbirth), and as an adjunct to psychological therapy and counseling.

157. (p. 165) In general, hypnosis is better at changing _____ _____ than at modifying behavior, such as smoking or overeating. Hypnotic effects are useful, but seldom amazing.

158. (p. 165) Authority T. X. Barber says that stage hypnotists make use of several factors excluding legitimate hypnosis to perform their act. For example, they employ _____ _____: On stage, people are unusually cooperative because they don't want to ruin the act.

159. (p. 165) Stage hypnotists are careful to select _____ subjects. Participants must volunteer thus ensuring that they are relatively uninhibited. They are hypnotized as a group and anyone who does not succumb is eliminated.

160. (p. 165) The hypnosis label _____. Once a person is labeled as hypnotized he or she can "perform" without fear of embarrassment.

161. (p. 165) The stage hypnotist acts as a "_____." Audience response to participants encourages their antics so that all the "hypnotist" need do is guide the action.

162. (p. 165) And finally, stage hypnotists use _____. Stage hypnosis is about 50 percent taking advantage of the situation and 50 percent deception.

163. (p. 165) _____ _____ refers to any major reduction in external stimulation. It has been one of the most frequently used means of altering consciousness.

164. (p. 166) Under such conditions of limited or monotonous stimulation, people have at times had bizarre _____, dangerous lapses in _____, and wildly distorted _____.

165. (p. 166) D. O. Hebb studied volunteers paid to lie on their backs in a small cubicle. They wore darkened goggles, and gloves and cardboard cuffs restricted touch. A constant hissing noise masked all sounds. Under such conditions, few subjects could take more than _____ or _____ days without "pushing the panic button."

166. (p. 166) The most consistent disturbances after sensory deprivation are a distortion of _____, heightened visual _____, slower _____, and a brief warping of visual lines and space. Some participants in early experiments also reported strange and vivid images.

167. (p. 166) We now know that true hallucinations are rare during sensory deprivation. The fanciful, dreamlike visions that sometimes do occur are actually _____ _____, similar to those that may occur just before you fall asleep.

168. (p. 166) Hypnogogic images may be vivid and surprising, but they are rarely mistaken for real objects. Such images are apparently linked to an increase in the number of _____ waves produced by the brain.

169. (p. 166) These brainwaves, in the _____- to _____-cycles-per-second range, are usually recorded just before sleep. Sensory deprivation also increases their occurrence.

170. (p. 166) One of the most consistent after-effects of sensory deprivation is increased _____ acuity. Some people report using this effect to aid creative thinking.

171. (p. 166) While most people find prolonged sensory deprivation stressful and uncomfortable, brief periods of restricted sensation are very relaxing and can produce a large drop in blood _____, muscle _____, and other signs of stress. It is one of the surest ways to induce deep relaxation.

172. (p. 166) Peter Suedfeld has found that sensory deprivation can help people change habitual behaviors. For example, of subjects exposed to standard anti-smoking messages combined with sensory deprivation, _____ percent less were smoking three months later when compared with controls.

173. (p. 166) Another study found similar prolonged benefits for people in a _____-_____ program based on using Suedfeld's REST technique—restricted environmental stimulation therapy.

174. (p. 167) Suedfeld's technique makes use of tape recorded suggestions played to subjects while they are isolated in a flotation tank. Deep _____ and mental confusion leading to the _____ of belief systems may make it easier to produce lasting changes.

175. (p. 167) After years of being viewed only as a disruptive state, sensory deprivation may yet prove to have other benefits. For example, REST also shows promise as a way to stimulate _____ thinking.

176. (p. 167) The surest way to alter human consciousness is to administer a _____ _____. Such substances are capable of altering attention, memory, judgment, time sense, self-control, emotion, and perception.

177. (p. 167) Most psychoactive drugs can be placed on a scale ranging from _____ to _____.

178. (p. 167) Drug dependence falls into two broad categories. When a person compulsively uses a drug to maintain bodily comfort a _____ dependence, commonly referred to as _____, exists.

179. (p. 167) Physical dependence occurs most often with drugs that cause _____ _____—extremely unpleasant reactions that take place when the drug is withheld.

180. (p. 167) Addiction is often accompanied by a drug _____, the need to take larger and larger doses to achieve the same effects initially supplied by smaller doses.

181. (p. 167) A _____ _____ is said to exist when an individual feels that a drug is necessary to maintain emotional or psychological well-being. Usually this is based on an intense craving for the drug and its rewarding qualities.

182. (p. 167) Psychological dependence may affect a drug user as powerfully as physical addiction does. This is why some psychologists prefer to define addiction more broadly as any _____ habit pattern. By this definition, a person who has lost control over his or her drug use, for whatever reason, is addicted.

183. (p. 170) The psychoactive drugs most associated with physical dependence are: heroin, morphine, codeine, methadone, barbiturates, alcohol, amphetamines and tobacco. All can lead to _____ _____.

184. (p. 170) Drug-taking behavior can be classified as: (1) _____, short-term use motivated by curiosity; (2) _____, occasional social use considered pleasurable by participants; (3) _____, used to cope with a specific problem such as boredom or staying awake for night work; (4) _____, daily use having elements of dependence; or (5) _____, intense use and extreme dependence.

185. (p. 170) Amphetamines form a large group of synthetic stimulants. Drugs commonly available in this group are _____, _____, and _____.

186. (p. 170) Amphetamines were once widely prescribed by doctors to aid _____ _____ or to combat _____ _____. Both practices are now discouraged because of drug dependency problems.

187. (p. 170) The only fully legitimate medical uses of amphetamines are to treat _____ and overdoses of _____ drugs.

188. (p. 170) Amphetamines rapidly produce a _____ _____, with abusers taking ever larger quantities of pills or switching to injections directly into the bloodstream to maintain the desired effect.

189. (p. 171) The true speed freak typically goes on _____ lasting several days, after which he or she "crashes" from lack of sleep and food.

190. (p. 171) Amphetamine use poses many dangers. To stay high, the abuser must take more of the drug as the body's tolerance grows. Higher doses can cause _____, _____, high blood _____, fatal heart _____, and crippling strokes.

191. (p. 171) Amphetamines speed the expenditure of _____ _____. They do not magically supply energy.

192. (p. 171) The after-effects of an amphetamine high may include _____, _____, terrifying nightmares, confusion, and uncontrolled irritation and _____.

193. (p. 171) Repeatedly overextending one's body with stimulants may lead to considerable _____ loss, sores and non-healing _____, brittle _____, toothgrinding, chronic chest _____, _____ disease, high blood pressure, and in some cases _____ hemorrhage.

194. (p. 171) Amphetamines can cause a loss of contact with reality known as _____ _____. Affected users feel threatened and suffer from paranoid delusions that someone is out to get them. Acting on these delusions, the speed-freak may become violent, resulting in self-injury or injury to others.

195. (p. 171) A potent new smokable form of crystal methamphetamine (known as "ice") has recently added to the problem of methamphetamine abuse. The drug is highly _____ and produces an intense _____ without the use of needles. It leads very rapidly to compulsive abuse and severe drug dependence.

196. (p. 171) Cocaine is a powerful central nervous system stimulant extracted from the leaves of the coca plant. Its subjective effects are sensations of _____, _____, well-being, power, boundless energy, and pleasure.

197. (p. 171) Until 1906 when the Pure _____ and _____ Act was passed, Coca-Cola contained cocaine (since replaced by caffeine), as did dozens of nonprescription potions and cure-alls.

198. (p. 171) Cocaine is one of the most widely abused drugs. An estimated _____ to _____ million Americans use it at least once a month, and _____ of all Americans between the ages of 25 and 30 have tried it.

199. (p. 171) Among college students, there has been a _____-fold increase in cocaine use, compared to 15 years ago.

200. (p. 171) Cocaine and amphetamines are very similar in their effect on the central nervous system. The main difference is that amphetamine effects may last several _____; cocaine is quickly metabolized, so its effects last only about _____ to _____ minutes.

201. (p. 171) Cocaine is one of the most dangerous drugs of abuse. Even casual or first-time users run a risk because cocaine can cause _____, heart attack, or a _____.

202. (p. 171) Just one hit of cocaine taken by a pregnant woman can cause defects in her fetus. At birth, "crack babies" are very _____ and _____ if their mother recently used cocaine. Otherwise, they are _____ and _____.

203. (p. 172) By the time crack babies start school, they often suffer from _____, _____, listlessness, slowed _____ learning, and disorganized thinking.

204. (p. 172) Rats and monkeys given free access to cocaine find it irresistible, some to the point of dying of _____ from self-administered overdoses.

205. (p. 172) Cocaine increases activity in brain pathways sensitive to the chemical messengers _____ and _____. One arouses the brain, while an increase in the other can produce a "rush" of pleasure.

206. (p. 172) Termination of cocaine usage does not produce physical withdrawal symptoms, but rather has its own withdrawal pattern. First, there is a jarring "crash" of _____ and _____.

207. (p. 172) Within a few days, the person enters a long period of _____, _____, paranoia, boredom, and _____ (an inability to feel pleasure).

208. (p. 172) During withdrawal, cravings for cocaine are intense. The person feels wretched and also vividly remembers the intense pleasure of previous cocaine highs. The urge to use cocaine grows overwhelming. Cravings may remain for _____ or _____ after last using it.

209. (p. 172) Because of the powerfully rewarding effects of cocaine, there is a high risk of becoming a dependent and compulsive abuser. Many authorities estimate that if cocaine were cheaper, _____ out of 10 users would progress to compulsive use. In fact, rock cocaine (or "crack"), which is cheaper, produces very high abuse rates among those who try it.

210. (p. 172) Serious signs of cocaine abuse include: (1) _____ use—when it is available, you can't say "no" to it. (2) Loss of _____—once you have had some cocaine, you keep using it until you are exhausted or the cocaine is gone. (3) Disregarding _____—you use cocaine no matter what happens or how serious the cost.

211. (p. 172) Anyone who thinks he or she may be developing a cocaine problem should seek advice at a drug clinic or a Cocaine Anonymous meeting. From _____ to _____ percent of cocaine abusers who remain in treatment programs succeed in breaking their coke addiction.

212. (p. 172) The most frequently used psychoactive drug in the U.S. is _____, a substance that stimulates the brain by blocking chemicals which normally inhibit or slow nerve activity.

213. (p. 172) Caffeine in doses as small as 100 to 200 milligrams has an effect. Psychologically, caffeine suppresses _____ or drowsiness, and increases feelings of _____.

214. (p. 172) It is common to think of _____ as the major source of caffeine, but it is also found in tea, soft drinks, chocolate, cocoa, and over 2000 non-prescription drugs.

215. (p. 172) Serious abuse of caffeine is known as _____. People with this condition commonly drink 15 to 20 cups of coffee a day and may suffer increased health risks.

216. (p. 172) Caffeinism can result in insomnia, irritability, loss of _____, chills, racing _____, and elevated body _____.

217. (p. 172) Caffeine encourages the development of breast _____ in women, and may contribute to insomnia, _____ problems, and _____ problems, and high blood pressure.

218. (p. 173) Health authorities urge pregnant women to give up caffeine entirely because of a suspected link between caffeine and _____ _____. A possible link between caffeine and _____ has also been detected.

219. (p. 173) Next to caffeine, _____, found mainly in tobacco, is the most widely used psychoactive drug.

220. (p. 173) In large doses nicotine causes stomach pain, _____ and diarrhea, cold sweats, _____, confusion, and tremors.

221. (p. 173) In very large doses nicotine may cause _____, respiratory failure, and _____.

222. (p. 173) For a non-smoker, 50-75 milligrams of nicotine could be lethal. In contrast, a heavy smoker may inhale 40 cigarettes a day without feeling ill. This difference indicates that regular smokers build a _____ for nicotine.

223. (p. 173) A 1988 report by the United States Surgeon General concluded that nicotine is addicting. Withdrawal may cause _____, _____, cramps, insomnia, _____ upset, irritability, and a sharp craving for cigarettes.

224. (p. 173) These symptoms may last from _____ to _____ weeks and may be worse than heroin withdrawal. Indeed, relapse patterns are nearly identical for alcoholics, heroin addicts, cocaine abusers, and smokers who try to quit.

225. (p. 173) A burning cigarette releases more than 6,800 different chemicals. Many of these, including nicotine, are potent _____, cancer-causing substances.

226. (p. 173) _____-_____ percent of lung cancers among men and 74 percent among women are caused by smoking. Altogether smoking is responsible for about one-third of all cancer deaths in the U.S.

227. (p. 173) Users of smokeless tobacco run a _____ to _____ times higher risk of developing oral cancer. Smokeless tobacco also causes shrinkage of the _____, contributes to _____ disease, and probably is as addicting as cigarettes.

228. (p. 174) Most smokers claim that smoking helps them concentrate, feel sociable, or calm down. However, psychologist Stanley Schachter asserts that smokers only smoke to prevent _____.

229. (p. 174) Schachter has shown that smoking does not improve mood or performance, but that heavy smokers who are _____ of nicotine feel and perform worse than non-smokers.

230. (p. 174) Also, smokers adjust their smoking to keep bodily levels of nicotine _____. Thus when smokers are given lighter cigarettes or when they are under stress (which speeds removal of nicotine) they smoke more.

231. (p. 174) Schachter's work shows that smokers who cut down are in a constant state of _____ causing irritability and discomfort without really ending smoking.

232. (p. 174) Smokers who switch to lighter cigarettes often smoke more and thus may expose themselves to more _____-_____ substances than before.

233. (p. 174) Quitting smoking is not easy. It helps if you get a spouse or partner to support your effort. Also anyone trying to quit should be prepared to make _____ attempts before succeeding.

234. (p. 174) Barbiturates are _____ drugs that produce a general depression of activity in the brain. They are used medically to calm patients or to induce sleep.

235. (p. 174) In mild doses, barbiturates have an effect similar to _____ intoxication, but an overdose of barbiturates can cause _____ or _____.

236. (p. 174) Barbiturates taken with alcohol are particularly dangerous as the combined effects of the two drugs are multiplied by a _____ _____ (one drug enhances the effect of another).

237. (p. 174) Barbiturates may be taken in excessive amounts because increasing consumption makes users uninhibited or forgetful. An overdose first causes unconsciousness and then so severely depresses brain centers controlling _____ and _____ that death results.

238. (p. 174) The most frequently abused downers are short-acting barbiturates such as _____ and _____ and the non-barbiturate _____ (Quaadlude, Sopor, and Parest are its trade names).

239. (p. 174) These drugs seem to be preferred because they take effect quickly and the rush of intoxication only lasts from _____ to _____ hours. Like the other depressants, repeated use can cause a physical dependence and emotional depression.

240. (p. 174) Alcohol is not a stimulant, but instead is a _____ which in small amounts produces relaxation, euphoria, and diminishes inhibition, but in larger amounts can impair brain functioning to the point of unconsciousness.

241. (p. 174) Alcohol is not an _____, usually it impairs sexual performance particularly in males.

242. (p. 174) When a person is drunk, thinking and perception become dulled or shortsighted, a condition that has been called _____ _____.

243. (p. 175) Behaviors become more _____ when a person is drunk because worries and "second thoughts" that would normally restrain behavior are diminished.

244. (p. 175) Alcohol reduces _____ and temporarily makes people feel _____ about themselves.

245. (p. 175) In America, alcohol is used by over _____ million people, _____ to _____ million of whom have a serious drinking problem.

246. (p. 175) A recent national survey found that _____ percent of college students are heavy drinkers. Among college males, the figure was _____ percent.

247. (p. 175) _____ of alcoholics and those who have other relatives who abuse alcohol are at greater risk for becoming alcohol abusers themselves.

248. (p. 176) There are several phases involved in the progression of a social drinker to a problem drinker. Four danger signs that signal excessive dependence during the initial phase are: _____ consumption; _____ drinking; _____ behavior; and _____.

249. (p. 176) During the second phase (crucial phase) there is usually control over when and where a first drink is taken, but one drink starts a _____ _____.

250. (p. 176) Finally, at the _____ phase, the alcoholic drinks compulsively and continuously.

251. (p. 176) Psychologists Roger Vogler and Wayne Bartz have studied the amount of alcohol per hour that can be consumed to maintain a level which makes you feel good. As long as blood alcohol remains below a level of about _____ people feel relaxed, euphoric, and sociable.

252. (p. 176) At blood alcohol levels above 0.05, drinkers may go from moderately intoxicated to thoroughly drunk. Later, as blood alcohol begins to _____, those who overdrink become sick and miserable.

253. (p. 176) Treatment for alcoholism begins by sobering the person up and cutting off the supply. This procedure is referred to as _____ and frequently produces all the symptoms of drug withdrawal.

254. (p. 176) The next step is to try to restore the alcoholic's _____ through food, vitamins, and medical care.

255. (p. 177) And finally the alcoholic may be treated with _____, _____, or psychotherapy. Unfortunately, the success of these procedures has been limited.

256. (p. 177) One mutual-help approach that has been fairly successful in treating alcoholics is _____ _____, which acts on the premise that it takes a former alcoholic to understand and help a current alcoholic.

257. (p. 177) One study has shown that of those who remain in AA over one year, _____ percent get through the following year without a drink.

258. (p. 177) The National Institute of Drug Abuse has found that one out of every _____ Americans has tried marijuana at least once. More than _____ million Americans may be regular users.

259. (p. 177) Marijuana and hashish are derived from the hemp plant _____ _____ containing the active chemical _____ (abbreviated THC), a mild hallucinogen.

260. (p. 177) Scientists have located a specific receptor site on the surface of brain cells where THC binds to produce its effects. These receptor sites are found in large numbers in the _____ _____, which is the seat of human consciousness.

261. (p. 177) While there have been no overdose deaths from marijuana, it cannot be considered harmless. One issue is that THC accumulates in the body's fatty tissues, especially in the _____ and _____ organs.

262. (p. 177) Studies of long-term heavy users of marijuana in Jamaica, Greece, and Costa Rica have failed to find evidence of _____ dependence. Its potential for abuse, therefore, lies primarily in the realm of psychological dependence, not addiction.

263. (p. 177) Marijuana's typical psychological effects are: a sense of _____ or well-being, _____, altered _____ sense and perceptual distortions. Marijuana also impairs short-term _____ and slows _____.

264. (p. 177) Although marijuana intoxication is relatively subtle by comparison to a drug such as alcohol, it is still extremely _____ to drive a car or operate machinery while high.

265. (p. 177) Marijuana has been charged with causing brain _____, mental illness, and loss of _____. Each of these effects has been criticized for being based on poorly done or inconclusive research.

266. (p. 178) Major studies in Jamaica, Greece, and Costa Rica failed to find any serious _____ problems or _____ impairment in long-term marijuana users.

267. (p. 178) There are several liabilities associated with marijuana. As is true of alcohol, some adults become highly _____ on marijuana. Frequent use of any psychoactive drug can seriously impair mental, physical, and emotional development.

268. (p. 178) Several potential risks have been identified for marijuana usage. In regular users it causes chronic _____ and pre- _____ changes in lung cells.

269. (p. 178) A recent study by Swiss researchers found that marijuana smoke contains _____ percent more cancer-causing hydrocarbons than does tobacco smoke. Some doctors estimate that smoking several "joints" a week is the equivalent of smoking a dozen cigarettes a day.

270. (p. 178) Other researchers have found that smokers of only a few joints a day have as much microscopic damage to the cells lining the _____ as smokers of more than a pack of cigarettes a day.

271. (p. 178) Marijuana temporarily lowers _____ production in males and may produce reproductive abnormalities. This effect could be a problem for a marginally fertile man who wants to have a family.

272. (p. 170) In experiments with female monkeys, THC causes abnormal _____ _____ and disrupts ovulation. Other animal studies have shown it causes a higher rate of _____ and can reach the fetus. The effect on human females is as yet unclear, but marijuana should be avoided during pregnancy.

273. (p. 178) THC can suppress the body's _____ system, possibly increasing the risk of disease.

274. (p. 178) In animals, marijuana causes _____ damage within cells of the body. It is not known, however, to what extent this happens in humans.

275. (p. 179) Freud identified four dream processes which help disguise hidden meanings of dreams. In the first, called _____, a single character in a dream represents several people at once.

276. (p. 179) A second means of disguising dream content is _____. The most important emotions of a dream may be redirected toward safe or seemingly unimportant images.

277. (p. 180) A third process is _____. Freud believed that dreams usually express symbolic images, rather than being literal in meaning.

278. (p. 180) A process called _____ _____ is the fourth method by which the meaning of dreams is disguised. This process refers to the tendency to reorganize a dream when remembering it.

279. (p. 180) Dream theorist Calvin _____ thinks of dreams as plays and the dreamer as a playwright. He feels much can be learned by simply considering the setting, cast, plot, and emotions portrayed in a dream.

280. (p. 180) Rosalind Cartwright suggests that one's everyday dream life can be a source of varied experience and personal enrichment. Emphasis is placed on the overall _____ _____ of the dream as a clue to its meaning.

281. (p. 180) Ann Faraday thinks of dreams as messages from yourself to yourself. She believes in the value of studying one's own dreams and suggests the following techniques to "catch a dream:"
    1) Before retiring, plan to _____ your dreams.
    2) If possible, arrange to awaken _____.
    3) If you rarely remember your dreams, set an alarm clock to wake you up earlier.
    4) Upon awakening, review the images with your _____ _____.
    5) Make your first _____ _____ with your eyes closed.
    6) Review the dream again and record as many additional details as possible.
    7) Keep a permanent "dream diary."
    8) Remember that a number of drugs _____ dreaming.

282. (p. 181) Fritz _____ feels that dreams are a special message about what is missing in our lives. They are a means of filling in gaps in personal experience.

283. (p. 181) An approach that Perls found helpful in understanding a dream is to "take the part of" each of the characters and objects in the dream. It is also revealing to set up dialogues between people or objects in the dream, especially those that stand in _____ to one another.

284. (p. 181) Dream theorist Gordon Globus believes that some of our most _____ moments take place during dreaming. Even unimaginative people, he notes, may create amazing worlds each night in their dreams.

285. (p. 181) The dream state is one of reduced _____, and may be helpful in _____ _____ that require a fresh point of view. Certainly individuals such as Otto Loewi, to whom the idea for a breakthrough experiment leading to the Nobel Prize came in a dream, have found them to be of value in the production of creative solutions.

286. (p. 182) During a _____ dream, the dreamer "wakes" within an ordinary dream and feels capable of normal thought and action. Such dreamers know they are dreaming, but feel fully conscious within the dream world.

287. (p. 182) Stephen _____ showed that lucid dreaming and voluntary action in dreams are possible by training lucid dreamers to make prearranged signs when they become aware they were dreaming.

288. (p. 182) La Berge found he could greatly increase lucid dreaming with this routine:
   1) When you awaken, _____ your dream.
   2) Next engage in 10 or 15 minutes of any activity requiring full _____.
   3) Then while lying in bed and returning to sleep, say to yourself, "Next time I'm dreaming, I want to remember I'm dreaming."
   4) Finally, visualize yourself lying in bed asleep, while in the dream just rehearsed, and simultaneously picture yourself realizing you are dreaming.

289. (p. 183) The best predictors of adolescent drug use and abuse are _____ drug use, _____ drug use, delinquency, parental maladjustment, poor _____-_____, social nonconformity, and stressful life changes.

290. (p. 183) For many young people, drug abuse is just one part of a general pattern of problem behavior. A study that followed children from preschool to age 18 found that adolescents who abuse drugs tend to be _____, alienated, _____, and _____ distressed. Drug abuse is a symptom, rather than a cause, of personal and social maladjustment.

291. (p. 183) A combination of immediate pleasure and delayed punishment allows abusers to feel good on demand. As a result, drug taking can become _____.

292. (p. 183) Closely related to a drug's actual effects are users' beliefs and expectations about drugs. For example, one study found that heavy drinkers expect far more _____ effects and fewer _____ consequences from drinking alcohol than light drinkers do.

293. (p. 183) There is a widespread tendency to think of drugs as a magic way to produce good feelings by avoiding, minimizing, or escaping negative situations. Some observers believe that drug use is so deeply ingrained in modern society that we are addicted to _____.

294. (p. 183) Some observers feel that the medical profession, well meaning but misguided, unnecessarily encourages legal drug use. Many _____ and _____ problems of living are now being redefined as medical problems, to be solved by physicians with prescription pads.

295. (p. 184) Drug abuse and drug-related problems once restricted to certain subcultures and the urban poor have spread widely. For example, one recent survey found that nearly _____ percent of doctors under age 40 admitted that they use marijuana or cocaine to get high with friends.

296. (p. 184) Psychiatrist Thomas Szasz and Consumer Reports have independently taken the position that current drug regulations encourage a black market, organized crime, disrespect for the law, and adulterated drugs. They believe it is futile for the government to "legislate _____."

297. (p. 184) There has been _____ _____ in use of marijuana in states that have relaxed penalties for possession to a fine.

298. (p. 184) In Amsterdam, drug addiction is treated as a medical rather than a criminal problem. Methadone is freely available to heroin addicts and little effort is made to prevent the use of "soft drugs" such as marijuana. In this situation, the proportion of younger addicts has _____ during the last decade.

299. (p. 184) Given such facts, some experts believe that prevention through _____ and early _____, rather than tougher enforcement is the answer to drug problems.

SELF-TEST

1.   (p. 150) Mental states related to fatigue, delirium, hypnosis, meditation, drugs, and ecstasy are referred to as _____ states of consciousness.
      a.   altered   c.   extrasensory
      b.   distorted   d.   psi

2.   (p. 151) _____ is a brief shift in brain activity to patterns normally found in sleep.
      a.   Minisleep   c.   Brain sleep
      b.   EEG sleep   d.   Microsleep

3.   (p. 152) True-False. The experiences of Peter Tripp and Randy Gardner demonstrate that a person must sleep at least 8 hours for each 24 hours of sleep deprivation to regain normal functioning.

4.   (p. 152) True-False. Moderate sleep loss affects motivation and influences performance of low-level, boring tasks much more than complex mental tasks.

5.   (p. 152) Extremely long periods without sleep can produce sleep-deprivation psychosis. Which of the following is *not* an element of this reaction that can occur?
      a.   confusion   c.   delusions
      b.   illusions   d.   hallucinations

6.   (p. 153) True-False. The average sleep time for adults is 8 hours, but the actual sleep time needed by various individuals may vary greatly from this average.

7.   (p. 153) Which age group averages the least sleep per night?
      a.   young infants   c.   adults
      b.   adolescents   d.   elderly adults

8.   (p. 154) Which of the following is *not* an area of the brain actively involved in generating sleep?
      a.   pituitary gland   c.   hypothalamus
      b.   reticular formation   d.   brainstem

9.   (p. 155) Which of the following pairings of brain waves and state of consciousness is *not* an accurate association?
      a.   beta brain waves—relaxed state or just prior to sleep
      b.   delta brain waves—deep sleep
      c.   beta brain waves—awake and alert state
      d.   alpha brain waves—relaxed state or just prior to sleep

10.   (p. 155) Which of the following is strongly associated with dreaming?
      a.   REMs   c.   Stage 2 sleep
      b.   NREMs   d.   Stage 3 sleep

11. (p. 156) True-False. Sleepwalking and sleeptalking occur during dream periods, as if the person is acting out dreams.

12. (p. 156) True-False. Night terrors are more intense, but basically similar to nightmares; they both occur during REM sleep.

13. (p. 156) Which of the following is *not* a sleep disorder?
    a. microsleep   c. insomnia
    b. narcolepsy   d. apnea

14. (p. 158) True-False. Drug-dependency insomnia may result from drug tolerance to prescription sedatives.

15. (p. 158) Which of the following is *not* an effective technique for reducing insomnia problems?
    a. Drink a glass of milk or eat something containing tryptophan.
    b. Establish your own schedule of sleeping—sleep when you want to, not on a fixed routine.
    c. Avoid fighting it—get up and do something useful or satisfying.
    d. Establish the pattern of only sleeping in bed.

16. (p. 159) Some doctors think SIDS is caused by:
    a. narcolepsy   c. cataplexy
    b. night terrors   d. apnea

17. (p. 160) About how many dreams do you have each night?
    a. 1 or 2   c. 4 or 5
    b. 3 or 4   d. 6 or 7

18. (p. 160) True-False. Dreams may seem to take hours, but actually occur in a flash.

19. (p. 160) When finally allowed to dream following periods of dream sleep deprivation, people will dream extra amounts. This reaction is known as:
    a. the REM myth   c. the REM rebound effect
    b. paradoxical sleep   d. displacement effect

20. (p. 160) Which of the following is *not* a possible function of REM sleep?
    a. provide stimulation for infant brain development
    b. process emotional events
    c. reduce sleep-inducing chemicals in the blood
    d. restore the brain's chemical balance

21. (p. 161) True-False. Unpleasant emotions such as fear, anger, and sadness are more frequent in dreams than pleasant emotions.

22. (p. 161) True-False. Sigmund Freud believed that many dreams represent wish fulfillment of repressed or unconscious desires or conflicts.

23. (p. 162) The activation-synthesis hypothesis proposed by Hobson and McCarley postulates that dreams:
    a. represent a way of filling in gaps in personal experience
    b. are a meaningless carry-over of waking thoughts or the result of indigestion
    c. are manufactured by the brain as a means of interpreting incoming information from cells aroused by "sleep center" cells in the brainstem
    d. represent a message from yourself to yourself that can be of value to understand and study

24. (p. 163) Which of the following statements is *not* true of hypnosis?
     a. Approximately 8 out of 10 people can be hypnotized, but only about 4 out of 10 are good hypnotic subjects.
     b. Hypnosis is not sleep, since brain wave recordings made during hypnosis are similar to those obtained when a person is awake.
     c. Many theorists feel hypnosis is really self-hypnosis guided by a hypnotist.
     d. Hypnosis is an altered state of consciousness, characterized by expansive attention and a decreased openness to suggestion.

25. (p. 163) True-False. The term hypnosis was coined by Franz Mesmer as an extention of his theories of animal magnetism.

26. (p. 163) Effective techniques of hypnotic induction have in common all but one of the factors below. Which does *not* apply?
     a. encouraging subjects to focus attention on what is being said
     b. decreasing imagination so as to focus on the hypnotist's instructions and control
     c. inducing relaxation and tiredness
     d. helping a person to "let go" and accept suggestions easily

27. (p. 164) Which of the following is true of human abilities under hypnosis?
     a. Hypnotic suggestions can be used to so convince subjects of their strength that they can perform superhuman acts.
     b. Hypnosis is helpful in the relief of pain, particularly where chemical painkillers cannot be used.
     c. Memory can be improved dramatically.
     d. Hypnotic suggestions concerning sensations seem to be at best mildly effective.

28. (p. 165) Stage hypnotists make use of tricks, deception, waking suggestibility, and _____ to perform their act.
     a. disinhibition of subjects labeled hypnotized
     b. psi abilities
     c. difficult to hypnotize subjects
     d. the same effective techniques used by non-stage hypnotists

29. (p. 166) Which of the following is *not* an effect reported by subjects in experiments of sensory deprivation?
     a. loss of time boundaries
     b. increased concentration
     c. inability to tolerate reduced stimulation for more than two or three days
     d. a variety of perceptual changes

30. (p. 166) Subjects severely deprived of sensory information while floating in a tank of water experience _____ similar to those that occur when one is falling asleep.
     a. hypnogogic images   c. hallucinations
     b. sleep distortions   d. subliminal perception

31. (p. 166) True-False. Peter Suedfeld has found that sensory deprivation can be used to help people quit smoking.

32. (p. 167) Which of the following is *not* associated with drug addiction?
     a. physical dependence   c. drug tolerance
     b. relaxation response   d. withdrawal symptoms

33. (p. 170) When drugs are used to cope with a specific problem such as boredom or staying awake for night work, such drug-taking behavior is classified as:
    a. recreational
    b. intensive
    c. situational
    d. compuisive

34. (p. 170) Dexedrine, Methedrine, and Benzedrine are all drugs from a large group of synthetic stimulants collectively referred to as:
    a. speed
    b. amphetamines
    c. barbiturates
    d. hallucinogens

35. (p. 171) Repeated use of which drug may lead to weight loss, ulcers, hypertension, liver disease, and/or cerebral hemorrhage?
    a. barbiturates
    b. hallucinogens
    c. alcohol
    d. amphetamines

36. (p. 172) True-False. Cocaine is so powerfully rewarding that animals given free access to the drug often end up dying of convulsions from self-administered overdoses.

37. (p. 172) Which of the following is *not* true of cocaine usage?
    a. Some scientists believe it may be physically addictive.
    b. Drug tolerance never develops.
    c. Physical and emotional depression may follow a high.
    d. Even first-time users may risk convulsions, heart attack, or a stroke.

38. (p. 172) _____ is the most frequently used psychoactive drug in America.
    a. Nicotine
    b. Alcohol
    c. Marijuana
    d. Caffeine

39. (p. 172) True-False. Tea, cocoa, soft drinks, and chocolate drinks are all good alternatives to coffee because they contain no caffeine.

40. (p. 172) Which of the following is *not* true of caffeine?
    a. It encourages the development of breast cysts in women.
    b. It may contribute to lung problems.
    c. It can stimulate high blood pressure.
    d. It may contribute to stomach problems.

41. (p. 173) True-False. A burning cigarette releases more than 6,800 different chemicals.

42. (p. 173) Which statistic is *not* associated with tobacco usage in the U.S.?
    a. Cigarette smoking is the cause of 97% of lung cancer deaths among men.
    b. Smoking is responsible for about one-third of all cancer deaths.
    c. Users of smokeless tobacco actually run a lower risk of developing oral cancer.
    d. Cigarette smoking is the cause of 74% of lung cancer deaths among women.

43. (p. 174) True-False. Psychologist Stanley Schachter believes it is better to cut down smoking gradually or switch to lighter cigarettes rather than suddenly quitting because quitting abruptly can place the body under tremendous physical stress.

44. (p. 174) The combined effects of two drugs may be multiplied by a _____ _____.
    a. dosage excess
    b. drug interation
    c. drug intolerance
    d. drug narcosis

45. (p. 174) An overdose of _____ first causes unconsciousness and then so severely depresses activity in brain centers controlling heartbeat and respiration that death results.
    a. amphetamines   c. barbiturates
    b. marijuana   d. cocaine

46. (p. 174) Which of the following is *not* a frequently abused "downer?"
    a. Seconal   c. Tuinal
    b. Tetrahydrocannabinol   d. Parest

47. (p. 174) True-False. Alcohol is a stimulant used by over 140 million Americans.

48. (p. 176) Which of the following does *not* signal excessive dependence on alcohol?
    a. morning drinking   c. regretted behavior
    b. blackouts   d. increased feelings of control over the drug

49. (p. 176) Treatment for alcoholism does *not* include which of the following?
    a. toxification
    b. restoring physical health
    c. use of tranquilizers, antidepressants, and psychotherapy
    d. gradual reduction of alcohol intake

50. (p. 177) Which of the following is *not* true of marijuana usage in the U.S.?
    a. About 40 to 50 million Americans consider themselves regular users of marijuana.
    b. The psychoactive ingredient in marijuana is tetrahydrocannabinol.
    c. Marijuana's potential for abuse lies primarily in the realm of psychological dependence.
    d. The drug's typical effects include a sense of euphoria, altered time sense, perceptual distortions, and relaxation.

51. (p. 177) True-False. A strong research base exists to support claims that marijuana causes brain damage, genetic damage, loss of motivation, and a reduction in the body's natural immunity to diseases.

52. (p. 178) The National Academy of Sciences concluded in 1982 that all of the following are long-term health risks associated with marijuana usage *except*:
    a. lowered sperm production in males
    b. chronic bronchitis and pre-cancerous changes in lung cells
    c. possible gynecological problems such as abnormal menstrual cycles and increased miscarriages
    d. brain damage, genetic damage, and possible reductions in disease immunity

53. (p. 179) Which of the following is *not* a Freudian dream process which disguises the meaning of consciously remembered dreams?
    a. symbolization   c. condensation
    b. displacement   d. archetype images

54. (p. 180) Which of the following pairs of dream theorists and dream theories is incorrect?
    a. Cartwright—dreams are feeling statements
    b. Hobson—dreams are messages from yourself to yourself
    c. Hall—dreams are plays and dreamers are playwrights
    d. Perls—dreams are special messages about what is missing in our lives

55. (p. 181) True-False. Scientists such as Loewi have used dreams to solve problems of major importance, thus demonstrating the potential value of dreams for the production of creative solutions.

56. (p. 182) During a _____ the dreamer "wakes" within an ordinary dream and feels capable of normal thought and action.
   a. lucid dream
   b. REM period
   c. secondary elaboration
   d. paradoxical sleep

57. (p. 183) Which of the following may be a factor in our society's increased use and dependence upon drugs?
   a. our society's apparent belief that everyone should be able to will themselves to be calm, cheerful, thin, industrious, and creative
   b. marketing and advertising campaigns directed to encourage overuse of drugs
   c. physicians rely more than ever upon the use of drugs to deal with a range of problems
   d. all of the above

58. (p. 184) True-False. Psychiatrist Thomas Szasz believes that current attempts to "legislate morality" through drug regulation encourages a black market, organized crime, and disrespect for the law.

59. (p. 184) True-False. Thanks to the billions of dollars spent on drug enforcement, the overall level of drug use by young adults in the United States has declined. Stricter laws and heavier penalties do work quite effectively.

APPLYING YOUR KNOWLEDGE

1. Chemical dependency is a major problem in the United States. To expand your knowledge of how mutual-help approaches work in treating dependency attend an AA, NA, or CA meeting. Describe what happened at the meeting. What did people talk about and how were those issues handled?

2. Use the suggestions from the Applications section on "How To Catch a Dream." Record your dreams for a few weeks. Do you find that your dreams show some of the same trends noted in Calvin Hall's analysis of over 10,000 dreams?

ANSWERS—PROGRAMMED REVIEW

1. hallucinate; sleep	20. memory	40. hypothalamus; reticular formation; brainstem
2. time	21. self-motivated	41. pattern
3. Consciousness	22. will to continue	42. electroencephalograph; EEG
4. waking	23. sleep-deprivation psychosis	43. beta; larger, slower; alpha
5. quality, patterning	24. disorientation; delusions	44. light
6. memory, suggestibility	25. visual; tactile	45. hypnic
7. overload; monotonous	26. 60	46. myoclonus; 15; 20
8. Sioux	27. hands; eyelids; pain	47. small, irregular
9. fasting; loss; pain; psychedelic	28. 25	48. sleep spindles
10. meaning	29. 8	49. 4
11. name	30. worry	50. delta; large, slow
12. electric shock	31. 6	51. deep sleep; delta
13 no evidence	32. 2; 4	52. Rapid eye movements; 85
14. coma; die	33. biological	53. REM; non-REM; NREM
15. microsleep	34. naps	54. 90
16. 11	35. two to one	55. REMs, dreams
17. single	36. 28	
18. age, personality	37. fatigue; Siamese twins	
19. complex; irritable; declines	38. spinal cord	
	39. asleep	

56. fatigue; exercise
57. 90
58. irregularly; waver
59. erection; genital; increases
60. REM behavior disorder
61. somnambulists
62. hereditary
63. no harm
64. 3, 4
65. NREM
66. REM
67. twice
68. Night terrors; 4
69. 15; 20
70. childhood
71. Narcolepsy
72. cataplexy
73. REM
74. brainstem
75. hereditary; stimulant
76. 40; insomnia
77. sedatives; 4; REM
78. drug-dependency
79. nightmares
80. triazolam
81. frustration
82. fighting
83. blood sugar
84. tryptophan
85. Chronic insomnia
86. history
87. caffeine, alcohol, tobacco
88. relaxation
89. Stimulus control
90. regular schedule
91. stimulants
92. early evening
93. progressive; meditation
94. sleepy; naps; nonsleep;510
95. paradoxical
96. sleep apnea
97. 20; 2
98. hypersomnia
99. brain; air passages
100. health; sleep clinic
101. Sudden Infant Death Syndrome; SIDS
102. 1
103. brainstem; heart
104. passive

105. 6
106. teenager, smoker; high-pitched; open mouth
107. Nathaniel Kleitman, Eugene Aserinsky
108. 4, 5
109. 90; 10; 30; 50
110. increased; 20; 30
111. rebound
112. suppresses
113. memory, concentration; anxious
114. REM myth
115. total amount
116. 50
117. increases
118. memories
119. deprivation; emotional
120. hippocampus
121. fears, ambitions; sexual, love
122. worse
123. everyday events
124. house; emotionally
125. half
126. more
127. thoughts; fantasies; emotions
128. wish fulfillment
129. images
130. dream symbols
131. activation-synthesis hypothesis
132. memories
133. deeper meaning
134. Hypnosis
135. conformity, relaxation, imagination
136. Mesmer; magnets
137. animal magnetism
138. James Braid; EEG
139. 8; 4
140. imaginative; fantasy
141. Stanford Hypnotic Susceptibility
142. stable
143. attention; tired; suggestions; imagination
144. willpower
145. self-hypnosis
146. floating; separation
147. basic suggestion

148. dissociation
149. hidden observer
150. superhuman
151. false memories
152. pain
153. phantom limb
154. regressed
155. sensations
156. relaxation; pain
157. subjective experience
158. waking suggestibility
159. responsive
160. disinhibits
161. director
162. tricks
163. Sensory deprivation
164. sensations; awareness; perceptions
165. 2; 3
166. colors; illusions; reactions
167. hypnogogic images
168. theta
169. 4; 7
170. sensory
171. pressure; tension
172. 40
173. weight-loss
174. relaxation; unfreezing
175. creative
176. psychoactive drug
177. stimulation, depression
178. physical; addiction
179. withdrawal symptoms
180. tolerance
181. psychological dependence
182. compulsive
183. psychological dependence
184. experimental; recreational; situational; intensive; compulsive
185. Dexedrine, Methedrine, Benzedrine
186. weight loss; mild depression
187. narcolepsy; depressant
188. drug tolerance
189. binges
190. nausea, vomiting; pressure; arrhythmias
191. bodily resources

192. fatigue; depression;
     aggression
193. weight; ulcers;
     fingernails; infections;
     liver; cerebral
194. amphetamine psychosis
195. addictive; high
196. alertness, euphoria
197. Food; Drug
198. 4, 5; half
199. 4
200. hours; 15; 30
201. convulsions; stroke
202. excitable, jittery;
     sluggish, depressed
203. tremors, hyperactivity;
     language
204. convulsions
205. dopamine,
     noradrenaline
206. mood, energy
207. fatigue, anxiety;
     anhedonia
208. months, years
209. 9
210. Compulsive; control;
     consequences
211. 30; 90
212. caffeine
213. fatigue; alertness
214. coffee
215. caffeinism
216. appetite; heart;
     temperature
217. cysts; stomach, heart
218. birth defects;
     miscarriages
219. nicotine
220. vomiting; dizziness
221. convulsions, death
222. tolerance
223. headaches, sweating;
     digestive
224. 2; 6

225. carcinogens
226. Ninety-seven; 74
227. 4; 6; gums; heart
228. withdrawal
229. deprived
230. constant
231. withdrawal
232. cancer-causing
233. several
234. sedative
235. alcohol; coma, death
236. drug interaction
237. heartbeat, respiration
238. Seconal, Tuinal;
     Methaqualone
239. 2; 4
240. depressant
241. aphrodisiac
242. alcohol myopia
243. extreme
244. anxiety; better
245. 140; 14; 18
246. 17; 25
247. Children
248. increased; morning;
     regretted; blackouts
249. chain reaction
250. chronic
251. 0.05
252. fall
253. detoxification
254. health
255. tranquilizers,
     antidepressants
256. Alcoholics Anonymous
257. 81
258. three; 18
259. Cannabis sativa;
     tetrahydrocannabinol
260. cerebral cortex
261. brain; reproductive
262. physical
263. euphoria; relaxation;
     time; memory; learning

264. hazardous
265. damage; motivation
266. health; mental
267. dependent
268. bronchitis; cancerous
269. 50
270. airways
271. sperm
272. menstrual cycles;
     miscarriages
273. immune
274. genetic
275. condensation
276. displacement
277. symbolization
278. secondary elaboration
279. Hall
280. emotional tone
281. remember; gradually;
     eyes closed; dream
     record; suppress
282. Perls
283. opposition
284. creative
285. inhibition; solving
     problems
286. lucid
287. LaBerge
288. memorize; wakefulness
289. peer, parental; self-
     esteem
290. maladjusted; impulsive;
     emotionally
291. compulsive
292. positive; negative
293. addiction
294. psychological; social
295. 40
296. morality
297. no increase
298. fallen
299. education; intervention

ANSWERS—SELF-TEST

1.	a	11.	False	21.	True	31.	True	41.	True	51.	False
2.	d	12.	False	22.	True	32.	b	42.	c	52.	d
3.	False	13.	a	23.	c	33.	c	43.	False	53.	d
4.	True	14.	True	24.	d	34.	b	44.	b	54.	b
5.	b	15.	b	25.	False	35.	d	45.	c	55.	True
6.	True	16.	d	26.	b	36.	True	46.	b	56.	a
7.	d	17.	c	27.	b	37.	b	47.	False	57.	d
8.	a	18.	False	28.	a	38.	d	48.	d	58.	True
9.	a	19.	c	29.	b	39.	False	49.	d	59.	False
10.	a	20.	c	30.	a	40.	b	50.	a		

ACROSS

2. sleep attack disorder
4. these occur about 90 min. apart at night
5. brain waves that occur in Stage 4
6. Freud believed dreams represent _____ fulfillment
8. momentary shift in brain wave patterns to that of sleep
12. most active chemical in cannabis (short term)
13. Sudden Infant Death Syndrome (abbr.)
15. rapid eye movement (abbr.)
16. Freud analyzed dreams through these
18. sleepwalking
19. cannot breathe and sleep at same time
20. difficulty going or staying asleep
21. English surgeon who used hypnosis

DOWN

1. these symptoms may occur when a drug is withheld
2. bad dreams
3. she says emotional tone clues one to dream meaning
7. to be aware
9. short burst of electrical brain activity
10. electroencephalograph (abbr.)
11. Freudian Dream Theory is _____ Approach
14. explained dreaming via activation-synthesis hypothesis
17. type of dream in which dreamer "wakes" within dream

Conditioning & Learning I

CONTENTS

TERMS AND CONCEPTS

learning
reinforcement
antecedents
consequences
classical conditioning (respondent conditioning)
operant conditioning (instrumental conditioning)
neutral stimulus (NS)
conditioned stimulus (CS)
unconditioned stimulus (US)
unconditioned response (UR)
conditioned response (CR)
acquisition
higher order conditioning
extinction
spontaneous recovery
stimulus generalization
stimulus discrimination
phobia
conditioned emotional response (CER)
desensitization
vicarious conditioning (secondhand conditioning)
law of effect
operant reinforcer
voluntary responses
conditioning chamber (Skinner box)
response contingent
shaping
successive approximations
operant extinction
negative attention seeking

positive reinforcement
punishment
response cost
primary reinforcer
intra-cranial stimulation (ICS)
secondary reinforcer
social reinforcer
tokens
generalized reinforcer
Premack principle
prepotent responses
delay of reinforcement
response chaining
superstitious behavior
schedules of reinforcement
continuous reinforcement
partial reinforcement
partial reinforcement effect
fixed ratio (FR)
variable ratio (VR)
fixed interval (FI)
variable interval (VI)
stimulus control
discriminative stimuli (S+, S-)
behavioral contracting
negative practice
fixed action pattern (FAP)
innate behaviors
reflex
instincts

species-specific behavior
species-typical behavior
biological constraints

prepared fear theory
instinctive drift

IMPORTANT INDIVIDUALS

Ivan Pavlov
Edward L. Thorndike
B. B. Skinner

David Premack
Melissa Bowerman
Martin Seligman

Keller Breland
Marion Breland

PROGRAMMED REVIEW

1. (p. 189) _____ is formally defined as a relatively permanent change in behavior that can be attributed to experience. This definition excludes changes caused by motivation, fatigue, maturation, disease, injury, or drugs.

2. (p. 189) _____ is any procedure that strengthens learning and makes a particular response more probable. It is the basis for both classical and operant conditioning.

3. (p. 189) Events before a response are called _____. Events that follow a response are called _____. An understanding of learning requires that careful attention be given to the "before and after" aspects of the situation.

4. (p. 189) In _____ conditioning, the focus is on what happens before a response. Learning involves an association between antecedent events. A stimulus that does not produce a response is associated with one that does. Learning is evident when the new stimulus also begins to elicit the response.

5. (p. 190) _____ conditioning involves learning affected by consequences. Each time a response is made, it may be followed by reinforcement, punishment, or nothing. These results determine whether or not a response is likely to be made again.

6. (p. 190) At the beginning of the twentieth century, Russian physiologist Ivan _____ discovered and began to research the concept of classical conditioning (also known as Pavlovian conditioning or _____ conditioning).

7. (p. 190) In his experiments, Pavlov found that dogs salivated to the sound of a bell consistently rung before meat powder was given them. The bell starts out as a _____ stimulus, abbreviated _____, because it is a stimulus that does not evoke a response.

8. (p. 191) In time, the bell becomes a _____ stimulus, abbreviated _____, because it is a stimulus to which the dog has learned to respond.

9. (p. 191) The meat powder is called an _____ stimulus, abbreviated _____, because the dog does not have to learn to respond to it.

10. (p. 191) Unconditioned stimuli typically produce "built in" reflex responses called _____ (non-learned) responses, abbreviated _____. In Pavlov's experiment, this was salivation.

11. (p. 191) When the bell alone causes salivation, the response can no longer be called a simple reflex. Instead, it is a _____ (learned) _____, abbreviated _____.

12. (p. 191) Applying these terms to the effects of the shower and flushing toilet described in the chapter "Preview" we get the following:

_____ response = reflex jump from the hot water

_____ stimulus = pain caused by the hot water

_____ stimulus = sound of a flushing toilet

13. (p. 192) During _____, or training, a conditioned response must be reinforced, or strengthened.

14. (p. 192) In classical conditioning, reinforcement occurs when the _____ _____ is followed by, or paired with, an _____ _____.

15. (p. 192) Conditioning will be most rapid if the US follows immediately after the CS. With most reflexes, for conditioning to occur the optimal delay between CS and US is from _____ second to _____ seconds.

16. (p. 192) In _____ _____ conditioning, a well-learned CS is used to reinforce further learning. Through this procedure, learning can be extended one or more steps beyond the original conditioned stimulus.

17. (p. 192) Many _____ try to use higher order conditioning by pairing images associated with good feelings with pictures of their products. The hope is that you will learn to feel good when you see their products.

18. (p. 192) If the US never again follows the CS, conditioning will _____. We say that the CR has been _____ (or suppressed).

19. (p. 193) Thus, classical conditioning can be weakened by removing reinforcement. This process is called _____.

20. (p. 193) The next day following extinction, presentation of the conditioned stimulus may initially elicit a response, a reaction called _____ _____.

21. (p. 193) Because of spontaneous recovery, several _____ sessions may be necessary to completely reverse learning.

22. (p. 193) Once a subject is conditioned to respond to a particular conditioned stimulus, other stimuli similar to the CS may also trigger a response. This effect is called _____ _____.

23. (p. 193) For instance, a child accidentally burned by matches may also show a healthy fear of flames produced by lighters, fireplaces, stoves, etc. Generalization tends to extend the effects of learning to _____ _____ and similar situations.

24. (p. 193) Stimulus generalization does have limits. There is a gradual decrease in generalization as test stimuli become _____ like the original CS.

25. (p. 193) Using the example of a child conditioned to salivate to a bell paired with lemon juice, suppose that we occasionally sound a buzzer instead of the bell, but never follow it with the US. At first, the buzzer produces salivation due to _____.

26. (p. 193) But after the buzzer has been presented several more times, the child ceases to respond to it. The child has now learned to _____, or respond differently to, the bell and the buzzer.

27. (p. 193) This process of _____ discrimination is an important element of learning. For example, most children quickly learn to discriminate voice qualities associated with pain from those associated with praise or affection.

28. (p. 194) In its simplest form, classical conditioning depends on responses called _____, dependable, inborn stimulus-and-response connections. Withdrawal of various parts of the body in response to pain would be one example.

29. (p. 194) Simple conditioning of human reflexes is a common occurrence. Of greater importance, perhaps, are more subtle kinds of conditioning involving complex emotional or "gut" responses. For instance, if your face reddened as a child, you may blush now as an adult when you are embarrassed or ashamed. Many such _____, autonomic nervous system responses, are linked with new stimuli and situations by classical conditioning.

30. (p. 194) Another common example of such conditioning is a _____—a fear that persists even when no realistic danger exists.

31. (p. 194) Reactions of fear to animals, water, heights, and so forth are called _____ _____ _____, abbreviated _____. They may be broadened into phobias by stimulus generalization.

32. (p. 194) Fortunately, phobias can be extinguished. In a therapy technique called _____, learning principles are used to extinguish or countercondition phobias, fears, or anxieties.

33. (p. 195) Undoubtedly, many of our likes, dislikes, and fears are acquired as conditioned emotional responses. For example, in one recent study, college students gave _____ ratings to shapes paired with pleasant music than to shapes associated with silence.

34. (p. 195) People can be conditioned to give an emotional response to a light, merely by watching another person get an electric shock each time the light comes on. Children can learn to fear thunder by watching their parents. These are examples of _____ classical conditioning.

35. (p. 195) Vicarious conditioning probably plays a part in _____ reactions to many situations including attitudes toward certain types of food, political parties, minority groups, and so forth.

36. (p. 195) _____ conditioning concerns how we learn to associate responses with their consequences. The basic principle behind this is simple: Acts that are _____ tend to be repeated.

37. (p. 195) Pioneer learning theorist Edward L. Thorndike called this the _____ of _____. According to Thorndike, learning is strengthened each time a response is followed by a satisfying state of affair.

38. (p. 196) While classical conditioning is passive and involuntary, in operant conditioning the learner actively "operates on" the environment. Thus, operant conditioning refers mainly to learning _____ responses.

39. (p. 196) "_____" do not always increase responding and are therefore not always the same as reinforcers. If you give licorice candy to a child as a "_____" for good behavior it will work only if the child likes licorice.

40. (p. 196) Psychologists therefore define an _____ _____ as any event that follows a response and increases its probability.

41. (p. 196) Most laboratory research on operant conditioning takes place in some form of _____ _____ also called a "Skinner box." It is usually a cagelike chamber with bare walls except for a metal lever and a tray from which food pellets may be dispensed.

42. (p. 196) This simplified environment increases the chances that subjects will make the response we are interested in rewarding. Hunger also insures that animals will be motivated to seek food and to actively _____, or give off, a variety of responses.

43. (p. 197) In operant conditioning _____ is used to alter the frequency of responses, or to mold them into new patterns or habits.

44. (p. 197) To be effective, operant reinforcement must be _____ _____. That is, reinforcement is given only after a desired response is made.

45. (p. 197) The importance of making reinforcement response contingent was demonstrated in an example of a severely disturbed child learning to say "Please" whenever he wanted something. Here, and in situations ranging from studying to working hard on the job, contingent reinforcement affects the _____ of responses.

46. (p. 197) In 1948, B. F. Skinner published *Walden Two*, a utopian novel about a model community based on _____ _____.

47. (p. 197) One "operant community" organized at the University of Kansas has been quite successful. Here, college students have taken part in an _____ _____ _____ in which work sharing is strongly reinforced.

48. (p. 198) Residents in this experimental community rated the project as _____ to dormitory living and similar alternatives. Most were highly _____ with the system.

49. (p. 198) When we reward responses that come closer and closer to the final desired pattern, the process is called _____.

50. (p. 198) The basic principle of shaping is that gradual or _____ _____ to the desired response are rewarded.

51. (p. 199) If a learned response is not reinforced, it gradually drops out of behavior. Such a process is called operant _____, just as in classical conditioning.

52. (p. 199) If a rat is removed from a Skinner box and allowed to rest after bar pressing is extinguished, he will begin pressing the bar when returned to the Skinner box. This brief return of an operant response following extinction is called _____ _____.

53. (p. 199) _____ and approval from parents are very powerful reinforcers for children. Parents may knowingly reinforce _____ _____ seeking in children by ignoring them when they are quiet or are playing constructively.

54. (p. 199) _____ reinforcement occurs when a pleasant or desired event follows a response. _____ reinforcement occurs when making a response removes an unpleasant event.

55. (p. 199) A rat could be taught to press a bar to get food (positive reinforcement) or the rat could be given a mild shock that continues until it is turned off by a bar press (negative reinforcement). Either way, bar pressing would _____.

56. (p. 199) _____ is any event that follows a response and decreases its likelihood of occurring again.

57. (p. 199) Punishment may occur when some unpleasant event follows a response and thereby decreases the frequency of that response in the future. It also occurs when a reinforcer or positive state of affairs is removed. This type of punishment is called _____ _____.

58. (p. 200) _____ reinforcers are unlearned rewards that apply almost universally to a species. They are usually biological in nature and produce comfort or end discomfort, such as _____, _____ or _____.

59. (p. 200) Rats wired for pleasurable intra-cranial stimulation (an unusual form of primary reinforcement) will bar press _____ of times per hour for 15 to 20 hours before collapsing. They will ignore _____, _____ and sex in favor of bar pressing.

60. (p. 200) _____ reinforcers are learned reinforcers, such as money, praise, attention, approval, success, affection, and grades. Reinforcers of this type become rewards through association with primary reinforcers.

61. (p. 200) This effect can be shown experimentally by associating bar pressing, food, and a tone. Once learned, rats transferred to a new test chamber will bar press to receive a _____ even when food is unavailable.

62. (p. 200) Learned desires for attention and approval, which are sometimes called _____ reinforcers, often influence human behavior. This was demonstrated in the example of students using class interest to shape a teacher to lecture from the right side of the room.

63. (p. 201) Secondary reinforcers may also gain their value more directly when they can be exchanged for primary reward. For example, _____ can be used with chimpanzees to reinforce behavior.

64. (p. 201) One problem with primary reinforcers is that people and animals receiving them quickly _____ (meaning they are fully satisfied or have reduced desire).

65. (p. 202) A major advantage of _____ is that they do not lose their reinforcing value as quickly as do primary reinforcers. They are particularly useful in work with troubled children, adolescents, adults in special programs, and in the education of the mentally retarded.

66. (p. 202) When a secondary reinforcer has become largely independent of its connection to primary reinforcers, it is called a _____ reinforcer.

67.   (p. 202) As one example, chimps working for tokens also tended to _____ them, even when hungry. For humans, money is a similar example of a generalized reinforcer.

68.   (p. 202) One way to discover what will serve as a reinforcer is to apply the _____ principle: any frequent (or "_____") response can be used to reinforce an infrequent response.

69.   (p. 202) If TV watching is a high-frequency response and studying is infrequent, TV watching can be used as a _____ to increase the frequency of studying.

70.   (p. 203) Reinforcement has its greatest effect on operant learning when the time lapse between a response and the reward is _____. Reward is most effective when given _____ after the response.

71.   (p. 203) Operant conditioning experiments with rats show that when reward follows responding by 50 seconds, very little occurs. When food delivery follows a bar press by more than _____ seconds, no learning occurs.

72.   (p. 203) Humans are less affected by delay of reinforcement because they are able to _____ future reward. Also, a single reward can often maintain a long _____ of responses.

73.   (p. 203) A simple example of _____ _____ is provided by Barnabus, a rat trained to perform a long series of complex behaviors.

74.   (p. 203) When behaviors develop as a result of reinforcement, but actually have nothing to do with bringing about reinforcement, they are called _____ behaviors.

75.   (p. 203) These behaviors develop because a reward will reinforce not only the last response that precedes it, but also other responses occurring shortly before the reward is given. Such responses tend to persist because they _____ to pay off.

76.   (p. 204) As an example, if pigeons initially trained to key peck for food then have food delivered at _____ intervals (independent of responding) they will still make thousands of responses a 20 minute period.

77.   (p. 204) When rewards are given in particular patterns, the patterns are called _____ of _____.

78.   (p. 204) _____ means that a reinforcer follows every response.

79.   (p. 204) Reinforcement which does not follow every response is called _____ _____.

80.   (p. 204) Partial reinforcement while acquiring a response makes the response very resistant to _____. This effect is called the _____ _____ effect and applies to both classical and instrumental conditioning.

81.   (p. 205) One reason for this effect is that acquisition on a schedule of partial reward includes long periods of nonreward. This fact makes it harder to discriminate between conditions of _____ and _____.

82.   (p. 205) If we follow every third, fourth, fifth, or other number of responses with reinforcement, the reinforcement schedule is _____ _____.

83. (p. 205) A fixed ratio schedule where every third response is rewarded would be symbolized _____.

84. (p. 205) The most prominent characteristic of FR schedules is that they produce very _____ rates of responding.

85. (p. 205) An example is illustrated when factory or farm workers are paid on a _____ basis. When a fixed number of items must be produced for a set amount of pay, work output is high.

86. (p. 205) If subjects receive reward every fourth response *on the average*, the schedule of reinforcement is _____ _____, which is symbolized _____.

87. (p. 205) Variable ratio schedules also produce high response rates. VR schedules tend to produce _____ resistance to extinction than FR schedules. Playing a slot machine is an example of behavior maintained by a VR schedule.

88. (p. 206) If reinforcement is given for the first correct response made after a fixed amount of time has passed, the reward pattern is called _____ _____, abbreviated _____.

89. (p. 206) FI schedules produce _____ response rates characterized by spurts of _____ mixed with periods of _____.

90. (p. 206) Having a paper due in a class every two weeks is one illustration of an FI schedule. Immediately after turning in a paper, your work probably drops to _____ until the next due date draws near.

91. (p. 206) When subjects are given reinforcement for the first correct response made after a varied amount of time, the schedule is _____ _____, abbreviated _____.

92. (p. 206) For example, a VI-30 sec. schedule means that reinforcement is available after an interval that _____ 30 seconds duration.

93. (p. 206) VI schedules produce _____, _____ rates of response and tremendous _____ to _____.

94. (p. 206) When you dial a phone number and get a busy signal, reward (getting through) is on a _____ schedule. People usually dial repeatedly until getting a connection.

95. (p. 206) In the "real world" two or more schedules of reinforcement may be in effect at once. For example, continued use of _____ _____ rewards (hourly wage or salary) would guarantee a basic level of income for employees. To reinforce extra effort, employers could add _____ _____ reinforcement (such as incentives, bonuses, etc.) to employees' pay.

96. (p. 206) Responses that are reinforced in a particular situation tend to come under the control of stimuli present during conditioning. This process is called _____ _____. A child who learns to ask for candy when her mother is in a good mood (but not at other times) is an example of this principle.

97. (p. 207) Responses followed by reinforcement tend to be made again when the stimuli that preceded them are present. As a result, similar antecedents also tend to bring forth a response. This process is called _____.

98. (p. 207) A good example of generalization is the way children use _____ _____. One child studied by psychologist Melissa Bowerman first used the word "snow" for several white objects.

99. (p. 207) To discriminate means to respond differently to different stimuli. When you have learned to discriminate between antecedent stimuli that signal reward and non-reward, your response pattern has shifted to match these _____
_____.

100. (p. 208) _____ _____ is illustrated by "sniffer" dogs trained to locate drugs and explosives. During operant discrimination training, these dogs are reinforced only for approaching contraband.

101. (p. 208) Psychologists symbolize a stimulus that precedes reinforced responses as an _____. Discriminative stimuli that precede unrewarded responses are symbolized as _____.

102. (p. 209) To increase the frequency of any behavior, several steps can be suggested. First, choose a _____ behavior; that is, identify what you want to change.

103. (p. 209) Then, record a _____ so you'll know how much time you currently spend performing the target behavior.

104. (p. 209) Next, establish _____. Make them realistic and set them daily so that they add up to a weekly total.

105. (p. 209) You also need to choose _____ that you can reward yourself with for making your daily goals.

106. (p. 210) Be sure to _____ your progress. Keeping accurate records of the amount of time spent each day on the desired activity can help.

107. (p. 210) _____ successes. If you meet your daily goal, collect your reward. But be honest and skip the reward if you fall short. Do the same for your weekly goal.

108. (p. 210) _____ your plan as you learn more about your behavior. Overall progress will reinforce your attempts at self-management.

109. (p. 210) The key to any self-management program is accurate _____ _____. This fact was demonstrated by an investigation in which students who recorded their study time and graphed their study behavior earned better grades than those who did no recording, even though no rewards were offered.

110. (p. 210) In a _____ _____, you state a specific goal to be achieved and the rewards you will receive for completion, along with the privileges you will forfeit or punishments you must accept if you fail to complete the goal. It should be signed by you and someone with whom you are close.

111. (p. 210) There are several techniques which you can use to break a bad habit. The place to begin is by discovering what is _____ the habit and remove, avoid, or delay the _____.

112. (p. 210) Another suggestion is to try to get the same reinforcement with _____ responses. For example, Alice often tells jokes at the expense of others. She could just as easily get the same social reinforcement by giving other people praise or compliments.

113. (p. 211) Another way to control the habit is to avoid or narrow down _____ that elicit the habit. To help reduce smoking, remove ashtrays, matches, and extra cigarettes. Also, try smoking only in one place, such as an uninteresting room at home.

114. (p. 211) Another strategy for controlling antecedents is to break _____ _____ that precede an undesired behavior. The key idea is to scramble the chain of events that leads up to the undesired response.

115. (p. 211) Making an _____ _____ in the presence of stimuli that usually precede the bad habit can also be useful. Persons who bite their nails in particular situations could learn to put their hands in their pockets, chew gum, comb their hair, etc.

116. (p. 211) Use _____ _____, that is, deliberately repeat a bad habit until it becomes boring, painful, or produces fatigue, to associate a bad habit with discomfort.

117. (p. 211) If you would like to break a bad habit, pay close attention to _____, the _____ itself, and the _____ that follow the behavior. Be familiar with the general plan, provided in this chapter, for breaking a bad habit.

118. (p. 212) Weaver birds raised in total isolation for several generations can still tie a special knot for nesting at the first opportunity. This phenomenon is an example of a _____ _____ _____, abbreviated _____.

119. (p. 212) FAPs are instinctual chains of movements found in all members of a species. Like other _____ (inborn) behaviors they help prepare animals to meet major needs in their lives.

120. (p. 213) To qualify as instinctual, a behavior must be complex, unlearned, and _____ _____ (it occurs with little variation in almost all members of a species).

121. (p. 213) All species, including humans, engage in a large number of clearly recognizable _____-_____ behaviors. For example, pigeons typically peck at things when they are hungry.

122. (p. 213) Training is easy when you want to train a pigeon to peck at a button to receive food or to flap its wings to escape an electric shock. However, little or no learning takes place in the reverse cases. This suggests that there are _____ _____, or limits, to learning.

123. (p. 213) Some _____ between stimuli and responses or between responses and consequences are easily learned. Others can be acquired only with great difficulty. Such biological constraints affect both classical and operant conditioning.

124. (p. 213) Through classical conditioning, it is possible to learn to fear or dislike just about anything. But Martin Seligman's _____ _____ theory holds that we are prepared by evolution to readily develop fears to certain stimuli, such as snakes and spiders.

125. (p. 213) According to Seligman's theory, such stimuli posed dangers earlier in human history and through _____ _____ have become highly effective conditioning stimuli.

126. (p. 214) Two psychologists, Keller and Marion _____, have found many examples of operant learning limitations in their business of training animals for television shows, zoo displays, and amusement parks.

127. (p. 214) As one example, they found it nearly impossible to condition a raccoon to place coins in a piggy-bank. Instead, the animal repeatedly rubbed the coins together (an innate food-washing response). They called this problem _____ _____: learned responses tend to "drift" toward innate ones.

128. (p. 214) An advantage of biologically programmed behavior is that it prepares animals and humans to survive in their natural environments. But change the environment in unexpected ways and behavior may suddenly look very "stupid." For example, even with silk glands removed, a spider will make _____ spinning movements and lay eggs in a non-existent cocoon.

SELF-TEST

1.   (p. 189) _____ is a relatively permanent change in behavior that can be attributed to experience.
    a. Instinct   c. Learning
    b. FAP   d. Memory

A young child is bitten by a particular dog and later fears all dogs, but not all animals. Answer Questions 2-7 with reference to this event.

2.   (p. 191) What is the unconditioned stimulus?
    a. pain from being bitten   c. seeing or being near any animal
    b. seeing or being near a dog   d. fear of any dog

3.   (p. 191) What is the conditioned stimulus?
    a. pain from being bitten   c. seeing or being near any animal
    b. seeing or being near a dog   d. fear of any dog

4.   (p. 191) What is the conditioned response?
    a. pain from being bitten   c. seeing or being near any animal
    b. seeing or being near a dog   d. fear of any dog

5.   (p. 193) The child's fear of all dogs illustrates:
    a. stimulus generalization   c. stimulus discrimination
    b. spontaneous recovery   d. vicarious conditioning

6.   (p. 193) The child's fear of all dogs, but not all animals, illustrates:
    a. stimulus generalization   c. stimulus discrimination
    b. successive approximation   d. resistance to extinction

7.   (p. 194) The child's fear of dogs illustrates a(n):
    a. instinct   c. spontaneous recovery
    b. conditioned emotional response   d. fixed action pattern

8.   (p. 191) Pavlov's dogs salivated to the presence of the meat powder because:
    a. they had learned to do so prior to the experiment
    b. they associated the meat powder with the presentation of the bell
    c. it was a naturally elicited, reflex response
    d. that was what Pavlov wanted them to do

9.   (p. 192) During acquisition, a conditioned response must be reinforced. In classical conditioning, reinforcement occurs when the CS is followed by a:
      a. US   c. UR
      b. CR   d. FAP

10.   (p. 192) After acquisition, if the CS is never again followed by the US, the CR will be inhibited. This process is called:
      a. reinforcement   c. desensitization
      b. generalization   d. extinction

11.   (p. 193) If on the next day following extinction, the CS is again presented, a response may occur. This reaction is called:
      a. reinforcement   c. vicarious conditioning
      b. spontaneous recovery   d. emitted responding

12.   (p. 194) A _____ is a fear which persists even when no realistic danger exists. Many are thought to be learned through classical conditioning.
      a. phobia   c. conditioned unemotional response
      b. reflex   d. fixed action pattern

13.   (p. 195) Children who learn to fear thunder by watching their parents have undergone:
      a. vicarious extinction   c. conditioned acquisition
      b. spontaneous conditioning   d. vicarious conditioning

14.   (p. 196) Classical conditioning involves _____, while instrumental conditioning involves _____.
      a. voluntary behaviors, learned reflexes
      b. learned reflexes, voluntary behaviors
      c. freely paced trials, individual learning trials
      d. stimulus generalization, stimulus discrimination

15.   (p. 197) University of Kansas students participated in an experimental living project which emphasized:
      a. interpersonal compatibility
      b. use of rewards to increase studying
      c. worksharing
      d. existence unencumbered by responsibilities

16.   (p. 198) Reinforcing successive approximations to the desired act, defines the basic principle of:
      a. vicarious conditioning   c. reinforcement scheduling
      b. shaping   d. stimulus control

17.   (p. 199) True-False. Extinction and spontaneous recovery are phenomena that occur in both classical and instrumental conditioning.

18.   (p. 200) Food, water, and sex are all examples of _____ reinforcers.
      a. secondary   c. stimulatory
      b. primary   d. generalized

19.   (p. 200) Which of the following are examples of secondary reinforcers?
      a. praise, attention, affection, grades
      b. food, water, sex
      c. stimulation of brain pleasure centers, money, sex
      d. pain, discomfort, fear

20. (p. 201) One problem with primary reinforcers is that subjects receiving them may satiate quickly. A valuable alternative is to use:
    a. punishment
    b. delayed reinforcement
    c. tokens
    d. food, water, or sex

21. (p. 202) Which of the following defines a generalized reinforcer?
    a. primary reinforcers that are effective across a general species population
    b. secondary reinforcers that facilitate stimulus generalization in operant conditioning experiments
    c. secondary reinforcers that have become independent of their connection with primary reinforcers
    d. any reinforcer that is effective across a wide (generalized) class of stimuli

22. (p. 202) The Premack principle refers to the fact that:
    a. animals will bar press for electrical stimulation of brain pleasure centers while ignoring food, water, or sex
    b. punishment normally only suppresses a response, it does not extinguish it
    c. in order for reinforcement to be effective it must be made contingent upon responding
    d. prepotent responses can be used to reinforce low-frequency responses

23. (p. 203) True-False. The longer the interval between a response and a reward, the greater the learning, since subjects have more time to think about the response.

24. (p. 203) True-False. A reward will reinforce only the last response which precedes it. This phenomenon is the principle behind superstitious behavior.

25. (p. 204) Schedules of partial reinforcement, as contrasted with continuous reinforcement, produce:
    a. equally fast learning
    b. more rapid shaping
    c. more rewards per time
    d. slower extinction

26. (p. 204) Which of the following is *not* true of the partial reinforcement effect?
    a. It occurs when acquisition of a response is reinforced on a continuous basis.
    b. It refers to the fact that partial reinforcement makes a response very resistant to extinction.
    c. Acquisition on a partial schedule makes it harder to discriminate between conditions of reward and extinction.
    d. For many people, gambling often involves the partial reinforcement effect.

27. (p. 205) Which schedule produces slow, steady of responding?
    a. FI
    b. FR
    c. VR
    d. VI

28. (p. 206) On an FI-10 sec. schedule, how is reward dispensed?
    a. The first response following an average interval of 10 seconds duration is reinforced.
    b. Reward follows every time the subject responds continuously for 10 seconds.
    c. During the first 10 second interval of each minute period, reward is available on a continuous basis.
    d. The first correct response following the passage of a 10 second interval is reinforced.

29. (p. 206) Which of the following characterizes responding on an FI schedule?
    a. extremely high rates of responding
    b. low rates of responding, but high resistance to extinction
    c. slow, steady rates of responding
    d. moderate response rates marked by bursts of activity mixed with periods of inactivity

30. (p. 206) True-False. Stimulus control refers to the fact that stimuli that precede a rewarded response tend to influence when and where the response will occur in the future.

31. (p. 207) Which of the following is *not* associated with both classical and instrumental conditioning?
     a. discrimination   c. learned reflexes
     b. extinction   d. generalization

32. (p. 210) True-False. Recording study time may be necessary before you can reward progress, but keeping records alone has no effect on behavior.

33. (p. 210) A _____ _____ involves a written agreement outlining a specific behavior to be changed and the rewards and punishments to be applied.
     a. token economy   c. behavior therapy
     b. behavioral contract   d. systematic record

34. (p. 210) When trying to break a bad habit, which of the following is *not* recommended?
     a. Remove, avoid, or delay what is reinforcing the habit.
     b. Increase the number of cues that elicit the bad habit to help remind you to stop.
     c. Make an incompatible response in the presence of stimuli that usually precede the bad habit.
     d. Seek the same reinforcement from new responses.

35. (p. 211) When you deliberately repeat a bad habit until it becomes boring, painful, or produces fatigue, so as to break the habit, the technique is called _____ _____.
     a. habit reversal   c. modified punishment
     b. negative practice   d. negative reinforcement

36. (p. 212) A fixed action pattern can be defined as:
     a. an instinctual chain of movements found in all members of a species
     b. a chain of responses learned through classical conditioning
     c. The pattern of responding usually observed when using fixed ratio schedules of reinforcement
     d. a type of conditioned response observed when certain conditioned stimuli are present

37. (p. 213) Which of the following is *not* a quality of instinctual behaviors?
     a. complex   c. unlearned
     b. spontaneous   d. species specific

38. (p. 213) The fact that honey bees can only learn the location of their hives in the morning is an example of:
     a. biological constraints on learning
     b. stimulus discrimination and generalization
     c. extinction and spontaneous recovery
     d. classical conditioning in the "real world"

39. (p. 213) True-False. Instinctive drift refers to the use of partial schedules to produce long chains of behavior.

APPLYING YOUR KNOWLEDGE

1. Do you have a pet, younger brother or sister, or willing friend with whom you can try a simple classical conditioning experiment? Design and conduct demonstration of Pavlovian conditioning. What are your US, CS, UR, and CR? How many trials were necessary to develop the CR? Can you manipulate the variables to demonstrate generalization, discrimination, response extinction, and spontaneous recovery?

2. Try another experiment using operant conditioning principles. Identify the various key factors and then demonstrate generalization, discrimination, response extinction, and spontaneous recovery.

3. Use the Applications section ("Behavioral Self-Management") to design a behavioral system to alter some habit you've been wanting to change. Execute your plan and keep a log of what you did. Check back with yourself periodically to see how your behavior has changed.

ANSWERS—PROGRAMMED REVIEW

1. Learning
2. Reinforcement
3. antecedents; consequences
4. classical
5. Operant
6. Pavlov; respondent
7. neutral; NS
8. conditioned; CS
9. unconditioned; US
10. unconditioned; UR
11. conditioned response; CR
12. unconditioned; unconditioned; conditioned
13. acquisition
14. conditioned stimulus; unconditioned stimulus
15. $1/2$; 5
16. higher order
17. advertisers
18. extinguish; inhibited
19. extinction
20. spontaneous recovery
21. extinction
22. stimulus generalization
23. new settings
24. less
25. generalization
26. discriminate
27. stimulus
28. reflexes
29. involuntary
30. phobia
31. conditioned emotional responses; CERs
32. desensitization

33. higher
34. vicarious
35. emotional
36. Operant; reinforced
37. law of effect
38. voluntary
39. Rewards; reward
40. operant reinforcer
41. conditioning chamber
42. emit
43. reinforcement
44. response contingent
45. performance
46. behavioral engineering
47. Experimental Living Project
48. superior; satisfied
49. shaping
50. successive approximations
51. extinction
52. spontaneous recovery
53. Attention; negative attention
54. Positive; Negative
55. increase
56. Punishment
57. response cost
58. Primary; food, water, sex
59. thousands; food, water
60. Secondary
61. tone
62. social
63. tokens
64. satiate
65. tokens
66. generalized

67. hoard
68. Premack; prepotent
69. reinforcer
70. short; immediately
71. 90
72. anticipate; chain
73. response chaining
74. superstitious
75. appear
76. random
77. schedules of reinforcement
78. Continuous reinforcement
79. partial reinforcement
80. extinction; partial reinforcement
81. reinforcemtn, extinction
82. fixed ratio
83. FR-3
84. high
85. piecework
86. variable ratio; VR-4
87. greater
88. fixed variable; VI
89. moderate; activity; inactivity
90. zero
91. variable interval; VI
92. averages
93. slow, steady; resistance to extinction
94. VI
95. fixed interval; fixed ratio
96. stimulus control
97. generalization
98. new words

99. discriminative stimuli
100. Stimulus discrimination
101. S+; S–
102. target
103. baseline
104. goals
105. reinforcers
106. record
107. Reward
108. Adjust
109. record keeping
110. behavioral contract

111. reinforcing; reinforcement
112. new
113. cues
114. response chains
115. incompatible response
116. negative practice
117. antecedents; response; consequences
118. fixed action pattern; FAP

119. innate
120. species-specific
121. species-typical
122. biological constraints
123. associations
124. prepared fear
125. natural selection
126. Breland
127. instinctive drift
128. 6400

ANSWERS—SELF-TEST

1.	c	8.	c	15.	c	22.	d	29.	d	36.	a
2.	a	9.	a	16.	b	23.	False	30.	True	37.	b
3.	b	10.	d	17.	True	24.	False	31.	c	38.	a
4.	d	11.	b	18.	b	25.	d	32.	False	39.	False
5.	a	12.	a	19.	a	26.	a	33.	b		
6.	c	13.	d	20.	c	27.	d	34.	b		
7.	b	14.	b	21.	d	28.	d	35.	b		

ACROSS

3. events before a response are called _____
6. this animal salivated a lot
7. Harvard psychologist B. F. _____
9. conditioned stimulus (abbr.)
12. training period used to make association between the CS and US
13. chimps were taught to work for these secondary reinforcers
14. unconditioned stimulus (abbr.)
16. this principle says a high frequency response can help reinforce a low frequency response
17. fears that persist when no real danger exists
19. avoiding black cats and walking under ladders exhibits this type of behavior

DOWN

1. his name should "ring" a bell
2. conditioned emotional response (abbr.)
4. events that follow a response are called _____
5. unconditioned response (abbr.)
8. removal of the reinforcement causes this to occur
10. sudden reappearance of learned response after apparent extinction describes _____ recovery
11. _____ ratio reinforcement is very easy to extinguish
15. gradual molding of desired response
18. conditional response (abbr.)

■ CHAPTER 8 ■
Conditioning and Learning II

CONTENTS

TERMS AND CONCEPTS

two-factor learning
informational view
expectancies
feedback (knowledge of results or KR)
programmed instruction
computer-assisted instruction (CAI)
branching program
drill and practice
instructional games
educational simulations
punishment
response cost
escape learning
avoidance learning
cognitive learning
cognitive map
latent learning

rote learning
discovery learning
modeling (observational learning)
biofeedback
alpha brain waves
electroencephalograph (EEG)
motor skill
motor program
mental practice
spaced practice
massed practice
transfer of training
positive transfer
negative transfer
negative practice
self-regulated learning

IMPORTANT INDIVIDUALS

Robert Rescorla
Albert Bandura
Tannis Williams
Elmer Green

Alyce Green
Joseph Kamiya
Barry Zimmerman

Rowell Huesmann
Neil Malamuth
Victor Cline

PROGRAMMED REVIEW

1. (p. 217) Video games often promote rapid learning. Such games provide two key elements that underlie learning: a _____ environment and _____. The same dynamic applies to many other learning situations.

2. (p. 218) _____-_____ learning refers to the fact that in the "real world" classical and operant conditioning are often intertwined.

3. (p. 218) An ice cream truck approaches with its bell ringing continuously; a boy runs to the truck, buys an ice cream, and eats it, salivating as he does. In this learning situation, _____ _____ is demonstrated because each time the ice cream truck approaches, the boy will salivate when he hears the bell.

4. (p. 218) Also, the bell is a _____ _____ signaling that reward is available if certain responses are made.

5. (p. 218) _____ _____ is demonstrated when the boy hears the bell, runs to the truck, then buys and eats the ice cream.

6. (p. 218) The boy's _____ responses are altered by classical conditioning while his _____ behavior is shaped by operant conditioning.

7. (p. 218) At one time psychologists considered conditioning a mechanical "stamping in" of responses. Now, many think of learning in terms of _____ _____.

8. (p. 218) According to this informational view, learning creates mental _____ (or expectations) about events which, once acquired, alter behavior.

9. (p. 218) Researcher Robert Rescorla explains classical conditioning this way: Because the CS consistently precedes the US, it _____ the US. When the CS is present, the brain _____ the US to follow and prepares the body to respond.

10. (p. 219) The CS gives valuable _____ about the US before the US appears. Pavlovian conditioning is not a "stupid" process that links any two stimuli that happen to occur together. Rather, conditioning occurs as we seek _____ about the world.

11. (p. 219) In operant conditioning we learn to _____ that a certain response will have a certain effect at certain times. Reward tells a person or animal which response was right and discriminative stimuli tell what response to make to get a reinforcer.

12. (p. 219) The _____ value of information helps explain why much human learning occurs without obvious reinforcement by food, water, and the like. Humans readily learn responses that merely have a desired effect or that bring a goal closer.

13. (p. 219) Particularly important to human learning is the value of _____ (information about what effect a response has had).

14. (p. 219) Increasing feedback (also called _____ of _____, abbreviated _____) almost always improves learning and performance.

15. (p. 219) There are numerous ways to apply feedback. For example, tape-recorded feedback can be very helpful. Videotapes are often useful in sports, but are most helpful when a skilled coach directs attention to _____ _____.

16. (p. 219) Feedback is valuable in education too. Feedback is most effective when it is _____, _____, and detailed.

17. (p. 219) Recently, operant learning and feedback have been combined in two interesting ways. One of these is _____ _____, which gives information to students in a format that requires precise answers about information as it is presented.

18. (p. 219) This arrangement supplies frequent feedback to keep learners from practicing _____. It also has the advantage of letting students work at their own _____.

19. (p. 219) In _____-_____ instruction, abbreviated _____, a computer transmits lessons to a display screen while the student responds by typing answers.

20. (p. 219) The computer can provide immediate feedback and can analyze each answer. This capacity allows use of a _____ _____ in which additional information and questions are given when an error is made.

21. (p. 219) The newest CAI programs, which use _____ _____ programs, can even give hints about why an answer was wrong and what is needed to correct it.

22. (p. 219) Elementary school children seem to do especially well with a "computor tutor" due to the rapid feedback and individualized pacing. Among adults, CAI has been found to speed training in the _____ and in _____.

23. (p. 219) CAI also accelerates learning for various _____ subjects (although the final level of skill or knowledge is no higher than that gained by conventional methods).

24. (p. 219) The simplest computerized instruction consists of self-paced _____ and _____. In this format, students answer questions similar to those found in printed workbooks. This has the advantage of instantly providing correct answers.

25. (p. 220) Higher-level CAI programs include _____ _____ which use stories, competition with a partner, sound effects, and game-like graphics to increase interest and motivation.

26. (p. 220) CAI programs also include _____ _____ where students face problems in an imaginary situation or "microworld" through which they can learn basic principles for a variety of subjects.

27. (p. 220) Punishment reduces the probability that a response will occur again. To be most effective, punishment must be given _____ or only after an undesired response occurs.

28. (p. 221) Punishers, like reinforcers, are best defined by observing their effect on behavior. Any consequence that reduces the occurrence of a target behavior is, by definition, a punisher. A punisher can be either the onset of an _____ event, or the removal of a _____ state of affairs (response cost).

29. (p. 221) Psychologists have learned that the effectiveness of punishment depends greatly on its _____, _____, and _____.

30. (p. 221) Punishment is most effective when it occurs while a response is being made, or _____ afterward and when it is given each time a response occurs.

31. (p. 221) _____ punishment can be extremely effective in stopping behavior. More often, however, punishment only temporarily _____ a response.

32. (p. 221) If the punished behavior is still reinforced, it will usually _____, especially if only mild punishment is used.

33. (p. 221) This effect has been shown experimentally with rats slapped on the paws while bar pressing during extinction. Compared with rats not punished, those whose paws were slapped temporarily _____ responding but their responding did not _____ more rapidly.

34. (p. 221) However, intense punishment may _____ _____ a response. For instance, animals severely punished while eating may never eat again.

35. (p. 222) Three tools useful in controlling simple learning are:
    1) _____, which strengthens a response;
    2) _____-_____, which causes a response to extinguish;
    3) _____, which suppresses a response.

36. (p. 223) These tools work best in combination. Punishment used without reinforcement is less effective, because punishment only tells a person or an animal that a response was "_____"; it provides no alternative. It does not teach new behaviors.

37. (p. 223) In a situation that poses immediate danger, punishment is most effective when it produces responses _____ with the undesirable response.

38. (p. 223) When punishment is necessary to manage the behavior of an animal, child, or even another adult, keep these tips in mind:
    1) Don't use punishment at all if you can discourage misbehavior in other ways.
    2) Apply punishment during or _____ after misbehavior.
    3) Use the _____ punishment necessary to suppress misbehavior.
    4) Be consistent.
    5) Expect _____ from a punished person.
    6) Punish with kindness and respect.

39. (p. 223) The basic problem with punishment is that it is usually _____. As a result, people and situations associated with punishment may also be feared or resented.

40. (p. 223) _____ learning reflects the operation of negative reinforcement. If a dog is placed in a two-compartment cage and shocked in one of the compartments, it will quickly learn to jump to the second compartment to escape the shock.

41. (p. 223) If a buzzer is sounded ten seconds before the shock is turned on, the animal will learn to jump before the shock begins. This response is known as _____ learning.

42. (p. 223) Psychologists have theorized that avoidance involves two-factor learning. An animal first learns to feel fear in the presence of the buzzer (a form of _____ _____). Then leaping from the compartment is rewarded by negative reinforcement in the form of a reduction in fear (a process involving _____ _____).

43. (p. 224) When drivers learn to fasten their seat belts in order to stop the unpleasant buzzer features in newer automobiles, this is an example of _____ conditioning.

44. (p. 224) _____ conditioning is evident when a driver learns to buckle up before the buzzer sounds.

45. (p. 224) Once avoidance is learned, it is very _____. This can be explained in informational terms given that once the dog has learned to expect that the buzzer is followed by shock, if the dog leaves before the shock would normally occur, it gets no new information to change the expectancy.

46. (p. 224) In any situation involving frequent punishment, desires to escape and avoid are activated. For example, children who run away from punishing parents (_____), may soon learn to lie about their behavior (_____).

47. (p. 224) Punishment can greatly increase _____. Researchers have shown that animals consistently react to pain by attacking whomever or whatever else is around.

48. (p. 224) Punishment may produce _____, which in turn leads to increased _____. For example, one study found that boys severely punished for aggression at home frequently were aggressive at school.

49. (p. 224) To summarize, the most common error in using punishment is to rely on it alone for training or discipline. The overall emotional adjustment of a child or pet disciplined mainly by _____ is usually superior to one disciplined mainly by punishment.

50. (p. 224) Frequent punishment makes a person or an animal _____, confused, anxious, _____, and fearful of the source of punishment. Children who are punished often learn not only to dislike the punishers, but also to dislike and to avoid the activities associated with punishment.

51. (p. 224) Parents and teachers should be aware that using punishment can be "_____ _____." The trouble is that punishment often works. When it does, a sudden end to the adult's feelings of irritation acts as a _____ reinforcer. This encourages the adult to use punishment more often in the future.

52. (p. 225) Humans can anticipate future reward or punishment and react accordingly. For example, extinction of a fear response to electric shock occurs almost _____ when subjects are told the shock will not occur again.

53. (p. 225) Human learning usually includes a large _____, or mental, dimension, being affected by expectations, information, perceptions, mental images, etc.

54. (p. 225) Cognitive learning, then, refers to understanding, knowing, anticipating, or otherwise making use of higher mental processes, and extends into the realms of _____, _____, problem solving, and _____.

55. (p. 225) A _____ _____ is an internal representation of relationships that act as a guide in gaining an overall mental picture of some stimulus complex. This principle applies when you must detour or take a new route while driving in a familiar area.

56. (p. 225) Animals are capable of cognitive learning as well. One experiment showed that chimpanzees permitted to watch fruit being hidden in different places could later return and collect about _____ pieces of fruit each.

57. (p. 225) Cognitive maps also apply to other kinds of knowledge. For instance, students develop a "map" of psychology while reading a textbook. This may be why students sometimes find it helpful to draw _____ of how they envision concepts fitting together.

58. (p. 225) Cognitive learning is also revealed by _____ (hidden) _____ where learning sometimes occurs with no obvious reinforcement at all. For example, rats allowed to explore a maze without reinforcement show no learning, but when later given food they perform as well as rats rewarded all along.

59. (p. 226) Learning in this situation may be related to satisfying curiosity or ending boredom. In humans, this phenomenon is probably related to higher-level abilities such as _____ future reward.

60. (p. 226) Much of what is meant by cognitive learning is summarized by the word _____. Specific skills are learned that can be applied to new situations.

61. (p. 226) Although ideas can be learned through _____ (repetition and memorization), many psychologists believe that learning is more lasting when people use _____ learning where skills are gained by insight and understanding.

62. (p. 226) As an example, one experiment showed that students taught to calculate the area of a parallelogram by modifying it into a triangle were _____ _____ to solve unusual problems than were students who simply memorized a rule.

63. (p. 226) Discovery learning is particularly valuable if a person has to try new strategies or discover new solutions to problems during _____.

64. (p. 226) Albert Bandura has studied learning through imitation, which is often called _____ learning or _____. It involves any process in which information is imparted by example, before direct practice is allowed.

65. (p. 227) Modeling can be used to: (1) learn new _____; (2) learn to carry out or avoid previously learned responses, depending on what happens to the model for doing the same things; or (3) learn a _____ _____ that can be applied to various situations.

66. (p. 227) For observational learning to occur, several things must take place. The learner must pay _____ to the model and _____ what was done. Then the learner must be able to _____ the learned behavior.

67. (p. 227) Also, if a model is _____ or _____, the learner is more likely to imitate the behavior.

68. (p. 227) In general, models who are _____, _____, _____ or high in status also tend to be imitated.

69. (p. 227) Once a new response is learned through modeling, normal _____ determines if it will be repeated thereafter.

70. (p. 227) This phenomenon was demonstrated in a classic experiment where children saw models displaying aggression toward a blow-up doll. When later frustrated and allowed to play with the doll, most imitated the attack. A cartoon was only _____ less effective in encouraging aggression than a live model or a filmed model.

71. (p. 228) Research shows that when parents tell a child to do one thing, but model a completely different response, children tend to imitate what the parents _____, and not what they _____.

72. (p. 228) There is reason to believe that television can serve as a model for observational learning. It may teach new antisocial actions and _____ dangerous impulses that viewers already have.

73. (p. 228) Many TV programs give the message that violence is normal, acceptable behavior. For some people, this message can lower _____ against acting out hostile feelings.

74. (p. 228) Disinhibition may even extend to _____-_____ impulses. There is evidence that after a television soap opera character commits suicide, real suicides increase among viewers.

75. (p. 228) TV also presents viewers with a distorted image of minorities, women, sex, alcohol, and authority figures. For example, stable, happy marriages are rarely portrayed on TV. Soap operas average _____ mentions of sexual intercourse per hour. Most workers shown are authority figures.

76. (p. 228) Televised violence is even more disturbing. There are about _____ hours of violence per week. Eighty-five percent of all programs contain violence, averaging 5.2 aggressive acts per hour.

77. (p. 229) More gunshots are fired in one evening of TV than in one year in a medium-sized American city. _____-_____ percent of these shots fail to hit their targets, which makes it seem like violence typically does not end in bloodshed.

78. (p. 229) Also disturbing is the finding that more than _____ of all music videos contain violence, and more than three-fourths of these violent videos include sexual imagery.

79. (p. 229) TV lawmen more often than not contribute to violence rather than prevent it. Murder, robbery, kidnapping, and assault comprise _____ percent of TV crimes.

80. (p. 229) The distortions and stereotypes of "TV land" are cause for concern, especially considering that over _____ percent of all United States households contain a TV. Also, average TV viewing in America now exceeds _____ hours per day.

81. (p. 229) Even _____-month-old infants will imitate actions they have seen on TV, which suggests that TV may begin to have an effect on children at a very early age.

82. (p. 229) Tannis Williams recently studied residents of a town in northwestern Canada before TV arrived and again two years later. Her research revealed reading development among children _____ when TV was introduced.

83. (p. 229) This natural experiment showed that children's scores on tests of creativity _____. Also, children's perceptions of sex roles became more _____.

84. (p. 229) Williams' study also demonstrated that there was a significant _____ in both verbal and physical aggression for both boys and girls regardless of whether they were high or low in aggression before they began watching TV.

85. (p. 230) Examples of "involuntary" functions which yoga and Zen masters can control include heart _____, _____ pressure, _____ consumption, and temperature of parts of the body.

86. (p. 230) These involuntary functions can now be self-controlled using _____, the application of the general principle of feedback to the control of bodily responses.

87. (p. 230) When you are given feedback, you can repeat successful responses, even if they are subtle. Biofeedback promotes learning by converting bodily processes into a clear signal that provides _____ about correct responses.

88. (p. 230) Biofeedback holds promise as a way to treat _____ problems (illnesses caused mainly by stress or psychological factors).

89. (p. 231) For example, Elmer and Alyce Green have had success in training people to prevent _____ _____ using biofeedback to redirect blood flow away from the head to the extremities.

90. (p. 231) Early successes with biofeedback led many to predict it would be a cure for a long list of ailments. In reality it has proven useful for a more limited set of problems including:
    1) relief of muscle-tension headaches and migraine headaches;
    2) lowering blood _____ and controlling heart rhythms;
    3) some control of _____ seizures;
    4) hyperactivity in children;
    5) insomnia.

91. (p. 231) Some researchers believe that many of biofeedback's benefits arise from _____ _____.

92. (p. 231) Also, the method simply acts as a "mirror" to help a person perform tasks involving _____-_____. Although it can help people make desired changes in their behavior, it does not do anything by itself.

93. (p. 231) Biofeedback has special promise for the rehabilitation of people suffering from _____ damage, _____ disorders, and stroke. For example, Neal Miller has reported on the use of biofeedback to help a child regain use of a paralyzed hand.

94. (p. 231) Alpha waves are one of several distinctive patterns of brain activity that can be recorded with the _____, abbreviated _____.

95. (p. 231) Joseph Kamiya developed a technique whereby subjects are signaled by a _____ or _____ whenever they produce alpha waves.

96. (p. 231) Subjects in early alpha-control experiments reported that high levels of alpha were linked with sensations of _____, _____, passive alertness, or peaceful images.

97. (p. 231) More recently, serious questions have been raised about the use of alpha training to promote deep relaxation. Research has shown that for some people increased alpha output is the product of relaxation; but for others, it occurs at times of _____ _____.

98. (p. 231) Low-cost home "alpha-feedback" machines are so inaccurate that many users are actually listening to _____ _____ from their house wiring rather than their own brain waves.

99. (p. 231) A _____ skill is a series of actions molded into a smooth and efficient performance. Typing, walking, and driving a car are examples.

100. (p. 231) Many such skills begin as simple response chains. However, as skills improve we typically develop _____ _____ for them—mental plans or models of what a skilled movement should be like.

101. (p. 232) Walking is a good example. We use feedback from the body and senses to compare our actions to an internal standard or program. Such monitoring, plus rapid _____, is what allows us to walk on varied surfaces.

102. (p. 232) Eventually skills become _____, or nearly automatic. This ability frees higher brain centers to make decisions and attend to other information.

103. (p. 232) The following points should be kept in mind for optimal skill learning:
   1) Begin by observing and imitating a _____ _____.
   2) Learn _____ _____to back up motor learning.
   3) Practice should be as _____ as possible so that artificial cues and responses do not become a part of the skill.
   4) Get feedback. Someone experienced should direct attention to correct responses when they occur.
   5) It is better to practice _____ _____than to break the task into artificial parts.
   6) Learn to evaluate and analyze your own performance.

104. (p. 232) Research has shown that merely thinking about or imagining a skilled performance can aid learning. This technique is called _____ _____.

105. (p. 232) Although mental practice is better than no practice at all, it is still not better than _____ practice. Also, the more familiar you are with a skill, the _____ mental rehearsal helps.

106. (p. 233) Since performance improves after a short rest, motor learning proceeds most efficiently using _____ practice rather than _____ practice.

107. (p. 233) Also, there is evidence that in the long run, new skills learned with _____ practice are retained better than those learned by _____ practice.

108. (p. 233) _____ _____ is said to have taken place when mastery of one task aids mastery of a second task. For example, learning to play the violin helps an individual to later learn the mandolin.

109. (p. 233) In _____ _____, skills developed in one situation conflict with those required for mastery of a new task. Learning to back a car with a trailer attached is a good example.

110. (p. 233) Negative transfer occurs _____ often than positive transfer and it is usually brief. It is most likely to occur when a _____ response must be made to an _____ stimulus.

111. (p. 234) Psychologist Barry Zimmerman calls the active pursuit of knowledge _____-_____ learning. Learners who use this approach employ planning and feedback to guide their efforts. They are self-starters who persist until they get it right.

112. (p. 234) The concept of self-regulated learning suggests that the best students are not always the _____ or even the hardest _____. Rather, they are people who have learned how to learn. Rather than being passive learners, they do whatever is necessary to master a topic or skill. They view learning as a process they can control.

113. (p. 235) In the last 10 years the broad features of self-regulated learning have come into focus. Self-regulated learners typically do all of the following:
    1) set specific, objective learning _____;
    2) plan learning efforts and use learning _____;
    3) use _____-_____ to guide studying;
    4) use feedback and record keeping to monitor progress;
    5) periodically evaluate their progress and goals;
    6) reinforce efforts and successes; and
    7) take corrective action.

114. (p. 237) Hundreds of studies involving over 10,000 children all point to the conclusion that if large groups of children watch a great deal of televised violence, they will be more prone to behave _____. The same conclusion also applies to violent videogames.

115. (p. 237) Children may learn new aggressive actions by watching violent behavior, or they may learn that violence is "okay." Younger children may simply remember that when TV heroes were bothered, they aggressed. TV dramas tend to give the message that violence leads to _____ and _____.

116. (p. 237) Psychologist Rowell Huesmann and Neil Malamuth believe that habitual aggression is mostly learned during the first _____ years of life. By then aggression becomes a set style of behavior that is very hard to change.

117. (p. 237) Not only does TV encourage violence, it may also lower _____ to violent acts. Victor Cline found that among groups of boys shown a brutal and bloody fight scene, those boys who averaged 42 hours per week of TV viewing showed much less emotion compared to those boys who watched little or no TV.

118. (p. 137) In another study, college men saw five R-rated slasher films that depicted violence against women. The men consistently reported _____ levels of anxiety when viewing the last film as compared with the first.

119. (p. 238) Televised violence can make aggression more likely, but it does not "cause" it to occur. Many factors affect the chances that hostile thoughts will be translated into actions. Among children, one such factor is the extent to which a child _____ with aggressive characters.

120. (p. 238) TV can also be a _____ model. Over 150 research reports evaluating the impact of educational programs such as "Sesame Street" and "The Electric Company" have been positive.

121. (p. 238) TV can be an effective model for "prosocial" attitudes and responses. Over 200 studies have shown that prosocial behavior on TV increases prosocial behavior by viewers. As one example, children in one experiment who watched a TV program that emphasized helping were _____ _____ than others to help a puppy in distress even when it meant skipping a chance to win prizes.

122. (p. 238) Children typically model _____ TV viewing habits, and they are guided by their reactions to programs. Be familiar with the TV guides provided for parents in this chapter.

123. (p. 238) There are several things that parents can do to be "TV Guides." The following guidelines can help children learn to enjoy television without being overly influenced by programs and advertisers:
    1) limit _____ _____ _____ so that television does not dominate your child's view of the world;
    2) closely monitor what your child does watch;
    3) actively seek programs your child will enjoy, especially those that model _____ behavior and social attitude;
    4) watch television with your child so that you can counter what is shown;
    5) discuss the social conflicts and violent solutions shown on television;
    6) show by your own disapproval that _____ TV heroes are not the ones to emulate.

SELF-TEST

1.   (p. 218) True-False. In the "real world" operant and classical conditioning often occur together.

2.   (p. 218) True-False. The information processing view of conditioning holds that a response is "stamped in" during conditioning.

3.   (p. 218) The information processing view of learning stresses that learning creates _____ about events that alter behavior.
     a.   predictions   c.   expectancies
     b.   instincts   d.   consistencies

4.   (p. 219) Which of the following is *not* directly involved in learning?
     a.   KR   c.   reinforcement
     b.   practice   d.   instinct

5.   (p. 219) Which of the following is *not* a factor in programmed instruction?
     a.   analyzes each answer and uses branching programs
     b.   breaks learning into a series of small steps
     c.   provides constant feedback to correct errors
     d.   requires precise answers about information as it is presented

6.   (p. 219) The simplest CAI consists of:
     a.   instructional games   c.   educational simulations
     b.   branch programming   d.   self-paced drill and practice

7.   (p. 221) Which of the following is *not* true of punishment?
     a.   Severe punishment can be extremely effective in stopping behavior.
     b.   The effectiveness of punishment depends greatly on its timing, consistency, and intensity.
     c.   Responses suppressed by mild punishment often reappear later.
     d.   Punishment is best delayed until well after an undesirable behavior has occurred.

8.   (p. 221) Which of the following conditions would *not* enhance the effectiveness of punishment?
     a.   punishment given on a partial schedule so that resistance to extinction is high
     b.   use of rewards to reinforce other responses while punishing the undesirable response
     c.   punishment that produces responses incompatible with the undesired response
     d.   punishment applied during or immediately after the undesired response

9.   (p. 221) Which of the following is *not* true of the use of punishment?
     a.   People and situations associated with punishment also tend to become aversive.
     b.   Aversive stimuli associated with punishment encourage escape and avoidance learning.
     c.   Weak punishment typically overwhelms the effects of even strong reinforcers.
     d.   Punishment can greatly increase aggression.

10. (p. 223) Escape and avoidance learning are maintained by:
     a.   positive reinforcement   c.   generalized reinforcement
     b.   primary reinforcement   d.   negative reinforcement

11. (p. 224) True-False. Children who receive a lot of physical punishment from parents or teachers tend to be well disciplined, good students who respect and like authority figures.

12. (p. 225) When humans or animals develop an overall mental picture of a stimulus complex (such as a town or a maze) it is referred to as:
     a.   superstitious behavior   c.   a cognitive map
     b.   observational learning   d.   response chaining

13. (p. 225) When no obvious reinforcement is available, yet learning occurs, we are probably speaking of the type of cognitive learning known as:
     a.   avoidance learning   c.   motor skill learning
     b.   latent learning   d.   learning to learn

14. (p. 226) In _____ learning, skills are acquired by insight and understanding.
     a.   rote   c.   discovery
     b.   latent   d.   generalized

15. (p. 227) Which of the following does *not* tend to facilitate observational learning?
     a.   model is rewarded for observed responses
     b.   model is engaged in constructive activities rather than violent ones
     c.   model is high in status
     d.   model is attractive, rewarding, or admired

16. (p. 228) True-False. In many situations modeling is more effective than verbal instruction.

17. (p. 228) Which of the following is *not* true about television?
     a.   Television may disinhibit dangerous impulses that viewers already have.
     b.   Most victims on TV are single women, young boys, or nonwhites.
     c.   Eighty-one percent of all programs contain violence.
     d.   Music videos can be especially prosocial because only a small number of them contain violence.

18. (p. 231) Biofeedback has been shown to be at least somewhat helpful in the treatment of all of the following *except*:
     a.   retinal blindness   c.   epileptic seizures
     b.   migraine headaches   d.   high blood pressure

19. (p. 231) Some researchers believe that many of the benefits of biofeedback may reflect:
    a. latent learning   c. transfer of training
    b. placebo effects   d. general relaxation

20. (p. 231) Brain wave patterns can be recorded using an _____ machine.
    a. EKG   c. EEG
    b. EMG   d. EGG

21. (p. 231) Motor skills usually first develop as response chains, but later are guided by mental models called:
    a. automated images   c. motor programs
    b. overlearned engrams   d. cognitive habits

22. (p. 232) Which of the following would *not* be expected to optimize skill learning?
    a. learning verbal rules to back up motor learning
    b. using mental practice to refine motor programs
    c. using negative practice to decrease knowledge of results
    d. practicing the task in natural units rather than artificial parts

23. (p. 233) Which of the following is *not* true about how the pattern of practice and rest periods affect learning and performance?
    a. Improvement in performance of a motor skill is most rapid when spaced practice is used.
    b. Massed practice lowers performance during training.
    c. In the long run, skills learned with massed practice are retained better than those learned by spaced practice.
    d. Both massed and spaced practice produce similar amounts of learning after a short break in training.

24. (p. 233) Learning to balance and turn on a bicycle should make it easier for you to learn riding a motorcycle. This fact is an example of:
    a. learning to learn   c. motor programming
    b. negative transfer   d. positive transfer

25. (p. 233) When mastery of one task adversely affects the acquisition of a new task, this is known as:
    a. learning set   c. negative transfer
    b. positive transfer   d. negative practice

26. (p. 234) Which of the following is *not* characteristic of self-regulated learners?
    a. They view learning as a process they can control
    b. They actively seek needed information.
    c. They are the brightest and hardest working students.
    d. They do whatever is necessary to master a topic or skill.

27. (p. 235) Self-regulated learning involves all of the following *except*:
    a. learning goals   c. self-reinforcement
    b. passive pursuit   d. self-instruction

28. (p. 237) True-False. Hundreds of studies have concluded that children who watch a great deal of television violence are more prone to behave aggressively.

29. (p. 237) In addition to encouraging imitation of violence, television also adds to tendencies toward aggression by:
    a. reducing emotional sensitivity to violence
    b. stimulating frustration among viewers
    c. romanticizing competition
    d. increasing the number of outlets for hostilities

30. (p. 238) Television can be a force for prosocial attitudes and responses. This was demonstrated by one study in which:
    a. children punished for watching violent shows became less violent and more helpful
    b. children watching a program that emphasized helping were more willing to assist an animal in distress
    c. children told they would be given prizes for helping other children were more likely to do so after viewing violent programs
    d. none of the above

APPLYING YOUR KNOWLEDGE

1. As you've learned, modeling has powerful effects on behavior. Behaviors modeled on television may certainly influence our perceptions and yet TV reality doesn't often match the real world. Keep a log of shows you randomly tune to for the next few days. How many different examples can you find of distortions, stereotypes, and bad modeling?

ANSWERS—PROGRAMMED REVIEW

1. responsive; information
2. Two-factor
3. classical conditioning
4. discriminative stimulus
5. Operant conditioning
6. involuntary; voluntary
7. information processing
8. expectancies
9. predicts; expects
10. information; information
11. expect
12. adaptive
13. feedback
14. knowledge of results; KR
15. key details
16. frequent; immediate
17. programmed instruction
18. errors; pace
19. computer-assisted; CAI
20. branching program
21. artificial intelligence
22. military; business
23. college
24. drill and practice
25. instructional games
26. educational simulations
27. contingently

28. unpleasant; positive
29. timing, consistency, intensity
30. immediately
31. Severe; suppresses
32. reappear
33. slowed; extinguish
34. permanently suppress
35. reinforcement; non-reinforcement; punishment
36. wrong
37. incompatible
38. immediately; minimum; anger
39. aversive
40. Escape
41. avoidance
42. classical conditioning; operant learning
43. escape
44. Avoidance
45. persistent
46. escape; avoidance
47. aggression
48. frustration; aggression
49. reward
50. unhappy; aggressive
51. habit forming; negative

52. immediately
53. cognitive
54. memory, thinking; language
55. cognitive map
56. 12
57. pictures
58. latent learning
59. anticipating
60. understanding
61. rote; discovery
62. better able
63. learning
64. observational; modeling
65. responses; general rule
66. attention; remember; reproduce
67. successful; rewarded
68. attractive, rewarding, admired
69. reinforcement
70. slightly
71. do; say
72. disinhibit
73. inhibitions
74. self-destructive
75. 1.5
76. 188; Eighty-one
77. Eighty-five

78. half
79. 85
80. 99; 7
81. 14
82. declined
83. dropped; stereotyped
84. increase
85. rate; blood; oxygen
86. biofeedback
87. information
88. psychosomatic
89. migraine headaches
90. pressure; epileptic
91. general relaxation
92. self-regulation
93. nerve; muscular
94. electroencephalograph; EEG

95. tone, light
96. pleasure, relaxation
97. heightened arousal
98. electrical noise
99. motor
100. motor programs
101. corrections
102. automated
103. skilled model; verbal rules; lifelike; natural units
104. mental practice
105. actual; more
106. spaced; massed
107. spaced; massed
108. Positive transfer
109. negative transfer
110. less; new; old

111. self-regulated
112. brightest; working
113. goals; strategies; self-instruction
114. aggressively
115. success; popularity
116. 10
117. sensitivity
118. lower
119. identifies
120. positive
121. more willing
122. parents'
123. total viewing time; positive; violent

ANSWERS—SELF-TEST

1.	True	6.	d	11.	False	16.	True	21.	c	26.	b
2.	False	7.	d	12.	c	17.	d	22.	c	27.	b
3.	c	8.	a	13.	b	18.	a	23.	c	28.	True
4.	d	9.	c	14.	c	19.	d	24.	d	29.	a
5.	a	10.	d	15.	b	20.	c	25.	c	30.	b

ACROSS

4. _____ learning is based on insight or understanding
5. observational learning
6. knowledge of results (abbr.)
9. punishment may cause this
10. opposite of spaced practice
12. he studied observational learning and imitating
14. brain waves denoting relaxation or heightened arousal
15. process of monitoring body processes
17. punishment should be intense, immediate, and _____

DOWN

1. Computer-Assisted Instruction (abbr.)
2. _____ instruction provides immediate feedback
3. it shows a lot of violence
7. learning remains hidden until reward is given
8. learning by watching
11. decreases likelihood of undesired response occurring again
13. common response to frustration
16. negative reinforcement increases responding by _____ discomfort

CHAPTER 9

Memory

CONTENTS

TERMS AND CONCEPTS

memory
encoding
storage
retrieval
sensory memory
icon
echo
short-term memory (STM)
working memory
long-term memory (LTM)
digit-span test
chunks of information
recoding
rehearsal
constructive processing
pseudo-memories
memory structure
network model
redintegration
tip-of-the-tongue state
feeling-of-knowing reactions
memory tasks
recall
verbatim memory
recognition
distractors
false positive
relearning
savings score
explicit memory

implicit memory
eidetic imagery
internal images
nonsense syllables
curve of forgetting
memory traces
memory decay
disuse
cue-dependent forgetting
state dependent learning
interference
retroactive interference
proactive interference
repression
suppression
flashbulb memories
retrograde amnesia
anterograde amnesia
consolidation
electroconvulsive shock (ECS)
hippocampus
engram
progressive part method
cognitive interview
mnemonics
keyword method
procedural memory (skill memory)
fact memory
semantic memory
episodic memory

IMPORTANT INDIVIDUALS

George Miller
Wilder Penfield
Elizabeth Loftus
Geoffrey Loftus
A. R. Luria

William Chase
Anders Ericsson
Herman Ebbinghaus
Roger Brown
James Kulik

Brenda Milner
Karl Lashley
Eric Kandel
R. Edward Geiselman
Ron Fisher

PROGRAMMED REVIEW

1. (p. 242) _____ is an active system that receives, stores, organizes, alters, and recovers information.

2. (p. 242) In some ways, memory acts like a computer. Information to be recorded is first _____, or changed into a usable form, then _____, or held in the system.

3. (p. 242) To be used, memories must be _____, or taken out of storage. In order to "remember" something all three of these processes must occur.

4. (p. 242) To be stored for a long time, information must pass through three stages of memory. Incoming information first enters _____ memory, where an exact copy of what is seen or heard is held.

5. (p. 242) If the information is seen, an _____, or fleeting image, persists for about one-half second afterward. Hearing is held as a brief _____ in sensory memory, lasting as long as 2 seconds.

6. (p. 242) _____ _____ determines what information moves from sensory memory to the second memory system.

7. (p. 242) This second system is called _____-_____ memory, abbreviated _____. Memories are also brief here, but longer than sensory memories.

8. (p. 243) Short-term memories can be stored as images, but more often they are encoded by _____, especially in remembering words and letters.

9. (p. 243) Short-term memory acts as a _____ storehouse for _____ amounts of information. Unless the information is important it is quickly removed from STM and forever lost.

10. (p. 243) While STM prevents our minds from being cluttered with trivia, it also provides a _____ _____ where we do much of our thinking, like dialing a phone number, remembering a shopping list, and the like.

11. (p. 243) STM is severely affected by any _____ or _____. You've probably experienced this when dialing a phone number, getting a busy signal, and not remembering the number when you try to redial.

12. (p. 243) Information that is important or meaningful is transferred to the third memory system called _____-_____ memory, abbreviated _____.

13. (p. 243) LTM acts as a _____ storehouse for information and appears to have almost _____ capacity to store information.

14. (p. 243) Information in LTM is stored on the basis of _____ and _____, not by sound as in STM.

15. (p. 243) When new information enters STM it is related to knowledge stored in LTM. This gives the new information _____, and makes it easier to store in LTM.

16. (p. 244) In studying short-term memory, George Miller found that we can normally retain about _____ _____ of information, the "magic number" for memory.

17. (p. 244) This number was determined through his use of the _____-_____ test in which subjects must remember a series of numbers.

18. (p. 245) Humans can retain more than seven individual bits (or single "pieces") of information by converting them into _____ of information. Through this process we combine several individual units into one "stack" of information.

19. (p. 245) Chunking _____ information into larger units. Most often it does so by taking advantage of units that already have meaning in LTM. For example, one memory experiment found that subjects remembered best when the letters used were read as familiar meaningful chunks such as TV, IBM, USN, and YMCA than when unconnected letters were employed.

20. (p. 245) Short-term memory traces appear to weaken and disappear very rapidly, but can be prolonged by _____, mentally repeating the information.

21. (p. 245) One experiment showed that when rehearsal is prevented, as little as _____ seconds after presentation of a stimulus, subjects could not recall the stimulus.

22. (p. 245) In Wilder Penfield's research, patients whose brains were electrically stimulated seemed to have _____ _____ of long-forgotten events.

23. (p. 246) This finding led Penfield to claim that all memories are absolutely permanent. However, this claim is exaggerated because many events never get past _____-_____ memory.

24. (p. 246) Also, brain stimulation only produces memory-like experiences in about _____ percent of cases. Most reports are more like dreams, and many are clearly fictional.

25. (p. 246) Memory experts Elizabeth and Geoffrey Loftus conclude that there is little evidence that long-term memories are absolutely permanent. Rather, it is more accurate to say that they are _____ permanent, or long-lasting.

26. (p. 246) There is another reason to doubt Penfield's claim. As new long-term memories are formed, older memories are often updated, changed, lost, or revised. This process is called _____ _____.

27. (p. 246) Research shows that gaps in memory may be filled in by logic, guesses, or new information. It is possible to have _____ _____ (or false memories) for things that never happened.

28. (p. 246) Other research has shown that being _____ about a memory tells little about the actual accuracy of the memory.

29. (p. 246) News stories often give the impression that hypnosis can be used to help recall lost or blocked memories. However, recent research has shown that a hypnotized person is more likely than normal to use _____ to fill in gaps in memory.

30. (p. 246) When hypnotized subjects are given _____ information, they tend to weave it into their memories. Also, "leading" questions asked during hypnosis can alter memories.

31. (p. 247) A further problem with the use of hypnosis in reviving memories is that even when a memory is completely false, the hypnotized person's confidence in it can be _____.

32. (p. 247) Hypnosis increases false memories more than it does true ones. For instance, _____ percent of the new memories produced by hypnotized subjects in one experiment were incorrect.

33. (p. 247) Long-term memory may record one _____ separate bits of information in a lifetime.

34. (p. 247) Long-term memories appear to be highly organized. The _____, or arrangement, of this organization may be based on rules, images, categories, symbols, similarity, formal meaning, or personal meaning.

35. (p. 247) The _____ _____ of memory proposed by Collins and Quillian hypothesizes that LTM is organized as a network of linked ideas. When ideas are farther apart, it takes a longer chain of associations to connect them.

36. (p. 248) Networks of associated memories may help explain the process of _____ in which one memory serves as a cue to trigger another. As a result, an entire past experience may be reconstructed from one small recollection.

37. (p. 248) The experience of having an answer or a memory just out of reach is sometimes called the _____-_____-_____-_____ state.

38. (p. 248) One study illustrating partial memory showed that students were often able to accurately guess the first and last letter and even the number of syllables of the word they were trying to remember. They were also able to give words that sounded like or meant the same as the defined word. This illustrates that memory is not an _____-_____-_____ event.

39. (p. 248) A related finding is that people can often tell beforehand if they are likely to remember something. This ability is based on a state called the _____ of _____. Such reactions are easy to observe on television game shows, where they occur just before contestants are allowed to answer.

40. (p. 248) There are three commonly used memory _____ employed to measure memory.

41. (p. 248) To _____ means to supply or reproduce important facts and information. Tests of this type usually require _____ (word-for-word) memory.

42. (p. 249) A type of recall is required when you take an _____ examination, or when you memorize a poem until you can recite it without looking.

43. (p. 249) The order in which information is memorized has an effect on recall because of the _____ _____ effect. The greatest number of errors occurs for items in the middle of a list.

44. (p. 249) The last items in a list appear to be remembered best because they are still in _____. The first items are also remembered because they entered an "empty" short-term memory where they could be _____.

45. (p. 249) A multiple-choice examination is based on a testing procedure called _____. It is a more sensitive measure of memory than recall.

46. (p. 249) Recognition memory can be amazingly accurate. Subjects shown 2560 photographs and then asked to pick those they had seen from each of 280 pairs of pictures could do so with _____ to _____ percent accuracy.

47. (p. 249) Recognition is usually _____ to recall. This fact explains why police departments use photographs or a lineup to identify criminal suspects.

48. (p. 249) Witnesses who disagree in their recall of a suspect's height, weight, age, or eye color often agree completely when recognition is all that is required. Identification is even more accurate when witnesses are allowed to hear suspects' _____ as well as see them.

49. (p. 250) While recognition is usually superior to recall, it depends greatly on the kind of _____ used. These elements are false items included along with an item to be recognized.

50. (p. 250) If the distractors are very similar to the correct item, memory may be poor. A reverse problem sometimes occurs when only one choice looks like it could be correct. This fact can produce a _____ _____, or false sense of recognition.

51. (p. 250) For example, witnesses describing a criminal as black, tall, or young might make a _____ _____ if the lineup only includes one suspect who is black among whites, tall among short individuals, or young among older persons.

52. (p. 250) In a classic memory experiment, a Greek passage was read daily to a young child. Years later, the child could recall nothing, but could memorize the same passage _____ percent faster than others of equal difficulty.

53. (p. 250) Thus, testing memory by _____ shows a savings in the time or effort necessary to remaster previously learned material.

54. (p. 250) Relearning is measured by a _____ _____. For example, if you memorize a list in 60 minutes and much later cannot recall any of it, but can relearn it in 45 minutes, your savings is 25 percent (15 divided by 60 times 100).

55. (p. 250) Psychologists have recently discovered that many memories remain outside of conscious awareness. Nevertheless, _____ memories, such as unconsciously knowing where the letters are on a typewriter, greatly influence our behavior.

56. (p. 250) Such memories are in contrast to _____ memories, which are past experiences that a person is aware he or she has brought to mind. Recall, recognition, and the tests you take in school rely on these memories.

57. (p. 250) Implicit memory was first noticed in studies of patients who were suffering memory loss as a result of brain injuries. As one example, a patient shown a list of common words may not be able to recall words from the original list. But if the first two letters of each word is given, the patient can repeat the list even though not aware that they are remembering the list. Apparently, the letters _____ (or activated) hidden memories, which then influenced their answers.

58. (p. 250) Similar effects have been found for people with normal memories. Implicit memories are often revealed by giving a person _____ _____ to which the person simply says whatever comes to mind. Quite often the person "remembers" the original items even though they are not aware that they are remembering.

59. (p. 251) _____ _____, known informally as photographic memory, occurs when a person has visual images clear enough to be scanned or retained for at least 30 seconds after viewing a picture.

60. (p. 251) Eidetic imagery is most often observed in childhood. About _____ children out of a hundred can give detailed descriptions of pictures they have viewed for only seconds.

61. (p. 251) Eidetic imagery appears to disappear with age. This change is no great loss, as the majority of eidetic memorizers have no better _____-_____ memory than average.

62. (p. 251) Eidetic memory depends on images projected on a surface in front of a person. A second type of "photographic" memory occurs in people who have very vivid _____ _____.

63. (p. 251) Researchers Kosslyn, Ball, and Reisler found that memories do exist as images. Subjects memorized a treasure map and then were asked to picture a black dot moving from one object to another. The time it took to mentally "move" the dot was _____ _____ to actual distances on the map.

64. (p. 252) Word memories sometimes impair our recall of remembered images. For example, subjects in one study were _____ _____ at recognizing a picture of a face they had seen on a videotape if asked to describe the face before choosing a picture of it on a test.

65. (p. 252) Some people may have such vivid internal images that they too have "photographic memory." Such was the case of Mr. S reported by A. R. Luria, who had practically unlimited memory for visual images. Unfortunately, Mr. S remembered so much that he could not separate _____ _____ from _____.

66. (p. 252) Another case of exceptional memory has been studied by William Chase and Anders Ericsson. Their subject, Steve, practiced memorizing longer lists of digits until he was able to remember around _____ digits.

67. (p. 253) Steve relied on association, such as ages or dates, to chunk digits. But his short-term memory did not improve, nor was he able to memorize more than seven _____.

68. (p. 253) Chase and Ericsson believe Steve's performance shows that exceptional memory may be merely a _____ extension of normal memory. However, in the case of Mr. S, this hypothesis is open to debate since he could memorize strings of digits, meaningless consonants, mathematical formulas, and poems in foreign languages.

69. (p. 253) In a series of famous early experiments, Herman Ebbinghaus learned long lists of _____ _____, meaningless three letter words like GEX or WOJ.

70. (p. 253) Ebbinghaus used nonsense syllables to prevent being swayed by prior learning. By waiting various amounts of time before testing his memory, he constructed a _____ of _____.

71. (p. 253) The curve shows that forgetting is _____ at first and then is followed by a slow decline.

72. (p. 253) The Ebbinghaus curve shows that less than _____ percent of nonsense syllables were remembered after only two days had passed. However, forgetting is not lost nearly as quickly for meaningful information.

73. (p. 254) For example, tests show that students of Spanish forget an average of _____ percent of their vocabulary during the first three years after they stop studying. After this early decline, however, little more forgetting occurs during the next 20 years.

74. (p. 254) The most obvious reason for forgetting is also the most commonly overlooked. In many cases we forget because we never _____ (formed a memory of) the information in the first place. This is illustrated by Nickerson and Adams' experiments in which it was found that very few students could accurately draw a penny or even recognize a drawing of a real one among fakes.

75. (p. 254) When 140 college professors were asked what strategies they use to improve their memory, the most frequently recommended technique was to _____ things down. This ensures that information will not be lost from STM before it can be stored more permanently.

76. (p. 254) One view of why forgetting occurs says that _____ _____ (changes in nerve cells or brain activity) fade or decay over a period of time.

77. (p. 254) Such decay appears definitely to be a factor in the loss of sensory memories and to STM and has appeal as an explanation for long-term forgetting. Perhaps long-term memory traces fade from _____ and eventually become so weak they cannot be retrieved.

78. (p. 254) Reasons exist to question this view. One is the seemingly forgotten memories recovered through _____, relearning, and priming. Another is that disuse fails to explain why some unused memories fade and others are carried for life.

79. (p. 254) A third contradiction is revealed by those elderly people who have vivid memories of trivial and long-forgotten events from the _____, while _____ memories are fading.

80. (p. 255) There appear to be several additional possibilities that explain LTM forgetting. One emphasizes that many memories appear to be available but not accessible, because _____ present at the time of learning are no longer present when the time comes to retrieve information.

81. (p. 255) In theory, memory will be best if you study in the _____ _____ where you will be tested. Since this is often impossible, it may be wise to vary your study environment so that memories are not tied too strongly to a particular place.

82. (p. 255) The bodily state that exists during learning can be a strong cue for later memory. For this reason, information learned under the influence of a drug is best remembered when the drugged state occurs again. This effect is known as _____-_____ _____.

83. (p. 255) A similar effect applies to _____ states. For instance, Gordon Bower found that people who learned a list of words while in a particular mood recalled the list better when experiencing that same mood.

84. (p. 255) Similarly, if you are in a _____ mood you are more likely to remember recent happy events. If you are in a _____ mood you will tend to have unpleasant memories. This helps explain why couples who quarrel often end up remembering, and rehashing, old arguments.

85. (p. 256) Another aspect of forgetting is demonstrated in an experiment in which one group of college students learned lists of nonsense syllables, then slept for eight hours and were retested. They performed better than a second group that remained awake for eight hours. This difference is based on the fact that new learning can _____ with previous learning.

86. (p. 256) In another supporting experiment, subjects were asked to memorize new lists of words only to be remembered until the next day. Subjects who learned only one list recalled _____ percent, while those who learned 20 lists (one each day) were only able to recall _____ percent of the last list one day later.

87. (p. 256) The sleeping college students remembered more because _____ interference was held to a minimum. This term refers to the tendency for new learning to inhibit retrieval of old learning.

88. (p. 256) Retroactive interference is demonstrated by this arrangement:
    Experimental group: Learn A   Learn B   Test A
    Control group: Learn A   _____   Test A
    When the experimental group does not remember as much when tested on Task A as the control group, retroactive interference has occurred.

89. (p. 257) A second basic type of interference is _____ _____. It is demonstrated when experimental subjects in this arrangement remember less of Task B than controls:
    Experimental group: Learn A   Learn B   Test B
    Control group: Rest   Learn B   Test B

90. (p. 257) Many people find that they tend to remember happy, positive events better than disappointments and irritations. A clinical psychologists would call this tendency _____, or motivated forgetting. Through this, painful, threatening, or embarrassing memories are actively held out of consciousness by forces within one's personality.

91. (p. 258) Repression can be distinguished from _____, a conscious attempt to put something out of mind.

92. (p. 258) By not thinking about something unpleasant, you have merely suppressed a memory. Clinicians consider true repression an _____ event. When a memory is repressed, we are unaware that forgetting has even occurred.

93. (p. 258) We have much evidence of the existence of repression, but do not understand why some traumatic events are frozen in memory at times of personal tragedy, accident, or other significant events. Psychologists Roger Brown and James Kulik refer to these as _____ _____.

94. (p. 258) One reason such memories can be so vivid is that the hormones _____ and _____, which have been shown to enhance memory formation, are secreted during times of emotion or stress.

95. (p. 258) Not all flashbulb memories are negative. In general, vivid memories are most likely when an event is _____, important, or _____.

96. (p. 258) The fact that flashbulb memories are vivid doesn't mean they are always _____. Some are entirely incorrect.

97. (p. 258) A head injury may cause a "gap" in memories preceding the accident. This effect is called _____ _____.

98. (p. 258) In contrast, _____ amnesia involves forgetting events that occur after an injury or trauma.

99. (p. 258) Retrograde amnesia can be understood by recognizing that transferring memories from short-term storage to long-term storage takes a certain amount of time. The process is called _____.

100. (p. 259) Support for the notion of memory consolidation comes from work showing that a mild electric shock to the brain, known as _____ _____ and abbreviated _____, can prevent consolidation.

101. (p. 259) For example, rats given a painful _____ for stepping off a platform would continue to step off if ECS was used to block consolidation immediately after each learning experience.

102. (p. 259) ECS has been employed as a psychiatric treatment for severe _____ in humans. Used in this way, electroshock therapy also causes memory loss.

103. (p. 259) If enough time is allowed to pass between learning and ECS, the memory is unaffected, apparently because consolidation is already complete. This is why people with head injuries usually only lose memories from _____ before the accident, while older memories remain intact.

104. (p. 259) In controlled dosages, various drugs can speed up consolidation, although they do not directly increase memory. These drugs include metrazol, strychnine, _____, _____ and _____.

105. (p. 259) However, if the dosage of a stimulant drug is too high by even a small amount, memory will be _____.

106. (p. 259) Memory losses are common when a person overindulges in _____. Blackouts may cause loss of memory for a few minutes to several hours.

107. (p. 259) Such losses appear to result because alcohol impairs _____ and _____ of memories. Research makes it clear that studying while drunk is an excellent way to lower test scores.

108. (p. 259) Even intoxicated eyewitnesses to crimes, which are usually memorable events, suffer _____ memory for what they saw.

109. (p. 259) An area of the brain of particular importance to memory is the _____. This structure, buried deep within the brain, seems to act as a sort of "switching station" between short-term and long-term memory.

110. (p. 259) Humans who have had the hippocampus damaged show a striking inability to store _____ _____, as in the case reported by Brenda Milner. Her patient suffered from anterograde amnesia and, therefore, lived eternally in the present.

111. (p. 260) At one time researchers sought to discover where in particular memory is stored in the brain. For instance, Karl Lashley, a pioneering brain researcher, began in the 1920s to search for an _____, or memory trace.

112. (p. 260) Lashley taught animals to run mazes and then removed parts of their brains to see how memory of the maze changed. He discovered that it mattered little which part of the cortex was removed. Only the _____ removed correlated to memory loss.

113. (p. 260) There is now extensive evidence that learning alters the electrical activity, structure, and chemistry of the brain. For example Eric Kandel has found that learning in the marine snail Aplysia occurs when certain nerve cells in a circuit alter the amount of _____ chemicals they release.

114. (p. 260) Such changes essentially determine which circuits get strengthened and which become weaker. Others have shown that an increase in _____ _____ for transmitter chemicals occurs during learning.

115. (p. 261) Several suggestions can be made for improving memory. One of these emphasizes the importance of _____ or knowledge of results.

116. (p. 261) Feedback can help you check to see if you are learning and can help identify material that needs extra practice. A prime means of providing feedback is _____, repeating to yourself what you have learned.

117. (p. 261) One experiment illustrating this point showed that the best memory score was earned by students who spent _____ percent of their time reciting and only _____ percent reading.

118. (p. 261) _____ is similar to recitation, but it can be done privately. It refers to mentally repeating, paraphrasing, and summarizing information. The more you do this as you read, the better you will remember it.

119. (p. 261) Another suggestion is to boil down paragraphs to one or two important terms or ideas. Such careful and _____ marking of a text makes memorization more manageable.

120. (p. 261) Organizing materials to be learned into more meaningful chunks can help with memorization. For example, students in one experiment who made up stories using long lists of words to be memorized learned the lists _____ than those who didn't.

121. (p. 261) _____ class notes can be extremely helpful. In fact, outlining your outlines so that the organization of ideas becomes clearer and simpler can also help.

122. (p. 261) It is generally better to practice whole packages of information rather than smaller parts. Try to study the largest _____ amount of information possible at one time.

123. (p. 261) For very long or complex material, try the _____ _____ method: Break a learning task into short sections, first study part "A," then parts "A" and "B," then "A," "B," and "C," and so forth.

124. (p. 261) Whenever you must learn something in order, remember the _____ _____ effect and give special attention to items in the _____ of the list, since they are most easily forgotten.

125. (p. 262) Remember that the best _____ for remembering are those that were present during encoding. You should elaborate information as you learn and form images that include the new information, and relate it to knowledge you already have.

126. (p. 262) This principle is demonstrated by one study where students were asked to give three words closely related in meaning to each of 600 words they were later asked to recall. They correctly recalled _____ percent of the original word list when the words supplied by the students were used as cues to jog memory.

127. (p. 262) Numerous studies have shown that memory is greatly improved by _____, that is, study continued beyond bare mastery.

128. (p. 262) _____ practice is generally superior to _____ practice. By scheduling your time into brief study sessions, you maximize your study skills.

129. (p. 262) Remember that _____ after study reduces interference. Also, include ample breaks between subjects.

130. (p. 262) _____ shortly before an exam to cut down the time during which you must remember details. However, hold the amount of new information you try to memorize to a minimum, as it will confuse you and interfere with what you already know.

131. (p. 262) Successful recall is usually the result of a planned _____ of memory. For example, one study found that students were most likely to recall a name that eluded them if they made use of partial information.

132. (p. 262) R. Edward Geiselman and Ron Fisher have developed a technique called the _____ _____ to help police detectives jog the memory of eye-witnesses.

133. (p. 262) Cognitive interviewing is a good example of how active probing often helps improve recall. When used properly, it produces _____ percent more correct information than standard questioning.

134. (p. 262) There are four simple steps you can use when searching for a "lost" memory. First, say or write down _____ you can remember that relates to the information you are seeking.

135. (p. 263) Secondly, try to recall events of information in different _____. Let your memories flow out backward or start with whatever impressed you the most.

136. (p. 263) As a third step, recall from different _____. Review events by mentally standing in a different place. Try to view information as another person would remember it.

137. (p. 263) And finally, mentally put yourself back in the situation where you learned the information. Try to mentally recreate the _____ _____ or relive the event. As you do, include sounds, smells, details of weather, nearby objects, other people present, etc.

138. (p. 264) _____ refers to any kind of memory system or aid. In some cases they can increase recall ten-fold.

139. (p. 264) Mnemonic techniques are effective alternatives to rote learning, as demonstrated by many studies. One experiment showed that subjects using mnemonics remembered an average of _____ items from a 100 item list, while those using simple or rote learning remembered an average of _____.

140. (p. 264) There are several basic principles of mnemonics. One is to use _____ _____, since visual memory is usually superior to verbal memory.

141. (p. 264) Another aid is to make things _____, since this technique facilitates the transfer of information from short-term to long-term memory.

142. (p. 264) Along with this, try to make information _____ by connecting it with information already stored in LTM.

143. (p. 264) Finally, try to form _____. _____, or exaggerated mental associations, since connecting two ideas, terms, or images in this way increases the likelihood you will remember them later.

144. (p. 264) Bizarre images can make stored information more distinctive and therefore easier to recall. They mainly help improve _____ memory, but this can be a first step toward retaining information.

145. (p. 265) Mnemonics can be used to avoid rote memorization. As one example, use the _____ method. To remember that pajaro means bird in Spanish, visualize a parked car full of birds.

146. (p. 265) Mnemonics are not a complete substitute for normal memory. They are not likely to be helpful unless you make extensive use of _____. Mnemonics can be thought of as a built-in hint in your memory.

147. (p. 265) There are three mnemonic techniques which can be used to help remember things in order. One of them is to _____ a _____. Connecting one item to the next can be quite useful for lists of twenty or more items.

148. (p. 265) Another suggestion is to take a _____ _____. By mentally "placing" objects or ideas along a familiar path, you can later retrace your steps mentally to remember the items.

149. (p. 266) A third tool is to use a _____. As an example, the first letter or syllable of words or ideas can be formed into another word which can serve as a reminder of the order you wish to remember.

150. (p. 267) Many psychologists have concluded that long-term memories fall into at least two categories. One of these, _____ memory (or "_____" memory), includes basic conditioned responses and response chains like those involved in typing, solving a puzzle, etc.

151. (p. 267) It is likely that skill memories register in "lower" brain areas, especially the _____, and that they appeared early in the evolution of the brain.

152. (p. 267) The second category of long-term memories is sometimes called _____ memory. It is the ability to learn specific information such as names, faces, words, dates, or ideas.

153. (p. 267) Most of our factual knowledge about the world is almost totally immune to forgetting. Such facts make up a part of LTM called _____ _____.

154. (p. 267) Semantic memory has no connection to time or places. In contrast, _____ _____ is autobiographical; it records life events in time sequences.

155. (p. 268) In general, episodic memories are more easily _____ than semantic memories because new information constantly pours into the system. (Flashbulb memories are an exception.)

SELF-TEST

1. (p. 242) The memory system that stores information as icons or echoes is:
   a. long-term memory
   b. short-term memory
   c. working memory
   d. sensory memory

2. (p. 243) Which of the following is *not* true of short-term memory?
   a. Most often memories are encoded on the basis of meaning and importance.
   b. Information that is lost from STM is gone forever.
   c. STM is brief, easily interrupted, and limited in capacity.
   d. It provides a working memory where we do most of our thinking.

3. (p. 243) Two weeks after memorizing a list of words you try to remember the word "wheat" and can't. You are more likely to say _____ because of the way in which memories are encoded in LTM.
   a. heat
   b. what
   c. grain
   d. brown

4. (p. 244) Which of the following is a test used to measure STM?
   a. Ishihara
   b. recoding
   c. digit-span
   d. relearning

5. (p. 245) George Miller has shown that humans can normally retain about how many bits of information in STM?
   a. 3
   b. 7
   c. 13
   d. 4 for numbers, 8 for words

6. (p. 245) The process of _____ allows us to organize information into larger, meaningful units so that greater STM storage is possible.
   a. rehearsing
   b. encoding
   c. construction
   d. chunking

7. (p. 245) A good way to keep information in STM or to increase the chances of transfer to LTM is through:
   a. frequent retrieval
   b. rehearsal
   c. repression
   d. consolidation

8.   (p. 246) True-False. There is little evidence that long-term memories are absolutely permanent, rather they are only relatively permanent, or long lasting.

9.   (p. 246) One example of constructive processing is:
     a.   peudo-memories   c.   consolidation
     b.   eidetic imagery   d.   mental scripts

10. (p. 247) Which of the following is *not* true of the relationship between hypnosis and memory?
     a.   Hypnosis decreases false memories more than it does true ones.
     b.   A hypnotized person is more likely than normal to use imagination to fill in gaps in memory.
     c.   "Leading" questions asked during hypnosis can alter memories.
     d.   When hypnotized subjects are given false information, they tend to weave it into their memories.

11. (p. 247) True-False. According to the network model proposed by Collins and Quillian, LTM is organized such that when ideas are "farther" apart, it takes a shorter chain of associations to connect them.

12. (p. 248) When you smell a perfume that triggers a reconstructive memory, you are experiencing:
     a.   recall   c.   relearning
     b.   recognition   d.   redintegration

13. (p. 248) True-False. While people used to think that partial memory existed, we now know that you either remember something or you don't.

14. (p. 249) The serial position effect indicates that the most easily forgotten material in a sequence is:
     a.   the first part   c.   the middle part
     b.   the last part   d.   not the items PER SE, but their order

15. (p. 149) Which of the following is *not* true of recognition?
     a.   It is a more sensitive testing procedure than recall.
     b.   Recognition yields a savings score based on the number of items initially identified correctly.
     c.   Recognition can be greatly influenced by the presence of distractors.
     d.   Exams involving multiple choice are an example of the recognition procedure.

16. (p. 250) When a person is tested by relearning, how do we know a memory still exists?
     a.   through the use of a savings score
     b.   through the use of essay tests
     c.   through the use of multiple-choice tests
     d.   because one memory can serve as a cue to trigger unother

17. (p. 251) True-False. The incidence of eidetic imagery is much greater among adults than children since adults have had more opportunity to develop memory skills.

18. (p. 251) Which of the following is *not* true of "photographic memory?"
     a.   It may involve eidetic images projected on a surface out in front of a person.
     b.   It may involve vivid internal images.
     c.   Complete "photographic memory," as in the case of Mr. S, may be more a liability an asset.
     d.   The majority of eidetic memorizers have much better than average long-term memory.

19. (p. 253) Ebbinghaus conducted a famous set of experiments to:
    a. develop a mnemonic system
    b. study relearning by teaching Greek passages to his child
    c. develop a curve of forgetting
    d. discover flashbulb memories

20. (p. 253) True-False. We forget relatively more information long periods after it has been learned than after short periods.

21. (p. 254) Which of the following facts supports the view that some forgetting occurs through decay or disuse of memories?
    a. Recovery of seemingly forgotten memories may occur through redintegration.
    b. Some memories fade away and others are carried for life.
    c. Among elderly people, recent memories may fade, while long past memories remain vivid.
    d. None of the above.

22. (p. 255) Which of the following is *not* a factor in forgetting?
    a. Cues present at the time of learning may not be available at the time of retrieval.
    b. New learning may interfere with memories of previously learned material.
    c. Previously learned material may interfere with the recall of new material.
    d. Through suppression, unpleasant memories may be held out of consciousness by forces within one's personality.

23. (p. 256) True-False. If on the same night, you cram for a psychology exam and then cram for a biology exam, memory for biology may be reduced due to proactive interference, while memory for psychology may suffer from retroactive interference.

24. (p. 258) True-False. Flashbulb memories are relatively short-lived memory traces that result from intense stimuli such as the temporary white images you see when a flashbulb is operated.

25. (p. 258) True-False. A person suffering from retrograde amnesia can learn new information, but has great difficulty remembering events prior to whatever caused the amnesia.

26. (p. 258) The process of consolidation refers to:
    a. how information gets into short-term memory
    b. how information in long-term memory is recalled
    c. how information in short-term memory is recalled
    d. how information is transferred from STM to LTM

27. (p. 259) Which of the following can be used to retard or prevent consolidation?
    a. amphetamines   c. caffeine
    b. ECS   d. nicotine

28. (p. 259) Damage to which area of the brain may result in a striking inability to store new memories?
    a. hypothalamus   c. amygdala
    b. hippocampus   d. cerebellum

29. (p. 261) Which of the following is *not* a useful aid to increasing memory?
    a. recitation   c. organization
    b. underlearning   d. knowledge of results

30. (p. 262) Which of the following will *not* tend to increase your ability to retain information in memory?
    a. using spaced versus massed practice to improve concentration
    b. studying the largest meaningful amount of information possible at one time
    c. learning in a novel environment to heighten your attention
    d. trying to sleep after study if possible, and using ample breaks between subjects

31. (p. 262) Which of the following is *not* true of the cognitive interview?
    a. This technique was designed by Geiselman and Fisher to help police detectives jog the memory of eyewitnesses.
    b. There are four steps involved, including the idea that you should say or write down everything you can remember that relates to the information you are seeking.
    c. One of the steps involved in this technique is the notion of trying to recall information from different viewpoints.
    d. The cognitive interview produces 85 percent more correct information than standard questioning when used properly.

32. (p. 264) Mnemonics are:
    a. memory traces linked with changes in RNA
    b. an example of the network model of LTM
    c. lasting images that are frozen in memory at times of personal tragedy
    d. memory systems or aids

33. (p. 264) Which of the following is *not* a basic principle of mnemonics?
    a. make things familiar
    b. form bizarre or unusual mental associations
    c. focus on words or verbal memories
    d. make things meaningful

34. (p. 267) Which of the following is *not* a true statement with respect to procedural memory?
    a. It includes basic conditioned responses and response chains.
    b. This is the memory that a person with amnesia lacks.
    c. It is registered in "lower" brain areas.
    d. It can be fully expressed only as actions.

35. (p. 267) Episodic memory refers to:
    a. occasions when one part of a larger memory will trigger thoughts of previous life episodes
    b. transient memories which usually decay before transfer into LTM
    c. the mental dictionary or encyclopedia of basic knowledge stored in LTM
    d. the autobiographical part of LTM which records life events involving times or places

APPLYING YOUR KNOWLEDGE

1. One measure of memory is relearning. Conduct a self-experiment to better understand this technique. Memorize a poem, a section of your textbook, and a story (make selections that are about the same amount of material) until you can recite each quite easily, then set them aside. Wait several weeks and test yourself again to see if you can still recite them perfectly. If not, relearn the materials and compute your savings scores. Does your savings score vary depending upon the type of material? Try a different time period next time to see if the amount of time you wait to relearn the materials really does affect the savings score.

2. Generate a list of nonsense syllables and memorize the list in order. Test your recall after various lengths of time and plot your results. Can you develop a curve of forgetting similar to that demonstrated by Ebbinghaus?

3. Design and execute a simple experiment to demonstrate proactive interference and retroactive interference. Try using different kinds of learning materials such as phone numbers, nonsense syllables, lists of words, etc. Does the meaningfulness of the materials make a difference in the amount of interference?

4. When you take your next test for a class, try using the basic principles of mnemonics discussed in the Applications section. Keep a log of what worked and didn't work for you. Did using the techniques help your test score? Did it take more or less time to study for the examination than what you might normally have needed?

ANSWERS—PROGRAMMED REVIEW

1. Memory
2. encoded; stored
3. retrieved
4. sensory
5. icon; echo
6. Selective attention
7. short-term; STM
8. sound
9. temporary; small
10. working memory
11. interruption, interference
12. long-term; LTM
13. permanent; limitless
14. meaning, importance
15. meaning
16. seven bits
17. digit-span
18. chunks
19. recodes
20. rehearsal
21. 18
22. vivid memories
23. short-term
24. 3
25. relatively
26. constructive processing
27. pseudo-memories
28. confident
29. imagination
30. false
31. unshakable
32. 80
33. quadrillion
34. structure
35. network model
36. redintegration
37. tip-of-the-tongue
38. all-or-nothing
39. feeling of knowing
40. tasks

41. recall; verbatim
42. essay
43. serial position
44. STM; rehearsed
45. recognition
46. 85; 95
47. superior
48. voices
49. distractors
50. false positive
51. false identification
52. 25
53. relearning
54. savings score
55. implicit
56. explicit
57. primed
58. limited cues
59. Eidetic imagery
60. eight
61. long-term
62. internal images
62. internal images
63. directly related
64. less accurate
65. important facts; trivia
66. 80
67. consonants
68. learned
69. nonsense syllables
70. curve of forgetting
71. rapid
72. 30
73. 30
74. encoded
75. write
76. memory traces
77. disuse
78. redintegration
79. past; recent
80. cues

81. same room
82. state-dependent learning
83. emotional
84. happy; bad
85. interfere
86. 80; 15
87. retroactive
88. Rest
89. proactive interference
90. repression
91. suppression
92. unconscious
93. flashbulb memories
94. adrenaline; ACTH
95. surprising, emotional
96. accurate
97. retrograde amnesia
98. anterograde
99. consolidation
100. electroconvulsive shock; ECS
101. shock
102. depression
103. immediately
104. nicotine, caffeine, amphetamines
105. disrupted
106. alcohol
107. encoding; consolidation
108. impaired
109. hippocampus
110. new memories
111. engram
112. amount
113. transmitter
114. receptor sites
115. feedback
116. recitation
117. 80; 20
118. Rehearsal
119. selective

120. better
121. Organizing
122. meaningful
123. progressive part
124. serial position; middle
125. cues
126. 90
127. overlearning
128. Spaced; massed
129. sleep
130. Review
131. search

132. cognitive interview
133. 35
134. everything
135. orders
136. viewpoints
137. learning environment
138. Mnemonics
139. 72; 28
140. mental pictures
141. meaningful
142. familiar
143. bizarre, unusual
144. immediate

145. keyword
146. images
147. form a chain
148. mental walk
149. system
150. procedural; skill
151. cerebellum
152. fact
153. semantic memory
154. episodic memory
155. forgotten

ANSWERS—SELF-TEST

1. d
2. a
3. c
4. c
5. b
6. d

7. b
8. True
9. a
10. a
11. False
12. d

13. False
14. c
15. b
16. a
17. False
18. d

19. c
20. False
21. d
22. d
23. True
24. False

25. True
26. d
27. b
28. b
29. b
30. c

31. d
32. d
33. c
34. b
35. d

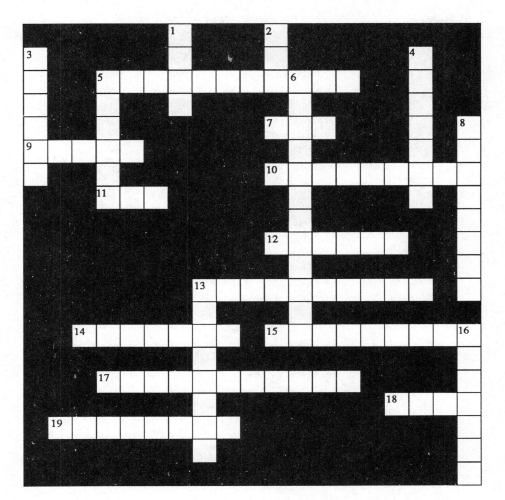

ACROSS

5. the multiple choice question is a common test for _____
7. short-term memory (abbr.)
9. memory traces may fade or _____ .
10. prior learning inhibiting recall of later learning leads to _____ interference
11. long-term memory (abbr.)
12. memory _____ are changes in nerve cells or brain activity
13. he developed a "curve of forgetting"
14. marine snail used in memory studies
15. _____ attention determines what goes into STM
17. brain area acting as "switchboard" between STM and LTM
18. information one hears and is held in sensory memory two seconds or less
19. _____ memory serves as mental dictionary

DOWN

1. image lasts $^1/_2$ second
2. tip-of-tongue (abbr.)
3. memories which are false
4. imagery yielding photographic memory
5. used to take an essay exam
6. much forgetting attributed to _____
8. any kind of memory system or aid
13. memory that records life events
16. to be remembered, information is _____, stored and retrieved

Cognition and Creativity

CONTENTS

TERMS AND CONCEPTS

thinking (cognition)
cognitive psychology
delayed response problems
insight
multiple-stick problem
mental imagery
synesthesia
stored images
created images
muscular imagery
kinesthetic sensations
micromovements
concepts
concept formation
conjunctive concept
relational concept
disjunctive concept
prototypes
denotative meaning
connotative meaning
semantic differential
semantics
symbols
phonemes
morphemes
grammar
syntax
transformational rules
American Sign Language (ASL)
conditional relationships

mechanical solutions
trial-and-error (rote) problem solving
solutions by understanding
general solutions
functional solutions
random search strategy
heuristic
ideal problem solving
selective encoding
selective combination
selective comparison
fixation
functional fixedness
inductive thinking
deductive thinking
logical thinking
illogical thinking
fluency
flexibility
originality
divergent thinking
convergent thinking
Unusual Uses Test
Consequences Test
Anagrams Test
stages of creative thought
representativeness
base rate
problem framing
mental set

syllogism
all-or-nothing thinking
stereotypes
brainstorming

cross-stimulation effect
artificial intelligence
computer simulations
expert systems

IMPORTANT INDIVIDUALS

Shakuntala Devi
Wolfgang Köhler
Donald Griffin
Stephen Kosslyn
Nancy Franklin
Barbara Tversky
Jerome Bruner
Charles Osgood
Noam Chomsky

Beatrice Gardner
Allen Gardner
David Premack
Roger Fouts
Debbi Fouts
Duane Rumbaugh
Sue Savage-Rumbaugh
Karl Duncker

John Bransford
Robert Sternberg
Janet Davidson
Eric Klinger
Donald MacKinnon
Daniel Kahneman
Amos Tversky
Kemal Ebcioglu

PROGRAMMED REVIEW

1. (p. 272) Thinking or _____ refers to the mental manipulation of images, concepts, words, rules, and symbols.

2. (p. 272) The challenge of studying thinking is similar to figuring out how a computer works by repeatedly asking, "I wonder what would happen if I did this?" In _____ psychology the "computer" is the brain, and thinking is the "programming" we seek to understand.

3. (p. 272) The incredibly complex thinking of humans is demonstrated in the remarkable feats of Shakuntala Devi. She holds the "world record" for mental calculation having once multiplied two _____ digit numbers in her head, giving the answer in 28 seconds.

4. (p. 272) In its most basic form, thinking is the _____ _____ of a problem or situation.

5. (p. 272) Animals demonstrate internal representation in _____ _____ problems. For example, a hungry animal allowed to watch as food is hidden under one of three goal boxes can usually pick the correct one if the choice can be made without too long a delay.

6. (p. 272) Wolfgang Köhler felt that the problem solving observed in chimpanzees revealed a capacity for _____, a sudden reorganization of the elements of a problem whereby the solution becomes evident.

7. (p. 272) One of Köhler's subjects, Sultan, was given a _____-_____ problem. Sultan had to use one stick to retrieve a second, slightly-longer stick, which could be used to retrieve an even longer stick which would reach a banana placed out of reach.

8. (p. 273) Evidence that animals are capable of intelligent thought is supported by the following findings:
    1) Monkeys can learn to select, from among three objects, the one that _____ from the other two;
    2) When sugar water is moved farther from a bee hive each day, the bees begin to look for the new location _____ the water is moved;
    3) Pigeons can learn to select photographs of humans from among various pictures;
    4) A chimpanzee can recognize itself in a _____.

9.   (p. 273) To verify animal thinking, Donald Griffin suggests that we must observe behavior that is _____ and _____ to changing circumstances. Thinking is implied by actions that appear to be planned with an awareness of likely results.

10. (p. 273) As one example, sea _____ select suitably sized rocks and use them to hammer shellfish loose for eating. They then use the rock to open the shell.

11. (p. 273) Such examples have been challenged. For instance, Epstein, Lanza, and Skinner have conditioned pigeons to duplicate seemingly insightful behavior. Other psychologists, however, reply that the pigeons only achieved the _____ of thinking, because their behavior was strongly guided by reinforcement.

12. (p. 274) The basic units of thought include images, muscular responses, concepts, and language or symbols. Grandmaster chess player Miguel Najdorf uses several of these when simultaneously playing 45 chess games while _____.

13. (p. 274) A survey of 500 people found that _____ percent have visual imagery and _____ percent auditory imagery. Over _____ percent had imagery that included movement, touch, taste, smell, and pain.

14. (p. 274) When we speak of images we are usually referring to a mental "_____." But as the results of this survey show, images may involve the other senses as well.

15. (p. 274) Some people experience a rare form of imagery called _____ in which images cross normal sensory barriers. For instance, hearing music may induce a burst of colors or tastes as well as sounds.

16. (p. 274) Stephen Kosslyn discovered that mental images are not _____, like photographs. Instead they can be moved about as needed.

17. (p. 274) Psychologists Nancy Franklin and Barbara Tversky believe that we don't merely remember words. Rather, we form a mental _____, or _____ image, of how objects are arranged.

18. (p. 275) They had subjects first read descriptions of realistic three-dimensional environments. Then they were asked about the locations of various objects. Even though subjects were not told to do so, all used _____ _____ to locate the objects.

19. (p. 275) Interestingly, subjects were quickest at locating objects _____ or _____ themselves. Next came objects in front, followed by objects behind themselves. Most difficult of all was finding objects placed to the _____ or _____.

20. (p. 275) _____ images can be used in problem solving to bring prior experience to bear. To generate more original solutions, _____ images may be used.

21. (p. 275) Research indicates that people who have good imaging ability also tend to score higher on tests of _____. Thus, an artist may completely picture a proposed sculpture before beginning work.

22. (p. 275) Stephen Kosslyn found that the _____ an image is, the harder it is to "see" its details. To apply this to problem solving, try forming over-sized images of things you want to think about.

23. (p. 275) It is surprising to note that we think with our bodies as well as our heads. Jerome Bruner believes that we often represent things in a kind of _____ _____ created by actions or implicit actions.

24. (p. 275) A great deal of information is contained in _____ sensations (sensations from the muscles and joints). As a person talks, these sensations help structure the flow of ideas.

25. (p. 276) Most thinking is accompanied by muscular tension and _____ throughout the body.

26. (p. 276) This fact has been demonstrated in one classic study where a subject was asked to imagine that he was hitting a nail with a hammer. As he did, there was a clearly discernible burst of activity in the muscles of his unmoving _____.

27. (p. 276) A concept is an idea that represents a _____ of objects or events. They allow us to think more _____, free from distracting details.

28. (p. 276) Concept _____ is the process by which we classify information into meaningful categories. At its most basic, this phenomenon involves experience with _____ and _____ instances of the concept.

29. (p. 276) Adults are more likely to acquire concepts by learning or forming _____. This process is generally more efficient than examples, but examples remain important.

30. (p. 276) Several general types of concepts have been identified. A _____ _____ refers to a class of objects having one or more features in common.

31. (p. 276) Conjunctive concepts are sometimes called "_____" concepts because to belong to the concept class, an item must have "this feature, and this feature, and this feature." For example, "motorcycles" have wheels, engines, and handle bars.

32. (p. 276) _____ concepts classify objects on the basis of their relationship to something else, or by the relationship between features of an object. Examples include "large," "above," "left," and "north."

33. (p. 276) _____ concepts refer to objects that have at least one of several possible features. They possess an either-or quality. For example, a "strike" is either a swing or a miss or a pitch down the middle, or a foul ball.

34. (p. 276) Most people do not picture a list of features when thinking of a concept. Rather, they think in terms of _____, or ideal models.

35. (p. 276) Reliance on prototypes suggests that not all instances of a concept are equally _____. That fact explains why concept identification becomes difficult when there is no prototype for comparison.

36. (p. 277) Generally speaking, concepts have two types of meaning. The _____ meaning of a word or concept is its explicit definition. The _____ meaning is its emotional or personal meaning.

37. (p. 277) Charles Osgood has used the _____ _____ to measure connotative meaning. He found that when words or concepts are rated on a series of scales, most of their connotative meaning boils down to the dimensions: _____-_____, _____-_____, and _____-_____.

38. (p. 278) While thought can take place without language, most thought does lean heavily on language because it allows us to _____ the world into easily manipulated _____.

39. (p. 278) Study of the meaning of words and language is called _____. It is here that the connection between language and thought becomes most evident.

40. (p. 279) True language must provide _____ which can be used to stand for objects and ideas.

41. (p. 279) The symbols we call words are built out of _____, the basic speech sounds, and _____, speech sounds collected into meaningful units.

42. (p. 279) A second requirement of true language is that it have a _____, or set of rules for the combination of sounds into words and words into sentences.

43. (p. 279) One part of grammar, known as _____, consists of rules pertaining to word order in sentences.

44. (p. 279) Rather than concentrating on the "surface" of language as does traditional grammar, linguist Noam Chomsky has emphasized _____ rules that allow us to change core ideas into a variety of sentences.

45. (p. 279) _____ Language (abbreviated _____) is a visually communicated true language. It has a spatial grammar, syntax, and semantics all its own. It is not understood by those who use other gestural languages.

46. (p. 279) There are similarities between speech and sign languages. Universal language _____ are evident in both. Also, signing children pass through the same stages of language development at about the same _____ as speaking children do.

47. (p. 280) The third, and perhaps most essential, characteristic of language is that it is _____. It can be used to produce new possibilities or to generate new ideas.

48. (p. 280) While animals do communicate, it is quite limited. Animal communication seems to lack the _____ quality of human language.

49. (p. 280) Early attempts to teach chimpanzees to talk were a failure. Even after six years of intensive training, one subject named Vicki could only say _____ words.

50. (p. 280) The first real success in this area came from the work of Beatrice and Allen Gardner who used a combination of _____ _____ and _____ to teach Washoe to use American Sign Language.

51. (p. 280) Washoe now has a vocabulary of about _____ signs and can construct _____-word sentences.

52. (p. 280) David Premack has taught another chimp, Sarah, to use _____ "words" consisting of _____ _____ arranged on a magnetized board.

53. (p. 280) Sarah has learned to answer questions, label things "same" or "different," classify things by color, shape, and size, and to construct _____ sentences.

54. (p. 280) One of Sarah's most outstanding achievements is use of sentences involving _____ _____. For example, "If Sarah take apple, then Mary give Sarah chocolate."

55. (p. 281) Several psychologists have recently expressed doubt that apes can really use language. For one thing, the chimps rarely "speak" without _____.

56. (p. 281) Also, many of their seemingly original sentences turn out to be responses to questions or _____ of signs made by the teacher.

57. (p. 281) Further, it often appears that the apes are simply performing chains of _____ _____ to get food or other rewards.

58. (p. 281) Roger and Debbi Fouts have recently countered such criticism. An analysis they performed of some 6000 conversations between chimps showed that only _____ percent had anything to do with food. Also, they have videotaped conversations between chimps that took place when no humans were present to _____ them.

59. (p. 281) Numerous chimps, a gorilla named Koko, and an assortment of dolphins and sea lions have learned to communicate with word symbols of various kinds. Yet, linguists such as Noam Chomsky remain unconvinced that animals can truly use language because problems with _____ (word order) have plagued almost all animal language experiments.

60. (p. 281) New evidence of primate language skills comes from Duane Rumbaugh and Sue Savage-Rumbaugh's work with Kanzi. Kanzi communicates using gestures and 250 different push-buttons on a computer keyboard. He can create primitive sentences several words long and can understand about _____ spoken sentences.

61. (p. 282) Kanzi's sentences follow correct syntax, even for new word combinations he has never made before. He has picked up some ordering rules from his caregivers, but has developed other patterns on his own. He uses symbols to _____ and _____ the order of actions.

62. (p. 282) Psycholinguist Patricia Marks Greenfield says that Kanzi's use of grammar is on a par with that of a _____-year-old child.

63. (p. 282) Primate language research promises to unravel some of the mysteries of language learning. It has already been helpful for teaching language to _____ children (those with serious language impairment) and severely retarded children.

64. (p. 282) A number of different approaches to thinking and reasoning in problem solving can be identified. _____ solutions may be achieved by trial and error, or by _____. Such problem solving is inefficient when more than a few alternative solutions exist.

65. (p. 282) When a solution is achieved by rote, we mean that thinking is guided by a learned set of _____.

66. (p. 282) Many problems are unsolvable by mechanical means or by the use of habitual modes of thought. In this case a higher level of thinking based on _____ is necessary.

67. (p. 282) This fact is demonstrated in the classic studies of Karl Duncker. He studied the problem-solving process of students and discovered two phases. First, the student had to discover the _____ _____ of a correct solution. The second stage was marked by _____ (workable) _____ from which a specific solution was selected.

68. (p. 283) Solving problems often requires a strategy. If the number of alternatives is small, a _____ _____ strategy may work. This is an example of trial-and-error problem solving in which all possibilities are tried.

69. (p. 283) A _____ of problem-solving strategy reduces the number of alternatives that a thinker must consider. In more complex problem solving they can be very helpful.

70. (p. 283) Some strategies that often work include:
    1) Try to identify how the current state of affairs differs from the desired goal;
    2) Try working _____ from the desired goal to the starting point or current state;
    3) If you can't reach the goal directly, try to identify an intermediate goal or subproblem that at least gets you closer;
    4) Represent the problem in other ways, with graphs, diagrams, or analogies, for instance;
    5) Generate a possible _____ and test it. This may eliminate many alternatives, or it may clarify what is needed for a solution.

71. (p. 283) Perhaps the most valuable heuristic of all is having a _____ thinking strategy. John Bransford has developed one based on five steps that can lead to effective problem solving.

72. (p. 283) To apply Bransford's "IDEAL" strategy you should _____ the problem, _____ it clearly, and then _____ possible solutions and relevant knowledge. Next, you must _____ by trying a possible solution or hypothesis. Finally, you should _____ at the results and learn from them.

73. (p. 283) _____ has occurred when an answer suddenly appears after a period of unsuccessful thought. It is usually so rapid and clear that we often wonder how such an "obvious" solution could have been missed.

74. (p. 283) You may be headed for a mistake if an insight is not _____. As an example, one study rated how "warm" (close to an answer) students felt while solving insight problems. Students who had insights usually jumped directly from "cold" to the correct answer. Those who _____ felt "warmer," and then "very warm," usually gave wrong answers.

75. (p. 283) Robert Sternberg and Janet Davidson have hypothesized that insight involves three abilities. The first is _____ _____ which refers to the ability to select information that is relevant to a problem while ignoring that which is not.

76. (p. 283) _____ _____ also produces insights by bringing together seemingly unrelated bits of useful information.

77. (p. 284) A third source of insights is _____ _____ which is the ability to compare new problems to old information or to problems already solved.

78. (p. 284) The ease with which a solution is achieved in problem solving is related to a variety of factors. A very important barrier to problem solving is _____—the tendency to get hung up on inappropriate solutions or to become blind to other alternatives.

79.   (p. 284) A prime example of this tendency is _____ _____ the inability to see new uses (functions) for familiar objects, or for objects that have been used in a particular way.

80.   (p. 284) Karl Duncker found functional fixedness to be a problem when experimental subjects were asked to mount a candle on a vertical board using a variety of common objects. When the objects were presented in boxes, solution was difficult because the boxes were seen as _____, rather than items necessary to complete the task.

81.   (p. 284) There are several other blocks that prevent creative thinking. One of these, _____ barriers, refers to inhibition and fear of making a fool of oneself, fear of making a mistake, inability to tolerate ambiguity, and/or excessive self-criticism.

82.   (p. 285) _____ barriers refer to values which hold that fantasy is a waste of time; playfulness is for children; reason, logic, and numbers are good, and/or feelings, intuitions, pleasure, and humor are bad or have no place in problem solving.

83.   (p. 285) _____ barriers include conventions about uses (functional fixedness), meanings, possibilities, and taboos.

84.   (p. 285) _____ barriers are habits leading to a failure to identify important elements of a problem.

85.   (p. 285) Creative thinking involves more than mechanical, insightful, or understanding modes of thinking. We must also add _____ thinking (going from specific facts or observations to general principles) or _____ thinking (going from general principles to specific situations).

86.   (p. 285) Thinking may also be _____ thinking (proceeding from given information to new conclusions on the basis of explicit rules) or _____ thinking (intuitive, associative, or personal).

87.   (p. 285) _____ is defined as the total number of suggestions to a problem you can produce.

88.   (p. 285) _____ is defined as the number of times you shift from one class of possible uses to another.

89.   (p. 285) _____ refers to how novel or unusual your suggestions in solving a problem are.

90.   (p. 286) By totaling the number of times you showed fluency, flexibility, and originality, we could rate the creativity of your thinking. Speaking more generally, we would be rating your capacity for _____ thinking.

91.   (p. 286) Divergent thinking is also a characteristic of _____, a unique mental state we experience every day.

92.   (p. 286) Psychologist Eric Klinger fitted volunteers with electronic pagers and asked them to record what they were doing or thinking whenever he "beeped" them. He found that about _____ of our waking thoughts are occupied by daydreams.

93.   (p. 286) Daydreams mirror our desires, fears, and anxieties in a fairly direct way. Because they are fairly straightforward in meaning, they can be a good source of _____ _____.

94. (p. 286) Sleeping dreams, in contrast, tend to be more _____ and _____ to analyze.

95. (p. 286) Two of the most common daydream "plots" are the _____ _____ and the _____ _____ themes.

96. (p. 286) Daydreams often fill a need for _____ when a person performs a routine or monotonous task and they improve the ability to delay immediate _____ so that future goals can be achieved.

97. (p. 286) Fantasy can be a valuable outlet for _____ impulses. Studies confirm that discharging hostility in fantasy can reduce the impulse to behave aggressively.

98. (p. 286) Perhaps the greatest value of fantasy is its contribution to _____ to which it is directly linked.

99. (p. 286) For most people, fantasy and daydreaming are associated with _____ adjustment, lower levels of _____ and greater mental flexibility or creativity.

100. (p. 286) _____ thinking is the most widely used measure of creative problem solving. It is the process by which many possibilities are developed from one starting place.

101. (p. 286) In routine problem solving, there is one correct answer, and the problem is to find it. This leads to _____ thought where lines of thought converge on the correct answer.

102. (p. 286) There are several tests of divergent thinking. In the _____ _____ _____ a person is asked to think of as many uses for an object as possible.

103. (p. 286) In the _____ _____ the object is to answer questions phrased in "what-if" form, where the subject tries to list as many reactions as possible.

104. (p. 286) In the _____ _____ subjects are given a word like "creativity" and asked to make as many new words as possible by rearranging the letters.

105. (p. 286) Tests of divergent thinking apparently tap something quite different from intelligence. Generally there is _____ _____ between such tests and IQ test scores.

106. (p. 287) Creativity is more than divergent thinking. To be creative, problem solutions must be more than novel, unusual, or original. They must also be _____ or _____, and must meet the demands of the problem.

107. (p. 287) A good summary of the sequence of events in creative thinking proposes five stages. The first step is _____, where the problem must be defined and important dimensions identified.

108. (p. 287) _____ is next, where individuals saturate themselves with as much information pertaining to the problem as possible.

109. (p. 287) The third stage, _____, involves a period during which all attempted solutions will have proven futile, and the person leaves the problem "cooking" in the background.

110. (p. 287) The stage of incubation is often ended by a rapid insight or series of insights which mark the fourth stage referred to as _____.

111. (p. 287) The final step, _____, is to test and critically evaluate the solution obtained during the stage of illumination. If the solution proves faulty, the thinker reverts to the stage of _____.

112. (p. 288) Psychologist David MacKinnon has discovered several important factors about creative people. First, for people of normal or above normal intelligence, there is _____ _____ between creativity and IQ.

113. (p. 289) Creative people have a greater than average range of _____ and _____, and they are more fluent in combining ideas from different sources.

114. (p. 289) The creative person has an _____ to experience, and shows a relative lack of inhibition about thoughts, feelings, and fantasies.

115. (p. 289) Creative people enjoy _____ _____, ideas, concepts, and possibilities. Their creative work is an end in itself.

116. (p. 289) Highly creative people value _____ and have a preference for _____. They are nonconforming in their work, but otherwise are not particularly unusual or bizarre.

117. (p. 289) It is widely accepted that people are often creative in particular areas of skill or knowledge. Perhaps this is because creativity favors a _____ mind. Those who are creative in a particular field often are building on a large store of existing knowledge.

118. (p. 290) We often make decisions on the basis of _____, rather than by logic. Doing so may provide quick answers, but it can also be misleading and sometimes disastrous.

119. (p. 290) Daniel Kahneman and Amos Tversky have studied how people make decisions in uncertain situations. They have found that human judgment is often seriously _____.

120. (p. 290) One error in thinking they have pointed out is the intuitive error called _____. That is, a choice that seems to be representative of what we already know is given greater weight.

121. (p. 290) A second common error in judgment involves ignoring the _____ _____ or underlying probability of an event. In many high-risk situations, ignoring this factor is the same as thinking you are an exception to the rule.

122. (p. 290) Kahneman and Tversky found that the way a problem is stated, or _____, affects decisions. People often give different answers to the same problem posed in slightly different ways.

123. (p. 291) There are several factors which can contribute to difficulties in thinking and problem solving. One of these factors is the limiting effects of a rigid _____ _____.

124. (p. 292) Another major thinking difficulty focuses on the process of _____ reasoning.

125. (p. 292) This process can be demonstrated in simple sequences involving a set of premises (assumptions) and a conclusion in the format known as a _____.

126. (p. 293) A syllogism can be evaluated for the _____ of its reasoning and for the _____ of its conclusion.

127. (p. 293) Another very basic source of thinking errors is over-simplification. In the first type, _____-_____-_____ thinking, things are classified as absolutely right or wrong, good or bad, or in other ways that prevent appreciation of the complexity of most life problems.

128. (p. 293) The other type of over-simplification, thinking in terms of _____ is particularly troublesome when human relationships are involved.

129. (p. 293) Several suggestions can be offered as to how to begin increasing creativity. One of these is to define the problem _____. Whenever possible, enlarge the definition of problems for which you seek creative solutions.

130. (p. 293) A variety of experiments show that people make more original, spontaneous, and imaginative responses when exposed to others (models) doing the same thing, so create the _____ _____.

131. (p. 294) Trying to hurry or force a problem solution may simply encourage fixation on a deadend, so always allow time for _____.

132. (p. 294) Creativity requires divergent thinking, so remember to seek _____ _____. Attempt to shift your mental "prospecting" to new areas.

133. (p. 294) Edward de Bono suggests a technique to help with this process. He recommends that you _____ look up words in the dictionary and _____ each to the problem.

134. (p. 294) Representing a problem in a variety of ways is often the key to solution. One way to do this is to look for _____.

135. (p. 294) Various studies suggest that people are most likely to be creative when they are free to play with ideas and solutions without having to worry about being _____. Especially in the first stages of creative thinking, it is important to avoid _____ your efforts.

136. (p. 295) _____ is an alternative approach to enhancing creativity that involves keeping production and criticism of ideas completely separate.

137. (p. 295) As ideas are freely generated an interesting _____-_____ effect takes place, in which one participant's ideas trigger ideas for others.

138. (p. 295) The four basic rules for successful brainstorming are:
    1) _____ of an idea is absolutely barred;
    2) _____ or combination with other ideas is encouraged;
    3) _____ of ideas is sought; and
    4) _____, remote, or wild ideas are sought.

139. (p. 295) As an aid to the brainstorming method, a creativity checklist is suggested. The key terms here include:
    1) Redefine
    2) _____
    3) _____
    4) _____
    5) Minify

    6) _____
    7) _____
    8) _____
    9) Combine

140. (p. 296) In 1988, Kemal Ebcioglu devised a computer program that writes harmonies remarkably similar to Bach's. Ebcioglu employed 350 rules that govern the harmonization process to produce a program that displays what is known as _____ _____.

141. (p. 296) Artificial intelligence (AI) refers to computer programs capable of doing things that require intelligence when done by people. AI is based on the fact that many tasks can be reduced to a set of _____ applied to a body of _____.

142. (p. 296) Increasingly, cognitive psychologists are using AI as a research tool in two basic ways. In _____ _____ programs are used as analogs to human behavior, especially problem solving. The computer acts as a "laboratory" for testing models of cognition.

143. (p. 296) _____ _____ are programs that display advanced knowledge of a specific topic or skill. Such programs have been created to predict the weather, to analyze geologic formations, to diagnose disease, etc.

144. (p. 296) Working with AI has helped especially to clarify differences between novices and experts. Research on chess masters, for example, shows that their skills are based on specific organized _____ and acquired _____.

145. (p. 296) Becoming a star performer does not come from some general strengthening of the mind or from better memory. Master players have superior ability to recognize _____ that suggest what lines of play should be explored next.

146. (p. 296) Expertise also allows more _____ processing, or fast, fairly effortless thinking based on experience with similar problems. This frees attention and "space" in short-term memory that can be used to work on the problem.

147. (p. 297) Experts in one area do not automatically become better _____ _____ elsewhere. Nor do they become generally smarter.

148. (p. 297) Likewise, expert systems are very adept with a narrow range of problem solving, but they are "idiots" at everything else. They process information without regard for the _____ of actions, which might be disastrous in unanticipated situations.

SELF-TEST

1. (p. 272) Of the following, which are problems that can be used to demonstrate representational thought in animals?
    a. delayed response problems
    b. response deprivation tasks
    c. Consequences Test
    d. Anagrams Test

2. (p. 272) Köhler tested insight among chimpanzees using:
    a. delayed response problems
    b. multiple-stick problems
    c. items from the Unusual Uses Test
    d. the Consequences Test

3. (p. 274) Of the following, which is *not* an internal representation you use in thinking?
    a. language
    b. muscular responses
    c. images
    d. photographs

4.   (p. 274) The ability to experience a given sensation in a totally different physical dimension is called:
  a.   kinesthesia   c.   anesthesia
  b.   synesthesia   d.   euthanasia

5.   (p. 275) Which of the following is *not* a type of imagery used in problem solving?
  a.   stored images   c.   transformational imagery
  b.   muscular imagery   d.   created images

6.   (p. 275) True-False. We often think with our bodies as well as our heads; that is, we often represent things in a kind of muscular imagery created by implicit actions.

7.   (p. 276) Which of the following is *not* true of concept formation?
  a.   In early childhood, much concept formation involves experience with positive and negative instances of the concept.
  b.   Rule learning in concept formation is generally less efficient than exposure to examples.
  c.   Concept formation is the process whereby we classify information into meaningful categories.
  d.   As adults, we are more likely to acquire concepts by learning or formulating rules.

8.   (p. 276) True-False. Conjunctive concepts refer to a class of objects having one or more features in common.

9.   (p. 276) _____ concepts refer to objects that have at least one of several possible features.
  a.   Conjunctive   c.   Relational
  b.   Disjunctive   d.   Conditional

10. (p. 276) "Left," "above," "north," and "up" are all examples of what type of concept?
  a.   conjunctive   c.   disjunctive
  b.   relational   d.   conditional

11. (p. 276) True-False. Most people tend to think of concepts in terms of prototypes since all instances of a concept are considered equally representative.

12. (p. 277) The explicit definition of a word or concept is its:
  a.   denotative meaning   c.   semantic differential
  b.   connotative meaning   d.   derogatory meaning

13. (p. 277) The connotative meaning of words can be measured using:
  a.   Osgood's Inventory   c.   the Denotative Scale
  b.   the Consequence Test   d.   the semantic differential

14. (p. 279) The basic speech sounds built into words are called:
  a.   symbols   c.   grammar
  b.   phonemes   d.   morphemes

15. (p. 279) Speech sounds collected into meaningful units are called:
  a.   symbols   c.   grammar
  b.   phonemes   d.   morphemes

16. (p. 279) Of the following, which is *not* a requirement that defines true language?
  a.   productivity   c.   grammar
  b.   symbols   d.   simplicity

17. (p. 279) True-False. One part of grammar, known as semantics, refers to rules pertaining to word order in sentences.

18. (p. 279) Noam Chomsky has argued that we do not learn all sentences we might ever utter, but rather we actively and creatively generate them by applying:
    a. transformation rules   c. divergent thinking
    b. syntax   d. semantics

19. (p. 280) Which of the following is *not* true of language learning in primates?
    a. The first breakthrough came with the learning of ASL by Washoe.
    b. One of the most outstanding achievements of Sarah was her use of sentences involving conditional relationships.
    c. Kanzi's biggest language-usage problem is his inability to follow correct word order.
    d. Viki, a chimp taught to speak, could only say four words after six years of intensive training.

20. (p. 280) Which of the following is *not* a criticism that has been leveled against the interpretation that primates actually use and understand true language?
    a. The primates rarely "speak" without prompting.
    b. Their vocabularies are quite small and they cannot master important features such as proper word order.
    c. Many of their seemingly original sentences turn out to be imitations of signs made by their trainer.
    d. It often appears they are simply performing instrumental responses to get food.

21. (p. 282) Which of the following is *not* true of problem solving?
    a. Problem solving by understanding involves first understanding the general properties of a correct solution and then selecting a correct solution from a number of functional solutions.
    b. Solution by insight occurs when an answer suddenly appears after a period of unsuccessful thought.
    c. Mechanical problem solving may be achieved by trial and error but is quite inefficient when more than a few alternative solutions exist.
    d. When solution is achieved by rote, we mean that thinking has proceeded erratically until insight is achieved.

22. (p. 283) Problem-solving strategies that reduce the number of alternatives that a thinker must consider are called:
    a. random searches   c. idea problem solving
    b. heuristics   d. insights

23. (p. 283) Which of the following is *not* an ability involved in solving problems that require insight as detailed by Sternberg and Davidson?
    a. selective attention   c. selective comparison
    b. selective combination   d. selective encoding

24. (p. 284) True-False. The point at which a useful idea or insight becomes set in one's mind is known as fixation.

25. (p. 285) Values which hold that fantasy is a waste of time, playfulness is for children only, or feelings, intuitions, pleasure, and humor have no place in problem solving all define _____ barriers to creative thinking.
    a. perceptual   c. cultural
    b. emotional   d. learned

26. (p. 285) Which of the following definitions regarding thinking is *not* true?
     a. Constructive thinking involves going from specific facts or observations to general principles.
     b. Thinking that is intuitive, associative, or personal is referred to as illogical.
     c. Deductive thinking involves going from general principles to specific situations.
     d. Logical thinking is thought which proceeds from given information to new conclusions on the basis of explicit rules.

27. (p. 285) Creative thinking involves all of the following *except*:
     a. fluency   c. fixation
     b. flexibility   d. originality

28. (p. 286) Which of the following is *not* a benefit of daydreaming?
     a. It contributes to creativity.
     b. It can be a valuable outlet for frustrated impulses.
     c. Fantasies can act as a substitute source of gratification during times of deprivation.
     d. It facilitates other types of more concrete or realistic thinking.

29. (p. 296) Of the following, which is *not* a test of divergent thinking?
     a. Anagrams Test   c. Consequences Test
     b. Unusual Uses Test   d. Semantic Differential Test

30. (p. 387) Which of the following sequences best describes the process of creative thinking?
     a. preparation, orientation, illumination, incubation, verification
     b. orientation, preparation, verification, illumination, incubation
     c. preparation, incubation, orientation, illumination, verification
     d. orientation, preparation, incubation, illumination, verification

31. (p. 288) Which of the following is *not* true of creative persons according to Donald MacKinnon?
     a. Creative people are usually talented in only one area; they have an average range of knowledge or interests.
     b. Creative people show a relative lack of inhibition about their thoughts, feelings, and fantasies.
     c. They do not have particularly unusual personalities.
     d. They tend to be interested in truth, form, and beauty rather than in recognition or success.

32. (p. 288) True-False. Most creative individuals have above average IQ, but not all above average IQ individuals are necessarily creative.

33. (p. 290) Which of the following is *not* a problem of intuition and problem solving as discussed by Kahneman and Tversky?
     a. The way in which problems are framed can affect the answers people give, even for problems identical in content.
     b. People do not always carefully consider the base rate of events.
     c. People do not always ignore probabilities in high risk situations. It's hard for them to believe they can be the exception to the rule.
     d. People demonstrate an intuitive error called representativeness.

34. (p. 291) Which of the following is *not* a difficulty in thinking and problem solving?
     a. rigid mental set   c. over-simplification
     b. disjunctive conceptual thinking d. problems with logic

35. (p. 292) The format for presenting simple sequences of logical thought involving premises and a conclusion is known as a(n):
    a. syntax
    b. semantic
    c. syllogism
    d. anagram

36. (p. 293) Which of the following is *not* a good suggestion for enhancing creativity?
    a. allow time for incubation
    b. seek varied input
    c. develop a narrow, but consistent chain of thoughts
    d. look for analogies

37. (p. 295) Which of the following is *not* a basic rule for successful brainstorming?
    a. Cross-stimulation through criticism is necessary.
    b. Unusual, remote, or wild ideas are sought.
    c. Modification or combination with other ideas is encouraged.
    d. Quantity of ideas is sought.

38. (p. 296) Which of the following is *not* a true statement about artificial intelligence?
    a. AI refers to computer programs capable of doing things that require intelligence when done by people.
    b. AI is based on the fact that many tasks cannot be reduced to a set of rules, instead intuition and insight (intelligence) are needed.
    c. AI will play an increasingly visible role in cognitive research and in our lives, but is not likely to soon replace human involvement.
    d. AI is valuable in situations where speed, vast memory, and persistence are required.

39. (p. 296) Expert systems are:
    a. programs that emulate human behavior and provide models of how we think.
    b. adept across a broad range of problem solving.
    c. potentially disastrous in unanticipated situations because they cannot anticipate an infinite number of possible events.
    d. unable to provide more automatic processing because such a precise set of rules must be followed.

APPLYING YOUR KNOWLEDGE

1. How much do *you* daydream? Set your wristwatch to go off at different times of the day. What were you doing when it went off? If you were daydreaming, keep a log of what you were thinking about. How does your log compare with the findings of Eric Klinger?

2. See if you can develop a Consequences Test for creativity. Try several different questions with a small group of friends or classmates. Does the percentage of answers each person produces vary depending upon the question asked or does the highest scorer always score highest, the lowest scorer always the lowest, and so forth?

3. Try developing an Anagrams Test and use it with the same people that took your Consequences Test. How do your subjects compare on the two tests?

ANSWERS—PROGRAMMED REVIEW

1.	cognition	4.	internal representation	7.	multiple-stick
2.	cognitive	5.	delayed response	8.	differs; before; mirror
3.	18	6.	insight	9.	versatile; appropriate

10. otters
11. appearance
12. blindfolded
13. 97; 92; 50
14. picture
15. synesthesia
16. flat
17. model; spatial
18. mental imagery
19. above; below; right; left
20. Stored; created
21. creativity
22. smaller
23. muscular imagery
24. kinesthetic
25. micromovements
26. arm
27. class; abstractly
28. formation; positive, negative
29. rules
30. conjunctive concept
31. and
32. Relational
33. Disjunctive
34. prototypes
35. representative
36. denotative; connotative
37. semantic differential; good-bad, strong-weak, active-passive
38. encode; symbols
39. semantics
40. symbols
41. phonemes; morphemes
42. grammar
43. syntax
44. transformation
45. American Sign; ASL
46. patterns; age
47. productive
48. productive
49. four
50. operant conditioning; imitation
51. 240; six
52. 130; plastic chips
53. compound
54. conditional relationships
55. prompting
56. imitation

57. instrumental responses
58. 5; cue
59. syntax
60. 650
61. plan; communicate
62. 2
63. aphasic
64. Mechanical; rote
65. rules
66. understanding
67. general properties; functional solutions
68. random search
69. heuristic
70. backward; solution
71. general
72. identify; define; explore; act; look
73. Insight
74. rapid; gradually
75. selective encoding
76. Selective combination
77. selective comparison
78. fixation
79. functional fixedness
80. containers
81. emotional
82. Cultural
83. Learned
84. Perceptual
85. inductive; deductive
86. logical; illogical
87. Fluency
88. Flexibility
89. Originality
90. divergent
91. daydreaming
92. half
93. personal insights
94. complex; difficult
95. conquering hero; suffering martyr
96. stimulation; gratification
97. frustrated
98. creativity
99. emotional; aggression
100. Divergent
101. convergent
102. Unusual Uses Test
103. Consequences Test

104. Anagrams Test
105. little correlation
106. practical; sensible
107. orientation
108. Preparation
109. incubation
110. illumination
111. verification; incubation
112. little correlation
113. knowledge, interests
114. openness
115. symbolic thought
116. independence; complexity
117. prepared
118. intuition
119. flawed
120. representativeness
121. base rate
122. framed
123. mental set
124. logical
125. syllogism
126. validity; truth
127. all-or-nothing
128. stereotypes
129. broadly
130. right atmosphere
131. incubation
132. varied input
133. randomly; relate
134. analogies
135. evaluating; criticizing
136. Brainstorming
137. cross-stimulation
138. Criticism; Modification; Quantity; Unusual
139. Adapt; Modify; Magnify; Substitute; Rearrange; Reverse
140. artificial intelligence
141. rules; information
142. computer simulations
143. Expert systems
144. knowledge; strategies
145. patterns
146. automatic
147. problem solvers
148. meaning

ANSWERS—SELF-TEST

1.	a	8.	True	15.	d	22.	b	29.	d	36.	c
2.	b	9.	b	16.	d	23.	a	30.	d	37.	a
3.	d	10.	b	17.	False	24.	False	31.	a	38.	b
4.	b	11.	False	18.	a	25.	c	32.	True	39.	c
5.	c	12.	a	19.	c	26.	a	33.	c		
6.	True	13.	d	20.	b	27.	c	34.	b		
7.	b	14.	b	21.	d	28.	d	35.	c		

ACROSS

2. going from specific facts or observations to general principles denotes _____thinking
4. sudden mental reorganization of elements of problem in which solution becomes obvious
5. American sign language (abbr.)
7. Washoe was a talking _____who used American sign language
10. problem-solving technique where participants are encouraged to produce ideas without criticism and evaluation
12. an idea that represents a class of objects or events
13. basic speech sounds are called _____
14. this stage of creative thought involves the "Aha" experience
15. first step of creative thought
16. creative thinking requires _____thought

DOWN

1. tendency to get stuck on wrong solutions creates a barrier to solving problems
3. _____meaning refers to emotional or personal meaning of a concept
6. rules for word order in sentences
8. with this stage of creative thought, problem solving proceeds at subconscious level
9. he challenged his chimp with a multiple-stick problem
11. going from general principles to specific situations exemplifies _____ thinking

Motivation

CONTENTS

TERMS AND CONCEPTS

motivation
need-drive-response-goal-need reduction
incentive value
primary motives
stimulus motives
learned (secondary) motives
homeostasis
hypoglycemia
hypothalamus
feeding system
ventromedial hypothalamus
satiety system
lateral hypothalamus
set point
weight cycling
metabolic rate
taste aversion
bait shyness
self-selection feeding
extracellular thirst
intracellular thirst
episodic drive
estrus
estrogen
Coolidge Effect

sensory deprivation
arousal
arousal theory
Sensation-Seeking Scale (SSS)
inverted U function
Yerkes-Dodson law
circadian rhythms
jet lag
shift work
biorhythm theory
opponent-process theory
social motives
need for achievement (nAch)
need for power
fear of success
hierarchy of human needs
basic needs
growth needs
meta-needs
intrinsic motivation
extrinsic motivation
behavioral dieting
anorexia nervosa
bulimia (binge-purge syndrome)

IMPORTANT INDIVIDUALS

Cannon and Washburn   Richard Soloman   Abraham Maslow
Judith Rodin   David McClelland   Janet Polivy
Albert Stunkard   Benjamin Bloom   Peter Herman
Marvin Zuckerman

PROGRAMMED REVIEW

1.   (p. 301) _____ "refers to the dynamics of behavior, the process of initiating, sustaining, and directing activities of the organism."

2.   (p. 301) In developing a model of motivation, we may begin with a _____, the starting point of many motivated activities.

3.   (p. 301) Needs cause a psychological state or feeling called a _____ to develop.

4.   (p. 301) Drives activate a _____ (or a series of actions) designed to attain a _____ that will relieve the need.

5.   (p. 301) Relieving the need temporarily ends the motivational sequence. This may be referred to as _____ _____.

6.   (p. 301) We need both "drive" and "need" to discuss motivation because the _____ of these two is not always the same. If you begin fasting, your bodily need for food increases daily, but you would probably find yourself less "hungry" the seventh day compared to the first.

7.   (p. 302) Motivated behavior can be energized by the "pull" of _____ _____ as well as by the "push" of internal needs.

8.   (p. 302) The pull exerted by a goal is called its _____ _____. Very desirable goals (strawberry pie) may motivate behavior in the absence of internal need, while undesirable goals (live grubs) may be rejected even though they might meet the internal need.

9.   (p. 302) In most instances it is helpful to recognize that actions are energized by both internal needs and external incentives, and that a strong state of _____ may make a less attractive goal into a desirable _____.

10. (p. 302) For the purpose of study, motives can be divided into three major categories. The first, referred to as _____ _____, are innate motives based on biological needs which must be met for survival.

11. (p. 302) The most important primary motives are hunger, _____, _____, avoidance, and needs for air, _____, elimination of wastes, and regulation of body _____.

12. (p. 302) _____ _____ are related to a second category of needs. Like the primary motives, they appear to be innate, but they are not necessary for mere survival of the organism.

13. (p. 303) Their purpose seems to be to provide useful information about the environment and stimulation to the nervous system. The stimulus motives include: activity, _____, _____, _____, and physical _____.

14. (p. 303) The third category, _____ or _____ motives, accounts for the great diversity of human activities.

15. (p. 303) The most important secondary motives are related to acquired needs for power, affiliation, _____, _____, _____, and achievement.

16. (p. 303) The important motives of _____ and _____ also appear to be subject to learning.

17. (p. 303) Biological drives are essential because they maintain bodily equilibrium or _____ (meaning standing steady, or steady state).

18. (p. 303) The body constantly attempts to maintain itself at an ideal level through automatic reactions that correct deviations. Homeostatic mechanisms are similar in operation to a _____ set at a particular temperature.

19. (p. 303) When you feel hungry you probably associate a desire for food with sensations from your stomach. This idea led _____ and _____ to investigate whether contractions of an empty stomach cause hunger.

20. (p. 304) Washburn trained himself to swallow a toy balloon which could be inflated through an attached tube so that stomach contractions could be recorded. They found that when Washburn's stomach contracted, he felt "_____ _____."

21. (p. 304) While it is true that eating is limited when the stomach is _____ (full), it can be shown conclusively that the stomach is not essential for experiencing hunger. For one thing, cutting the _____ _____ from the stomach (so that stomach sensations can no longer be felt) does not abolish hunger.

22. (p. 304) Also, people who have had their stomachs removed surgically continue to feel hungry and eat regularly. This fact leads us to believe that some _____ factor must be the cause of hunger.

23. (p. 304) One important factor in hunger appears to be the level of _____ in the blood. For example, if insulin is injected in a human it produces _____ (low blood sugar) and stimulates feelings of hunger and stomach contractions.

24. (p. 304) It now appears that the _____ may be responsible for hunger since it responds to a lack of bodily "fuel" by sending nerve impulses to the brain that trigger eating.

25. (p. 304) When you are hungry, many brain areas are affected, so no single "hunger center" exists. However, one area of importance is the _____, a small structure near the base of the brain.

26. (p. 304) Cells in the hypothalamus are sensitive to levels of sugar (and perhaps other substances) in the blood. The hypothalamus also receives messages from the _____ and the _____ which all combine to produce hunger.

27. (p. 304) One area of the hypothalamus seems to be part of a feeding system in the brain—the _____ hypothalamus (meaning it is located at the sides of the hypothalamus).

28. (p. 304) If the lateral hypothalamus is activated electrically, even a well-fed animal will immediately begin _____. If this same area is destroyed, the animal will refuse to eat and will _____ if not force-fed.

29. (p. 304) A second area within the hypothalamus seems to be part of a satiety system—the _____ hypothalamus (meaning it is found on the bottom of the hypothalamus).

30. (p. 305) If the ventromedial hypothalamus is destroyed, dramatic overeating results. Normal-sized rats weighing about 180 grams will balloon up to weights of _____ grams or more and become so totally obese that they can barely move.

31. (p. 305) While it is clear that the hypothalamus plays a role in hunger, there are no simple "hunger control centers." The effects of damage to the hypothalamus, for example, may simply reflect the fact that a large amount of _____ and _____ activity passes through this area.

32. (p. 305) There is more to hunger than "start" and "stop" systems in the brain. Recent evidence suggests that _____ stored in the body also influences hunger.

33. (p. 305) The body acts as if there is a _____ _____ for the proportion of body fat it maintains. When your body goes below this level, you are likely to feel hungry most of the time.

34. (p. 305) People do appear to have different set points, partially _____ and partially determined by _____ early feeding patterns.

35. (p. 305) Adopted children whose birth _____ are overweight are much more likely to be overweight themselves. This shows that a person's genes greatly influence adult weight.

36. (p. 305) The set point may be lastingly altered when a child is overfed. If a weight problem begins in childhood, the person will, as an adult, have _____ fat cells and _____ fat cells in the body.

37. (p. 305) If the person does not become overweight until adulthood, his or her fat cells will be _____, but their number will not increase.

38. (p. 306) The sight or aroma of food often makes people want to eat, even when they do not feel hungry. Such observations suggest that many people are sensitive to _____ eating _____.

39. (p. 306) For those sensitive to the wide variety of signs and signals linked with food, eating is _____, highly _____, and easy to obtain.

40. (p. 306) Even the time of day can influence eating. In one experiment obese subjects ate more crackers when a clock was set closer to mealtime than it actually was. Subjects of normal weight _____ their eating when they thought it was closer to mealtime.

41. (p. 306) People of all weights can be found who are unusually sensitive to external eating cues, so this is not strictly a problem of the _____. Eating cues are a factor in some overeating, but they are not the sole cause.

42. (p. 306) Just the same, eating cues do appear to be a factor in some overeating. For example, Judith Rodin found that externally responsive girls were _____ _____ to gain weight at a 2-month summer camp.

43. (p. 306) For many people, _____ also contributes to overeating. In general, sweetness, high fat content, and variety tend to encourage overeating.

44. (p. 306) In one experiment, rats given a junk food diet gained almost _____ times as much weight as controls who ate only standard laboratory "rat chow." It seems that our culture may provide the worst possible kinds of foods for those with a tendency toward obesity.

45. (p. 306) Fatness does not come from constant overeating. Studies by Albert Stunkard and Judith Rodin show that overeating occurs mainly when a person is gaining weight. Once excess weight is gained, it can be _____ with a normal diet.

46. (p. 306) As people gain weight, many reduce their _____ _____ and burn fewer calories. Consequently, some overweight persons may continue to gain weight while consuming _____ calories then their slimmer neighbors.

47. (p. 306) People with overweight problems are just as likely to eat when anxious, angry, bored, or distressed. Furthermore, _____ often accompanies obesity in our fat-conscious culture. This can set up a pattern of overeating that leads to emotional distress and still more overeating.

48. (p. 306) While dieters do lose weight, most regain it soon after the diet ends. Many people experience a _____ that can push weight higher than before the diet began.

49. (p. 306) Many theorists now believe that dieting alters the physiology of the body. In effect, dieting causes the body to become highly efficient at conserving _____ and storing them as _____.

50. (p. 306) Frequent weight cycling caused by dieting tends to slow the body's _____ _____ (the rate at which energy is used up). This makes it harder to lose weight each time a person diets and easier to regain weight when the diet ends.

51. (p. 307) Frequent changes in weight may also increase susceptibility to _____ _____ and premature _____.

52. (p. 307) Hunger is affected by a number of factors in addition to actual bodily needs for food. _____ values are certainly important since what our society thinks are desirable foods or revolting edibles has much to do with eating habits.

53. (p. 307) Another important factor is _____. It has been demonstrated that the hungrier a person is, the more "pleasant" a sweet-tasting food is judged to be.

54. (p. 307) If a food causes sickness or if it simply precedes sickness caused by something else, we quickly learn to avoid such foods. This process is referred to as _____ _____.

55. (p. 307) Taste aversions are a type of _____ _____. Since a long time delay normally prevents conditioning, it is theorized that there is a _____ tendency to associate an upset stomach with food eaten earlier.

56. (p. 307) While such learning is usually protective, many human cancer patients suffer taste aversions long after the _____ of the drug treatment has passed.

57. (p. 307) This phenomenon is also seen in animals. In a pioneering experiment, coyotes given lamb treated with lithium chloride became nauseated and vomited. After one or two such treatments, they developed _____ _____, a lasting distaste for the tainted food.

58. (p. 307) Taste aversions may also help people avoid severe _____ imbalances. If you overeat something until you feel ill, your discomfort could create an aversion and restore some balance to your diet.

59. (p. 307) In one classic experiment on _____-_____ _____, infants selected a balanced diet, and their health and growth were normal. However the babies could only select from nutritious foods. If candy had been a choice, they might not have done so well.

60. (p. 308) Humans seem to have an innate preference for _____ and _____ food. Thus, an appetite for candy and junk food can easily override the weaker tendency to eat a balanced diet.

61. (p. 308) Thirst is only partially related to dryness of the mouth and throat. When drugs are given that produce constantly wet or dry mouths, thirst and water intake remain normal. Like hunger, thirst appears to be controlled through the _____ where separate thirst and thirst-satiety systems are found.

62. (p. 308) There are actually two kinds of thirst. _____ thirst occurs when there is a loss of water from the fluids surrounding the cells of your body due to bleeding, vomiting, diarrhea, sweating, or drinking alcohol.

63. (p. 308) When a person loses both water and minerals in any of these ways, especially by perspiration, a slightly _____ liquid may be more satisfying than plain water.

64. (p. 308) Before the body can retain water, minerals lost through perspiration (mainly salt) must be replaced. Thus, research shows that animals greatly prefer _____ _____ when body salt levels are lowered. Similarly, some nomadic peoples of the Sahara Desert prize _____ as a beverage, probably because of its saltiness.

65. (p. 308) A second type of thirst occurs when you eat a salty meal. In this case excess salt within the body causes fluid to be drawn out of the cells. This produces _____ thirst.

66. (p. 308) Drives like hunger, thirst, and sleepiness come and go in a fairly consistent cycle each day. Pain, by contrast, is an _____ drive since it is aroused only when damage to the tissues of the body takes place.

67. (p. 308) Most of the primary drives cause a person to actively seek a desired goal. Pain is different in this respect, because the pain drive has as its goal the _____ or _____ of pain.

68. (p. 308) Surprisingly, avoiding pain appears to be partially _____. This fact was demonstrated in an experiment in which dogs reared in isolation acted like they did not know the meaning of pain or how to avoid it.

69. (p. 308) Human pain avoidance is also affected by learning. Persons who feel they must be "tough" and not show any discomfort have increased _____ _____.

70. (p. 308) Sexual motivation is quite unusual by comparison to other biological motives. Many psychologists do not think of sex as a primary motive because it is not necessary for _____ _____.

71. (p. 308) In lower animals the sex drive is directly related to the action of bodily _____. For example, females are only interested in mating when their fertility cycle is in the stage of _____ or "heat," caused by secretion of _____ into the bloodstream.

72. (p. 308) Hormones are important in the male animal as well. In most lower animals, _____ will abolish the sex drive.

73. (p. 309) In contrast to the female, the normal male animal is always ready to mate. His sex drive is primarily aroused by the behavior of a receptive female. In animals, mating is therefore closely tied to the _____ _____ of the female.

74. (p. 309) The link between hormones and the sex drive grows weaker as we ascend the biological scale. Hormones do affect the human sex drive, but only to a limited degree. For example, one study found no connection between female sexual activity and the monthly _____ _____.

75. (p. 309) In humans, mental, cultural, and emotional factors determine sexual expression. However, hormones do affect human sex drive. Males show a loss of sex drive after _____, and some women lose sexual desire when using _____ _____ _____.

76. (p. 309) Sex drive shows no clear relationship to deprivation. It is therefore considered to be largely _____.

77. (p. 309) The sex drive is also unusual in that its _____ is as actively sought as its _____.

78. (p. 309) The non-homeostatic quality of the sex drive is demonstrated by the _____ _____. An animal allowed to copulate until apparently satiated will immediately resume sexual activity when a new partner is provided.

79. (p. 310) Stimulus needs encompass drives for exploration, manipulation, and curiosity. Curiosity drive was demonstrated in experiments showing that monkeys would learn tasks for stimulation when no external _____ was offered.

80. (p. 310) Closely related to curiosity is the drive for sensory stimulation. The nervous system seems to require varied, patterned stimulation to respond normally. This fact is apparently why people who have undergone severe _____ _____ often report sensory distortions and disturbed thinking.

81. (p. 310) The drive for stimulation can even be observed in infants. When babies are shown patterns of varying complexity, they spend more time looking at _____ patterns.

82. (p. 310) _____ refers to variations in activation of the body and nervous system. It is zero at death, low during sleep, moderate during normal daily activities, and high at times of excitement, emotion, or panic.

83. (p. 310) The position known as the _____ _____ of motivation assumes that there is an ideal level of arousal for various activities and that individuals behave in ways that keep arousal near this ideal level.

84. (p. 310) According to arousal theory, _____ and the drive to seek _____ can be interpreted as an attempt to raise the level of arousal when it is too low.

85. (p. 311) Marvin Zuckerman has devised a test called the _____-_____ _____ (SSS) to measure individual differences in preferred arousal levels.

86. (p. 311) High and low sensation seeking probably reflects differences in how a person's _____ responds to new, unusual, surprising, or intense stimulation.

87. (p. 311) People who score high on the SSS tend to be _____, _____, and to value change. They also report more _____ partners, are more likely to _____, and prefer spicy, sour, and crunchy foods over blander foods.

88. (p. 311) Low sensation seekers are _____, _____, _____, and enjoy the company of others.

89. (p. 311) Performance of a task is usually best when arousal is _____. The relationship between arousal and efficiency of behavior can be expressed as an _____ _____ function.

90. (p. 311) The optimal level of arousal also depends on the complexity of the particular task. If a task is relatively simple, the optimal level of arousal will be _____. When difficult or complicated, the best performance occurs at _____ levels of arousal.

91. (p. 311) This relationship is called the _____-_____ law. It applies to a wide variety of tasks and to measures of motivation other than arousal.

92. (p. 312) Studies of anxious students show that they are typically most anxious when they don't know the material. One of the best ways to overcome test anxiety is to be _____.

93. (p. 312) Guided by internal "biological clocks," the body undergoes a complex cycle of changes every 24 hours called _____ _____.

94. (p. 312) Throughout the day, large changes take place in body _____, _____ pressure, _____ volume, amino acid level, and in activity of the liver, kidneys, and endocrine glands.

95. (p. 312) Especially important is the output of the hormone _____, which causes general arousal. It is often 3 to 5 times greater during the day.

96. (p. 312) Differences in such peaks are so basic that when a "day person" rooms with a "night person," both are more likely to give their relationship a _____ rating.

97. (p. 312) The effects of sleep-waking cycles become especially noticeable whenever there is major shift in time schedules. For example, it is well documented that people who travel through many time zones often make errors or perform poorly when their body rhythms are disturbed by _____ _____.

98. (p. 313) _____ work has the same effect causing a loss of efficiency, as well as _____, _____, upset stomach, nervousness, depression and a decline in mental agility.

99. (p. 313) For major time zone shifts (5 hours or more), it can take from several days to _____ weeks to resynchronize.

100. (p. 313) Adaptation to jet lag is _____ when you get outside where you must sleep, eat, and socialize on the new schedule. Staying in a hotel room (where sleeping and eating can be done on the old schedule) slows the process.

101. (p. 313) The direction of travel also affects adaptation. Westerly flights take an average of _____ to _____ days adaptation. Easterly flights take _____ percent longer, or more.

102. (p. 313) When you fly west, the sun comes up _____. This combined with the fact that the circadian rhythm naturally runs _____ than 24 hours explains why adaptation is easier. It's more like staying up late and sleeping in.

103. (p. 313) Work shifts that "rotate" _____ are more disruptive than those that _____. If work shifts must change, those lasting only three days are less disruptive than week-long shifts.

104. (p. 313) Consistent work shifts are the best. Even continuous _____ work is less disruptive than changing shifts.

105. (p. 313) If you can anticipate an upcoming body rhythm change, it is best to _____ yourself to your new schedule beforehand. For instance, before traveling you should go to sleep one hour later (or earlier) each day until your sleep cycle matches the time at your destination.

106. (p. 313) If you cannot preadapt, it at least helps to fly early in the day when you fly _____. When you fly _____, it is better to fly late.

107. (p. 314) _____ _____ states that we all are subject to three separate cycles: a physical cycle lasting _____ days, an emotional cycle of _____ days, and a 33-day intellectual cycle.

108. (p. 314) Biorhythm theory states that the three cycles begin at birth and continue throughout life. When your cycles line up on "critical days," you are supposedly more likely to have an _____ or other problems.

109. (p. 314) The strongest evidence against biorhythm theory comes from attempts to match cycles with outcomes. For instance, one researcher compared 100 no-hit baseball games pitched in the major leagues to biorhythm charts for the pitchers. He found _____ _____ between cycles and these performances.

110. (p. 314) The Workmen's Compensation Board of British Columbia studied over 13,000 occupational accidents. They found that accidents are no more likely to occur on "_____" days than at any other time.

111. (p. 314) Other studies have found absolutely _____ _____ between aviation accidents and pilots' biorhythms, or between biorhythms and death by suicide, homicide, or natural causes.

112. (p. 314) Psychologist Richard Soloman has offered an intriguing explanation for drug addiction and other learned motives using his _____-_____ theory.

113. (p. 314) According to this theory, a stimulus that causes strong emotion, such as fear or pleasure, is often followed by an _____ emotion when the stimulus ends.

114. (p. 314) Soloman assumes that when a stimulus is repeated, our response to it _____. In contrast, emotional after effects get _____ with repetition.

115. (p. 315) _____ _____ or goals such as success, status, approval, power, and so forth are acquired in complex ways through socialization and cultural conditioning.

116. (p. 315) A dominant social motive in American culture is need for achievement (nAch), the desire to meet some _____ _____ of excellence. The person with high needs for achievement strives to do well in any situation where evaluation takes place.

117. (p. 315) The need for achievement differs from a need for _____, which is a desire to have impact or control over others.

118. (p. 315) In researching nAch, psychologist David McClelland found that 14 years after graduation, students shown high, versus low, in need for achievement, were found more often in careers involving an element of _____ and _____.

119. (p. 315) Scores for achievement motivation have _____ for students in recent years. Some psychologists believe this may help account for the dramatic decline in Scholastic Aptitude Test scores observed in the last decade.

120. (p. 315) Those high in nAch are _____ risk-takers. They avoid goals that are too easy because they offer no sense of satisfaction. They also avoid long shots because there is no hope of success, or success is more due to luck than skill.

121. (p. 315) Persons low in nAch select either sure things or impossible goals where there is no risk of _____ _____ for failure.

122. (p. 315) People high in nAch do better on various laboratory tasks, are more likely to complete _____ tasks, make better _____ in school, and tend to excel in their _____.

123. (p. 315) College students high in nAch tend to attribute success to their own _____, and failure to _____ _____. High nAch students are more likely to renew their efforts when faced with a poor performance.

124. (p. 316) Each year, consumers spend millions of dollars on "_____" self-help audiotapes, which supposedly contain messages presented below the level of conscious awareness.

125. (p. 316) Russell, Rowe, and Smouse studied the benefits of such tapes using three groups of students who took part in a 10-week evaluation. The results were clear: A comparison of average final exam grades and semester grade point averages for all three groups revealed _____ effects or benefits from listening to the tapes.

126. (p. 316) Fear of success most often occurs because:
    1) success can require a stressful shift in _____-_____
    2) many people fear _____ when they stand out in a group
    3) some people fear the extra _____ of being a "successful person."

127. (p. 317) Both men and women appear to be equally subject to success fears. But in our culture there is often an extra conflict for women. By adulthood, many men and women have learned to consider it "unfeminine" for a woman to excel. Successful women, then, are most often those who define achievement as an _____ feminine quality.

128. (p. 317) Benjamin Bloom recently completed a study of America's top performers in six fields. He found that _____ and _____, not great natural talent, led to success in the lives of the high achievers studied.

129. (p. 317) The upshot of Bloom's work is that talent is nurtured through dedication and hard work. It appears that this is most likely to happen when parents give their wholehearted _____ to a child's special interest, and when they place emphasis on doing one's _____ at all times.

130. (p. 317) Abraham Maslow has proposed a _____ (or ordering) of needs in his attempt to place human motivation in perspective.

131. (p. 317) The bottom or first level needs are _____. They are necessary for survival and tend to be prepotent or dominant over the higher needs.

132. (p. 317) The higher needs are expressed only when the prepotent physiological needs are satisfied. This tendency is true of the next level of needs, those for _____ and _____.

133. (p. 317) Maslow described these first two levels of needs as _____ needs, with the next broad level known as _____ needs. These include needs for love and belonging, needs for _____ and _____-_____ (recognition and self-respect) and the need for _____-_____.

134. (p. 318) According to Maslow, there is a tendency to move up the hierarchy to the _____-_____, the less powerful, but humanly important motives.

135. (p. 318) When survival needs are met, but meta-needs are unfulfilled, a person falls into a "_____ of _____" and experiences despair, apathy, and alienation.

136. (p. 319) Maslow estimated that only one person in _____ is primarily motivated by self-actualization needs. Most are concerned with esteem, love, or security.

137. (p. 319) _____ _____ occurs when there is no obvious external reward or ulterior purpose behind your actions. In contrast, _____ _____ stems from obvious external factors like pay, grades, rewards, obligations, or approval.

138. (p. 319) Research with children shows that excessive rewards can undermine spontaneous interest. Children lavishly rewarded for drawing showed _____ interest on subsequent occasions when allowed to draw spontaneously.

139. (p. 319) On the job, the _____ of work may be increased by salaries and bonuses. However, the _____ of work is tied more to intrinsic factors, such as interest, freedom of action, and constructive feedback.

140. (p. 319) When a person is _____ motivated, a certain amount of challenge, surprise, and complexity makes a task rewarding. When _____ motivation is stressed, complexity, surprise, and challenge just become barriers to reaching a goal.

141. (p. 319) Motivation can't always be intrinsic since every worthwhile activity is not intrinsically satisfying. Extrinsic motivation is often needed if we are to develop enough _____ or _____ for an activity to become intrinsically rewarding.

142. (p. 319) Greene and Lepper summarized their findings by pointing out that:
    1) If there is no _____ interest in an activity to begin with, there is nothing to lose by using extrinsic rewards
    2) If needed skills are lacking, _____ rewards may be necessary to begin
    3) Extrinsic rewards may focus _____ on an activity so that real interest can develop
    4) If extrinsic rewards or incentives are to be used, they should be as _____ as possible, used only when absolutely necessary and faded out as soon as possible.

143. (p. 320) Many people think the basic approach to controlling weight is to diet. What is really needed to control weight is a complete overhaul of _____ _____ and control of _____ for eating.

144. (p. 320) This approach has been called _____ _____ and involves a number of techniques and suggestions. The first of these is to have a physical check-up since about _____ percent of all weight problems are physical.

145. (p. 321) Keeping a diet _____ can be useful as a means of learning your eating habits. Along with this, count _____.

146. (p. 321) Develop techniques to control the act of eating by taking smaller _____ carrying only what you plan to eat to the table, putting all food away before leaving the kitchen, eating slowly, leaving food on your plate, and avoid eating alone.

147. (p. 321) Learn to weaken your personal eating cues by _____ when and where you do the most eating. Require yourself to _____ what you are doing in order to eat and be aware of the "_____-_____ syndrome."

148. (p. 321) Avoid snacks by fixing only a single portion using low-calorie foods. _____ the impulse to eat using a timer or by filling up on raw carrots, bouillon, water, coffee, or tea.

149. (p. 321) Exercise burns calories. Contrary to popular opinion, regular exercise does not increase appetite, and may lower the body's _____ _____ for fat storage.

150. (p. 321) Many psychologists are now convinced that no diet can succeed for long without an increase in exercise. Burning as little as _____ extra calories a day can play a major role in preventing regain of weight.

151. (p. 321) Get yourself committed to weight loss by involving as many _____ in your program as you can. Formal programs such as Overeaters Anonymous or Take Off Pounds Sensibly can be a good source of social support.

152. (p. 321) Make a list of _____ you will receive if you change your eating habits and _____ that will occur if you don't.

153. (p. 321) _____ your progress daily. Record your weight, the number of calories eaten, and whether you met your daily goal.

154. (p. 321) Try to identify specific high risk situations in which you are likely to overeat. Then form a plan to help you cope with the risk of _____.

155. (p. 321) You should set a "threshold" for weight control. A study of Weight Watchers members found that those who successfully maintained their weight loss had a regain limit of _____ pounds or less which, if exceeded, alerted them to immediately begin making corrections in their diet and exercise.

156. (p. 322) Serious cases of undereating are called _____ _____. Victims of this condition are mostly adolescent females (5 percent are males) who suffer devastating weight loss from self-inflicted starvation.

157. (p. 322) Anorexia nervosa is not a simple loss of desire for food. Many anorexics continue to feel hunger and struggle to starve themselves. The problem can best be described as a relentless pursuit of _____ _____.

158. (p. 322) Persons who suffer from anorexia nervosa have an obsessive fear of gaining weight. Often the problem starts with normal _____ that gradually begins to dominate the person's life.

159. (p. 322) In time, anorexics suffer physical weakness, absence of _____ _____, and a dangerous risk of infection. Five to _____ percent die of malnutrition or related health problems.

160. (p. 322) _____, also known as the binge-purge syndrome, is a second major eating disorder. Victims gorge on food, then induce vomiting or take laxatives to avoid gaining weight.

161. (p. 322) Bulimia, too, is far more prevalent in women than in men. A recent study of college women found that _____ percent are bulimic. As many as _____ percent have milder eating problems.

162. (p. 323) Typical risks associated with bulimia include sore _____, _____ loss, _____ spasms, _____ damage, dehydration, tooth decay, swelling of the _____ _____, menstrual irregularity, loss of sex drive, and even heart attack.

163. (p. 323) Close to _____ percent of anorexics are also bulimic. However, they are separate problems. Anorexics suffer a weight loss of at least _____ percent of their original body weight. Bulimics may be from any weight group (most are only slightly below average weight).

164. (p. 323) Bulimia is indicated if any three of the following conditions are present: _____ eating; hiding the amount eaten during a binge; gorging on food, followed by self-induced vomiting or abdominal pain; repeated attempts to lose weight by severe dieting; use of vomiting, laxatives, or diuretics to lose weight; frequent weight changes of more than _____ pounds; awareness that one's eating is abnormal, coupled with an inability to change; _____ or _____ following binges.

165. (p. 323) Both anorexics and bulimics have exaggerated fears of becoming fat. Anorexics, especially, have distorted body images. Most overestimate their body size by _____ percent or more.

166. (p. 323) Anorexics are usually described as "perfect" daughters. Many are would-be high
_____ who frantically try to be "perfect" in one area—to have complete
control over their weight and to be perfectly slim.

167. (p. 323) Bulimics are obsessed with weight, food, etc., and feel guilt, shame, and anxiety after a binge.
_____ reduces the anxiety triggered by a binge and thus is highly reinforcing.

168. (p. 323) Recent research suggests that _____ may actually encourage binging since
most bulimics go through this phase before they begin to purge.

169. (p. 324) Janet Polivy and Peter Herman have found that dieters eat _____ after first eating a large
meal than they do if they ate nothing beforehand. It's as if once they have "broken" their diet,
the suppressed urge to eat is released and a binge follows. This effect can occur even when
dieters are merely told they ate a high calorie meal.

170. (p. 324) Treatment for anorexia usually begins with admitting the person to a _____.
As a second step, the client enters counseling to work on the personal conflicts and family
issues that led to weight loss.

171. (p. 324) For bulimia, psychologists have had some success with behavioral counseling that includes
careful _____-_____ of food intake and work on extinguishing the urge
to vomit after eating.

172. (p. 324) Although much progress is being made in treating eating disorders, most
_____ do not seek help, and many actively resist it. _____ will
sometimes seek treatment, but usually not until their eating habits become intolerable.

SELF-TEST

1. (p. 301) The concept of motivation can be related to a sequence of activities. Which of the following
shows the proper order of a model of motivation?
   a. need, drive, response, goal, need reduction
   b. need, need reduction, goal, drive, response
   c. need, response, drive, goal, need reduction
   d. drive, need, goal, response, need reduction

2. (p. 302) Motivated behavior can be energized by external stimuli as well as by the push of internal
needs. The "pull" exerted by a goal is called its:
   a. drive reduction   c. incentive value
   b. goal attainment   d. primary motivation

3. (p. 302) Motives based on biological needs which must be met for survival are called:
   a. primary   c. secondary
   b. stimulus   d. learned

4. (p. 303) Within the body there are ideal levels for body temperature, concentration of various chemicals
in the blood, etc. When the body deviates from these ideal levels, automatic reactions restore
equilibrium. This process is known as:
   a. Yerkes-Dodson Law   c. thermostasis
   b. homeostatsis   d. biological calibration

5. (p. 304) True-False. Stomach contractions are the main source of food regulation and control of hunger.

6.   (p. 304) Which of the following areas of the brain is most important to the regulation of hunger and
      eating?
      a.   hypothalamus   c.   thalamus
      b.   cerebellum   d.   pituitary gland

7.   (p. 304) True-False. The drive to initiate eating and the desire to stop eating are regulated by separate
      centers located respectively in the right and left brains.

8.   (p. 305) Which of the following is *not* true of body set points for fat?
      a.   The set point may be lastingly altered when a child is overfed.
      b.   The set point appears to be entirely inherited, being linked with feeding patterns of parents.
      c.   The set point acts like a "thermostat" for body fat, maintaining a proportion of fat
      d.   When an overweight person loses weight, the body goes below the set point, and the
           person feels hungry most of the time.

9.   (p. 306) Which of the following is *not* true of obesity?
      a.   The overweight are unusually sensitive to external cues for eating.
      b.   For many people, diet contributes to obesity.
      c.   Overeating occurs mainly when a person is gaining weight.
      d.   People with weight problems are just as likely to eat when emotionally aroused as when
           hungry.

10.   (p. 307) Which of the following is *not* true of taste aversions?
      a.   They are a type of classical conditioning.
      b.   They can be learned if a food causes sickness or simply precedes sickness caused by
           something else.
      c.   It has been theorized that there is a biological tendency to associate an upset stomach with
           food eaten earlier.
      d.   Bait shyness is a related, but distinctly different phenomenon in which animals actively
           seek a bait laced with addictive drugs.

11.   (p. 308) Extracellular thirst occurs when:
      a.   there is an increase in water levels surrounding body cells
      b.   intracellular thirst has reached homeostasis
      c.   bleeding, vomiting, diarrhea, sweating, or alcohol consumption occurs
      d.   you eat a salty meal

12.   (p. 308) True-False. Avoiding pain is an entirely unlearned motive basic to survival.

13.   (p. 308) Pain is called a(n) _____ since it is aroused only when damage to the tissues of the body takes
      place.
      a.   primary drive   c.   chronic drive
      b.   episodic drive   d.   secondary motive

14.   (p. 308) Which of the following is *not* true of sexual motivation?
      a.   In lower animals and humans the sex drive is exclusively related to the action of hormones
           in the body.
      b.   Human males may show a loss of sex drive after castration.
      c.   Some women show loss or sexual desire when using birth control pills.
      d.   Sex is not necessary for individual survival, but is a necessity for group survival.

15. (p. 309) The drive which is non-homeostatic in nature is:
     a. hunger   c. sex
     b. thirst   d. oxygen intake

16. (p. 309) In animal research, the Coolidge effect refers to:
     a. learned avoidance of pain
     b. maze exploration for curiosity
     c. the resumption of sexual activity following satiation when a new partner is introduced
     d. the inverted U function relating arousal level and performance

17. (p. 309) Motives which provide useful information about the environment and stimulation to the nervous
     system are called:
     a. primary needs   c. secondary needs
     b. stimulus needs   d. learned needs

18. (p. 311) Zuckerman developed which of the following to measure differences in preferred stimulus
     arousal level?
     a. SSS   c. Yerkes-Dodson law
     b. SST   d. nAch

19. (p. 311) According to the Yerkes-Dodson law, when a task is relatively simple, the optimal level of
     arousal will be:
     a. low   c. high
     b. moderate   d. unimportant

20. (p. 312) Circadian rhythms refer to:
     a. the cycles of our bodies' internal clocks
     b. the body's ever-changing levels of blood sugar
     c. the female sexual cycle
     d. the need-drive-response-goal attainment cycle

21. (p. 314) Which of the following is *not* one of the cycles postulated by biorhythm theory?
     a. intellectual cycle lasting 33 days
     b. physical cycle lasting 23 days
     c. critical day cycle lasting 13 days
     d. sensitivity cycle lasting 28 days

22. (p. 314) Which of the following is *not* a true statement with regard to the merits of biorhythm theory?
     a. There is absolutely no correlation between aviation accidents and pilot biorhythms.
     b. There is no relationship between occupational accidents and biorhythm cycles.
     c. Biorhythm theory makes logical sense and is based on scientific evidence.
     d. There is no connection between biorhythms and recovery from surgery.

23. (p. 314) Which of the following is *not* true of Soloman's opponent-process theory?
     a. Emotional aftereffects get stronger with repetition.
     b. When a stimulus is repeated, our response to it habituates, or gets weaker.
     c. A stimulus that causes strong emotion is often followed by a similar emotion when the
         stimulus ends.
     d. The opponent-process theory has been used to explain the maintenance of drug addiction,
         and the reinforcing effects of sky-diving, and other hazardous pursuits.

24. (p. 315) Which of the following is true of the need for achievement (nAch)?
    a. It is essentially the same as need for power.
    b. Those high in nAch are more often found in careers involving very little risk.
    c. College students high in nAch tend to view success as the result of forces outside themselves.
    d. Those high in nAch are generally moderate risk-takers.

25. (p. 316) Which of the following is *not* true of fear of success?
    a. Both men and women are prone to act as if there is a conflict between success and femininity.
    b. Fear of success is more likely to occur among women than men.
    c. Fear of success seems related to requirements to shift self-concept, fear of rejection, and fear of extra demands.
    d. Successful women are most often those who define achievement as contradictory to femininity, but learn to live with the conflict.

26. (p. 317) True-False. According to Maslow, biological needs tend to be prepotent over psychological motives or needs.

27. (p. 317) Maslow's hierarchy of needs places the order of needs as:
    a. basic, growth, meta   c. growth, basic, meta
    b. meta, basic, growth   d. basic, meta, growth

28. (p. 319) True-False. Research with children has demonstrated that excessive rewards can undermine spontaneous interest in an activity.

29. (p. 321) Which of the following is *not* a behavioral dieting technique?
    a. observe your eating habits and keep a diet diary
    b. eat snacks frequently rather than preparing long meals
    c. weaken personal eating cues
    d. make a list of rewards you will receive for change

30. (p. 322) Which of the following is *not* true of anorexics?
    a. Most are adolescent females.
    b. Five to 18 percent die of malnutrition or related health problems.
    c. Close to 90 percent are also bulimics.
    d. They suffer a weight loss of at least 15 percent of their original body weight.

31. (p. 323) Typical health risks for bulimics include all of the following *except*:
    a. loss of sex drive   c. sore throat
    b. swelling of the salivary glands   d. added hair growth

32. (p. 323) The single most common personal issue involved in anorexia and bulimia is:
    a. feelings of unreality   c. needs for complete control
    b. desires to rebel against society d. overinflated self-worth

APPLYING YOUR KNOWLEDGE

1. Try investigating your daily circadian rhythm. What kinds of measures might you use? Plot the results of the data you collect on yourself. Is one measure more accurate than another? Is there a trend you can see in your charting towards certain highs and lows?

Chapter 11

ANSWERS—SELF-TEST

1. Motivation
2. need
3. drive
4. response; goal
5. need reduction
6. strength
7. external stimuli
8. incentive value
9. need; goal
10. primary motives
11. thirst, pain; sleep; temperature
12. Stimulus motives; innate
13. curiosity, exploration, manipulation; contact
14. learned, secondary
15. approval, status, security
16. fear, aggression
17. homeostasis
18. thermostat
19. Cannon, Washburn
20. hunger pangs
21. distended; sensory nerves
22. central
23. sugar; hypoglycemia
24. liver
25. hypothalamus
26. liver, stomach
27. lateral
28. eating; die
29. ventromedial
30. 1,000
31. sensory; motor
32. fat
33. set point
34. inherited; early
35. parents
36. more; larger
37. larger
38. external; cues
39. available; visible
40. decreased
41. obese
42. most likely
43. diet
44. three
45. maintained
46. activity level; fewer

47. unhappiness
48. rebound
49. calories; fat
50. metabolic rate
51. heart disease; death
52. Cultural
53. taste
54. taste aversion
55. classical conditioning; biological
56. nausea
57. bait shyness
58. nutritional
59. self-selection feeding; nutritious
60. sweet; fatty
61. hypothalamus
62. extracellular
63. salty
64. salt water; blood
65. intracellular
66. episodic
67. avoidance, elimination
68. learned
69. pain tolerance
70. individual survival
71. hormones; estrus; estrogen
72. castration
73. fertility cycle
74. menstrual cycle
75. castration; birth control pills
76. non-homeostatic
77. arousal; reduction
78. Coolidge effect
79. reward
80. sensory deprivation
81. complex
82. Arousal
83. arousal theory
84. curiosity; stimulation
85. Sensation-Seeking Scale
86. body
87. extroverted, independent; sexual; smoke
88. orderly, nurturant, giving
89. moderate; inverted U

90. high; low
91. Yerkes-Dodson
92. overprepared
93. circadian rhythms
94. temperature; blood; urine
95. adrenaline
96. negative
97. jet lag
98. Shift; fatigue; irritability
99. 2
100. faster
101. 4; 5; 50
102. later; longer
103. backwards; advance
104. night
105. preadapt
106. east; west
107. Biorhythm theory; 23; 28
108. accident
109. no connection
110. critical
111. no correlation
112. opponent-process
113. opposite
114. habituates; stronger
115. Social motives
116. internalized standard
117. power
118. risk, responsibility
119. declined
120. moderate
121. personal responsibility
122. difficult; grades; occupations
123. ability; insufficient effort
124. subliminal
125. no
126. self-concept; rejection; demands
127. acceptable
128. drive, determination
129. support; best
130. hierarchy
131. physiological
132. safety, security

133. basic; growth; esteem; self-esteem; self-actualization
134. meta-needs
135. syndrome of decay
136. ten
137. Intrinsic motivation; extrinsic motivation
138. little
139. quantity; quality
140. intrinsically; extrinsic
141. skill, knowledge
142. intrinsic; extrinsic; attention; small
143. eating habits; cues
144. behavioral dieting; 5
145. diary; calories
146. portions; alone
147. avoiding; interrupt; night-eating
148. Delay
149. set point
150. 200
151. people
152. rewards; punishments
153. Chart
154. relapse
155. 3
156. anorexia nervosa
157. excessive thinness
158. dieting
159. menstrual cycles; 8
160. Bulimia
161. 5; 61
162. throat; hair; muscle; kidney; salivary glands
163. 50; 15
164. binge; 3; anxiety, depression
165. 25
166. achievers
167. Vomiting
168. dieting
169. more
170. hospital
171. self-monitoring
172. anorexics; Bulimics

ANSWERS—SELF-TEST

1.	a	7.	False	13.	b	19.	c	25.	d	31.	d
2.	c	8.	b	14.	a	20.	a	26.	True	32.	c
3.	a	9.	a	15.	c	21.	c	27.	a		
4.	b	10.	d	16.	c	22.	c	28.	True		
5.	False	11.	c	17.	b	23.	c	29.	b		
6.	a	12.	False	18.	a	24.	d	30.	c		

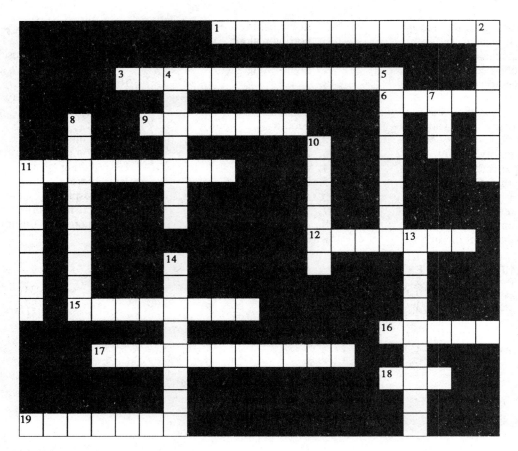

ACROSS

1. _____ hypothalamus is "satiety" center of brain
3. brain area regulating hunger
6. aversion learned if food causes sickness
9. changing eating habits leads to behavioral _____
11. learned motives
12. may present major health risk and low self-esteem
15. pain avoidance is an _____ drive
16. organ that sends signals to brain to encourage eating
17. body equilibrium
18. sensation seeking scale (abbr.)
19. binge-purge syndrome

DOWN

2. _____ hypothalamus is "feeding" center of brain
4. motives based on biological survival needs
5. curiosity and exploration are examples of these motives
7. in humans, this drive is largely nonhomeostatic
8. _____ value is the "pull" exerted by a goal
10. he offered hierarchy of motives
11. prolonged _____ deprivation may cause disturbed thinking and sensory distortion
13. _____ motivation comes from within
14. serious eating disorder—lose much body weight

CHAPTER 12

Emotion

CONTENTS

TERMS AND CONCEPTS

voodoo deaths
adaptive behaviors
physiological changes
adrenaline
emotional expressions
primary emotions
moods
autonomic nervous system (ANS)
sympathetic branch
parasympathetic branch
parasympathetic rebound
polygraph (lie detector)
kinesics
illustrators
emblems
commonsense theory of emotion
James-Lange theory
Cannon-Bard theory
Schachter's cognitive theory
attribution

facial feedback hypothesis
contemporary model of emotion
primary appraisal
secondary appraisal
problem-focused coping
emotion-focused coping
anxiety
defense mechanism
denial
repression
reaction formation
regression
projection
rationalization
compensation
sublimation
learned helplessness
mastery training
triangular theory of love

IMPORTANT INDIVIDUALS

Walter Cannon
Robert Plutchik
Eckhard Hess
George Engel
David Lykken
Charles Darwin
Paul Ekman

William James
Carl Lange
Phillip Bard
Stanley Schachter
Stuart Valins
Carrol Izard
Richard Lazarus

Joseph Spiesman
Sigmund Freud
Bruno Bettelheim
Martin Seligman
Aaron Beck
Robert Sternberg

PROGRAMMED REVIEW

1.   (p. 327) Voodoo deaths can partially be explained by the victim's strong belief in the power of the curse. Walter Cannon believes that the real cause lies in changes that occur in the body which accompany strong _____.

2.   (p. 327) More recent research indicates that such deaths are more likely the result of the body's reaction to strong emotion, rather than fear itself. The cursed person's emotional response is so intense that the _____ _____ system overreacts and eventually slows the heart to a stop.

3.   (p. 328) Emotions have a powerful influence on everyday behavior. For example, it is easier to make decisions when you are in a _____ mood. Likewise, people who are feeling _____ are more likely to help others in need.

4.   (p. 328) The root of the word emotion means "to _____," and indeed emotions do. First, the body is _____ aroused during emotion.

5.   (p. 328) Second, we are often motivated by emotions such as fear, anger, or joy. Underlying this is the fact that emotions are linked to such basic _____ behaviors as attack, retreat, seeking comfort, helping others, reproduction, etc.

6.   (p. 328) At times human emotions can be disruptive, but in general they aid in _____. This fact seems to explain why emotional reactions were retained in evolution.

7.   (p. 328) Physiological changes within the body are a major element of many emotions. These changes include alterations in heart _____, blood _____, perspiration, and other bodily stirrings.

8.   (p. 328) Most such reactions are caused by release of _____ into the bloodstream. This hormone stimulates the sympathetic nervous system, which in turn activates the body.

9.   (p. 328) _____ _____, or outward signs of what a person is feeling, are a major element of emotion. These are particularly important because they communicate emotion from one person to another. A marked shift in voice tone or modulation is one familiar example.

10. (p. 329) A final major element of emotion consists of _____ _____, or a person's private emotional experience. This is the part of emotion with which we are typically most familiar.

11. (p. 329) Based on his research, Robert Plutchik believes there are eight _____ emotions which include fear, surprise, sadness, disgust, anger, anticipation, joy, and acceptance (receptivity).

12. (p. 329) Each of these emotions can vary in _____ to produce a variety of other emotions.

13. (p. 329) The mildest forms of various emotions are called _____. They act as a subtle emotional undercurrent that affects much day-to-day behavior.

14. (p. 329) According to Plutchik, primary emotions can also be _____ to yield another, more complex emotion. For example, joy and fear may combine to produce guilt.

15. (p. 329) To a large degree the physical aspects of emotion are _____, or built into the body.

16. (p. 329) Unpleasant emotions produce especially consistent reactions including pounding heart, muscular tension, irritability, and so forth. This consistency is tied to the fact that they are generated by the _____ _____ _____ (ANS).

17. (p. 329) The reactions of the ANS are automatic and not normally under voluntary control. There are two divisions to the ANS, the _____ branch and the _____ branch.

18. (p. 330) The _____ branch prepares the body for emergency action: for "_____ or _____" by arousing a number of bodily systems and inhibiting others.

19. (p. 330) Most of the sympathetic reactions increase the chances that an organism will survive an emergency. _____ is released into the bloodstream for quick energy, the heart beats faster to distribute blood to the _____, _____ is temporarily inhibited, and blood flow in the skin is restricted to reduce _____.

20. (p. 330) The actions of the _____ branch generally reverse emotional arousal and calm and relax the body. The heart is slowed, the pupils return to normal size, blood pressure drops, and so forth.

21. (p. 330) In addition to restoring balance, the parasympathetic system helps build up and conserve _____ _____.

22. (p. 330) The parasympathetic branch responds much more _____ than the sympathetic. This finding explains why emotions do not subside until _____ or _____ minutes after the threat has passed.

23. (p. 330) After a strong emotional shock, the parasympathetic system may overreact and lower _____ _____ too much. This is why people sometimes become dizzy or faint at the sight of blood and other such shocks.

24. (p. 330) Eckhard Hess has studied the relationship between emotion and the size of a person's _____. Emotional effects such as arousal, interest, or attention can activate the sympathetic nervous system and cause dilation (enlargement).

25. (p. 330) Dilation of the pupils can occur during both pleasant and unpleasant emotions. However, most people tend to interpret _____ pupils as a sign of pleasant feelings, and _____ pupils as a sign of negative feelings.

26. (p. 330) To illustrate this, Hess demonstrated that men describe photos of a woman with _____ pupils as "soft," "feminine," or "pretty." The same woman with _____ pupils was described as "hard," "selfish," and "cold."

27. (p. 331) This effect was shown in an experiment where subjects were introduced to two potential partners (one of whom used eye drops to enlarge their pupils) and asked to choose one. Subjects of both sexes tended to select the person with the _____ _____.

28. (p. 331) The parasympathetic system may overreact during intense fear and in rare cases cause death. This reaction, called a _____ _____, has been noted in voodoo curses and under the pressures of combat during war.

29. (p. 331) Another example of such deaths is provided by the young woman admitted to a hospital because she felt she was going to die. She strongly believed in a midwife's prediction that she would die before her twenty-third birthday. Indeed, she did die two days before this birthday, an apparent victim of her own _____.

30. (p. 331) In the case of older individuals or people with heart problems, the direct effects of _____ _____ may be enough to bring about heart attack and collapse. Such was the case with the widow of Louis Armstrong.

31. (p. 331) Psychiatrist George Engel has studied hundreds of similar deaths. He found that almost _____ were associated with the extremely traumatic disruption of a close human relationship.

32. (p. 332) Because bodily changes caused by the autonomic nervous system are good indicators of emotion, a number of techniques for measuring them have been developed. One of these is the _____ or lie detector.

33. (p. 332) Many businesses use lie detectors to check the honesty of employees. However, this practice must be questioned for two reasons: First, the detector's accuracy is _____; and second, such testing is often a serious invasion of _____.

34. (p. 332) A polygraph is a device that draws a record of changes in heart _____, blood _____, breathing _____, and the _____ _____ _____ (GSR).

35. (p. 332) To be more accurate, a polygraph is not a lie detector at all, it only records general _____ _____. There is no unique "lie response."

36. (p. 332) When attempting to detect a lie, the polygraph operator begins by asking a number of _____ (nonemotional) questions. This process establishes a "_____," or normal emotional responsiveness.

37. (p. 332) To minimize the problem of general subject nervousness, a polygraph examiner asks a series of questions with _____ questions mixed among them.

38. (p. 332) As an alternative, subjects may be asked _____ questions that can be compared to critical questions. Such questions are designed to make almost anyone anxious and, therefore, allow the examiner to see how a person reacts to doubt or misgivings.

39. (p. 333) Even when questioning is done properly, lie detection may be _____. Such was the case with Floyd Fay convicted of murdering his friend Fred Ery. Psychologist David Lykken has documented three such cases like this in which innocent people were convicted and imprisoned based on a polygrapher's testimony.

40. (p. 333) Proponents of lie detection claim _____ to _____ percent accuracy, but in one laboratory experiment, accuracy was lowered to _____ percent by subjects who intentionally thought exciting or upsetting thoughts during questioning.

41. (p. 333) The polygraph can be thrown off by self-inflicted pain, _____ drugs, or by people who can lie without anxiety.

42. (p. 333) The test's most common error is to label an innocent person guilty, rather than a guilty person innocent. In field studies involving real crimes and criminal suspects, an average of approximately _____ innocent person in _____ was rated as guilty by the "lie detector." In some instances, the "false positives" reached _____ percent.

43. (p. 333) In 1988 the United States Congress passed a law strictly limiting the use of lie detector tests for _____ _____ and employees of _____ _____. However, there are still certain circumstances in which a polygraph may be given. You should be familiar with these and if given a lie detector test remain calm, then challenge the outcome if the machine wrongly questions your honesty.

44. (p. 333) Even the basic reactions of anger, fear, and joy, which appear to be unlearned, take time to develop. General _____ is the only emotional response newborn infants clearly express.

45. (p. 334) Bridges observed a large number of babies and found that all of the basic human emotions (both learned and unlearned) appear before age _____.

46. (p. 334) Bridges found that there is a consistent order in which emotions appear, and that the first basic split is between _____ and _____ emotions.

47. (p. 334) More recent research suggests that by the end of year _____, babies can express happiness, surprise, fear, anger, sadness, disgust, and interest.

48. (p. 334) When new parents see and hear a crying baby they feel annoyed and unhappy and their blood _____ and _____ increase. Such reactions encourage parents to tend to a baby's needs, thus increasing its chances for survival.

49. (p. 334) Development of the ability to express emotion is probably related to maturation of the _____ since children of all cultures show a similar pattern.

50. (p. 334) Charles _____ believed that emotional expressions were a carryover from more primitive and animal-like stages of evolution retained because communicating one's feelings to others is an aid to survival.

51. (p. 334) The most basic expressions do appear to be fairly universal. Children born _____ and _____ use the same facial gestures as others to display joy, sadness, disgust, etc.

52. (p. 335) By adulthood, many facial gestures are unique to various cultures. For example, among the Chinese sticking out the tongue is a gesture of _____, not of disrespect or teasing.

53. (p. 335) Despite such cultural differences, facial expressions of fear, surprise, sadness, disgust, anger, and happiness are recognized by people of all cultures. A _____ is the most universal and easily recognized facial expression of emotion.

54. (p. 335) The study of communication through body movement, posture, gestures, and facial expressions is called _____ and informally referred to as body language.

55. (p. 335) While popular books on body language tend to list particular meanings for various gestures, researchers in the field emphasize that gestures are rarely this fixed in meaning. Instead an overall _____ _____ is communicated.

56. (p. 336) The most expressive and frequently noticed part of the body is the face, capable of producing some 20,000 different expressions. Most of these are _____ _____ involving a mixture of two or more basic expressions.

57. (p. 336) Facial expressions can be boiled down to three basic dimensions of _____-_____, and _____-_____ and _____ (or arousal).

58. (p. 336) Other emotional qualities are transmitted with the body, the most general being _____ or _____, and _____ or _____.

59. (p. 336) _____ is expressed by casual position of the arms and legs, leaning back (if sitting), and spreading the arms and legs. _____ is expressed mainly by leaning toward a person or object.

60. (p. 336) Recent research suggests that overall posture can indicate one's emotional state. When a person is _____, his or her posture is likely to be more erect. It remains debatable whether this tendency is a product of emotion or is simply learned.

61. (p. 336) Because most people learn to maintain careful control over their facial expressions, detecting deception may be difficult. Deception is best revealed by the _____ _____.

62. (p. 336) Most people assume that _____ eyes and _____ are clear signs of lying. Not so according to Paul Ekman. Also _____ _____ that involve touching one's own body (rubbing, grooming, etc.) are not consistently related to lying.

63. (p. 337) The gestures people use to illustrate what they are saying may reveal lying. These gestures, called _____, tend to decrease when a person is telling a lie.

64. (p. 337) Other movements, called _____, can also reveal lying. These gestures have clear meanings within a particular culture and tend to increase when a person is lying.

65. (p. 337) Among the best clues to lying are the signs of strong emotion produced by the ANS. These include _____, blushing, blanching, _____ dilation, rapid or irregular _____, perspiration, frequent swallowing, _____ errors, and a louder, higher-pitched voice.

66. (p. 337) There are several theories that attempt to explain what takes place during emotion. Common sense tells us that we perceive a stimulus, are aroused, and then respond. But the _____-_____ theory proposes the reverse. It postulates that bodily changes precede emotion and only later are we aware of the emotional experience.

67. (p. 337) Another theory, which opposes that of James and Lange, proposes that emotional feelings and bodily arousal occur at the same time. This theory is the _____-_____ theory.

68. (p. 337) The Cannon-Bard theory proposed that the thalamus simultaneously activates both the _____ (responsible for emotional feelings and emotional behavior), and the _____ (responsible for arousing the body).

69. (p. 337) While the previous theories are mostly concerned with emotion as a physical response, Stanley Schachter's _____ theory of emotion stresses that mental factors also enter into emotion.

70. (p. 337) According to Schachter, emotion occurs when a particular _____ is applied to general physical arousal.

71. (p. 337) In support of his theory, Schachter showed that subjects given _____ before viewing a slapstick movie, rated the movie funniest. Subjects given a _____ were least amused, while a placebo group fell in the middle.

72. (p. 338) Stuart Valins has added an interesting refinement to the cognitive theory. According to Valins, perception of emotion depends upon what you _____ your feelings of physical arousal to.

73. (p. 338) To demonstrate attribution, Valins showed male students a series of slides of nude females, some paired with an amplified artificial heartbeat subjects believed to be their own. Asked to rate which females they found most attractive, they consistently chose the ones associated with a "_____ _____."

74. (p. 338) Attribution theory predicts that adding fear, anger, frustration, or rejection to a relationship tends to _____ a couple's feelings for each other.

75. (p. 338) In support of this, one study found that men interviewed on a swaying suspension bridge 230 feet above ground were _____ likely to later contact their woman interviewer than men interviewed on a wooden bridge ten feet above ground.

76. (p. 339) According to psychologist Carrol Izard, emotional activity causes innately programmed changes in facial expression. The face then provides cues to the brain that help us determine what emotion we are feeling. This idea is known as the _____ _____ hypothesis.

77. (p. 339) This hypothesis states that having facial expressions and becoming aware of them is what leads to emotional experience. _____, for instance, arouses the body, but this arousal is not experienced as emotion because it does not trigger emotional expressions.

78. (p. 339) Paul Ekman monitored bodily reactions while subjects arranged their faces, muscle by muscle, into expressions of surprise, disgust, sadness, anger, fear, and happiness. "Making faces" brought about changes in the _____ nervous system, as reflected by heart rate and skin temperature.

79. (p. 339) Each facial expression produced a different pattern of activity. An angry face, for instance, _____ heart rate and skin temperature, whereas disgust _____ heart rate and skin temperature.

80. (p. 339) Ekman also found that subjects holding a pen crosswise in their mouths rated cartoons as funnier than did people who held the pen in their lips. The reason is that holding a pen with your teeth forces you to form a _____. Thus, subjects' emotional experiences were influenced by their facial expression.

81. (p. 339) Emotions determine expressions, and expressions may determine emotions. This could explain why when you are feeling sad, forcing yourself to _____ will sometimes cause an actual improvement in your mood.

82. (p. 341) Psychologists are increasingly aware that the _____ of a situation greatly affects the course of emotion. This refers to evaluating the personal meaning of a stimulus.

83.   (p. 341) As an example of the contemporary model of emotions, when you see a snarling dog (an emotional stimulus), it is _____ (judged) as a threat. Your emotional appraisal gives rise to _____ _____ (your heart pounds and your body becomes stirred up).

84.   (p. 341) The appraisal also releases _____ _____ expressions (your face twists into a mask of fear and your posture becomes tense).

85.   (p. 341) At the same time, the appraisal leads to _____ behavior (running from the dog). It also causes a change in consciousness that you recognize as the _____ experience of fear. (The intensity of this emotional feeling is directly related to the amount of ANS arousal.)

86.   (p. 341) The original emotional stimulus can be _____, like the attacking dog, or it can be _____, such as a memory of being chased by a dog.

87.   (p. 342) According to Richard Lazarus, there are two important steps in the process of coping with a threatening situation. The first is _____ _____, in which you decide if a situation is threatening or not. Then you make a _____ _____ during which you choose a means of meeting the threat.

88.   (p. 342) The emotional effects of appraisal have been demonstrated by Joseph Spiesman through an experiment using a graphic film called _____. The film shows a painful operation being performed on the penises of adolescent boys from a tribe of Australian Aborigines.

89.   (p. 342) Viewers watched the film under one of _____ different versions, ranging from no sound track to an emphasis on the pain, etc.

90.   (p. 342) Recordings of heart rate and GSR showed that the film emphasizing _____ aspects of the operation produced an _____ in emotion over that caused by the silent film.

91.   (p. 342) In contrast, the intellectual and denial sound tracks _____ emotion.

92.   (p. 342) After a person makes a secondary appraisal, coping attempts can be one of two types. _____-_____ coping is aimed at managing or altering the distressing situation itself. In _____-_____ coping, the person tries instead to control emotional reactions.

93.   (p. 343) Sometimes problem-and emotion-focused coping aid one another. It is also possible for the two types to clash or impede one another. For example, when suffering emotional distress over an important decision, you may make a premature choice to end the distress. While this may allow you to cope with your emotions, it can short-change _____-_____ coping.

94.   (p. 343) In general, problem-focused coping tends to be especially useful when you are facing a _____ stressor, that is, a situation you can actually do something about. Emotion-focused efforts are best suited to managing stressors that you cannot _____.

95.   (p. 343) Test anxiety refers to a combination of heightened _____ _____ (uneasiness, tension, sweating, pounding heart, nervousness) plus excessive _____ during test taking.

96. (p. 343) Worries arise when taking a test that is appraised as a _____. Worries are the real heart of test anxiety because they directly interfere with thinking about the test. Some test anxious students actually spend as much time worrying as they do working on the test.

97. (p. 343) The most direct antidote for test anxiety is _____ _____. Many test anxious students simply study too little and too late for exams.

98. (p. 343) One solution for test anxiety is to _____ by studying well in advance of the test day. Those who are well prepared score higher, worry less, and are less likely to become overly aroused.

99. (p. 343) As in other stressful situations, learning to _____ can help lower test anxiety. Anxiety is also lowered by support for others—so discuss any problems with your professors.

100. (p. 343) Nervousness during tests can often be lessened by carefully _____ in your imagination how you will cope with upsetting events.

101. (p. 343) Because worries are such a major part of test anxiety, changing _____-_____ thinking patterns can be the best solution of all. Learn to counter worries with calming, rational replies (coping statements).

102. (p. 343) Threatening situations are often accompanied by an unpleasant emotional state known as _____, characterized by tension, uneasiness, apprehension, and worry.

103. (p. 344) Anxiety caused by stressful situations or by our own shortcomings and limitations, may be lessened by the use of psychological _____ _____.

104. (p. 344) A defense mechanism is any technique used to avoid, deny, or distort sources of threat or anxiety. They are also used to maintain an idealized _____-_____ so that we can comfortably live with ourselves.

105. (p. 344) Many of the defense mechanisms were first identified by Sigmund Freud, who assumed they operate _____ creating large "blind spots" in awareness.

106. (p. 344) One of the most basic defense mechanisms is _____—to protect oneself from an unpleasant reality by refusing to accept or believe it.

107. (p. 344) Denial is closely associated with _____, _____, and similar painful and threatening experiences.

108. (p. 344) Freud noticed that his patients had tremendous difficulty recalling shocking or traumatic events from childhood. It seemed that powerful forces were holding these painful memories from awareness. Freud called this _____.

109. (p. 344) _____ _____ is a defense in which impulses are not only repressed, they are also held in check by exaggerated opposite behavior. For example, a mother who unconsciously resents her children may become absurdly overprotective and overindulgent.

110. (p. 345) In its broadest meaning, _____ as a defense mechanism refers to any return to earlier, less demanding situations or habits. For example, parents who have a second child find that the older child, frustrated by a new rival for attention, may demonstrate childish _____, bed-_____, or infantile _____.

111. (p. 345) _____, another defense mechanism, is the unconscious process whereby an individual tends to see his or her own shortcomings or unacceptable impulses in others. By exaggerating these unacceptable traits in others, the individual lessens his or her own failings.

112. (p. 345) When the explanations offered for our behavior are reasonable and convincing, but not the real reasons, we say a person is _____. This defense mechanism unconsciously provides us with reasons for behavior we ourselves find somewhat questionable.

113. (p. 345) Overuse of defense mechanisms requires great amounts of _____ energy. However, they do have value since they may prevent a person from being overwhelmed by immediate threats and give him or her time to learn to _____ in a more effective manner with continuing frustrations.

114. (p. 345) There are two defense mechanisms that have a decidedly more positive quality to them than those previously described. One of these, _____, is a form of behavior whereby a person tries to make up for some personal defect or fault.

115. (p. 345) _____ reactions are defenses against feelings of inferiority. If directed at overcoming the deficiency itself, they may be constructive.

116. (p. 345) _____ is defined as working off frustrated desires in substitute activities that are constructive and accepted by society.

117. (p. 346) Freud believed that almost any strong desire can be sublimated, but that the most easily and widely sublimated motives are _____.

118. (p. 346) Bruno Bettelheim has described a reaction called "give-up-itis" which he observed among Nazi concentration camp prisoners who developed a "zombie-like" detachment from their situations. Martin Seligman has described a similar reaction in Vietnam prisoner of war camps. Recent attempts to understand such events have focused on the concept of _____ _____.

119. (p. 346) Learned helplessness has been demonstrated in the laboratory with animals. If placed in one side of a divided box, dogs will quickly learn to leap to the other to _____ an electric shock or to _____ the electric shock when given a warning in advance.

120. (p. 346) In learned helplessness, dogs first given several painful shocks which they were _____ to prevent, later would not escape or avoid shock when given the chance.

121. (p. 346) Similar effects occur when humans are made to fail or receive punishment they cannot predict or prevent. However, where humans are concerned, _____ have a large effect on helplessness. Helplessness in one situation can produce helplessness in other situations if people attribute their failure to lasting, general factors.

122. (p. 347) Seligman has drawn attention to the similarities between learned helplessness and _____. Symptoms that occur in both include feelings of powerlessness and hopelessness, decreased _____, lowered _____, loss of _____ drive and appetite, and a tendency to see oneself as failing, even when this is not the case.

123. (p. 347) With dogs, the most effective technique for eliminating learned helplessness has been to forcibly drag them away from the _____ into the "safe" compartment. After this is done several times, the animals regain "hope" and feelings of control over the environment.

124. (p. 347) When animals are given _____ _____ they become more resistant to learned helplessness. For example, animals that first learn to successfully escape shock are more persistent later in trying to escape inescapable shock.

125. (p. 347) Perhaps programs such as the _____ _____ schools might help immunize people against helplessness by giving them experience at mastering seemingly impossible challenges.

126. (p. 348) Hope is among the most important of all human emotions. In general, having positive beliefs, such as optimism, hope, and a sense of _____ and _____ is related to personal well-being.

127. (p. 348) Recent studies show that during the school year, up to _____ percent of the students enrolled at American colleges suffer some of the symptoms of depression.

128. (p. 348) At any given time, roughly _____-_____ of the student population is involved.

129. (p. 348) In a more recent survey, college students reported that they got depressed from one to two times a _____. These episodes lasted from a few hours to several days.

130. (p. 349) A variety of problems seem to be associated with this problem. Four common issues include: (1) stresses from increased difficulty of college work and pressures to make a _____ choice; (2) _____ and loneliness; (3) problems with studying and _____; and (4) breakups of intimate _____.

131. (p. 349) Aaron Beck points out five monitors of depression. These signals include: (1) a consistently _____ opinion of yourself; (2) frequent self-criticism and self-blame; (3) placing _____ interpretations on events; (4) the _____ looks bleak and negative; and (5) your _____ feel overwhelming.

132. (p. 349) As solutions for dealing with "college blues," Beck and Greenberg suggest that you start by making a _____ _____. Keeping busy often helps.

133. (p. 349) Also, try writing down self-critical and negative thoughts, especially those that immediately precede feelings of sadness. Then write a _____ answer to each.

134. (p. 349) Attacks of the college blues are common and should be distinguished from more serious cases of depression. The National Association for Mental Health lists _____ "danger signals" which can help distinguish normal from severe depression. Be familiar with them.

135. (p. 350) According to psychologist Robert Sternberg's triangular theory of love, love is made up of _____, _____, and commitment.

136. (p. 351) A relationship has intimacy, or closeness, if _____, sharing, _____, and support are present.

137. (p. 351) Intimacy grows _____ at first, but in time it _____ _____. After it does, people in long-term relationships may gradually lose sight of the fact that they are still very close and mutually dependent.

138. (p. 351) Passion refers mainly to _____ _____. It may be sexual, but it includes other sources too. Passion is the primary source of love's intensity.

139. (p. 351) Passionate love often occurs against a backdrop of danger, adversity, or frustration. Perhaps because of this, _____ inspires the strongest feelings of love, while love for _____ is least intense.

140. (p. 351) The third side of the love triangle, commitment, starts at zero before you meet a person and grows steadily as you get acquainted. Like intimacy, commitment tends to level off. It _____ rapidly when a relationship is in serious trouble.

141. (p. 351) The presence or absence of each factor in love produces eight different triangles. The first defines _____, a total absence of all three elements.

142. (p. 351) In _____, you feel close to a person and communicate well with her or him. However, you do not feel any passion or deep commitment to the person.

143. (p. 351) _____ love mixes intimacy with passion. Despite its intensity, it does not involve much commitment at first.

144. (p. 351) _____ love describes commitments made rapidly on the basis of physical attraction, but without much emotional intimacy. Relationships started this way risk failure because lovers make a commitment before they really get to know one another well.

145. (p. 351) _____ is a very superficial form of love in which a person is inflamed with passion but shares no intimacy or commitment with the beloved. In time, it may lead to more lasting kinds of love.

146. (p. 352) _____ love refers to affection and deep attachment that is built on respect, shared interests, and firm friendship. It is lower-key emotionally, steady, long-term, and tends to grow in time.

147. (p. 352) Couples sometimes reach a point where there is little passion or intimacy left in their relationship. If they stay together merely out of commitment or habit, they experience _____ love.

148. (p. 352) _____ love occurs when two people are passionate, committed to one another, and emotionally close. Complete, balanced love of this kind occurs only in very special relationships.

149. (p. 352) Other theorists have noted that Sternberg's theory may place too much emphasis on _____. In most relationships, intimacy and commitment are a bigger part of love.

150. (p. 352) Our culture also tends to place much emphasis on passion as the main basis for "falling" in love. However, this overlooks the fact that the passionate, breathless state of love typically lasts only about _____ to _____ months.

151. (p. 352) Sternberg and Michael Barnes found that relationships are generally _____ if you think the other person feels about you as you would like for her or him to feel about you.

SELF-TEST

1. (p. 327) Voodoo deaths are now thought to be caused by:
   a. witchcraft
   b. sympathetic nervous system arousal
   c. overreaction of the parasympathetic nervous system
   d. peripheral nervous system reversals

2. (p. 328) Emotions seem to have been retained in evolution because:
   a. they are simply residual behaviors transmitted from our animal heritage serving little purpose
   b. they underlie adaptive behaviors and generally are an aid to survival
   c. they primarily serve as universal communication facilitating cross-cultural interactions
   d. they are a by-product of our nervous system and as such evolved along with our neural structure

3. (p. 328) Physiological changes which underlie fear, anger, joy, and other emotions are primarily caused by:
   a. release of pituitary hormones into the bloodstream
   b. parasympathetic nervous system arousal
   c. the shutdown of the sympathetic nervous system
   d. release of adrenaline into the bloodstream

4. (p. 329) Which of the following is *not* true of Robert Plutchik's ideas concerning emotion?
   a. Primary emotions are primitive, less desirable emotions which are combined with more sophisticated elements in the higher species.
   b. Primary emotions can blend to produce a different more complex emotion.
   c. Each primary emotion can vary in intensity to produce other related emotions.
   d. There are eight primary emotions including fear, surprise, sadness, etc.

5. (p. 329) Unpleasant emotional reactions are all generated by the:
   a. peripheral nervous system
   b. autonomic nervous system
   c. automatic nervous system
   d. voluntary nervous system

6. (p. 330) True-False. The sympathetic branch of the ANS responds much more slowly than the parasympathetic branch.

7. (p. 330) Which of the following is *not* associated with the parasympathetic nervous system?
   a. preparations for "fight or night"
   b. reverses emotional arousal
   c. builds up and conserves bodily energy
   d. calm, and relax, the body

8. (p. 330) True-False. Not only is the notion that enlarged pupils occur with pleasant emotions untrue, people actually prefer the appearance of individuals with constricted pupils.

9. (p. 332) Which of the following is true of lie detectors?
   a. There are several unique lie responses they can measure.
   b. They are 90 to 95 percent accurate.
   c. The test's most common error is to label a guilty person innocent.
   d. Only a few states require polygraph operators to be licensed.

10. (p. 332) Of the following bodily changes, which is *not* usually measured by the polygraph?
     a. heart rate   c. blood pressure
     b. GSR   d. brain waves

11. (p. 334) Which of the following emotions appear to be unlearned?
     a. remorse, sadness, frustration   c. surprise, awe, excitement
     b. guilt, grief, greed   d. joy, rage, fear

12. (p. 334) Bridges has found that among human infants, all of the basic emotions appear before age:
     a. 6 months   c. 24 months
     b. 12 months   d. 36 months

13. (p. 334) True-False. Charles Darwin felt that human emotional expression was a carry-over from more primitive and animal-like stages of human evolution.

14. (p. 335) True-False. The ability to express emotion is highly learned and culturally dependent. For example, infants in China stick out their tongue as a gesture of surprise.

15. (p. 335) The most universal facial expression of emotion is:
     a. smiling   c. frowning
     b. grimacing   d. winking

16. (p. 335) Which of the following isnot true of kinesics?
     a. It is the study of communication through body movement, posture, gestures, and facial expressions.
     b. Generally, it can be accurately used to predict particular meanings from particular gestures.
     c. An overall emotional tone is usually communicated by body language.
     d. It is informally referred to as "body language."

17. (p. 336) Of the following, which is *not* a basic dimension of emotion conveyed by facial expressions?
     a. activation   c. attention-rejection
     b. pleasantness-unpleasantness   d. hope-disappointment

18. (p. 336) True-False. Because most people learn to maintain careful control over their facial expressions, a deception is better revealed by the lower body.

19. (p. 337) Which theory of emotion first stressed that emotional feelings follow bodily arousal?
     a. James-Lange theory
     b. Schachter-Singer cognitive theory
     c. attribution theory
     d. Cannon-Bard theory

20. (p. 337) The Cannon-Bard theory of emotion states that:
     a. emotional feelings follow bodily arousal
     b. the thalamus simultaneously activates the cortex and the hypothalamus
     c. perception of emotion depends on what feelings of physical arousal are attributed to
     d. emotion occurs when a particular label is applied to general physical arousal

21. (p. 337) True-False. According to Schachter's view of emotion it is the interpretation of physical arousal that determines the emotion experienced.

22. (p. 338) True-False. According to the idea of attribution, adding fear, anger, or frustration to a relationship tends to diminish a couple's feelings for each other.

23. (p. 342) Recordings of heart rate and GSR showed that viewers watching a graphic film called *Subincision* demonstrated the greatest emotional response when the film's soundtrack:
   a. was totally absent (silent)
   b. emphasized the painful and traumatic aspects of the operation
   c. treated the operation in an intellectual and distant way
   d. glossed over the threatening aspects of the operation and denied that it was painful

24. (p. 343) Test anxiety does *not* involve which of the following?
   a. overpreparation leading to superficial competency
   b. heightened physiological arousal
   c. excessive worry
   d. lowered test scores

25. (p. 343) Which of the following is a useful technique to use in lowering test anxiety?
   a. being overprepared
   b. changing self-defeating thinking patterns
   c. rehearsing how to cope with upsetting events
   d. all of the above

26. (p. 344) Which of the following is *not* true of psychological defense mechanisms?
   a. They prevent us from facing reality and should be actively avoided at all times.
   b. Many were first identified by Freud who assumed they operate unconsciously.
   c. They are used to avoid, deny, or distort sources of anxiety.
   d. They are commonly used to maintain an idealized self-image.

27. (p. 344) When you protect yourself from an unpleasant reality by refusing to perceive it, this process is called:
   a. repression   c. denial
   b. fantasy   d. sour grapes

28. (p. 344) When painful and dangerous thoughts are prevented from entering consciousness, this process is called:
   a. sublimation   c. delusion
   b. repression   d. projection

29. (p. 344) Reaction formation involves:
   a. preventing dangerous impulses from being expressed by exaggerating opposite behaviors
   b. reacting to the formation of anxiety-producing mental images by denying they exist
   c. attempts to overcome a deficiency or weakness by excelling in other areas
   d. working off frustrated desires in substitute activities that are constructive and accepted by society

30. (p. 345) Retreating to an earlier level of development or to earlier, less demanding habits or situations is called:
   a. suppression   c. projection
   b. repression   d. regression

31. (p. 345) _____ as a defense mechanism means attributing to others one's own shortcomings or unacceptable feelings.
   a. Projection   c. Sublimation
   b. Compensation   d. Rationalization

32. (p. 345) Counteracting a real or imagined weakness by emphasizing desirable traits or by seeking to excel in others defines the process of:
     a. compensation   c. reaction formation
     b. rationalization   d. sublimation

33. (p. 345) _____ is defined as working off frustrated desires in substitute activities that are constructive or socially acceptable.
     a. Sublimation   c. Rationalization
     b. Compensation   d. Projection

34. (p. 345) Learned helplessness may result when unpleasant events frequently occur which:
     a. cannot be controlled by the individual
     b. are attributed to the negative behaviors of the individual
     c. produce high fear levels in the individual
     d. are not adapted to by the individual

35. (p. 345) Which of the following is a reasonable example of learned helplessness?
     a. Concentration camp survivors suffering what Bettelheim called "give-up-itis."
     b. Laboratory animals which do not escape or avoid shocks when possible after first receiving unavoidable shocks.
     c. Depression in humans accompanied by feelings of powerlessness and marked by passive endurance of psychological shocks.
     d. All of the above.

36. (p. 348) True-False. Mild depression among college students is relatively common since roughly one-quarter of the student population is involved at any given time.

37. (p. 349) Which of the following is *not* a common reason for depression among college students?
     a. lack of financial resources and tight budgets
     b. breakup of an intimate relationship
     c. isolation and loneliness
     d. pressures to make career choices

38. (p. 350) Which of the following is *not* an element defined by Sternberg as part of his triangular theory of love?
     a. commitment   c. arousal
     b. passion   d. intimacy

39. (p. 351) Sternberg refers to _____ love as affection and deep attachment that is built on respect, shared interests, and firm friendship.
     a. consummate   c. romantic
     b. companionate   d. fatuous

40. (p. 351) Which of the following is *not* true of Sternberg's concept of passion?
     a. It refers mainly to physiological arousal and is the primary source of love's intensity.
     b. It is the main element of infatuation where neither intimacy nor commitment is involved.
     c. Couples who have only strong passion left in their relationships are said to experience empty love.
     d. Other theorists have suggested that Sternberg's theory places too much emphasis on passion.

APPLYING YOUR KNOWLEDGE

1.   Now that you've learned about psychological defense mechanisms do you see examples of them in yourself and others? Keep a log of different examples you find in your own behavior and that your observe among other people. Are some defenses more common than others? Do certain types of situations tend to prompt one type or another?

2.   Martin Seligman has drawn attention to the similarities between learned helplessness and depression. Research in this area suggests that mastery training may help. The Outward Bound schools are one such type of mastery training program. See what you can find out about what Outward Bound schools actually do. Are there other programs like this that you can find information about?

ANSWERS—PROGRAMMED REVIEW

1.   emotion
2.   parasympathetic nervous
3.   good; happy
4.   move; physically
5.   adaptive
6.   survival
7.   rate; pressure
8.   adrenaline
9.   Emotional expressions
10. emotional feelings
11. primary
12. intensity
13. moods
14. mixed
15. innate
16. autonomic nervous system
17. sympathetic; parasympathetic
18. sympathetic; fighting; fleeing
19. Sugar; muscles; digestion; bleeding
20. parasympathetic
21. bodily energy
22. slowly; 20; 30
23. blood pressure
24. pupils
25. large; small
26. large; small
27. larger pupils
28. parasympathetic rebound
29. terror
30. sympathetic activation
31. half
32. polygraph
33. doubtful; privacy

34. rate; pressure; rate; galvanic skin response
35. emotional arousal
36. irrelevant; baseline
37. critical
38. control
39. inaccurate
40. 90; 95; 25
41. tranquilizing
42. 1; 5; 75
43. job applicants; private business
44. excitement
45. two
46. pleasant, unpleasant
47. one
48. pressure; perspiration
49. brain
50. Darwin
51. deaf, blind
52. surprise
53. smile
54. kinesics
55. emotional tone
56. facial blends
57. pleasantness-unpleasantness; attention-rejection; activation
58. relaxation, tension; liking, disliking
59. Relaxation; Liking
60. successful
61. lower body
62. shifty; squirming; nervous movements
63. illustrators
64. emblems
65. blinking; pupil; breathing; speech

66. James-Lange
67. Cannon-Bard
68. cortex; hypothalamus
69. cognitive
70. label
71. adrenaline; tranquilizer
72. attribute
73. pounding heart
74. increase
75. more
76. facial feedback
77. Exercise
78. autonomic
79. raised; lowered
80. smile
81. smile
82. appraisal
83. appraised; ANS arousal
84. innate emotional
85. adaptive; subjective
86. external; internal
87. primary appraisal; secondary appraisal
88. Subincision
89. four
90. traumatic; increase
91. reduced
92. Problem-focused; Emotion-focused
93. problem-focused
94. controllable; control
95. physiological arousal; worry
96. threat
97. hard work
98. overprepare
99. relax
100. rehearsing
101. self-defeating
102. anxiety

103. defense mechanisms
104. self-image
105. unconsciously
106. denial
107. death, illness
108. repression
109. Reaction formation
110. regression; speech; wetting; play
111. Projection
112. rationalizing
113. emotional; cope
114. compensation
115. Compensatory
116. Sublimation
117. sexual
118. learned helplessness
119. escape; avoid

120. helpless
121. attributions
122. depression; activity; aggression; sexual
123. shock
124. mastery training
125. Outward Bound
126. meaning, control
127. 78
128. one-quarter
129. month
130. career; isolation; grades; relationships
131. negative; negative; future; responsibilities
132. daily schedule
133. rational
134. ten

135. intimacy; passion
136. affection; communication
137. steadily; levels off
138. physiological arousal
139. romance; siblings
140. drops
141. nonlove
142. liking
143. Romantic
144. Fatuous
145. Infatuation
146. Companionate
147. empty
148. Consummate
149. passion
150. 6, 30
151. satisfying

ANSWERS—SELF-TEST

1.	c	8.	False	15.	a	22.	False	29.	a	36.	True
2.	b	9.	d	16.	b	23.	b	30.	d	37.	a
3.	d	10.	d	17.	d	24.	a	31.	a	38.	c
4.	a	11.	d	18.	True	25.	d	32.	a	39.	b
5.	b	12.	c	19.	a	26.	a	33.	a	40.	c
6.	False	13.	True	20.	b	27.	c	34.	a		
7.	a	14.	False	21.	True	28.	b	35.	d		

ACROSS

1. American college students may suffer from symptoms of _____
4. justifying one's own behavior by giving reasonable, yet false reasons for it
6. branch of ANS prepares one for "fight or flight"
9. American functionalist believed one experiences an emotion after reacting
10. galvanic skin response (abbr.)
11. autonomic nervous system (abbr.)
14. "don't believe it"—a defense mechanism
15. hormone that stimulates sympathetic nervous system

DOWN

2. working off frustrated desires in a socially acceptable manner
3. study of communication via body movements
4. return to an earlier behavior
5. attributing one's own feelings, shortcomings, or unacceptable impulses to others
7. gestures that have clear meanings within a particular culture
8. defense mechanism used to make up for personal defect or weakness
12. he described cognitive theory of emotions
13. lie detector

Health, Stress, & Coping

CONTENTS

TERMS AND CONCEPTS

frustration
stress
stress reaction
pressure
job burnout
external frustration
social obstacles
nonsocial obstacles
personal frustration
displaced aggression
scapegoating
conflict
approach-approach conflicts
avoidance-avoidance conflicts
approach-avoidance conflicts
ambivalence
partial approach
double approach-avoidance conflicts
multiple approach-avoidance conflicts
Social Readjustment Rating Scale (SRRS)
life change unit (LCU)
hassles (microstressors)
acculturative stress
psychosomatic disorders

hypochondria
Type A personality
Type B personality
hardy personality
general adaptation syndrome (G.A.S.)
alarm reaction
stage of resistance
stage of exhaustion
psychoneuroimmunology
health psychology
behavioral medicine
behavioral risk factors
community health campaigns
stress management
progressive relaxation
stress inoculation
coping statements
negative self-statements
stereotyped response
concentrative meditation
receptive meditation
mantra
relaxation response

IMPORTANT INDIVIDUALS

Christina Maslach
Thomas Holmes
Richard Lazarus
Meyer Friedman

Ray Rosenman
Redford Williams
Salvatore Maddi
Suzanne Kobasa

Hanse Selye
Donald Meichenbaum
Herbert Benson

PROGRAMMED REVIEW

1. (p. 355) _____ is defined as a negative emotional state that occurs when one is prevented from reaching a _____.

2. (p. 356) _____ occurs whenever a challenge or a threat forces a person to adjust or adapt. While it is a normal part of life, it can do tremendous damage to one's health when it is severe or prolonged.

3. (p. 356) It is common to assume that stress is always _____, or that a complete _____ of stress is ideal. While unpleasant events do produce stress, so do travel, sports, dating, and other pleasant activities. A healthy lifestyle may include a fair amount of stress.

4. (p. 356) Your body's stress _____ begins with the same autonomic nervous system arousal that occurs during emotions. ANS responses include a rapid surge in your heart rate, blood pressure, respiration, muscle tension, etc.

5. (p. 356) _____-term stresses can be uncomfortable, but they rarely do any damage. _____-term physical changes can accompany prolonged stress. These changes can do much harm.

6. (p. 356) A major factor in stress is _____. This factor was shown in a laboratory experiment in which rats given shocks without warning developed severe ulcers.

7. (p. 356) _____ is another element in stress. It occurs when activities must be speeded up, when deadlines must be met, when extra work is added unexpectedly, or when a person must work at, or near, capacity for long periods.

8. (p. 356) People generally feel more stress in situations over which they have little _____. For example, DeGood found that among students subjected to an unpleasant shock-avoidance learning task, those subjects allowed to select their own rest periods showed _____ stress levels (as measured by blood pressure) than those who could not.

9. (p. 357) Ultimately, stress depends on how a situation is perceived. Whenever a stressor is appraised as a _____, a powerful stress reaction follows.

10. (p. 357) The concept of "threat" does not mean that you believe your life is in danger. Rather threat has more to do with the idea of control. _____ control is just as important as _____ control in causing us to feel threatened by events.

11. (p. 357) Your personal sense of control in any situation comes from believing that you have the power to reach desired goals. It is threatening for a person to feel that he or she lacks _____ to meet a particular demand.

12. (p. 357) The _____ of the body's stress reaction often depends on what we think and tell ourselves about stressors. This is why it can be valuable to train yourself to think in ways that avoid triggering the body's stress response.

13. (p. 357) At work, prolonged stress sometimes results in job _____, a condition that exists when an employee is physically, mentally, and emotionally drained.

14. (p. 357) Christina Maslach has identified three aspects of this problem. First, burnout involves _____ _____. Affected persons are fatigued, tense, apathetic, and suffer from various physical complaints.

15. (p. 357) A second aspect of burnout is _____, or detachment from others. "Burned-out" workers coldly treat clients as if they were objects and find it difficult to care about them.

16. (p. 357) The third aspect of burnout is a feeling of reduced _____ _____. Workers who have burned out do poor work, their self-esteem suffers, and they yearn to change jobs or careers.

17. (p. 357) Burnout may occur in any job but is a marked problem in emotionally-demanding _____ professions, such as nursing, teaching, social work, counseling, or police work.

18. (p. 358) To help prevent burnout, a good start might include redesigning jobs, workloads, and responsibilities to create a better balance between demands and satisfactions. Building stronger _____ _____ systems at work could also help.

19. (p. 358) A good example of social support systems is the growing use of _____ _____ by nurses and other caregivers. These allow workers to give and receive emotional support as they talk about feelings, problems, and stresses.

20. (p. 358) _____ frustration is based on conditions outside of the individual which impede progress toward a goal. They are based upon delay, _____, _____, _____, and other direct blocking of motives.

21. (p. 358) External obstacles can be either _____ (in which case other people's behavior is the source) or _____ (in which case events or situations are the source).

22. (p. 358) The amount of frustration experienced usually increases as the _____, _____, or _____ of the blocked motive increases.

23. (p. 358) _____ becomes stronger as we near a goal. Therefore, frustration is more intense when a person encounters an obstacle very close to a goal.

24. (p. 358) _____ frustrations can accumulate in their effect until a small irritation unleashes an unexpectedly violent response.

25. (p. 358) _____ frustrations are based on an individual's personal characteristics. They are ultimately based on personal limitations, although the resulting failures may be perceived as externally caused frustrations.

26. (p. 358) Although aggression is a common response to frustration, there are several others. The first response is usually _____, characterized by more vigorous efforts and more variable responses.

27. (p. 359) Increased persistence can be very adaptive. The same is true of aggression that removes or destroys a barrier. However, since aggression can be disruptive and is generally discouraged, it is frequently _____.

28. (p. 359) Targets of displaced aggression tend to be "safer" or less likely to retaliate than the original source of frustration. Sometimes long _____ of displaced aggression, in which one person displaces aggression to the next, can be observed.

29. (p. 359) Psychologists attribute much hostility and destructiveness in our society to displaced aggression. A disturbing example is the finding that when unemployment increases, so does _____ _____.

30. (p. 359) A particularly damaging form of displaced aggression is _____, in which a person becomes a habitual target of redirected aggression. For example, between 1880 and 1930 there was a strong correlation between the price of _____ and the number of _____ in the South.

31. (p. 359) Another major reaction to frustration is _____ or withdrawal—either physically or psychologically leaving the frustrating situation.

32. (p. 359) Two common forms of psychological escape are _____ (pretending not to care) and the use of _____.

33. (p. 359) _____ occurs whenever a person must choose between incompatible or contradictory needs, desires, motives, wishes, or external demands.

34. (p. 359) The simplest conflict comes from having to choose between two positive, or desirable, alternatives and is called _____-_____ conflict.

35. (p. 360) Approach-approach conflicts tend to be the _____ to resolve. When both options are positive, the scales of decision are _____ tipped in one direction or the other.

36. (p. 360) When forced to choose between two negative, or undesirable, alternatives an _____-_____ conflict develops.

37. (p. 361) These conflicts can be defined only on the basis of a personal _____ and _____.

38. (p. 361) When faced with severe avoidance-avoidance conflict in which there is no escape, people often _____, finding it impossible to make a decision or to take action.

39. (p. 361) In cases where escape is possible, people may react to avoidance-avoidance conflicts by _____ the _____ so as to pull out of avoidance situations entirely.

40. (p. 361) In an _____-_____ conflict a person is attracted to, and repelled by, the same goal or activity.

41. (p. 361) In these situations, a person will feel _____ (mixed positive and negative feelings) toward the goal. This experience is usually translated into _____ approach.

42. (p. 361) The most typical of the choices we usually must make is known as _____ _____-_____ conflicts because each alternative has both positive and negative qualities.

43. (p. 361) When faced with this situation, people tend to _____ or waiver between the alternatives.

44. (p. 361) In real life it is common to face _____ approach-avoidance conflicts in which several alternatives each have positive and negative features. Most of these are little more than an annoyance, but when they involve major life decisions, they can add greatly to the amount of stress experienced.

45. (p. 362) Thomas Holmes has demonstrated that stressful events reduce the body's natural defenses against disease and increase the likelihood of _____. Disaster and sorrow often precede illness.

46. (p. 362) More surprising is the finding that almost any major _____ in one's life requires adjustment and increases susceptibility to accident and illness.

47. (p. 362) Holmes and his associates have developed the _____ _____ _____ _____ (SRRS) to help determine the health hazards faced when stresses accumulate.

48. (p. 362) The SRRS expresses the effect of life events in _____ _____ _____ (LCUs).

49. (p. 362) If the total LCUs for events experienced during the past year exceeds _____, there is a high chance of illness or accident in the near future. A more conservative rating can be obtained by totalling LCUs for just the past six months.

50. (p. 363) The SRRS tends to be more appropriate for _____, more established adults. However, recent research has shown that entering college, changing majors, or breaking up a steady relationship can affect the health of younger adults.

51. (p. 363) The SRRS is not a foolproof way to rate stress and does have limitations. Some studies have _____ to confirm the LCU-illness link. Also, it is debatable whether _____ life events are always stressful. Another very important criticism is that people differ greatly in their reactions to the same event.

52. (p. 363) Richard Lazarus has studied the impact of minor but frequent stresses referred to as _____, or _____.

53. (p. 364) In a year-long study involving _____ men and women, Lazarus found that frequent and severe hassles were better predictors of day-to-day psychological and physical health than were major life events.

54. (p. 364) Major life events, however, did predict changes in health _____ or _____ years after the events took place.

55. (p. 364) Thus, it appears that daily hassles are closely linked to _____ health and psychological well-being. Major life changes have more of a _____-_____ impact.

56. (p. 364) Lazarus found that the personal importance of hassles affects the amount of stress they produce. Hassles that are _____ to one's self worth (such as work, family, and relationships) are most likely to cause trouble.

57. (p. 364) Stress occurs in people, not in the environment. Stress is always related to _____, _____, perceptions, and personal resources.

58. (p. 364) Around the world, an increasing number of emigrants and refugees must adapt to dramatic changes in language, dress, values, and social customs. For many, the result is a period of culture shock or _____ stress, marked by confusion, anxiety, hostility, depression, alienation, physical illness, or identity confusion.

59. (p. 364) The severity of acculturative stress is related, in part, to how a person adapts to a new culture. Four main patterns are: (1) _____—maintain your old cultural identity but participate in the new culture; (2) _____—maintain your old cultural identity and avoid contact with the new culture; (3) _____—adopt the new culture as your own and have contact with its members; and (4) _____—reject your old culture but suffer rejection by members of the new culture.

60. (p. 364) Those who feel marginalized tend to be _____ stressed; those who seek to remain separate are also _____ stressed; those who pursue integration into their new culture are _____ stressed; and those who assimilate are _____ stressed.

61. (p. 365) Prolonged stress reactions are related to a large number of _____ _____ in which psychological and emotional factors are associated with actual damage to tissues of the body.

62. (p. 365) Psychosomatic problems, such as ulcers, are not the same as _____ where a person imagines that they suffer from diseases.

63. (p. 365) The most common psychosomatic problems are gastrointestinal and _____, but other major problems include _____ (skin rash), hives, migraine headaches, rheumatoid arthritis, _____ (high blood pressure), _____ (ulceration of the colon), and heart disease.

64. (p. 365) Lesser health complaints that may be stress-related include muscle _____, headaches, neckaches, backaches, _____, constipation, fatigue, insomnia, and sexual _____.

65. (p. 365) It is estimated that at least _____ of all patients who go to a doctor either have a psychosomatic problem, or have a problem complicated by psychosomatic symptoms.

66. (p. 365) Usually several other factors combine with stress to produce physical damage. These factors include _____ differences, specific _____ weaknesses, and _____ reactions to stress.

67. (p. 365) Two noted cardiologists, Meyer Friedman and Ray Rosenman, have conducted long-term studies of personality and _____ problems.

68. (p. 365) They classified people into two categories: _____ _____ personalities (those who run a high risk of heart attack), and _____ _____ personalities (those unlikely to have heart attacks).

69. (p. 365) After an eight year follow-up, they found that the rate of heart disease among Type A's was more than _____ that among Type B's.

70. (p. 365) Type A people are hard-driving, ambitious, highly competitive, achievement oriented, and striving. Type A's work closer to their actual limits of endurance (on a treadmill), but say they are _____ _____ than do Type B people.

71. (p. 365) Type A's are characterized by _____ _____. They seem unsatisfied with the normal pace of events. They race the clock in self-imposed urgency.

72. (p. 365) Another characteristic of Type A's is their chronic _____ or _____. These feelings are strongly related to increased risk of heart attack.

73. (p. 365) One study found that _____ percent of a group of 25-year-old doctors and lawyers who scored high on a hostility test were dead by age 50.

74. (p. 365) While it is true that some recent studies have failed to show a link between Type A behavior and heart attacks, _____ of studies have supported the validity of the Type A concept. Many researchers believe it is possible that those studies which failed may not have accurately classified people as Type As and Bs in the first place.

75. (p. 365) There is growing evidence that _____ or _____ may be more important than other aspects of Type A behavior. Whatever the factors, it seems that Type A's would be wise to take their increased health risks seriously.

76. (p. 366) A large-scale study of heart attack victims found that modifying Type A behavior significantly _____ the rate of repeat heart attacks.

77. (p. 366) Many of the destructive habits of Type A people are summarized in the self-identification test presented in the text. The best way to avoid the self-made stress caused by Type A personality is to adopt behavior that is the _____ of these destructive habits.

78. (p. 366) According to Redford Williams, reducing hostility involves three goals: (1) You must stop _____ the motives of others; (2) You must find ways to _____ how often you feel anger, indignation, irritation, and rage; and (3) You must learn to be kinder and more _____ of others. Williams recommends 12 strategies for reducing hostility and increasing trust. You should be aware of them.

79. (p. 367) For the last 10 years, psychologists Salvatore Maddi and Suzanne Kobasa have studied people with a _____ _____. Such people seem to be unusually resistant to stress.

80. (p. 367) People with hardy personalities seem to hold a world view that consists of the following:
     1) They have a personal _____ to self, work, family, and other stabilizing values.
     2) They feel they have _____ over their lives and their work
     3) They have a tendency to see life as a series of _____ rather than as threats or problems.

81. (p. 367) The answer to how stress causes physical damage seems to lie in the body's defense against stress, a pattern of reactions known as the _____ _____ _____, abbreviated _____.

82. (p. 367) Study of the G.A.S. began when physiologist Hans Selye noticed that the initial symptoms of almost any disease or trauma are almost _____.

83. (p. 367) The first stage of the G.A.S. is called the _____ _____. During this stage the body mobilizes its defenses against stress.

84. (p. 367) During this first phase, the pituitary gland secretes a hormone that causes the adrenal glands to increase their output of _____ and _____, which speed up some bodily processes and slow down others to concentrate resources where needed.

85. (p. 367) During the alarm reaction, people experience such symptoms as headache, fever, fatigue, sore _____, shortness of _____, diarrhea, upset _____, loss of _____ and lack of _____.

86. (p. 367) If stress continues, the second stage, called the _____ of _____, begins. At this point the body's defenses are stabilized and symptoms disappear, but resistance to other stresses may be lowered.

87. (p. 367) Research demonstrates that animals placed in an extremely cold environment become more resistant to the cold, but more susceptible to _____.

88. (p. 367) It is during this second stage that the first signs of _____ disorders begin to appear.

89. (p. 368) If stress continues, the _____ of _____ may be reached. In this stage, the body's resources are exhausted and a psychosomatic disorder, organ failure, or complete collapse results.

90. (p. 368) Animals examined by Selye during the latter stages of the G.A.S. showed enlargement and discoloration of their _____ _____, intense shrinkage of the _____, spleen and lymph nodes, and deep bleeding _____ _____.

91. (p. 368) In addition to such direct effects, there is growing evidence that stress can disrupt the body's _____ _____, making people more susceptible to illness.

92. (p. 368) The area of research called _____ is beginning to uncover evidence that the body and the brain work together as a kind of "health care system."

93. (p. 368) The body's immune system is regulated, in part, by the brain. Stress, upsetting _____, and _____ may affect this link in ways that increase susceptibility to disease.

94. (p. 368) _____ appears to be an important factor in how stress affects us. For instance, one recent study found that immune system response was suppressed in rats given inescapable shocks but not in rats given escapable shocks.

95. (p. 368) Other studies have found that the immune system was _____ in students during major exam times, and by _____, bereavement, a troubled marriage and similar stresses. Such findings suggest that part of the link between stress and illness may be traced to changes in the immune system.

96. (p. 369) Almost one-half of all deaths in the United States are primarily due to unhealthy behavior or lifestyles. A new specialty called _____ _____ aims to do something about it by using psychological principles to promote health and prevent illness.

97. (p. 369) Psychologists working in the allied field of _____ _____ apply psychological knowledge to medical problems. Their interests include the control of pain, adjustment to chronic illness, adherence to doctors' instructions, psychosomatic disease, and similar topics.

98. (p. 369) Around the turn of the century, people primarily died from infectious diseases and accidents. Today, people generally suffer and die from "lifestyle" illnesses such as _____ disease, stroke, _____ cancer, and similar problems.

99. (p. 369) Health psychologists have identified a number of major _____ _____ factors such as stress, untreated high _____ pressure, cigarette smoking, abuse of alcohol or other drugs, overeating, Type A behavior, _____, and driving at excessive speeds.

100. (p. 369) There may also exist a general _____ _____ personality style, marked by depression, anxiety, and hostility.

101. (p. 369) Unhealthy lifestyles almost always create _____ _____. That is, people who smoke are also likely to drink excessively. Those who overeat usually do not get enough exercise, and so on.

102. (p. 370) To help prevent disease and promote well-being, health psychologists first try to remove behavioral risk factors. They are also interested in _____ behaviors that actively promote health including such practices as getting regular _____ maintaining a balanced _____, managing stress, etc.

103. (p. 370) In a major study, nearly 7000 people were given a detailed health questionnaire that focused on seven basic health practices. The outcome showed that men who engaged in all seven health practices had a death rate almost _____ times lower than that of men who engaged in zero to three practices.

104. (p. 370) The death rate for women who engaged in all seven practices was _____ times lower than that for women who engaged in zero to three practices.

105. (p. 370) Smoking provides a good example of the behavioral possibilities of preventing illness. Smoking has been called "the largest preventable cause of death in the U.S." It is clearly the single most _____ behavioral risk factor.

106. (p. 370) Only 1 smoker in _____ has long-term success in quitting. Thus, the best way to deal with smoking may be to prevent it before it becomes a lifelong habit.

107. (p. 370) A study of 7th, 9th, and 10th grade students found that habitual smoking develops _____. This makes it possible to expose young people to refusal skills training and other prevention efforts.

108. (p. 370) In one prevention program, junior high students were given "standard" information on the unhealthy effects of smoking. Then, the students role played ways to resist pressures to smoke. These students were only _____ as likely to begin smoking as were students in a control group.

109. (p. 370) Psychologists have had some success with _____ _____ campaigns— educational projects designed to lessen a combination of major risk factors.

110. (p. 370) A good example is the Stanford Heart Disease Prevention Program. A media campaign about risk factors in heart disease was combined with special group workshops for high-risk individuals. After two years, the number of smokers had decreased by _____ percent in the test community, compared with a _____ percent increase observed in untreated communities.

111. (p. 371) While the progress of the Stanford program may seem modest, it is worthwhile, cost-effective, and highly promising. Overall, results of the project show a _____ percent reduction in risk of heart disease in the target cities.

112. (p. 372) Stress triggers _____ effects, upsetting _____ and _____ behavior. Each element worsens the others in a vicious cycle. This is why learning to manage stress is so important.

113. (p. 372) Much of the immediate discomfort of stress is caused by the body's fight-or-flight emotional response. When action is prevented, we merely remain "uptight." A sensible remedy is to learn a reliable, drugfree way of _____.

114. (p. 372) Relaxing might be accomplished through vigorous exercise, meditation, or a technique called _____ relaxation in which people learn to relax systematically, completely, and by choice.

115. (p. 372) Stress also triggers ineffective behavior. Suggestions which may help you deal with stress more effectively include slow down, _____, strike a _____, recognize and accept your _____ and seek _____ support.

116. (p. 374) Recent studies have shown that close, positive relationships with others facilitate good _____ and _____. Support serves as a buffer to cushion the impact of stressful events.

117. (p. 374) A recent study found that students who merely wrote down their thoughts and feelings about starting college were _____ _____ to cope with stress. They also experienced fewer _____.

118. (p. 374) One further effect stress has is to trigger upsetting thoughts. This problem can be treated using the technique developed by Donald Meichenbaum called _____ _____.

119. (p. 374) Meichenbaum's method helps clients first learn to identify and monitor negative _____- _____ and then to develop an internal monologue of positive _____ statements.

120. (p. 375) A psychologist studying frustration forced rats to jump off a platform toward two elevated doors, one of which was randomly locked and caused the animal to bounce off and fall into a net, the other of which led to safety. Most rats adopted a _____ _____ of choosing the same door every time, even when this door was later permanently locked.

121. (p. 375) Persistence is different from stereotyped responding. Persistence that is not _____ can lead to stereotyped responses. It is important to know when to quit and establish a new direction.

122. (p. 375) There are several suggestions to help avoid needless frustration:
     1) Try to identify the _____ of your frustration.
     2) Is it something that can be changed?
     3) If it can be changed, is the effort worth it?
     4) Is there a real or imagined _____?

123. (p. 375) There are four additional suggestions which apply to conflict:
     1) Don't be _____ when making important decisions.
     2) Try out important decisions _____ when possible.
     3) Look for workable _____.
     4) When all else fails, make a decision and live with it.

124. (p. 376) _____ refers to a family of mental exercises designed to focus attention in a way that interrupts the typical flow of thoughts, worries, and analysis. People who regularly use it as a stress-reduction technique often report less daily physical arousal and anxiety.

125. (p. 376) In _____ meditation, attention is given to a single focal point, such as an object, a thought, or one's own breathing.

126. (p. 376) More difficult to attain is _____ meditation, wherein attention is widened to include a nonjudgmental awareness of one's total subjective experience and presence in the world.

127. (p. 376) In one experiment, college students were instructed to concentrate on breathing. At the end of a two-week period, many reported experiences of deep _____, pleasant _____ sensations, and extreme detachment from outside worries and distractions.

128. (p. 376) An alternative approach involves the use of a _____—smooth, flowing words that are easily repeated. Like breathing, this approach is basically used as a focus for attention.

129. (p. 376) Herbert Benson believes that the benefits of meditation are the same no matter what word is used for a mantra. He believes that the core of meditation is production of the _____ _____, an innate physiological pattern that opposes the stressful activation of the body's fight-or-flight mechanisms.

130. (p. 377) Many extravagant claims have been made about meditation. For example, members of the Transcendental Meditation movement have stated that _____ minutes of meditation are as restful as a night's sleep. However, one recent study found that merely "_____" for 20 minutes produces the same bodily effects as meditation.

131. (p. 377) Long-term meditators have also claimed improvements in memory, alertness, creativity, and intuition. However, a recent study by Warrenburg and Pagano found no improvements in _____, _____, or _____ skills that could be linked to TM.

132. (p. 377) There is some evidence that those who meditate regularly react _____ _____ to stressful stimuli during laboratory testing. However, they recover faster than nonmeditators, and say they feel less stressed.

133. (p. 377) Benson believes that the key elements for producing the relaxation responses are: (1) a _____ environment; (2) decreased _____ tension; (3) a mental device that helps shift thoughts away from ordinary, rational concerns; and (4) a _____ attitude toward whether you are "succeeding" at becoming relaxed.

Self-Test

1. (p. 356) Which of the following is *not* true of stress?
    a. A healthy lifestyle may include a fair amount of stress.
    b. Stress occurs anytime we must adjust or adapt to the environment.
    c. Stress may become harmful in threatening situations that are unpredictable.
    d. Stress is almost always harmful; complete lack of stress is ideal.

2. (p. 356) Which of the following can produce stress?
    a. pressure   c. lack of control
    b. unpredictability   d. all of the above

3. (p. 357) Which of the following is *not* an aspect of job burnout as identified by Christina Maslach?
    a. depersonalization   c. reduced personal accomplishment
    b. stereotyped responding   d. emotional exhaustion

4. (p. 358) You have been preparing for an examination on very difficult material. You have wisely scheduled your time so as to have just enough and then your teacher moves up the date of the examination. You will probably suffer which type of frustration?
    a. external   c. conflicted
    b. personal   d. impersonal

5. (p. 358) Which of the following is *not* true of factors affecting frustration?
    a. External obstacles that produce frustration may be either social or non-social.
    b. Repeated frustrations can accumulate in their effect until a small irritation produces a violent response.
    c. Frustration usually increases as the strength, urgency, or importance of a blocked motive increases.
    d. Frustration is usually less intense as we near a goal.

6. (p. 358) Personal frustrations refer to:
    a. specific frustrations you personally experience because of other people's behavior
    b. how you personally interpret an event—some people find certain situations frustrating, while others do not
    c. frustrations based on an individual's personal characteristics
    d. intense frustrations produced by those to whom you are closest—family, friends, etc.

7. (p. 358) True-False. Aggression followed by persistence is usually how people react to frustration.

8. (p. 359) When you get an "F" on a test and then insult the person sitting next to you, you are showing _____ aggression.
    a. repressed   c. displaced
    b. suppressed   d. replaced

9. (p. 359) Minorities have often served as _____ for the aggressions of whole societies.
    a. examples   c. facilitators
    b. scapegoats   d. primers

10. (p. 359) When you can't decide whether to attend a particular movie or play because both are very good, you may experience:
    a. approach-avoidance conflict   c. avoidance-avoidance conflict
    b. approach-approach conflict   d. double approach conflict

11. (p. 360) Which of the following is *not* true of avoidance-avoidance conflicts?
     a. They may occur when people are forced to choose between two negative alternatives.
     b. They tend to be the easiest conflicts to resolve even though they are usually stressful.
     c. When faced with such conflicts, people often freeze.
     d. People sometimes react to this situation by leaving the field.

12. (p. 361) Ambivalence expressed in partial approach is often seen in:
     a. approach-approach conflicts   c. avoidance-avoidance conflicts
     b. approach-avoidance conflicts   d. double approach-avoidance conflicts

13. (p. 361) Faced with a double approach-avoidance conflict we would most likely observe that people:
     a. partially approach   c. leave the field
     b. freeze   d. vacillate

14. (p. 362) A high number of LCUs on the _____ indicates increased chance of illness or accident.
     a. G.A.S.   c. S.R.R.S.
     b. S.S.S.   d. none of the above

15. (p. 363) Which of the following is *not* true of hassles as studied by Richard Lazarus?
     a. They are distressing, daily annoyances.
     b. Central hassles are most likely to cause significant stress.
     c. Hassles are better predictors of day-to-day psychological and physical health than are major life events.
     d. Hassles can produce a ripple effect—that is, countless daily frustrations and irritations can spring from an original hassle.

16. (p. 365) True-False. Psychological stress can cause psychological problems, but rarely causes physical illness.

17. (p. 365) Which of the following is *not* true of psychosomatic disorders?
     a. The most common are gastrointestinal and respiratory.
     b. About one-half or more of all medical patients either have a psychosomatic disorder or a condition complicated by them.
     c. Stress is not the sole cause of psychosomatic disease.
     d. Hypochondria is a form of psychosomatic illness.

18. (p. 365) True-False. Type A personalities frequently suffer from a sense of time urgency.

19. (p. 365) There is now growing evidence that which of the following may be the most important aspect of Type A behavior?
     a. The Type A's inability to slow down and accommodate to the normal pace of events.
     b. The Type A's constant state of anger and hostility.
     c. The fact that Type A's are overly competitive and achievement oriented.
     d. The fact that Type A's are hard-driving, ambitious, and push themselves to their limits of endurance.

20. (p. 367) The hardy personality as defined by Maddi and Kobasa is characterized by all of the following *except*:
     a. personal commitment to self, work, family, and other stabilizing values
     b. tendency to see life as a series of challenges
     c. lack of Type A personality characteristics
     d. feelings of control over their lives and work

21. (p. 367) The three stages of the G.A.S. are:
    a.   alarm reaction, psychosomatic stage, stage of exhaustion
    b.   burnout, alarm reaction, stage of exhaustion
    c.   alarm reaction, stage of resistance, stage of exhaustion
    d.   burnout, psychosomatic stage, stage of adaptation

22. (p. 367) Which of the following is *not* a correct association?
    a.   alarm reaction—secretion of pituitary hormone that increases adrenal gland output of adrenaline and noradrenaline
    b.   stage of exhaustion—stress hormones depleted, psychosomatic disease, organ failure, or serious loss of health may occur
    c.   stage of resistance—job burnout with chronic fatigue and apathy
    d.   stage of resistance—body coping with original stressor but more susceptible to effects of other stressors

23. (p. 368) True-False. Psychoneuroimmunology is a new field of research that seeks to discover how various personality characteristics associated with poor stress tolerance can be altered by neurological techniques or immunological alterations.

24. (p. 369) All of the following are associated with health psychology *except*:
    a.   community health campaigns
    b.   identification of behavioral risk factors
    c.   use of behavioral methods to promote health and treat disease
    d.   facilitation of peak performances

25. (p. 370) Which of the following is *not* a factor that has been identified as a basic health-promoting behavior associated with increased life expectancy?
    a.   Engaging in regular physical exercise.
    b.   Eating three meals a day.
    c.   Using alcohol moderately or not at all.
    d.   Sleeping seven to eight hours a night.

26. (p. 370) Which of the following is *not* an effective approach to coping with stress?
    a.   vigorous exercise   c.   progressive relaxation
    b.   meditation   d.   developing a Type A personality

27. (p. 374) Stress innoculation is a technique effective in treating:
    a.   upsetting thoughts   c.   physical tension
    b.   disorganization   d.   poor time management

28. (p. 377) Meditation has been shown to produce which of the following?
    a.   increased oxygen consumption, greater respiration, increased alpha brain wave activity
    b.   improved sexual response, increased alertness, and improved intellectual capacity
    c.   improvement in verbal, musical, and spatial skills
    d.   reductions in heart rate, blood pressure, and muscle tension

29.   (p. 377) Herbert Benson supports which of the following statements?
      a.   Any individual practicing meditation should make use of a person-specific mantra.
      b.   Meditation elicits the relaxation response that opposes stressful activation of the body's fight-or-flight mechanisms.
      c.   Meditators should presume an aggressive role in seeking to become relaxed during meditation.
      d.   Meditation should involve a temporary increase in muscle tension indicative of enhanced mental concentration on the body.

APPLYING YOUR KNOWLEDGE

1.   What can you find out about prevention and health campaigns going on in your community? Try calling local hospitals and health facilities. Do they have any health psychologists working with their programs?

2.   The Exploration section of your text talks about an experiment in which college student were instructed to concentrate on breathing. Try this experiment on yourself for a 2-week period. Did the exercise have any effect on your concentration, bodily sensations, frustration tolerance, etc.?

ANSWERS—PROGRAMMED REVIEW

1.   Frustration; goal
2.   Stress
3.   bad; lack
4.   reaction
5.   Short; Long
6.   unpredictability
7.   Pressure
8.   control; lower
9.   threat
10. Perceived; actual
11. competence
12. intensity
13. burnout
14. emotional exhaustion
15. depersonalization
16. personal accomplishment
17. helping
18. social support
19. support groups
20. External; failure, rejection, loss
21. social; nonsocial
22. strength, urgency, importance
23. Motivation
24. Repeated
25. Personal
26. persistence
27. displaced
28. chains
29. child abuse
30. scapegoating; cotton; blacks

31. escape
32. apathy; drugs
33. Conflict
34. approach-approach
35. easiest; easily
36. avoidance-avoidance
37. needs, values
38. freeze
39. leaving the field
40. approach-avoidance
41. ambivalence; partial
42. double approach-avoidance
43. vacillate
44. multiple
45. illness
46. change
47. Social Readjustment Rating Scale
48. life change units
49. 300
50. older
51. failed; positive
52. hassles; microstressors
53. 100
54. 1; 2
55. immediate; long-term
56. central
57. personality, values
58. acculturative
59. Integration; Separation; Assimilation; Marginalization

60. highly; highly; minimally; moderately
61. psychosomatic disorders
62. hypochondria
63. respiratory; eczema; hypertension; colitis
64. tension; indigestion; dysfunction
65. half
66. hereditary; organ; learned
67. heart
68. Type A; Type B
69. twice
70. less fatigued
71. time urgency
72. anger, hostility
73. 15
74. hundreds
75. anger; hostility
76. reduces
77. opposite
78. mistrusting; reduce; considerate
79. hardy personality
80. commitment; control; challenges
81. general adaptation syndrome; G.A.S.
82. identical
83. alarm reaction
84. adrenaline, noradrenaline

85. muscles; breath; stomach, appetite; energy
86. stage of resistance
87. infection
88. psychosomatic
89. stage of exhaustion
90. adrenal glands; thymus; stomach ulcers
91. immune system
92. psychoneuroimmunology
93. thoughts; emotions
94. Control
95. weakened; divorce
96. health psychology
97. behavioral medicine
98. heart; lung
99. behavioral risk; blood; underexercise

100. disease prone
101. multiple risks
102. increasing; exercise; diet
103. 4
104. 2
105. lethal
106. 10
107. slowly
108. half
109. community health
110. 17; 12
111. 15
112. bodily; thoughts; ineffective
113. relaxing
114. progressive
115. organize; balance; limitations; social

116. health, morale
117. better able; illnesses
118. stress innoculation
119. self-statements; coping
120. stereotyped response
121. flexible
122. source; barrier
123. hasty; partially; compromises
124. Meditation
125. concentrative
126. receptive
127. concentration; bodily
128. mantra
129. relaxation response
130. 20; resting
131. verbal, musical, spatial
132. more strongly
133. quiet; muscle; passive

ANSWERS—SELF-TEST

1.	d	6.	c	11.	b	16.	False	21.	c	26.	d
2.	d	7.	False	12.	b	17.	d	22.	c	27.	a
3.	b	8.	c	13.	d	18.	True	23.	False	28.	d
4.	a	9.	b	14.	c	19.	b	24.	d	29.	b
5.	d	10.	b	15.	d	20.	c	25.	b		

ACROSS

2. this specialty of psychology is concerned with improving one's well-being
5. one who suffers from imaginary diseases
7. a psychological escape in which one pretends not to care
10. General Adaptation Syndrome (abbr.)
11. results when one is prevented from reaching a goal
15. it can be effective in combatting stress
16. this occurs when demands are placed on an organism to adjust

DOWN

1. in this stage the body's stress hormones are depleted
3. the _____ personality seems to be resistant to stress
4. a wavering between alternatives
6. these disorders are related to the "mind and body"
8. the _____ reaction mobilizes the body's resources to cope with added stress
9. mixed positive and negative feelings
12. target of displaced aggression
13. distressing daily annoyances
14. Social Readjustment Rating Scale (abbr.)

Child Development

CONTENTS

TERMS AND CONCEPTS

developmental psychology
neonate
reflex
grasping reflex
rooting reflex
sucking reflex
Moro reflex
looking changer
maturation
principle of motor primacy (principle of readiness)
nature versus nurture controversy
heredity
chromosomes
genes
Deoxyribonucleic acid (DNA)
polygenetic
dominant genes
recessive genes
X chromosome
Y chromosome
sex-linked traits
human growth sequence
intrauterine environment
congenital problems
fetal alcohol syndrome
medicated birth
natural (prepared) childbirth
Lamaze method
birthing rooms
gentle birth

maternal influences
paternal influences
self-awareness
social referencing
critical period
imprinting
emotional attachment
separation anxiety
emotional bond
motherless monkeys
affectional needs
cooing
babbling
single-word stage
telegraphic speech
biological predisposition
psycholinguist
transformations
stages of intellectual development
assimilation
accommodation
sensorimotor stage
object permanence
preoperational stage
concrete operational stage
formal operations stage
conservation
moral dilemmas
preconventional level
conventional level

261

postconventional level
feral children
deprivation dwarfism
hospitalism
surrogate mother
contact comfort
colostrum
enriched environments
early childhood education programs

artificial insemination
in vitro fertilization
genome
genetic counseling
amniocentesis
chorionic villus sampling
eugenics (selective breeding)
genetic engineering
cloning

IMPORTANT INDIVIDUALS

Andrew Meltzoff
Keith Moore
Jerome Bruner
Robert Fantz
Ferdinand Lamaze
Frederick Leboyer
Konrad Lorenz
Mary Ainsworth

Harry Harlow
Marshall Klaus
John Kennel
Louis Sander
William Condon
Noam Chomsky
Jean Piaget
Charles Croll

Renee Baillargeon
Burton White
Lawrence Kohlberg
Carol Gilligan
René Spitz
Paul Chance
Morris Holland

PROGRAMMED REVIEW

1.   (p. 380) _____ _____ can be described as the study of progressive changes in behavior and abilities from conception to death.

2.   (p. 381) At birth the human _____ is completely helpless and will die if not cared for. While their senses are less acute, babies are immediately responsive to their surroundings. In fact, they will follow a moving object with their eyes and will turn in the direction of sounds.

3.   (p. 381) Just one day after they are born, babies begin to prefer seeing their _____ face rather than a stranger's.

4.   (p. 381) A number of adaptive reflexes can be observed in the newborn. For example, an object pressed to its palm will be grasped with surprising strength. This reflex is appropriately called the _____ reflex and enhances survival by helping to prevent falling.

5.   (p. 381) The _____ reflex is demonstrated by touching the baby's cheek. The baby will immediately turn toward your finger as if searching for something. This reflex helps the infant find a bottle or breast.

6.   (p. 381) When a nipple touches the infant's mouth, the _____ reflex helps it to obtain the food it needs.

7.   (p. 381) Obtaining food rewards _____, which rapidly increases in vigor during the first days after birth. Thus, we see that learning begins immediately in the newborn.

8.   (p. 381) Also of interest is the _____ reflex. If a baby's position is changed abruptly or the infant is startled by a loud noise, the infant will make movements similar to an embrace.

9.   (p. 381) Andrew Meltzoff and Keith Moore have found that babies are born _____ that is, they consistently imitate adult facial features.

10. (p. 381) As early as _____ months of age, infants can also imitate other actions and they can repeat them the next day. Such mimicry is obviously an aid to rapid learning in infancy.

11. (p. 381) Jerome Bruner showed that _____ to _____-week old babies demonstrate signs of understanding that a person's voice and body are _____. If babies heard their mother's voice coming from where she was standing, they remained calm. If her voice came from a loudspeaker several feet away, the babies cried.

12. (p. 382) To test infant vision, Robert Fantz invented a device called a _____ _____.

13. (p. 382) Fantz places a child on its back inside the chamber and places two objects overhead. By observing the movements of the infant's eyes, and the images reflected from their surface, Fantz found that three-day-old babies preferred _____ patterns to _____ colored rectangles.

14. (p. 382) Other researchers have learned that infants are more excited by _____ and _____ in figures, and that they will look longer at _____ and _____ than they will at other colors.

15. (p. 382) By the age of _____ months infants can even perceive shapes traced by a moving light.

16. (p. 382) Infants spend more time looking at a _____ face pattern than a scrambled one or a colored oval.

17. (p. 382) When real human faces were used, Fantz found that _____ faces were preferred to _____ faces.

18. (p. 382) This preference reverses at about age _____, when unusual objects begin to hold greater interest. For example, Jerome Kagan found that children at this age were fascinated by a face mask with eyes on the chin and a nose in the middle of the forehead.

19. (p. 382) _____ refers to growth and development of the body—especially the nervous system. It underlies the orderly sequence observed in the unfolding of many basic abilities, particularly motor abilities.

20. (p. 382) While the _____ of maturation varies from child to child, the _____ is virtually universal. For instance, the strength and coordination needed for sitting appears before that needed for crawling.

21. (p. 383) Typically, infants sit before they crawl (and crawl before they stand, etc.). A few children substitute rolling, creeping, or shuffling for crawling. A very small percentage move directly from sitting to _____ and _____.

22. (p. 383) In general, increased motor control usually proceeds from _____ to _____ and from the _____ of the body to the _____.

23. (p. 383) Maturation often creates a condition of readiness for learning. This principle, known as the _____ of _____ _____, states that until the necessary physical structures are mature, no amount of practice will be sufficient to establish a skill.

24. (p. 383) Readiness is not an all-or-nothing effect. Training that comes too early will be _____; training that is only a little early may succeed, but will be _____; and training when a child is maturationally ready produces rapid _____.

25. (p. 384) Much needless grief can be avoided by respecting a child's rate of growth. For instance, eager parents who toilet trained an 18-month-old child in 10 weeks might have done it in 3 weeks by waiting until the child was 24 months old to begin. Parents may control when toilet training starts, but maturation tends to determine when it will be completed. Around _____ months is average for completion.

26. (p. 384) For many years psychologists have debated the _____ versus _____ controversy, trying to determine the relative importance of heredity and environment in the development of human beings.

27. (p. 384) Heredity is certainly an important factor in development. It has been estimated that the _____ information carried in each human cell would fill thousands of 1000-page books if translated into words.

28. (p. 384) The nucleus of every cell in the body contains 46 threadlike structures called _____ which transmit coded instructions of heredity.

29. (p. 384) Each sperm cell and each ovum contains only _____ chromosomes. Thus, humans normally receive half their chromosomes from their mother and half from their father.

30. (p. 384) Chromosomes are made up of _____ _____, abbreviated _____. It is a long ladder-like chemical molecule that is made up of smaller molecules. The order of these smaller molecules, or organic bases, acts as a code for genetic information.

31. (p. 384) _____ are small areas of the DNA molecule. They carry instructions that affect a particular process or personal characteristic. There are 50,000 to 100,000 such areas in every human cell.

32. (p. 385) In some cases a single gene is responsible for a particular inherited characteristic, but most characteristics are _____, or determined by many genes working in combination.

33. (p. 385) When a gene is _____, the trait it controls will be present every time the gene is present; when _____, it must be paired with an identical gene before its effect will be expressed.

34. (p. 385) We receive one-half of our chromosomes (and genes) from each parent. If each parent has two brown-eye genes, the couple's children will all be brown-eyed. But if each parent has one brown-eye gene and one blue-eye gene, the parents would both have brown eyes, but there is one chance in _____ that their children will have blue eyes.

35. (p. 385) The sex of a child is genetically determined. When two "_____" chromosomes are inherited the child will be a female, but an "_____" chromosome paired with a "_____" chromosome yields a male.

36. (p. 385) Some traits are _____-_____, that is carried only by genes on either the X or Y chromosome. Color blindness, which is carried on the X chromosome, is a good example.

37. (p. 385) Heredity instructions carried by the chromosomes influence development throughout life by affecting the sequence of growth, the timing of puberty, and the course of aging. Thus, the broad outlines of the human _____ _____ are universal.

38. (p. 385) In addition, heredity determines _____ and _____ color, the order of motor development, and susceptibility to some diseases. Heredity also exerts considerable influence over body size and shape, height, intelligence, athletic potential, personality traits, and a host of other details.

39. (p. 386) _____ (or the nurture side of the learning vs. heredity controversy) by no means takes a back seat in development. As Aldous Huxley noted, humans today are physically very similar to cave-dwellers of 20 or 30 thousand years ago. However, today's baby could become almost anything, while the Upper Paleolithic baby could only grow into a hunter or food-gatherer.

40. (p. 386) While both heredity and environment are separately important in development, the recognition that both are important and, in fact, _____ represents a more realistic approach. There is a constant interplay or _____ between the forces of nature and nurture.

41. (p. 387) Children show individual difference almost immediately after birth. Newborn babies may differ noticeably in activity, irritability, distractibility, and other aspects of _____ (the physical foundations of personality, such as prevailing mood, sensitivity, and energy levels).

42. (p. 387) Babies can be separated into three major categories of temperament, including _____ children who are relaxed and agreeable (about _____ percent of those observed); _____ children who tend to overreact to most situations (about _____ percent), and _____-to-_____-_____ children who are restrained and unexpressive (about _____ percent).

43. (p. 387) Because of inborn differences in temperament, babies rapidly become _____ _____ in their own development—especially their social development. They change their environment at the same time they are changed by it.

44. (p. 387) Consistent differences in temperament can be detected for at least the first 2 years of life. Yet by age 10, children's personalities show little connection to _____, _____, or _____ observed in infancy.

45. (p. 388) Thus, there appear to be at least three factors which combine to determine a person's developmental level at any stage in life. These elements are _____, _____, and the individual's own _____.

46. (p. 388) In considering the effects of environment on behavior, we must go back as far as the _____ environment of the womb. If a mother's health or nutrition is poor, if she contracts certain diseases such as German measles or syphilis, uses drugs, or is exposed to x-rays or atomic radiation, the resultant damage to the fetus is referred to as a _____ _____.

47. (p. 388) Congenital problems, or "_____ _____" as they are sometimes called, are distinct from _____ problems which are difficulties inherited from one's parents.

48. (p. 388) Even though there is no direct intermingling of blood between mother and fetus, some substances still reach the fetus. Most common prescription drugs reach the fetus and if the mother is addicted to _____, _____, or _____ the infant may be born with a drug addiction.

49. (p. 388) Even one dose of _____ taken by a pregnant woman can damage her fetus. Frequent use does horrible, irreversible damage to the unborn baby's brain.

50. (p. 388) Other potentially damaging substances which if ingested by the mother can adversely affect the fetus include: general anesthetics, _____, _____, excessive amounts of vitamins _____, _____, B_6, and K, cocaine, some barbiturates, opiates, tranquilizers, synthetic sex hormones, and possibly even caffeine and aspirin.

51. (p. 389) Repeated heavy drinking by a pregnant woman can produce a pattern known as the _____ _____ _____, characterized by miscarriage or premature birth, low birth weight, and a variety of bodily defects and facial deformations. Many affected infants are mentally retarded.

52. (p. 389) During the first 3 months of pregnancy, frequent drinking of even small amounts of alcohol may significantly lower a child's _____.

53. (p. 389) Four-year-old children who were exposed to alcohol before birth have been found to have impaired _____ _____ and balance.

54. (p. 389) Smoking also has an adverse effect on prenatal development. A pregnant woman who smokes 2 packs of cigarettes a day blocks off about _____ percent of the oxygen supply to the fetus.

55. (p. 389) Heavy smokers run a higher risk of _____ or giving premature birth to _____ babies.

56. (p. 389) The infant death rate immediately before, during, or after birth is _____ percent higher if a woman smokes during pregnancy.

57. (p. 389) Children exposed to smoking prenatally score _____ in language development and on general mental tests.

58. (p. 389) Until recently, _____ births in hospital delivery rooms were the rule in Western nations. In such births, the mother is assisted by a physician and given drugs ranging from local analgesics (painkillers) to general anesthetics that cause a loss of consciousness.

59. (p. 389) Increasingly, doctors and parents have come to realize that general anesthesia during birth has major drawbacks. They can dull or block the mother's _____ of birth. Also, they reduce _____ flow to the fetus and can cause the infant to be born partially anesthetized.

60. (p. 389) Studies show that babies whose mothers were given heavy doses of anesthetic tend to lag in _____ and _____ development.

61. (p. 389) In the last 5 years there has been a marked move away from use of general anesthesia during birth. Nevertheless, some form of painkiller is used in _____ percent of all deliveries in the United States.

62. (p. 389) Many psychologists are convinced that _____ or _____ childbirth is an effective way to minimize the discomfort of birth while giving babies the best possible start in life.

63. (p. 389) The most widely used approach to natural childbirth is the _____ _____ named after its French physician developer.

64. (p. 389) The Lamaze method begins by teaching couples what will happen _____ during birth. This helps to reduce fears and lessen anxiety.

65. (p. 389) Couples are also taught methods of _____ and _____ control to minimize pain. Further, the father or a friend is trained to give support to the mother during birth.

66. (p. 389) Natural childbirth typically shortens _____ and minimizes _____. In addition, it treats birth as a celebration of life, rather than a medical problem or a disease.

67. (p. 389) Parents are more likely to experience birth as a time of great happiness when natural childbirth is used and the _____ is present.

68. (p. 389) The emotional intensity of birth magnifies its impact. Many fathers form _____ at the time of birth that may make a difference later in the father's willingness to care for the child, or his reaction when the child angers him.

69. (p. 389) Researchers have found that fathers generally make a better transition to parenthood when they participate in preparing for childbirth. While participation may be valuable, it is not essential. The father's _____ toward the birth of his child is probably more important.

70. (p. 389) Psychologists have found that fathers who wanted to be present during delivery showed _____ interest in their infants during the first year and were _____ likely to help care for the baby. This was true whether or not the father was actually able to attend the birth.

71. (p. 390) Many hospitals now have _____ _____ that allow the father to room-in in a homelike atmosphere. This allows him to participate in the birth and to share in caring for the newborn.

72. (p. 390) Even traditional delivery rooms are allowing fathers to be present during birth. In some cases the father cuts the _____ _____ and gives the infant its first bath. In many hospitals the baby spends its first night with the parents in the _____ _____.

73. (p. 390) The French obstetrician Frederick _____ advocates a system of gentle birth that purportedly makes it pleasant for both mother and baby. It involves delivery in a silent, dimly lit room. Immediately after birth the baby is placed on its mother's stomach and gently massaged, then the umbilical cord is cut and the baby bathed in warm water.

74. (p. 390) Many obstetricians have been skeptical of Leboyer's methods. Doctors working in a darkened delivery room have had trouble detecting a "_____ _____."

75. (p. 390) Another point to consider is that stress during birth may be normal and perhaps even desirable. There is some evidence that babies born by caesarean section (surgical birth) have a _____ survival rate.

76. (p. 390) Leboyer claims that gentle births produce children who are happier, healthier, more relaxed, and more emotionally stable. However, evidence in support of this claim is not very convincing. While Leboyer babies are more relaxed than other newborns during the first _____ or _____ minutes after birth, from then on there is no measurable difference.

77. (p. 390) The quality of mothering during the first few years of life is very important. One study of maternal influences showed that whether children were unusually competent or had a low degree of competence was set by age _____.

78. (p. 391) To understand how this finding was possible, children and their mothers were observed at home. Five types of caregiving styles were identified. One of these, _____ _____, went out of their way to provide educational experiences for their children and allowed them to initiate some activities.

79. (p. 391) Super mothers produce an A child, _____ in most areas of development.

80. (p. 391) The _____-_____ mother gave her children good physical care, but interacted with them very little; her childcare routines were rigid and highly structured. Her children tended to be of below-average competence and to approach problems inflexibly.

81. (p. 391) A more recent study found that _____ maternal involvement (warm, educational interactions between mother and child) is strongly related to an absence of behavioral problems in 4-year-olds.

82. (p. 391) Optimal caregiving is also related to the _____ of _____ between parents and children. For instance, a slow-to-warm-up child who has impatient parents may have more difficulty adjusting than if the same child had easy-going parents.

83. (p. 391) Another recent study found that children's intellectual abilities at age 6 can be predicted, to some extent, by their mothers' _____ to them during infancy. Effective mothers are those who are sensitive to their children's needs.

84. (p. 391) Paternal influences also contribute to the infant's development, but in different ways. Generally, the father's main role tends to be that of a _____ for the infant. They spend _____ or _____ times as much time playing with their infants as they do in caretaking.

85. (p. 391) Fathers pay more visual _____ to the child, are much more _____, more physically arousing, and more likely to engage in _____ _____. Mothers speak to the infant more, play more conventional games, and spend more time in caretaking activities.

86. (p. 391) Such differences in mothers' and fathers' behavior continue until at least _____ childhood.

87. (p. 391) Infants can get very different views of males and females. Females, who offer comfort, nurturance, and _____ stimulation, also tend to be close at hand. Males come and go, and when they are present, action, _____ and risk-taking prevail.

88. (p. 392) The growth of _____-_____, the recognition of your own image, depends on maturation of the nervous system.

89. (p. 392) One experiment in which rouge was placed on children's noses before being brought in front of a mirror showed that the probability that children would touch their nose was very low at _____ months, but jumped dramatically through the _____ year.

90. (p. 392) Infants shown their own videotaped images usually had to be _____ months old before they could tell their own images from those of other children.

91. (p. 392) Adults sometimes glance at the facial expressions of others in order to decide how to respond. This sort of _____ _____ can also be observed in babies.

92. (p. 392) By _____ months of age, most babies reference (glance at) their mothers when placed in an unfamiliar situation. Such was the finding with tests involving the visual cliff.

93. (p. 392) When mothers posed faces of _____ or _____, most babies crossed the deep side of the cliff. When they posed _____ or _____, few babies crossed.

94. (p. 392) Thus, by the end of their _____ year, infants are aware of the facial expression of others and seek guidance from them—especially from mother.

95. (p. 392) _____ _____ are times when susceptibility to environmental influences (both positive and negative) are increased.

96. (p. 393) For example, the critical period for mastering a second language is before _____—the earlier the better.

97. (p. 393) Often, certain events must occur during a critical period in order for organisms to develop normally. Konrad Lorenz has demonstrated this fact in his experiments with _____ where a permanent behavior pattern is rapidly learned early in development.

98. (p. 393) Lorenz found that infant geese learned to follow moving objects seen early in development. This imprinting process occurs during a very brief critical period. For instance, Hess found that if ducklings are not allowed to imprint on their mother or some other object within _____ hours after hatching, they never will.

99. (p. 393) While true cases of imprinting are limited to birds and other animals, human infants do form an _____ _____ to their primary caregivers (usually parents).

100. (p. 393) There is a critical period for this attachment (roughly the first year of life). Around 8 to 12 months of age, babies display _____ _____ (crying and signs of fear) when their parents leave them alone, or alone with strangers.

101. (p. 393) Mary Ainsworth has proposed three types of attachment revealed by how babies act when their mothers return after a brief separation. Infants who are _____ attached are upset by the mother's absence and they seek to be near her when she returns.

102. (p. 393) _____-_____ infants turn away from their mother when she returns. _____-_____ attachment is revealed when an infant both seeks to be near the returning mother and resists contact with her.

103. (p. 393) Studies of several cultures support the idea that these three types of attachment are _____.

104. (p. 393) The key to secure attachment is a mother who is accepting and sensitive to her baby's signals and rhythms. Poor attachment occurs when a mother's actions are _____, _____, intrusive, or overstimulating.

105. (p. 393) Infants who are securely attached to their parents at age one later show more _____, curiosity, problem solving ability and _____ competence in preschool.

106. (p. 393) Authorities generally agree that high-quality _____ does not have harmful effects on preschool children. Poor-quality care, however, can be risky.

107. (p. 394) Small group size (12-15 children) and a ratio of 1 caregiver to _____ children (or better) is very important.

108. (p. 394) Parents should look for caregivers trained in _____ _____. Ideally, children should be cared for by the same people day to day since stable relationships promote positive social and mental development.

109. (p. 394) Daycare has no ill effects until it exceeds _____ or more hours a week. Then there often are signs of insecurity in children's relationships with their mothers.

110. (p. 394) Insecurity is especially likely if the child is under _____ year of age, if the mother works full time, if the father helps little in caring for the child, and if the parents' marriage is troubled.

111. (p. 394) Studies by Marshall Klaus and John Kennel suggest that mother-child pairs who spend extra time together form a stronger _____ _____ to one another. This is especially true if skin-to-skin touching is part of early contact.

112. (p. 394) They have reported that "bonded" babies are more _____ and _____, healthier, and brighter than those who are denied extra contact. However, the majority of studies have failed to support the idea that extended, early contact is crucial to bonding.

113. (p. 394) Critics point out that _____ children, _____ babies, and babies born by _____ section all develop normal, affectionate bonds with their mothers.

114. (p. 394) Research with rhesus monkeys suggests that infant attachments have lasting effects. Harry Harlow has shown that baby monkeys separated from their mothers and raised in isolation never develop normal _____ behaviors and make very poor mothers if mated.

115. (p. 394) These "motherless monkeys" are coldly _____ or _____ to their babies and may brutalize or injure them. It has been suggested that a similar pattern may exist among humans. Most abusive parents were themselves rejected or mistreated as children.

116. (p. 394) Some psychologists believe that _____ behavior can often be traced to a lack of attachment in infancy. Children with severe attachment problems do not learn to trust and care about others and are cruel, angry, and self-destructive.

117. (p. 394) Meeting a baby's affectional needs is an important factor in early development. An important task of the first year of life is creation of a bond of trust and affection between the infant and at least one other person. A later capacity to experience _____ and _____ relationships may depend on it.

118. (p. 395) The development of language is also closely tied to maturation. By _____ _____ of age, the infant can control crying enough to use it as an attention-getting device.

119. (p. 395) Around 6 to 8 weeks of age, babies begin _____—the repetition of vowel sounds like "oo" and "ah."

120. (p. 395) By age _____ months, the nervous system has matured enough to allow the child to grasp objects, to smile, laugh, sit up, and to babble.

121. (p. 395) In the babbling stage, _____ sounds are added to produce a continuous outpouring of repeated language sounds. It increases when parents talk to the child.

122. (p. 395) At about _____ _____ of age, the child can stand alone for a short time and can respond to words. Soon afterward, the first connection between words and objects is formed.

123. (p. 395) Between the ages of 1$^1/_2$ and _____ years, the child becomes able to stand and walk alone. By this time, the child's vocabulary may include from 24 to _____ words.

124. (p. 395) At first there is a _____-_____ stage during which the child says only one word at a time. Soon after, words are arranged in simple two-word sentences called _____ _____: "Want Teddy."

125. (p. 395) From this point on, growth of vocabulary and language skills proceeds at a phenomenal rate. By first grade the child can understand around _____ words and can use about _____.

126. (p. 395) Louis Sander and William Condon filmed newborn infants as they listened to various sounds. They found that infants as young as one day old move their arms and legs in synchrony to the rhythms of _____ _____.

127. (p. 395) Linguist Noam Chomsky has long claimed that humans have a _____ _____ to develop language; he believes language is inborn like a child's ability to coordinate walking.

128. (p. 395) If such inborn language recognition exists, it may explain why children universally use a limited number of _____ in their first sentences.

129. (p. 396) Many psychologists feel that Chomsky underestimates the importance of learning. _____ (specialists in the psychology of language) have recently shown that language learning involves imitation of adults, rewards for correctly using words, and early, shared communication.

130. (p. 396) From this point of view, infants' behavior reflects a readiness to interact _____ with parents, not innate language recognition.

131. (p. 396) To elicit smiles and vocalizations from babies, parents quickly learn to change their actions to keep the infant's attention, arousal, and activity at optimal levels. A system of shared _____ is created which helps lay a foundation for later language use and establishes a pattern of "conversational" turn taking.

132. (p. 396) A baby's vocalizations and attention provide a way of interacting emotionally with parents. Even infants as young as _____ months make more speechlike sounds when an adult engages them in a turn-taking pattern of interacting.

133. (p. 397) A child's thinking is less _____ than that of an adult; they use fewer generalizations, categories, or principles. They also tend to base their understanding of the world on particular examples, tangible sensations, and material objects.

134. (p. 397) An indication of the concrete nature of thinking can be found in the fact that before age 6 or 7, children are unable to make _____. If you show a child a full, short, wide glass and a full, tall, narrow glass, the child will consider the taller glass to contain more fluid.

135. (p. 397) Perhaps this is why age _____ has been called the "age of reason." After this age, we see a definite trend toward more abstract thought.

136. (p. 398) Jean Piaget investigated the series of _____ that children progress through intellectually. He believed that intellect grows through _____—the use of existing patterns in new situations, and through _____—the modification of existing ideas to fit new requirements.

137. (p. 398) Piaget's first stage, known as the _____ stage, includes the first _____ years of life.

138. (p. 398) During the first stage, the child shows a gradual emergence of the concept of _____ _____. At about age 1 the child begins to pursue disappearing objects. By age 2, the child can anticipate the movement of an object behind a screen. These developments indicate that the child's conceptions are becoming more stable.

139. (p. 398) During the _____ stage (ages 2-7), the child is developing an ability to think _____ and to use language.

140. (p. 398) During this stage, the child's thinking is very intuitive. Judging weight is an example. Among 4-to 6-year olds, _____ percent say that a Styrofoam cup has no weight after lifting it.

141. (p. 398) The use of language is not as sophisticated as it might seem. Children have a tendency to confuse _____ with the _____ they represent.

142. (p. 398) During this stage, children are also quite _____, or unable to take the viewpoint of other people. This fact helps us understand why children of this stage can seem so selfish or uncooperative at times.

143. (p. 399) By _____ to _____ years of age, the child enters the _____ _____ stage. An important development here is the mastery of the concept of _____.

144. (p. 399) During this period, a child's thoughts begin to include the concepts of _____, _____, and number. Categories and principles are used, and the child can think _____ about concrete objects or situations.

145. (p. 399) Usually children at this stage stop believing in Santa Claus. Similarly, Charles Croll found that _____ percent of children aged 5 to 7 believe that the Tooth Fairy is real. Around the ages of 7 to 8, however, most children begin to realize that this is a fantasy.

146. (p. 399) Another important development during the concrete operational stage is the ability to _____ thoughts or operations. Older children recognize that if 4 x 2 = 8, then 2 x 4 does, too. Younger children must memorize each relationship separately.

147. (p. 399) The final stage, the _____ _____ stage, includes ages _____ years and up. Here, thinking is based more on _____ _____. The child in this stage has come to consider hypothetical possibilities also.

148. (p. 399) In this last stage, full adult intellectual ability is attained. The older adolescent is capable of inductive and deductive reasoning and can comprehend abstract systems. From this point on, improvements in intellectual ability are based on gaining _____, _____, and wisdom, rather than on a boost in basic thinking capacity.

149. (p. 400) Today, many psychologists are convinced that Piaget gave too little credit to the effects of _____. For example, children of pottery-making parents can correctly answer questions about the conservation of clay at an earlier age than Piaget would have predicted.

150. (p. 400) According to learning theorists, children continuously gain _____ _____; they do not undergo stage-like increases in general mental ability.

151. (p. 400) Numerous studies do show that children make _____ mental gains at about the ages Piaget stated. In fact, researchers have recently found evidence that cycles of _____ growth occur at times that correspond with Piaget's stages.

152. (p. 400) Piaget believed that infants under the age of _____ year cannot think. Babies, he said, have no memory of people and objects that are out of sight.

153. (p. 400) However, researchers have shown that babies as young as _____ months of age know that objects are solid and do not disappear when out of view.

154. (p. 400) Other researchers have found that babies have memories at age _____ to _____ months that Piaget didn't see until 18 months.

155. (p. 400) Piaget may have underestimated the abilities of infants by mistaking their limited _____ skills for mental incompetence. His tests required babies to search for objects or reach out and touch them.

156. (p. 401) Psychologist Renee Baillargeon has taken advantage of the fact that babies, like adults, act surprised when they see something "impossible" or unexpected occur. He found that some _____-month-old infants act surprised and look longer at impossible events, such as solid objects seeming to pass through each other.

157. (p. 401) Evidence continues to mount that some of the memory and thinking abilities Piaget believed emerged only after a long sensorimotor period actually occur much sooner. It seems that babies are born with the capacity to form _____ about the world or acquire this ability early in life.

158. (p. 401) To study moral development, Lawrence Kohlberg posed _____ _____ to children of different ages. By classifying the reasons children gave for their answers he identified three levels and six stages of moral development.

159. (p. 401) The first level, _____, includes a _____ _____ (stage 1) where actions are evaluated in terms of possible punishment, not goodness or badness. Here, obedience to power is emphasized.

160. (p. 402) A second stage of the preconventional level involves a _____- _____ orientation. At this stage, proper action is determined by one's own needs.

161. (p. 402) The second level of moral development, the _____ level, includes stage 3 development called good boy/good girl orientation. Good behavior is that which brings approval or pleases others.

162. (p. 402) Stage 4 (conventional level), _____ orientation, involves an emphasis on upholding law, order, and authority, doing one's duty, and following social rules.

163. (p. 402) The third level is called the _____ level. It includes stage 5, _____-_____ orientation, where support of laws and rules is based on rational analysis and mutual agreement.

164. (p. 402) Also included is stage 6, _____ of _____ _____, where behavior is directed by self-chosen ethical principles that tend to be general, comprehensive, or universal.

165. (p. 402) Kohlberg found that people advance through the stages at different rates. Stages 1 and 2 are most characteristic of young _____ and _____. Conventional group-oriented morals of stages 3 and 4 are characteristic of older _____ and most of the _____ population.

166. (p. 402) Kohlberg estimated that postconventional morality, representing self-direction and higher principles, is characteristic of only about _____ percent of the adult population.

167. (p. 403) Psychologist Carol Gilligan has pointed out that Kohlberg's system is concerned mainly with the ethics of _____. But Gilligan argues that there is also an ethic of _____ and responsibility to be considered.

168. (p. 403) Gilligan has studied women who face real-life dilemmas. She has concluded that male psychologists have defined moral maturity in terms of justice and autonomy. From this perspective, women's concern with _____ can look like a weakness rather than a strength.

169. (p. 403) Gilligan believes that caring is also a major element of moral development and suggests that _____ may lag in achieving it.

170. (p. 403) Several recent studies have found little or no _____ in men's and women's moral reasoning abilities. Both men and women may use caring and justice to make moral decisions.

171. (p. 403) However, some researchers continue to find evidence that _____ are more likely to value caring.

172 (p. 403) While the existence of so-called _____ _____ (raised in the wild) have rarely been documented, there are numerous cases of children who have spent the first 5 or 6 years of life in closets, etc. These children demonstrate the destructive effects of early _____, since they are usually mute, severely retarded, and emotionally damaged.

173. (p. 403) Some of these children suffer from _____ _____—stunted growth associated with isolation, rejection, or general deprivation in the home environment.

174. (p. 403) Examples, such as these early deprived children, suggest that in many ways all of infancy is a relatively _____ _____ in development.

175. (p. 404) René Spitz investigated the damaging effects of deprivation in early childhood. He used the term _____ to refer to a group of foundling-home babies suffering from a pattern of deep depression marked by weeping and sadness, long periods of immobility or mechanical rocking, and a lack of normal response to other humans.

176. (p. 404) Spitz discovered that the foundling home had an unusually high rate of infant _____ and development of the living babies was severely _____. He considered this "wasting away" to be due to a lack of dependable "mother figures."

177. (p. 404) Recent work supports the idea that lack of _____ is a major element in early deprivation. For example, improving living conditions failed to reverse declining mental health at one Canadian institution. Children improved only when placed with caring foster or adoptive parents.

178. (p. 404) A second major factor in many cases of deprivation is a lack of _____ _____. Foundling-home babies studied by Spitz were kept in bare rooms, in cribs with white sheets hung on the sides.

179. (p. 404) Experiments with animals have confirmed the destructive effects of a lack of stimulation in infancy. Harry Harlow found that infant rhesus monkeys separated from their real mothers always preferred surrogate mothers with a soft terry cloth surface. Harlow concluded from this finding that an important dimension of early stimulation is _____ _____ supplied by touching, holding, and stroking an infant.

180. (p. 404) Researchers working with humans have found much the same thing. For instance, just _____ minutes of extra touching a day can affect the developmental rate of infants in an institution.

181. (p. 405) Many psychologists have advocated breast feeding of infants as a means of assuring contact comfort. In addition, the breast-feeding mother produces _____, a protein-rich fluid containing antibodies, for the first few days after birth. However, the advantages of breast feeding are not overriding.

182. (p. 405) Contact comfort may underlie the tendency of many children to become attached to _____ objects. This appears not to be a cause for alarm, however. A recent study of 2- to 3-year-old "blanket-attached" children found that they were no more _____ than others.

183. (p. 405) An _____ environment is one that has been deliberately made more novel, complex, and richly stimulating. Rats raised in such environments dramatically out-perform those raised in stimulus-poor environments. Also, they have larger and heavier brains with a thicker cortex.

184. (p. 405) One study of environmental enrichment effects upon human development involved giving newborn infants several kinds of extra stimulation each day for several months. These conditions did cause _____ _____ reaching to occur an average of six weeks early.

185. (p. 405) One of the most encouraging examples of the benefits of enrichment is Program _____ _____. Such early childhood education programs produce real improvements in later school performance, especially for the most needy children.

186. (p. 407) "Enrichment" that is poorly matched to a child's needs is of little value. It helps to have appropriate goals for infancy. Burton White believes that for the first year or so of life the three goals for healthy development are: (1) Giving the infant a feeling of being _____ and cared for; (2) Encouraging interest in the _____ _____; and (3) Helping the infant develop specific skills.

187. (p. 407) The importance of giving good physical care to a baby is self-evident. Beyond that, parents should touch, hold, and handle their infant _____.

188. (p. 407) Parents should also attend _____ to a baby's cries as often as possible. Infants are better off in the long run if they are tended to and comforted in a loving way. This helps them feel secure and strengthens their _____ bonds with parents.

189. (p. 407) Spoiling very young infants is nearly impossible. But from about age _____ on, parents are asking for trouble if they overindulge their child. What spoils a child is a lack of firm age-appropriate limits and guidelines for acceptable behavior.

190. (p. 407) Parents can help encourage interest in the world by seeing that their baby is regularly involved in activities that interest her or him. To encourage exploration, try to minimize the use of _____ devices. These can stifle a child's natural curiosity when used for long periods.

191. (p. 407) Parents can contribute greatly to intellectual growth through their attitudes toward a child's _____ of the world. Placing virtually all common objects off limits for a child is a serious mistake.

192. (p. 407) A major element of good child rearing in infancy consists of knowing what the _____ _____ of emerging skills is and facilitating their emergence. If an infant lags far behind expected milestones in development, parents should take note and find out why.

193. (p. 407) In considering maturation rates, it is wise for parents to recognize the difference between the _____ child and the _____ child. Developmental norms specifying ages at which particular abilities appear are based on _____; there is always a wide range of normal variation around this figure.

194. (p. 408) Parents can do much to provide opportunities for varied sensory experience during infancy. Stimulation through contact is quite helpful. For instance, the more time babies spend interacting with parents, the faster they develop _____ and _____ abilities.

195. (p. 408) Throughout a baby's _____ year it is very important to watch for signs of hearing loss. To test this, the baby's mother should call to the infant in a normal voice from 6-10 feet away. Within a minute, the baby should turn accurately toward the voice.

196. (p. 408) The _____ of enrichment rather than its quantity is important in infant development. The presence of stimulating play materials, together with _____ parents, is strongly related to how quickly children progress.

197. (p. 408) The concept of responsiveness applies to toys and objects, as well as to parents' behavior. Particularly effective are experiences like those pointed out by psychologist Paul Chance that allow children to see _____-and-_____ results from their own behavior.

198. (p. 408) Many authorities are concerned about parents who try to push their children's intellectual development. Forced teaching of physical and intellectual skills can bore or oppress a child. True enrichment is responsive to the child's _____ and _____. It does not make the child feel pressured to perform.

199. (p. 408) Piaget's concept of accommodation suggests that the ideal way to stretch a child's intellect is to provide experiences that are only slightly _____, _____, or _____. This gradual expansion helps minimize the frustration and withdrawal that experiences too far beyond the familiar may cause.

200. (p. 409) Effective parents typically follow a sort of _____-_____-ahead strategy when adapting their instructions to their infants' current level of ability.

201. (p. 409) Morris Holland offers several suggestions on how to relate to children at different stages of intellectual development. He suggests that during the sensorimotor stage _____ play is most effective.

202. (p. 409) During the preoperational phase, the child should be encouraged to _____ things in different ways.

203. (p. 409) During the concrete operational stage the child is beginning to use generalizations, but expect a degree of _____ in the child's ability to apply concepts of time, space, quantity, and volume to new situations.

204. (p. 409) During the formal operations stage, it becomes more realistic to explain things verbally or symbolically. Encourage the child to create _____ and to imagine how things could be.

205. (p. 410) Couples now have an array of new options available to deal with infertility. With _____ _____, sperm from an anonymous donor is used to impregnate the woman. Donors are selected so that their eye and hair color, height, and so on, match the husband's as closely as possible.

206. (p. 410) To produce a "test-tube" baby using _____ _____ _____, egg cells are surgically collected from the mother's ovary. The egg cells are then placed in a petri dish of nutrients and the father's sperm cells are added. After the egg cell is fertilized and begins dividing, it is implanted in the mother's womb where it develops normally.

207. (p. 410) In a new variation, an _____ woman may donate an egg cell to the infertile couple. The egg cell is then fertilized with the husband's sperm and implanted in the wife's uterus.

208. (p. 410) Infertile couples who are considering this new technique should be warned. The average first-time success rate is only _____ percent and the cost ranges from $5000 to $7000.

209. (p. 410) Many donors for artificial insemination are used _____ (one clinic reported that a single donor fathered 50 babies). Should rules of testing and record-keeping be applied here? This is but one of many unanswered questions raised by the new biological procedures now available to couples.

210. (p. 410) The possibility of selecting an infant's sex prior to conception may have an impact on parenthood. The procedure involves separating X-and Y-bearing sperm and then _____ _____ the egg cell with all male-producing, or female-producing, sperm.

211. (p. 411) At present, sex selection techniques cannot _____ to produce a child of the desired sex. The procedure is also relatively expensive and some couples dislike the need for artificial insemination.

212. (p. 411) A further worry is that _____-_____ of all childless American couples say they would prefer to have a boy as a first child. If large numbers of couples select their children's sex, would there be an excess of male births?

213. (p. 411) It is now possible to identify a large number of genetic disorders. Prospective parents who suspect that they may be carriers of genetic disorders may seek _____ _____ to help calculate the risk of a genetic disorder.

214. (p. 411) Within another decade scientists may be able to complete a map of the human _____, or entire complement of genes, by identifying, in order, every gene on every human chromosome. This will allow advanced identification of genetic diseases and new tests to detect those diseases in people.

215. (p. 411) Parents who are potential carriers of genetic disorders may elect to have a child but then have a test performed about the fifth week of pregnancy to detect the presence or absence of the genetic defect. Such prenatal testing is done by _____, which involves taking amniotic fluid from the mother's womb.

216. (p. 411) Amniocentesis is usually done at about the fifteenth week of pregnancy. An alternate procedure, called _____ _____ _____, can be done between 6 and 8 weeks of pregnancy.

217. (p. 411) Chorionic villus sampling takes a small piece of the _____ for analysis. Either method allows couples who do not object to abortion to terminate the pregnancy when a serious genetic defect is detected. Parents who consider abortion unacceptable still have the advantage of forewarning so that they may prepare the best possible care for the child.

218. (p. 411) Plants and animals have been improved more in the past 50 years than in the previous 5000. This progress is primarily due to _____, or selective breeding for desirable characteristics.

219. (p. 411) Through the use of _____ _____ it may someday become possible to remove defective genes and replace them with normal ones. This process will soon be possible with one or two genes, but tampering on a major scale is not likely in the near future.

220. (p. 411) _____, the production of an entire organism from a single cell, is also unlikely, at least where humans are concerned.

221. (p. 412) It has also been predicted that ultimately people will carry "gene identity cards" based on _____ _____ made during childhood. These cards would show what hereditary diseases a person is predisposed to, or which may be passed on in childbearing when combined with the gene pattern of a mate.

SELF-TEST

1. (p. 380) Developmental psychology is the study of progressive changes in behavior and abilities:
   a. during infancy
   b. during adolescence
   c. during old age
   d. throughout life

2. (p. 381) Of the following, which is *not* an adaptive, human neonatal reflex?
   a. rooting
   b. imprinting
   c. Moro
   d. grasping

3. (p. 382) The looking chamber was devised by Robert Fantz to study:
   a. development of infant vision
   b. critical periods in monkey development
   c. the principle of motor primacy
   d. how infants establish preferences for certain auditory stimuli

4. (p. 382) Of the following, which sequence represents the progression in infant visual interest?
   a. attraction to complex patterns—preference for the familiar—interest in the unusual
   b. preference for the unusual—interest in complex patterns—attraction to the unfamiliar
   c. indifference to complex patterns—preference for the unusual—attraction to the familiar
   d. preference for simple rectangles—attraction to scrambled faces—preference for novel stimuli

5. (p. 382) True-False. In general, increased muscular control develops at an equal rate throughout the body as maturation proceeds.

6. (p. 383) Of the following, which is *not* defined by the phrase, "until the necessary physical structures are mature, no amount of practice will be sufficient to establish a skill?"
   a. principle of readiness
   b. maturation
   c. principle of motor primacy
   d. principle of accommodation

7. (p. 385) True-False. The nature versus nurture debate refers to controversy regarding proper parenting styles (letting the child develop naturally at its own pace versus pushing or nurturing the child to succeed through special and early practice).

8. (p. 385) True-False. Recessive genes determine particular traits only when paired with dominant genes.

9. (p. 385) Traits that are carried only by genes on either the X or Y chromosome are referred to as:
   a. polygenetic
   b. recessive genes
   c. sex-linked
   d. monogenetic

10. (p. 387) Research studying children with easy, difficult, and slow-to-warm-up temperaments indicates that:
    a. different mothering styles can produce children with varying personalities
    b. children move through various stages of personality development of which these three classes are representative
    c. newborn babies differ in temperament and thus are active participants in determining the course of their own development
    d. children from foster homes where emotional attachments are encouraged tend to be easy children while children from foundling-homes tend to be difficult or slow-to-warm-up

11. (p. 388) True-False. Environmental effects on development do not occur until after birth.

12. (p. 388) True-False. Congenital problems are those which result from the transmission of abnormal genes during conception.

13. (p. 389) Repeated heavy drinking by a pregnant woman can produce a pattern known as the fetal alcohol syndrome. It includes all of the following *except*:
    a. miscarriage or premature birth
    b. infants with low birth weight and a variety of bodily defects and deformations
    c. children with mental retardation, poor coordination, or learning disabilities
    d. adolescents and adults who are prone to alcoholism

14. (p. 389) Which of the following statements is *not* true of the Lamaze method?
    a. It teaches couples what will happen physically during birth.
    b. The mother is taught methods of breathing and muscle control.
    c. The father is trained to give support to and coach the mother.
    d. Painkillers are regularly used to help reduce anxiety.

15. (p. 389) Which of the following is *not* true of fathers' involvement with birth?
    a. Fathers generally make a better transition to parenthood when they participate in preparing for childbirth.
    b. Many hospitals now have birthing rooms that allow the father to room-in, participate in the birth and share in caring for the newborn.
    c. While more hospitals now provide birthing rooms, traditional delivery rooms still exclude fathers.
    d. A recent study found that fathers who wanted to be present during delivery showed greater interest in their infants during the first year.

16. (p. 391) Which of the following is *not* usually a paternal influence in child development?
    a. being a playmate for the infant
    b. being an equal to the mother in caretaking responsibilities
    c. being tactile and physically arousing
    d. engaging in unusual play

17. (p. 392) True-False. Children tested for self-awareness show low probability of self-recognition at nine months. The probability increases through the second year.

18. (p. 393) True-False. Imprinting is an instinctive, innate ability that can take place at any time the appropriate environmental stimuli are present.

19. (p. 393) Separation anxiety indicates the existence of:
    a. human imprinting   c. biological predispositions
    b. acquired fears   d. emotional attachments

20. (p. 394) Which of the following is *not* true of "motherless monkeys?"
    a. They develop abnormal sexual behaviors.
    b. If mated they make very poor mothers who are coldly rejecting or indifferent to their babies.
    c. They make excellent mothers because of their own needs for increased physical contact.
    d. They are infant monkeys separated from their mothers and raised in isolation.

21. (p. 395) True-False. Telegraphic speech refers to the period of language development marked by a continuous outpouring of connected and repeated language sounds.

22. (p. 395) Which of the following is *not* true of the roots of language?
    a. Sander and Condon found that even day-old infants move their limbs in synchrony to human speech.
    b. Children universally use a limited number of patterns in their first sentences.
    c. Children and parents develop a system of shared signals which establishes a "conversational" turn-taking pattern even prior to the child's first words.
    d. Infants quickly display a pattern of mutual monitoring with each other that facilitates social readiness for language between peers.

23. (p. 395) True-False. Noam Chomsky believes that humans have a biological predisposition to develop language.

24. (p. 398) According to Piaget, _____ refers to using existing patterns in new situations, while _____ involves modifying existing ideas to fit new requirements.
    a. conversation, transformation   c. concreteness, abstractness
    b. assimilation, accommodation   d. accommodation, assimilation

25. (p. 398) According to Piaget, the development of the concept of object permanence takes place during the:
    a. sensorimotor stage   c. concrete operational stage
    b. preoperational stage   d. formal operations stage

26. (p. 399) Mastery of the concept of conservation usually occurs during the:
    a. sensorimotor stage   c. concrete operational stage
    b. preoperational stage   d. formal operations stage

27. (p. 399) True-False. Reversibility of thoughts or operations is usually an ability acquired during the preoperational stage.

28. (p. 402) Which of the following is *not* a correct association according to Kohlberg's study of moral development?
    a. preconventional level—moral thinking determined by the consequences of actions
    b. anticonventional level—moral thinking is directed by self-chosen ethical principles
    c. postconventional level—advanced moral development directed by self-accepted moral principles
    d. conventional level—moral actions are directed by desire to conform to the expectations of others or to uphold socially accepted rules and values

29. (p. 402) True-False. Kohlberg found that everyone goes through six stages of moral development, but not necessarily at the same rate.

30. (p. 403) Children raised in extremely isolated or restricted environments often suffer:
    a. telegraphic speech   c. deprivation dwarfism
    b. congenital problems   d. stranger anxiety

31. (p. 404) René Spitz found that foundling-home infants who lacked emotional attachments suffered from all of the following *except*:
    a. depression   c. overdependency
    b. hospitalism   d. high mortality rate

32. (p. 404) True-False. Harlow's work with surrogate mothers has shown that contact comfort is an important dimension of early stimulation.

33. (p. 405) True-False. Experiments have shown that rats raised in stimulus-enriched environments have the same brain size as control subjects, but significantly better temperaments.

34. (p. 405) True-False. While sensory deprivation can seriously affect development, environmental richness seems to have little influence.

35. (p. 407) True-False. In most cases a child can be considered abnormal if he or she has not demonstrated a certain ability during the developmental norm established for children in general.

36. (p. 410) Which of the following is *not* true of the present state of sex selection techniques?
    a. The procedure can guarantee to produce a child of the desired sex.
    b. It involves separating X-and Y-bearing sperm.
    c. It involves artificially inseminating the mother.
    d. The procedure is relatively expensive, costing about $300.

37. (p. 411) True-False. Amniocentesis is the process of genetic engineering responsible for sex selection prior to conception.

38. (p. 411) Selective breeding for desirable characteristics is called:
    a. eugenics   c. cloning
    b. genetic engineering   d. DNA control

APPLYING YOUR KNOWLEDGE

1. If you have access to a infant, try researching the various reflexes of a neonate. Try making different facial gestures. Does the infant show mimicry? How do these various traits help in survival?

2. Conduct a demonstration of Piaget's theory of cognitive development by testing children of various ages using the kinds of tasks Piaget discusses. Can you find examples of the operations most children can perform at the different stages?

3. Use the moral dilemma example discussed in your text (e.g., the husband who steals a drug from a pharmacist needed to save his wife from cancer) to demonstrate Kohlberg's stages of moral development. Give the example to children of different ages and use the sample answers listed in the text to rate the stage and level of each child's moral development.

ANSWERS—PROGRAMMED REVIEW

1.	Developmental psychology	14.	circularity, curves; red, blue	25.	30
2.	neonate	15.	6	26.	nature; nurture
3.	mother's	16.	human	27.	genetic
4.	grasping	17.	familiar; unfamiliar	28.	chromosomes
5.	rooting	18.	2	29.	6
6.	sucking	19.	Maturation	30.	deoxyribonucleic acid; DNA
7.	nursing	20.	rate; order	31.	Genes
8.	Moro	21.	standing, walking	32.	polygenetic
9.	mimics	22.	head, toe; center, extremities	33.	dominant; recessive
10.	9	23.	principle of motor primacy	34.	4
11.	3; 8; connected			35.	X; X, Y
12.	looking chamber	24.	unsuccessful; inefficient; learning	36.	sex-linked
13.	complex; simpler			37.	growth sequence

38. eye, skin; motor; diseases
39. Environment
40. inseparable; interaction
41. temperament
42. easy; 40; difficult; 10; slow-to-warm-up; 15
43. active participants
44. irritability; activity; attentiveness
45. heredity, environment; behavior
46. intrauterine; congenital problem
47. birth defects; genetic
48. morphine, heroin, methadone
49. cocaine
50. cortisone, tetracycline; A, D
51. fetal alcohol syndrome
52. intelligence
53. muscular coordination
54. 25
55. miscarrying; underweight
56. 27
57. lower
58. medicated
59. awareness; oxygen
60. muscular, neural
61. 95
62. natural, prepared
63. Lamaze method
64. physically
65. breathing; muscular
66. labor; pain
67. father
68. memories
69. attitude
70. greater; more
71. birthing rooms
72. umbilical cord; birthing room
73. Leboyer
74. blue baby
75. lower
76. 15; 20
77. 3
78. super mothers
79. competent
80. zoo-keeper
81. proactive

82. goodness of fit
83. responsiveness
84. playmate; 4, 5
85. attentive; tactile; unusual play
86. middle
87. verbal; exploration
88. self-awareness
89. 9; second
90. 15
91. social referencing
92. 12
93. joy, interest; fear, anger
94. first
95. Critical periods
96. puberty
97. imprinting
98. 30
99. emotional attachment
100. separation anxiety
101. securely
102. Insecure-avoidant; Insecure-ambivalent
103. universal
104. inappropriate, insufficient
105. resiliency; social
106. daycare
107. 3
108. child development
109. 20
110. 1
111. emotional bond
112. alert; responsive
113. adopted; premature; caesarean
114. sexual
115. rejecting; indifferent
116. antisocial
117. warm, loving
118. 1 month
119. cooing
120. 6
121. consonant
122. 1 year
123. 2; 200
124. single-word; telegraphic speech
125. 8,000; 4,000
126. human speech
127. biological predisposition
128. patterns

129. Psycholinguists
130. socially
131. signals
132. 3
133. abstract
134. transformations
135. 7
136. stages; assimilation; accommodation
137. sensorimotor; 2
138. object permanence
139. symbolically
140. 75
141. words; objects
142. egocentric
143. 7, 11; concrete operational; conservation
144. time, space; logically
145. 65
146. reverse
147. formal operations; 11; abstract principles
148. knowledge, experience
149. learning
150. specific knowledge
151. swift; brain
152. 1
153. 3
154. 6; 8
155. physical
156. 3
157. concepts
158. moral dilemmas
159. preconventional; punishment orientation
160. pleasure-seeking
161. conventional
162. authority
163. postconventional; social-contract
164. morality of individual principles
165. children; delinquents; children; adult
166. 20
167. justice; caring
168. relationships
169. males
170. difference
171. women
172. feral children; deprivation

173. deprivation dwarfism
174. critical period
175. hospitalism
176. deaths; retarded
177. attachment
178. perceptual stimulation
179. contact comfort
180. 20
181. colostrum
182. inanimate; insecure
183. enriched
184. visually directed
185. Head Start
186. loved; outside world
187. frequently
188. promptly; emotional
189. 2
190. restrictive

191. investigation
192. normal pattern
193. statistical; particular; averages
194. language; thinking
195. second
196. quality; responsive
197. cause-and-effect
198. curiosity, interests
199. novel, unusual, challenging
200. one-step-ahead
201. active
202. classify
203. inconsistency
204. hypotheses
205. artificial insemination
206. in vitro fertilization

207. unrelated
208. 6
209. repeatedly
210. artificially fertilizing
211. guarantee
212. two-thirds
213. genetic counseling
214. genome
215. amniocentesis
216. chorionic villus sampling
217. placenta
218. eugenics
219. genetic engineering
220. Cloning
221. blood tests

ANSWERS—SELF-TEST

1. d	8. False	15. c	22. d	29. False	36. a
2. b	9. c	16. b	23. True	30. c	37. False
3. a	10. c	17. True	24. b	31. c	38. a
4. a	11. False	18. False	25. a	32. True	
5. False	12. False	19. d	26. c	33. False	
6. d	13. d	20. c	27. False	34. False	
7. False	14. d	21. False	28. b	35. False	

ACROSS

2. environment that is richly stimulating
5. he studied institutionalized babies
6. unable to take another's viewpoint
9. growth and development of the body—especially the nervous system
11. environment
13. reflex which helps infant find bottle or breast
14. simple two-word sentences describe this speech
15. specialists in psychology who study language

DOWN

1. first stage of Piaget's Cognitive Theory
3. babies suffering from this condition are sad and depressed
4. Piaget's final stage of cognitive development
7. physical foundations of personality such as sensitivity, moodiness, etc.
8. in this stage consonant sounds are added to vowels
10. heredity
12. babies repeating vowel sounds like "oo" and "ah"

CHAPTER 15

Birth to Death: Life-Span Development

CONTENTS

TERMS AND CONCEPTS

life-span psychologist
life stages
developmental tasks
psychosocial dilemma
authoritarian parents
overly permissive parents
effective parents
overprotection (smother love)
sibling rivalry
eneuresis
encopresis
anorexia nervosa
pica
delayed speech
stuttering
learning disabilities
dyslexia
attention-deficit hyperactivity disorder (ADHD)
behavior modification
autism
echolalia
sensory blocking
sensory "spin-out"
operant shaping
child abuse
Parents Anonymous
adolescence
puberty
social markers

imaginary audiences
career development
    exploration phase
    fantasy stage
    tentative stage
    realistic stage
    establishment phase
    midcareer phase
    later career phase
vocational aspiration
vocational counselor
career centers
menopause
climacteric
biological aging
gerontologist
fluid abilities
crystallized abilities
maximum lifespan
life expectancy
disengagement theory
activity theory
ageism
thanatologist
power assertion
withdrawal of love
child management
self-esteem
Parent Effectiveness Training (PET)

I-messages   living will
natural consequences   passive euthanasia
logical consequences   active euthanasia
hospice   cryonics

IMPORTANT INDIVIDUALS

Erik Erickson   Irving Janis   Stanley Coopersmith
Diana Baumrind   Dan Wheeler   Don Dinkmeyer
Ivar Lovaas   Alex Comfort   Gary McKay
David Elkind   Bernice Neugarten   Haim Ginott
Roger Gould   Carol Ryff   Thomas Gordon
Daniel Levinson   Elizabeth Kübler-Ross

PROGRAMMED REVIEW

1.   (p. 415) The challenges of development extend from beyond childhood and into old age. _____-_____ psychologists study both continuity and change in behavior during a lifetime.

2.   (p. 416) There are six universal life stages which share certain broad similarities. These phases include _____, _____, _____, _____ _____, _____ _____, and _____ _____.

3.   (p. 416) Each stage confronts a person with a new set of _____ _____ to be mastered. These tasks are skills that must be acquired or personal changes that must take place for optimal development.

4.   (p. 416) Personality theorist Erik Erikson suggests that we face a specific _____ dilemma at each stage of life. Resolving these crises creates a new balance between a person and the social world. An unfavorable outcome makes it harder to deal with later crises.

5.   (p. 416) During stage one, the first year of life, _____ is established by regular satisfaction of a baby's needs so that the world is seen as a safe and predictable place. _____ is caused by inadequate or unpredictable care and may become the core of later insecurity, suspiciousness, or inability to relate to others.

6.   (p. 416) During stage two (1-3 years), parents help their children develop a sense _____ of when they encourage them to try new skills. Consistent overprotection may limit development, and teasing and ridicule may result in feelings of _____ and _____, the unfavorable outcome of this stage.

7.   (p. 417) During stage three (3-5 years), the child moves from simple self-control to an ability to take initiative. Parents can reinforce _____ by giving freedom to play, to ask questions, to use imagination, and to choose activities. If children learn to feel that their play, ideas, or questions are silly or stupid, they also learn to feel ashamed and _____ about the activities they initiate.

8.   (p. 417) _____ play during this period helps children practice more mature social skills and roles.

9.   (p. 417) During stage four (years 6-12), the major tasks surround introduction to school. The major crisis involves the development of _____ versus _____. The first develops if the child is praised for building, painting, and other productive activities. The second develops if a child's accomplishments are regarded as messy, childish, or inadequate.

10. (p. 417) Adolescence is the next major life stage. During stage five (12-18 years), the adolescent must build a consistent _____ out of self-perceptions and relationships with others. Failure to do so causes _____ _____ which may cause the person to seek identity by emulating musicians, athletes, etc.

11. (p. 417) Stage six, young adulthood, involves the psychological crisis of developing _____ versus _____. The former refers to an ability to care about others and a willingness to share experiences with them, the latter makes a person feel alone and uncared for in life.

12. (p. 417) In line with Erickson's view, _____ percent of college-age men and women rank a good marriage and family life as their primary adult goal.

13. (p. 417) Successful adjustment during middle adulthood, stage seven, centers on the development of _____, which is expressed by caring about oneself, one's children, and the future. It may also be achieved through productive or creative work.

14. (p. 417) Failure to develop an interest in guiding the next generation during stage seven is marked by a _____ concern with one's own needs and comforts. Life loses meaning, and the person feels bitter, dreary, and trapped.

15. (p. 418) According to Erikson, the previous seven stages of life become the basis for successful aging during stage eight, late adulthood. The person who has lived richly and responsibly develops a sense of _____ which allows aging and death to be faced with dignity. However, if previous life events are viewed with regret, the elderly person falls into _____ with a feeling that life has been a series of missed opportunities.

16. (p. 418) Erikson's description is not an exact map of the future. The dilemmas he described do not inevitably occur at the listed ages. Also, they may be _____ at various points in life.

17. (p. 419) Psychologist Diana Baumrind has studied the effects of three major styles of parenting. She describes _____ parents as those who view children as having few rights but adult-like responsibilities.

18. (p. 419) Children of authoritarian parents are expected to stay out of trouble and to accept without question what the parents regard as right and wrong behavior. Such children are typically _____ and self-controlled, but they also tend to be emotionally stiff, _____, _____ and lacking in _____.

19. (p. 419) _____ _____ parents view children as having few responsibilities, but rights similar to adults. Such parents require little responsible behavior, and rules are not enforced.

20. (p. 419) Overly permissive parents tend to produce _____, _____ children who misbehave frequently. Such children tend to "run amok" and to be aimless in their approach to life.

21. (p. 420) _____ parents are seen as those who balance their own rights with those of their children. Such parents are authoritative, but not authoritarian.

22. (p. 420) Effective parents are firm and consistent, not harsh or rigid in discipline. They encourage children to act responsibly. This parenting style produces children who tend to be _____, self controlled, _____, _____, and inquiring.

23. (p. 420) It is important for parents to remember that stress is a normal part of life. There is no point in trying to completely shield children from stressful stimulation. In fact, _____ (sometimes called "smother love") can be as damaging as overstressing a child or being excessively strict or permissive.

24. (p. 420) Most children do a good job of keeping stress at comfortable levels when _____ initiate an activity. If no immediate danger is present, it is reasonable to let children solve their own problems. This can help prepare them to cope with later stresses.

25. (p. 420) Researchers Chess, Thomas, and Birch have discussed several normal problems which may occur during childhood as reactions to stress. One of these, _____ _____, is a common problem. All children experience occasional wakefulness, frightening dreams, or a desire to get into the parents' bed.

26. (p. 420) _____ _____ of the dark, dogs, school, or of a particular room or person are also common.

27. (p. 420) Most children will be _____ _____ at times, allowing themselves to be bullied by other children. There may also be temporary periods of _____ _____ when nothing pleases the child.

28. (p. 420) Children also normally display periods of general _____ marked by tantrums or refusal to do anything requested. This trait is particularly characteristic of _____-year-olds and may be a sign of growing independence.

29. (p. 420) Another normal problem is _____, in which the child refuses to leave the side of his or her mother.

30. (p. 420) Development does not always advance smoothly. Every child will show occasional _____ or _____ to more infantile behavior.

31. (p. 420) An additional problem common to the elementary school years is _____ _____ where jealousy, competition, and even hostility may develop between brothers and sisters.

32. (p. 420) Some sibling conflict may be constructive. A limited amount of aggressive give-and-take between siblings provides an opportunity to learn emotional _____, self-_____, and good sportsmanship. Parents should be careful not to play favorites or compare one child with another.

33. (p. 421) Parents should also expect school-age children to _____ at times against the rules and limitations of the adult world. Being with peers can offer a chance to do some of the things the adult world forbids. It is normal for children to be messy, noisy, hostile, or destructive to a moderate degree.

34. (p. 421) Significant emotional difficulties may develop during toilet training or over bowel and bladder habits. The two most common problems are _____ (lack of bladder control) and _____ (lack of bowel control).

35. (p. 421) Enuresis is more common than encopresis and many times more common among males than females. They can both represent a means of expressing _____ or pent-up _____.

36. (p. 421) Delays in toilet training or a few "accidents" are no cause for alarm. The average age for completing toilet training is _____ months, and it is not unusual for some children to take _____ months longer.

37. (p. 421) Many bed wetters have difficulties because they become extremely _____ when asleep. Limiting fluids during the evening, encouraging and rewarding "dry" nights, and taking an understanding and sympathetic attitude can all help.

38. (p. 421) Feeding disturbances are another area of emotional difficulty. _____ may be encouraged by an overprotective mother who compensates for feeling unloved by showering the child with "love" in the form of food.

39. (p. 421) Serious cases of undereating, or self-starvation, are called _____ _____. The victims are mostly adolescent females experiencing conflicts about maturing sexually. By starving themselves, they limit figure development, prevent menstruation, and delay the time when they must face adult responsibilities.

40. (p. 421) Another childhood problem associated with eating difficulties is a condition called _____, during which children go through a period of intense appetite and eat or chew on all sorts of inedible substances.

41. (p. 421) Speech disturbances may be another source of emotional difficulties. One of two common speech problems is _____ _____. This difficulty may result from a general lack of stimulation, parents who discourage growing up, childhood stresses, mental retardation, or emotional disturbances.

42. (p. 421) The other common problem, _____, was once held to be primarily a psychological disturbance, but now believed to be more _____ in origin. For example, it is _____ times more common in males than females, and there seem to be hereditary factors underlying its occurrence. However, learned fears, anxieties, and speech patterns probably add to the problem as well.

43. (p. 421) Stuttering occurs most when a person _____ that he or she is going to stutter. Therefore, parents must be careful not to add to a child's anxiety and frustration by being angry or critical.

44. (p. 421) If a child begins speech therapy before _____, there is a chance that stuttering will disappear. In some cases it may even disappear on its own. But if it doesn't disappear, or isn't treated, stuttering can become a _____ problem.

45. (p. 422) _____ _____ include problems with thinking, perception, language ability, control of attention, or activity levels. For example, _____ is an inability to read with understanding.

46. (p. 422) Approximately _____ to _____ percent of school-age children have some degree of dyslexia. These children often reverse letters or try to read from right to left.

47. (p. 422) Dyslexia appears to be caused by a malfunction of language processing areas on the _____ side of the brain. It is typically treated by special educational programs that use exercises in hearing, touch, and vision to improve reading comprehension.

48. (p. 422) One of the most significant learning disorders is _____-_____ _____ disorder, a condition in which the child is constantly in motion and cannot concentrate.

49. (p. 422) An ADHD child's problem may be primarily _____ (poor attention) or _____ (hyperactivity). Usually it is both.

50. (p. 422) ADHD affects _____ to _____ percent of all children, 5 times as many boys as girls. Unless it is carefully managed, it frequently leads to school drop-outs and life-long learning problems.

51. (p. 422) ADHD is believed to result from a brain condition present at birth. Specific areas of the brain associated with language, motor control, and attention are _____ than normal in ADHD children.

52. (p. 422) Treatment for ADHD includes drugs, behavioral management approaches, and family counseling. Physicians typically use the stimulant drug _____ (methylphenidate) to control ADHD. While it might seem that stimulants would make hyperactivity worse, such drugs actually have a calming effect, probably because they lengthen the ADHD child's attention span and reduce impulsiveness.

53. (p. 422) Ritalin remains controversial because it can retard _____ growth, at least temporarily. Also, many experts believe that some of the 800,000 American children who take stimulants are wrongly given such drugs for ordinary _____.

54. (p. 422) Today, drugs are not usually used to treat ADHD without also providing therapy for behavioral and emotional problems. For many children, _____ _____ (the application of learning principles to human problems) is as effective as drug treatment.

55. (p. 423) The basic idea of behavior modification is to reward the child when he or she is calm and paying attention. Children are also taught how to monitor their own behavior and how to ignore distractions. When they learn self-control in this way, improvements are _____ _____ than they are with drug treatment alone.

56. (p. 423) Childhood autism is a problem which affects 1 in 2500 children, boys _____ times more often than girls. It is one of the most severe childhood problems.

57. (p. 423) In addition to being extremely _____, the autistic child may throw gigantic temper tantrums including self-destructive behavior. Many autistic children are _____, evidencing no speech.

58. (p. 423) If they speak at all, they often parrot back everything said, a reaction known as _____. Autistic children also engage in frequent repetitive actions like rocking, flapping their arms, or waving their fingers in front of their eyes.

59. (p. 423) Additionally, the child may show no response to an extremely loud noise (_____ _____) or may spend hours watching a water faucet drip (_____ _____- _____).

60. (p. 423) At one time, experts blamed autism on parents. It is now recognized that autism is caused by _____ defects in the _____ _____.

61. (p. 423) Even as babies, autistic children are aloof and do not cuddle or mold to their parents' arms. Recent research suggests that the defect may lie in the _____, which affects attention and motor activity.

62. (p. 423) Even with help, only about 1 autistic child in _____ approaches normalcy. Nevertheless, almost all autistic children can make progress with proper care. When treatment is begun early, behavior modification has been particularly successful.

63. (p. 423) Teaching Billy (the autistic child described in the chapter preview) to talk began with his learning to blow out a match. Next he was rewarded for babbling meaningless sounds, then for accidentally saying a word. Notice that this process is basically an example of _____ _____.

64. (p. 423) In a behavior modification program such as that pioneered by Ivar Lovaas, each of the autistic child's maladaptive behaviors is altered using combinations of reward and punishment. In addition to food, sensory stimulation, such as _____ or _____, is often very reinforcing.

65. (p. 423) Researchers have found that following actions such as head banging and hand biting by _____ can bring a swift end to self-destructive behavior.

66. (p. 423) Estimates on the number of children who are physically abused by parents range from _____ percent to _____ percent. At a minimum, 1.7 million children are physically battered each year in the U.S.

67. (p. 423) In about _____-_____ of all such cases, the child is seriously injured. Every hear hundreds of children are killed by their parents.

68. (p. 423) Abusive parents are usually young (under _____ years old) and more are from _____ income levels. They often have a high level of stress and frustration in their lives. Typical problems include loneliness, marital discord, unemployment, drug or alcohol abuse, divorce, family violence, and work anxieties.

69. (p. 424) Some parents are aware they are mistreating a child, but are unable to _____; others may hate their child because the child's diapers, crying, or needs are unbearable to them. Often these parents expect the child to love them and make them _____ and respond with violence when these unrealistic demands are not met.

70. (p. 424) In addition to being highly reactive to stress, abusive mothers are more likely to believe that their children are acting _____ to annoy them.

71. (p. 424) The core of much child abuse is a _____ of _____ established when parents were themselves mistreated as children. As an estimate, roughly 30 percent of all parents who were abused as children will mistreat their own children.

72. (p. 424) In one study, abused children were observed as they interacted with playmates. In almost every instance, they responded to distress with _____, _____, or physical assault.

73. (p. 424) Adults who are able to break the abusive cycle are more likely to have received _____ support from a nonabusive adult during childhood, to have received _____, and to have had an emotionally supportive relationship with a _____.

74. (p. 424) Legal "cures" for child abuse are not very satisfying. Parents need help such as that available through _____ _____, a national organization staffed by former child abusers who are determined to help each other stop abusing children.

75. (p. 424) Another way of preventing child abuse is by changing _____. One recent survey found that corporal punishment is widely accepted in this country, even punishment that hovers on the threshold of abuse.

76. (p. 425) _____ refers to the period during which we move from childhood to acceptance as an adult. This change is recognized in almost all cultures.

77. (p. 425) The _____ of adolescence varies greatly from culture to culture. Most 14-year-old girls in America live at home and go to school. But in rural villages of the Near East many are married and have children.

78. (p. 425) _____ refers to rapid physical growth coupled with hormonal changes that bring sexual maturity. This phenomenon is a biological event, while adolescence is a culturally defined period.

79. (p. 426) The peak growth spurt during puberty occurs earlier for girls than for boys. This accounts for the 1 to 2 year period when girls tend to be taller than boys. For girls, the onset of puberty typically occurs between _____ and _____, while for boys the range is _____ to _____.

80. (p. 426) Puberty tends to dramatically increase body awareness and concerns about physical appearance. About one-_____ of all boys and one-_____ of all girls report being dissatisfied with their appearance during early adolescence.

81. (p. 426) When puberty comes unusually early or late, its impact may be magnified. For boys, early maturation typically enhances their self-image. They tend to be more _____, _____, _____, self-assured, and popular with their peers.

82. (p. 426) Many late maturing boys are anxious about being behind in development. However, after they catch up they tend to be more _____, _____, self-assertive, and _____ of themselves.

83. (p. 426) Developmentally advanced girls in elementary school tend to have _____ prestige among peers. By junior high, however, early development leads to _____ peer prestige and adult approval.

84. (p. 426) Later maturing girls have the possible advantage of usually growing _____ and _____ than early maturing girls.

85. (p. 426) Early maturing girls date _____, are more independent, and are more active in school. They are also more often in _____ at school.

86. (p. 426) One added cost of early maturation is that it may force premature _____ _____. When a teenager begins to look like an adult, he or she may be treated like an adult. If not emotionally ready for this, the search for identity may end too soon, leaving the person with a distorted, poorly formed sense of self.

87. (p. 426) Psychologist David Elkind believes that a large number of American parents are hurrying their children's development causing more children than ever to show serious _____ _____.

88. (p. 426) Elkind's main point is that today's teenagers have _____ thrust on them too soon. Too many teenagers are left without the guidance, direction, and support they need to become healthy adults. There is no place for teenagers in today's society.

89. (p. 426) According to Elkind, the traditional social _____ of adolescence have all but disappeared. These are signs that tell where a person stands socially.

90. (p. 427) Another interesting pattern Elkind has noted in adolescent thought is their preoccupation with _____ _____. They act like others are as aware of their thoughts and feelings as they are themselves.

91. (p. 427) This tendency can lead to painful _____-_____, as in everyone staring at you. It also seems to underlie attention-seeking "performances" involving outlandish _____ or _____.

92. (p. 427) The adolescent search for identity often results in increased conflict with _____. Some of this is necessary for growth of a separate identity. A complete lack of conflict may mean that the adolescent is afraid to seek independence.

93. (p. 428) Adolescents and their parents usually agree on most basic topics. The largest conflicts tend to be over more superficial differences in styles of _____, _____, social behavior, etc. In general, adolescents tend to overestimate differences between themselves and their parents.

94. (p. 428) Increased identification with _____ groups is quite common during adolescence. This gives a measure of security and a sense of identity apart from the family. It also provides practice in belonging to a social network.

95. (p. 428) Conformity to peer values peaks in early adolescence, but it remains strong at least through high school. Throughout this period there is always a danger of allowing group pressure to _____ personal growth.

96. (p. 428) By the end of high school, many adolescents have not yet sufficiently explored various aspects of personal identity. Perhaps this is why many students view moving on to work or college as a chance to _____ _____ of earlier roles.

97. (p. 428) For many who choose college, the effect may be more a matter of placing further changes in identity on hold. Typically, commitment to an emerging adult identity grows _____ in later college years.

98. (p. 428) Minority adolescents often face a barrage of prejudice and negative stereotypes from the majority culture. For such reasons, these adolescents run a high risk of adopting a personal identity _____.

99. (p. 428) The danger in foreclosed identities is that it severely limits the exploration of various life paths. Minority youth share the hopes, dreams, and aspirations of mainstream society, but frequently do not share the _____ to attain their goals.

100. (p. 428) The search for identity may be intensified during adolescence, but it does not end there. For example, the process of selecting a _____ often starts in childhood and continues into young adulthood.

101. (p. 428) Vocational decisions are neither permanent nor easily undone. Usually, by the time a person has selected a career path, it takes a big effort to change course. This reality is illustrated by a survey in which _____ percent of those polled said that for better or worse, they felt "locked into" their current jobs.

102. (p. 428) For most people who enter professions, career development tends to flow through four broad phases: (1) the _____ phase, during which an initial search for career possibilities is made; (2) the _____ phase, during which the person finds a job, enters a career, develops competence, and gains status; (3) the _____ phase, which is a time of high productivity and acceptance by co-workers; and (4) the _____ career phase, when the individual serves as a respected expert and often as a mentor for younger workers.

103. (p. 429) During the exploration phase, most people go through a recognizable series of stages as they choose a vocation. In the _____ stage, children under age 10 simply imagine what they want to be when they grow up.

104. (p. 429) During the _____ stage (roughly, ages 10 to 18) adolescents begin to form more realistic, if somewhat general, ideas about what they want to do. However, their plans may shift several times during this period.

105. (p. 429) After high school, various social and practical pressures lead most people to narrow their range of vocational options. During this _____ stage, the first steps are taken to find out what specific jobs are like and to prepare for them.

106. (p. 429) By the early 20s, most people begin to carry out their vocational plans. While it may seem that most people carefully choose a vocation or career, there is evidence that vocational choice is often rather _____.

107. (p. 429) To improve the quality of a vocational choice it helps to recognize that our attraction to certain jobs or careers is influenced by such important influences as _____ status, _____, school achievement, _____ background, gender, and personal interests.

108. (p. 429) It is also important to realize that you have the potential to succeed in a variety of occupations. This is reflected by the fact that the best single predictor of what job category you will enter is your _____ _____.

109. (p. 429) To make sure that your vocational choice will be realistic and personally rewarding, you must (1) gain an accurate understanding of various _____ and (2) get a clear picture of your own interests, needs, and goals.

110. (p. 429) The easiest way to improve occupational choice is to consult a _____ _____. These professionals are counseling psychologists who have specialized in the skills and knowledge needed to match people with jobs.

111. (p. 429) A vocational counselor can help you clarify your career goals, and can administer vocational _____ and _____ tests to guide your choice.

112. (p. 429) Many colleges now offer vocational counseling at campus _____ _____. These facilities also typically hold a wealth of information about various jobs and careers.

113. (p. 429) A good way to be your own vocational counselor is to consult the _____ _____ _____. This book, published yearly by the U.S. Department of Labor, provides objective information about the outlook for various occupations. It includes job descriptions, information on training requirements, average earnings, and the number of jobs likely to be available in coming years.

114. (p. 430) In many occupations the nature of the work is not what it seems from the outside. To find out beforehand what an occupation is really like, it is advisable to _____ to several people in that line of work or even spend a day _____ them.

115. (p. 430) Recent research by Roger Gould has identified several important substages in adult development. According to Gould, the age group 16-18 is marked by a struggle to escape from _____ _____ which may cause anxiety about the future and conflict about dependency.

116. (p. 430) By the early 20s, leaving the _____ is usually associated with building new friendships with other adults who serve as substitutes.

117. (p. 430) Building a workable life summarizes ages 22-28 during which the two dominant activities are striving for _____ and reaching out to _____.

118. (p. 430) By age 30 many people experience a minor life crisis, questioning what life is all about. _____ are particularly vulnerable during this time of dissatisfaction. _____ _____ and _____ are common symptoms of this "crisis of questions."

119. (p. 430) People in the age 35-43 stage of life are typically beginning to become more aware of the reality of _____. Attempts to succeed at a career, or to achieve one's life goals become more _____.

120. (p. 431) The urgency of the previous stage gives way to a calmer acceptance of one's fate in the _____ to _____ year age range. The predominant feeling is that former decisions can be lived with.

121. (p. 431) After age _____, a noticeable mellowing occurs. Emphasis is placed on sharing day-to-day joys and sorrows.

122. (p. 431) Psychologist Daniel Levinson carried out an in-depth study of adult lives and identified five periods when people typically experience a _____ period when one life pattern ends and opens the door to new possibilities.

123. (p. 431) He found that most men went through a period of instability, anxiety, and change between the ages of _____ and _____. He believes this also applies to women.

124. (p. 431) Roughly _____-_____ of the men studied by Levinson defined the midlife period as a last chance to achieve their goals, often stated as a key event.

125. (p. 432) A smaller percentage of men experienced a serious midlife _____, often based on having chosen a dead-end job or lifestyle.

126. (p. 432) Levinson characterized a third pattern as "_____ _____." In this case, the person had earlier established a seriously flawed life structure. The midlife decision to "start over" was typically followed by 8 to 10 years of rebuilding.

127. (p. 432) One way to improve career decisions is to examine how you approach them. Irving Janis and Dan Wheeler have described four basic _____ styles by which people typically deal with work dilemmas.

128. (p. 432) The _____ style is the most effective of the four. It describes individuals who evaluate information objectively and make decisions with a clear understanding of the alternatives.

129. (p. 432) Persons with the _____ style drift along with a nonchalant attitude toward job decisions. They tend to let chance direct their careers and to take whatever comes along without really making plans.

130. (p. 432) People with the _____-_____ style are fully aware of the risks and opportunities presented by career choices and dilemmas. However, they are uncomfortable making decisions. This leads them to procrastinate, rationalize, and to make excuses for their inaction and indecision.

131. (p. 432) People with the _____ style more or less panic when forced to make career decisions. They may collect hundreds of job announcements and brochures, but they become so frantic that making logical decisions is nearly impossible.

132. (p. 432) In the forties and fifties, declining strength, physical vigor, and youthfulness make it clear to individuals that more than half of their time is gone. But, there is a letting go of the "_____ _____" and an increased attempt to be _____ with the direction one's life has taken.

133. (p. 432) For most women during this era, _____ represents the first real encounter with aging. This process ends monthly menstruation. Also, the level of the hormone estrogen drops, sometimes causing drastic changes in mood or appearance and the occurrence of physical symptoms such as "hot flashes."

134. (p. 432) While many women experience anxiety, irritability, or depression at this time, most postmenopausal women feel that menopause was not as bad as they expected and that their anxiety came from _____ _____ what to expect.

135. (p. 432) Males do not undergo any abrupt physical change directly comparable to menopause, but often experience _____, or significant physiological change, with symptoms similar to those experienced by women in menopause.

136. (p. 433) During the climacteric, decreases in male hormone output may cause psychological symptoms similar to those experienced by women in menopause. However, men remain _____ at this time, and many of their symptoms are more likely related to self-doubts caused by declining vigor and changing physical appearance.

137. (p. 433) Currently, there are an estimated _____ million Americans over the age of 65; by the year 2020, there will be some _____ million people 65 and older, or one out of every five people.

138. (p. 433) _____ _____ is a gradual process that begins early in life. Peak functioning in most physical capacities reaches a maximum by about _____ to _____ years of age and then gradually declines.

139. (p. 433) For those who are still young, the prospect of physical aging may be the largest threat of old age. However, only about _____ percent of the elderly are in nursing homes.

140. (p. 433) The length of our lives is limited by a boundary called the _____ _____. Current estimates of the average human lifespan place it around 95 to 110 years.

141. (p. 434) For most people, _____ _____ (the actual number of years the average person lives) is shorter than a lifespan. In the 1800's the average was 36. Currently, it is _____ for males and _____ for females.

142. (p. 434) While there is no known way to extend human lifespan, the following rules can help increase life expectancy: (1) Do not _____; (2) Use _____ in moderation or not at all; (3) Avoid becoming _____; (4) Have high blood pressure treated; (5) Remain socially and economically active in retirement; (6) _____ regularly throughout life; (7) Get married; (8) Learn to manage _____; (9) Choose long-lived parents.

143. (p. 434) _____ (those who study aging) estimate that only _____ percent of the disabilities of old people are medical, the rest are social, political, and cultural.

144. (p. 434) Little overall decline occurs in intelligence test scores with aging. Although "_____" abilities (those requiring speed or rapid learning) may decline, "_____" abilities, such as vocabulary and accumulated knowledge, actually improve at least into the 70s.

145. (p. 434) Many elderly persons are at least as mentally able as the average young adult. On intellectual tests, top scorers over the age of 65 match the average for men under _____. These are typically people who have continued to work and remain intellectually active.

146. (p. 434) Two principal theories have been proposed to explain successful adjustment to the physical and social changes that accompany aging. The _____ _____ of aging assumes that it is normal and desirable that people will withdraw from society as they age.

147. (p. 434) The second view, _____ _____, predicts that people who remain active physically, mentally, and socially will adjust better to aging.

148. (p. 435) The majority of studies conducted on aging support the _____ _____, although successful aging probably requires a combination of activity and disengagement. For example, one researcher has shown that the elderly tend to disengage from activities that are no longer satisfying while maintaining those that are.

149. (p. 435) _____ refers to discrimination or prejudice on the basis of age. It can be positive (as in Japan, where increased age brings increased status and respect), but in most western nations it tends to have a negative impact on older individuals.

150. (p. 435) Another facet of ageism is _____ of the aged. Popular images, especially as seen in movies and television, help perpetrate the myths underlying ageism.

151. (p. 435) One of the best ways to combat ageism is to counter stereotypes with facts. As one example, studies show that in many occupations older workers perform better at jobs requiring both _____ and _____.

152. (p. 435) Gradual slowing with age is a reality, but it is often countered by experience, skill, or expertise. For example, one study showed that while older typists responded _____ on reaction time tests, there was _____ _____ in the actual typing speeds of younger and older typists.

153. (p. 436) Bernice Neugarten conducted a study of 200 people between the ages of 70 and 79. She found that _____ percent were satisfied with their lives after retirement. She also found that most prefer to live apart from their children and few are placed in mental hospitals because of mental senility or uncaring children.

154. (p. 436) Carol Ryff has pointed out six criteria of well-being in old age: (1) self-_____; (2) _____ relations with others; (3) _____ (personal freedom); (4) _____ mastery; (5) A purpose in _____; (6) Continued personal growth.

155. (p. 436) In a public opinion poll of 1500 adults, only about _____ percent showed evidence of directly fearing their own deaths.

156. (p. 436) Older people actually have fewer death fears than younger people. They more often fear the _____ of dying, such as pain or helplessness, rather than death itself.

157. (p. 436) While these findings seem to indicate a general lack of fear about death, it may be more accurate to say that they reflect a deeply ingrained _____ of death.

158. (p. 436) The average person's exposure to death consists of the artificial and unrealistic portrayals of death on TV. By the time the average person is 17 years old, he or she will have witnessed roughly _____ TV deaths, mostly homicides.

159. (p. 436) A more direct indication of emotional responses to death comes from the work of Elizabeth Kübler-Ross, a _____ (one who studies death) who has spent hundreds of hours at the bedsides of the terminally ill.

160. (p. 436) She has found that dying people display at least five basic reactions as they prepare for death. These include: (1) _____ and _____; (2) _____; (3) _____; (4) _____; (5) _____.

161. (p. 437) Not all terminally ill persons display all these reactions, nor do they always occur in this order. Individual styles of dying vary greatly according to _____ maturity, religious belief, _____, _____, the attitudes of relatives, etc. In general, one's approach to dying will mirror his or her style of living.

162. (p. 437) It is a mistake to think of Kübler-Ross' list as a fixed series of stages to go through in order or to assume someone who does not show all the list emotional reactions is somehow deviant or immature. Rather, the list describes _____ reactions to impending death.

163. (p. 437) Understanding the emotional reactions involved in the process of dying can help the dying individual cope. Also, it is helpful to realize that close friends or relatives of the dying person may feel many of the same _____ _____ before or after the person's death because they, too, are facing a loss.

164. (p. 437) Perhaps the most important thing to recognize is that the dying person may have a need to _____ _____ with others or to discuss death openly.

165. (p. 437) _____ is a natural and normal reaction to loss and an essential part of adjusting to death. It tends to follow a predictable pattern beginning with a period of _____ or numbness when the bereaved may remain in a dazed state showing little emotion.

166. (p. 437) This reaction is followed by sharp _____ of _____, episodes of yearning for the dead person and sometimes anguished outbursts of anger.

167. (p. 438) The first powerful reactions of grief gradually give way to weeks or months of _____, _____, and depression. Life seems futile.

168. (p. 438) The mourner is usually able to resume work or other activities after _____ or _____ weeks, but insomnia, loss of energy and appetite, and similar signs of depression may continue.

169. (p. 438) Slowly the bereaved person accepts what cannot be changed, makes a new beginning, and moves toward _____. Reaching this point can take many months, or longer.

170. (p. 438) Individual reactions to grief vary considerably. Generally, a _____ or _____ typically passes before the more intense stages of grief run their course.

171. (p. 438) It has long been assumed that suppressing grief may later lead to more severe and lasting _____. However, research shows that a lack of intense grief does _____ usually predict later problems.

172. (p. 439) As a single problem area in development, the question of how to be a good parent has probably attracted more attention than any other. Two key ingredients are _____ and _____.

173. (p. 439) Effective discipline is authoritative yet _____. The goal is to socialize a child without destroying the _____ of love and trust between parent and child.

174. (p. 439) One 22-year-long study found that children whose parents are critical, harsh, or authoritarian often become _____-_____ adults. They also have a higher than average record of _____ and substance abuse.

175. (p. 439) Discipline should give children freedom to express their deepest feelings through speech and actions. It should permit the child to move freely within well-defined _____ for acceptable behavior.

176. (p. 439) Individual parents may choose limits that are more "strict" or less "strict." This choice is less important than the _____ of parental standards, which gives a child a sense of security and stability. Without it the child's world seems unreliable and unpredictable.

177. (p. 440) Parents tend to base discipline on one or more of three techniques. Power _____ refers to physical punishment or to a show of force in which parents take away toys or privileges. Such power-oriented techniques are associated with fear, hatred

of parents, and a lack of spontaneity and warmth. Severely punished children also tend to be defiant, rebellious and aggressive.

178. (p. 440) Some parents use _____ of _____ by refusing to speak to a child, by threatening to leave, or by rejecting the child. This tends to produce children who are self-disciplined, but also anxious, insecure, and dependent on adults for approval.

179. (p. 440) The third technique, child _____, combines praise, recognition, approval, etc., to encourage desirable behavior. However, younger children may not always see the connection between rules, explanations, and their own behavior.

180. (p. 440) The term _____-_____ refers to a quiet confidence that comes from regarding oneself a worthwhile person. A high amount is essential for emotional health. Low amounts are associated with individuals who have a low estimation of their value as people.

181. (p. 440) Stanley Coopersmith has found that _____ self-esteem was related to the use of physical punishment or withholding of love. _____ self-esteem was related to management techniques which emphasized clear and consistent discipline coupled with high parental interest and concern for the child.

182. (p. 440) In using physical punishment and withdrawal of love the following guidelines should be observed:
    1) Separate disapproval of the _____ from disapproval of the _____.
    2) State specifically what misbehaviors you are punishing.
    3) Punishment should never be harsh or injurious to a child.
    4) Punishment is most effective when it is administered _____.
    5) Physical punishment is not particularly effective with children under age _____ or older than age _____.
    6) Reserve physical punishment for situations that pose an immediate danger to the younger child.
    7) Remember too that it is usually more effective to reinforce children when they are being good than it is to punish them for misbehavior.

183. (p. 441) Don Dinkmeyer and Gary McKay point out four basic ingredients of a positive parent-child relationship: (1) Mutual _____; (2) Shared _____; (3) Love; and (4) Encouragement.

184. (p. 441) In practice, encouragement means: (1) Valuing and _____ children; (2) Pointing out _____ aspects of a child's behavior; (3) Showing _____ in children; (4) Giving _____ for effort and improvement; (5) Showing appreciation for the child's contributions to the family.

185. (p. 441) Haim Ginott has suggested that it is essential to make a distinction between a child's _____ and a child's _____. He encourages parents to teach their children that all _____ are appropriate, only actions are subject to disapproval.

186. (p. 442) Thomas Gordon, who has developed a program called _____ _____ _____ program called (PET), believes that parents should send _____ messages instead of _____ messages.

187. (p. 442) Children are greatly influenced by the consequences of their actions. Sometimes _____ consequences arise which tend to discourage misbehavior. For example, the child who refuses to eat dinner will get uncomfortably hungry if snacking is not allowed.

188. (p. 442) An alternative are those defined by parents. These are sometimes called _____ consequences because they should be rational and reasonable. For example, a parent might say, "You can play with your dolls as soon as you've taken your bath."

189. (p. 442) The concept of logical, parent-defined consequences can be combined with I-messages to handle many day-to-day instances of misbehavior. The key idea is to use an I-message to set up _____ and then give the child a _____ to make.

190. (p. 444) A _____ is basically a hospital for the terminally ill, modeled after a pioneering English facility. The development of such facilities is one of the reactions to the fact that more than 70 percent of the people in our country die outside their homes, much the reverse of how things were at the beginning of this century.

191. (p. 444) A hospice is different from a hospital in several ways. For one, there are lots of _____ present. Secondly, the _____ is pleasant, informal, and has a sense of continued living. And thirdly, the patient is allowed _____ of _____.

192. (p. 444) The "right to die" concept has been most recently focused by the Karen Ann Quinlan case. In most states it is illegal to remove life-supporting equipment as was done in her case. One solution gaining support is the _____ _____ made out when the person is healthy, saying that should the person become irreversibly ill, they do not want life sustained by medical machines or heroic measures.

193. (p. 445) The right to die won for Karen Quinlan by her parents may be thought of as _____ _____ in which death is allowed to occur but is not actively caused. In _____ _____, steps would be taken to administer drugs that induce death painlessly.

194. (p. 445) _____ involves freezing a person's body upon death. The idea is to keep them frozen until medical science perfects ways to thaw, restore, and revive the person. However, freezing does serious damage to the body and would severely cripple the brain.

SELF-TEST

1. (p. 416) There are certain broad similarities in the universal life stages of each individual. Each represents a milestone in physical maturation and psychological development, and each confronts a person with a new set of:
   a. developmental tasks
   b. life enhancements
   c. developmental modifications
   d. psychosocial outcomes

2. (p. 416) Which of the following is *not* a correct association according to Erikson's life stages?
   a. stage 2—autonomy versus shame and doubt
   b. stage 6—intimacy versus isolation
   c. stage 4—industry versus inferiority
   d. stage 1—generativity versus stagnation

3. (p. 417) A favorable outcome to the life crisis of adolescence would include:
    a. faith in the environment and others
    b. concern for family, society, and future generations
    c. an integrated image of oneself as a unique person
    d. confidence in productive skills, learning how to work

4. (p. 417) If the psychosocial dilemma of middle adulthood is favorably resolved, the outcome is a(n):
    a. concern for family, society, and/or future generations
    b. confidence in productive skills, learning how to work
    c. feelings of self-control and adequacy
    d. ability to form bonds of love and friendship with others

5. (p. 419) Which of these is a correct match of parenting styles and effects upon children's behaivor according to Baumrind's studies?
    a. effective parents—inquiring, assertive, self-controlled children
    b. authoritarian parents—dependent, immature children who misbehave frequently
    c. overly permissive parents—obedient, emotionally stiff, apprehensive children
    d. all of the above

6. (p. 420) True-False. Stress during childhood should always be avoided since the infant has little ability to deal with it at that age.

7. (p. 420) Of the following, which is *not* considered a normal reaction to the unavoidable stress of growing up?
    a. sibling rivalry   c. specific fears of the dark, school, etc.
    b. anorexia   d. reversals to more infantile behaviors

8. (p. 421) Which of the following is *not* true of enuresis?
    a. It is more common than encopresis.
    b. It is many times more common in females due to slower muscular development.
    c. It may represent expression of frustration or pent-up hostility.
    d. It may simply result because children are extremely relaxed when they sleep.

9. (p. 421) Which of the following is true of anorexia nervosa?
    a. Most victims are adolescent males.
    b. It is possibly related to distortions in body image or conflicts about maturing sexually.
    c. It is often associated with encopresis or enuresis.
    d. The condition refers to excessive overeating leading to significant overweight problems.

10. (p. 421) Which of the following is a type of eating disorder in which inedible objects are chewed or eaten?
    a. anorexia nervosa   c. autism
    b. enuresis   d. pica

11. (p. 421) True-False. The two most common speech problems among children are stuttering and echolalia.

12. (p. 422) Which of the following is a learning disability?
    a. dyslexia   c. climacteric change
    b. pica   d. crystallized intelligence

13. (p. 422) ADHD is believed to result from
    a. poor diet occurring during specific learning critical periods
    b. lack of parental discipline and family dysfunction
    c. a condition present at birth in which certain brain areas are smaller than normal
    d. environmental factors such as lighting

14. (p. 423) Which of the following does *not* characterize childhood autism?
    a. extreme isolation   c. retarded language development
    b. sensory spin-out   d. hyperactivity

15. (p. 423) Which of the following is a behavior disturbance in which spoken words are simply repeated in a parroting, stereotyped manner?
    a. encopresis   c. echolalia
    b. stuttering   d. glossalalia

16. (p. 423) Autism, hyperactivity, and other extreme behavioral problems of childhood can be effectively treated through:
    a. severe and consistent punishment
    b. behavior modification techniques
    c. increased parental attention
    d. proper diet

17. (p. 423) Which of the following is *not* a characteristic frequently seen among abusive parents?
    a. most do not begin abusing their child until the child reaches the rebellious teen years
    b. many were themselves abused as children
    c. they often have a high level of stress and frustration in their lives
    d. more come from lower income levels

18. (p. 424) Parents Anonymous seeks to:
    a. assist courts in supervising foster home placements of abused children
    b. use volunteers and former child abusers to create a network of support in helping parents to stop abusing their children
    c. promote legislation setting criteria for who can and cannot become parents
    d. study abusive parents, collect statistical data, and make suggestions to professionals treating abusive parents

19. (p. 425) True-False. While the onset of adolescence may vary from culture to culture, the length is fairly consistent—usually about five years.

20. (p. 425) Which of the following is *not* true of puberty?
    a. It is a biological process that refers to rapid physical growth, coupled with hormonal changes that bring sexual maturity.
    b. The onset for girls typically occurs between 11 and 14.
    c. It tends to dramatically increase body image and concerns about physical appearance.
    d. The peak growth spurt during puberty occurs earlier for boys than for girls.

21. (p. 427) True-False. David Elkind has theorized that teenagers are preoccupied with imaginary audiences which can lead to painful self-consciousness or attention-seeking "performances."

22. (p. 430) True-False. In Roger Gould's analysis of personality changes and psychological developments during adulthood, he found that people 29-34 years of age experience a mellowing of desires and an emphasis on sharing day-to-day joys and sorrows.

23. (p. 431) Which of the following is *not* a pattern of response to the midlife crisis as discussed by Daniel Levinson?
     a. People mellow out, accept their recognition of inevitable death, and place strong emphasis on family and friends.
     b. A serious decline may occur related to obvious failure or feelings of pointlessness.
     c. People break out of seriously flawed life structures and may literally start over.
     d. It is seen as a last chance to achieve life goals and can be a period of stress.

24. (p. 433) True-False. Only about five percent of the elderly are placed in nursing homes.

25. (p. 434) An expert on the problems of aging and the aged is called a:
     a. thanatologist   c. obstetrician
     b. gerontologist   d. pediatrician

26. (p. 434) It is estimated that only about _____ percent of the disability of old people is medical.
     a. 5   c. 20
     b. 10   d. 25

27. (p. 434) True-False. Although there may be declines in crystallized abilities with aging, there is an improvement in fluid abilities.

28. (p. 434) Which of the following postulates that people who remain psychologically, physically, and socially involved are better able to adjust to the aging process?
     a. activation-arousal theory   c. disengagement theory
     b. engagement theory   d. activity theory

29. (p. 436) True-False. One researcher found that older people more often fear the circumstances of death rather than death itself.

30. (p. 436) A person who studies death and dying is referred to as a:
     a. thanatologist   c. cerebrologist
     b. gerontologist   d. mortician

31. (p. 436) Which of the following is *not* a basic stage in preparation for death as described by Kübler-Ross?
     a. positioning   c. anger
     b. depression   d. acceptance

32. (p. 437) After the period of shock or numbness, the next predictable pattern a mourner usually experiences is:
     a. acceptance of what cannot be changed, and the start of a new beginning
     b. weeks or months of apathy, dejection, and depression
     c. the absence of emotion accompanied by difficulties accepting the reality of loss
     d. pangs of grief in which the mourner experiences painful yearnings for the dead person

33. (p. 437) Which of the following is *not* true of grief?
   a. It is a natural and normal reaction to loss.
   b. Initial shock is followed by sharp pangs of grief.
   c. A person who avoids grief by suppressing feelings usually later experiences a much more severe and lasting depression.
   d. It is important for those around the mourner to support their grief and allow its expression.

34. (p. 440) Which of the following parental styles results in children who tend to be self-disciplined and frequently anxious, insecure, and dependent on adults for approval?
   a. power assertion   c. withdrawal of love
   b. child management   d. power-oriented

35. (p. 440) Which of the following is *not* true of punishment as a parenting technique?
   a. Physical punishment should be reserved for situations that pose an immediate danger to the younger child.
   b. Spanking is not particularly effective for children under age two.
   c. Spanking is most effective for children over age five.
   d. Punishment should involve separating disapproval of the act from disapproval of the child.

36. (p. 441) True-False. Haim Ginott encourages parents to teach their children that all feelings are appropriate, only actions are subject to disapproval.

37. (p. 442) True-False. Thomas Gordon recommends that parents learn to send "I" messages rather than "you" messages, to their children.

38. (p. 444) True-False. A hospice is a hospital for the terminally ill where the dying person receives specialized care to improve the quality of life in the person's final days.

39. (p. 445) True-False. Passive euthanasia involves passively freezing a body immediately after death.

APPLYING YOUR KNOWLEDGE

1. Contact a vocational counselor or campus career center if available and arrange to discuss your occupational interests and choices. Take a vocational interest or aptitude test if available.

2. Become familiar with the *Occupational Outlook Handbook*. Look up several careers you might be interested in and examine the kinds of education, skills, and experience you might need for each of these occupations. See if you can interview any people who are already working in these fields. Are their comments in line with the information from the *Handbook*?

3. Is there a hospice in your area? If so, visit the facility and talk to one of the counselors from the staff. Learn more about how a hospice functions, the kinds of problems that they try to help patients and their families deal with, and the approaches they use in working with the kinds of reactions to impending death discussed by Kübler-Ross.

ANSWERS—PROGRAMMED REVIEW

1. life-span
2. infancy; childhood, adolescence; young adulthood, middle adulthood; old age
3. developmental tasks
4. psychosocial
5. trust; Mistrust
6. autonomy; shame, doubt
7. initiative; guilty
8. Pretend
9. industry; inferiority
10. identity; role confusion
11. intimacy; isolation
12. 75
13. generativity
14. stagnant
15. integrity; despair
16. repeated
17. authoritarian
18. obedient; withdrawn, apprehensive; curiosity
19. Overly permissive
20. dependent, immature
21. Effective
22. competent, independent, assertive
23. overprotection
24. they
25. sleep disturbances
26. Specific fears
27. overly timid; general dissatisfaction
28. negativism; two
29. clinging
30. reversals, regressions
31. sibling rivalry
32. control; assertion
33. rebel
34. enuresis; encopresis
35. frustration; hostility
36. 30; 6
37. relaxed
38. Overeating
39. anorexia nervosa
40. pica
41. delayed speech
42. stuttering; physical; 4
43. fears
44. adolescence; lifelong

45. Learning disabilities; dyslexia
46. 10;15
47. left
48. attention-deficit hyperactivity
49. cognitive; behavioral
50. 3; 5
51. smaller
52. Ritalin
53. physical; misbehavior
54. behavior modification
55. more lasting
56. 4
57. isolated; mute
58. echolalia
59. sensory blocking; sensory spin-out
60. congenital; nervous system
61. cerebellum
62. 4
63. operant shaping
64. tickling, music
65. punishment
66. 3.5; 14
67. one-third
68. 30; lower
69. stop; happy
70. intentionally
71. cycle of violence; 30
72. fear; threats
73. emotional; therapy; mate
74. Parents Anonymous
75. attitudes
76. Adolescence
77. length
78. Puberty
79. 11; 14; 13; 16
80. half; third
81. poised; relaxed; dominant
82. eager; talkative; tolerant
83. less; greater
84. taller, thinner
85. sooner; trouble
86. identity formation
87. stress symptoms
88. adulthood
89. markers

90. imaginary audiences
91. self-consciousness; dress, behavior
92. parents
93. dress; manners
94. peer
95. foreclose
96. break out
97. stronger
98. prematurely
99. means
100. career
101. 44
102. exploration; establishment; mid-career; later
103. fantasy
104. tentative
105. realistic
106. haphazard
107. socioeconomic; intelligence; family
108. vocational aspiration
109. occupations
110. vocational counselor
111. interest; aptitude
112. career centers
113. *Occupational Outlook Handbook*
114. talk; observing
115. parental dominance
116. family
117. accomplishment; others
118. Marriages; Extramarital affairs; divorces
119. death; urgent
120. 45, 50
121. 50
122. transition
123. 37; 41
124. one-half
125. decline
126. breaking out
127. coping
128. vigilant
129. complacent
130. defensive-avoidant
131. hypervigilant
132. impossible dream; satisfied
133. menopause

134. not knowing
135. climacteric
136. fertile
137. 30; 50
138. Biological aging; 25, 30
139. 5
140. maximum lifespan
141. life expectancy; 73; 81
142. smoke; alcohol; overweight; Exercise; stress
143. gerontologists; 25
144. fluid; crystallized
145. 35
146. disengagement theory
147. activity theory
148. activity theory
149. Ageism
150. stereotyping
151. speed; skill
152. slower; no difference
153. 75
154. acceptance; positive; autonomy; environmental; life

155. 4
156. circumstances
157. denial
158. 18,000
159. thanatologist
160. denial and isolation; anger; bargaining; depression; acceptance
161. emotional; age; education
162. typical
163. emotions
164. share feelings
165. Grief; shock
166. pangs of grief
167. apathy, dejection
168. 2; 3
169. resolution
170. month; two
171. depression; not
172. communication, discipline
173. sensitive; bond
174. self-absorbed; violence
175. guidelines

176. consistency
177. assertion
178. withdrawal of love
179. management
180. self-esteem
181. low; High
182. act; child; immediate; two; five
183. respect; enjoyment
184. accepting; positive; faith; recognition
185. feelings, behavior; feelings
186. Parent Effectiveness Training; I; you
187. natural
188. logical
189. consequences; choice
190. hospice
191. people; atmosphere; freedom of choice
192. living will
193. passive euthanasia; active euthanasia
194. Cryonics

ANSWERS—SELF-TEST

1.	a	8.	b	15.	c	22.	False	29.	True	36.	True
2.	d	9.	b	16.	b	23.	a	30.	a	37.	True
3.	c	10.	d	17.	a	24.	True	31.	a	38.	True
4.	a	11.	False	18.	b	25.	b	32.	d	39.	False
5.	a	12.	a	19.	False	26.	d	33.	c		
6.	False	13.	c	20.	d	27.	False	34.	c		
7.	b	14.	d	21.	True	28.	d	35.	c		

ACROSS

4. _____ parents are the most effective parents according to Diana Baumrind
6. form of euthanasia—steps taken to speed up death
7. he felt we experienced psychosocial crisis
8. form of euthanasia—no steps taken to hasten death
11. rapid physical growth and hormones cause this condition of sexual maturity
12. severe condition of undereating
14. one who studies aging
15. severe childhood problem—child is locked into a private world

DOWN

1. freezing one's body at death
2. this theory says withdrawal from society is necessary and desirable in old age
3. lack of bowel control
4. Erikson's shame and doubt vs. _____
5. attention-deficit hyperactivity disorder (abbr.)
9. lack of bladder control
10. inability to read with understanding
13. prejudice on basis of age

CHAPTER 16

Dimensions of Personality

CONTENTS

TERMS AND CONCEPTS

hypothetical construct
personality
character
temperament
traits
personality types
introvert
extrovert
self-concept
personality theory
trait theorist
common traits
individual traits
cardinal traits
central traits
secondary traits
surface traits
clusters
source traits
factor analysis
Sixteen Personality Factor Questionnaire (16 PF)
trait profile
five-factor model
trait-situation interactions
birth order (ordinal position)
androgyny
Bem Sex Role Inventory (BSRI)
interview
structured interview

unstructured interview
halo effect
direct observation
rating scales
behavioral assessment
situational testing
personality questionnaires
reliability
validity
Minnesota Multiphasic Personality Inventory (MMPI-2)
hypochondriasis
psychasthenia
hypomania
MMPI-2 profile
validity scales
honesty tests
projective tests
Rorschach Inkblot Test
Thematic Apperception Test (TAT)
test battery
sudden murderers
shyness
social skills
social anxiety
mental bias
private self-consciousness
public self-consciousness
behavioral genetics

IMPORTANT INDIVIDUALS

Carl Jung	Henry Murray	Jonathan Cheek
Gordon Allport	Melvin Lee	Arnold Buss
Raymond Cattell	Philip Zimbardo	Michel Girodo
Sandra Bem	Minerva Bertholf	Chris Kleinke
Hermann Rorschach		

PROGRAMMED REVIEW

1. (p. 449) A _____ _____ is an explanatory concept that is not directly observable. Personality is such a concept.

2. (p. 449) Most psychologists regard personality as one's unique and enduring _____ _____.

3. (p. 449) Personality, then, refers to the _____ in who a person is, has been, and will become. It also refers to the special blend of talents, attitudes, values, hopes, loves, hates, and habits that mark each person as a unique individual.

4. (p. 449) Many people confuse personality with what is known as _____, a term that implies that a person has been judged or evaluated, not just described.

5. (p. 449) Personality can also be distinguished from _____, which is the raw material from which personality is formed. It refers to the hereditary aspects of one's emotional nature: sensitivity, prevailing mood, etc.

6. (p. 450) In general, psychologists think of traits as _____ _____ within a person that are inferred from observed behavior. We often use traits to predict future behavior from past behavior, since they imply some consistency in behavior.

7. (p. 450) A personality _____ represents a category of individuals who have a number of traits or characteristics in common.

8. (p. 450) Over the years, psychologists have proposed various ways to categorize personalities. For example, Carl Jung proposed that a person is either an _____ (shy, self-centered person) or an _____ (bold, outgoing person). In reality, people are usually both, to some degree, depending upon the situation.

9. (p. 450) Even though types tend to _____ personality, they do have value. Most often, types are used by psychologists as a shorthand way of labeling people who share similar personality traits, for example Type A or Type B personalities.

10. (p. 450) Another way of understanding personality is to focus on a person's _____-_____. That is, a person's perception of his or her own personality traits.

11. (p. 451) Your self-concept consists of all your ideas and feelings about who you are. It tends to shape our subjective world by guiding what we _____ to, _____, and _____ about.

12. (p. 451) An individual's self-concept can greatly affect personal adjustment—especially when the self-concept is _____ or _____. A negative self-concept can result in depression or anxiety no matter how well a person does.

13. (p. 451) A personality _____ is a system of assumptions, ideas, and principles proposed to explain personality.

14. (p. 452) There are over 18,000 English words which refer to personal characteristics. Many of these words describe personality _____ (relatively permanent and enduring qualities that a person shows in most situations).

15. (p. 452) Splitting people into introverted and extroverted types is an oversimplification. But many psychologists regard one's _____ of introversion/extroversion as one of several important personality traits.

16. (p. 452) For example, one recent study found that students scoring high in _____ chose study locations that provided more chances for socializing, and higher noise levels.

17. (p. 452) In general, the trait approach attempts to identify traits which best describe a particular individual. To understand personality, _____ _____ attempt to classify traits and to discover which are most basic.

18. (p. 452) Gordon Allport has analyzed several kinds of traits. He identifies _____ traits (those shared by most members of a culture which help reveal the similarities among people) and _____ traits (those which define unique personal characteristics).

19. (p. 453) Allport has also distinguished three other types of traits, including _____ traits (those so basic that all of a person's activities can be traced to the existence of the trait).

20. (p. 453) _____ traits are the basic building blocks that make up the core of personality. A surprisingly small number of these are sufficient to capture the essence of a person. For example, college students asked to write a short description of someone they knew well mentioned an average of only _____ central traits.

21. (p. 453) _____ traits are less consistent and less important aspects of a person. They include such things as food preferences, attitudes, political opinions, and reactions to particular situations.

22. (p. 453) A second major approach to the study of personality traits is illustrated by the work of Raymond _____, who was dissatisfied with merely classifying traits, but instead wanted to learn how traits are organized and interlinked.

23. (p. 453) Through the use of questionnaires, direct observation, and life records, Cattell assembled data on _____ traits (those characteristics making up the visible portions of personality).

24. (p. 453) He then noted that surface traits often appear in _____, or groupings. Some traits appeared together so often they seemed to represent a single more basic trait Cattell called _____ traits.

25. (p. 453) While Allport classified traits subjectively, Cattell used a statistical technique called _____ _____ reduce surface traits to source traits. This procedure uses _____ to identify interrelated traits.

26. (p. 453) Cattell's list of source traits forms the basis of a personality test called the _____ _____ _____ _____ (often referred to as the 16 PF).

27. (p. 453) Like many personality tests of its type, the 16 PF can be used to produce a _____ _____. This tool is a graphic representation of the scores obtained by an individual on each trait.

28. (p. 453) Attempts to further reduce Cattell's 16 factors have resulted in the _____-factor model of personality. This model proposes that there are _____ universal dimensions of personality.

29. (p. 453) The universal dimensions suggested by the five-factor model include: (1) Extroversion; (2) _____—how friendly, nurturant, and caring a person is, as opposed to cold, indifferent, self-centered, or spiteful; (3) _____—how self-disciplined, responsible, and achieving a person is, as opposed to being irresponsible, careless, and undependable; (4) _____—refers to the presence of negative, upsetting emotions; (5) Openness to experience—how intelligent, open to new ideas, and interested in cultural pursuits a person is.

30. (p. 455) There is now little doubt that personality traits remain _____ over long periods of time. And yet, _____ also exert a powerful influence on behavior.

31. (p. 455) This is why most psychologists now agree that both factors are interrelated in determining behavior. Therefore, trait-situation _____ must be examined in order to fully understand behavior.

32. (p. 455) Birth order, or _____ _____, in a family can leave a lasting imprint on adult personality, the clearest differences being between firstborn and later-born children.

33. (p. 455) Firstborn (and only) children seem to have a higher chance of achieving _____ than later-born persons. For example, more firstborns become National Merit Scholars, and more are medical students or graduate students.

34. (p. 455) However, firstborns also tend to be more shy, _____, _____, and likely to need attention and admiration from others. They also have more Type A personality traits.

35. (p. 455) Later-born persons tend to excel in _____ _____. They are affectionate, friendly, and at ease with others. They also tend to be more _____ and _____ than firstborns.

36. (p. 455) Later-borns are typically more popular with their _____. They are also more skillful at interacting with _____.

37. (p. 455) The reason for these differences seems to lie in the "_____ _____" parents bring to each child.

38. (p. 456) The firstborn often get more attention, praise, and concern, are talked to more, punished more, and get more stimulation and affection. They also are more likely to be a planned child and are breast-fed longer. Higher parental expectations are translated into high _____-_____.

39. (p. 456) For example, women business executives who have excelled in traditional, male dominated occupations tend to be firstborn children. It may be that these firstborn men were especially encouraged to _____ by their parents.

40. (p. 456) However, the inexperienced parents of the firstborn are more _____ and _____, which results in higher levels of anxiety and a tendency to conform to adult values among firstborn children.

41. (p. 456) Parents consistently report that they used _____ discipline and were more relaxed with second or later children. The youngest child is particularly prone to be _____ and to have fewer responsibilities than older siblings.

42. (p. 456) Countless factors, including the _____ of children in a family, their _____ and age differences, and the age of the parents, can modify birth-order effects. Still, when large samples of people are considered, small birth-order effects do emerge.

43. (p. 456) Sandra Bem has used the _____ _____ _____ _____ (BSRI) to classify individuals as traditionally masculine, feminine, or _____ (literally meaning "man-woman").

44. (p. 456) She found that _____ percent of those surveyed fell into traditional masculine or feminine categories, _____ percent scored higher on traits characteristic of the opposite gender, and _____ percent were androgynous, getting roughly equal scores on the masculine and feminine items.

45. (p. 456) _____ individuals are more adaptable and less hindered by sex roles or images of what is appropriate "masculine" or "feminine" behavior.

46. (p. 445) For example, in one experiment Bem gave people the choice of performing either a "masculine" activity or a "feminine" activity. Masculine men and feminine women consistently chose sex-appropriate activities, even when the opposite choice _____ _____.

47. (p. 456) Bem's conclusion from a number of studies is that rigid sex roles can seriously restrict behavior, especially for _____. They have great difficulty expressing warmth, playfulness, and concern.

48. (p. 457) The overall picture which has emerged from research on androgyny is that having "masculine" traits primarily means a person is _____ and _____, which is related to high self-esteem and to success in many situations.

49. (p. 457) Having "feminine" traits primarily means a person is _____ and _____ _____. Such people tend to experience greater social closeness with others and more happiness in marriage.

50. (p. 458) Psychologists use various tools to assess personality. A very direct way to learn about a person's personality is to engage in conversation. An interview is described as _____ if the conversation is informal and the interviewee determines what subjects are discussed.

51. (p. 458) In a _____ interview, information is obtained by asking a series of planned questions.

52. (p. 458) Interviews are used to select persons for employment, college, or special programs, and for research on the dynamics of personality, and to provide information for _____ or _____. An advantage is that they allow observation of a person's tone of voice, hand gestures, posture, and facial expressions.

53. (p. 458) They also have certain limitations. Interviewers can be swayed by _____. A person identified by a title (i.e., housewife) may be misjudged because of an interviewer's attitudes toward a particular lifestyle.

54. (p. 458) Also, the interviewer's own _____ may cause him or her to accentuate or distort qualities of the interviewee. A third problem in interviewing is the halo effect, the tendency to generalize a favorable or unfavorable impression to unrelated details of personality.

55. (p. 459) When used as an assessment procedure, _____ _____ is a simple extension of the natural interest in "people watching." It is a useful technique but is subject to the same problems of misperception as an interview.

56. (p. 459) For this reason, _____ _____ are used which limit the chance of overlooking some traits while exaggerating others.

57. (p. 459) An alternative to rating scales is to do a _____ _____ in which observers record how often various actions occur, rather than what traits they think a person has.

58. (p. 459) Behavioral assessments are not strictly limited to _____ behavior. In one study, students high in math anxiety were asked to think aloud while doing math problems. Then their thoughts were analyzed to pinpoint the causes of their anxiety.

59. (p. 459) A specialized form of direct observation is called _____ _____. It is based on the premise that the best way to learn how a person would react to a certain situation is to simulate that situation.

60. (p. 459) An interesting example of situational testing is the "_____-_____ _____" training now done by many police departments. As various high-risk scenes are acted out live, or on videotape, officers must decide whether or not to fire their guns.

61. (p. 460) Most personality _____ are paper-and-pencil tests requiring people to answer questions about themselves. As measures of personality they are more _____ than interviews or observation.

62. (p. 461) To ensure a test's accuracy, it must be _____ (it yields close to the same score each time it is given to the same individual) and have _____ (it measures what it claims to measure).

63. (p. 461) Many personality tests have been created, including tests such as the Guilford-Zimmerman Temperament Survey, the California Psychological Inventory, the Allport-Vernon Study of Values, and the 16 PF. One of the best known and most widely used objective tests of personality is the _____ _____ _____ _____-2 (usually referred to as the MMPI-2).

64. (p. 461) The MMPI-2 is composed of _____ items to which a subject must respond _____ or _____ or cannot say.

65. (p. 461) The answer to a single item of the MMPI-2 tells nothing about personality. It is only through _____ of responses that personality is revealed.

66. (p. 461) Items on the MMPI-2 were selected for their ability to correctly identify persons with particular _____ problems. If items are consistently answered in a particular way by depressed patients, it is assumed that others who answer the same way are also prone to depression.

67. (p. 461) The MMPI-2 measures 10 major aspects of personality. Each is represented by a separate subscale on the test. Examples include:
   1) the _____ subscale reflects exaggerated concern about one's physical health
   2) the _____ _____ subscale shows a disregard to social and moral standards and emotional shallowness in relationships
   3) _____ which suggests the presence of irrational fears (phobias) and compulsive (ritualistic) action
   4) _____ which suggests emotional excitability, manic moods or behavior, and excessive activity. Other scales include depression, hysteria, masculinity/femininity, etc.

68. (p. 461) After the MMPI-2 is scored, results are charted as an _____ _____. This procedure allows comparison of a person's scores to those produced by normal adults, thus pinpointing various personality disorders.

69. (p. 461) Because truthful answers are important, the MMPI-2 has additional _____ _____ to detect attempts of subjects to "fake good" (make themselves look good) or "fake bad" (make it look like they have problems).

70. (p. 462) Other scales within the MMPI-2 help adjust final scores that are affected by personal _____ or by tendencies to _____ shortcomings and troubles.

71. (p. 462) It is necessary to consider information from interviews and other sources in connection with classifying people using the MMPI-2. If the test alone were used large numbers of _____ people would be classified as neurotic, severely depressed, or schizophrenic.

72. (p. 462) Most psychologists are well aware of the limitations of psychological tests, but many other organizations routinely use them, and errors or abuses sometimes occur. As a result, the U.S. Supreme Court handed down a decision limiting the use of tests as conditions of _____ or _____.

73. (p. 462) Each year, millions of job-seekers take paper-and-pencil _____ tests. These tests assume that poor attitudes toward various dishonest acts predispose a person to dishonest behavior.

74. (p. 462) Most honesty tests also ask people how honest they think the average person is, and how honest they are in comparison. They also ask about prior brushes with the _____, past acts of _____ or deceit, and attitudes toward use of illicit _____ and alcohol.

75. (p. 463) The question of whether honesty testing is _____ is still very much in dispute. Some psychologists believe that the best honesty tests are sufficiently valid to be used for making employment decisions. Others remain unconvinced.

76. (p. 463) To date, studies have _____ to demonstrate that honesty tests can accurately predict if a person will be a poor risk on the job. Also, even if the validity of such tests can be fully verified, there are many other ethical and practical questions to consider.

77. (p. 463) Because of the controversy about honesty tests, some states have _____ their use as the sole basis for deciding whether to hire a person.

78. (p. 463) In contrast to personality assessments that provide information on observable traits, _____ tests attempt to uncover deep-seated or _____ wishes, thoughts, and needs.

79. (p. 463) A projective test provides _____ _____ which subjects must describe, or about which they must make up a story. You must organize and interpret what you see in terms of your own life experiences.

80. (p. 463) Since projective tests have no _____ or _____ answers, the ability of subjects to fake or "see through" the test is greatly reduced. Projective tests can be a rich source of information, since responses are not restricted to simple true/false or yes/no answers.

81. (p. 463) One of the oldest and most widely used projective tests is the _____ _____ _____. It consists of a set of 10 standardized inkblots which vary in color, shading, form, and complexity.

82. (p. 463) The Rorschach is administered by first showing subjects each blot and asking them to _____ what they see in it. Later, subjects may be asked to identify specific _____ of a blot, to elaborate on previous descriptions, or to suggest a completely new story about a blot.

83. (p. 464) Obvious differences in content are important for identifying a subject's conflicts and fantasies. However, content is considered less important than what _____ of the inkblot are used to form an image and how the image is _____.

84. (p. 464) Another popular projective test is the _____ _____ _____ (TAT) developed by Henry Murray.

85. (p. 464) The TAT consists of _____ sketches depicting various scenes and life situations. The subject is shown each sketch and is asked to make up a story about the people in it. This procedure may be repeated several times.

86. (p. 464) Scoring of the TAT is restricted to analyzing the _____ of the stories. Interpretation focuses on how people feel, how they interact, what events led up to the incidents depicted in the sketch, and how the story will end.

87. (p. 464) Although projective tests have been popular with clinical psychologists, their _____ (their ability to measure what they claim to measure) is considered lowest among tests of personality.

88. (p. 464) Because of the subjectivity involved in scoring, _____ (consistency) of judgments among different users of the TAT and Rorschach is also low.

89. (p. 464) Despite the drawbacks of projective tests, many psychologists attest to their value, especially as part of a _____ of tests and interviews.

90. (p. 465) Researchers like Melvin Lee, Philip Zimbardo, and Minerva Bertholf have investigated the personalities of "_____ _____"—those who explode and commit violent crimes without warning.

91. (p. 465) Prison inmate studies showed that sudden murderers were passive, shy, and _____ (restrained) individuals. Their attacks are usually triggered by a minor irritation or frustration, but based on years of unexpressed feelings of anger and belittlement.

92. (p. 465) When sudden murderers finally release the strict controls they maintain on their behavior, a furious attack ensues, usually out of proportion to the offense against them. Often, such individuals experience _____ for some or all of their violent acts.

93. (p. 465) In contrast, those previously violent murderers studied tended to be "masculine" (aggressive), _____ (impulsive), and _____ likely to view themselves as shyer than the average person. Their violence was moderate and they typically felt they had been cheated or betrayed and were doing what was necessary to remedy the situation or to maintain their manhood.

94. (p. 466) _____ percent of American college students consider themselves to be shy. As a personality trait, shyness refers to an avoidance of others, plus feelings of social inhibition (uneasiness and strain when socializing).

95. (p. 466) There are at least three basic elements of shyness. The first involves a lack of _____ _____. Many shy persons simply have not learned how to meet others or how to start conversation and keep it going.

96. (p. 466) _____ _____ is a second common element. For the shy, nervousness in social situations is more frequent or intense. It is based on _____ fears (fears of being embarrassed, ridiculed, rejected, etc).

97. (p. 466) A third problem for shy persons is a _____-_____ bias in their thinking. They almost always blame themselves when a social encounter doesn't go well.

98. (p. 466) Shyness is most often triggered by _____ or unfamiliar social situations. It may be magnified by formality, meeting someone of _____ status, being noticeably _____ from others, or being the focus of attention.

99. (p. 466) Jonathan Cheek and Arnold Buss found no connection between shyness and _____ self-consciousness (attention to inner feelings, thoughts, and fantasies).

100. (p. 466) Persons who rate high in _____ self-consciousness are intensely aware of themselves as social objects. They think that they are being rejected even when they are not. Such feelings trigger anxiety or outright fear during social encounters, leading to awkwardness and inhibition.

101. (p. 466) Shy persons tend to label their social anxiety a lasting _____ _____, while non-shy persons believe that _____ _____ cause their occasional feelings of shyness.

102. (p. 466) In general, non-shy persons tend to have higher _____-_____ than shy persons. This is because nonshy persons give themselves credit for their social successes and they recognize that failures are often due to circumstances.

103. (p. 467) In America, many children seem to "outgrow" shyness as they gain social skills and wider social experience. Some adults overcome shyness with the aid of a shyness _____ or similar program.

104. (p. 467) Psychologist Michel Girodo directs such a shyness clinic. She observed that shyness is often maintained by _____ or _____-_____ beliefs. Be familiar with the examples discussed.

105. (p. 467) There is nothing "innate" about learning social skills. They can be directly practiced in a variety of ways to help people learn to put more animation and skill into their self-presentation. As one example, get a _____ _____ and listen to several of your conversations.

106. (p. 467) Psychologist Chris Kleinke reported a study of 1,000 men and women rating a collection of typical "opening lines." An analysis revealed that the statements fell into three categories: cute-flippant, _____, and _____ (mild or harmless).

107. (p. 468) By a large margin, both men and women preferred opening lines that were direct or innocuous. Cute or flippant statements were least liked, especially by _____.

108. (p. 468) One of the simplest ways of becoming a better conversationalist is by learning to ask questions. The best questions are often _____-_____; they require more than one or two words to answer and often give you "free information" that will help further stimulate conversation.

109. (p. 469) _____ _____ is the study of inherited behavioral traits. This is the basis for selectively breeding animals, leading to striking differences in social behavior, emotionality, learning ability, aggression, activity, and other behaviors.

110. (p. 469) Genetic studies of humans rely mainly on comparisons of _____ _____ and other close relatives. Such studies show that intelligence, some mental disorders, temperament, and other complex qualities are influenced by heredity.

111. (p. 470) Psychologists at the University of Minnesota have studied twins who grew up in separate homes. Extensive testing indicates that when identical twins are reunited, they are astonishingly similar in _____ and _____ quality.

112. (p. 470) Observers are also struck by how often the twins display identical _____ gestures, _____ movements, and nervous _____, such as nail biting or finger tapping.

113. (p. 470) Reunited twins are quite similar on many physical tests, have highly correlated IQ scores, and tend to share similar talents. However, where personality is concerned, similarities exist, but are not as strong. For instance, identical twins frequently differ in _____ and _____.

114. (p. 470) The longer twins have been apart, and the more different their experiences have been, the more different they become. Still, it seems reasonable to conclude that there is a _____ factor in personality, although it is relatively small in comparison to the great physical similarity of identical twins.

115. (p. 470) The "Jim twins" are a good example of similarities found in twin studies that seem to go beyond what one would expect on the basis of heredity. However, many of the similarities shown by them are found with unrelated people. For example, the odds of any two people driving a Chevrolet are 1 in _____.

116. (p. 470) Strong, albeit coincidental, similarities can exist between nontwins. In fact, one recent study compared twins with unrelated pairs of students of the same age and sex. The unrelated pairs were almost as alike as twins are with respect to _____ beliefs, _____ interests, religious preferences, jobs held, hobbies, favorite _____, and so on.

117. (p. 471) Much of the seemingly "astounding" coincidences shared by reunited twins may be a special case of the _____ of _____ _____.
Similarities blaze brightly in the memories of reunited twins, while differences are ignored.

118. (p. 471) A variety of studies suggest that heredity may be responsible for as much as _____ to _____ percent of the variation in some personality traits. Even so, there is danger in overstating the role of heredity in human behavior.

119. (p. 471) It is wise to remember that we do not inherit specific behavioral traits. Rather, we inherit certain _____ and _____ ways of reacting to the environment. These, in turn, can be greatly altered by experience.

SELF-TEST

1. (p. 449) One's enduring and unique behavior patterns defines which of the following?
   a. disposition
   b. character
   c. personality
   d. temperament

2. (p. 449) True-False. Personality is a hypothetical construct and is thus not directly observable.

3. (p. 449) Of the following, which is personality evaluated?
   a. disposition
   b. character
   c. temperament
   d. trait

4. (p. 450) Of the following, who first proposed that people are either introvert or extrovert types?
   a. Carl Jung
   b. Gordon Allport
   c. Raymond Cattell
   d. Henry Murray

5. (p. 451) Which of the following is *not* true of a person's self-concept?
   a. It is a person's perception of his or her own personality traits and consists of all their ideas and feelings about who they are.
   b. An inaccurate or inadequate self-concept can greatly affect personal adjustment in a negative manner.
   c. We creatively build our self-concepts out of daily experience, then we slowly revise them as we have new experiences.
   d. It is most important in early stages. Once a stable self-concept exists, it tends to have little ability to shape our subjective world.

6. (p. 453) Of the following, which traits are defined by Allport as ones that are so basic that all of a person's activities can be traced to the existence of that trait?
   a. common
   b. secondary
   c. central
   d. cardinal

7. (p. 453) True-False. Central traits are defined as those shared by most members of a given society.

8. (p. 453) Traits such as food preference, political opinions, and reactions to particular situations are classified by Allport as which of the following types?
   a. cardinal
   b. central
   c. secondary
   d. unique

9. (p. 453) True-False. Cattell formed his surface traits from certain core traits of the individual known as source traits.

10. (p. 453) The 16 PF was developed by which of the following?
   a. Allport   c. Cattell
   b. Freud   d. Jung

11. (p. 455) Which of the ordinal positions of birth is most likely to produce a child with high self-expectations, anxiety, and conformity?
   a. first   c. last
   b. middle   d. they are all about equal

12. (p. 456) The Bem Sex Role Inventory is used to:
   a. classify individuals into feminine, masculine, and androgynous sex-role categories
   b. assess unconscious sexual desires through use of ambiguous stimuli
   c. classify direct observations; it is a type of behavioral assessment
   d. measure sex-role competence under situational testing conditions

13. (p. 456) True-False. Androgynous individuals score high in both masculine and feminine traits.

14. (p. 456) True-False. Androgynous individuals are usually less adaptable because they do not know how to implement sex-role appropriate behaviors.

15. (p. 458) Of the following, which is *not* a disadvantage associated with the interview technique of assessing personality?
   a. interviewer can be swayed by preconceptions
   b. interviewee may be influenced by actions of the interviewer
   c. halo effect
   d. technique is rigid and inhibits feelings

16. (p. 459) Of the following, which make use of rating scales and behavioral assessments to limit bias?
   a. interviews   c. direct observations
   b. projective tests   d. personality questionnaires

17. (p. 459) Situational testing is a special form of:
   a. interviews   c. personality inventories
   b. projective tests   d. direct observations

18. (p. 461) One of the best known and most widely used objective tests of personality is the:
   a. 16 PF   c. Rorschach Inkblot Test
   b. MMPI-2   d. TAT

19. (p. 461) Which of the following is *not* true of the MMPI-2?
   a. It is composed of 567 items to be answered true, false, or cannot say.
   b. Items were selected for their ability to correctly identify persons with particular psychiatric problems.
   c. It was designed to measure ten major areas of personality.
   d. It contains a "Lie Scale" which can be used to judge a person's character and determine his or her tendencies to disregard social and moral standards.

20. (p. 463) Which of the following is *not* true of the Rorschach Inkblot Test?
   a. It consists of 10 standardized blots varying in color, shading, form, and complexity.
   b. It is administered by showing each card to subjects and recording their response to a standardized list of questions.
   c. Responses are scored according to content, determinants, and location.
   d. It was developed by Swiss psychologist Hermann Rorschach in the 1920s.

21. (p. 464) True-False. The location and organization of responses to the Rorschach are considered less important than content.

22. (p. 464) Which of the following is *not* true of the TAT?
    a. Scoring is done objectively by simply counting the total number of responses to each card and dividing by the number of cards.
    b. It was developed by Henry Murray.
    c. It consists of 20 sketches depicting various scenes and life situations.
    d. Test administration usually involves asking subjects to make up a story about the people depicted in the card pictures.

23. (p. 464) Which of the following is *not* true of projective tests?
    a. They are usually scored with a high degree of objectivity among different test users.
    b. They provide ambiguous stimuli which subjects must describe or incorporate in a story.
    c. Their validity is lowest among tests of personality.
    d. They attempt to uncover deep-seated or unconscious wishes, thoughts, and needs.

24. (p. 465) True-False. "Sudden murderers" are more likely to be habitually violent individuals who feel cheated or betrayed and are very impulsive.

25. (p. 466) Which of the following is *not* a basic element of shyness?
    a. underdevelopment of social skills
    b. awkwardness and inhibition with friends and family
    c. social anxiety
    d. confidence-lowering mental bias in thinking

26. (p. 466) Which of the following is *not* true of shyness?
    a. As a personality trait it combines social inhibition with a tendency to avoid others.
    b. It can be magnified by formality, meeting someone of higher status, or being the focus of attention.
    c. Nearly 20 percent of American college students consider themselves shy—a highly significant figure.
    d. It is most often triggered by unfamiliar or novel social situations.

27. (p. 466) True-False. Cheek and Buss found that shy people have a tendency to be wrapped up in their own feelings and thoughts. They demonstrate heightened private self-consciousness.

28. (p. 467) Which of the following is *not* a good suggestion for overcoming shyness?
    a. Learn to use open-ended questions in engaging others in conversations.
    b. Become involved in social situations where better social skills can be learned.
    c. Practice with a tape recorder or mirror to learn how you come across to other people.
    d. Take responsibility for all social failures and recognize that social successes may just result from the situation.

29. (p. 467) True-False. Recent studies show that when men initiate conversations, women prefer that they begin with cute or flippant opening lines.

30. (p. 469) Behavioral genetics is:
    a. an effort on the part of behaviorists to downplay the role of genetics in determining behavior.
    b. the study of acquired behavioral traits.
    c. the study of inherited behavioral traits.
    d. the study of how behavior affects genetic transmission.

31.   (p. 470) Which of the following is *not* true of identical twins?
      a.   Their appearance and voice quality are astonishingly similar.
      b.   They have high correlated IQs.
      c.   Their personalities are as similar as their physical features.
      d.   They tend to share similar talents.

32.   (p. 471) True-False. Striking similarities which appear to go beyond what one would expect on the basis of heredity are probably best understood as examples of how powerful genes really are in determining even very specific traits.

ANSWERS—PROGRAMMED REVIEW

1.   hypothetical construct
2.   behavior patterns
3.   consistency
4.   character
5.   temperament
6.   lasting qualities
7.   type
8.   introvert; extrovert
9.   oversimplify
10.   self-concept
11.   attend; remember; think
12.   inaccurate; inadequate
13.   theory
14.   traits
15.   degree
16.   extroversion
17.   trait theorists
18.   common; individual
19.   cardinal
20.   Central; 7.2
21.   Secondary
22.   Raymond Cattell
23.   surface
24.   clusters; source
25.   factor analysis;
      correlations
26.   Sixteen Personality
      Factor Questionnaire
27.   trait profile
28.   five; five
29.   Agreeableness;
      Conscientiousness;
      Neuroticism
30.   consistent; situations
31.   interactions
32.   ordinal position
33.   eminence
34.   conforming; anxious
35.   social relationships;
      original, creative
36.   peers; strangers

37.   emotional set
38.   self-expectations
39.   achieve
40.   anxious, inconsistent
41.   lighter; pampered
42.   number; sex
43.   Bem Sex Role
      Inventory; androgynous
44.   50; 15; 35
45.   Androgynous
46.   paid more
47.   men
48.   independent, assertive
49.   nurturant;
      interpersonally oriented
50.   unstructured
51.   structured
52.   counseling, therapy
53.   preconceptions
54.   personality; halo effect
55.   direct observation
56.   rating scales
57.   behavioral assessment
58.   visible
59.   situational testing
60.   Shoot-Don't Shoot
61.   questionnaires;
      objective
62.   reliable; validity
63.   Minnesota Multiphasic
      Personality Inventory
64.   567; true, false
65.   patterns
66.   psychiatric
67.   hypochondriasis;
      psychopathic deviancy;
      Psychasthenia;
      Hypomania
68.   MMPI-2 profile
69.   validity scales

70.   defensiveness;
      exaggerate
71.   normal
72.   employment, promotion
73.   honesty
74.   law; theft; drugs
75.   valid
76.   failed
77.   banned
78.   projective; unconscious
79.   ambiguous stimuli
80.   right, wrong
81.   Rorschach Inkblot Test
82.   describe; sections
83.   parts; organized
84.   Thematic Apperception
      Test
85.   20
86.   content
87.   validity
88.   objectivity
89.   battery
90.   sudden murderers
91.   overcontrolled
92.   amnesia
93.   undercontrolled; less
94.   Fifty
95.   social skills
96.   Social anxiety;
      evaluation
97.   self-defeating
98.   novel; higher; different
99.   private
100. public
101. personality trait;
      external events
102. self-esteem
103. clinic
104. unrealistic; self-
      defeating
105. tape recorder

106. direct; innocuous
107. women
108. open-ended
109. Behavioral genetics
110. identical twins
111. appearance; voice
112. facial; hand; tics
113. dominance, extroversion
114. genetic
115. 7
116. political; musical; foods
117. fallacy of positive instances
118. 20; 45
119. potentials; general

ANSWERS—SELF-TEST

1.	c	7.	False	13.	True	19.	d	25.	b	31.	c
2.	True	8.	c	14.	False	20.	b	26.	c	32.	False
3.	b	9.	False	15.	d	21.	False	27.	False		
4.	a	10.	c	16.	c	22.	a	28.	d		
5.	d	11.	a	17.	d	23.	a	29.	False		
6.	d	12.	a	18.	b	24.	False	30.	c		

ACROSS

5. one's unique, enduring behavior patterns
7. Bem Sex-Role Inventory (abbr.)
8. Thematic Apperception Test (abbr.)
12. bold, outgoing person
13. he described introverts and extroverts
14. _____ position refers to one's birth order
15. shy, self-centered person

DOWN

1. test consisting of 10 standardized ink blots
2. Minnesota Multiphasic Personality Inventory (abbr.)
3. these children often are high achievers
4. tests providing ambiguous stimuli for subjects to describe
6. these are relatively permanent and enduring qualities a person shows most of the time
9. he studied surface traits of personality
10. possessing both male and female traits
11. he identified "common traits"

■ CHAPTER 17 ■

Theories of Personality

CONTENTS

TERMS AND CONCEPTS

psychoanalytic theory
id
ego
superego
pleasure principle
psyche
libido
life instincts (Eros)
death instinct (Thanatos)
primary process thinking
reality principle
conscience
ego ideal
displacement
sublimation
neurotic anxiety
ego-defense mechanisms
unconscious
conscious
preconscious
socialization
psychosexual stages
oral stage
anal stage
phallic stage
genital stage
erogenous zone
fixations
oral-dependent personality
oral-aggressive personality
anal-retentive personality
anal-expulsive personality
phallic personality

Oedipus conflict
identification
Electra conflict
latency
neo-Freudians
striving for superiority
feelings of inferiority
style of life
creative self
basic anxiety
persona
introversion
extroversion
personal unconscious
collective unconscious
archetypes
anima
animus
self-archetype
mandalas
learning theories
situational determinants
habits
drive
cue
response
reward
social learning theorists
psychological situation
expectancy
reinforcement values
self-reinforcement
radical behaviorism

social reinforcement
imitation
humanistic theory
human nature
free choice
subjective experience
self-actualization
peak experience
fully functioning person
self
phenomenal field

self-image
symbolized
incongruent
congruence
ideal self
possible selves
conditions of worth
positive self-regard
organismic valuing
self-monitoring
Self-Monitoring Scale

IMPORTANT INDIVIDUALS

Sigmund Freud
Alfred Adler
Karen Horney
Carl Jung
John Dollard
Neal Miller

Julian Rotter
B. F. Skinner
Elaine Heiby
Lisa Serbin
Daniel O'Leary

Abraham Maslow
Carl Rogers
Hazel Markus
Paula Nurius
Mark Snyder

PROGRAMMED REVIEW

1. (p. 475) _____ theory, the best-known psychodynamic approach, grew out of Sigmund Freud's clinical study of disturbed individuals and evolved from 1890 until his death in 1939.

2. (p. 475) Freud became interested in the treatment of mental disorders when he determined that many of his patients' problems seemed to lack _____ _____.

3. (p. 475) Freud conceived of personality as a dynamic system of energies directed by three structures usually involved in any behavior. One structure, the _____, is made up of innate biological instincts and urges present at birth. It is self-serving, irrational, impulsive, and totally _____.

4. (p. 475) The id operates on a _____ _____, meaning that pleasure-seeking impulses of all kinds are freely expressed.

5. (p. 475) The energy for the entire psyche, or personality, was called the _____, derived from the _____ _____ (Eros) which promote survival and underlie sexual desires.

6. (p. 475) Freud also postulated a death instinct (_____) which he said is responsible for aggressive and destructive urges.

7. (p. 475) Most id energies are aimed at discharge of tensions related to _____ and _____.

8. (p. 475) The second structure, the _____ (sometimes described as the "executive"), draws energies supplied by the _____. It wins power to direct our behavior by matching the desires of the id with _____ _____.

9. (p. 475) The id can only produce mental images of things it desires (called _____ _____ _____). It must rely on others to carry out its orders.

10. (p. 475) Whereas the id operates on the pleasure principle, the ego is guided by the _____ _____, delaying action until it is practical or appropriate.

11. (p. 475) The ego is the system of thinking, planning, problem solving, and deciding. It is in _____ control of the personality.

12. (p. 475) The _____ acts as a judge or censor for the thoughts and actions of the ego. It is composed of a number of different aspects.

13. (p. 475) One part of the superego, called the _____, represents all actions for which a person has been punished.

14. (p. 475) If you act contrary to standards of the conscience, you are punished internally by _____ feelings.

15. (p. 475) The _____ _____ represents all behavior one's parents approved or rewarded. It is a source of goals and aspirations. When the standards of the ego-ideal are met, pride is felt.

16. (p. 475) In Freudian terms, a person with a _____ superego will be a delinquent, criminal, or antisocial personality. In contrast, an overly _____ superego may cause inhibition, rigidity, or unbearable guilt.

17. (p. 476) Freud did not picture the id, ego, and superego as parts of the brain, or as "little people" running the human psyche. Rather, they are separate and conflicting _____ _____ requiring a delicate balance of power.

18. (p. 476) To reduce tension, the ego could bring actions leading to friendship, romance, courtship, and marriage. If the id is unusually powerful, the ego may direct an attempted seduction. If the superego prevails, the ego may be forced to _____ or _____ sexual energies to other activities.

19. (p. 476) When the ego is threatened or overwhelmed, the person feels anxiety. Impulses from the id cause _____ _____ when the ego can barely keep them under control. Threats of punishment from the superego cause _____ _____.

20. (p. 476) Everyone develops habitual ways of reducing these anxieties and many resort to use of _____-_____ _____ to lessen internal conflicts.

21. (p. 476) A major principle of psychoanalytic theory is that behavior often expresses _____ (or hidden) internal forces within the personality including repressed memories and emotions as well as the instinctual drives of the id.

22. (p. 477) Modern scientists are beginning to identify brain areas that seem to have the kinds of unconscious effects Freud described. Especially important are areas linked with emotion and memory such as the _____ in the limbic system.

23. (p. 477) The ego and superego may operate on two other levels besides the unconscious. The _____ level includes everything we are aware of at a given moment. The _____ contains material that can be easily brought to awareness.

24. (p. 477) The operation of the superego gives another sign of the levels of awareness. At times a person may feel guilty without knowing why due to the _____ workings of the superego. Freudian psychology holds that such events cannot be easily brought to awareness or directly known by the individual.

25. (p. 477) Every society must _____ its children by teaching them language, customs, rules, roles, and morals. While carrying out this process, parents leave traces of their own personality in their children.

26. (p. 478) Freud theorized that the core of personality is formed before age six in a series of _____ _____.

27. (p. 478) His account holds that childhood urges for erotic pleasure have lasting effects on development. While controversial, he used the term _____ very broadly to refer to several different physical sources of pleasure.

28. (p. 478) At each stage a different part of the body becomes an _____ _____ (an area capable of producing pleasure). It serves as the principle source of pleasure, frustration, and self-expression.

29. (p. 478) Freud believed that many adult personality traits can be traced to _____ (an unresolved conflict or emotional hang-up caused by overindulgence or by frustration) in one or more of the stages.

30. (p. 478) During the first year of life, most of an infant's pleasure comes from stimulation of the mouth. If a child is overfed or frustrated, _____ traits may be created. Adult expressions of these needs include gum chewing, nail biting, smoking, kissing, overeating, and alcoholism.

31. (p. 478) Fixation early in the oral stage produces an _____-_____ personality who is gullible, passive and needs lots of attention.

32. (p. 478) Fixation later in the oral stage causes an _____-_____ adult who is argumentative, cynical, and exploitive of others.

33. (p. 478) Fixation during the anal stage (age 1-3 years) can lead to the _____-_____ personality, who is obstinate, stingy, orderly, and compulsively clean. It may also lead to the _____-_____ personality who is disorderly, destructive, cruel, or messy.

34. (p. 478) Adult traits of the _____ personality are vanity, exhibitionism, sensitive pride, and narcissism (self-love).

35. (p. 478) During the phallic stage (age 3-6 years), increased sexual interest causes the child to become physically attracted to the parent of the opposite sex. In males this generates the _____ _____, in which the boy feels rivalry with his father for the affection of the mother.

36. (p. 478) To ease his anxieties of the rival father (especially fear of _____), the boy must _____ with the father, and form a _____.

37. (p. 478) With girls, there is a competition for the father which produces the _____ _____. Freud believed that females already feel castrated and are, therefore, less driven to identify with their mothers than boys are with their fathers. The girl's identification with the mother is more gradual and less effective in creating a conscience.

38.   (p. 479) According to Freud, there is a period of _____ from age six to puberty during which psychosexual development is temporarily interrupted.

39.   (p. 479) At puberty an upswing in sexual energies activates all the unresolved conflicts of earlier years, the reason why adolescence can be filled with emotion and turmoil. During this _____ stage, personality is marked by a growing capacity for mature and responsible social-sexual relationships culminating in heterosexual love.

40.   (p. 479) Freud's theory has been widely influential for a number of reasons:
      1) it pioneered the idea that the first years of life help shape _____ _____;
      2) it identified _____, _____ _____, and early _____ experiences as critical events in personality formation;
      3) Freud was among the first to propose that development proceeds through a series of _____.

41.   (p. 479) Freud's theory remains controversial. His portrayal of the elementary school years, _____, as free from sexuality and unimportant for personality development is hard to believe.

42.   (p. 479) Studies challenging Freud's view, show that an affectionate and accepting father is more likely than a stern one to create a strong _____ in a son.

43.   (p. 479) Freud also overemphasized _____ in personality development; other motives and cognitive factors are of equal importance.

44.   (p. 479) Freud's ideas quickly attracted a brilliant following. Those who stayed closest to the core of Freud's thought are now referred to as _____-_____.

45.   (p. 479) Alfred Adler broke away from Freud because he disagreed with Freud's emphasis on the _____, on instinctual drives, and on the importance of _____. Adler believed that we are social creatures governed by social urges—not by biological instincts.

46.   (p. 479) In Adler's view, the main driving force in personality is a striving for _____ —a struggle to overcome imperfections, an upward drive for competence, completion, and mastery of shortcomings.

47.   (p. 479) Adler felt that everyone experiences _____ of _____ mainly because we begin life as small, weak and relatively powerless children surrounded by larger and more powerful adults. They may also come from our personal limitations. The struggle for superiority arises from such feelings.

48.   (p. 479) While everyone strives for superiority, each person tries to _____ for different limitations and each chooses a different pathway to superiority.

49.   (p. 479) Adler believed that this process creates a unique of _____ of _____, or personality pattern, for each individual.

50.   (p. 479) According to Adler, the core of each person's style of life is formed by age _____. He later emphasized the existence of a _____ _____, the ability of humans to create personality through choice and experience.

51.   (p. 480) According to Adler, valuable clues to a person's style of life are revealed by the _____ _____ that can be recalled.

52. (p. 480) Karen Horney remained faithful to most of Freud's ideas, but rejected the claim that "_____ is destiny." She was among the first to counter the obvious male bias in Freud's thinking.

53. (p. 480) She also disagreed with Freud about the causes of _____. Horney's view was that a core of _____ _____ occurs when people feel isolated and helpless in a hostile world. This dilemma causes troubled individuals to exaggerate a single mode of interacting with others.

54. (p. 480) According to Horney, each of us can move _____ others, _____ from others, or _____ others. Emotional health requires a balance of each. Emotional problems lock people into overuse of only one of the three modes.

55. (p. 480) Carl Jung was a student of Freud's, but the two parted ways as Jung began to develop his own ideas. Like Freud, Jung called the conscious part of the personality the _____, but noted that between the ego and the outside world we often find a _____, or mask: the "public self" presented to others when we adopt particular roles.

56. (p. 480) Actions of the ego may reflect attitudes of _____ (in which energy is mainly directed inward) or _____ (in which energy is mainly directed outward).

57. (p. 480) Jung used the term _____ _____ to refer to what Freud simply called the unconscious. It is a storehouse for personal experiences, feelings, and memories that are not directly knowable.

58. (p. 480) Jung also proposed a deeper _____ _____, shared by all humans. It is at this level that _____ (original ideas, patterns or prototypes) exist. They are unconscious images that cause us to respond emotionally to symbols of birth, death, energy, animals, evil, and the like.

59. (p. 481) Two particularly important archetypes are the _____ (representing the female principle) and the _____ (representing the male principle). Each person has both.

60. (p. 481) Jung considered the _____-_____ the most important because it represents unity. He believed it is symbolized in every culture by _____ (magic circles).

61. (p. 481) Jung was the first to use the term "_____-_____" to describe a striving for completion and unity.

62. (p. 481) The behaviorist position is not nearly as mechanistic as some critics would have us believe, and its value is well established. For one thing, the behaviorists have shown repeatedly that children can learn things like _____, _____, generosity, or destructiveness.

63. (p. 481) Learning theories of personality and the behaviorist position stress that personality is no more (or less) than a collection of _____ _____ _____ acquired through conditioning principles.

64. (p. 482) Strict learning theorists reject the idea that personality is made up of consistent _____. For instance, they would assert that there is no such thing as a trait of "honesty."

65. (p. 482) A good example of how situations influence behavior is provided by the role-playing experiment in which students were assigned one of three reasons why an assigned paper was late. Most students lied to their professor when they had an _____ excuse (hangover). None lied when their excuse was _____ (the flu).

66. (p. 482) By drawing our attention to _____ determinants of behavior, learning theorists have not entirely removed the "person" from personality. They agree that external events interact with each person's unique learning history to produce behavior in any given situation.

67. (p. 482) Trait theorists also believe that situations affect behavior. But in their view, situations interact with traits. Learning theorists favor replacing the concept of "traits" with "_____ _____" in order to explain behavior.

68. (p. 483) Learning theorists John Dollard and Neal Miller consider _____ the basic structure of personality.

69. (p. 483) As for the dynamics of personality, they believe habits are governed by four elements of the learning process: (1) _____, any stimulus strong enough to goad a person to action; (2) _____, signals from the environment that guide response so they are most likely to bring about reinforcement; (3) response; (4) reward

70. (p. 483) The new breed of behavioral psychologists—who include perception, thinking, and other "mental" events in their view of personality—are called _____ _____ theorists (because they also emphasize social relationships and modeling).

71. (p. 483) The "cognitive behaviorism" of social learning theory is illustrated by three concepts proposed by Julian Rotter. Rotter points out that it is not enough to know the setting in which a person responds, we must also know the person's _____ _____ (how the person interprets or defines the situation).

72. (p. 483) Rotter's term _____ refers to anticipation that will produce reinforcement. To predict a response, we must know if the person expects their efforts to pay off. Expected reinforcement may be more important than actual past reinforcement.

73. (p. 483) Rotter's third concept, _____ _____ states that humans attach different values to various activities or rewards which must be considered in understanding personality.

74. (p. 483) Social learning theory adds to the behavioristic viewpoint the concept of _____-_____, personal reward we give ourselves in response to a positive evaluation of our actions.

75. (p. 484) Elaine Heiby has developed a scale to evaluate self-reinforcement. Work in this area shows that high rates of self-reinforcement are related to high _____-_____.

76. (p. 484) Numerous studies have shown that mildly _____ college students tend to have low rates of self-reinforcement. Learning to be more self-reinforcing appears to lessen _____.

77. (p. 484) The most extreme view of personality is held by _____ behaviorist B. F. Skinner who believes "personality" is a convenient fiction we invent to pretend we have explained behavior that is actually controlled by the environment.

78. (p. 484) Skinner believes that everything a person does is ultimately based on past and present _____ and _____.

79. (p. 485) Rather than thinking in terms of psychosexual urges and fixations, modern learning theory emphasizes that childhood is a time of urgent and tearing drives, powerful rewards and punishments, and crushing frustrations. Also important is _____ _____ based on the effects of attention and approval from others.

80. (p. 485) Dollard and Miller consider four developmental situations to be of critical importance: _____, _____ or _____ training; _____ training; and learning to express _____ or _____.

81. (p. 485) A basic _____ or _____ orientation toward the world may be established by early feeding experiences. Feeding can also affect later social relationships because a child learns to associate people with satisfaction and pleasure, or frustration and discomfort.

82. (p. 485) Many attitudes toward cleanliness, conformity, and bodily functions are formed during toilet and cleanliness training. Studies show that severe, _____, or _____ toilet training can have undesirable effects on personality development.

83. (p. 485) When, where, and how a child learns to express anger and sexuality can leave an imprint on personality. Specifically, permissiveness for sexual and aggressive behavior in childhood is linked to adult needs for _____ probably because permitting such behaviors allows children to get pleasure from asserting themselves.

84. (p. 485) Behaviorists tend to stress two processes that contribute greatly to personality development in general, and particularly to sex training. _____ refers to the child's emotional attachment to admired adults, especially to those the child depends on for love and care.

85. (p. 485) Identification typically encourages _____, a desire to be like the valued and admired adult. Many of a child's "male" or "female" traits come from conscious or unconscious attempts to imitate the behavior of a same-sex parent with whom they identify.

86. (p. 485) Psychologist Albert Bandura and others have shown that learning takes place _____ as well as directly. This fact means we can learn without direct reward by observing and remembering the actions of others.

87. (p. 485) An example of differential sex role learning is provided by the study of Lisa Serbin and Daniel O'Leary. They found that teachers were _____ times more likely to pay attention to boys who were aggressive or disruptive than to girls acting the same way.

88. (p. 485) Boys who hit other students or broke things typically got attention through loud scoldings, while girls got more attention when they were clinging to the teacher (therefore being reinforced for submissive, _____, and _____ behavior).

89. (p. 485) Similar differences in reinforcement probably explain why males are responsible for much more aggression in society than females are. _____ and _____ rates, for example, are consistently higher for men.

90. (p. 486) Humanists reject the pessimism of psychoanalytic theory and the Freudian view that personality is a battleground for biological instincts and unconscious forces. Instead, they view _____ _____ as inherently good and they seek ways to allow our positive potentials to emerge.

91. (p. 486) Humanists also oppose the mechanism of learning theory. They say we are creative beings capable of _____ _____.

92. (p. 486) The humanistic viewpoint also places greater emphasis on immediate _____ _____ rather than on prior learning. To understand behavior we must learn what is "real" for her or him.

93. (p. 487) Abraham Maslow studied the lives of people who seemed to be using almost all of their talents and potentials. He referred to this tendency as _____-_____.

94. (p. 487) Maslow's primary contribution was to draw attention to the _____ of continued personal growth. He considered self-actualization an _____ process, not a simple end point to be attained only once.

95. (p. 487) Maslow found that such persons shared a number of similarities. These included:
    1) _____ perceptions of reality;
    2) comfortable _____ of self, others, and nature;
    3) spontaneity;
    4) _____-centering;
    5) autonomy;
    6) continued freshness of appreciation;
    7) fellowship with _____;
    8) profound _____ relationships;
    9) unhostile sense of _____.

96. (p. 487) Also, all of Maslow's subjects reported the frequent occurrence of _____ _____—occasions marked by feelings of ecstasy, harmony, and deep meaning.

97. (p. 487) Carl _____ is a contemporary psychotherapist who, like Freud, based his theory on clinical experience. Unlike Freud, who portrayed the normal personality as "adjusted" to internal conflict, he sees greater possibility for inner harmony.

98. (p. 487) Rogers sees the _____ _____ person as one who has achieved an openness to feelings and experiences, and who has learned to trust inner urges and intuitions.

99. (p. 487) Rogers' theory of personality centers on the concept of the _____, a flexible and changing perception of personal identity that emerges from the _____ _____.

100. (p. 488) The phenomenal field is a person's total subjective experience of reality. One's _____-_____ is made up of those experiences identified as "I" or "me" which are separated from "not me" experiences.

101. (p. 488) According to Rogers, experiences that match the self-image are _____ (admitted into consciousness) and contribute to gradual changes in the self.

102. (p. 488) Information or feelings inconsistent with the self-image are said to be _____.

103. (p. 488) Experiences seriously incongruent with the self-image can be threatening, and they are often distorted or denied conscious recognition. This prevents the self from changing and creates a gulf between the self-image and reality. As the self-image grows more unrealistic, the _____ _____ becomes confused, vulnerable, dissatisfied, or seriously maladjusted.

104. (p. 488) Recent studies have confirmed that people who know themselves well tend to like and feel good about themselves. Poor self-knowledge is associated with low _____-_____.

105. (p. 488) When your self-image is consistent with what you really think, feel, do, and experience, you are best able to actualize your potentials. Rogers also considers it essential to have congruence between the self-image and the _____ _____—the image of the person you would most like to be.

106. (p. 488) In accord with Roger's thinking, researchers have found that people with a close match between their self-image and ideal self tend to be socially _____, _____, and _____. Those with a poor match tend to be _____, insecure, and lacking in social skills.

107. (p. 489) Psychologists Hazel Markus and Paula Nurius believe that each of us harbors images of many _____ _____ including the ideal self, as well as other selves we could become, or are afraid of becoming.

108. (p. 489) Possible selves translate our hopes, fears, fantasies, and goals into specific images of who we _____ be. They also give meaning to _____ behavior and help us evaluate it.

109. (p. 489) From the humanists' viewpoint, the development of one's self-image is highly dependent on information from the environment and contributes to later personality functioning. Rogers holds that positive and negative evaluations by others cause a child to develop internal standards of evaluation called _____ of _____.

110. (p. 490) By this term he means that we learn that some actions win our parents' love and approval while others are rejected. This process is directly related to a later capacity for self-esteem, positive self-evaluation, or _____ _____-_____.

111. (p. 490) He believes congruence and self-actualization are encouraged by substituting _____ _____ (direct, gut-level response to life experiences that avoids the filtering and distortion of incongruence) for conditions of worth.

112. (p. 490) None of the major theories can be fully proved or disproved. While they are neither true nor false, their implications or predictions may be. The best way to judge a theory is in terms of its _____.

113. (p. 490) In evaluating the different theories of personality, psychoanalytic theory seems to over-emphasize _____ and _____. These distortions were corrected somewhat by the neo-Freudians, but problems remain.

114. (p. 490) One of the most telling criticisms of Freudian theory is that it can be used to explain any psychological event _____ it has occurred, but offers little help in predicting _____ behavior.

115. (p. 490) Of the three major perspectives, the _____ have made the best effort to rigorously test and verify their ideas.

116. (p. 490) However, behavioristic theories tend to _____ the importance of temperamental, emotional, and subjective factors in personality. Social Learning theory is an attempt to answer such criticisms.

117. (p. 490) A great strength of the humanists is the light they have shed on _____ dimensions of personality. However, they can be criticized for using imprecise concepts that are difficult to _____ or study _____.

118. (p. 492) While self-actualization offers the promise of personal growth, creativity, and fullness of life, it requires hard work, patience, and commitment. It is primarily a _____, not a goal or an end point.

119. (p. 492) Several points can be gleaned from the writings of Abraham Maslow as suggestions on how to achieve self-actualization. One is to be willing to _____.

120. (p. 492) You must learn to _____ _____. You can become an architect of self by acting as if you are personally responsible for every aspect of your life.

121. (p. 492) Another point is to examine your _____. Use self-discovery to try to make each life decision a choice for growth, not a response to fear or anxiety.

122. (p. 492) Try to see things as they are, not as you would like them to be. In other words, experience things _____ and _____.

123. (p. 492) Make use of positive experiences to promote growth. You might actively repeat activities that cause "_____ _____" (temporary moments of self-actualization).

124. (p. 492) Actualizing potentials may place you at odds with cultural expectations. This situation may produce fear which keeps many people from becoming what they might. You must be prepared to be _____.

125. (p. 493) Maslow found that self-actualizers tend to have a _____ or "_____" in life. Therefore, get involved and committed to problems outside yourself.

126. (p. 493) Self-awareness takes time to develop. Slow down and avoid _____ or over-_____ your time.

127. (p. 493) A valuable means of promoting self-awareness is to start a _____. Keeping records of experiences, daily thoughts, feelings, and attitudes can help make growth-oriented life changes.

128. (p. 493) As a final note, _____ your progress. It is important to gauge your progress and to renew your efforts. _____ is a good sign you are in need of further growth and change.

129. (p. 494) _____-_____ refers to differences in how people monitor (observe, regulate, and control) the image of themselves they display to others in public.

130. (p. 494) Some of us are _____ self-monitors, who are very sensitive to situations and expectations. In contrast, _____ self-monitors are less interested in controlling the impression they make.

131. (p. 494) Persons _____ in self-monitoring take a flexible approach to defining themselves. They are very interested in their public "image." _____ self-monitors try to accurately present their beliefs and principles no matter what the situation is.

132. (p. 494) Psychologist Mark Snyder has studied self-monitoring extensively. He found that in social settings _____ self-monitors preferred to join clearly defined groups.

133. (p. 494) Snyder developed the _____-_____ _____ to measure high and low self-monitors. You should be familiar with the comparisons that have come from the use of this test.

134. (p. 494) In general, _____ self-monitors are adaptable and present themselves well in social situations. However, they tend to reveal little about their private feelings, beliefs, and intentions.

135. (p. 495) The primary drawback to being _____ in self-monitoring is a tendency to be unresponsive to the demands of different situations. Such individuals want to "just be themselves" even when adjustments in self-presentation would make them more effective.

136. (p. 495) Studies of self-monitoring raise questions about the idea that each person has a "_____ _____." High self-monitors, in particular, act as if they have many selves.

SELF-TEST

1.   (p. 475) Which of the following is *not* a structure which directs the dynamic system of energies composing personality as proposed by Freud?
      a.   superego   c.   id
      b.   self   d.   ego

2.   (p. 475) Which of the following is *not* true of the id?
      a.   It is totally unconscious.
      b.   It operates on the pleasure principle.
      c.   It is associated with secondary process thinking.
      d.   Most id energies are directed toward discharge of tensions associated with sex and aggression.

3.   (p. 475) Of the following, which is in conscious control of the personality and acts as an executive for action?
      a.   id   c.   ego
      b.   libido   d.   superego

4.   (p. 475) The conscience and the ego-ideal are parts of the:
      a.   id   c.   ego
      b.   superego   d.   libido

5.   (p. 476) Neurotic anxiety is caused by:
      a.   threats of punishment from the superego
      b.   a breakdown of the ego's functions
      c.   impulses from the id that threaten a loss of control
      d.   overuse of ego-defense mechanisms

6.   (p. 476) True-False. According to Freud, the preconscious is a level of awareness in which repressed memories and emotions are stored along with instinctual drives.

7.   (p. 478) According to Freud, a personality characterized as argumentative, cynical, and exploitive of others is:
      a.   anal-retentive   c.   oral-dependent
      b.   oral-aggressive   d.   anal-expulsive

8. (p. 478) According to Freud, a person whose personality is characterized as obstinate, stingy, orderly, and compulsively clean would be classified as:
   a. oral-aggressive
   b. anal-expulsive
   c. anal-compulsive
   d. anal-retentive

9. (p. 478) According to psychoanalysis, which of the following does *not* occur during the phallic stage of development?
   a. Electra conflict
   b. elimination fixation
   c. Oedipus conflict
   d. conscience formation

10. (p. 479) True-False. One of the reasons psychoanalysis has been most influential in later psychological theories is because it pioneered the idea that the first years of life shape adult personality.

11. (p. 479) In the view of Alfred Adler, the main force in personality is:
    a. libido
    b. striving for superiority
    c. feelings of inferiority
    d. basic anxiety

12. (p. 480) According to Karen Horney, the result when people feel isolated and helpless in a hostile world is:
    a. incongruence
    b. organismic devaluing
    c. basic anxiety
    d. feelings of inferiority

13. (p. 480) The view that emotional health requires a balance in moving toward, away from, and against others was first proposed by:
    a. Sigmund Freud
    b. Carl Rogers
    c. Alfred Adler
    d. Karen Horney

14. (p. 481) Which of the following is *not* an important archetype in Jung's theory of personality?
    a. Eros
    b. self
    c. animus
    d. anima

15. (p. 482) True-False. Learning theorists reject the idea that personality is made up of consistent traits.

16. (p. 483) According to Dollard and Miller of the behaviorist camp, which of the following is the basic structure or component of personality?
    a. response
    b. needs
    c. habits
    d. self-image

17. (p. 483) Which of the following is *not* a concept developed by the "cognitive behaviorism" of social learning theory as illustrated in the work of Julian Rotter
    a. expectancy
    b. reinforcement value
    c. psychological situation
    d. organismic valuing

18. (p. 485) According to Dollard and Miller, which of the following contribute greatly to personality development in general, and particularly to sex training?
    a. identification, imitation
    b. fixations, urges
    c. life instincts, death instincts
    d. self-image, ideal self

19. (p. 486) Of the following, which describes the emphasis of the humanistic approach to personality?
    a. subjective experience
    b. objective experience
    c. previous learning
    d. stages of psychosexual development

20. (p. 487) The humanists' term for fulfillment of potential is:
     a. self-actualization   c. condition of worth
     b. growth fulfillment   d. congruence

21. (p. 487) Which of the following is *not* a characteristic of Maslow's self-actualizers?
     a. task-centering   c. efficient perceptions of reality
     b. dependency   d. profound interpersonal relationships

22. (p. 487) True-False. All of Maslow's self-actualized subjects reported the frequent occurrence of peak experiences, that is, occasions marked by strong feelings of confidence resulting from the fulfillment of some important task.

23. (p. 487) A person's total subjective experience of reality is called (the):
     a. self-image   c. conscious understanding
     b. reality perception   d. phenomenal field

24. (p. 488) When your self-image is consistent with what you really think, feel, do and experience, you are best able to actualize your potential. Rogers calls this:
     a. incongruence   c. a position of worth
     b. congruence   d. the ideal self

25. (p. 490) According to Rogers, a direct, gut-level response to life experiences that avoids the filtering and distortion of incongruence is called:
     a. self-actualization   c. conditions of worth
     b. organismic valuing   d. ideal self

26. (p. 490) Which of the following is *not* a criticism that has been directed at psychoanalytic theory?
     a. preoccupied with sex and aggression
     b. overemphasizes biological instincts
     c. offers little help in predicting future behavior
     d. suggests a treatment procedure for psychological disorders

27. (p. 490) Of the following approaches, which has done the best job to rigorously test and verify their concepts?
     a. humanism   c. behaviorism
     b. psychoanalysis   d. cognitivism

28. (p. 490) True-False. The chief criticism of humanistic theory is its overly optimistic view of humanity.

29. (p. 492) True-False. According to Abraham Maslow, self-actualization is more a process than a goal or endpoint.

30. (p. 492) Which of the following does *not* indicate that a person is moving toward greater self-actualization?
     a. better being able to live up to standards set by others
     b. greater acceptance of yourself and others
     c. greater confidence
     d. less strain or conflict in accomplishing daily routines

31. (p. 494) Which of the following is *not* true of high self-monitors?
     a. They are flexible, adaptable, and display different behavior from situation to situation.
     b. They believe it is possible to love two people at the same time.
     c. They choose friends who are skilled or knowledgeable in various areas.
     d. They identify themselves in terms of their beliefs, emotions, values, and personality.

32. (p. 494) Which of the following is *not* true of low self-monitors?
     a. They are keenly interested in the actions of others and in trying to "read" their motives, attitudes, and traits.
     b. They are more interested in a potential date's personality than appearance.
     c. They value a match between who they believe they are and what they do.
     d. They prefer jobs where they can "just be themselves."

33. (p. 495) True-False. Using the Self-Monitoring Scale, psychologist Mark Snyder found that the main drawback to being low in self-monitoring is a tendency to be unresponsive to the demands of different situations.

APPLYING YOUR KNOWLEDGE

1. Select an important figure responsible for helping develop a theory of personality. Do some additional reading on your own to find out more about the theory and the theorist. Are there factors in that person's own personality, their background, or the place or period when the theory was first developed that relate to the theory?

ANSWERS—PROGRAMMED REVIEW

1. Psychoanalytic
2. physical causes
3. id; unconscious
4. pleasure principle
5. libido; life instincts
6. Thanatos
7. sex, aggression
8. ego; id; external reality
9. primary process thinking
10. reality principle
11. conscious
12. superego
13. conscience
14. guilt
15. ego ideal
16. weak; strict
17. mental processes
18. displace, sublimate
19. neurotic anxiety; moral anxiety
20. ego-defense mechanisms
21. unconscious
22. hippocampus
23. conscious; preconscious
24. unconscious

25. socialize
26. psychosocial stages
27. sex
28. erogenous zone
29. fixations
30. oral
31. oral-dependent
32. oral-aggressive
33. anal-retentive; anal-expulsive
34. phallic
35. Oedipus conflict
36. castration; identify; conscience
37. Electra conflict
38. latency
39. genital
40. adult personality; feeding; toilet training; sexual; stages
41. latency
42. conscience
43. sexuality
44. neo-Freudians
45. unconscious; sexuality
46. superiority
47. feelings of inferiority

48. compensate
49. style of life
50. 5; creative self
51. earliest memory
52. anatomy
53. neurosis; basic anxiety
54. toward; away; against
55. ego; persona
56. introversion; extroversion
57. personal unconscious
58. collective unconscious; archetypes
59. anima; animus
60. self-archetype; mandalas
61. self-actualization
62. kindness, hostility
63. learned behavior patterns
64. traits
65. illegitimate; legitimate
66. situational
67. past learning
68. habits
69. drive; cue
70. social learning

71. psychological situation
72. expectancy
73. reinforcement value
74. self-reinforcement
75. self-esteem
76. depressed; depression
77. radical`
78. rewards; punishments
79. social reinforcement
80. feeding; toilet, cleanliness; sex; anger, aggression
81. active, passive
82. punishing, frustrating
83. power
84. Identification
85. imitation
86. vicariously
87. three
88. dependent, passive
89. Murder; assault
90. human nature
91. free choice
92. subjective experience
93. self-actualization

94. possibility; ongoing
95. efficient; acceptance, task; humanity; interpersonal; humor
96. peak experiences
97. Rogers
98. fully functioning
99. self; phenomenal field
100. reality; self-image
101. symbolized
102. incongruent
103. incongruent person
104. self-esteem
105. ideal self
106. poised; confident; resourceful; anxious
107. possible selves
108. could; current
109. conditions of worth
110. positive self-regard
111. organismic valuing
112. usefulness
113. sexuality; instincts
114. after; future
115. behaviorists

116. underestimate
117. positive; measure; objectivity
118. process
119. change
120. take responsibility
121. motives
122. honestly, directly
123. peak experiences
124. different
125. mission; calling
126. hurrying; over-scheduling
127. journal
128. assess; Boredom
129. Self-monitoring
130. high; low
131. high; Low
132. high
133. Self-Monitoring Scale
134. high
135. low
136. true self

ANSWERS—SELF-TEST

1.	b	7.	b	13.	d	19.	a	25.	b	31.	d
2.	c	8.	d	14.	a	20.	a	26.	d	32.	a
3.	c	9.	b	15.	True	21.	b	27.	c	33.	True
4.	b	10.	True	16.	c	22.	False	28.	False		
5.	c	11.	b	17.	d	23.	d	29.	True		
6.	False	12.	c	18.	a	24.	b	30.	a		

ACROSS

2. Freudian theory of personality
4. he said strive to reach your potentials
5. he believed personality is a striving for superiority
7. he proposed an unconscious level exists and influences one's personality
9. energy derived from life instincts (Eros)
10. the "executive" component of one's personality—Freudian term
11. acts as a judge or censor for thoughts and actions of ego
13. principle by which ego functions
15. humanist who developed self theory
16. found in collective unconscious according to Jung

DOWN

1. he and Miller look at personality from behavioral viewpoint
2. at this stage Oedipus or Electra conflicts arise
3. death instinct proposed by Freud
6. principle under which the id operates
8. contents of mind beyond one's awareness
12. Freud's first stage of psychosexual theory
14. part of one's personality demanding immediate gratification

Intelligence

CONTENTS

TERMS AND CONCEPTS

savant syndrome
intelligence
operational definition
reliability
test-retest reliability
split-half reliability
equivalent forms reliability
validity
criterion validity
objective
standardization
Stanford-Binet Intelligence Scale
mental age (MA)
chronological age (CA)
intelligence quotient (IQ)
deviation IQ
Wechsler Adult Intelligence Scale—Revised (WAIS-R)
Wechsler Intelligence Scale for Children—Third Edition (WISC-III)
performance intelligence
verbal intelligence
individual intelligence tests

group intelligence tests
Army Alpha
normal curve
GATE programs
g-factor
mental retardation (developmentally disabled)
levels of mental retardation
organic mental retardation
familial retardation
phenylketonuria (PKU)
microcephaly
hydrocephaly
cretinism
Down's Syndrome (mongolism)
eugenics
fraternal twins
identical twins
confluence model
Instrumental Enrichment
culture-fair tests
educable mentally retarded (EMR)
System of Multicultural Pluralistic Assessment (SOMPA)

IMPORTANT INDIVIDUALS

Alfred Binet
David Wechsler
Lewis Terman
Howard Gardner
Steven Ceci

Reuven Feuerstein
Robert Zajonc
Adrian Dove
Arthur Jensen

David McClelland
Robert Glaser
Jane Mercer
June Lewis

PROGRAMMED REVIEW

1.   (p. 498) The _____ _____, in which "an island of brillance is found in a sea of retardation," occurs when a person of subnormal intelligence shows highly developed mental abilities in one or more very limited areas.

2.   (p. 499) The first "intelligence" test was developed by _____ _____ who established questions an "average" child could answer which could then be used to distinguish slower students from the more capable.

3.   (p. 499) A general description of intelligence given by David Wechsler defines it as the global capacity of the individual to act _____, to think _____, and to deal effectively with the _____.

4.   (p. 499) A recent survey of 1,020 experts on intelligence shows that at least three-quarters of this group agree that the following elements are important parts of intelligence: _____ thinking or reasoning; problem-solving ability; capacity to acquire _____; memory; and adaptation to one's _____.____.

5.   (p. 500) Beyond this, intelligence is usually defined using an _____ definition, that is the procedures used to measure it have been specified. In this case, intelligence is what an intelligence test measures.

6.   (p. 500) For a test to be _____ it must yield the same score, or close to the same score, each time it is given to the same individual. In other words, the scores should be consistent and highly correlated.

7.   (p. 500) One way to assess reliability is to administer the test to a large group of people and then test them again at a later date. This method is known as _____-_____ reliability.

8.   (p. 500) Reliability is sometimes determined by comparing the score on one-half of the test items to the score on the other half. This method is known as _____-_____ reliability.

9.   (p. 500) Also, if two versions of the test were given, we could compare scores on one to scores on the other for each person. This method is known as _____ _____ reliability.

10. (p. 500) A test has _____ when it measures what it claims to measure. This capacity can be established in various ways.

11. (p. 500) Validity is usually demonstrated by comparing test scores to actual performance. This procedure is known as _____ validity.

12. (p. 500) For example, a test of legal aptitude might be validated by comparing scores on the test to grades in law school. If high scores _____ with high grades or some other standard of success, the test may be considered valid.

13. (p. 500) A test is said to be _____ if it gives the same score when different people correct it.

14. (p. 501) Test _____ means that the same procedures are used in giving the test to all people and that the norm or average score is determined for a large group of people like those for whom the test is designed.

15. (p. 501) In 1916, Lewis Terman and others at Stanford University revised Binet's original test for use in this country. It is still widely in use today after several more revisions and is known as the _____-_____ Intelligence _____.

16. (p. 501) Since the Stanford-Binet assumes that intellectual ability in childhood improves with increasing _____, it is really a graded set of more difficult tests, one for each _____ _____.

17. (p. 501) The age-ranked questions of the Stanford-Binet allow a person's _____ _____ to be determined. This capacity gives a good indication of one's actual abilities but says nothing about whether overall intelligence is high or low. To know this, one must also consider chronological age (age in years).

18. (p. 501) Using these two age values, an IQ or _____ _____ can be determined. It is defined as _____ _____ divided by _____ _____ multiplied by 100.

19. (p. 501) An advantage of the IQ is that it allows comparison of intelligence among children with different combinations of _____ and _____ ages.

20. (p. 502) The IQ equals 100 when MA = CA, thus 100 is defined as _____ intelligence. While 100 is the mathematical average (or mean) for such scores, average intelligence is usually defined as any score from _____ to _____.

21. (p. 502) It is no longer actually necessary to calculate IQs for many modern tests. Instead, a _____ IQ score is used.

22. (p. 502) Finding a deviation IQ is determined by how far above or below _____ a person's "raw" score is, relative to others taking the test.

23. (p. 502) Tables supplied with the test are then used to convert a person's _____ _____ in the group to an IQ score. This approach avoids certain troublesome errors that occur when IQ is calculated directly.

24. (p. 503) IQ scores are not very dependable until about age _____. The correlation obtained at age 2 and those obtained at age 18 is only _____.

25. (p. 503) The average change in IQ on retesting is approximately _____ points in either direction, however changes of 15 points or more are not uncommon during intellectual development.

26. (p. 503) Studies of IQ have shown a gradual increase in intellectual capacity until about age _____. In general, persons who showed the largest IQ increases had been exposed to stimulating intellectual experiences during early adulthood. Those who declined most typically suffered from chronic illness, drinking problems, or unstimulating life-styles.

27. (p. 503) After middle age, some studies of IQ have recorded _____ declines, while others indicate little or no change due to aging.

28. (p. 504) When _____ _____ or _____ is emphasized, there is little decline until advanced age. But test items requiring _____, rapid _____, or perceptual _____ show earlier losses and a rapid decline after middle age.

29. (p. 504) Overall, age-related losses are _____ for most healthy, well-educated individuals.

30. (p. 504) An intriguing link between IQ and aging centers around the observation that _____ _____ may be signalled as much as five years in advance by significant changes in brain function. This terminal decline in IQ can be measured even when the person appears to be in good health.

31. (p. 504) A widely used alternative to the Stanford-Binet is the _____ _____ Intelligence Scale—Revised, abbreviated _____. The form adopted for children is called the _____ Intelligence Scale for _____—Third Edition, abbreviated _____.

32. (p. 504) The Wechsler tests are generally similar to the Stanford-Binet, but differ in some important ways. The WAIS-R is specifically designed to test _____ intelligence.

33. (p. 504) The Stanford-Binet only gives an overall IQ, whereas both the WISC-III and WAIS-R rate _____ (non-verbal) intelligence in addition to verbal intelligence.

34. (p. 504) Both the Stanford-Binet and the Wechsler tests are _____ intelligence tests which must be administered by a trained specialist.

35. (p. 504) Other tests of intelligence have been designed for use with large groups of people. Group intelligence tests are usually in paper-and-pencil form and require test-takers to read, to follow instructions, and to solve problems of logic, mathematics, or spatial skills. The first group intelligence test was the _____ _____ developed for use in rating World War I military inductees.

36. (p. 504) Other examples of group intelligence tests include the _____ _____ _____ (or SAT), the _____ _____ _____ (or ACT), and the _____ _____ _____ (or CQT).

37. (p. 505) The distribution of IQs in the population approximates a _____ (bell-shaped) curve in which the majority of scores fall close to the _____, and relatively few at the _____.

38. (p. 505) It seems safe to assume that men and women do not differ in overall intelligence. However, on the WAIS-R women do better on _____ ability, _____, and _____ learning, whereas men are best in visualization of _____ relationships and _____ reasoning.

39. (p. 505) Such male-female differences have almost _____ in recent years among children and young adults. The small differences that still exist appear to be based on a tendency for parents and educators to encourage males, more than females, to learn _____ and _____ skills.

40. (p. 505) There are meaningful relationships between IQ scores and school "success." The correlation between IQ and school grades is _____—a sizable association. However, it is wise to remember that many factors influence school grades and success.

41. (p. 506) IQ is not as good a predictor of out-of-school achievements such as art, music, creative writing, dramatics, science, and leadership. Tests related to _____, such as tests of ideational fluency, are much more strongly related to such achievements.

42.   (p. 506) There is also a relationship between IQ and job classification. Persons holding white-collar professional positions average _____ IQs than those in blue-collar occupational settings. However, there is a range of IQ scores in all occupations.

43.   (p. 506) It is tempting to conclude that professional jobs require more intelligence. However, higher status jobs often demand an academic degree which requires much the same type of intelligence as that measured by IQ tests. Therefore, selection procedures for professional jobs appear to be _____ in favor of a particular type of intelligence.

44.   (p. 506) When variations in IQ are extreme, below 70 or above 140, influences on adjustment become unmistakable. Only _____ percent of the population falls in these ranges.

45.   (p. 506) Only about _____ percent of the population scores above 140 on IQ tests. A person scoring this high is at least "gifted" and depending on the standards used, he or she may be considered a "genius."

46.   (p. 506) Lewis Terman investigated some 1500 "gifted" children with IQs of 140 or higher. Terman's study makes it clear that the very bright tend to be gifted in many ways. He found the following results:
      1)   Gifted subjects were socially well adjusted and showed above average _____ capacity.
      2)   Children with high IQs also had high IQs when tested as adults.
      3)   As a group, the gifted were above average in _____, _____, and physical appearance.
      4)   The gifted have better than average mental health records, indicating a greater resistance to mental illness.
      5)   As a group, the gifted were considered to be very professionally _____ as adults.

47.   (p. 507) Terman round that the gifted have greater resistance to mental illness. However, the very intelligent (IQ of over _____) may have social and behavioral adjustment problems as children.

48.   (p. 507) Not all of the gifted children Terman studied were superior as adults. Some had committed _____, were _____, or were poorly adjusted.

49.   (p. 507) There are two factors that greatly influence eventual success for the gifted. One is parental _____. Highly educated parents place a high value on learning and encourage their children to pursue educational achievement.

50.   (p. 507) The other important factor for the gifted is intellectual _____, referring to perseverance, a desire to excel, and a desire to know.

51.   (p. 507) Such findings tell us that highly successful gifted persons tend to be those who are more _____ and _____ to learn and to succeed.

52.   (p. 507) Early signs frequently observed in gifted children include: a tendency to seek out and identify with older children and adults; an early fascination with explanations and problem solving; talking complete sentences as early as _____ or _____ years of age; an unusually good _____; precocious talent in art, music, or number skills; an early interest in books along with early reading (often by age _____); showing of kindness, understanding, and cooperation towards others.

53. (p. 507) An unusually bright child may be gifted in ways other than that reflected by a high IQ score. If artistic talent, mechanical aptitude, etc. are considered, _____ out of 20 children could be considered "gifted" in some respect.

54. (p. 508) Psychologist Howard Gardner has theorized that there are actually several different kinds of intelligence. These include abilities in: _____, logic and math, _____ and _____ thinking, music, bodily-kinesthetic skills (such as dance or athletics), _____ skills (self-knowledge), and _____ skills (leadership, social abilities).

55. (p. 508) If Gardner's theory is correct, traditional IQ tests measure only a part of real world intelligence. An implication is that our _____ may be wasting human potential. Some children might learn math or reading more easily if these topics were tied into art, music, dance, drama, etc.

56. (p. 508) Gardner's view is at odds with studies which suggest that scores on IQ tests mainly reflect an underlying "general intelligence" factor. This _____-_____ is said to explain the high correlations found among scores on various tests of intellectual ability and achievement.

57. (p. 509) Having a high IQ is not without its problems. Boredom with classes and classmates can lead to behavioral problems. In recognition of these difficulties, many school systems now provide special classes under _____ and _____ _____ (GATE) programs, which combine classroom enrichment with fast-paced instruction.

58. (p. 509) An individual with intellectual abilities significantly below average is termed _____ _____ or _____ _____. An IQ of _____ or below is regarded as the dividing line for retardation.

59. (p. 509) A person's ability to perform _____ _____, such as dressing, eating, communicating, shopping, and working also figures into evaluating retardation.

60. (p. 509) The severity of retardation is classified into one of four degrees along with a general educational classification. For example, an individual with an IQ ranging on the low end from roughly 50-55 to a high of 70 would be considered to have a _____ degree of retardation and to be educable. You should be familiar with the other categories.

61. (p. 509) Total care is only necessary for the _____. The _____ and _____ retarded are capable of mastering basic language skills and routine self-help skills. Many become self-supporting by working in _____ _____ (special simplified work environments).

62. (p. 509) The _____ retarded (about 85 percent of all those affected) benefit from carefully structured and supervised education. As adults, these persons, as well as the borderline retarded, are capable of living alone and may marry (although they tend to have difficulties with many of the demands of adult life).

63. (p. 509) In 30 to 40 percent of cases, no known biological problem can be identified. In such cases the degree of retardation is usually mild, in the _____ to _____ IQ range, and quite often other family members are also mildly retarded.

64. (p. 509) _____ _____, as it is called, occurs most often in very poor households. In some such homes nutrition, early stimulation, medical care, intellectual stimulation, and emotional support are inadequate.

65. (p. 510) About 50 percent of all cases of mental retardation are _____, or related to known physical disorders including:
    1) _____ injuries, such as lack of oxygen;
    2) _____ damage caused by maternal drug abuse, disease or infection contracted by the mother before birth, or by the child after birth;
    3) _____ disorders, such as cretinism or phenylketonuria;
    4) _____ abnormalities.

66. (p. 510) There are several distinctive forms of organic retardation, including _____, abbreviated _____, which results from the build-up of phenylpyruvic acid. This condition can now be detected by medical testing during the first _____ of life and can be controlled by special _____.

67. (p. 510) PKU is genetically induced lack of an important enzyme. If PKU goes untreated, severe retardation typically occurs by age _____.

68. (p. 510) The _____ suffers a rare abnormality in which the skull is extremely small or fails to grow, thus forcing the brain to develop in a severely limited space.

69. (p. 510) Microcephaly causes severe retardation that usually requires the individual to be in an institution. They are typically _____, _____ behaved, and easy to work with.

70. (p. 510) _____ is caused by excess production of cerebrospinal fluid within the brain which forces the brain against the skull, grossly enlarging the head and damaging brain tissue. It affects about 8000 babies every year in the U.S.

71. (p. 510) A new medical treatment in which a tube is surgically implanted to drain fluid from the brain to the abdomen can now be used to avoid retardation if performed within the first _____ months of life.

72. (p. 510) _____ develops in infancy due to insufficient secretion of thyroid hormone. In some parts of the world it is caused by too little _____ in the diet.

73. (p. 510) Cretinism causes stunted physical and intellectual growth that cannot be corrected unless detected early. However, it is easily and routinely detected in infancy and may be treated by thyroid hormone _____.

74. (p. 510) _____ _____ (once known as mongolism) causes moderate to severe retardation and a shortened life expectancy in 1 out of 800 babies. Distinctive features include almond-shaped eyes, a slightly protruding tongue, stubby hands, a stocky build, and sometimes a deep crease on the palm of the hand.

75. (p. 510) It is now known that the Down child has an extra chromosome resulting from flaws in the parent's egg or sperm cells. Thus, the syndrome is _____, but not usually _____ (it does not "run" in the family).

76. (p. 510) Mothers in their early twenties have about one chance in _____ of giving birth to a Down syndrome baby. After age _____, the odds increase to about one in 105. By age 48 the risk reaches one in _____.

77. (p. 510) The age of the father is also linked to an increased risk of Down syndrome. In about _____ percent of cases, the father is the source of the extra chromosome.

78. (p. 510) Down syndrome children are usually _____ and _____, and they can do most of the things that other children can do, only slower. There is evidence that they continue to learn and make slow mental progress well into adulthood. While there is no "cure" for Down syndrome, specially tailored educational programs can enable them to lead fuller lives.

79. (p. 511) In a classic study of genetic factors in learning, Tryon managed to breed separate strains of "_____-_____" and "_____-_____" rats.

80. (p. 511) This experiment and other studies of _____ (selective breeding for desirable characteristics) suggest that some traits are highly influenced by heredity.

81. (p. 511) The Tryon study seemed to show that intelligence is inherited, but later researchers found "maze-bright" rats weren't actually smarter, just more motivated by _____ and less easily _____ during testing.

82. (p. 511) In assessing the relative importance of heredity and environment on the development of intelligence, studies have looked at the similarity in IQ between relatives of varying closeness in genetic association. It is typically found that the similarity grows in _____ to the closeness in genetic association.

83. (p. 511) But relatives often share similar environments as well as heredity, so some select comparisons must be made. For example, _____ _____ come from two separate eggs fertilized at the same time; they are no more genetically alike than ordinary siblings, but their IQ scores tend to be more similar.

84. (p. 511) The reason for this increased similarity must be _____: Parents treat twins more alike than ordinary siblings, which results in a closer match in IQs.

85. (p. 511) More striking similarities are observed with _____ _____ who develop from a single egg and therefore have identical genes. When reared in the same home environment, highly correlated IQs result. But when reared apart, the correlation drops from _____ to _____ showing the effects of less similar environments.

86. (p. 512) Psychologists who emphasize genetics believe these figures show that intelligence is _____ to _____ percent hereditary.

87. (p. 512) Environmentalists point out that some separated twins differ by as much as _____ IQ points. Also, separated twins are almost always placed in homes socially and educationally similar to their biological parents. This fact tends to _____ the apparent genetic effects.

88. (p. 512) Strong evidence for an environmental view of intelligence comes from families having one _____ child and one _____ child. Recent studies show that children reared by the same mother resemble her in IQ to the same degree, in spite of differences in heredity.

89. (p. 512) Trans-racially adopted children are as _____ in IQ to their adoptive brothers and sisters as biologically related siblings are.

90. (p. 512) Also, the rate of _____ failures for adopted children matches the adoptive parents' social class, not that of the biological parents.

91. (p. 513) Further support for the role of environment in intelligence is seen in one study where 25 children considered mentally retarded were transferred to a more stimulating environment. The result was an average gain of _____ IQ points. A second group of initially less retarded children who remained in the orphanage lost an average of _____ IQ points.

92. (p. 513) Data from 14 nations have shown average IQ gains of from _____ to _____ points during a single generation (the last 30 years). These IQ boosts, averaging 15 points, have occurred in far too short a time for genetics to explain them.

93. (p. 513) Steven Ceci found that those who miss school lose anywhere from _____ point to _____ points in IQ per year. Conversely, IQ rises as people spend more time in school.

94. (p. 513) _____ has little positive effect on aptitude and intelligence test scores. But there is increasing evidence that _____, in-depth training in thinking skills can increase tested intelligence.

95. (p. 513) Reuven Feuerstein has developed a program called "_____ _____" which involves hundreds of hours of guided problem solving. Research has shown that such training can raise IQ scores.

96. (p. 513) Similarly, over 400 seventh grade students in _____ have taken special classes over the last six years under a program designed by American psychologists. Results have shown that the course had sizable, beneficial effects on students.

97. (p. 513) The difficulty with such training, however, is that it is very time consuming. Psychologists are now developing _____ _____ to teach problem solving, effective thinking, and other elements of intelligence.

98. (p. 513) Robert Zajonc believes that IQ _____ as family size grows. That is, the brightest children come from the _____ families. In addition, the brightest children are, on the average, those who are born _____ in a family.

99. (p. 513) Zajonc has developed the _____ _____ to explain these findings. According to this theory, each arriving baby temporarily lowers the "average intellectual level" in the family, thus making it a less stimulating environment.

100. (p. 513) Even if Zajonc is right, the average IQ score for the older of two children is only _____ points higher than the average for the last of nine children. Such differences may mean little in terms of what a person can actually do.

101. (p. 513) Judith Blake has provided strong evidence that it's not birth order that's important. Only the overall _____ of families appears to make a difference.

102. (p. 514) Blake also found that children from smaller families tend to be more intelligent. However, she feels this is because in large families parents have less _____, _____ and physical energy, and _____ resources for each child.

103. (p. 514) There is probably no limit to how far _____ intelligence can go in a poor environment, but heredity may impose some limits on how far _____ IQ can go, even under ideal conditions.

104. (p. 514) Interestingly, _____ children tend to come from homes where parents encourage intellectual exploration, answer their children's questions, and spend time with their children.

105. (p. 516) There are many problems involved in the use and interpretation of IQ tests. One such problem is the language that is used. This is illustrated by the _____ Counterbalance Intelligence Test which was developed by sociologist Adrian _____. This "half serious" test is slanted in favor of urban African American culture just as he believes the typical intelligence test is biased toward a white middle-class background.

106. (p. 516) In recognition of this problem, some psychologists are trying to develop _____-_____ tests that do not disadvantage certain groups.

107. (p. 516) The issue of environmental versus genetic factors involved in IQ has been strongly raised regarding the IQs of blacks. Most psychologists do not support the genetic emphasis espoused by Arthur Jensen. Instead, psychologists have responded with several counter-arguments:
    1) blacks are more likely than whites to live in intellectually _____ environments;
    2) even if the gap in IQ between blacks and whites is hereditary, it is small enough to be corrected by _____;
    3) assumptions, biases, and content of IQ _____ do not always allow meaningful comparisons between ethnic, cultural, or racial groups;
    4) the logic Jensen used in reaching his conclusions is faulty.

108. (p. 517) Differences in IQ scores are not a fact of _____, but a decision by the test makers. That is why whites do better on IQ tests written by whites, and blacks do better on IQ tests devised by blacks.

109. (p. 517) Another example of this fact is an intelligence test made up of 100 words selected from the *Dictionary of Afro-American Slang*. Williams gave the test to 100 black and 100 white high school students and found that the black group averaged _____ points higher than the white group.

110. (p. 517) Only when black children are raised in exactly the same conditions as white children can hereditary factors be clearly assessed. Along this line, one study investigated the IQs of black children raised in white families. These children had IQ scores averaging _____, which is comparable to the national average for white children.

111. (p. 517) Criticism of intelligence tests used in public schools has also become an issue. Recent court decisions have led some states to _____ use of IQ tests in public schools.

112. (p. 517) Criticism of intelligence testing has also come from the academic community. David McClelland believes IQ is of little value in predicting real _____ to deal effectively with the world.

113. (p. 517) McClelland concedes that IQ predicts school performance, but when he compared a group of college students with straight A's to another group with poor grades he found no differences in later _____ _____.

114. (p. 517) Widespread reliance on standardized intelligence tests and aptitude tests raises questions about the relative good and harm they do. On the positive side, tests can open _____ as well as close them. A high test score may allow a disadvantaged youth to enter college, or it may identify a child who is bright but emotionally disturbed.

115. (p. 518) Test scores may also be _____ and more _____ than arbitrary judgments made by admissions officers of employment interviewers.

116. (p. 518) Also, tests do accurately predict _____ performance. The fact that grades do not predict later success may call for overhaul of college course work, not an end to testing.

117. (p. 518) On the negative side, mass testing can occasionally_____ people of obvious ability. Other complaints relate to the frequent appearance of bad or _____ questions, overuse of class time to prepare students for the tests, and in the case of intelligence tests, the charge that tests are often _____.

118. (p. 518) Also, most standardized tests demand _____ recognition of facts assessed with a multiple-choice format. They do not, for the most part, test a person's ability to think _____ or _____ or to apply knowledge to solve problems.

119. (p. 518) In considering the positive and negative aspects of standardized tests, Robert Glaser points out that they are now used primarily to _____ people rather than to _____ instruction to the strengths, weaknesses, and needs of each student.

120. (p. 518) In considering the use of IQ tests, it is wise for the individual to remember that IQ is not intelligence—it is only an _____ of intelligence as defined by a particular test. If you change the test, you change the score.

121. (p. 518) Some psychologists are seeking ways to teach necessary intellectual skills to all children. For example, one experiment divided 40 children from extremely disadvantaged families into two groups. Experimental subjects received a wide variety of stimulation and special attention, while control subjects did not. When tested at age $5\frac{1}{2}$, the average IQ for the control group was _____, but the experimental group showed an encouraging average of _____.

122. (p. 519) In the case of *Larry P.* vs. *The California State Superintendent of Education* it was ruled that IQ test scores alone can no longer be used for _____ _____ _____ (EMR) placement.

123. (p. 519) Jane Mercer, a sociologist who gave key testimony in the case, believes that schools often label children retarded, when they really lack _____ tied knowledge.

124. (p. 520) A child who does poorly in the classroom or on an IQ test may function perfectly well at home and in the community. Mercer refers to such children as "_____-_____ _____"—youngsters who are "retarded" only during the school day.

125. (p. 520) Mercer and her associate June Lewis believe that the _____ of _____ _____ _____ (SOMPA) can be effectively used in place of IQ testing to assess intellectual functioning.

126. (p. 520) SOMPA combines three ways of assessing a child:
    1) It looks for any _____ problems that may be causing low school performance.
    2) The child's behavior _____ the classroom is evaluated to avoid the mistake of creating a "six-hour retardate" on the basis of a test score.
    3) It assumes that when everything else is held constant the child who has learned the most probably has the most "learning potential."

127. (p. 520) SOMPA assumes that true potential can be masked by a child's cultural background. To avoid this problem, SOMPA compares each child's WISC-R score with that of children from _____ _____.

128. (p. 520) In December 1986, Judge Robert Peckham reiterated the California IQ test ban with a directive that appears to _____ even the use of alternatives like SOMPA.

129. (p. 520) Understandably, some psychologists object to the courts making educational decisions. Others point out that they must now resort to _____-_____ measures which may be subjective and open to potential abuse.

130. (p. 520) Critics of IQ testing reply that IQ gives little information about the _____ of a low score. It tells little about what corrective action should be taken.

SELF-TEST

1. (p. 499) Alfred Binet was responsible for
   a. developing SOMPA for testing minority youngsters
   b. developing the Army Alpha group intelligence test
   c. key testimony in the California court case involving the use of IQ tests in EMR placement
   d. developing the first "intelligence" test in which age-related items could be used to distinguish intellectually slower students from the more capable

2. (p. 500) Intelligence is usually defined using a(n) _____ definition.
   a. subjective
   b. physiological
   c. mathematical
   d. operational

3. (p. 500) When we administer a test to a large group of people, retest them at a later date and then compare the scores for similarity, we are investigating
   a. split-half reliability
   b. equivalent forms reliability
   c. test-retest reliability
   d. construct validity

4. (p. 500) Which of the following is *not* a test of reliability?
   a. test-retest
   b. face
   c. split-half
   d. equivalent forms

5. (p. 500) A test has _____ when it measures what it claims to measure.
   a. split-half reliability
   b. validity
   c. equivalent form reliability
   d. culture fairness

6. (p. 500) When we compare test scores to actual performance, we are measuring
   a. face validity
   b. test-retest reliability
   c. split-half reliability
   d. criterion validity

7. (p. 501) A test is said to be _____ when it gives the same score when corrected by different people.
   a. objective
   b. standardized
   c. reliable
   d. valid

8. (p. 501) When norms are used in interpreting test scores and the test is administered the same way to everyone taking it, we say the test is
   a. objective
   b. standardized
   c. reliable
   d. valid

9. (p. 501) Of the following, which is *not* associated with the Stanford-Binet Intelligence Scale?
   a. chronological age
   b. mental age
   c. separate subscales
   d. intelligence quotient

10. (p. 501) According to the Stanford-Binet Intelligence Scale, if Jill is 15 years old and her MA is 18, her intelligence quotient is
   a. 78
   b. 100
   c. 120
   d. 16.5

11. (p. 503) True-False. IQ scores are not very dependable until about age six. After middle childhood, changes in IQ are usually quite small.

12. (p. 504) Which of the following is *not* associated with the WAIS-R?
   a. It is specifically designed to test adult intelligence.
   b. It can be administered as either a group test or an individual test.
   c. Test scores can be broken down into various areas to reveal strengths and weaknesses.
   d. It rates both verbal and performance intelligence.

13. (p. 505) Which of the following is *not* true of IQ scores?
   a. When graphically displayed the distribution approximates a normal curve.
   b. IQ is positively correlated with educational level.
   c. IQ differences of even a few points can tell much about intellectual potential.
   d. IQ is positively correlated with job classification.

14. (p. 505) True-False. Women tend to excel on IQ test items that require arithmetic reasoning, verbal ability, and rote learning.

15. (p. 506) According to Terman's work with mentally gifted children, which of the following is *not* correct?
   a. Gifted children were more susceptible to mental health problems.
   b. The gifted were considered quite successful in their later educational and professional endeavors.
   c. Gifted children were above average in height, weight, and physical appearance.
   d. The gifted tend to be especially well adjusted and above average in leadership capacity.

16. (p. 507) True-False. The difference between gifted individuals who succeed and those who do not seems strongly tied to persistence and motivation to succeed.

17. (p. 510) Which of the following is *not* an organic cause of mental retardation?
   a. fetal damage
   b. familial retardation
   c. metabolic disorders
   d. birth injuries

18. (p. 510) The genetically inherited lack of an important bodily enzyme which causes the build-up of a destructive chemical defines the condition known as
   a. PKU
   b. microcephaly
   c. cretinism
   d. mongolism

19. (p. 510) True-False. Microcephaly can now be effectively treated by surgically implanting a tube that drains excess cerebrospinal fluid into the abdomen.

20. (p. 510) _____ is a form of retardation that develops in infancy due to the insufficient secretion of thyroid hormone.
   a. PKU
   b. Microcephaly
   c. Cretinism
   d. Mongolism

21.   (p. 510) Which of the following is *not* true of Down syndrome?
      a.   Victims of this disorder have one less chromosome than normal.
      b.   The condition has been linked to the age of the mother.
      c.   The condition has been linked to the age of the father.
      d.   It was once known as mongolism and is characterized by almond-shaped eyes and an overly large, protruding tongue.

22.   (p. 511) Selective breeding for desirable characteristics is referred to as
      a.   euthanasia   c.   genetics
      b.   eugenics   d.   Army Alpha

23.   (p. 512) Which of the following is *not* evidence for environmental influence in IQ?
      a.   Fraternal twins reared together have IQs more similar than those of ordinary siblings.
      b.   Separated twins with large differences in IQs have been exposed to large educational and environmental differences.
      c.   Apparent genetic effects in separated twin studies may be inflated because the twins are almost always placed in homes socially and educationally similar to their biological parents.
      d.   Identical twins have IQs more similar than any other comparison of relatives, regardless of whether they are raised apart or together.

24.   (p. 512) Which of the following cannot be counted as evidence that environment can alter intelligence?
      a.   Arthur Jensen's claim that the lower IQ scores of blacks can be primarily attributed to "genetic heritage."
      b.   Children reared by the same mother resemble her in IQ to the same degree regardless of whether they are biological or adopted children.
      c.   One study found that children considered mentally retarded showed an average gain of 29 points when placed in more stimulating environments.
      d.   One study found that adopted children reared by more highly educated, professionally employed parents had higher IQs than siblings who remained with their biological parents.

25.   (p. 513) True-False. Robert Zajonc believes that IQ decreases as family size grows and has developed the confluence model to explain this effect.

26.   (p. 516) True-False. Psychological tests that disadvantage minority groups are called culture-free tests.

27.   (p. 516) Which of the following is *not* a criticism that psychologists have leveled at the extreme hereditarian view of Arthur Jensen?
      a.   Black children in the U.S. do not score significantly below white on standard IQ tests.
      b.   Blacks are more likely to live in intellectually impoverished environments that may affect intelligence.
      c.   The assumptions, biases, and content of standard IQ tests do not allow meaningful comparisons between ethnic groups.
      d.   The logic of their argument is faulty.

28.   (p. 517) True-False. David McClelland believes IQ is of little value in predicting real competence to deal effectively with the environment.

29.   (p. 518) True-False. Providing extra stimulation and special teaching attention can raise the IQ of young children above that of children not receiving such special treatment.

30. (p. 519) The case of *Larry P.* vs. *The California State Superintendent of Education* revolved around
    a. the use of standardized tests to determine whether a person is admitted to college
    b. the use of IQ tests alone to determine EMR placement
    c. the validity of IQ tests to assess racial differences
    d. whether culture-fair IQ tests are as valid and reliable as more commonly used standard IQ tests

31. (p. 520) True-False. The idea of SOMPA is to keep average kids out of classes for the mentally retarded, and to identify gifted children who might otherwise be passed over as average.

APPLYING YOUR KNOWLEDGE

1. Contact a psychologist at your school who does intelligence testing and ask if he or she to administer you an IQ test. Ask them to show you how they score the test and how they arrive at an actual IQ score. Discuss with the tester what strengths and weaknesses you may have shown on the test.

2. Lewis Terman conducted an interesting study of children with high IQ scores. Go to your library and read the original report. Can you find follow-up studies that have been conducted since the original work that analyzes how these same gifted children have progressed at later stages of life?

3. There are probably some agencies in your area that work with the developmentally disabled. Contact a psychologist at one of these facilities and ask to talk with them about how they assess intellectual and behavioral functioning. How does their program work differently with people at different levels of retardation?

4. What are the laws governing the use of IQ tests in the schools within your state? Contact a school psychologist in your area and find out. Discuss with them how they deal with cultural differences when assessing minority youngsters.

ANSWERS—PROGRAMMED REVIEW

1. savant syndrome
2. Alfred Binet
3. purposefully; rationally; environment
4. abstract; knowledge; environment
5. operational
6. reliable
7. test-retest
8. split-half
9. equivalent forms
10. validity
11. criterion
12. correlate
13. objective
14. standardization
15. Stanford-Binet Intelligence Scale
16. age; age group

17. mental age; chronological age
18. intelligence quotient; mental age; chronological age
19. chronological, mental
20. average; 90, 109
21. deviation
22. average
23. relative standing
24. six; 31
25. 5
26. 40
27. slow
28. general information; comprehension; speed; insight; flexibility
29. small
30. impending death

31. Wechsler Adult Intelligence Scale—Revised; WAIS-R: Wechsler Intelligence Scale for Children—Third Edition; WISC-III
32. adult
33. performance
34. individual
35. Army Alpha
36. Scholastic Aptitude Test; American College Test; College Qualification Test
37. normal; average; extremes
38. verbal; vocabulary; rote; spatial; arithmetic

39. disappeared; math, spatial
40. .50
41. creativity
42. higher
43. biased
44. 3
45. 1
46. leadership; height, weight; successful
47. 180
48. crimes; unemployed
49. education
50. determination
51. persistent; motivated
52. 2; 3; memory; 3
53. 19
54. g-factor
55. Gifted and Talented Education
56. language; visual, spatial; intrapersonal; interpersonal
57. schools
58. mentally retarded; developmentally disabled; 70
59. adaptive behaviors
60. mild
61. profoundly; severely, moderately; sheltered workshops
62. mildly
63. 50; 70
64. Familial retardation
65. organic; birth; fetal; metabolic; genetic
66. phenylketonuria; PKU; month, diet

67. 3
68. microcephalic
69. affectionate; well
70. Hydrocephaly
71. 3
72. Cretinism; iodine
73. replacement
74. Down syndrome
75. genetic; hereditary
76. 2,000; 40; 12
77. 25
78. loving, responsive; adulthood
79. maze-bright, maze-dull
80. eugenics
81. food; distracted
82. proportion
83. fraternal twins
84. environmental
85. identical twins; .86; .72
86. 50; 75
87. 20; inflate
88. adopted, biological
89. similar
90. school
91. 29; 26
92. 5; 25
93. .25; 6
94. Coaching; extended
95. Instrumental Enrichment
96. Venezuela
97. computer programs
98. decreases; smallest; first
99. confluence model
100. 10
101. size

102. time; emotional; financial
103. down; up
104. gifted
105. Dove; Dove
106. culture-fair
107. impoverished; environment; tests
108. nature
109. 36
110. 106
111. outlaw
112. competency
113. career success
114. opportunities
115. fairer; objective
116. academic
117. exclude; ambiguous; biased
118. passive; critically, creatively
119. select; adapt
120. index
121. 95; 124
122. educable mentally retarded
123. culturally
114. six-hour retardates
125. System of Multicultural Pluralistic Assessment
126. medical; outside
127. similar backgrounds
128. eliminates
129. non-standard
130. cause

ANSWERS—SELF-TEST

1.	d	7.	a	12.	b	17.	b	22.	b	27.	a
2.	d	8.	b	13.	c	18.	a	23.	d	28.	True
3.	c	9.	c	14.	False	19.	False	24.	a	29.	True
4.	b	10.	c	15.	a	20.	c	25.	True	30.	b
5.	b	11.	True	16.	True	21.	a	26.	False	31.	True
6.	d								

ACROSS

3. small headedness
5. classification of IQ from 90-109
6. portion of WAIS-R measures vocabulary, arithmetic etc.
7. classification of IQ from 120-129
11. he once said IQ's of blacks are lower due to genetics
12. degree of retardation for an IQ range 50-55 (educable)
13. degree of retardation for an IQ range 35-40 (trainable)
14. Weschler Adult Intelligence Scale (abbr.) —Revised

DOWN

1. test is _____ if it yields similar scores on retest
2. condition of water on the brain
4. retardation resulting from insufficient thyroid hormone
8. Phenylketonuria (abbr.)
9. he developed first successful IQ test
10. global capacity of person to act purposefully, think rationally and deal well with environment

CHAPTER 19

Maladaptive Behavior: Deviance and Disorder

CONTENTS

TERMS AND CONCEPTS

psychopathology
Diagnostic and Statistical Manual of Mental
   Disorders (DSM-III-R)
psychotic disorders
organic mental disorders
psychoactive substance use disorders
mood disorders
  mania
  depression
anxiety disorders
  phobic disorders
  panic disorder
  generalized anxiety disorder
  post-traumatic stress disorder
  obsessive-compulsive disorder
somatoform disorders
  hypochondriasis
  somatoform pain
  conversion reaction
    glove anesthesia
dissociative disorders
  amnesia
  fugue
  multiple personalities
  depersonalization
personality disorders
  paranoid personality
  narcissistic personality
  dependent personality

compulsive personality
borderline personality
antisocial personality
sexual disorders
  gender identity
  transsexualism
  paraphilias
  psychosexual dysfunctions
neurosis
psychosis
insanity
expert witness
subjective discomfort
statistical definitions
normal curve
social nonconformity
cultural relativity
sociopathy, psychopathy (antisocial personality)
pedophilia
incest
fetishism
exhibitionism
voyeurism
transvestic fetishism
sexual sadism
sexual masochism
frotteurism
rape
anxiety

adjustment disorders
free floating anxiety
anxiety attack
phobias
   simple (or specific) phobia
   social phobia
   agoraphobia
obsessions
compulsions

la belle indifférence
avoidance learning
anxiety reduction hypothesis
insanity defense
M'Naghten rule
irresistible impulses
diminished capacity
Twinkie Defense
expert witness

IMPORTANT INDIVIDUALS

Marcie Kaplan
James Check

Neil Malamuth
Sigmund Freud

Carl Rogers
David Rosenhan

PROGRAMMED REVIEW

1. (p. 524) Some of the facts of psychopathology are startling:
    1) One out of every _____ persons will become so severely disturbed as to require hospitalization at some point in his or her lifetime.
    2) Some 3 to 6 percent of the aged suffer from organic psychoses.
    3) In any given week, _____ percent of the population is experiencing an anxiety-related disorder.
    4) One out of every _____ school-age children is seriously maladjusted.
    5) Ten to 20 percent or more of all adults will suffer a major depression in their lifetime.
    6) Each year over _____ persons are admitted or readmitted to out-patient services or psychiatric treatment in general hospitals.

2. (p. 524) _____ may be defined as the inability to behave in ways that foster the well-being of the individual and ultimately of society. This definition covers not only obviously maladaptive behavior such as drug addiction, compulsive gambling, or loss of contact with reality, but also any behavior that interferes with personal growth and self-fulfillment.

3. (p. 525) Psychological problems are grouped into broad categories of maladaptive behavior. The most widely accepted system of classification is found in the _____ and _____ _____ of _____ _____, abbreviated _____.

4. (p. 525) The purpose of DSM-III-R is to provide a common _____ for various professionals. It helps _____ and classify problems and aids in the selection of appropriate therapies.

5. (p. 526) _____ disorders are among the most severe type of psychopathology, often requiring hospitalization. Here there is a loss of contact with reality with a major loss of ability to control thoughts and actions.

6. (p. 526) _____ mental disorders are problems caused by brain pathology; that is, by senility, drug damage, diseases of the brain, injuries, the toxic effects of poisons, and so on.

7. (p. 526) These disorders are often accompanied by severe emotional disturbances, impaired _____, _____ loss, _____ changes, and delirium. Psychotic features are also possible in this category.

8.   (p. 526) Psychoactive _____ _____ disorders are defined as abuse or dependence on mood- or behavior-altering drugs: alcohol, barbiturates, opiates, cocaine, amphetamines, hallucinogens, cannabis, tobacco, and others.

9.   (p. 526) Problems in this category usually center on damaged of _____ or occupational functioning and inability to _____ using the drug.

10. (p. 526) _____ disorders primarily involve disturbances in affect or emotion. Individuals with this disorder may be _____, meaning agitated, euphoric, and hyperactive, or they may be _____, running a high risk of suicide.

11. (p. 526) _____ disorders may take the form of _____ (irrational fears of objects, activities, or situations), panic (in which the person suffers unexplainable feelings of total panic), _____ _____ (chronic and persistent anxiety), or post-traumatic stress disorder (high anxiety that surfaces after an extremely distressing event). Also associated with this disorder is a pattern known as _____-_____ behavior.

12. (p. 526) _____ disorders are indicated when a person has physical symptoms that mimic physical disease or injury (paralysis, blindness, illness, chronic pain, etc.) for which there is no identifiable cause.

13. (p. 526) _____ disorders include cases of temporary amnesia and instances of _____ _____, like that displayed by Ohio State "university rapist" William Milligan.

14. (p. 526) Also included are frightening episodes of _____-feelings of being outside one's body, of behaving like a robot, or of being in a dream world.

15. (p. 526) _____ disorders are deeply ingrained, unhealthy personality patterns usually apparent by adolescence and continued throughout most of the individual's adult life.

16. (p. 526) They include _____ (overly suspicious), narcissistic (self-loving), dependent, _____, and antisocial and other personality types.

17. (p. 526) _____ disorders include _____ _____ disorders (where sexual identity does not match physical gender), _____ (a persistent discomfort about one's sex and a desire to change to the opposite sex), and a wide range of deviations in sexual behavior known as _____ (fetishism, voyeurism, etc.).

18. (p. 526) Also found in this category are a variety of sexual _____ (problems in sexual desire or sexual response).

19. (p. 526) DSM-III-R discourages the use of the term _____ because it tends to lump together too many separate problems. Such behavior is now listed as an anxiety, somatoform, or dissociative disorder.

20. (p. 526) Many professionals continue to use the term to loosely refer to problems associated with excessive anxiety. It still makes sense to separate these milder problems from _____, because they do not involve a major loss of contact with reality.

21. (p. 527) Insanity refers to legal responsibility for one's _____ or to the legal designation required for _____ commitment to a mental institution. It is usually established through the testimony of psychologists and psychiatrists who serve as expert witnesses in a court of law.

22. (p. 527) Defining normality is difficult. We can begin by saying that _____ _____ is characteristic of psychopathology. That is, the unhealthy personality will be marked by unhappiness, anxiety, depression, or other signs of emotional upset.

23. (p. 527) A problem with this definition of abnormality is that in some cases a person's behavior may be quite maladaptive without producing subjective discomfort. Additionally, in some cases a _____ of discomfort may indicate a problem.

24. (p. 527) Some psychologists have tried to define normality more objectively by using _____ definitions. For example, we could develop a test to learn how many people show low, medium, or high levels of anxiety. Usually this type of measurement will produce a _____ (bell-shaped) _____.

25. (p. 527) Unfortunately, a statistical definition of abnormality tells us nothing about the meaning of a _____ from the norm and does not help us draw the line between _____ and _____.

26. (p. 528) _____ _____ may also serve as a basis for judging normality. Abnormal behavior can sometimes be viewed as a failure in _____. Here we refer to the person who has not adopted the usual minimum rules for social conduct or who has learned to engage in socially destructive behavior.

27. (p. 528) Before any behavior can be defined as normal or abnormal, we must consider the _____ in which it occurs. Almost any imaginable behavior can be considered normal in some situation.

28. (p. 529) One of the most influential contexts in which any behavior is judged is that of culture. There is a high degree of _____ _____ in perceptions of normality and abnormality. Still, all known cultures classify people as abnormal if they either fail to communicate with others or are consistently unpredictable in their actions.

29. (p. 529) There are several possibilities as to why more women than men are treated for psychological problems: (1) Due to _____ _____ training, women may be more willing to reveal distress and to seek help. (2) Because women are often denied power, responsibility, and independence in our society, they may more often feel depressed, anxious, or hopeless. (3) There may be a male bias to traditional _____ of normality.

30. (p. 529) This last possibility has been explored by psychologist Marcie Kaplan. She believes that women are penalized both for conforming to female _____ and for ignoring them.

31. (p. 529) All definitions of abnormality are _____. Still, there are various standards which help define abnormality.

32. (p. 529) In addition, a core feature of all abnormal behavior is that it is _____. Rather than helping a person to cope successfully, abnormal behaviors make it more difficult for the person to meet the demands of day-to-day life.

33. (p. 529) In practice, the judgment that a person needs help usually occurs when the person does something that _____ or gains the _____ of a person in a position of power who then does something about it.

34. (p. 530) Personality disorders involve deeply ingrained maladaptive personality patterns. For example, the _____ personality is overly suspicious, mistrusting, hypersensitive, guarded, and disrustful of the loyalty and honesty of others.

35. (p. 530) _____ personalities are preoccupied with their own self-importance, need constant admiration, and are absorbed in fantasies of power, wealth, brilliance, etc.

36. (p. 530) The _____ personality is marked by an extreme lack of self-confidence in which others are allowed to run the person's life, and the person places his or her own needs second to others.

37. (p. 530) Persons with a _____ personality disorder are capable of working, but repeatedly lose jobs because of turbulent relationships. They can be friendly and charming, but also extremely unpredictable, moody, and even suicidal.

38. (p. 530) The individual with an antisocial personality, sometimes referred to as a _____ or _____, typically has a long history of conflict with society. They are irresponsible, impulsive, selfish, lacking in judgment and morals, and unable to learn from experience.

39. (p. 530) Antisocial persons are also incapable of deep feelings, including guilt, shame, fear, loyalty, and love. They are poorly _____, have a general disregard for the _____, and seem to lack a _____.

40. (p. 530) Many sociopaths are delinquents or criminals who may pose a threat to the general public. Studies show that more than _____ percent of all antisocial personalities have been arrested, usually for crimes such as robbery, vandalism, and rape.

41. (p. 530) Sociopaths are _____ the crazed murders that have been portrayed on TV and in movies. Many create a good impression and are frequently described as "charming." Their lying, self-serving manipulation, and lack of dependability only gradually become evident to their "friends."

42. (p. 530) People with antisocial personalities usually have a childhood history of emotional _____, _____ and physical abuse. Some psychologists believe that infants who fail to form a healthy emotional attachment to a caregiver later may be prone to antisocial behavior.

43. (p. 531) Adult sociopaths display some subtle physical differences. For example, they produce unusual _____ patterns suggesting _____-_____ of the brain. This may explain why many are thrill seekers—they are searching for stimulation strong enough to overcome their "boredom."

44. (p. 531) Interestingly, sociopaths tested in situations where they must learn to avoid an electric shock show much less _____ than normal. They might therefore be described as emotionally cold.

45.   (p. 531) Antisocial personality disorders are _____ treated with success since sociopaths manipulate therapy as they might any other situation. There is, however, some evidence that antisocial behavior declines somewhat after age _____.

46.   (p. 531) From a psychological point of view, the mark of true sexual deviations is that they are _____ or _____. Typically, they cause guilt, anxiety, or discomfort for one or both participants.

47.   (p. 531) Deviations fitting this definition are related to a wide variety of behaviors including:
      _____, Sex with children
      _____, Sex with blood relatives
      _____, Sexual arousal associated with inanimate objects
      _____, Displaying the genitals to unwilling viewers
      _____, Viewing the genitals of others
      _____ _____, Achieving sexual arousal by wearing clothing
          of the opposite sex
      sexual _____, Deriving sexual pleasure from inflicting pain
      sexual _____, Desiring pain as part of the sex act
      _____, Sexually touching or rubbing against a non-consenting person, usually
          in a public place such as a subway.

48.   (p. 531) At least some sexual deviations are related to sexual abuse or emotional traumas experienced in _____. Thus, while such behavior may harm others, many of its perpetrators are themselves victims.

49.   (p. 531) Roughly _____ percent of all sexual arrests are for exhibitionism. These individuals are typically male, married, and most come from strict and repressive backgrounds.

50.   (p. 531) Exhibitionists have the _____ repeat rate among sexual offenders. Most of them feel a deep sense of _____, which produces a compulsive need to prove their "manhood" by frightening women. While they are usually harmless, those who approach closer than arm's reach may be dangerous.

51.   (p. 531) In general, a woman confronted by an exhibitionist can assume that his goal is to _____ and _____ her. By becoming visibly upset she actual encourages him.

52.   (p. 532) Child molesters are usually males. Most are _____ and two-thirds are _____. Many are rigid, passive, puritanical, or religious. In one-half to two-thirds of all cases of molestation, the offender is a friend, acquaintance, or relative of the child. Most molestations rarely exceed fondling.

53.   (p. 532) Many authorities feel that a _____ incident of molestation is unlikely to cause severe psychological harm to a child. For most children the event is frightening, but not a lasting trauma. This is why parents are urged not to overreact. Doing so only further frightens the child.

54.   (p. 532) Unfortunately, most sexual abuse tends to involve _____ incidents. Parents should not ignore hints from a child that molestation may have occurred.

55.   (p. 532) There are several hints of trouble that parents should watch for when there is suspicion of molestation. These include:
      1)   The child fears being seen _____ (for instance, during bathing), when such fears were absent before;

2) The child develops physical complaints, such as headaches, stomachaches, and other stress symptoms;

3) The child displays anxiety, fidgeting, shame, or discomfort when any reference to sexual behavior occurs;

4) The child becomes markedly _____ and _____;

5) The child engages in hazardous risk taking, such as jumping from high places or riding a bicycle dangerously in traffic;

6) The child reveals self-destructive or suicidal thoughts, self-blame;

7) The child shows a loss of self-_____ or self-_____.

56. (p. 532) Repeated molestations, those that involve force or threats, incidents that exceed fondling, and especially victimization that involves a molester the child deeply trusts can leave lasting emotional scars. As adults, many molest victims develop _____ _____ where lovemaking may evoke vivid and terrifying memories.

57. (p. 532) Most authorities no longer think of _____ as a sexual act; rather it is an act of brutality or aggression based on the need to debase others.

58. (p. 532) Many rapists are _____ _____ who impulsively take what they want without concern for others or guilt about their deed. Others harbor deep-seated resentment or outright hatred of women.

59. (p. 532) A number of writers have suggested that rape is in some ways related to sex role _____. That is, many people learn to believe that women should not show direct interest in sex. Men on the other hand are taught to take the initiative and to persist in attempts at sexual intimacy even when the woman says no.

60. (p. 532) Psychologists James Check and Neil Malamuth believe that such attitudes create a "_____-_____ _____." In their view, rape is only an extreme expression of a system that condones coercive sexual intimacy.

61. (p. 532) To test the hypothesis that _____ _____ contribute to rape, male college students were classified as either high or low in sex-role stereotyping. Each student then read one of three stories.

62. (p. 533) College males high in sex-role stereotyping were more aroused by the rape stories. Their arousal patterns, in fact, were similar to those found among actual rapists. Moreover, _____ percent of those tested indicated they would consider rape, especially if they could be sure of not being caught.

63. (p. 533) In another study of rape, over _____ of a sample of adults agreed with the statement, "A woman who goes to the home or apartment of a man on the first date implies she is willing to have sex."

64. (p. 533) In view of the continuing widespread belief that when a woman says no she means yes, it is little wonder that rape occurs every _____ minutes in the United States.

65. (p. 533) Typical aftereffects for the victim include rage, _____, _____, loss of _____-_____, shame, and in many cases, a lasting mistrust of male-female relationships.

66. (p. 533) The impact of rape is so great that most women who successfully avoid a rape attempt are just as _____ as rape survivors.

67. (p. 533) Anxiety is similar to fear, except that anxiety is a response to an unclear or _____ threat. Compared to anxiety, fear is more _____ and _____. Typically it is the result of a specific, identifiable threat.

68. (p. 533) Problems once called neuroses are now classified separately as anxiety disorders, dissociative disorders, and somatoform disorders. In general, these problems include: (1) high levels of _____ and/or restrictive, self-defeating behavior patterns; (2) a tendency to use elaborate _____ _____ or avoidance responses to maintain minimal functioning; and (3) pervasive feelings of stress, insecurity, inferiority, unhappiness, and dissatisfaction with life.

69. (p. 534) Anxiety, fears, and phobias are probably the most common psychological disturbances today. Roughly _____ percent of the adult population is so affected by these emotions that they could be diagnosed as having an anxiety disorder.

70. (p. 534) The term "nervous breakdown" has no formal meaning. It seems to imply some sort of disease of the nervous system, but there is nothing physically wrong with the nerves of an anxious or emotionally troubled individual. What many people have in mind when they use the term is properly called an _____ _____.

71. (p. 534) The presence of an adjustment disorder is signaled by extreme _____, _____ disturbances, loss of _____, physical complaints, and apathy, anxiety, or depression. Often, these problems are successfully treated with rest, sedation, supportive _____, and a chance to "talk through" fears and anxieties.

72. (p. 534) The outward symptoms of adjustment disorders and anxiety disorders can be similar. However, adjustment disorders typically disappear when life circumstances _____. This demonstrates their link to stressful events.

73. (p. 534) Significant distress that seems greatly out of proportion to the situation is a key element in anxiety disorders. Many psychologists believe that it also underlies _____ and _____ disorders, where maladaptive behavior serves to reduce anxiety and personal discomfort.

74. (p. 534) At least 6 months of unrealistic or excessive anxiety and worry is the essential feature of the anxiety disorder known as _____ _____ disorder.

75. (p. 534) The discomfort felt in this disorder is sometimes described as _____ _____ anxiety, because the anxiety is so general and related to many different worries.

76. (p. 534) Affected individuals typically complain of _____, racing heart, _____ hands, dizziness, upset stomach, rapid breathing, and other symptoms of _____ nervous system activity.

77. (p. 534) The individual is continually preoccupied by worries, which makes them irritable and unable to concentrate. Typical worries involve adequacy at _____, acceptance by others, desertion by a loved one, feelings of _____, and anticipation of disasters.

78. (p. 534) The presence of _____ _____ differentiates what is known as panic disorder. This disorder is characterized by continuous tension, worry, and anxiety that occasionally explodes into sudden, unexpected episodes of intense panic.

79. (p. 535) Victims of a panic attack experience _____ palpitations or _____ pain, choking or smothering sensations, vertigo, feelings of _____, trembling, and fear of dying, going crazy, or losing control during the attack.

80. (p. 535) _____ are exaggerated, irrational fears that persist even when there is no real danger to a person.

81. (p. 535) In phobic disorders, persistent fears, anxiety, and avoidance are focused on various objects, activities, or situations. Affected persons recognize that their fear is unreasonable and excessive, but they cannot _____ it. For a phobic disorder to exist, the person's fear must _____ his or her daily life.

82. (p. 535) Phobias fall into three main categories. Some examples of simple phobias (those that may be attached to nearly any object or situation) are:
     _____—fear of lightning
     _____—fear of spiders
     _____—fear of heights
     _____—fear of closed spaces
     _____—fear of blood
     _____—fear of darkness
     _____—fear of disease
     _____—fear of animals

83. (p. 535) A phobic disorder differs from ordinary fears in that it produces overwhelming anxiety that may cause _____, wild climbing and running, or _____. Such individuals are so threatened that they will go to almost any length to avoid the feared object or situation.

84. (p. 535) _____ phobias involve fear of situations in which one can be observed, evaluated, embarrassed, or humiliated by others. There is an avoidance of certain social situations, such as eating, writing, blushing, or speaking in public.

85. (p. 535) The most disruptive phobic disorder is agoraphobia. One expert estimates one out of every _____ people has this problem to a degree serious enough to restrict his or her life. They may have an intense fear of leaving the familiar setting of the home, becoming literally "housebound."

86. (p. 535) Agoraphobia often starts after a stressful life event, such as an interpersonal conflict. This may trigger a _____ _____ that seems to come from nowhere.

87. (p. 536) The agoraphobic begins to find ways of avoiding areas of insecurity—such as crowds, open roads, and so on. They depend heavily on others to carry out everyday tasks and may have such an intense fear of leaving the familiar setting of the home that they become literally _____.

88. (p. 536) _____ are thoughts or images that intrude into consciousness against a person's will. They are so disturbing that they cause anxiety or extreme discomfort.

89. (p. 536) The common obsessions are about _____ (such as poisoning one's spouse or stabbing a child), about being "dirty" or "unclear," about whether one has performed some action (such as turning off the stove), and about committing _____ acts.

90. (p. 536) Obsessions usually give rise to _____, irrational acts a person feels driven to repeat. Typically, these acts help control or block out anxiety caused by obsessions.

91. (p. 536) Many people with compulsions can be classified as _____ or _____. For example, they may repeatedly wash their hands hundreds of times a day or frequently count household items to see that they are present. Doing this is strongly motivated by a need to reduce anxieties, at least temporarily.

92. (p. 536) Not all obsessive-compulsive disorders are dramatic. Many simply involve extreme _____ and rigid _____. This focus helps the highly anxious person feel more secure by keeping activities totally structured and under control.

93. (p. 536) When compulsive patterns are long-standing, but less intense, they may be classified as a _____ disorder.

94. (p. 536) Most anxiety disorders are relatively lasting patterns. A notable exception is found in _____-_____ _____ disorders. These problems occur when stresses outside the range of normal human experience cause a significant psychological and emotional disturbance.

95. (p. 536) PTSD reactions frequently follow sudden _____, such as floods, tornadoes, earthquakes, or serious accidents. Research shows that it also affects many political _____, _____veterans, prisoners of war, and victims of terrorism, violent crime, child _____, or rape.

96. (p. 536) Characteristic symptoms of PTSD include repeatedly reliving the traumatic event, _____ stimuli associated with the event, and a numbing of _____.

97. (p. 536) Also common are _____, nightmares, guardedness, an inability to _____, irritability, and explosions of anger or aggression, all of which may surface long after the stress has passed.

98. (p. 537) A dissociative reaction is marked by striking episodes of _____ (the inability to recall one's name, address, or past) or _____ (fleeing to escape threat or conflict). These phenomena are often triggered by highly traumatic events.

99. (p. 537) Dissociative disorders may also involve _____ _____, a relatively rare condition in which two or more separate personalities exist in an individual. Such was the case with Sybil, a woman who had 16 complete and totally different personalities.

100. (p. 537) Sybil's alternate personalities developed during childhood when she was regularly beaten, locked in closets, perversely tortured, sexually abused and almost killed. Sybil's first dissociations allowed her to _____ by creating another person who would suffer torture in her place.

101. (p. 537) Multiple personality often begins with unbearable childhood experiences. A history of childhood trauma, especially sexual abuse, is found in over _____ percent of persons suffering from multiple personality disorder.

102. (p. 537) Therapy for multiple personality is often aided by _____, which allows contact with the various personalities. The goal of therapy is integration and fusing of the various personalities into a single, balanced entity.

103. (p. 537) Somatoform disorders are noted in individuals who are continually distracted by fears of having a serious _____. Such individuals are preoccupied with bodily functions or minor physical problems, despite the fact that there is no medical basis for their complaints.

104. (p. 538) In _____, the person interprets normal sensations and small bodily signs as proof that he or she has a terrible disease.

105. (p. 538) Persons who have a related problem called _____ disorder, express their anxieties in the form of various bodily complaints such as vomiting or nausea, shortness of breath, difficulty swallowing, or painful menstruation.

106. (p. 538) Persons with somatization disorder feel ill much of the time and visit doctors repeatedly. Most are taking medicines or other treatments, but no _____ cause can be found for their distress.

107. (p. 538) A person suffering from _____ _____ disorder is disabled by pain that has no identifiable physical basis.

108. (p. 538) A rarer somatoform disorder (or "body-form" disorder) is called a _____ _____, said to occur when anxiety or severe emotional conflicts are converted into symptoms that actually disturb physical functioning or closely resemble a physical disability.

109. (p. 538) An example of a conversion reaction is _____ _____, a loss of sensitivity in the areas of skin that would normally be covered by a glove.

110. (p. 538) Glove anesthesia shows that conversion symptoms often contradict known _____ facts. The system of nerves in the hands does not form a glove-like pattern and could not cause the observed symptoms.

111. (p. 538) Conversion symptoms typically disappear when the victim is asleep, _____, or _____. This shows that they have no physical basis.

112. (p. 538) Conversion disorders usually serve to excuse the person from a _____ situation.

113. (p. 538) Victims of conversion disorders usually show a lack of concern for their disability. This sign is referred to as _____ _____ _____,_____.

114. (p. 538) Conversion reactions probably account for many of the so-called miracle cures attributed to faith _____ or medical _____. Though "cured," new symptoms usually develop later.

115. (p. 538) Susceptibility to anxiety-based disorders appears to be partly inherited. Studies of parents suffering from panic disorder, for instance, show that _____ percent of their children are born with a fearful, inhibited temperament.

116. (p. 538) Such children are irritable and wary as infants, shy and fearful as toddlers, and by school age they are quiet and cautious introverts. Authorities believe that such children are at _____ risk for anxiety problems, such as panic attacks, in adulthood.

117. (p. 538) At least three major psychological perspectives on the causes of dissociative, anxiety, and somatoform disorders can be identified. The first comprehensive explanation of neurosis was proposed by Sigmund _____ and is called the _____ approach.

118. (p. 539) According to Freud, neurosis (as it was called then) represents a raging conflict between the three subparts of the personality. The _____ becomes overwhelmed by anxiety caused by forbidden _____ impulses and guilt generated by the _____ in response to these impulses, resulting in rigid defense mechanisms and inflexible behavior.

119. (p. 539) Psychologist Carl Rogers, exemplifying the humanistic-existential approach, interprets emotional disorders as the end-product of a faulty _____-_____. He feels that anxious individuals build up an unrealistic picture of themselves which leaves them vulnerable to contradictory information.

120. (p. 539) Some psychologists take a more existential point of view, emphasizing that unhealthy anxiety reflects a loss of _____ in one's life.

121. (p. 539) According to this view, humans must show _____ and _____ in their choices if life is to have meaning, but too often we back away from life-enhancing choices.

122. (p. 539) This hesitancy occurs because we experience "_____ _____," the anguish that comes from knowing that we are personally responsible for our lives, hence, that we have a crushing responsibility to choose wisely and courageously.

123. (p. 539) From the existential view, people who are unhappy and anxious are living in "_____ _____." That is, they have collapsed in the face of the awesome responsibility to choose a meaningful existence. In short, they have lost their way in life.

124. (p. 539) Behaviorists assume that the "symptoms" of these disorders are _____ just as other behaviors are. For example, phobias can be acquired through classical conditioning. Anxiety attacks may reflect the generalization of conditioned emotional responses to new situations. The hypochondriac's "sickness behavior" may be reinforced by the sympathy and attention he or she gets.

125. (p. 540) One point that all theorists agree upon is that it is ultimately self-defeating and _____ (contradictory): it makes people more miserable in the long run, but its immediate effect is to temporarily lower anxiety.

126. (p. 540) The behavioristic explanation of the origins of this paradox is that self-defeating behavior begins with _____ _____. The powerful reward of immediate relief from anxiety keeps self-defeating avoidance behavior alive. This view is known as the _____ _____ _____.

127. (p. 541) David Rosenhan gained entrance to mental hospitals by complaining of hearing voices. In _____ out of 12 tries, he and his colleagues were admitted with a diagnosis of _____. None of the researchers was ever recognized by hospital staff as a phony patient.

128. (p. 541) Rosenhan spent from one to seven weeks in hospitals before being discharged and found that contact between staff and patients was very limited. Attendants and staff only spent an average of _____ percent of their time out of the glassed-in central compartment in the ward.

129. (p. 541) Daily contact of patients with psychiatrists, psychologists, or physicians averaged about _____ minutes. On the other hand, the researchers were given a total of _____ pills to swallow.

130. (p. 542) Patients tended to be treated as non-persons. It was as if they were invisible. Because they were seen in the context of a mental ward, and because they had been _____ schizophrenic, anything they did was seen as a symptom of their psychotic "illness." For example, Rosenhan took notes at will and was simply ignored.

131. (p. 542) In a follow-up study, the staff of another hospital was warned that one or more pseudo-patients were going to try to gain admission. Among 193 candidates, _____ were labeled "fakes" and _____ more "suspicious" despite the fact that Rosenhan never sent any patients.

132. (p. 542) All of the normal people who served as pseudo-patients in the original studies were discharged as schizophrenics "in _____" (temporarily free of symptoms). The label that prevented hospital staff from seeing the normality of the researchers stayed with them when they left.

133. (p. 542) These findings carry an important message: _____ can be dangerous. It is more productive to label _____ than to label people.

134. (p. 542) Even careful usage of labels can cause difficulties. Some people are _____ to learn that their problem has a name and that it is shared by others.

135. (p. 542) Others, however, may be upset to learn that they are considered "_____ _____." The stigma that still clings to this term discourages some people from seeking needed professional help.

136. (p. 543) The insanity defense entered western law as the _____ _____ based on an 1843 ruling by the English House of Lords. This decision indicated that persons suffering from mental disease or other defects that prevent them from knowing right from wrong are insane.

137. (p. 543) Defendants may also claim they knew their act was wrong, but they had an _____ _____ they could not control.

138. (p. 543) A related defense claims _____ _____ to control actions or to know right from wrong. A person who commits a crime while under the influence of drugs might make this plea.

139. (p. 544) The problems posed by the insanity defense are vividly shown by three recent cases. In Darlin June Cromer's case, he was found sane in the racial killing of a 5-year-old boy despite the fact that one psychiatrist testified that Cromer was "the _____ _____ person" he'd ever seen.

140. (p. 544) In Dan White's case the defense pleaded diminished capacity claiming, among other things, that White was deranged from eating too much "junk food." This argument became known as the _____ _____. California now bans claims of diminished capacity.

141. (p. 544) "Vampire Killer" Richard _____ was convicted of killing six people and drinking the blood of some of his victims. He was declared sane.

142. (p. 544) Criminal trials involving insanity have a typical pattern. Psychiatrists serving as _____ _____ for defense and prosecution present conflicting views leaving the jury to decide who is right.

143. (p. 544) More often, this "battle of the experts" never takes place. In _____ out of 5 cases, prosecutors, defense attorneys, medical experts, and judges agree before trial that the defendant is mentally ill.

144. (p. 544) The states of _____, _____, and _____ have banned the insanity plea, but in most states it remains intact. Several other states now allow only a "guilty, but mentally ill" plea.

145. (p. 544) Pleas of insanity are used in only about 1 out of every _____ court cases and succeed as a defense in only about _____ percent of those cases.

146. (p. 544) Verdicts of innocence by reason of insanity do not set defendants free. Rather they are committed to a _____ _____ and thereafter must prove they are no longer a danger in order to be released.

147. (p. 544) In some cases, persons declared "insane" have been hospitalized longer than they would have been imprisoned for a criminal conviction. Then again, on the average insane offenders are now held for about _____ years.

148. (p. 544) At present there is no way to accurately predict which individuals are likely to be dangerous. Follow-ups of arrests and mental hospital records show that from _____-_____ to _____-_____ of the time, experts are wrong in predicting violent behavior.

SELF-TEST

1.   (p. 524) What percent of the U.S. population will become so severely disturbed as to require hospitalization at some point in time?
     a.   1   c.   8
     b.   5   d.   10

2.   (p. 526) Which of the following would *not* be a possible cause of organic mental disorders?
     a.   toxic effects of poisons   c.   diseases of the brain
     b.   senility   d.   chronic depression

3.   (p. 526) Which of the following is *not* a type of anxiety disorder?
     a.   conversion reactions   c.   panic disorder
     b.   obsessive-compulsive disorder   d.   phobias

4.   (p. 526) _____ disorders are indicated when a person has physical symptoms suggesting disease or injury for which there is no identifiable cause.
     a.   Organic   c.   Anxiety
     b.   Dissociative   d.   Somatoform

5.   (p. 526) Which of the following is *not* a type of personality disorder?
     a.   paranoid personality   c.   antisocial personality
     b.   senile personality   d.   narcissistic personality

6.   (p. 527) True-False. Psychosis is the same as insanity.

7.   (p. 527) Of the following, which has been used in attempts to define abnormality?
     a.   subjective discomfort   c.   social nonconformity
     b.   statistical definitions   d.   all of the above

8.   (p. 530) People who are selfish, impulsive, unable to feel guilt, manipulative, and lacking in moral
      values are classified as
      a.   psychotic   c.   traumatized
      b.   sociopathic   d.   schizophrenic

9.   (p. 530) The early history of sociopaths is usually marked by
      a.   parental double-bind communication
      b.   tension and stress
      c.   emotional deprivation and disregard
      d.   sexual perversion and obscenity

10.   (p. 531) Which of the following is *not* a correct match?
      a.   pedophilia—sex with children
      b.   voyeurism—displaying the genitals
      c.   frotteurism—sexually touching a non-consenting person, usually in a public place
      d.   sadism—inflicting pain as part of the sex act

11.   (p. 532) Which of the following is *not* true of child molesters?
      a.   They are typically married and two-thirds are fathers.
      b.   Many are rigid, passive, puritanical, or religious.
      c.   Their acts rarely exceed fondling.
      d.   In almost every case, force or threats are used.

12.   (p. 532) Which of the following is *not* true of rape?
      a.   Psychologists no longer think of it as a sexual act.
      b.   It is in some ways related to sex role socialization.
      c.   Aftereffects can include rage, guilt, depression, and loss of self-esteem.
      d.   Many rapists are psychotics who do not recognize the seriousness of their behavior.

13.   (p. 534) True-False. The term nervous breakdown has no formal meaning.

14.   (p. 534) Which of the following characterizes panic disorders?
      a.   anxiety attacks   c.   hallucinations
      b.   amnesia   d.   obsessions

15.   (p. 535) Which of the following is *not* a correct match?
      a.   arastraphobia—fear of lightning
      b.   zoophobia—fear of animals
      c.   claustrophobia—fear of darkness
      d.   acrophobia—fear of heights

16.   (p. 535) True-False.Agoraphobia is the most common and debilitating of the phobic reactions. Persons
      suffering this disorder may literally become "housebound."

17.   (p. 536) Thoughts or images that intrude into consciousness against a person's will which may cause
      anxiety or extreme discomfort are called
      a.   phobias   c.   compulsions
      b.   obsessions   d.   hallucinations

18.   (p. 536) Irrational acts a person feels driven to repeat are called
      a.   phobias   c.   compulsions
      b.   obsessions   d.   hallucinations

19. (p. 536) _____ disorders can occur when stresses outside the range of normal human experience cause a significant psychological and emotional disturbance.
    a. Affective   c. Phobic
    b. Post-traumatic stress   d. Adjustment

20. (p. 537) Amnesia, fugue, and multiple personality are examples of
    a. conversion reactions   c. traumatic disorders
    b. dissociative disorders   d. anxiety disorders

21. (p. 538) Which of the following is *not* true of conversion reactions?
    a. They occur when anxiety or severe emotional conflicts are converted into physical symptoms resembling disease or disability.
    b. An example is multiple personality development in which a pathological splitting of the person's basic personality occurs.
    c. They usually serve to excuse a person from a threatening situation.
    d. They probably account for many so-called miracle cures attributed to faith healers and medical quacks.

22. (p. 539) Which of the following produces neurosis according to Freud?
    a. anxiety caused by id impulses for sex or aggression which threaten to break through into behavior
    b. guilt generated by the superego in response to id impulses
    c. the development of rigid defense mechanisms by the ego in response to conflicting demands of the id and superego
    d. all of the above

23. (p. 539) Humanist Carl Rogers believes that emotional disorders are the end product of a faulty
    a. childhood   c. self-image
    b. communication skill   d. id

24. (p. 541) David Rosenhan and his associates found it very difficult to gain admission to mental hospitals by faking symptoms.

25. (p. 543) The M'Naghten rule refers to
    a. the court case decision that introduced the insanity defense into Western law
    b. the psychological law relating degree of anxiety to degree of pathology
    c. the legal statute which prevents use of the insanity plea in Montana and Idaho
    d. the standard procedures psychiatrists use as expert witnesses in reporting to the courts

26. (p. 543) Which of the following is *not* a court pleading in which the person claims psychological constraints precluded normal behavior or reasoning?
    a. insanity   c. diminished capacity
    b. irresistible impulse   d. cultural relativity

APPLYING YOUR KNOWLEDGE

1. Locate a copy of the *Diagnostic and Statistical Manual of Mental Disorders* (DSM-III-Revised). What are the five axes used to make a complete diagnosis? What is a V code? What are the predisposing factors associated with a Conduct Disorder diagnosis? What is the prevalence of Bipolar Disorder? What is the familial pattern associated with Alcohol Dependence? What are the associated features of Histrionic Personality Disorder?

2. What are the laws in your state regarding the use of insanity pleas? There are usually psychologists that work with the adult and juvenile criminal systems to assist the courts in understanding the nature of a person's functioning and ability to stand trial. See if you can locate one and talk to them about how they assess factors related to sanity. If a person is found insane or incapable of understanding the trial process, to what facilities in your area would that person be sent?

ANSWERS—PROGRAMMED REVIEW

1. 100; 7; 8; 2 million
2. Psychopathology
3. Diagnostic and Statistical Manual of Mental Disorders; DSM-III-R
4. language; diagnose
5. Psychotic
6. Organic
7. thinking; memory; personality
8. Substance use
9. social, occupational; stop
10. Mood; manic; depressed
11. Anxiety; phobias; generalized anxiety; obsessive-compulsive
12. Somatoform
13. Dissociative; multiple personalities
14. depersonalization
15. Personality
16. paranoid; compulsive
17. Sexual; gender identity; transsexualism; paraphilias
18. dysfunctions
19. neurosis
20. psychosis
21. actions; involuntary
22. subjective discomfort
23. lack
24. statistical; normal curve
25. deviation; normality; abnormality
26. Social nonconformity; socialization
27. context
28. cultural relativity
29. cultural training; bias
30. stereotypes
31. relative
32. maladaptive

33. annoys; attention
34. paranoid
35. Narcissistic
36. dependent
37. borderline
38. sociopath, psychopath
39. socialized; truth; conscience
40. 65
41. rarely
42. deprivation; neglect
43. brainwave; under-arousal
44. anxiety
45. rarely; 40
46. compulsive; destructive
47. pedophilia; incest; fetishism; exhibitionism; voyeurism; transvestic fetishism; sadism; masochism; frotteurism
48. childhood
49. 35
50. highest; inadequacy
51. shock; alarm
52. married; fathers
53. single
54. ongoing
55. nude; emotional, irritable; esteem, worth
56. sexual phobias
57. rape
58. antisocial personalities
59. socialization
60. rape-supportive culture
61. stereotyped images
62. 44
63. half
64. 6
59. guilt, depression; self-esteem
66. depressed
67. ambiguous; focused; intense

68. anxiety; defense mechanisms
69. 7
70. adjustment disorder
71. irritability; sleep; appetite; counseling
72. improve
73. dissociative; somatoform
74. generalized anxiety
75. free floating
76. sweating; clammy; autonomic
77. work; inadequacy
78. anxiety attacks
79. heart; chest; unreality
80. Phobias
81. control; disrupt
82. Arastraphobia; Arachnephobia; Acrophobia; Claustrophobia; Hemophobia; Nyctophobia; Pathophobia; Zoophobia
83. vomiting; fainting
84. Social
85. 100
86. panic attack
87. housebound
88. Obsessions
89. violence; immoral
90. compulsions
91. checkers, cleaners
92. orderliness; routine
93. personality
94. post-traumatic stress
95. disasters; hostages; combat; molestation
96. avoiding; emotions
97. insomnia; concentrate
98. amnesia; fugue
99. multiple personalities
100. escape
101. 95

102. hypnosis
103. disease
104. hypochondriasis
105. somatization
106. organic
107. Somatoform pain
108. conversion reaction
109. glove anesthesia
110. medical
111. hypnotized,
     anesthetized
112. threatening
113. la belle indifférence
114. healers; quacks
115. 60
116. high
117. Freud; psychodynamic

118. ego; id; superego
119. self-image
120. meaning
121. courage, responsibility
122. existential anxiety
123. bad faith
124. learned
125. paradoxical
126. avoidance learning;
     anxiety reduction
     hypothesis
127. 11; schizophrenia
128. 11
129. 7; 2100
130. labeled
131. 43; 19
132. remission

133. labels; problems
134. relieved
135. mentally ill
136. M'Naghten rule
137. irresistible impulse
138. diminished capacity
139. most psychotic
140. Twinkie Defense
141. Chase
142. expert witnesses
143. 4
144. Montana, Idaho, Utah
145. 500; two
146. mental hospital
147. 2
148. two-thirds; nine-tenths

ANSWERS—SELF-TEST

1. a	6. False	11. d	15. c	19. b	23. c
2. d	7. d	12. d	16. True	20. b	24. False
3. a	8. b	13. True	17. b	21. b	25. a
4. d	9. c	14. a	18. c	22. d	26. d
5. b	10. b				

ROBYN YASONI

ACROSS

2. inability to behave in ways that foster the well-being of an individual and society
6. billionaire with fear of contamination
7. with this disorder one has brief moments of *intense* anxiety
9. inability to recall one's name, address, or past events
11. this personality may consider actions of others as threatening
12. sexual arousal associated with inanimate objects
13. he and his colleagues had themselves committed to a mental hospital
14. sex with children

DOWN

1. most common phobia—fear of losing control in public places
2. these psychopathological disorders often require hospitalization
3. _____mental disorders are caused by brain pathology (e.g., senility, injuries)
4. persistent intrusion of unwelcome thoughts
5. irrational act a person feels driven to repeat
7. irrational fears that persist even when there's no real danger
8. this personality is sometimes referred to as a psychopath
10. Sybil had this personality condition

ROBIN YASONi

Major Mental Disorders

CONTENTS

TERMS AND CONCEPTS

delusions
   depressive
   somatic
   grandeur
   influence
   persecution
   reference
hallucinations
anesthesia
flat effect
brief reactive psychosis
organic psychosis
   general paresis
   senile dementia
   Alzheimer's disease
functional psychosis
delusional disorders
   erotomanic type
   grandiose type
   jealous type
   persecutory type
   somatic type
paranoid psychosis
schizophrenia
   disorganized (hebephrenic)
   catatonic
   paranoid
   undifferentiated
schizotypal personality disorder
waxy flexibility
catatonic episode
mutism
double-bind communication

phenothiazine
dopamine
CT (computed tomography) scan
PET (positron emission tomography) scan
mood disorders
   depressive disorders
     dysthymia
     major depression
   bipolar disorders
     cyclothymia
     bipolar types
       mixed
       manic
       depressed
   unipolar disorder
reactive depression
maternity blues
postpartum depression
affective psychosis
endogenous
seasonal affective disorder
phototherapy
psychotherapy
somatic (bodily) therapy
   chemotherapy
     minor tranquilizers
     major tranquilizers (anti-psychotics)
     energizers
   electroconvulsive therapy (ECT)
   psychosurgery
     prefrontal lobotomy
     deep lesioning
tardive dyskinesia

hospitalization   paraprofessional
deinstitutionalization   medical model
community mental health center

IMPORTANT INDIVIDUALS

Ronald Laing
Aaron Beck   Edwin Schneidman
Norman Rosenthal   Thomas Szasz

PROGRAMMED REVIEW

1.   (p. 548) _____—a major loss of contact with shared views of reality—is among the most serious of all mental problems.

2.   (p. 548) One of the major characteristics of psychosis is the presence of _____—false beliefs that are held even when the facts contradict them.

3.   (p. 548) Some common types of delusion are:
     1) _____ delusions in which people feel they have committed some horrible crime or sinful deed;
     2) _____ delusions, such as belief that one's body is "rotting" away or emitting foul odors;
     3) delusions of _____ in which individuals think they are extremely important persons;
     4) delusions of _____ in which people feel that they are being controlled by other persons or unseen forces;
     5) delusions of _____ , in which people feel others are "out to get" them; and
     6) delusions of _____, in which unrelated events are given personal significance (as when it is assumed that a newspaper article or a TV program is giving a special personal message to the person).

4.   (p. 548) _____ are sensory experiences that occur in the absence of a stimulus. The most common psychotic hallucination is _____ _____, but people may also feel "insects crawling under their skin," taste "poison" in their food or smell "gas" their "enemies" are using to "get" them.

5.   (p. 548) Sensory changes may bring about extreme sensitivity to heat, cold, pain, or touch, or _____, a loss of normal sensitivity.

6.   (p. 548) _____ emotions also accompany psychosis. Emotions may swing violently between extremes, or the person may be chronically hyperemotional, depressed, or emotionally "flat" or apathetic. In _____ affect, there are virtually no signs of emotion.

7.   (p. 548) An almost universal symptom of psychosis is difficulty in _____ communicating with others. Psychotic speech tends to be garbled and chaotic.

8.   (p. 549) These major disturbances coupled with additional problems in thought, speech, memory, actions, and attention bring about _____ _____ and a break with reality.

9.   (p. 549) When psychotic disturbances and a shattered personality are evident for weeks or months (often including a period of _____, an active phase, and a _____ phase), then the person has suffered a psychosis.

10. (p. 549) It is rare to find all these changes occurring at once; usually psychotic behavior occurs in brief _____.

11. (p. 549) Psychosis does not usually occur without warning. Symptoms such as _____, emotional changes, or feeling "high" signal a coming crisis.

12. (p. 549) Most patients are aware of their symptoms and try to fight off the coming psychotic break. An exception to this observation is a pattern called a _____ _____ psychosis. Here, psychotic symptoms typically appear after an extremely stressful event. The onset tends to be sudden and the episode rarely lasts more than a month.

13. (p. 549) Psychotics are not necessarily totally unresponsive to their surroundings. One experiment found that psychotics who liked the hospital acted very _____ and _____ when interviewed under pretext of possible discharge, while a second group became amazingly free of _____ when interviewed regarding possible open ward privileges.

14. (p. 549) This experiment shows that psychotic symptoms can be considered a primitive form of _____, the message being "I need help."

15. (p. 549) A psychosis based on known brain pathology caused by disease, gunshot wound, accident, etc., is termed an _____ _____, while a psychosis based on unknown or psychological factors is called a _____ _____.

16. (p. 549) One example of organic psychosis is _____ _____, which occurs in some cases of untreated syphilis. In advanced stages, syphilis attacks brain cells and gradually brings about a deterioration in behavior.

17. (p. 549) One characteristic of general paresis is a loss of _____, occasionally leading to inappropriate comments, shocking profanity, and obscenity—the "dirty old man" syndrome.

18. (p. 549) A second source of organic psychosis is _____ and _____ poisoning. This problem is of special concern since children who eat old-style paint may become psychotic or retarded.

19. (p. 550) Leaded paints also release powdered lead into the air, where children may breathe it. Testing shows that inhaled lead can lead to difficulties in _____ and _____.

20. (p. 550) Yet another source of lead is old _____ _____ in schools. Many are contaminated by lead solder or lead-lined coolers.

21. (p. 550) Probably the most common organic problem is _____ dementia. Here, we see major disturbances in memory, reasoning, judgment, impulse control, and personality.

22. (p. 550) Senile demential usually leaves the person confused, _____, apathetic, or _____. This condition is closely related to physical deterioration of the brain.

23. (p. 550) The most common cause of senile dementia is _____ disease. Other common causes are circulatory problems, repeated strokes, or general shrinkage and atrophy of the brain.

24. (p. 550) Alzheimer's disease afflicts about 5 to 10 percent of Americans over age 65. Its victims at first have difficulty _____ recent events. They slowly become more disoriented, _____, and confused. As their condition worsens, they become unable to read, write, and calculate. Eventually they are _____, _____, and unable to walk, sit up, or smile.

25. (p. 550) Researchers are urgently seeking the causes of Alzheimer's disease. Especially important is the presence of unusual webs and tangles in nerve cells leading to and from the _____—an important area for learning and memory.

26. (p. 550) Important changes also take place in an area called the _____ _____ and in _____ necessary for carrying messages within the brain.

27. (p. 550) In roughly _____ percent of all cases of Alzheimer's disease the cause is genetic.

28. (p. 550) Hereditary Alzheimer's disease runs in families and strikes its victims early between the ages of _____ and _____.

29. (p. 550) By the year 2000, it is estimated that 1 of every _____ adults over 65 will be a victim of Alzheimer's disease. Yet, there is no established treatment. Although the disease tends to progress slowly, it is ultimately fatal.

30. (p. 550) Three major types of functional psychoses are _____ disorders, psychotic _____ disorders, and schizophrenia. There is also a general category called psychotic disorders not elsewhere classified.

31. (p. 550) People with _____ disorders usually do not suffer from hallucinations, emotional excesses, or personality disintegration. The main feature of this problem is the presence of deeply held false beliefs.

32. (p. 550) The content of delusions may involve the following types:
     1) _____—marked by erotic delusions that one is loved by another, especially by someone famous or of higher status;
     2) _____—feeling that one has some great, unrecognized talent, knowledge, or insight or a special relationship with an important person or with God or that one is a prominent person;
     3) _____—an all-consuming, unfounded belief that one's spouse or lover is unfaithful;
     4) _____—feeling that one is being conspired against, cheated, spied on, followed, poisoned, maligned, or harassed;
     5) _____—belief that one's body is diseased or infested with insects or parasites, or that it is emitting foul orders, or that parts of the body are misshapen or defective.

33. (p. 550) The most common delusional disorder, often called _____ _____, centers on delusions of persecution. The evidence such people find to support their beliefs is usually unconvincing to others.

34. (p. 551) Persons suffering paranoid delusions are _____ treated, because it is almost impossible for them to accept that they need help. Anyone who suggests that they have a problem simply becomes part of the "conspiracy" to "persecute" them.

35. (p. 551) Paranoids frequently lead lonely, isolated, and humorless lives marked by constant _____ and _____ towards others. Paranoids are not necessarily dangerous to others, but they can be.

36. (p. 551) _____ accounts for approximately half of all admissions to mental hospitals. One person in 100 will develop this psychosis. Most are young adults, but it can occur at any age.

37. (p. 551) In schizophrenia, there is a split between thought and emotions, which may become blunted or _____, or very _____.

38. (p. 551) In addition, schizophrenia is marked by by _____ from contact with others and a loss of interest in _____ activities; a breakdown of personal _____ and ability to deal with daily events; and delusions, hallucinations, and thought abnormalities.

39. (p. 551) Recent studies suggest that many symptoms of schizophrenia are related to an impaired ability to maintain _____ _____. It is hard for schizophrenics to focus on one item of information at a time.

40. (p. 552) Schizophrenic delusions can be bizarre. They often include the idea that the person's thoughts and actions are being _____, that his or her thoughts are being _____ so others can hear them, that thoughts have been "_____" into the person's mind, or that thoughts have been _____.

41. (p. 552) Schizophrenia does not refer to having more than one personality. Multiple personality is a non-psychotic, _____ disorder.

42. (p. 552) Schizophrenia is often confused with a personality disorder that somewhat resembles it. The _____ _____ develops gradually, usually starting in adolescence. The individual becomes ever more withdrawn and isolated from his or her surroundings, displaying dulled emotions and peculiar behavior.

43. (p. 552) The schizotypal personality, like other personality disorders, does not involve a psychotic "break with _____." Many individuals with a schizotypal personality simply live colorless and isolated lives on the fringes of society as vagrants, eccentrics, derelicts, or prostitutes.

44. (p. 552) In _____ schizophrenia (also called hebephrenic schizophrenia) the individual's personality disintegrates almost completely, resulting in silliness, laughter, bizarre and often obscene behavior. It typically develops in early adolescence or young adulthood, often preceded by serious personality disorganization in earlier years. Chances of improvement are limited and social impairment is usually extreme.

45. (p. 553) In _____ _____ the person seems to be in a state of total panic. This situation brings about a stuporous condition in which odd positions may be held for hours or days.

46. (p. 553) In catatonic schizophrenia, _____ _____ may occur in which the person can be arranged into any position like a mannequin. This immobility suggests that catatonic individuals are struggling desperately to control their inner turmoil because stupor occasionally gives way to outbursts of agitated and sometimes violent behavior.

47. (p. 553) _____ plus a marked decrease in responsiveness to the environment makes the catatonic patient difficult to "reach."

48. (p. 553) The most common form of schizophrenic disorder is _____ _____. Like a paranoid delusional disorder, this condition centers around delusions of grandeur and persecution, but there is a major personality disintegration not evident in paranoid psychosis.

49. (p. 553) The paranoid schizophrenic also experiences _____ and has _____ that are more bizarre, fragmented, and unconvincing than those of the paranoid. Such individuals may sometimes feel forced into violence to protect themselves.

50. (p. 553) There is considerable overlap among the types of schizophrenia, with patients often shifting from one pattern of behavior to another at different times during the course of the psychosis. Many are simply classified as suffering from _____ _____.

51. (p. 553) The diagnosis of schizophrenia is fairly subjective and open to considerable error. For example, when 72 "schizophrenic" patients in a state hospital were reevaluated, only _____ were confirmed to be schizophrenic.

52. (p. 554) Some experts suspect that early _____ _____ may contribute to the later development of schizophrenia. Case studies have found a greater than average degree of childhood stress among schizophrenics.

53. (p. 554) An unanswered question is why early trauma leaves some individuals emotionally crippled and others not. Also, why is it that severely disturbed and more mildly disturbed adults appear to have experienced _____ levels of stress prior to the onset of their illness.

54. (p. 554) Many psychologists theorize that a _____ _____ environment is another risk factor in schizophrenia. For example, Ronald Laing suggests that schizophrenia is an escape from unsolvable emotional conflicts.

55. (p. 554) Laing claimed that the families of schizophrenics frequently engage in _____-_____ communication where the listener is in a "no-win" situation.

56. (p. 554) Support for this comes from a recent 15-year follow-up study of disturbed adolescents which found that the families of persons most likely to become disturbed interacted in ways that were laden with _____, conflict, _____, prying, criticism, negativity, and emotional _____.

57. (p. 554) Although attractive, environmental explanations of schizophrenia are incomplete. When the children of schizophrenic parents are raised away from their home environment, they are just as likely to become psychotic. Thus, children may inherit a _____ for schizophrenia.

58. (p. 554) This tendency is shown by studies with identical twins. If one twin becomes schizophrenic, there is a _____ percent chance the other will also.

59. (p. 554) If both parents are schizophrenic, a child has a _____ percent chance of developing the disorder; persons with a brother or sister and one parent who are schizophrenic run a _____ percent risk themselves; with a brother or sister the risk is _____ percent, and for fraternal twins the chances of mutual schizophrenia is about _____ percent.

60. (p. 555) These figures can be compared to the risk of developing schizophrenia for the population in general, which is _____ percent.

61. (p. 555) The _____ quadruplets are an interesting example of how heredity and environment can influence the chances of schizophrenia. All four girls became ill before age 25 and have since been in and out of mental hospitals. A nightmarish family life and possible susceptibility to schizophrenia both seem to have been present.

62. (p. 556) The fact that LSD, PCP and similar drugs produce effects that mimic the symptoms of psychosis has led many scientists to believe that psychosis may be based on _____ _____ which cause the body to produce some substance similar to a psychedelic (mind-altering) drug.

63. (p. 556) This notion is further supported by the fact that _____ which are effective in treating an LSD overdose are effective in treatment of schizophrenia.

64. (p. 556) Many researchers now believe that schizophrenia is directly related to overactivity in brain systems involving _____, an important chemical messenger.

65. (p. 556) In support of this link, it is known that large doses of _____ which raise dopamine levels produce symptoms almost identical to paranoid schizophrenia. Also, all major _____ drugs block the action of dopamine at receptor areas in the brain.

66. (p. 556) No extra or abnormal amounts of dopamine exist in the brains of schizophrenics, but they do have nearly _____ the normal number of dopamine _____. Many are found in the limbic system (a major emotional system of the brain).

67. (p. 556) Many scientists now believe that dopamine activation triggers a flood of unrelated thoughts, feelings, and perceptions, and directly accounts for the _____, _____, _____, and other disturbances of schizophrenia. Because of the extra receptors, schizophrenics may get psychedelic effects from normal levels of dopamine in the brain.

68. (p. 556) Two new medical techniques are making it possible to directly observe the schizophrenic brain. The CT (_____ _____) scan provides an x-ray picture of the brain.

69. (p. 556) The brains of schizophrenics have wider surface _____. They also tend to have enlarged _____. The areas that appear to be abnormal in brain scans are considered crucial for regulating motivation, emotion, perception, and attention.

70. (p. 556) A second new technique, a PET (_____ _____ _____) scan, provides an image of brain activity by measuring how much of a radioactive sugar solution is used in each area of the brain.

71. (p. 556) These measurements are translated into a colored map, or _____, of brain activity. Distinct patterns linked with schizophrenia, affective disorders, and other problems have been found using this technique.

72. (p. 556) There is evidence that the _____ side of the brain is overactive in schizophrenia.

73. (p. 559) Mood disorders are among the most serious of all. Studies show that between _____ and _____ percent of the adult population has had a major depressive episode at some time.

74. (p. 559) At any given time, roughly _____ percent of the population is suffering from a mood disorder.

75. (p. 559) Although mood disorders include manic behavior, depression is by far the more common problem. In _____ disorders, sadness and despondency are exaggerated, prolonged, or unreasonable.

76. (p. 559) Indications of a depressive disorder are sadness, hopelessness, inability to feel _____ or to take interest in anything, fatigue, limited _____, sleep and eating disturbances, feelings of worthlessness, an extremely negative self-image, and recurrent thoughts of _____.

77. (p. 559) If a person is depressed more days than not, for at least 2 years, the problem is termed _____.

78. (p. 559) If depression alternates with periods when the person's mood is elevated, expansive, or irritable, the problem is called _____.

79. (p. 559) If a loved one dies or a person suffers a major failure or setback, a period of mourning or depression is to be expected. But in _____ depression the person is unprepared to cope with a major loss because of a long series of former disappointments, or because the person is emotionally dependent or immature.

80. (p. 559) Many women are surprised to learn that they run an increased risk of depression after giving birth. The two most common forms of the problem are _____ _____ and _____ depression (which refers to the time period following childbirth).

81. (p. 559) An estimated _____ to _____ percent of all women undergo a temporary disturbance in mood, usually lasting from 24 to 48 hours after childbirth.

82. (p. 559) These "third-day" maternity blues are marked by _____, fitful _____, tension, _____, and irritability. For most women, this reaction is a normal part of adjusting to childbirth.

83. (p. 559) However, the maternity blues can be the beginning of a more lasting depression. As many as _____ percent of all women who give birth may develop a mild to moderate depressive disorder.

84. (p. 559) Typical signs of postpartum depression are _____ _____, despondency, feeling of _____, and feeling unable to cope with the new baby. Depression of this kind may last anywhere from 2 months to about a year.

85. (p. 559) The risk of postpartum depression is increased by high levels of _____ or depression during pregnancy, by poor marital adjustment, and by _____ attitudes toward child rearing. The occurrence of stressful life events before birth is also a major factor. Also, the amount of social support a woman receives seems to be an important part of the problem.

86. (p. 560) Major mood disorders are marked by lasting extremes of emotion. About _____ percent of patients admitted to mental hospitals suffer from these problems.

87. (p. 560) In bipolar disorders, persons go "up" or "down" emotionally. The individual may be continuously loud, elated, hyperactive, and energetic (called _____ type) or may swing between this and deep depression (called _____ type).

88. (p. 560) Even when a person is sad and guilt-ridden, the problem is considered a bipolar disorder (_____ type) if the person has ever been manic in the past.

89. (p. 560) The person who only goes "down" emotionally suffers from a _____ _____. If severe depression occurs without any history of mania, it is called a _____ _____.

90. (p. 560) Major mood disorders can be limited primarily to emotional extremes. When persons with major mood disorders also have psychotic symptoms, it is called an _____ _____.

91. (p. 560) Manic individuals throw themselves into fits of activity characterized by extreme distractability, "_____ of ideas," constant _____, and restless _____. Eating or sleeping may be ignored, leading to states of total delirium.

92. (p. 560) Depressive reactions show a reverse pattern in which feelings of failure, sinfulness, worthlessness, and total despair predominate. Such reactions pose a serious threat since _____ attempted during a psychotic depression is rarely a "plea for help."

93. (p. 561) Manic and depressive reactions often appear to be related in bipolar disorders. Manic behavior may be considered an attempt to escape feelings of worthlessness and _____ in an unending rush of activity.

94. (p. 561) Major mood disorders and affective psychosis usually involve more severe mood distortions than other affective disorders and also involve psychotic delusions and hallucinations. In addition, they appear to be _____ (produced from within), rather than a reaction to external events.

95. (p. 561) Some scientists have focused on the biology of mood changes in efforts to explain mood disorders. These researchers are interested in brain chemicals and transmitter substances, especially, serotonin, noradrenaline, and _____ levels.

96. (p. 561) Their findings are complex and inconclusive, but progress has been made. For example, the chemical _____ _____ can be effective for treating some cases of depression, particularly those also showing manic behavior.

97. (p. 561) Other researchers have sought psychological explanations. Psychoanalytic theory, for instance, holds that depression is caused by repressed _____ that is displaced and turned inward as self-blame and self-hate.

98.   (p. 561) Behavioral theories of depression emphasize learned _____.

99.   (p. 561) Other psychologists, such as Aaron Beck, believe that negative, distorted, and self-defeating _____ underlie many cases of depression.

100. (p. 561) Clearly, life _____ can trigger some mood disorders, especially if a person has a personality and thinking patterns that make her or him vulnerable.

101. (p. 561) Overall, women are _____ as likely as men to experience depression. Factors that contribute to this include women's conflicts between work and parenting, reproductive stresses, the strain of providing emotional support for others, marital strife, sexual and physical abuse, and poverty.

102. (p. 561) Nationwide, poverty is concentrated among women and children. As a result, poor women frequently suffer the stresses associated with single _____, loss of _____ over their lives, poor housing, and dangerous neighborhoods.

103. (p. 561) Genetics has a role in the causation of major mood disorders, especially bipolar disorders. For example, among children of depressed parents, the rate of depression is _____ even if the children are adopted.

104. (p. 561) If one identical twin is depressed, the other has an _____ percent of suffering depression, too. For non-twin siblings, the correlation is _____ percent.

105. (p. 561) Researcher Norman Rosenthal has recently found that some people suffer depression only during the fall and winter months. When these symptoms are lasting and disabling, the problem is called _____ _____ _____ (abbreviated SAD).

106. (p. 561) Starting in the fall, people with SAD sleep _____but more poorly. They feel tired and drowsy and tend to _____. They become more sad, anxious, irritable, and socially withdrawn.

107. (p. 561) Although their depressions are usually only moderately severe, many victions of SAD face winter with foreboding. SAD affects _____ times more women than men, and most victims show signs of suffering from a bipolar disorder.

108. (p. 561) Experts believe that SAD may be related to an increased release of _____ during the winter. This hormone is secreted by the pineal gland to regulate the body's response to changing light conditions.

109. (p. 561) SAD patients can be helped by exposure to very bright, full-spectrum fluorescent light, a treatment called _____. This has relieved depression with 3 to 7 days for 80 percent of those treated.

110. (p. 562) An organic psychosis cannot be "cured" in the usual sense, but it may be controlled with _____ and other techniques.

111. (p. 562) With functional psychoses the outlook is still rather negative, but many people are _____ cured. A psychotic episode does not inevitably lead to a lifelong maladjustment.

112. (p. 562) Two basic forms of treatment for psychosis can be distinguished. The first, called _____, can be described as two people talking about one person's problems. It may be applied to anything from a brief crisis to a full-scale psychosis. However, psychoanalysts do not tend to treat patients with major depressive disorders, schizophrenia, or similarly severe conditions using this mode. Rather they are more often treated medically.

113. (p. 562) A second major approach to treatment is _____ (or _____) therapy. One such treatment is _____, the use of drugs to control or alleviate the symptoms of emotional disturbance.

114. (p. 563) Chemotherapy is more frequently used to combat _____, but may also be used to relieve the anxiety attacks and other discomforts of nonpsychotic disorders.

115. (p. 563) The three major classes of drugs include _____ _____ used to calm anxious or agitated persons, _____ used to improve the mood of those who are depressed, and _____ used to control the hallucinations and other symptoms of psychosis.

116. (p. 563) While drugs have improved the chances of recovery from a psychiatric disorder, there are some drawbacks. First of all, drugs generally do not _____ mental illness. Patients may separate temporary improvement caused by a drug from improvement they consider genuine.

117. (p. 563) Also, there is the problem of side effects. For example, as many as _____ percent of patients taking major tranquilizers for extended periods develop _____ _____, a neurological condition where patients develop rhythmical facial and mouth movements, as well as unusual movements of the arms and restless movements of other parts of the body.

118. (p. 563) Perhaps the most valid criticism of chemotherapy is the simple observation that it is _____. Only about _____ of the victims of disabling mental illness are helped by drugs, but nearly all receive them. Many critics feel that the locks that came off the doors of old-style asylums have simply been replaced by "chemical locks."

119. (p. 563) Another major problem is that the ease with which drugs can be given may discourage the use of _____.

120. (p. 563) Another principal somatic treatment is _____ _____, abbreviated ECT, a rather drastic medical treatment used mainly for depression, in which convulsions are produced by electric current.

121. (p. 563) About _____ volts of electrical current are passed through the brain for slightly less than a second over a series of 6 to _____ sessions spread over 3 to _____ weeks. Muscle relaxants and sedative drugs are given before to soften ECT's impact.

122. (p. 564) Proponents of ECT claim that shock-induced seizures alter the _____ balance in the brain, bringing an end to severe depression and suicidal behavior.

123. (p. 564) Others have charged that ECT works only by _____ patients so they can't remember why they were depressed.

124. (p. 564) Critics claim that ECT causes permanent _____ losses and occasional _____ damage. Proponents argue that detailed brain scans show no evidence of damage.

125. (p. 546) It has been reported recently that if electrodes are applied to only _____ _____ of the head, memory loss is greatly reduced. However, this may not end depression.

126. (p. 564) As is true of chemotherapy, the major problem with ECT seems to lie in _____ and _____. ECT is still considered by many to be a valid treatment for selected cases of depression.

127. (p. 564) Most experts seem to agree on the following:
    1) At best, ECT produces only _____ improvement.
    2) ECT does cause permanent _____ losses in many patients.
    3) ECT should be used as a last resort after _____ therapy has failed.

128. (p. 564) The most extreme type of somatic therapy is _____, a general term applied to any surgical alteration of the brain.

129. (p. 564) The best known psychosurgery is the _____ _____, where the frontal lobes are surgically disconnected from other areas of the brain.

130. (p. 564) The original goal of this procedure when introduced in the 1940s was to _____ a person who had not responded to any other type of treatment. But later studies showed that the effects are quite inconsistent and that it produces a high rate of undesirable side effects, such as seizures, extreme lack of emotional response, and even stupor.

131. (p. 564) While the lobotomy has been abandoned, psychosurgery is still considered a valid treatment by many neurosurgeons. Most now use _____ _____ techniques in which small target areas are destroyed in the brain's interior.

132. (p. 564) The appeal of deep lesioning is that it can have fairly specific effects. For instance, a patient with uncontrollable _____ impulses may be calmed by psychosurgery.

133. (p. 564) It is worth remembering that all forms of psychosurgery are _____. Because of continued controversy over psychosurgery, it is perhaps most accurate, even after decades of use, to describe it as an "experimental" technique.

134. (p. 564) Somatic therapy, psychotherapy, and other techniques may require a special setting or special control for a period of time. Traditionally, this has meant _____, which may itself be considered a form of treatment since it removes a troubled individual from situations that may be provoking or maintaining the problem.

135. (p. 564) Research indicates that most psychiatric patients do as well with short-term (_____- to _____- week) stays as they do with longer (3-to 4-month) periods. Therefore, hospital stays are held to a minimum through the use of revolving-door policies, in which patients are released as soon as possible and readmitted only if necessary.

136. (p. 564) In the last 20 years the population in large mental hospitals has been reduced by two-thirds, a process called _____. It was intended to improve the odds that hospitalization would be constructive.

137. (p. 564) Many long-term patients become so "institutionalized" that they have difficulty returning to the community. Long-term hospitalization can produce _____, isolation, and continued emotional _____.

138. (p. 565) The success of this policy has been limited. Many states have welcomed a reduction in mental hospital populations as a way to save _____. However, many chronic patients are discharged to a lonely existence in hostile communities without adequate care.

139. (p. 565) Many former patients have joined the ranks of the _____. Others are repeatedly jailed for minor crimes such as trespassing, vagrancy, and disturbing the peace.

140. (p. 565) Large mental hospitals may no longer be warehouses for society's unwanted, but many former patients are no better off consigned to bleak lives in nursing homes, single-room hotels, and _____-and-_____ homes, etc. As much as anything, a simple lack of sufficient _____ prevents large numbers of people from getting the care they need.

141. (p. 565) It would be especially helpful if better rehabilitation programs were offered as a follow-up to hospital treatment. One approach that has been helpful is the use of _____ _____ that ease the patient's return to the community.

142. (p. 565) Halfway houses provide a short-term _____ _____ situation combined with some supervision and support. They help keep people near their _____ and they are less restrictive and medically-slanted than hospitalization. They provide cost-effective therapy and can reduce a person's chances of being readmitted to a hospital

143. (p. 565) A bright spot in the area of mental health care has been the creation of _____ _____ _____ centers. They have two primary goals: to directly aid troubled citizens and to promote _____ through consultation, education, and crisis intervention.

144. (p. 565) Some centers attempt to raise the general level of mental health in target areas by combating problems such as _____, delinquency, and _____ abuse. Most have concentrated much more on providing clinical services due to wavering government support.

145. (p. 565) These centers have made mental health services more accessible than ever before. Much of their work is made possible by _____, individuals who work under the supervision of more highly trained staff.

146. (p. 566) Suicide ranks as the _____ cause of death in the United States with approximately 1 person out of _____ attempting suicide at some time in their life.

147. (p. 566) Several factors appear related to suicide; other popular beliefs appear untrue. For example, rates are lower on major holidays such as Christmas. The peak actually occurs in early _____.

148. (p. 567) _____ times as many men as women complete suicide, but women make more attempts, the difference being due to the type of technique selected (men typically use guns, women typically attempt a drug overdose).

149. (p. 567) Suicide rates gradually rise during adolescence. They then sharply _____ during young adulthood (ages 20-24). From then until age 84, the rate continues to gradually _____ with advancing age.

150. (p. 567) More than half of all suicides are committed by individuals over _____ years old, although there has been a steady increase in the total number of suicides by adolescents and young adults.

151. (p. 567) Part of this increase comes from the ranks of college students where suicide is the _____ cause of death, the most dangerous period being the first 6 weeks of a semester, not during final exams.

152. (p. 567) Factors important in student suicide appear to include a sense of not living up to extremely high self-imposed standards, chronic _____ problems, and _____ difficulties.

153. (p. 567) There has been a recent dramatic increase in adolescent suicides. At present, about 1 million teenagers attempt suicide each year in the U.S. and 7000 of those die. This total is _____ the number reported 20 years ago.

154. (p. 567) Some professions, particularly _____ and _____ show higher than average suicide rates, but generally suicide is not related to income.

155. (p. 567) The highest suicide rates are found among the _____; the next highest rates occur among the _____; lower rates are recorded for single persons; and _____ individuals have the lowest rate of all.

156. (p. 567) The best explanation for suicide may simply come from a look at conditions which precede it. Usually there is a history of interpersonal troubles with family, in-laws, or a lover or spouse. Often there is a _____ problem, _____ adjustment problem, or _____ difficulties.

157. (p. 567) A combination of factors can lead to severe depression and preoccupation with death as the "answer" to the person's suffering. There is usually a break in _____ with others that causes the person to feel isolated and misunderstood.

158. (p. 567) Self-image becomes very _____. The person feels worthless and helpless and wants to die. Severe feelings of _____ are a warning the risk of suicide is very high.

159. (p. 567) People who attempt suicide are not necessarily "mentally ill." Anyone may temporarily reach a state of depression severe enough to attempt suicide. Most dangerous for the average person are times of _____, separation, _____, and bereavement.

160. (p. 567) The causes of increased adolescent suicide remain unclear. As with adults, there is often a backdrop of problems with drugs, depression, school, peers, family, divorced parents, or the break-up of a romance. Many cases seem to result from _____ expectations and an unusual sensitivity to hurt and disappointment.

161. (p. 568) It is a major fallacy to believe that people who talk about or threaten suicide are rarely the ones who try it. Of every 10 potential suicides, _____ give warning beforehand.

162. (p. 568) It is also not true that suicide cannot be prevented. It is estimated that about _____-_____ of all suicide attempts fall into the "to be" category, with another third characterized by a "to be or not to be" attitude. Only about _____ to _____ percent of cases represent individuals who definitely want to die.

163. (p. 568) As Edwin Schneidman points out, "Suicidal behavior is often a form of _____, a cry for help born out of pain, with clues and messages of suffering and anguish and pleas for response."

164. (p. 568) Schneidman has identified several common characteristics of suicidal thoughts and feelings. They include (1) escape, (2) unbearable psychological _____, (3) frustrated psychological _____, and (4) constriction of _____.

165. (p. 568) In talking to a suicidal person, your most important task may be to establish _____ with the person. You should offer support, acceptance, and legitimate caring.

166. (p. 569) You can help by getting the person to commit themselves to daily schedules, even on a small scale. Also, don't end your efforts too soon. One of the most dangerous times is when a person suddenly seems to get better after a severe _____.

167. (p. 569) There are over _____ centers for suicide prevention in the U.S., and most sizable cities have mental health crisis intervention teams. Urge a suicidal person to call one of these resources if he or she becomes frightened or impulsive.

168. (p. 569) If a person actually threatens suicide, has a concrete, workable plan, and has the means to carry it out, you should ask that person to accompany you to a _____.

169. (p. 569) If a person seems on the verge of attempting suicide, don't worry about _____. Call the police, crisis intervention, or a rescue unit.

170. (p. 570) Thomas Szasz has charged that medical concepts of disease have been wrongly applied to emotional problems. The _____ _____, as this is called, treats such problems as "diseases" with "symptoms" that can be "cured."

171. (p. 570) Szasz believes that "mental illness" is just an idea used when trying to deal with _____ _____. He thinks such labels are used mainly to transform people from being responsible for their actions to non-responsible "patients" who need pity and therapy.

172. (p. 570) Szasz points out that "mental illness" labels do not explain anything. They are merely used to deal with persons whose behavior creates a _____ _____ or violates social rules.

173. (p. 570) It follows that if a person acts in a way that "offends" society and a law exists against such acts, the person may be jailed. If no law exists, the person may be "treated." Thus the distinction between madness and badness is a _____ judgment, not a medical reality.

174. (p. 570) He prefers to view emotional disturbances as "_____ in _____," making the goal of therapy "change" and the individual a "client."

175. (p. 570) Szasz's views have led him to question the handling of the civil rights of psychiatric "patients." He estimates that _____ percent of all patients in mental hospitals are there involuntarily. He feels it is indefensible to commit people because they *might* be dangerous.

176. (p. 570) According to Szasz, the only legitimate reason for depriving a person of freedom is for being "_____ to _____," but then only if the person has broken the law by committing violence or by threatening to do so.

SELF-TEST

1. (p. 548) Which of the following is *not* a correct match?
    a. delusion of reference—individuals think they are extremely important
    b. somatic delusion—individuals feel their bodies are rotting away and emitting foul odors
    c. depressive delusion—persons feel they have committed some horrible crime or sinful deed
    d. delusion of influence—persons feel they are being controlled by other persons or unseen forces

2. (p. 548) Among psychotics, the most common hallucination is
    a. hearing voices.
    b. seeing objects fly around the room.
    c. seeing places or people related to the source of the psychosis.
    d. feeling vibrations.

3. (p. 548) A characteristic feature of psychosis, _____ _____, means that there are virtually no signs of emotion.
    a. personality disintegration   b. depressive episodes
    c. emotional anesthesia   d. flat affect

4. (p. 549) True-False. Typically, psychotic behavior occurs in brief episodes rather than patients displaying bizarre behaviors nearly all the time.

5. (p. 549) General paresis is an example of
    a. organic psychosis.   c. senile psychosis.
    b. functional psychosis.   d. paranoid psychosis.

6. (p. 549) True-False. A psychosis produced by mercury poisoning would be classified as a functional disorder since it is produced by an environmental factor.

7. (p. 550) Which of the following is *not* true of senile dementia?
    a. It is probably the most common form of organic psychosis.
    b. It is associated with a loss of inhibition leading to shocking profanity and obscenity.
    c. It is closely associated with brain deterioration due to circulatory problems or repeated strokes.
    d. The person is usually confused, suspicious, apathetic, or withdrawn.

8. (p. 550) Which of the following is *not* true of persons suffering paranoid delusions?
    a. They are rarely treated or admitted to mental hospitals.
    b. They suffer from hallucinations, emotional excesses, or personality disintegration.
    c. Most often, paranoid delusions center on feelings of persecution.
    d. Paranoids are not necessarily dangerous to others, but they can be.

9. (p. 551) Approximately _____ of all admissions to mental hospitals are diagnosed as schizophrenic.
    a. $^1/_3$ c. $^2/_3$
    b. $^1/_2$ d. $^3/_4$

10. (p. 552) Which of the following is *not* true of the schizotypal personality?
    a. It is often confused with schizophrenia.
    b. Affected individuals gradually become withdrawn and isolated.
    c. Such individuals are usually seen as colorful or exotic; they display an exaggerated range of emotions.
    d. This disorder develops slowly, usually starting in adolescence.

11. (p. 552) Which type of schizophrenia is marked by almost complete personality disintegration resulting in silliness, laughter, bizarre and often obscene behavior?
    a. simple   c. catatonic
    b. disorganized   d. paranoid

12. (p. 553) In _____ schizophrenia, the person seems to be in a state of panic which produces a stuporous condition.
    a. simple   c. catatonic
    b. disorganized   d. paranoid

13. (p. 553) True-False. Waxy flexibility refers to the glassy-eyed look of catatonic schizophrenia.

14. (p. 553) The most common form of schizophrenic disorder is
    a. simple.   c. catatonic.
    b. disorganized.   d. paranoid.

15. (p. 553) True-False. There are only minor differences between the symptoms of a paranoid delusional disorder and paranoid schizophrenia.

16. (p. 553) True-False. Although difficult to treat, the symptoms used in classifying schizophrenic patients are very straightforward. Patients can be easily classified into one or the other of the categories.

17. (p. 554) True-False. Schizophrenia is caused solely by psychological trauma at an early age.

18. (p. 554) If one identical twin becomes schizophrenic, the chances of the other twin becoming schizophrenic are
    a. 23%.   c. 79%.
    b. 46%.   d. 10%.

19. (p. 556) Which of the following drugs are effective in the treatment of schizophrenia?
    a. amphetamines   c. adrenochromes
    b. phenothiazines   d. psychedelics

20. (p. 556) Evidence is mounting that the biochemical basis for schizophrenia may be linked with which system?
    a. noradrenaline-cortical   c. tardive dyskinesia
    b. dopamine-limbic   d. prefrontal lobes

21. (p. 556) True-False. It now appears that schizophrenics may have an overabundance of dopamine in their limbic systems, thus accounting for their bizarre abnormal behavior.

22. (p. 556) True-False. Observations of the brain using a CT scan shows that schizophrenic brains have wider surface fissures and enlarged ventricles.

23. (p. 556) The PET scan is
    a. a technique which produces an x-ray picture of the brain.
    b. a type of psychosurgery considered far more effective and reliable than a prefrontal lobotomy.
    c. a term used by Laing to describe the dysfunctional family systems of many schizophrenics.
    d. a technique which produces a colored map illustrating brain activity.

24. (p. 559) In _____ depression, the person is unable to cope with a major loss because of a long series of former disappointments, or because the person is emotionally dependent or immature.
    a. incongruent   c. reactive
    b. affective   d. phobic

25. (p. 559) Crying, fitful sleep, tension, anger, and irritability following childbirth are characteristics which mark
    a. postpartum depression   c. psychogenic pain
    b. reactive depression   d. maternity blues

26. (p. 560) Which of the following is *not* true of major mood disorders?
    a. They account for about 14 percent of patients admitted to mental hospitals.
    b. They are characterized by persistent and excessive changes in mood or emotion.
    c. They appear to be a reaction to external events rather than endogenous.
    d. Three types include manic, depressive, and mixed.

27. (p. 560) Constant talking, flights of ideas, extreme distractibility, restless movements, failure to eat or sleep, and incoherent, agitated, out of control behavior characterizes
    a. manic type bipolar disorder.   c. schizotypal personality disorders.
    b. disorganized schizophrenia.   d. senile dementia.

28. (p. 561) True-False. Manic behavior can be viewed as a reaction of individuals trying to escape depression and therefore produces symptoms commonly associated with depression.

29. (p. 563) Which of the following is *not* a major class of drugs used in chemotherapy?
    a. psychedelics   c. antipsychotics
    b. minor tranquilizers   d. energizers

30. (p. 563) Which of the following is a neurological side effect of extended major tranquilizer usage?
    a. deep lesioning   c. senility
    b. mutism   d. tardive dyskinesia

31. (p. 563) Which of the following is *not* a criticism that has been directed at chemotherapy?
    a. does not "cure," only temporarily relieves symptoms
    b. adverse drug side-effects
    c. overuse
    d. has no advantages over long-term hospitalization

32. (p. 563) ECT is used primarily in treating
    a. mania.   c. paranoia.
    b. depression.   d. psychosis.

33. (p. 564) True-False. Prefrontal lobotomies are still widely performed in cases of chronic, agitated schizophrenia.

34. (p. 564) True-False. Studies have shown that patients do as well with 3-4 weeks of hospitalization as they do with 3-4 month periods.

35. (p. 565) True-False. The aim of community mental health centers is to provide direct treatment services and prevention programs.

36. (p. 566) Which of the following is true of suicide?
    a. More men attempt suicide, but more women complete suicide.
    b. More than half of all suicides are committed by individuals under 30 years of age.
    c. The highest suicide rates are found among single, never married persons.
    d. At present, the number of adolescent suicides is double the number reported ten years ago.

37. (p. 568) Which of the following is *not* a useful suggestion in helping prevent suicide?
    a. Tell suicidal persons they really don't want to kill themselves; list reasons why they shouldn't.
    b. Talk about suicide directly; don't avoid the issue or the use of the term suicide.
    c. Continue your efforts even when the person suddenly seems better after a severe depression.
    d. Give the person a sense of acceptance not reassurance.

38. (p. 570) Which of the following is *not* true of the position taken by Thomas Szasz?
    a. He believes emotional disturbances should be viewed as problems in living.
    b. Involuntary commitment involves a serious loss of civil rights.
    c. A medical model should be applied to our treatment of the mentally ill.
    d. People should not be hospitalized just because they might be dangerous to themselves.

APPLYING YOUR KNOWLEDGE

1. Is there a psychiatric hospital in your area? If so, contact them and ask if you could have a tour of their facility. Are there particular programs or psychiatric populations they deal with in particular? What types of therapeutic approaches do they offer? You might ask to speak with a psychologist and interview them about what they do at the hospital.

2. Is there a community mental health center in your area? If so, contact them and ask if you could have a tour of their facility. What types of treatment programs do they offer? Do they work with particular kinds of problems and patients? You might ask to speak with a psychologist and interview them about what they do at the center.

3. Is there a suicide hotline or prevention center in your area. If so, contact them and learn more about their program. How many cases do they deal with in a year? What kinds of approaches do they use? Are there psychologists working there? If so, what role do they play in the program?

ANSWERS—PROGRAMMED REVIEW

1. Psychosis
2. delusions
3. depressive; somatic; grandeur; influence; persecution; reference
4. Hallucinations; hearing voices
5. anesthesia
6. Disturbed; flat
7. verbally
8. personality disintegration
9. deterioration; residual
10. episodes
11. insomnia; emotional

12. brief reactive
13. bizarre, disturbed; symptoms
14. communication
15. organic psychosis; functional psychosis
16. general paresis
17. inhibition
18. lead, mercury
19. thinking, attention
20. drinking fountains
21. senile
22. suspicious; withdrawn
23. Alzheimer's

24. remembering; suspicious; mute; bedridden
25. hippocampus
26. nucleus basilis; chemicals
27. 20
28. 45; 55
29. 10
30. delusional; mood
31. delusional
32. erotomanic; grandiose; jealous; persecutory; somatic
33. paranoid psychosis

34. rarely
35. suspicion; hostility
36. Schizophrenia
37. flat; inappropriate
38. withdrawal; external; habits
39. selective attention
40. controlled; broadcast; inserted; removed
41. dissociative
42. schizotypal personality
43. reality
44. disorganized
45. catatonic schizophrenia
46. waxy flexibility
47. Mutism
48. paranoid schizophrenia; personality disintegration
49. hallucinations; delusions
50. undifferentiated psychosis
51. 45
52. psychological trauma
53. similar
54. disturbed family
55. double-bind
56. confusion; guilt; attacks
57. potential
58. 46
59. 46; 17; 10; 14
60. 1
61. Genain
62. biological abnormalities
63. phenothiazines
64. dopamine
65. amphetamines; antipsychotic
66. double; receptors
67. voices, hallucinations, delusions
68. computed tomography
69. fissures; ventricles
70. positron emission tomography
71. scan
72. left
73. 10; 20
74. 5
75. depressive
76. pleasure; movement; suicide

77. dysthymia
78. cyclothymia
79. reactive
80. maternity blues; postpartum
81. 50; 80
82. crying; sleep; anger
83. 20
84. mood swings; inadequate; 2
85. anxiety; negative
86. 14
87. manic; mixed
88. depressed
89. unipolar disorder; major depression
90. affective psychosis
91. flights; talking; movement
92. suicide
93. depression
94. endogenous
95. dopamine
96. lithium carbonate
97. anger
98. helplessness
99. thoughts
100. stresses
101. twice
102. parenthood; control
103. higher
104. 80; 35
105. seasonal affective disorder
106. longer; overeat
107. 4
108. melatonin
109. phototherapy
110. drugs
111. permanently
112. psychotherapy
113. somatic; bodily; chemotherapy
114. psychosis
115. minor tranquilizers; energizers; antipsychotics
116. cure
117. 10; tardive dyskinesia
118. overused; 50
119. psychotherapy
120. electroconvulsive therapy; ECT

121. 150; 8; 4
122. biochemical
123. confusing
124. memory; brain
125. one side
126. overuse; misuse
127. temporary; memory; drug
128. psychosurgery
129. prefrontal lobotomy
130. calm; side effects
131. deep lesioning
132. aggressive
133. irreversible
134. hospitalization
135. 3; 4
136. deinstitutionalization
137. dependency; disturbance
138. money
139. homeless
140. board-and-care; funding
141. halfway houses
142. group living; family
143. community mental health; prevention
144. unemployment; drug
145. paraprofessionals
146. seventh; 100
147. spring
148. Three
149. increase; rise
150. 45
151. leading
152. health; interpersonal
153. triple
154. medicine, psychiatry
155. divorced; widowed; married
156. drinking; sexual; job
157. communication
158. negative; hopelessness
159. divorce; failure
160. unrealistic
161. 8
162. two-thirds; 3, 5
163. communication
164. pain; needs; options
165. rapport
166. depression
167. 300
168. hospital
169. overreacting

170. medical model
171. disturbing behavior
172. social disturbance

173. moral
174. problems in living

175. 90
176. dangerous to others

ANSWERS—SELF-TEST

1.	a	8.	b	15.	False	21.	False	27.	a	33.	False
2.	a	9.	b	16.	False	22.	True	28.	False	34.	True
3.	d	10.	c	17.	False	23.	d	29.	a	35.	True
4.	True	11.	b	18.	b	24.	c	30.	d	36.	d
5.	a	12.	c	19.	b	25.	d	31.	d	37.	a
6.	False	13.	False	20.	b	26.	c	32.	b	38.	c
7.	b	14.	d								

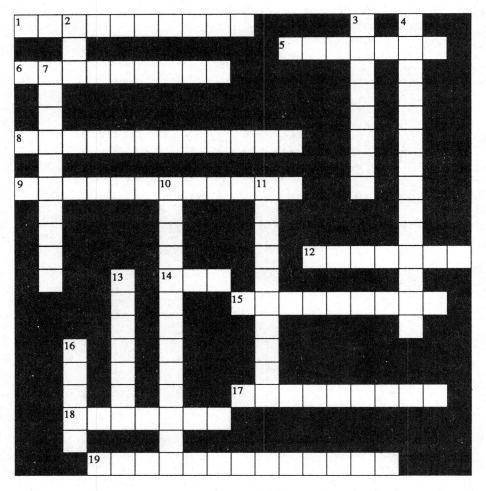

ACROSS

1. these drugs improve the mood of those who are depressed
5. with this disorder a person goes up or down emotionally
6. _____ schizophrenic characterized by body positions held for hours or days
8. use of drugs to alleviate symptoms of emotional disturbance
9. _____ schizophrenia characterized by silliness, laughter, and often obscene behavior
12. it ranks as 7th cause of death in U.S.
14. positron emission tomography (abbr.)
15. false beliefs held even when facts contradict them
17. a severe mental disturbance characterized by a break in contact with reality, delusions, etc.
18. _____ or bodily therapy (e.g. chemo-therapy, ECT)
19. surgical alteration of the brain

DOWN

2. electroconvulsive therapy (abbr.)
3. chemical messenger in brain related to schizophrenia
4. sensory experiences that occur in absence of a stimulus
7. victims of this disease may not remember recent events and become confused
10. drugs used to control hallucinations
11. affective psychoses appears to be _____ (produced from within)
13. drug used to treat depression in some cases
16. he views emotional disturbances as "problems in living"

CHAPTER 21

Insight Therapies

CONTENTS

TERMS AND CONCEPTS

psychotherapy
individual therapy
group therapy
insight therapy
action therapy
directive therapy
non-directive therapy
time-limited therapy
trepanning
demonology
exorcism
ergotism
hysteria
psychoanalysis
free association
dream analysis
manifest content
latent content
dream symbols
analysis of resistance
analysis of transference
short-term dynamic therapy
spontaneous remission
humanistic therapies
client-centered therapy
non-directive approach
unconditional positive regard
empathy
authenticity
reflection

existential therapy
logotherapy
confrontation
Gestalt therapy
directive approach
psychodrama
role playing
role reversals
family therapy
sensitivity groups
encounter groups
large group awareness training
therapy placebo effect
transactional analysis (TA)
ego-states
Child
Parent
Adult
crossed transactions
ulterior transactions
games
therapeutic alliance
emotional rapport
catharsis
eclectic therapist
paraprofessional
peer counselors
peer-led self-help groups
culturally skilled counselor

IMPORTANT INDIVIDUALS

Philippe Pinel	Victor Frankl	Eric Berne
Sigmund Freud	Frederick (Fritz) Perls	Derald Sue
H. J. Eysenck	Jacob L. Moreno	David Sue
Carl Rogers		

PROGRAMMED REVIEW

1. (p. 575) _____ is any psychological technique used to to facilitate positive changes in a person's personality, behavior, or adjustment. The term most often refers to verbal interaction between trained mental health professionals and their clients.

2. (p. 575) _____ therapy is defined by therapy sessions involving only one client and one therapist.

3. (p. 575) _____ therapy involves therapy sessions in which several clients participate at one time with one or more therapists.

4. (p. 575) _____ therapy is any psychotherapy whose goal is to lead clients to a deeper understanding of their thoughts, emotions, and behavior.

5. (p. 575) _____ therapy is any therapy designed to bring about direct changes in troublesome thoughts, habits, feelings, or behavior.

6. (p. 575) _____ therapy is any approach in which the therapist provides strong guidance during therapy sessions.

7. (p. 576) _____-_____ therapy is a style of therapy in which clients assume responsibility for solving their own problems; the therapist assists but does not guide or give advice.

8. (p. 576) _____-_____ therapy is any therapy begun with the expectation that it will last only a certain limited number of sessions.

9. (p. 576) Popular accounts tend to depict psychotherapy as a complete personal transformation. But as Bernie Zilbergeld points out, therapy is not equally effective for all problems. Chances of improvement are fairly good for _____, low self-esteem, some _____ problems, and _____ conflicts.

10. (p. 576) More complex problems can be difficult to treat. Therapy usually does not bring about dramatic changes in behavior or an end to personal problems. For many people, therapy's major benefit is that it provides _____, _____, and a way to make constructive changes.

11. (p. 576) Psychotherapy need not be undertaken only as a means of solving a deep psychological problem or an immediate crisis; some therapies are designed to encourage _____ _____ and enrichment for people who are already functioning effectively.

12. (p. 576) Attempts to cure psychological problems have occurred throughout history. During the Stone Age, spirits were released from the head by a process called _____, where a hole was bored, chipped, or bashed into the skull.

13. (p. 576) Trepanning may have simply been an excuse to kill people who were _____, since many of the "patients" didn't survive the "treatment."

14. (p. 576) During the Middle Ages, treatment for the mentally ill in Europe focused on _____. Abnormal behavior was attributed to supernatural forces. As treatment, _____ was used to drive out such evil.

15. (p. 576) One explanation for the rise of demonology may lie in a condition called _____. Eating bread made from tainted rye containing ergot fungus may have produced pinching sensations, convulsions, muscle twitches, facial spasms, delirium and hallucinations which made people appear "possessed."

16. (p. 577) Finally, a more compassionate view of the mentally ill emerged after 1793 when Philippe _____ changed the Bicetre Asylum in Paris from a "mad house" to a mental hospital by personally unchaining the inmates.

17. (p. 577) The first true psychotherapy was developed around the turn of the century by Sigmund _____. He called it _____.

18. (p. 577) Freud sought to understand and treat cases of _____, where physical symptoms like paralysis or numbness occur without known physical cause. Such problems are now called somatoform disorders.

19. (p. 578) Freud's patients usually reclined on a couch during therapy as a means of encouraging _____ and a free flow of thoughts and images from the _____. This procedure is the least important characteristic of psychoanalysis and one that has been abandoned by many modern analysts.

20. (p. 578) Freud's theory stressed that _____ memories, motives, and conflicts—especially instinctual drives for sex and aggression—are the cause of neurosis. These factors force a person to develop rigid defense mechanisms and to devote excessive amounts of time and energy to compulsive and self-defeating behavior.

21. (p. 578) Freud relied on four basic techniques to uncover the unconscious roots of neurosis. One of these, _____ _____, required the patient to say whatever came to mind without regard for whether it made sense, or was painful or embarrassing.

22. (p. 578) Freud considered a second technique, _____ _____, to be especially helpful because supposedly forbidden desires and unconscious feelings are more freely expressed in dreams.

23. (p. 578) In analyzing dreams, Freud distinguished between the _____ (obvious, visible) content and the _____ (hidden) content. The latter he sought to reveal by interpreting dream _____.

24. (p. 578) When associating or describing dreams, the patient may _____ talking or thinking about certain topics. Such _____ are said to reveal particularly important unconscious conflicts.

25. (p. 578) The individual undergoing psychoanalysis may _____ feelings to the therapist that relate to important past relationships with others. This process is considered a prime opportunity to help the patient undergo an emotional _____, where repressed emotions can be recognized and understood.

26. (p. 579) Psychoanalysts have become relatively rare since most people cannot afford _____ to _____ therapy sessions a week for up to _____ years.

27. (p. 579) Today, most psychoanalytic therapists have switched to doing short-term _____ therapy. They rely on _____ _____ to more rapidly uncover unconscious conflicts. They also seek to actively provoke emotional reactions that lower defenses and provide insights.

28. (p. 579) The development of newer, more streamlined dynamic therapies is in part due to questions about the _____ of traditional psychoanalysis.

29. (p. 579) Psychologist H. J. Eysenck has suggested that psychoanalysis takes so long that patients improve due to the mere passage of time. This improvement is called _____ _____.

30. (p. 579) To support his argument, Eysenck cites research showing that people placed on waiting lists _____ at the same rate as those who begin therapy. However, more recent work affirms that psychoanalysis is usually _____ than no treatment at all.

31. (p. 580) The goal of traditional psychoanalysis is _____. The humanistic therapies assume that it is possible for people to live rich and rewarding lives and to make full use of their _____. Psychotherapy is seen as a means of giving natural tendencies toward mental health a chance to emerge.

32. (p. 580) Psychoanalysts delve into childhood, dreams, and the unconscious. Humanistic psychologist Carl Rogers, creator of _____-_____ therapy, has found it more productive to explore _____ thoughts and feelings.

33. (p. 580) Rogers believes that the psychoanalyst tends to take a position of authority about what is wrong with the patient that may not be right or valuable to the client. Thus, Rogers uses a _____-_____ approach in that the client determines what will be discussed during each session.

34. (p. 580) The therapist's job is to create an "atmosphere of growth" by maintaining four basic conditions. First, the therapist offers the client _____ _____ _____— the client is accepted totally.

35. (p. 580) Second, the therapist attempts to achieve genuine _____ for the client by trying to view the world through the client's eyes.

36. (p. 580) As a third condition, the therapist strives to be _____ in his or her relationship with clients.

37. (p. 580) Fourth, rather than making interpretations, posing solutions, or offering advice, the therapist _____ the client's thoughts and feelings and serves as a psychological "mirror."

38. (p. 581) _____ therapy focuses on problems of existence or "being in the world." Its goals are self-knowledge and self-actualization.

39. (p. 581) While client-centered therapy seeks to uncover a "true self," existential therapy emphasizes the idea of _____ _____. Through choices one can become the person he or she wants to be.

40. (p. 581) Existential therapy attempts to restore meaning and vitality to life so that the individual has the _____ to make rewarding and socially constructive choices.

41. (p. 581) Typically, existential therapy focuses on the "ultimate concerns" of human existence: death, _____, _____, and _____.

42. (p. 581) One example of existential therapy is Victor Frankl's _____ developed on the basis of experiences in a _____ _____ camp. Frankl felt that those who survived with their sanity did so because they had managed to hold on to a sense of _____ (logos).

43. (p. 581) Like most existential therapists, Frankl uses a very flexible approach centered around _____ in which the person is challenged to examine the quality of his or her existence and choices, and to _____ the unique and intense here-and-now interaction of two human beings.

44. (p. 582) _____ therapy, which is most often associated with Frederick (Fritz) Perls, is built around the idea that perception or awareness becomes disjointed and incomplete in the maladjusted individual.

45. (p. 582) The Gestalt approach is more _____ than either client-centered therapy or existential therapy, and it places a special emphasis on immediate experience.

46. (p. 582) The German word Gestalt means _____, or complete. The Gestalt therapist seeks to help the individual rebuild thinking, feeling, and acting into connected wholes. This is achieved by expanding personal awareness, by accepting responsibility for one's thoughts, feelings, and actions, and by filling in gaps in experience.

47. (p. 582) Gestalt therapists believe that we often shy away from expressing or "owning" upsetting feelings. This creates a _____ in self-awareness that may become a barrier to personal growth. The Gestalt therapist encourages the individual to become more aware of his or her _____ _____.

48. (p. 582) In all his work, Perls emphasized that emotional health comes from getting in touch with what you _____ to do, not dwelling on what you _____ do, _____ to do, or should want to do.

49. (p. 582) Above all else, Gestalt therapy emphasizes _____ experience. Clients are urged to stop intellectualizing and talking *about* feelings.

50. (p. 583) In _____ _____, a person can act out or directly experience problems in addition to talking about them. Also, support is provided by other members who share similar problems.

51. (p. 583) Groups also help form a bridge between _____ and _____-_____ problems by providing a situation that is more realistic than the protected atmosphere of individual therapy. A number of specialized group techniques have emerged.

52. (p. 583) One of the first group approaches was developed by Jacob L. Moreno, who called his technique _____. Through this technique, an individual _____ _____ (acts out) dramatic incidents resembling those that cause problems in real life.

53.   (p. 583) Therapists using the role-playing technique of psychodrama often find _____ _____ especially helpful. For example, a teenage boy could be asked to role play his father or mother in order to better understand their feelings.

54.   (p. 583) In _____ therapy, husband, wife, and children work as a group to resolve the problems of each family member. This approach tends to be brief and focused on specific problems.

55.   (p. 584) Family therapists believe that problems are rarely limited to a _____ family member: a problem for one is considered a problem for all. That is, families often contribute to and maintain maladaptive behavior.

56.   (p. 584) If changes are not made in the _____ _____, changes in any single family member may not last. Thus, family members work together to improve communication, to change destructive patterns, and to see themselves and each other in new ways.

57.   (p. 584) Sensitivity groups tend to be less _____ than encounter groups; the focus is more on extending sensitivity to oneself and others. As one example, the "_____ _____," in which blindfolded participants are led about by "guides," is a typical exercise used to develop trust and confidence in others.

58.   (p. 584) In _____ groups, more intense emotion and communication may take place. Here, the emphasis is on tearing down defenses and false fronts through discussion that can be brutally honest.

59.   (p. 584) Because there is a danger of hostile confrontation and psychological damage, encounter group participation is safest when members are carefully _____ and a _____ leader guides the group.

60.   (p. 584) The basic principles of sensitivity and encounter groups are still used by many _____ to improve employee morale and relationships. Specially designed encounter groups for _____ couples are also widely held.

61.   (p. 584) Lifespring, Actualizations, est, the Forum, etc. are examples of _____ _____ awareness training. They combine psychological exercises, confrontation, new viewpoints, and group dynamics to promote personal change.

62.   (p. 584) While such groups may fill some need not met by society or traditional psychotherapy, there is little evidence that these experiences are truly _____.

63.   (p. 584) Many of the claimed benefits may simply result from a kind of _____ _____ effect related to positive expectations, a break in daily routine, and an excuse to act differently.

64.   (p. 584) The importance of such factors is easily illustrated: Participants in a weekend "retreat" that featured nothing more than volleyball, charades, and ballroom dancing also reported enhanced _____ _____.

65.   (p. 584) A danger in some large group training programs is that participants may be verbally _____ by a "trainer" as part of the "educational" process. This can create an emotional crisis that did not exist before. Unwary participants then resolve this crisis by _____ to the organization that promotes the training.

66. (p. 584) A recent study detected only _____ short-term benefits and _____ long-term benefits after participants completed one well-known large group training program.

67. (p. 585) Talk-radio psychology raises some important questions. In defense of themselves, such psychologists point out that listeners may learn solutions to their own problems by hearing others talk. Many also stress that their work is _____, not _____.

68. (p. 585) The American Psychological Association has taken the position that media psychologists should discuss only problems of a _____ _____ instead of actually _____ a person.

69. (p. 585) _____ _____ (TA) is a therapy that blends humanistic thought with some updated elements of psychoanalysis.

70. (p. 585) TA teaches people a model of behavior to use in becoming more aware of themselves and their interactions with others—especially those involving various "_____." Because TA emphasizes relationships, it is often conducted as a _____ therapy .

71. (p. 585) The personality scheme of TA proposed by Eric Berne postulates three basic parts or _____-_____ that can be distinguished from each other by distinct behaviors, words, tones, gestures, attitudes, and expressions.

72. (p. 585) The _____ a carry-over from youth that can be primitive, impulsive, demanding, creative, playful, or manipulative.

73. (p. 585) The _____ ego-state is an internal record of all the messages received from one's parents or other authority figures as personality developed. It can be evaluative and restrictive, or nurturing and allowing.

74. (p. 585) The _____ is a mature and rational decision-making part of the personality that, when in charge, allows an individual to explore alternatives and their consequences and decide which ego-state is needed.

75. (p. 585) TA holds that trouble comes in relationships when _____ transactions (exchanges) occur, where a message sent from one ego-state is answered by statements from another ego-state.

76. (p. 586) Also, in an _____ transaction, the exchange appears to take place on one level, but actually takes place on another.

77. (p. 586) Ulterior transactions form the basis of _____, indirect ways of communicating such as the "if it weren't for you" game that is very common in marriage.

78. (p. 586) To discover therapy's true impact, the placebo effect is controlled by assigning some people to a "placebo therapy" control group that mimics some aspects of psychotherapy, but lacks key elements of the real thing. Studies of this type show that the benefits of psychotherapy do _____ improvement based on the placebo effect alone.

79. (p. 586) In hundreds of studies of psychotherapy and counseling, a modest but consistent _____ _____ for therapy has been found to exist. Though based on averages, overall it was effective for more people than not.

80. (p. 586) An analysis of over 2400 patients found that about _____ percent felt better after only 8 therapy sessions (or in about 2 months of weekly one hour sessions). After 26 sessions, roughly _____ percent had improved.

81. (p. 586) One author writing in 1959 counted at least 36 major systems of psychotherapy. The count could easily exceed _____ today.

82. (p. 587) All of the psychotherapies discussed include some combination of the following goals: insight, resolution of _____, an improved sense of _____, a change in unacceptable patterns of _____, better _____ relationships, and an improved picture of oneself and the world.

83. (p. 587) All psychotherapies include some combination of several important goals. To accomplish these goals, all psychotherapies offer:
    1) a_____ _____, sometimes called the therapeutic alliance, between client and therapist based on emotional rapport
    2) a protected setting in which emotional _____ (release) can take place
    3) some _____ or _____for the suffering the client has experienced, and proposed action which if followed will end this suffering
    4) a new perspective for clients about themselves and their situations.

84. (p. 588) Because therapies have much in common, a majority of psychologists in the U.S. have become _____ in their work. They use whatever methods best fit a particular problem. In addition, some seek to combine the best elements of various therapies into more general systems.

85. (p. 589) In determining when you should seek professional help, several guidelines can be suggested. The first is: if your level of psychological discomfort becomes comparable to a level of _____ discomfort that would cause you to see a dentist or physician.

86. (p. 589) Another sign is the occurrence of significant _____ in observable behavior like the quality of your work, your rate of absenteeism, your use of drugs, or your relationships with others who are important to you.

87. (p. 589) If you find friends or relatives making suggestions that you seek professional help, they may be seeing things more _____ than you.

88. (p. 589) Definitely seek help if you have persistent or disturbing _____ thoughts or impulses._____

89. (p. 589) There are several ways of seeking professional help. One of these avenues is to look in the "_____ _____." These listings will put you in touch with individuals in private practice.

90. (p. 589) Most counties and many cities offer services through community or county _____ _____ _____ listed in the phone book.

91. (p. 589) Many cities have _____ _____ _____ organized to keep listings of therapists and services.

92. (p. 589) If you are a student, many schools have special counseling facilities. Also, some psychologists and low-cost "outreach" clinics make their presence known to the public through _____ _____.

93. (p. 589) For information concerning a wide range of mental health problems, you could call a _____ _____. Most of these telephone services are staffed by community volunteers who have lists of organizations, services, and other resources in the community to which they can refer you.

94. (p. 589) The choice between a psychiatrist and a psychologist is somewhat arbitrary. Both are trained to do psychotherapy. Fees for _____ are usually higher.

95. (p. 590) If fees are a problem, consider that many individual therapists and almost all community mental health centers charge on a _____ _____, or ability-to-pay basis.

96. (p. 590) Some communities and college campuses have counseling services staffed by sympathetic _____ or _____ counselors. These services are free or very low cost. Studies show that for minor problems these counselors are often as effective as professionals.

97. (p. 590) _____ therapy is much less expensive because the therapist's fee is divided among several people.

98. (p. 590) Don't overlook peer-led _____-_____ groups which can add valuable support to professional treatment. These groups exist for hundreds of specific problems and in some cases may be the best choice.

99. (p. 590) You can usually get information about the training and qualifications of a therapist simply by asking. If you have any doubts, _____ may be checked with a variety of organizations. You should be familiar with these groups.

100. (p. 590) The best way to pick a particular therapist is to start with one short _____. This will allow the person you consult to evaluate the nature of your difficulty and recommend an appropriate type of therapy, or a therapist who is likely to be helpful.

101. (p. 590) A balanced look at psychotherapies suggests that all _____ are about equally successful, but all _____ are not. The most successful psychotherapists are those who use whatever method seems most helpful and whose personal characteristics include _____, integrity, sincerity, and _____.

102. (p. 590) Since the relationship between a client and therapist is the therapist's basic tool, you must trust and easily relate to a therapist for therapy to be effective. Clients who _____ their therapist and are well-matched in personal characteristics with him or her are generally more successful in therapy.

103. (p. 590) An especially important part of the therapeutic alliance is agreement about the _____ of therapy. It is therefore a good idea to think about what you would like to accomplish by entering therapy. Discuss this with your therapist during the first session.

104. (p. 591) Several points may help you when a friend wants to talk about a problem. First, you should practice _____ _____; a person with a problem needs to be heard. Try to accept the person's message without judging it or immediately leaping to conclusions. Let the person know you are listening through eye contact, posture, your tone of voice, and your replies.

105. (p. 591) Try to understand the problem from the person's point of view. As you do, check your understanding often. This may help to _____ the problem and provide the person with a better position to discover solutions.

106. (p. 591) By focusing on the person's _____ you can avoid making him or her defensive. This process helps permit the free outpouring of emotion that is the basis for catharsis.

107. (p. 591) Avoid giving _____. It is not unreasonable to do so when asked, but beware of the trap described by 591Eric Berne, "Why don't you? Yes, but . . ."

108. (p. 591) Accept the person's frame of _____ and avoid contradicting the person with your point of view. If individuals feel that their point of view is understood, they will feel freer to examine it objectively and to question their perspective.

109. (p. 592) One of the most productive things you can do is to give _____ by simply reflecting (restating) thoughts and feelings said by the person.

110. (p. 592) To encourage the person to feel unhurried and to speak freely, be sure to listen patiently. Studies of counselors show that pauses of _____ seconds or more are not unusual, and interrupting is rare.

111. (p. 592) Because your goal is to encourage free expression, use _____ questions (those that call for an open-ended reply) rather than _____ (those which can be answered yes or no).

112. (p. 592) Your efforts to help should include maintaining _____. Avoid the temptation to gossip.

113. (p. 593) Western nations are rapidly moving toward cultural _____. Such a society combines the traditions of many racial and ethnic groups in a rich and varied tapestry. Our own multicultural society increasingly calls for therapists who can work with clients from varied cultural backgrounds.

114. (p. 593) Traditional theories of counseling and psychotherapy tend to emphasize values that are generally consistent with American culture. However, not all cultures or ethnic groups share these same values. As a result, therapists are learning that they need to use strategies and techniques that are consistent with the _____ _____ and cultural values of their clients.

115. (p. 593) When a client and therapist come from different cultural backgrounds, _____ _____ are common. The culturally aware therapist must be careful not to make false assumptions about a client's personal history, values, goals for therapy, or expectations.

116. (p. 593) Psychologists Derald Sue and David Sue believe there are four main cultural barriers to effective counseling. These include differences in _____, social _____, cultural values, and non-verbal communication.

117. (p. 594) In most Native-American cultures, you show respect by not making eye contact. American Indians who enter therapy may often avoid looking at the therapist, giving the impression (to the culturally uninformed counselor) that they have poor self-esteem. Not surprisingly, over _____ of all Native Americans do not return after a first therapy session with non-native therapists.

118. (p. 594) A _____ _____ counselor needs to be aware of issues faced by almost everyone, but in addition must know about the special conflicts and problems typical of members of various racial or ethnic groups.

119. (p. 594) A major step toward competence as a culturally skilled counselor is to become more aware of one's own cultural values and _____. He or she must try to avoid thinking of clients in terms of _____.

120. (p. 594) They must affirm that minority cultural beliefs and values are different, but not _____ to their own. They need to gain knowledge about the history and culture of diverse groups of people, often by direct experience in the community.

121. (p. 594) Cross-cultural counseling can be quite successful. Cultural barriers are transcended on a regular basis by counselors who can achieve _____ with their clients. This is aided by being able to mentally take the role of the client.

122. (p. 594) Many ethnic groups make little distinction between _____ and _____ life. For this reason, therapists sometimes work with clergy or tribal healers to bridge the gap between cultures.

123. (p. 594) Effective therapists need to be sensitive not only to racial and ethnic differences, but also to differences related to _____, _____ orientation, religious beliefs, handicaps, and other such dimensions.

SELF-TEST

1.   (p. 575) Which of the following is *not* a correct match?
        a. insight therapies—foster a deeper understanding of the assumptions, beliefs, emotions, and conflicts underlying a problem
        b. directive therapies—places responsibility for the course of therapy on the client
        c. action therapies—focus on directly changing troublesome habits and behavior
        d. individual therapies—proceed on a one-to-one basis between client and therapist

2.   (p. 576) True-False. Trepanning was used in the Stone Ages to treat ergotism.

3.   (p. 576) During the Middle Ages, treatment for the mentally ill in Europe focused on
        a. demonology
        b. ego-states
        c. unconscious motives
        d. physiological abnormalities

4.   (p. 577) A compassionate view of the mentally ill slowly emerged after 1793, facilitated by the work of _____ at the Bicetre Asylum in Paris.
        a. Freud   c. Charcot
        b. Pinel   d. Frankl

5.   (p. 578) Which of the following techniques was *not* used by Freud as part of psychoanalysis?
        a. analysis of transference   c. analysis of resistance
        b. analysis of irrational beliefs   d. dream analysis

6.   (p. 579) True-False. Psychoanalysis as originally conducted by Freud is still in widespread use today.

7. (p. 579) True-False. When psychotherapy has been effective in changing human thinking or behavior, we speak of spontaneous remission.

8. (p. 580) The goal of traditional psychoanalysis is
    a. adjustment
    b. to achieve here-and-now experiences
    c. self-actualization
    d. to rebuild connected wholes

9. (p. 580) Which of the following is *not* true of client-centered therapy?
    a. It focuses on conscious thoughts and feelings.
    b. The client determines what will be discussed during each session.
    c. The therapist's job is to create an "atmosphere of growth."
    d. It was developed by humanistic psychologist H. J. Eysenck.

10. (p. 580) Which of the following is *not* a basic condition for effective therapists as outlined by Carl Rogers?
    a. The therapist makes positive regard conditional upon therapeutic progress.
    b. The therapist strives to be authentic in his or her relationship with clients.
    c. The therapist attempts to achieve genuine empathy for the client.
    d. The therapist does not make interpretations, but instead reflects thoughts and feelings.

11. (p. 581) Which of the following is *not* true of existential therapy?
    a. It tries to promote self-knowledge and self-actualization.
    b. It seeks to uncover a "true self" hidden behind an artificial screen of defenses.
    c. It emphasizes the idea of free will.
    d. It focuses on ultimate human concerns such as death, isolation, and meaningfulness.

12. (p. 581) Which of the following is *not* true of logotherapy?
    a. It was developed by Victor Frankl on the basis of experiences in a Nazi concentration camp.
    b. It uses a flexible approach centered around confrontation.
    c. When it is successful, it brings about a reappraisal of what's important in life.
    d. It attempts to restore meaning and vitality to life through such experiences as the "trust walk" and the "blind mill."

13. (p. 582) According to Fritz Perls, emotional health comes from getting in touch with what you
    a. should do   c. want to do
    b. ought to do   d. should want to do

14. (p. 583) An advantage to group therapy is that
    a. it permits a therapist to provide a greater depth of empathy to clients
    b. it allows clients to experience the here-and-now more directly
    c. it provides a more realistic situation than the protected atmosphere of individual therapy
    d. it doesn't really provide any special advantages, but it does allow psychologists to work with more people at one time

15. (p. 583) A teenager would most likely act out a typical family fight in
    a. psychodrama   c. client-centered therapy
    b. Gestalt therapy   d. logotherapy

16. (p. 583) A primary technique in psychodrama is
    a. dream analysis
    b. role playing
    c. crossing transactions
    d. large group awareness training

17. (p. 584) True-False. Family therapists believe that problems within a family can usually be traced to a single individual who must be helped through therapy to "own" his or her problems.

18. (p. 584) Which of the following is *not* true of sensitivity groups?
    a. Participants take part in exercises that gently enlarge awareness of oneself and others.
    b. While different from traditional psychotherapy, they have been shown to be therapeutic.
    c. They are less confrontive than encounter groups.
    d. Their principles are used by many businesses to improve employee morale and relationships.

19. (p. 584) Encounter groups are designed to
    a. enhance adjustment through nondirective therapeutic techniques
    b. bolster the ego through group unconditional positive regard
    c. enhance self-awareness through "trust walks" and "blind mills"
    d. tear down defenses and facades in order to facilitate greater self-awareness

20. (p. 584) True-False. There are no dangers involved in participating in an encounter group.

21. (p. 584) True-False. Encounter and sensitivity groups may comfort, but they do not cure anything.

22. (p. 585) Of the following therapies, which focuses on the analysis of personality ego-states?
    a. Gestalt therapy
    b. transactional analysis
    c. logotherapy
    d. client-centered therapy

23. (p. 585) True-False. The Parent is a mature and rational decision-making part of the personality according to TA.

24. (p. 586) According to TA, when communication exchange appears to take place on one level but actually takes place on another, this is called a(n)
    a. ulterior transaction
    b. crossed transaction
    c. role reversal
    d. life script alteration

25. (p. 586) True-False. According to Berne, one way to overcome destructive transactions is to develop new ways of communicating called "games."

26. (p. 587) All psychotherapies have as their goals which of the following?
    a. an improved sense of self
    b. better interpersonal relations
    c. resolution of conflicts
    d. all of the above

27. (p. 589) Which of the following is *not* a sign that you should seek professional help?
    a. You find friends or relatives making the suggestion that you seek professional help.
    b. You have persistent or disturbing suicidal thoughts or impulses.
    c. Your psychological discomfort is comparable to a level of physical discomfort that would make you seek medical treatment.
    d. There have been no significant negative changes in your observable behavior for some time.

28. (p. 590) True-False. A balanced look at psychotherapies suggests that all techniques are about equally successful.

29. (p. 590) Which of the following is *not* true of successful therapists and effective therapy?
    a. Clients who dislike their therapists do better because they are forced to consider a strongly opposing point of view.
    b. Successful therapists are distinguished by warmth, integrity, sincerity, and empathy.
    c. Successful therapists are willing to use whatever method seems most helpful for a client.
    d. Since the relationship between a client and therapist is the therapist's most basic tool, clients must trust and easily relate to a therapist.

30. (p. 590) True-False. Psychotherapy is an art, not a science.

31. (p. 591) Which of the following is *not* a useful guideline to consider when "counseling" a friend?
    a. maintain confidentiality
    b. challenge the person's frame of reference
    c. reflect thoughts and feelings
    d. avoid giving advice

32. (p. 593) Which of the following is *not* true of a culturally skilled counselor?
    a. They are sensitive to cultural differences through reliance upon stereotypes.
    b. They use existing helping resources within a cultural group to support efforts to resolve problems.
    c. They adapt traditional theories and techniques to meet the needs of clients from non-European ethnic or racial groups.
    d. They are aware of a client's ethnic identity and degree of acculturation to the majority society.

33. (p. 593) Which of the following is identified by Sue and Sue as cultural barriers to effective counseling?
    a. language
    b. non-verbal communication
    c. social class
    d. all of the above

APPLYING YOUR KNOWLEDGE

1. A 36-year-old man is having problems at home and his job. His work performance has deteriorated and he misses too many days of work. He seems depressed, anxious, and lonely. He argues constantly with his wife and has become distant from his children. How might each of the various insight therapies discussed in your text approach the treatment of these problems?

2. Select one of the insight approaches to therapy and do some additional reading on this subject. What are the important features of the approach? Are there particular techniques used by practioners of this approach? How did this approach develop and who are some of the important individuals who have helped develop the approach. Are there certain kinds of problems the approach best seeks to treat?

3. Contact a counseling or clinical psychologist in your area who provides therapy as a part of their work. Interview that person about the kinds of problems they treat and the approaches they use. Do they rely on one or a few approaches or are they more eclectic in the techniques and styles they use? Where did they receive their training and what types of insight therapies do they have experience in using?

ANSWERS—PROGRAMMED REVIEW

1. Psychotherapy
2. Individual
3. Group
4. Insight
5. Action
6. Directive
7. Non-directive
8. Time-limited
9. phobias; sexual; marital
10. comfort, support
11. personal growth
12. trepanning
13. unusual
14. demonology; exorcism
15. ergotism

16. Philippe Pinel
17. Sigmund Freud; psychoanalysis
18. hysteria
19. relaxation; unconscious
20. repressed
21. free association
22. dream analysis
23. manifest; latent; symbols
24. resist; resistances
25. transfer; reeducation
26. 3; 5; 7
27. dynamic; direct interviewing
28. effectiveness
29. spontaneous remission
30. improve; better
31. adjustment; potential
32. client-centered; conscious
33. non-directive
34. unconditioned positive regard
35. empathy
36. authentic
37. reflects
38. Existential
39. free will
40. courage
41. freedom, isolation, meaningulness
42. logotherapy; Nazi concentration; meaning
43. confrontation; encounter
44. Gestalt
45. directive
46. whole
47. gap; immediate experience
48. want; should; ought
49. present

50. group therapy
51. therapy; real-life
52. psychodrama; role plays
53. role reversals
54. family
55. single
56. family system
57. confrontive; trust walk
58. encounter
59. screened; trained
60. businesses; married
61. large group
62. therapeutic
63. therapy placebo
64. mental health
65. attacked; converting
66. small; no
67. educational; therapeutic
68. general nature; counseling
69. Transactional analysis
70. games; group
71. ego-states
72. Child
73. Parent
74. Adult
75. crossed
76. ulterior
77. games
78. exceed
79. positive effect
80. 50; 75
81. 200
82. conflicts; self; behavior; interpersonal
83. caring relationship; catharsis; explanation, rationale
84. eclectic
85. physical
86. changes

87. objectively
88. suicidal
89. yellow pages
90. mental health centers
91. mental health associations
92. newspaper advertisements
93. crisis hotline
94. psychiatrists
95. sliding scale
96. paraprofessionals; peer
97. Group
98. self-help
99. credentials
100. consultation
101. techniques; therapists; warmth; empathy
102. like
103. goals
104. active listening
105. clarify
106. feelings
107. advice
108. reference
109. feedback
110. 5
111. open; closed
112. confidentiality
113. pluralism
114. life experiences
115. misunderstandings
116. language; class
117. half
118. culturally skilled
119. biases; stereotypes
120. inferior
121. empathy
122. religious; secular
123. age; sexual

ANSWERS—SELF-TEST

1.	b	7.	False	13.	c	19.	d
2.	False	8.	a	14.	c	20.	False
3.	a	9.	d	15.	a	21.	True
4.	b	10.	a	16.	b	22.	b
5.	b	11.	b	17.	False	23.	False
6.	False	12.	d	18.	b	24.	a

25.	False	31.	b
26.	d	32.	a
27.	d	33.	d
28.	True		
29.	a		
30.	True		

ACROSS

2. any psychological technique used to facilitate positive changes in a person's personality or behavior
7. capacity to feel and see what another is experiencing
9. practice of driving off an "evil spirit" of one who is "possessed"
10. Transactional analysis (abbr.)
13. emotional _____ (release) in a protected setting is useful in many psychotherapies
14. with this therapy individuals play roles resembling their real-life problems
15. in psychoanalysis, an emotional attachment to therapist by a patient

DOWN

1. he is connected with logotherapy
3. process of drilling or chipping holes in skull to release evil spirits
4. he unchained the "mentally ill"
5. this technique is "granddaddy" of most modern psychotherapies
6. repeating or restating what a client has said —a psychological "mirror"
8. he proposed transactional analysis theory
11. _____ means whole
12. he is a client-centered therapist

CHAPTER 22

Behavior Therapy

CONTENTS

TERMS AND CONCEPTS

behavior therapists
behavior modification
cognitive behavior therapy
classical conditioning
conditioned stimulus (CS)
unconditioned stimulus (US)
unconditioned response (UR)
conditioned response (CR)
aversion
aversion therapy
conditioned aversion
rapid smoking
Antabuse
response-contingent
transfer
generalization
desensitization
hierarchy

reciprocal inhibition
vicarious desensitization
eye-movement desensitization
operant conditioning
positive reinforcement
non-reinforcement
extinction
punishment
shaping
stimulus control
time out
tokens
target behaviors
token economy
cognitive behavior therapists
rational-emotive therapy
covert sensitization

IMPORTANT INDIVIDUALS

Ivan Pavlov
Roger Vogler
Joseph Wolpe

Francine Shapiro
B. F. Skinner
Aaron Beck

Albert Ellis
Scott Hamilton
David Waldman

PROGRAMMED REVIEW

1.   (p. 598) Behavioral approaches include behavior _____ (the use of learning principles to change behavior) and _____ behavior therapy (the use of learning principals to change upsetting thoughts and beliefs).

2.   (p. 599) Behavior therapists believe that insight, or deep understanding of one's problems, is often unnecessary for improvement. Instead, they try to directly alter troublesome thoughts and _____.

3.   (p. 599) Behavior therapy involves more _____-oriented approaches than previously discussed therapies that are based on insight, or self-awareness.

4.   (p. 599) Behavior therapy is based on the basic assumption that people have learned to be the way they are. Consequently, they can change their problematic responses or _____ more appropriate behaviors.

5.   (p. 599) Broadly speaking, behavior modification refers to any attempt to use the learning principles of _____ (respondent) and _____ conditioning to change human behavior.

6.   (p. 599) Classical conditioning is the process of learning originally studied by Russian psychologist Ivan _____.

7.   (p. 599) Through this process a previously neutral stimulus, the _____ _____, is followed by a stimulus, the _____ _____, which always produces a response, the _____ _____.

8.   (p. 599) Eventually the conditioned stimulus begins to produce the response directly. The response is then called a _____ _____.

9.   (p. 599) Classical conditioning can be used to associate discomfort, called an _____ with a bad habit. This procedure is called _____ _____.

10.   (p. 599) When an aversion (or negative emotional response) is paired with a bad habit such that the habit no longer occurs or is replaced by a competing response, a _____ _____ has developed.

11.   (p. 600) Aversion therapy has been used to treat smoking, drinking, and gambling, as well as hiccups, _____, _____, vomiting, bed-wetting, marijuana smoking, and compulsive hair-pulling. It is also used in the treatment of fetishism, _____, and other "maladaptive" sexual behaviors.

12.   (p. 600) Aversion therapy can be an aid to persons who want to quit smoking. _____ smoking is the most widely used method. Subjects smoke continuously, taking a puff every 6 to 8 seconds.

13.   (p. 600) A number of studies suggest that rapid smoking is the most _____ behavior therapy for smoking. Also, health risks of rapid smoking are _____. However, without the help of a therapist, most people quit too soon for the procedure to succeed.

14.   (p. 600) The most basic problem with rapid smoking is that about _____-_____ of those who quit smoking begin again.

15. (p. 600) Relapse is especially likely for smokers who have strong _____
symptoms.

16. (p. 600) During at least the first _____ after quitting, there is no "safe point" after which relapse becomes less likely. But, former smokers who get encouragement from others are much more likely to stay smoke free. In contrast, former smokers whose social groups include many smokers are more likely to begin smoking again.

17. (p. 600) Psychologist Roger Vogler uses aversion therapy with alcoholics who have tried almost everything to stop drinking, including therapy with _____, a drug that causes an alcoholic to become violently nauseated after drinking.

18. (p. 600) While Antabuse makes alcoholics ill after drinking, they don't develop an aversion to drinking because there is too great a _____ between drinking and becoming ill. This prevents discomfort from being closely associated with drinking.

19. (p. 600) Vogler associates painful, but noninjurious _____ _____ with the intake of alcohol. This condition takes the pleasure out of drinking and causes the patient to develop a conditioned aversion to drinking.

20. (p. 600) The shock is presented most of the time when the patient is beginning to take a drink. This _____ _____ (or response connected) association helps develop a conditioned aversion to alcohol.

21. (p. 600) One problem with successful treatment is getting aversive conditioning to _____ or _____ from the therapy situation to the "real world."

22. (p. 600) One way to improve transfer is to make the therapy situation resemble the normal site of drinking as much as possible. Vogler has accomplished this feat by having patients undergo aversion therapy in a simulated _____ or in other simulated sites.

23. (p. 601) Aversion therapy is used as a last resort. Vogler also trains alcoholics to discriminate _____ _____ levels (so clients can tell how drunk they are), teaches them alternatives to drinking, and offers alcohol education and general counseling.

24. (p. 601) Also, alcohol abusers are _____ as they go from sober to drunk; later they are shown the tape. Apparently, few people have any idea of how unattractive they are when drunk.

25. (p. 601) To add to the effect, the bartender is trained to provoke clients into becoming _____ and obnoxious. In the videotape self-confrontation held later, grossly drunken behaviors are replayed. Seeing themselves as obnoxious drunks adds to the aversion people feel for drinking, and it increases their determination to quit.

26. (p. 601) Commercial aversion programs for _____, _____, and alcohol abuse have attracted large numbers of willing customers.

27. (p. 601) For mild problems, it is not always necessary that a person receive shocks. For example, merely _____ a trained actor who appears to get _____ while biting his nails can effectively curb the problem.

28. (p. 601) When psychologists use aversion therapy, they often back it up with _____ _____.

29.   (p. 601) _____, a reduction in fear or anxiety, is usually brought about by gradually approaching a feared stimulus while maintaining complete relaxation.

30.   (p. 601) An ordered set of steps called a _____ is used to allow the individual to _____ to gradual approximations of the end, desired behavior.

31.   (p. 601) Desensitization is also based on a principle, developed by Joseph Wolpe, called _____ _____, which means that one emotional state can prevent the occurrence of another.

32.   (p. 602) Desensitization is primarily used to help people unlearn or counter-condition strong and or _____ such as fear of heights, water, snakes, and so forth.

33.   (p. 602) Desensitization usually involves three steps:
      1)   the client and therapist _____ a _____, a list of fear-provoking situations involving the phobia, and ranging from the least disturbing to the most;
      2)   the client is taught exercises that produce total _____; and
      3)   the client performs the least disturbing item on the list until no _____ is felt, then moves on to the next most fearful item, and so on through the hierarchy.

34.   (p. 602) In situations where it is impractical for the client to act out the steps, clients can observe models performing the feared behavior. This process is known as _____ _____.

35.   (p. 602) Desensitization also works well when a person vividly _____ each step in the hierarchy. If the steps can be visualized without anxiety, fear in the actual situation is reduced.

36.   (p. 603) Victims of accidents, natural disasters, molestations, muggings, rape, or emotional abuse often complain of anxiety, _____ thoughts, flashbacks, _____ disturbances, low _____-esteem, or relationship problems. Such problems can be successfully treated using traditional desensitization.

37.   (p. 603) Dr. Francine Shapiro has developed a technique called _____-_____ desensitization to treat traumatic memories. The traumatized person is asked to concentrate on the upsetting thoughts while an object is moved rapidly from side to side in front of the person's eyes. Watching the moving object causes the person's eyes to dart swiftly back and forth while the disturbing memory is held in mind.

38.   (p. 604) Results of initial studies indicate that a single session of eye-movement desensitization _____ anxieties and takes the _____ out of traumatic memories. At the moment, no one knows how Shapiro's technique works.

39.   (p. 604) The principles of _____ conditioning have been developed by B. F. _____ and his associates mostly through laboratory research with animals.

40.   (p. 604) There are several principles used to deal with human behavior. One of these principles is _____ _____, the process whereby an action that is followed by reward will occur more frequently.

41.   (p. 604) The principle of _____ means that an action not followed by reward will occur less frequently.

42. (p. 604) If the response is not followed by reward after it has been repeated many times, it will go away. This phenomenon defines the process of _____.

43. (p. 604) If a response is followed by discomfort, or an undesirable effect, the response will be suppressed (but not necessarily extinguished). This phenomenon defines the process of _____.

44. (p. 604) _____ means rewarding actions that are closer and closer approximations to a desired response.

45. (p. 604) Responses tend to come under the control of the situation in which they occur. When they do we speak of _____ _____.

46. (p. 604) A _____ _____ procedure usually involves removing the individual from a situation in which reinforcement occurs, thus preventing reward from following an undesirable response.

47. (p. 605) The most frequently occurring human behaviors lead to some form of reward. An undesirable response can be eliminated by _____ and _____ the rewards which maintain it.

48. (p. 605) Most of the rewards which maintain human behavior are more subtle than food, money, etc. Rather they include _____, _____, and concern.

49. (p. 605) Examples of these reinforcers are often seen in classrooms. Frequently, misbehaving children are surrounded by others who giggle and pay attention to them. If seating is rearranged so that the disruptive children are surrounded by less responsive students, misbehavior _____.

50. (p. 605) Attention from a teacher can also be a reinforcer. An experiment showed that when teachers paid extra attention to classroom misbehavior, it _____.

51. (p. 605) Also, misbehavior _____ when attention took the form of scolding such as the teacher saying, "Sit down!"

52. (p. 605) Nonreward and extinction can eliminate many of these problem behaviors. For example, in the classroom example when misbehaving children were _____ and attention was given to children not misbehaving, misbehavior _____.

53. (p. 605) A typical strategy used in institutions to deal with a particular disturbing response is _____ _____, refusing to reward maladaptive responses by refusing to play the attention game.

54. (p. 605) Another form of time out is to _____ an individual immediately from the setting in which an undesirable response occurs so that the response will not be rewarded.

55. (p. 606) An approach that has been widely used with the severely disturbed is based on _____, symbolic rewards that can be exchanged for real rewards. Such symbolic rewards are being used in mental hospitals, halfway houses for drug addicts, schools for the retarded, programs for delinquents, and ordinary classrooms. Their use is usually associated with dramatic improvements in behavior and overall adjustment.

56. (p. 606) Using tokens, a therapist can immediately reward a _____ response. This allows a therapist to use _____ _____ to influence behavior directly, instead of vaguely urging patients to "get themselves together."

57. (p. 606) For maximum impact, the therapist selects specific _____ _____ and then reinforces them with tokens. Gradually, patients are required to do more or better responses in order to receive rewards.

58. (p. 606) Full-scale use of tokens in an institutional setting produces a _____ _____. In such programs, patients are rewarded with tokens for a wide range of socially desirable or productive activities. They must pay tokens for privileges and for engaging in problem behavior.

59. (p. 606) Generalization to the outside world can be a problem in token economies. The most effective token economies are those that gradually switch from tokens to _____ _____ such as recognition and approval.

60. (p. 606) In recent years a new breed of behavior therapists has appeared. _____ behavior therapists, as they are called, are interested in thoughts, as well as visible behavior.

61. (p. 606) Rather than looking only at maladaptive actions, cognitive therapists try to learn what people think, believe, and feel. They then help clients change _____ _____ that lead to trouble.

62. (p. 607) Cognitive therapy has been especially effective in the treatment of _____ which Aaron Beck believes is a result of negative, self-defeating thoughts.

63. (p. 607) Depressed persons see themselves, the world, and the future in negative terms. According to Beck this situation occurs because of several major distortions in thinking. The first is _____ _____. For example, if five good things happen during the day and three bad, the depressed person will focus only on the bad.

64. (p. 607) _____ is another thinking error underlying depression. An example would be considering yourself a total failure, or worthless, if you were to lose a job or fail a class.

65. (p. 607) Also, Beck says that depressed persons tend to _____ the importance of undesirable events, and they engage in _____-_____-_____ thinking (seeing events, or themselves, as completely good or bad, right or wrong, successful or a failure).

66. (p. 607) Cognitive therapists make a step-by-step effort to correct negative thoughts that underlie depression or similar problems. At first, clients are taught to _____ and keep _____ of their own thoughts (especially those linked to depression).

67. (p. 608) Next, clients are asked to collect information to _____ their beliefs. For instance, a depressed person's weekly list of activities might be used to challenge the all-or-nothing thought, "I had a terrible week."

68. (p. 608) In an alternative approach, the cognitive therapist looks for an absence of effective _____ skills and thought patterns, not for the presence of self-defeating _____. The aim in this case is to teach clients how to _____ with anger, depression, and similar problems.

69. (p. 608) In addition to depression, cognitive behavior therapy is being used to treat panic, _____, agoraphobia, _____ disorders, couples problems, and even schizophrenia.

70. (p. 608) One widely used form of cognitive therapy is that which Albert Ellis calls _____-_____ therapy, abbreviated _____.

71. (p. 608) Ellis assumes that people become unhappy and develop self-defeating habits because of _____ beliefs.

72. (p. 608) Ellis analyzes the situation using the letters "A-B-C." The person assumes the cause of the emotional _____ (C) to be the _____ experience (A). Rational-emotive therapy shows the client the true cause of the difficulty is the client's irrational and unrealistic belief (B).

73. (p. 608) RET holds that events cannot _____ us to have feelings. We feel as we do because of our beliefs and expectations.

74. (p. 608) Ellis believes that most irrational beliefs come from three core ideas, each of which is unrealistic:
    1) I must _____ well and be _____ of by significant others.
    2) You must treat me _____.
    3) Conditions must be the way I want them to be.

75. (p. 608) Rational-emotive therapy takes a very _____ approach, since the therapist may directly attack clients' logic, challenge their thinking, or confront them with evidence contrary to their beliefs.

76. (p. 608) RET has been criticized by some as superficial and argumentative, but Ellis' basic insight has merit. For instance, one recent study found that having irrational beliefs, like those discussed by Ellis, is related to feelings of _____, _____, and low self-esteem.

77. (p. 610) The technique of _____ _____ can be applied by writing on cards a series of disturbing or disgusting scenes related to the problem and then frequently imagining those scenes during the day.

78. (p. 610) In using covert sensitization, the trick is to get yourself to imagine or picture vividly each of these disturbing scenes several times a day. By reviewing your cards each time you do something frequently each day (such as getting a cup of coffee) you can bring your task under _____ _____.

79. (p. 611) At least two _____-_____ techniques can be suggested (given that thoughts alone can cause trouble). One is to snap a rubber band attached to your wrist each time you catch yourself thinking the upsetting image or thought.

80. (p. 611) Another thought-stopping technique is to reserve privacy and time each day (at first) to deliberately think the unwanted thought. As you begin to form the thought, shout "stop!" Repeat this _____ to 20 times the first two or three days, then switch to shouting "stop!" covertly rather than aloud.

81. (p. 611) While punishing images can be linked to undesirable responses to decrease their occurrence, many people also find it helpful to covertly _____ desired actions.

82. (p. 611) For many people actual direct reinforcement is the most powerful way to alter behavior. Nevertheless, covert or "_____" reinforcement can have similar effects.

83. (p. 611) The key to desensitization is _____. One way to achieve deep muscle relaxation is to practice tightening different muscles for five seconds and then letting go.

84. (p. 612) As an alternative, you might try imagining a very safe, pleasant, and relaxing scene. Some people find such images as relaxing as the tension-release method. Another possibility is to use soothing _____ to produce relaxation.

85. (p. 612) In developing a hierarchy to overcome a fear by relaxation, make a list of situations related to the fear that makes you anxious. Try to list at least _____ situations, some should be very frightening and others only mildly frightening.

86. (p. 612) If you can vividly picture and imagine yourself in the first situation of your hierarchy without a noticeable increase in muscular tension at least _____, proceed to the next card you have constructed. Be sure to relax yourself between cards.

87. (p. 612) Each day, stop when you reach a card that you cannot visualize without tension after _____ attempts. On each successive day, begin one or two cards before the one on which you stopped the previous day. Eventually you can learn to control the fear.

88. (p. 612) Don't be discouraged if you are unable to relax completely while imagining the upsetting scenes. Research shows that in many instances your fear will still lessen after _____ _____ to the feared situation.

89. (p. 613) Scott Hamilton and David Waldman conducted a case study involving a psychology student (Al) with a 4-year history of depression. Al had tried group therapy and other efforts, but continued to engage in frequent _____-_____ and _____ thinking, which almost always made him depressed.

90. (p. 613) In designing a strategy for modifying Al's depression, an initial _____ level of depressive thinking was determined by having Al record how often he had negative thoughts (and how intense they were) during an initial 18-day period.

91. (p. 613) Al's first plan focused on solving the problems he worried about most. However, his use of a reinforcement system did not consistently lessen his depressive thinking. So, Al dropped the reinforcement system after 2 weeks and concentrated on directly changing his _____ _____.

92. (p. 613) Al's cognitive program had three elements. First, he kept a _____ of events and thoughts that immediately preceded his becoming depressed. He then reevaluated the event and restated his thoughts about it in a more rational form.

93. (p. 613) Second, he administered daily covert _____ to himself. This took the form of reading written, positive statements about himself while engaging in pleasant activities.

94. (p. 613) The third element involved setting aside times each day when he would relax and mentally rehearse coping with _____ situations. He tried to imagine the worst possible turn of events and to picture himself dealing with the situation _____.

95.   (p. 613) Hamilton and Waldman report that Al's original reinforcement system did eliminate many of the sources of his self-critical thoughts, but new depressive thoughts began to replace the old worries. In Al's case it proved more effective to _____ _____ his depressive thinking.

96.   (p. 614) When behavior therapy was first developed, many observers feared that it would be used to control people against their _____. By now, most fears of behavior therapy have faded. For one thing, it is clear that _____ psychotherapies modify behavior in one way or another.

97.   (p. 614) A second reason is that studies show that behavior therapists are rated just as _____ and _____ as traditional therapists.

98.   (p. 614) Like other approaches, success in behavior therapy depends greatly on building a _____ _____ between the client and therapist.

99.   (p. 614) Some critics still object to the use of behavior modification with "_____" groups, such as in schools, prisons, mental institutions, etc. Proponents of behavior modification consider it _____ to withhold treatment from such individuals.

SELF-TEST

1.   (p. 599) Behavior therapy is based upon which of the following assumptions?
      a.   Conflicts between the conscious and unconscious produce maladaptive behaviors.
      b.   People learn problem behaviors and can change them or relearn more appropriate responses.
      c.   The thwarting of self-actualization produces abnormal ego-states.
      d.   Insight is the key to normal adjustment.

In aversion therapy, an aversive event such as an electric shock is presented when an undesirable behavior such as drinking alcohol occurs.

2.   (p. 599) The electric shock could be called a(n)
      a.   conditioned stimulus   c.   conditioned response
      b.   unconditioned stimulus   d.   unconditioned response

3.   (p. 599) The pain of the shock and its physiological consequences could be called a(n)
      a.   conditioned stimulus   c.   conditioned response
      b.   unconditioned stimulus   d.   unconditioned response

4.   (p. 599) In this example, alcohol could be called a(n)
      a.   conditioned stimulus   c.   conditioned response
      b.   unconditioned stimulus   d.   unconditioned response

5.   (p. 599) When a conditioned aversion to alcohol develops, discomfort in drinking the alcohol could be called a(n)
      a.   conditioned stimulus   c.   conditioned response
      b.   unconditioned stimulus   d.   unconditioned response

6.   (p. 600) The above example exemplifies the work of which of the following?
      a.   Roger Vogler   c.   Ivar Lovaas
      b.   Joseph Wolpe   d.   B. F. Skinner

7.   (p. 600) The most widely used aversion therapy for smoking is
     a.   use of Antabuse which makes smokers vomit whenever they inhale a cigarette
     b.   electric shock paired with videotapes of cancerous lungs
     c.   rapid smoking method
     d.   overgeneralization technique

8.   (p. 600) Aversion therapy is usually arranged so that the aversion is _____ contingent.
     a.   response   c.   solution
     b.   problem   d.   stimulus

9.   (p. 600) Which of the following can be a problem in aversion therapy?
     a.   getting the aversion to be response non-contingent
     b.   finding effective aversions
     c.   getting patients to overcome their aversions so that therapy can proceed
     d.   generalization of aversion conditioning to the "real world"

10. (p. 601) True-False. Desensitization allows patients to adapt to a hierarchy of feared stimuli.

11. (p. 601) Desensitization is based partly on the principle of
     a.   retroactive inhibition   c.   reactive inhibition
     b.   proactive inhibition   d.   reciprocal inhibition

12. (p. 602) When acting out feared responses is impractical, clients can observe models who are performing the feared behavior. This procedure is called
     a.   counterconditioning   c.   vicarious desensitization
     b.   implosive therapy   d.   generalized desensitization

13. (p. 602) True-False. Desensitization in which the patient imagines each of the steps in the hierarchy is almost as effective as actually experiencing each step.

14. (p. 604) True-False. Punishment extinguishes behavior.

15. (p. 604) True-False. The process of gradually rewarding closer approximations to a final desired response is called sensitization.

16. (p. 604) When responses come under the control of the situation in which they occur, we speak
     a.   stimulus dominance   c.   stimulus cueing
     b.   response control   d.   stimulus control

17. (p. 604) True-False. A variation of non-reinforcement is the time out procedure whereby an individual is removed from a situation in which reinforcement occurs.

18. (p. 605) True-False. Most human behavior is maintained by primary reinforcers like food and water.

19. (p. 605) When children misbehave in order to gain attention, an effective way of decreasing this misbehavior is to
     a.   ignore children when they misbehave
     b.   be reinforcing and kind to children when they misbehave
     c.   direct negative statements at children when they misbehave
     d.   give children what they want so they will no longer misbehave

20. (p. 606) One behavioral approach to therapy is based on the use of _____, symbolic rewards that can be exchanged for real rewards.
  a. tokens   c. points
  b. symbolia   d. chips

21. (p. 606) Tokens are used in reward and punishment procedures to change specific actions called
  a. sequential acts   c. contingent responses
  b. target behaviors   d. unconditioned responses

22. (p. 606) When full-scale use of tokens is employed in an institutional setting, the program is called a
  a. behavioral community   c. reinforcer program
  b. token economy   d. secondary reward setting

23. (p. 606) Of the following, which is a challenging problem in the use of behavior modification techniques?
  a. ineffectiveness with some personality types
  b. lack of sound theoretical base
  c. poorly defined connections between applications and basic research
  d. difficulties of generalization of results from the therapy setting to the real world

24. (p. 606) Cognitive behavior therapists are interested in
  a. understanding the dynamics of cognitive mental illness
  b. applying traditional psychotherapies to cognitive problems
  c. helping clients change thinking patterns
  d. using cognitive tokens to enhance personal sensitivity

25. (p. 607) According to cognitive behavior therapists, which of the following is not associated with depression?
  a. Depressed clients tend to minimize the importance of undesirable events.
  b. The depressed demonstrate selective perception of unpleasant events or situations.
  c. The depressed engage in all-or-nothing thinking, seeing events or themselves as completely good or bad, right or wrong, successful or a failure.
  d. Depression is associated with overgeneralization in which the person feels a total failure, or worthless, due to a single loss or failure.

26. (p. 608) According to Albert Ellis, RET seeks to identify and alter
  a. emotional consequences   c. rational assumptions
  b. activating experiences   d. unrealistic beliefs

27. (p. 608) True-False. Rational-emotive therapists are very directive and may directly attack clients' logic, challenge their thinking, and confront them with evidence contrary to their beliefs.

28. (p. 610) When you systematically imagine a series of disturbing or disgusting scenes in order to reduce undesirable behaviors associated with the scenes, you are using
  a. counterconditioning   c. covert sensitization
  b. vicarious desensitization   d. implosive therapy

29. (p. 611) True-False. Snapping a rubber band worn on the wrist can be an effective thought-stopping technique when applied each time an upsetting or undesirable thought or image occurs.

30.   (p. 613) Hamilton and Waldman reported a case study of a change in depressive thinking accomplished through behavior modification. Which of the following was not an element of the effective system used by the subject Al?
  a. He set aside times each day when he would relax and mentally rehearse coping with stressful situations.
  b. He kept a record of events and thoughts that immediately preceded his becoming depressed —then he reevaluated the event and restated his thoughts about it in a more rational form.
  c. He focused on solving the problems he worried about most; he earned points for accomplishments and reinforced himself for constructive behavior.
  d. He administered daily covert reinforcement to himself by reading written, positive statements about himself while engaging in pleasant activities.

31.   (p. 614) True-False. While many observers feared that behavior therapy would be used to control people against their will, everyone has always agreed that it is the ideal therapy for "captive" groups.

APPLYING YOUR KNOWLEDGE

1.   There are probably any number of programs going on in your area that make use of behavior therapy —smoking cessation clinics, weight reduction programs, phobia alleviation programs, prison or hospital token economies, etc. Contact one of these programs and learn more about how they use behavioral principles to help change behavior. Which particular behavioral principles and techniques do they tend to rely upon? What degree of success do they have in their treatment?

2.   Is there a problem you have you'd like to work on using behavioral principles? Use the Applications section and keep a log of the self-management program you develop to help yourself. Monitor your progress and see how much progress you can make while you're finishing your psychology class.

ANSWERS—PROGRAMMED REVIEW

1. modification; cognitive	22. tavern	46. time out
2. actions	23. blood alcohol	47. identifying; removing
3. action	24. videotaped	48. attention, approval
4. relearn	25. argumentative	49. decreases
5. classical; operant	26. overeating, smoking	50. increased
6. Ivan Pavlov	27. watching; shocks	51. increased
7. conditioned stimulus; unconditioned stimulus; unconditioned response	28. supportive counseling	52. ignored; decreased
	29. Desensitization	53. time out
	30. hierarchy; adapt	54. remove
8. conditioned response	31. reciprocal inhibition	55. tokens
9. aversion; aversion therapy	32. phobias	56. positive; operant shaping
	33. construct a hierarchy; relaxation; anxiety	
10. conditioned aversion		57. target behaviors
11. sneezing, stuttering; transvestism	34. vicarious desensitization	58. token economy
	35. imagines	59. social rewards
12. Rapid	36. intrusive; sleep; self	60. Cognitive
13. effective; small	37. eye-movement	61. thinking patterns
14. one-half	38. lowers; pain	62. depression
15. withdrawal	39. operant; B. F. Skinner	63. selective perception
16. year	40. positive reinforcement	64. Overgeneralization
17. Antabuse	41. non-reinforcement	65. magnify; all-or-nothing
18. delay	42. extinction	66. recognize; track
19. electric shock	43. punishment	67. test
20. response contingent	44. Shaping	68. coping; thinking; cope
21. transfer, generalize	45. stimulus control	69. anxiety; eating

70.	rational-emotive; RET	80.	10; 20	90.	baseline
71.	faulty	81.	reinforce	91.	depressive thoughts
72.	consequence; activating	82.	visualized	92.	record
73.	cause	83.	relaxation	93.	reinforcement
74.	perform; approved; fairly	84.	music	94.	stressful; calmly
75.	directive	85.	10	95.	directly attack
76.	anger; unhappiness	86.	twice	96.	will; all
77.	covert sensitization	87.	three	97.	warm, caring
78.	stimulus control	88.	repeated exposures	98.	therapeutic alliance
79.	thought-stopping	89.	self-criticism; negative	99.	captive; unethical

ANSWERS—SELF-TEST

1.	b	7.	c	12.	c	17.	True	22.	b	27.	True
2.	b	8.	a	13.	True	18.	False	23.	d	28.	c
3.	d	9.	d	14.	False	19.	a	24.	c	29.	True
4.	a	10.	True	15.	False	20.	a	25.	a	30.	c
5.	c	11.	d	16.	d	21.	b	26.	d	31.	False
6.	a										

ACROSS

4. in _____ therapy one associates a negative emotional response with undesirable habits
7. a reduction in fears
9. with this conditioning CS and US are paired
12. RET gets rid of this kind of beliefs
13. he is associated with Rational-Emotive Therapy
14. behavior _____ refers to changing one's behavior with learning principles of classical or operant conditioning
15. therapist selects specific _____ behaviors that could or should be improved

DOWN

1. use of tokens in an institutional setting leads to development of a token _____
2. if shock is used to control drinking, it must be _____ contingent
3. symbolic rewards that can be exchanged for real rewards
5. ordered set of steps forms this
6. Rational-Emotive Therapy (abbr.)
8. key to desensitization is _____
10. he and his dog are associated with classical conditioning
11. _____ means rewarding actions that are closer and closer approximations to a desired response

■ CHAPTER 23 ■
Social Psychology I

CONTENTS

TERMS AND CONCEPTS

social psychology
culture
roles
ascribed roles
achieved roles
role conflict
status
group structure
group cohesiveness
norms
autokinetic effect
personal space
proxemics
intimate distance
personal distance
social distance
public distance
attribution
attribution theory
situational demands
self-handicapping
fundamental attribution error
need to affiliate
social comparisons
social comparison theory
interpersonal attraction
homogamy
self-disclosure

reciprocity
overdisclosure
social exchange theory
comparison level
romantic attraction
mutual absorption
attachment styles
social influence
conformity
groupthink
group sanctions
social power
reward power
coercive power
legitimate power
referent power
referent power
expert power
authority
obedience
passivity
compliance
foot-in-the-door effect
door-in-the-face effect
low-ball technique
assertiveness training
social trap
tragedy of the commons

IMPORTANT INDIVIDUALS

Stanley Milgram	Elliot Aronson	Thomas Moriarty
Philip Zimbardo	Zick Rubin	Joseph Wolpe
Muzafer Sherif	Soloman Asch	Robert Alberti
Steven Berglas	Irving Janis	Michael Emmons
Leon Festinger	Robert Cialdini	Garrett Hardin

PROGRAMMED REVIEW

1. (p. 617) Stanley Milgram conducted an interesting social psychology experiment to see how many messages could be delivered through the mail from one side of the continent to the other if each "link" had to be a first-name acquaintance. Amazingly, about one message in _____ made it with the number of intermediary "links" averaging about _____.

2. (p. 618) _____ _____ is the scientific study of how people behave, think, and feel in the presence (actual or implied) of others.

3. (p. 618) _____ is an ongoing pattern of life that is passed from one generation to the next.

4. (p. 618) In each group an individual belongs to, they occupy a _____ in the structure of the group. _____ are expected behavior patterns linked with various social positions.

5. (p. 618) Roles that are not under the individual's control—male or female, etc.—are called _____ roles, while _____ roles are those which are attained voluntarily, or by special effort—wife, teacher, scientist, bandleader, etc.

6. (p. 618) Roles can be useful because they streamline many of our daily interactions. However, it is not unusual for a person to occupy two or more opposing roles which results in _____ _____, an uncomfortable or frustrating situation.

7. (p. 618) The impact of roles is dramatically illustrated by Philip Zimbardo's "prison" experiment. Male college students paid to serve as "inmates" or "guards" assumed their roles so quickly that the experiment was halted after _____ days due to brutality by the "guards" and problems of hysterical crying, confusion, and severe depression among "inmates."

8. (p. 618) Zimbardo's interpretation of the prison experiment is that the roles assigned were so powerful that in just a matter of days the experiment had become "_____" for those involved.

9. (p. 619) After the experiment, many guards found it hard to believe their own behavior. It would seem that the source of many destructive human relationships can be found in _____ _____.

10. (p. 619) Position in a group also determines one's _____. This factor can operate very subtly to influence behavior in many situations.

11. (p. 619) For example, in one experiment, subjects approached by a well-dressed researcher, and asked to return a dime left in a phone booth, did so in _____ percent of the cases, while only _____ percent returned it when the researcher was poorly dressed.

12. (p. 619) Touching is a privilege of power and high status. For instance, _____ persons are more likely to touch _____ persons than the reverse.

13. (p. 619) People of _____ socioeconomic status are more likely to touch those of _____ status. Such differences, however, tend to disappear when people greet or take leave of one another. Then touches follow highly ritualized patterns.

14. (p. 619) As far as gender differences, _____, by virtue of their higher status and greater power in American society, are more likely to touch _____ than the reverse.

15. (p. 620) Groups are made up of people who are in some way interrelated. There are two very important dimensions of any group. Group _____ is the organization of roles, communication pathways, and power in the group.

16. (p. 620) _____ groups have a high degree of structure. _____ friendship groups may or may not be highly structured.

17. (p. 620) Group _____ is basically an indication of the degree of attraction between group members. Members are more likely to stand or sit close together and focus attention on one another. They also show more signs of mutual affection and their behavior tends to be closely coordinated.

18. (p. 620) Cohesiveness is the basis for much of the _____ groups exert over their members.

19. (p. 620) A very important aspect of the functioning of any group is its _____—standards of conduct which prescribe appropriate behavior in various situations.

20. (p. 620) The impact of norms on behavior was illustrated in an experiment on littering. Subjects walking into a public parking garage were given a handbill. The more litter there was in the garage, the _____ likely people were to drop their handbill on the floor. Apparently, seeing that others have already littered implies a lax norm about whether littering is acceptable.

21. (p. 620) One early study of how group norms are formed made use of a striking illusion called the _____ _____. Here a stationary pinpoint of light appears to move in a completely darkened room.

22. (p. 620) Using this effect, psychologist Muzafer Sherif found that when two or more people give estimates of the amount of drift, their judgments rapidly _____.

23. (p. 620) People extend effort to regulate the space around their bodies. Each person has an invisible "spatial envelope" that defines his or her _____ _____ and extends "I" or "me" boundaries past the skin.

24. (p. 620) There are unspoken rules covering the interpersonal distance considered appropriate for formal business, casual conversation, waiting in line with strangers, etc. The study of rules for the personal use of space is called _____.

25. (p. 621) Hall identified four basic zones related to personal space. These norms apply to face-to-face interactions in North American culture. Norms for personal distance may vary greatly in other cultures. For instance, in many Middle Eastern countries, people hold their faces _____ apart when conversing.

26. (p. 621) One of the basic zones identified by Hall is called _____ _____ which extends about 18 inches out from the skin. Entry here is reserved for special people or circumstances.

27. (p. 621) _____ _____ is the distance maintained in comfortable interaction with friends. It extends from about $1\frac{1}{2}$ to 4 feet from the body.

28. (p. 621) _____ _____ involves separation of about 4 to 12 feet. This distance is used in conducting impersonal business and at casual social gatherings.

29. (p. 621) _____ _____ involves separation by more than 12 feet. Here interactions take on a decidedly formal quality.

30. (p. 622) Attribution is the process of making inferences about behavior. For example, if a person tastes food, then salts it, you might assume the food needed salt. You have attributed the person's actions to an _____ cause. If a person salts food before tasting it, you might assume the person really likes salt. You have attributed the person's actions to an _____ cause.

31. (p. 622) Several factors greatly influence attribution, for example _____. If a person always avoids you, coincidence is ruled out and you may attribute that person's actions to a dislike for you.

32. (p. 622) However, the individual's avoidance of you may simply reflect shyness if that person avoids others too. Here is where _____ enters the picture. If the person only avoids you, you will probably assume that the individual dislikes you.

33. (p. 622) To infer cause, we typically have to take into account the behavior of the _____, the _____ of the action, and the _____ in which the action occurs. For example, how you interpret a compliment will depend on each of these factors.

34. (p. 622) In making attributions, we are very sensitive to _____ demands. When a person is quiet and polite in church, It tells us little about the individual's personality because the environment demands such behavior.

35. (p. 622) When situational demands are quite strong, we tend to _____ claims that a person's actions are internally caused. For example, you may question the sincerity of professional athletes who endorse commercial products.

36. (p. 622) _____ (or agreement) is another factor affecting attribution. When many people engage in the same behavior, it implies that behavior has an external cause.

78. (p. 623) Steven Berglas has done studies showing that _____-_____ occurs when a person does not feel very confident about succeeding. In order to protect a fragile self-image, people sometimes arrange to be evaluated while "handicapped" so that they can attribute failure to the handicap.

38. (p. 622) If they succeed, their self-image gets a boost because they succeeded under conditions that everyone knows hinder performance. Thus, self-handicappers try to arrange a _____-_____ situation.

39. (p. 622) There are many ways to arrange self-handicapping. Procrastination on school assignments may be one. However, drinking _____ is among the most popular—and dangerous.

40. (p. 623) Most of us have used self-handicapping at times when we faced a difficult challenge and were doubtful about success. It becomes a problem when it turns into a _____, rather than a way of coping with life's harshest demands.

41. (p. 623) We tend to infer causes for behavior from circumstantial evidence. In doing so we often make mistakes. The most common error, called the _____ _____ error, is to attribute the actions of others to _____ causes, while attributing our own behavior to _____ causes.

42. (p. 623) Psychologists have found that we consistently attribute the behavior of others to their _____, motives, and _____ traits. We tend to find external explanations for our own behavior.

43. (p. 623) Attribution research has uncovered an interesting double standard for men and women. In a study by Deaux and Emswiller, male and female subjects were asked to rate the cause of success for a male or female whom they overheard perform extremely well on a perception task. Both men and women attributed male success to _____ and female performances mainly to _____.

44. (p. 624) We have already observed that the need to _____ appears to be a basic human characteristic. This fact is probably true because it helps us meet needs for approval, support, friendship and information. We also seek company to alleviate fear or anxiety.

45. (p. 624) This notion was experimentally demonstrated in a study of subjects waiting to participate in an experiment using painful electric shock. Most subjects chose to wait with other people in circumstances similar to their own. Here, as with other threatening or unfamiliar situations, _____ _____ serve as a guide for behavior.

46. (p. 624) Social psychologist Leon Festinger was among the first to point out that _____ _____ fills needs for social comparison and that when there are no objective standards, we turn to others to evaluate our feelings, actions, opinions, or abilities.

47. (p. 625) Festinger emphasized that social comparisons are not made randomly, or on some ultimate scale. Useful personal evaluation requires comparison with people of _____ _____.

48. (p. 625) _____ _____ theory holds that a desire for self-evaluation determines what groups are joined, and provides a general motive for associating with others.

49. (p. 625) _____ _____ is the basis for most voluntary social relationships.

50. (p. 625) Social psychologist Elliot Aronson lists several things that determine with whom you are likely to become friends. One of these factors is simple _____ _____. Our friends are selected more on the basis of opportunity.

51. (p. 625) Nearness plays a powerful role in making friends. For example, in one study of friendship patterns in a campus married-student housing complex, it was found that the _____ people lived to each other, the more likely they were to be friends.

52. (p. 625) A main reason for proximity's effect is that it increases _____ of _____ between people. A variety of experiments show that we are generally attracted to people with whom we have had frequent contact.

53. (p. 625) Another important factor is _____ _____. Beautiful people are consistently rated more attractive than those of average appearance. This is an example of the halo effect.

54. (p. 625) This factor seems to be more an influence for women than men. For instance, there is a strong relationship between physical beauty in women and their frequency of _____. Such is not the case for men.

55. (p. 625) Among older married couples there is a tendency for attractive women to be paired with highly _____ men with high _____.

56. (p. 625) For men, however, there is _____ relationship between attractiveness and the achievement of status.

57. (p. 625) Beauty is a factor mainly in _____ _____. Later, more substantial personal qualities become important. It takes more than appearance to make a lasting relationship.

58. (p. 625) Even first impressions are less affected by beauty if we are given information about a person that helps us see her or him as an _____.

59. (p. 626) _____ is another quality which leads to interpersonal attraction. We are attracted to those who are talented, but human. This was demonstrated in an experiment in which students listened to a supposed candidate for the "College Quiz Bowl" who was either intelligent or average and who was either clumsy or not. The superior but clumsy student was rated as most attractive.

60. (p. 626) A fourth important factor in attraction is _____. Three important dimensions of this are commonality in age, sex, and race.

61. (p. 626) One of the most consistent findings about interpersonal attraction is that people with similar _____, interests, attitudes, _____, and personalities are attracted to each other. This is probably at least partially due to the reinforcing value of seeing our beliefs and attitudes affirmed by others.

62. (p. 626) _____ percent of all people in Western societies marry at some point. We tend to marry someone who is like us in almost every way, a pattern called _____.

63. (p. 626) A variety of studies show that people who marry are highly similar in _____, _____, race, religion, and _____ background.

64. (p. 626) In addition, the correlation of attitudes and opinions for married couples is _____. For mental abilities it is _____. And for socioeconomic status, height, weight, and eye color it is _____.

65. (p. 626) You are more likely to choose someone similar to yourself as a mate than someone very different. This is probably a good thing, because personality traits tend to be closely matched for husbands and wives whose marriages are most _____.

66. (p. 626) In the United States both men and women agree that the following qualities are most important when looking for a mate: kindness and understanding, _____, _____ personality, good _____, adaptability, and _____ attractiveness.

67. (p. 626) Men rank physical attractiveness as the _____ most important feature, whereas women rank it _____. Men rank good earning capacity _____, while women rank it _____.

68.   (p. 626) A major step toward friendship usually involves _____-_____, the process of letting yourself be known to others.

69.   (p. 626) The ability to reveal your thoughts and feelings to others is a basic skill for developing close relationships. Lack of self-disclosure is frequently associated with _____ and _____.

70.   (p. 626) Experimental work confirms that we more often reveal ourselves to people we _____ than to those we find less attractive.

71.   (p. 626) There are definite norms about when self-disclosure is acceptable and when it is not. Moderate self-disclosure leads to _____ (a return in kind) while _____ gives rise to suspicion and reduced attraction.

72.   (p. 627) When self-disclosure proceeds at a _____ pace, it is accompanied by growing trust and intimacy. Thus, as friends talk, they influence each other in ways that gradually deepen the level of liking, trust, and self-disclosure.

73.   (p. 627) As relationships progress, quite often they can be understood in terms of maximizing rewards while minimizing "costs." According to _____ _____ theory, we unconsciously weigh such rewards and costs. For a relationship to last, it must be profitable for both parties.

74.   (p. 627) Generally, the balance between rewards and costs in a relationship is judged in comparison with what we have come to expect from past experience. The personal standard used to evaluate rewards and costs is called the _____ _____.

75.   (p. 627) The comparison level is _____ for a person who has had a history of satisfying and rewarding relationships. It is _____ for someone whose relationships have been unsatisfying.

76.   (p. 627) The decision to continue a relationship is affected by one's personal comparison level. For example, a lonely person, or one whose friendships have been marginal, might stay in a relationship that others would consider _____.

77.   (p. 627) Zick Rubin has provided some answers to the similarities and differences between love and liking. He found that scores for love of partner and love of friend _____ more than those for liking.

78.   (p. 627) Dating couples liked and loved their partners, but most liked their friends. Women, however, were a little more "_____" of their friends than were men.

79.   (p. 627) Romantic love, in contrast to simple liking, usually involves deep _____ _____ of the lovers. In other words, lovers (unlike friends) attend almost exclusively to one another.

80.   (p. 627) Consistent with this idea, Rubin found that couples scoring high, compared to low, on the love scale spend _____ time gazing into each other's eyes.

81.   (p. 628) There is growing evidence that early attachments to caregivers can have a lasting impact on how we relate to others. For example, recent studies of dating couples have identified secure, _____, and _____ attachment patterns similar to those seen in early development.

82. (p. 628) A _____ attachment style is marked by caring, intimacy, supportiveness, and understanding in love relationships.

83. (p. 628) Secure persons regard themselves as _____, good-natured, and likable and they think of others as generally well-intentioned, _____, and trustworthy.

84. (p. 628) People with a secure attachment style find it relatively easy to get close to others. They are comfortable _____ on others and having others _____ on them. In general, they don't worry too much about being abandoned or about having someone become too emotionally close to them.

85. (p. 628) An _____ attachment style reflects a fear of intimacy and a tendency to pull back when things don't go well in a relationship. Such individuals are suspicious, aloof, and skeptical about love.

86. (p. 628) People with an avoidance attachment style tend to see others as either unreliable or overly eager to _____ to a relationship. As a result, they find it hard to completely _____ and depend on others. Basically, they want to avoid intimacy.

87. (p. 628) Persons who have an _____ attachment style are marked by mixed emotions about relationships. Conflicting feelings of affection, anger, emotional turmoil, physical attraction, and doubt leave them in an unsettled, ambivalent state.

88. (p. 628) Often, ambivalent persons regard themselves as _____ and _____. They tend to see their friends and lovers as unreliable and unable or unwilling to commit themselves to lasting relationships.

89. (p. 628) Ambivalent persons worry that their romantic partners don't really love them or may leave them. While they want to be extremely _____ to their partners, they are also preoccupied with doubts about the partner's dependability and trustworthiness.

90. (p. 629) It appears that we use early attachment experiences to build _____ _____ about affectionate relationships. Later, we use these models as a sort of blueprint for forming, maintaining, and breaking bonds of love and affection.

91. (p. 629) One of the most heavily researched topics in social psychology concerns the effects of _____ _____. When people interact, they almost always effect another's behavior.

92. (p. 629) As one example of social influence, consider the street-corner experiment in which either a well-dressed man or one dressed in shabby clothes crossed against the light. _____ people followed the well-dressed man than the other.

93. (p. 629) In another sidewalk experiment, groups of various sizes all looked at a sixth-floor window across the street on cue. A camera recorded the number of passersby who also stopped to stare. The _____ the influencing group, the more people were swayed to join in staring at the window.

94. (p. 629) Social influence ranges from simple suggestions to intensive indoctrination (brainwashing). Everyday behavior is probably most influenced by group pressures for _____.

95. (p. 629) Conformity situations develop when individuals become aware of differences between themselves and group actions, norms, or values. One of the better known experiments on group pressures for conformity was staged by Soloman _____ in the early 195Os.

96. (p. 630) In Asch's experiment, subjects were asked to select a comparison line that was closest in length to a standard. Six other people gave their answers prior to the subject. It was found that subjects conformed to the answers of the accomplices on about _____-_____ of the critical trials.

97. (p. 630) Furthermore, _____ percent of those tested yielded at least once. This result is underscored by the fact that other people tested alone erred in less than _____ percent of their judgments.

98. (p. 630) A variety of experiments have shown that people with high needs for _____ or certainty are more likely to be influenced. People who are _____, low in self-_____, or who are concerned with the opinions or _____ of others are also more susceptible.

99. (p. 630) Psychologist Irving Janis blames the Bay of Pigs and similar fiascoes on _____—a compulsion by decision makers to maintain each other's approval, even at the cost of critical thinking.

100. (p. 630) The core of groupthink is misguided group _____, which prevents members from "rocking the boat" or questioning weak arguments and sloppy thinking. The resulting _____ _____ and self-censorship causes members to believe that there is a greater agreement and unanimity than actually exists.

101. (p. 630) To prevent groupthink fiascoes Janis suggests that group leaders should:
    1) define each group member's role as that of _____ _____.
    2) avoid stating their _____ in the beginning;
    3) state the problem _____, and without bias;
    4) invite outside colleagues or different members each meeting to play _____ _____.

102. (p. 630) In addition, Janis suggests that there should be a "_____-_____" meeting to reevaluate important decisions. That is, each decision should be reached twice.

103. (p. 630) In most of our experiences with groups, we have been rewarded with acceptance and approval for conformity, and threatened with rejection or ridicule for non-conformity. These reactions are called _____ _____.

104. (p. 630) This notion is illustrated by later experiments in which Asch made up groups of six real subjects and one trained dissenter. When "Mr. Odd" announced his wrong answers, he was greeted with _____ and sidelong _____.

105. (p. 631) Several factors, besides importance of the group, can affect the degree of conformity. In Asch's experiment, the _____ of the majority made a difference. The number of conforming subjects increased dramatically as the majority increased from 2 to _____ people, but beyond this, an increase in numbers produced little effect.

106. (p. 631) Even more important than the size of the majority is its _____. Having at least one person in your corner can greatly reduce pressures to conform. In terms of numbers, a unanimous majority of 3 is _____ powerful than 8 with 1 dissenting.

107. (p. 631) In understanding the ways in which people are able to influence each other, it is helpful to distinguish among five types of social power:
    1) _____ power lies in the ability to reward a person for complying with desired behavior
    2) _____ power is based on the ability to punish a person for failure to comply
    3) _____ power comes from acceptance of a person as an agent of an established social order
    4) _____ power is based on respect for, or identification with, a person or a group
    5) _____ power is based upon recognition that another person has knowledge or expertise necessary for achieving a goal

108. (p. 631) A person who has power in one situation may have very little in another. In those situations where a person has power, he or she is described as an _____.

109. (p. 632) Psychologist Stanley Milgram has conducted a provocative series of studies on _____. The experiment involved "teachers" who gave "learners" progressively more intense shocks for errors in list memorization.

110. (p. 632) "Teachers" thought that "learners" were actually being shocked using voltage ranging from 15 to 450 volts. In the first experiment, Milgram found that _____ percent of those tested obeyed his instructions to continue shocking learners up to 450 volts. Virtually no one stopped short of 300 volts.

111. (p. 633) In a follow-up experiment, Milgram conducted the same study in a shabby office building to control for the prestige of Yale University. Here _____ percent of the "teachers" obeyed his instructions.

112. (p. 633) Milgram found that distance between the "teacher" and the "learner" was important. When subjects were in the same room as the "learner," only _____ percent were fully obedient.

113. (p. 633) When they were face-to-face with the "learner" and required to force his hand down on a shock plate, only _____ percent obeyed.

114. (p. 633) Milgram also found that distance from the authority had an effect. When the experimenter delivered his orders over the phone, only _____ percent obeyed.

115. (p. 634) On a more positive note, when real subjects saw two other "teachers" (both actors) resist orders and walk out of the experiment, only _____ percent continued to obey.

116. (p. 634) In conformity situations the pressure to "get in line" is usually indirect. When an authority commands obedience, the pressure is direct and difficult to resist. A third possibility involves the term _____ which has been used to describe situations in which a person with little or no authority makes a direct request to another person.

117. (p. 634) A person who agrees to a small request is later more likely to comply with a larger demand. This is the formal definition of the _____-_____-_____-_____ effect.

118. (p. 634) As an example of this principle, if someone asked you to put a large, ugly sign in your front yard you would refuse. If, however, you had first agreed to put a small sign in your window, you would later be much _____ _____ to allow the big sign to be placed in your yard.

119. (p. 634) Robert Cialdini and his associates coined the term _____-_____-_____-_____ effect to describe the reverse of the foot-in-the-door effect. On some occasions the best way to get a person to agree to a small request is to first make a major request.

120. (p. 635) The _____-_____ technique consists of getting a person committed to act and then making the terms of acting less desirable. Automobile dealers are notorious for using this method. They get the customer to agree to buy at an attractively low price, then use various techniques to bump the price up before the sale is concluded.

121. (p. 636) Thomas Moriarty has demonstrated excessive, passive compliance under realistic conditions. Two subjects (one an accomplice) were placed in a small room and given a difficult task to complete. The accomplice turned on a tape-player at full volume for 17 minutes and would turn it off only after a third request. In this experiment, _____ percent of the subjects said nothing.

122. (p. 636) It is possible that the passivity observed in Moriarty's study is limited to the experimental setting. However, when Moriarty and his students staged loud conversations in theaters or libraries, very _____ protested.

123. (p. 636) In other _____ experiments, people were accosted in phone booths. The experimenter explained that he had left a ring in the booth and asked if the subject had found it. When the subject said "no," the experimenter demanded that the subject empty his pockets. Most did.

124. (p. 637) Joseph Wolpe, and others, have pioneered a therapeutic technique called _____ _____ using group exercises, videotapes, mirrors, and staged conflicts.

125. (p. 637) The first step to becoming more assertive is to convince yourself of three basic rights: the right to _____, to _____, and to right a wrong.

126. (p. 637) A basic distinction can be made between _____-_____ and _____ behavior. Aggression is an attempt to get one's own way no matter what. Assertion techniques emphasize firmness, not attack.

127. (p. 638) To improve your assertiveness, begin by _____ how you would confront a situation. Practice is the key.

128. (p. 638) Working in front of a mirror or _____ _____ the scene with a friend (where they take the part of the person or situation you wish to confront) can help.

129. (p. 638) Another important principle is _____; continue practice until your responses become almost automatic. Such practice will help prevent becoming flustered in the actual situation.

130. (p. 638) One more technique is the _____ _____. Simple persistence through repeating a request as many times and as many ways as necessary is often all that is needed for successful self-assertion.

131. (p. 638) Responding assertively to verbal aggression (a "put-down") is a real challenge. A good way to respond is offered by psychologists Robert Alberti and Michael Emmons:
    1) if you are wrong _____ it;
    2) acknowledge the other person's _____;
    3) assert yourself about the other person's _____; and
    4) briskly end the interchange.

132. (p. 639) A _____ _____ is any social situation that rewards actions that have undesired effects in the long run. For instance, many people are enticed into drinking too much at parties because their pleasure is immediate and their discomfort comes later.

133. (p. 639) Behavioral traps that involve _____ of people, or social traps, are especially interesting. In a social trap no one individual acts against the group interest, but if many people act alike, collective harm is done.

134. (p. 640) Social traps are especially damaging when we are enticed into overuse of _____ resources. This is what happened a few years ago to crab fishermen in Alaska.

135. (p. 640) Garrett Hardin calls situations like the one involving the Alaskan crab fishermen the _____ of the _____: each person acts in his or her self-interest, which causes the resource to be used up so that everyone suffers.

136. (p. 640) In some situations it might be possible to dismantle social traps by rearranging rewards and costs. There is evidence that in real social traps people are _____ _____ to restrain themselves when they believe others will to.

SELF-TEST

1. (p. 618) Social psychology is
    a. the study of how people behave in the presence (actual or implied) of others
    b. the study of how intrapsychic factors affect social organization
    c. a branch of psychology primarily interested in cross-cultural social studies
    d. a division of psychology closely aligned with economics that seeks to understand how the economy affects social behavior

2. (p. 618) True-False. Ascribed roles are those which are attained voluntarily, such as wife, teacher, scientist, etc.

3. (p. 618) Which of the following was *not* true of Philip Zimbardo's simulated "prison" experiment?
    a. Normal, healthy, male college students were paid to serve as "inmates" and "guards" in a simulated prison.
    b. Each day the guards tormented the prisoners with more frequent commands, insults, and demeaning tasks.
    c. After a month the experiment had to be halted, so the final results were never known.
    d. Zimbardo interpreted problems during the experiment to be a result of the powerful roles prisoners and guards assumed.

4. (p. 618) Which of the following is *not* true of groups and their members?
    a. Position in a group determines a member's status.
    b. Group structure is the organization of roles, communication pathways, and power in the group.
    c. Group norms are standards of conduct that prescribe appropriate behavior in a given situation.
    d. Group cohesiveness refers to ongoing patterns of group life where such representations as language, marriage customs, and sex roles are passed from one generation to another.

5. (p. 619) True-False. In an experiment on group norms, Sherif found that when two or more people were asked to observe the autokinetic effect and give judgments on the degree of light drift, their answers tended to rapidly converge.

6. (p. 620) The study of the interpersonal use of space is called
    a. spacology   c. proxemics
    b. kinesthetics   d. distances

7. (p. 620) Which of the following is *not* a correct match?
    a. public distance—formal interactions such as speeches, lectures, and business meetings
    b. social distance—maintained in comfortable interactions with friends
    c. intimate distance—the most private personal space reserved for special people or circumstances
    d. personal distance—extends from about $1^1/_2$ to 4 feet from the body; basically keeps people within "arm's reach" of each other

8. (p. 622) Which of the following is *not* true of attribution?
    a. When situational demands are quite strong we tend to more easily accept that a person's actions are internally caused.
    b. Attributions can be either external or internal.
    c. Distinctiveness and consistency are two factors that greatly influence attribution.
    d. To infer causes, we typically take into account the behavior of the actor, the object of the action, and the setting in which the action occurs.

9. (p. 623) True-False. Psychologists have found that we consistently attribute the behavior of others to internal causes, while attributing our own behavior to external causes.

10. (p. 623) In a study by Deaux and Emswiller, subjects who overheard a man or a woman perform extremely well on a perception task
    a. attributed male success to luck and female success to skill
    b. attributed success for both sexes to luck when they themselves were female
    c. attributed success for both sexes to skill when they themselves were male
    d. attributed male success to skill and female success to luck

11. (p. 624) True-False. When a situation is threatening or unfamiliar, we tend to rely more upon our own judgment rather than making social comparisons.

12. (p. 625) Which of the following is *not* a factor in interpersonal attraction?
    a. physical reciprocity   c. physical proximity
    b. similarity   d. physical attractiveness

13. (p. 626) True-False. In an experiment studying the role of competency in degree of interpersonal attraction, Aronson found that superior but clumsy individuals were more attractive than individuals who were only superior.

14. (p. 626) Which of the following is *not* true of self-disclosure?
    a. Moderate self-disclosure leads to reciprocity and is a major step toward friendship.
    b. Rapid and unexpected self-disclosure produces immediate trust and intimacy.
    c. Overdisclosure gives rise to suspicion and reduced attraction.
    d. We more often reveal ourselves to persons we like than to those we find less attractive.

15. (p. 627) According to social exchange theory, a relationship must be _____ to endure.
    a. meaningful   c. profitable
    b. reasonable   d. positive

16. (p. 627) True-False. Dating couples like and love their partners, but mostly like their friends, according to the research of Zick Rubin.

17. (p. 627) True-False. Men tend to rate their friends higher on the love scale than do women.

18. (p. 629) Which of the following is *not* true of Soloman Asch's experiments on conformity?
    a. It was found that 75 percent of all subjects yielded to group judgment at least once.
    b. The tendency to agree with the group's judgment continued to increase as the size of the group increased, even up to as many as 8 people.
    c. It showed that even more important than the size of the group was the unanimity.
    d. Punishment for conformity as seen in the experiment are referred to as negative sanctions.

19. (p. 630) When decision making compulsively maintains personal status and conformity at the expense of critical thinking, we speak of
    a. proxemics   c. role conflict
    b. obedience   d. groupthink

20. (p. 631) Of the following, which is *not* a type of social power?
    a. coercive   c. referent
    b. legitimate   d. adaptive

21. (p. 632) Milgram's original study of obedience to authority found that _____ percent of those tested obeyed by going all the way up to the 450 volt shock level.
    a. 25   c. 65
    b. 50   d. 75

22. (p. 633) True-False. Milgram found in the obedience experiment that distance from the "learner" and the experimenter had less effect on subjects' tendency to obey than did the setting where the experiment was conducted.

23. (p. 634) Which of the following is *not* a factor that helps explain whether a person will comply with a request?
    a. the door-in-the-face effect   c. the passivity effect
    b. the low-ball technique   d. the foot-in-the-door effect

24. (p. 634) When the best way to get a person to agree to a small request is to first make a major request, this situation involves
    a. the door-in-the-face effect   c. external cause attribution
    b. obedience through authority   d. the foot-in-the-door effect

25. (p. 636) True-False. Investigators such as Thomas Moriarty have discovered that passivity is a relatively minor problem in our society today.

26. (p. 637) Convincing yourself that you have the right to refuse, to request, and to right a wrong is a basic principle of
    a. conformity
    b. assertiveness training
    c. groupthink
    d. proxemics

27. (p. 637) True-False. Assertion is a direct, honest expression of feelings and desires that is not exclusively self-serving. Aggression is an attempt to get one's own way no matter what and does not take into account the feelings or rights of others.

28. (p. 638) You simply restate your request as many times and as many ways as necessary in an assertiveness technique called
    a. the broken record
    b. redundant rehearsal
    c. overlearning
    d. the perpetual motion machine

29. (p. 639) A _____ _____ is any situation that rewards actions that have undesired effects in the long run.
    a. role conflict
    b. coercive power
    c. social trap
    d. situational demand

30. (p. 640) When people share a scarce resource, each person may act in his or her self-interest, which causes the resource to be used up so that everyone suffers. Garrett Hardin has called such situations
    a. groupthink
    b. tragedy of the commons
    c. overdisclosure
    d. polarized cooperation

APPLYING YOUR KNOWLEDGE

1. Get together with several of your classmates and friends and try the "chain letter" experiment first conducted by Stanley Milgram. Can you manage to get a letter delivered to a person about whom you know only their name, address, and occupation? Set up a system so you can keep track of how many "links" were required to complete the mailing.

2. Get together with classmates and design a test situation similar to the Asch experiments to measure conformity. You can use students from another class who are unfamiliar with these experiments to be your subjects. Manipulate the number of "subjects" who give their responses prior to the real subject's. What happens when you arrange things so that there isn't unanimity before the real subject gives his or her response?

ANSWERS—PROGRAMMED REVIEW

1. 5; seven
2. Social psychology
3. Culture
4. position; Roles
5. ascribed; achieved
6. role conflict
7. six
8. reality
9. destructive roles
10. status
11. 77; 38
12. older; younger
13. high; lower
14. men; women
15. structure
16. Organized; Informal
17. cohesiveness
18. power
19. norms
20. more
21. autokinetic effect
22. converge
23. personal space
24. proxemics
25. inches
26. intimate distance
27. Personal distance
28. Social distance
29. Public distance
30. external; internal
31. consistency
32. distinctiveness
33. actor; object; setting
34. situational
35. discount
36. Consensus
37. self-handicapping
38. no-lose
39. alcohol
40. habit
41. fundamental attribution; internal; external
42. wants; personality
43. skill; luck
44. affiliate

45.	social comparisons
46.	group membership
47.	similar backgrounds
48.	Social comparison
49.	Interpersonal attraction
50.	physical proximity
51.	closer
52.	frequency of contact
53.	physical attractiveness
54.	dating
55.	educated; incomes
56.	little
57.	initial acquaintance
58.	individual
59.	Competence
60.	similarity
61.	backgrounds; beliefs
62.	Ninety; homogamy
63.	age, education; ethnic
64.	.5; .4; .3
65.	stable
66.	intelligence; exciting; health; physical
67.	third; sixth; eleventh; eighth
68.	self-disclosure
69.	unhappiness; loneliness
70.	like
71.	reciprocity; overdisclosure
72.	moderate
73.	social exchange
74.	comparison level
75.	high; lower
76.	unacceptable

77.	differed
78.	loving
79.	mutual absorption
80.	more
81.	avoidant; ambivalent
82.	secure
83.	friendly; reliable
84.	depending; depend
85.	avoidant
86.	commit; trust
87.	ambivalent
88.	misunderstood; unappreciated
89.	close
90.	mental models
91.	social influence
92.	More
93.	larger
94.	conformity
95.	Soloman Asch
96.	one-third
97.	75; 1
98.	structure; anxious; confidence; approval
99.	groupthink
100.	loyalty; conformity pressures
101.	critical evaluator; preferences; factually; devil's advocate
102.	second-chance
103.	group sanctions
104.	laughter; glances
105.	size; 3
106.	unanimity; more

107.	reward; coercive; legitimate; referent; expert
108.	authority
109.	obedience
110.	65
111.	48
112.	40
113.	30
114.	22
115.	10
116.	compliance
117.	foot-in-the-door
118.	more likely
119.	door-in-the-face
120.	low-ball
121.	80
122.	few
123.	naturalistic
124.	assertiveness training
125.	refuse; request
126.	self-assertion; aggressive
127.	rehearsing
128.	role playing
129.	overlearning
130.	broken record
131.	admit; feelings; aggression
132.	social trap
133.	groups
134.	scarce
135.	tragedy of the commons
136.	more likely

ANSWERS—SELF-TEST

1.	a	6.	c	11.	False	16.	True	21.	c	26.	b
2.	False	7.	b	12.	a	17.	False	22.	False	26.	True
3.	c	8.	a	13.	True	18.	b	23.	c	28.	a
4.	d	9.	True	14.	b	19.	d	24.	a	29.	c
5.	True	10.	d	15.	c	20.	d	25.	False	30.	b

ACROSS

1. he was "shocked" by his findings on obedience
5. group _____ is the degree of attraction among group members
6. _____-in-door effect used by sales people
7. in describing personal space one's _____ extends about 18" from skin
9. study of rules for personal use of space
11. people look "flat"—lectures, formal speeches are made at _____ distance
14. he studied role playing in prison
15. he used lines in his conformity experiment

DOWN

2. this "effect" occurs with pinpoint of light in darkened room
3. distance maintained in interacting with friends
4. this conformity factor has been blamed for Susan B. Anthony dollar and Bay of Pigs invasion
8. "important people" keep _____ distance by using a desk in their offices
10. an ongoing pattern of life passed from one generation to the next
12. after slamming this in your face one may be more willing to agree to a lesser demand
13. assuming attractive people are intelligent, honest, etc., may exemplify this effect

Social Psychology II

CONTENTS

TERMS AND CONCEPTS

attitude
misdirected letter technique
"mean" world view
conviction
open-ended interview
social distance scale
attitude scales
reference group
persuasion
role playing
cognitive dissonance
brainwashing
cults
love bombing
prejudice
discrimination
racism
scapegoating
personal prejudice
group prejudice
authoritarian personality
ethnocentric
F scale

dogmatism
social stereotypes
symbolic prejudice (modern prejudice)
status inequalities
equal-status contact
superordinate goals
nuclear winter
jigsaw classroom
aggression
frustration-aggression hypothesis
aggression cues
weapons effect
social learning theory
aggressive pornography
anger control
prosocial behavior
bystander apathy
empathic arousal
empathy-helping relationship
multiculturalism
individuating information
social competition
sociobiology

IMPORTANT INDIVIDUALS

Christine Hansen
Ranald Hansen
Theodore Newcomb
James McConnell
Margaret Singer

Gordon Allport
Theodore Adorno
Milton Rokeach
Jane Elliot
Gerald Clore

Muzafer Sherif
Elliot Aronson
Konrad Lorenz
Neil Malamuth
Ed Donnerstein

Leonard Eron   John Darley   Patricia Devine
Bibb Latané   John Dovido   Edward Wilson

PROGRAMMED REVIEW

1. (p. 645) An _____ is a mixture of belief and emotion that predisposes a person to respond to other people, objects, or institutions in a positive or negative way. They summarize past experience and predict or direct future actions.

2. (p. 645) For example, wrongly-addressed letters have been sent to households in an approach known as the _____ _____ technique; the number of letters returned to the post office demonstrates that actions are closely connected to attitudes.

3. (p. 645) There are three ways in which attitudes are expressed. Most attitudes have a _____ component, an _____ component, and an _____ component.

4. (p. 645) Attitudes are acquired in several basic ways. Sometimes attitudes come from _____ _____ with the object of the attitude. Attitudes are also learned through _____ with others holding the same attitude.

5. (p. 645) Attitudes are also acquired through the effects of _____ _____. For example, if both parents belong to the same political party, chances are _____ out of 3 that the child will belong to the same party as an adult.

6. (p. 646) Group membership certainly influences attitudes. In one classic study, discussion groups were formed to discuss the case of a juvenile delinquent. As a test of group pressures on attitudes, a person was introduced into the group who advocated extreme punishment. At first the group directed _____ of the comments to him.

7. (p. 646) If the deviate stuck to his position, he was almost completely _____ from further conversation. And later, the deviate was strongly _____ in ratings made by other group members.

8. (p. 646) Attitudes are also influenced by the _____ _____. Ninety-nine percent of American homes have a television set, which is on an average of almost 7 hours a day.

9. (p. 646) The values and information thus channeled into homes exerts a powerful influence on attitudes. For instance, the heavy dose of violence on television may lead viewers to develop a "mean" world view. That is, frequent viewers _____ their chances of being involved in a violent incident. Also, heavy viewers are _____ likely to feel that most people can be trusted.

10. (p. 646) Some attitudes are formed quite inadvertently through _____ _____. If you have limited contact with an event and it is negative, you will tend to take an unduly dim view of all such events.

11. (p. 647) Christine and Ranald Hansen staged an experiment to assess whether watching _____ _____ _____ affect viewers' attitudes toward antisocial behavior.

12. (p. 647) College students watched videos that were either high in antisocial content or neutral. Afterward, they "accidentally" saw one of two "job applicants" make an obscene gesture. On later evaluations, subjects who saw the neutral videos liked the questionable job applicant _____ and gave him _____ ratings.

13. (p. 647) As the Hansens point out, music elicits positive emotional responses. If these good feelings are repeatedly associated with antisocial themes, quite likely _____ _____ will strengthen positive attitudes toward antisocial behavior.

14. (p. 647) Attitudes are only one of the many determinants of actions in a particular situation. The _____ _____ of one's actions weigh heavily on the choices that are made.

15. (p. 647) Also important is our expectation of how others will _____ our actions. By taking this factor into account, researchers have been able to predict family planning choices, adolescent alcohol use, reenlistment in the National Guard, voting on a nuclear power plant initiative, and so forth.

16. (p. 647) Finally, we must consider the effect that long-standing _____ have on action. There are often large differences between attitudes and behavior—particularly between privately held attitudes and public behavior.

17. (p. 647) Barriers to action typically fall when a person holds an attitude with _____— meaning that an attitude is of central importance to a person.

18. (p. 647) The issues about which you have conviction are those that you feel strongly about (emotionally), that you believe are important, that you frequently think about and discuss, and that you feel knowledgeable about. Such attitudes often lead to major changes in _____ _____.

19. (p. 647) Attitudes can be measured in several different ways. For example, a person might be asked in an _____-_____ _____ some question that requires the statement of an attitude.

20. (p. 647) Another approach which has been very useful as a measure of attitudes towards groups is a _____ _____ _____. This tool measures the degree to which a person would be willing to have contact with another person.

21. (p. 647) Use of _____ _____ is one of the most common approaches to attitude measurement. These scales consist of statements expressing various possible attitudes on an issue. By computing scores on all items, people can be rated for overall acceptance or rejection of a particular issue.

22. (p. 647) Although attitudes are relatively stable, they are subject to change. Some attitude change can be understood in terms of the concept of _____ _____ whose values and attitudes are seen by individuals as being relevant to their own.

23. (p. 648) In the 1930s, Theodore Newcomb studied real life attitude change among students at Bennington College. He found that most students shifted significantly toward more _____ attitudes (in line with those of the college) during their 4 year stay. Those who did not change kept parents and hometown friends as their primary reference group.

24. (p. 649) While all students could count the college and their families as membership groups, only one or the other tended to become their _____ group.

25. (p. 649) _____ refers to any deliberate attempt to change attitudes by imparting information. It can range from the daily blitz of media commercials to personal discussion among friends.

26. (p. 648) In most cases the success or failure of attempted persuasion can be understood by considering the characteristics of the _____, the _____, and the _____.

27. (p. 648) Research on persuasion suggests that attitude change is encouraged when:
   1) the communicator is likable, trustworthy, an expert on the topic, and similar to the audience in some respect;
   2) the message appeals to emotions, particularly to _____ or _____;
   3) the message also provides a clear course of action that will, if followed, reduce fear or anxiety;
   4) the message states clear-cut _____;
   5) The message is backed up by facts and statistics;
   6) _____ sides of the argument are presented (for a well-informed audience);
   7) only one side of the argument is presented (for a poorly informed audience);
   8) the persuader appears to have nothing to _____ if the audience accepts the message;
   9) the message is repeated as frequently as possible.

28. (p. 648) Emotional experiences can drastically alter attitudes. To actively bring about attitude change, psychologists have experimented with creating similar experiences through _____ _____.

29. (p. 648) For example, women who were known smokers and asked to play the role of a cancer patient drastically _____ their smoking. Control subjects who listened to a tape recording of similar information showed _____ change.

30. (p. 649) The influential theory of _____ _____ states that contradicting or clashing thoughts cause discomfort. If individuals can be made to act in a way that is inconsistent with their attitudes, they may change their thoughts to bring them into agreement with their actions.

31. (p. 649) Cognitive dissonance theory suggests that people _____ information contradictory to their attitudes and _____ new information that contradicts ideas they already hold.

32. (p. 649) The amount of _____ or _____ for acting contrary to one's attitudes and beliefs can influence the amount of dissonance created.

33. (p. 649) An example is shown in the now classic study where college students performed an extremely boring task. Students paid $20.00 for lying to others about the experiment rated the experiment as boring. But those paid only $1.00 actually rated the experience as being _____ and _____.

34. (p. 649) Other studies indicate that we are especially likely to experience dissonance when we _____ an event to occur that we would rather hadn't.

35. (p. 650) Many people associate brainwashing with techniques used by the Chinese on American prisoners during the Korean War. Through various types of "thought reform," the Chinese were able to coerce approximately _____ percent of these prisoners to sign false confessions.

36. (p. 650) James McConnell has studied brainwashing and notes that it requires a _____ audience. Complete control over the environment allows a degree of psychological manipulation that would be impossible in a normal setting.

37. (p. 651) Furthermore, McConnell has identified three techniques used for brainwashing: (1) the target person is _____ from other people who would support his original attitudes; (2) the target person is made completely _____ on his or her captors for satisfaction of need; (3) the indoctrinating agent is in a position to _____ the target person for changes in attitude or behavior.

38. (p. 651) Brainwashing typically begins with an attempt to make the target feel completely helpless. Physical and psychological abuse serve to _____ former values and beliefs. _____ comes about when exhaustion, etc., become unbearable. When prisoners break, they are suddenly rewarded with praise, food, etc. This condition serves to _____ new attitudes.

39. (p. 651) In most cases, the dramatic shift in attitudes brought about by brainwashing is _____. Most "converted" prisoners of the Korean War eventually reverted to their original beliefs and repudiated their indoctrinators.

40. (p. 651) A _____ is a religious group in which the leader's personality is more important than the beliefs he or she preaches. Members of such groups give their allegiance to this person and follow his or her dictates almost without question.

41. (p. 651) Psychologist Margaret Singer has studied and aided hundreds of former cult members. Her interviews reveal that, in recruiting new members, such groups make use of a powerful blend of guilt, manipulation, _____, deception, _____, and escalating commitment.

42. (p. 651) She found that some of those interviewed were suffering from marked psychological distress when they joined a cult, but most were simply undergoing a period of mild _____, indecision, or _____ from family and friends.

43. (p. 651) Cult members try to catch potential converts at a time of need, especially when a sense of _____ will be attractive to the convert.

44. (p. 651) Many converts were approached just after a romance had broken up, or when they were struggling with exams, were trying to choose a major, or were simply at loose ends. Another dangerous time is when young adults are having difficulty becoming _____ from their family.

45. (p. 651) Conversion is achieved through various steps. Often it begins with intense displays of affection and understanding called "_____ _____."

46. (p. 651) Next comes _____ from non-cult members along with drills, _____, and _____ to wear down physical and emotional resistance and to generate commitment.

47. (p. 651) At first recruits make small commitments, then larger commitments are encouraged, with making a major commitment usually the final step. Such major public commitments create such a powerful _____ _____ effect it becomes virtually impossible for converts to admit that they have made a mistake.

48. (p. 651) Once in the group, members are cut off from former _____ groups, and the cult can control the flow and interpretation of information to them. Members are physically and psychologically _____ from their former value systems and social structure.

49. (p. 651) Most former members mention _____ and _____ as the main reasons for not leaving even when they wished they could.

50. (p. 652) _____ is a negative attitude or a prejudgment tinged with unreasonable suspicion, fear, or hatred.

51. (p. 652) Prejudice that is institutionalized and backed by social power structures is referred to as _____, _____, or _____ depending on the group affected.

52. (p. 652) Both racial prejudice and institutionalized racism may lead to _____, behavior that prevents individuals from doing things they might reasonably expect to be able to do.

53. (p. 652) Discrimination is often deeply woven into society. For instance, in one study 15 college students who had received no traffic citations in the previous year attached bumper stickers supporting a militant black organization to their cars. During the next 17 days the group received a total of _____ traffic citations.

54. (p. 652) One theory suggests that prejudice is a form of _____, a type of displaced aggression in which hostilities generated by frustration are redirected to other targets.

55. (p. 652) This notion was demonstrated in a study in which subjects at a summer camp were asked to rate Mexicans and Japanese before and after a frustrating test. Subjects in this study consistently rated members of these two groups _____ after being frustrated.

56. (p. 652) Like other attitudes, the development of prejudice sometimes can be traced to _____ _____ with members of the rejected group. The tragedy in such cases is that once such antipathy is established, it prevents accepting additional, more positive experiences which could reverse the damage.

57. (p. 652) Psychologist Gordon Allport has concluded that there are two important sources of prejudice. _____ _____ occurs when members of another racial or ethnic group represent a threat to the individual's security or comfort.

58. (p. 652) Another type of prejudice occurs simply through the individual's adherence to _____ _____. You may have no personal reason for disliking out-group members but do so because you are expected to.

59. (p. 652) Theodore Adorno has conducted extensive research on what he calls the _____ _____.

60. (p. 653) Originally this work was directed at studying anti-Semitism as a means of understanding the social climate of World War II Germany. In the process, Adorno discovered that people who are prejudiced against one group tend to be prejudiced against all _____-_____.

61. (p. 653) This personality has a collection of personal attitudes and values marked by rigidity, inhibition, and oversimplification. Authoritarians tend to be very _____, considering their own national, ethnic, or religious group to be superior to others.

62. (p. 653) To measure these qualities, the "_____" scale was created. (F stands for facism.) It is made up of statements concerning power, authority, and obedience with which the person can agree or disagree.

63. (p. 653) As children, authoritarians were usually severely _____ and learned to fear _____ (and to covet it) at an early age.

64. (p. 653) The "F" scale tends to list statements slanted toward politically conservative authoritarians, but as noted by psychologist Milton Rokeach, rigid and authoritarian personalities can be found at both ends of the political spectrum. For this reason, Rokeach prefers to describe rigid and intolerant thinking as _____—an unwarranted positiveness or certainty in matters of belief or opinion.

65. (p. 653) It is still true that racial prejudice runs deep in many nations. For example, one experiment showed that liberal white male college students were _____ _____ to give shocks (under laboratory conditions) to a black victim than to a white victim.

66. (p. 654) An unfortunate by-product of group membership is that it often limits contact with people in other groups. Also, groups themselves may come into conflict. In many cases, intergroup conflict is accompanied by _____ images of out-group members and by bitter prejudice.

67. (p. 654) A social stereotype is an oversimplified image of people who fall into a particular category. They may be either _____ or _____ images.

68. (p. 654) Over the past 34 years the overall trend has been toward a _____ in negative stereotypes. However, belief in the existence of some negative traits has _____.

69. (p. 654) In the years since 1967, there have been further declines in negative stereotypes, but also some recent _____. Some observers believe that racial and ethnic prejudice is on the upswing in the United States.

70. (p. 655) Today's racism often takes the form of _____ _____ (also called "modern prejudice"). That is, many people realize that crude and obvious racism is socially unacceptable. However, this may not stop them from expressing prejudice in disguised forms.

71. (p. 655) Stereotypes held by the prejudiced tend to be unusually _____. When given a list of negative statements about other groups, prejudiced individuals agree with most of them, even though they are often _____ statements.

72. (p. 655) In one study, prejudiced subjects even expressed negative attitudes towards two _____ groups, the "Piraneans" and the "Danirians."

73. (p. 655) When a prejudiced person meets a pleasant or likable member of a rejected group, the out-group member tends to be perceived as "an _____ to the _____," not as a denial of the stereotype.

74. (p. 655) In times of war, _____ images are used to make it seem that a nation's enemies deserve hatred and even death. For many soldiers such images provide a degree of emotional insulation that makes it easier to harm another human.

75. (p. 655) During times of peace such images can lead to dangerous misperceptions of the motives and actions of other nations. For example, a study found that college students thought that actions (both good and bad) supposedly performed by the Soviet Union were based on _____ motives; when the same actions were attributed to the U.S., students assumed the motives were _____.

76. (p. 655) In a unique experiment, teacher Jane Elliot sought to give pupils a direct experience with prejudice. Brown-eyed children were discriminated against while blue-eyed children received special rewards. Within two days there was a very clear effect. It was possible to get children to hate each other because of their eye color and _____ _____— differences in the power, prestige, or privileges of two or more persons or groups.

77. (p. 656) Progress has been made through attempts to educate the general public about the lack of justification for prejudicial attitudes. Changing the _____ component of an attitude has long been known to be one of the most direct means of changing the entire attitude. Thus, when people are made aware that minority group members share the same goals, feelings, etc. as they do, intergroup relations may be improved.

78. (p. 656) Several lines of thought suggest that more frequent _____-_____ contact between groups in conflict should reduce prejudice and stereotypes.

79. (p. 656) Much evidence suggests it does. For example, in one early study white women living in integrated and segregated housing projects were compared for changes in attitude toward their black neighbors. In the integrated project, whites showed a _____ change in attitude toward members of the other racial group. Those in the segregated project showed no change or actually became _____ prejudiced than before.

80. (p. 656) Other studies of mixed race groups have concluded that personal contact with a disliked group will induce friendly interracial behavior, respect, and liking. However, these benefits occur only personal contact is on an _____ footing.

81. (p. 656) Gerald Clore and his associates set up a unique children's summer camp to further this idea. Blacks and whites were equally divided in number, power, privileges, duties. Testing showed that the children had significantly more _____ attitudes toward opposite-race children after the camp than they did before.

82. (p. 656) Psychologist _____ _____ and his associates conducted an ingenious experiment with ll-year-old boys at a summer camp to study prejudice and how to overcome it.

83. (p. 656) After strong intragroup loyalties had been established, it was found that having leaders from each group meet did nothing to reduce hostilities. Also, just getting the groups together did little. It was only when the boys had to work together that hostilities subsided. This result indicates that the creation of _____ _____ serves to help restore relations between groups.

84. (p. 657) A superordinate goal exceeds or overrides all others. One such example on a global scale might be desire to avoid nuclear holocaust and _____ _____—the devastating drop in global temperature that would follow the fire storms, dust, and smoke of a nuclear strike and result in global crop failure, famine, and death on a large scale.

85. (p. 657) Contrary to the hopes of many, _____ public schools often has little positive effect on racial prejudice. In fact, prejudice may be made worse, and the self-esteem of minority students frequently decreases.

86. (p. 657) Minority group children often enter newly integrated schools unprepared to compete on an equal footing. This fact, plus the intense competition in classrooms, almost guarantees that children will _____ learn to like and understand each other.

87. (p. 657) Elliot Aronson has pioneered a way to apply the concept of superordinate goals to ordinary classrooms by making people mutually _____.

88. (p. 657) Aronson has successfully created "_____" classrooms that emphasize cooperation rather than competition. Each child is given a "piece" of the information needed to prepare for a test which he or she must teach to the other members of five and six children groups.

89. (p. 657) Compared to children in traditional classrooms, children in jigsaw groups were _____ prejudiced, they liked their classmates _____, they had _____ positive attitudes toward school, their _____ improved, and their self-esteem increased.

90. (p. 658) Also, brighter students are not sacrificed by this method. High achievers working in cooperative groups never do _____ than they do when learning alone, and often they do _____.

91. (p. 658) The human capacity for aggression is staggering. It has been estimated that during the 125-year period ending with World War II, _____ million humans were killed by other humans (an average of nearly one person per minute).

92. (p. 658) Furthermore, _____ now ranks as a major cause of death in the United States. Also, more than 1.4 million American children are subjected to physical _____ by parents each year.

93. (p. 658) Over _____ percent of all married American men and women have physically attacked their spouse.

94. (p. 658) Ethologists such as Konrad Lorenz feel that humans are naturally aggressive, having inherited a "_____ _____" from our animal ancestors.

95. (p. 658) Lorenz believes that aggression is a _____ rooted behavior observed in all animals, including humans. Also, he feels that humans lack certain innate patterns that in other animal species _____ aggression.

96. (p. 658) Despite problems with this instinctive view, there is evidence that a biological basis for aggression may exist. Physiological studies have shown that there are brain areas capable of triggering or ending aggressive behavior. Also, there is a relationship between aggression and such physical factors as _____ (low blood sugar), _____, and specific _____ injuries and disorders.

97. (p. 658) None of the above conditions can be considered a direct cause of aggression. Instead they probably lower the _____ for aggression, making hostile behavior more likely to occur.

98. (p. 658) The effects of alcohol and other drugs provide another indication of the role of the brain and biology in violence and aggression. A variety of studies show that alcohol is involved in large percentages of _____ and _____ crimes.

99. (p. 659) The fact that we are biologically _____ of aggression does not mean that aggression is _____, or "part of human nature." This point was made in 1986 by a group of 20 eminent scientists.

100. (p. 659) The _____-_____ hypothesis states that frustration is closely associated with aggression. However, frustration does not always lead to aggression.

101. (p. 659) Frustration may lead to _____ responding, or perhaps to a state of "learned helplessness." Also, aggression can occur in the absence of frustration.

102. (p. 659) Frustration probably encourages aggression because it is _____ (uncomfortable). Many experiments have shown that unpleasant stimuli tend to increase aggression.

103. (p. 659) Aversive stimuli probably raise overall arousal levels so that we become more sensitive to _____ _____. Such signals may be internal (angry thoughts for instance) or external (for example, a raised middle finger).

104. (p. 660) One study showed that even inanimate objects may serve as cues for aggression. Subjects were ridiculed and shocked by another person. Just before they got a chance to "return the favor," they saw either a couple of badminton rackets, or a shotgun and a revolver. The latter subjects gave _____ shocks to the person who had angered them.

105. (p. 660) The implication of this _____ _____ seems to be that the symbols and trappings of aggression encourage aggression.

106. (p. 660) The simplest and one of the most widely accepted explanations of aggression comes from _____ _____ theory which holds that we learn to be aggressive by observing aggression in others.

107. (p. 660) According to this view, aggression must be learned. This, quite likely, is why being physically abused as a child is strongly related to _____ behavior in adulthood.

108. (p. 660) Considered in such terms, it is no wonder there is so much violence in America. A _____ crime occurs every 54 seconds, 40 percent of the population own _____, _____ percent agree that "when a boy is growing up, it is very important for him to have a few fist-fights," and _____ percent of the population admit to having slapped or kicked another person.

109. (p. 660) Until recently, most evidence regarding the effects of pornography suggested it has no major adverse effects when stimuli involved are merely erotic or sexual in content. However, in the last 10 years there has been an increase in _____ pornography in the mass media (referring to depictions in which violence, threats, or obvious power differences are used to force someone to engage in sex).

110. (p. 660) Researchers Neil Malamuth and Ed Donnerstein have concluded that a principal finding of such studies is that aggressive-pornographic stimuli do _____ aggression by males against females.

111. (p. 660) Social learning theory implies that watching violence may _____ aggression, rather than _____ _____ aggressive urges. This is supported by Leonard Eron's finding that one of the best predictors of how aggressive a young man would be at age 19 was the violence of the TV programs he preferred when he was 8 years old.

112. (p. 660) Other researchers have found that viewers who watch violent videotapes have _____ aggressive thoughts. This is significant since we know that violent thoughts often precede violent actions.

113. (p. 660) Some psychologists have succeeded in teaching people to control their anger and aggressive impulses. The key to _____ _____ is the fact that people who respond calmly to upsetting situations tend to see them as problems to be solved.

114. (p. 661) To limit anger, people are taught to:
    1) define the problem as _____ as possible.
    2) make a _____ of possible solutions.
    3) _____ the likely success of each solution.
    4) choose a solution and try it.
    5) assess how successful the solution was and make adjustments if necessary.

115. (p. 661) In studying the Kitty Genovese case, psychologists Bibb Latané and John Darley reached several conclusions. Failure to help (bystander apathy) was related to the _____ of people present.

116. (p. 661) Everyone thought someone else would help. Personal responsibility was spread so thin that no one took action. This result indicates that the more potential helpers present, the _____ the chances that help will be given.

117. (p. 662) There are four "decision pints" individuals must pass through before giving help. First, they must _____ that something is happening. Next, they must _____ the event as an emergency. Then they must take _____, and finally they must select a course of _____.

118. (p. 662) Latané and Darley suggest that if a sidewalk is crowded and you are in trouble, few people will even see you because of widely accepted norms to carefully "keep their eyes to themselves." Laboratory experiments show that _____ students working in groups exposed to a thick cloud of smoke actually noticed it, while _____ students working alone noticed it immediately.

119. (p. 662) After subjects in groups noticed the smoke, they coolly surveyed the reactions of others while being surveyed themselves. Until someone acts, _____ _____ acts.

120. (p. 662) Groups limit assuming responsibility by causing a _____ of _____. They produce a feeling that no one is personally responsible for helping.

121. (p. 663) This idea was demonstrated in an experiment in which students took part in a group discussion from separate rooms over an intercom system. Actually there was only one real subject, the others were confederates. During the discussion one of the confederates simulated an epileptic-like seizure and called out for help. In the six-person groups, over one-_____ of the subjects took no action at all. Some subjects in the three-person groups failed to respond, but those who were alone took action immediately.

122. (p. 663) It is not always clear how all the group factors combine in emergency situations however. In one naturalistic experiment, when a "victim" "passed out" in a subway car, he received _____ help when carrying a cane than a liquor bottle. However, most people were willing to help in either case.

123. (p. 663) Psychologist John Dovido has summarized some of the major factors that affect helping behavior. Many studies suggest that when we see a person in trouble, this tends to cause heightened _____.

124. (p. 663) This aroused, keyed-up feeling can motivate us to give aid, but only if the rewards of helping outweigh the costs. Higher costs almost always _____ helping.

125. (p. 663) Potential helpers may also feel _____ arousal. This means that they empathize with the person in need or feel some of the person's pain, fear, or anguish. Helping is much more likely when we are able to take the perspective of another person and feel sympathy for their plight.

126. (p. 663) Recent research has shown that empathy really does unleash altruistic motivation based on _____ and _____. Most helping, including such altruistic acts as making donations or being kind, are motivated by a true desire to relieve the distress of others.

127. (p. 663) Empathic arousal also motivates helping. In fact, feeling a connection to the victim may be one of the most important factors in helping. This, perhaps, is why being in a good mood also increases helping. When we are feeling successful, happy, or fortunate, we may also feel more _____ to others.

128. (p. 663) In summary, there is a strong _____-_____ relationship. We are most likely to help someone in need when we "feel for" that person and experience emotions such as empathy, sympathy, and compassion.

129. (p. 663) There is also evidence that people who see others helping are more likely to offer help themselves. For example, motorists were much _____ _____ to stop to help a woman fix a tire when they had just passed another woman being helped by someone.

130. (p. 663) Also, persons who give help in one situation tend to perceive themselves as _____ people. This change in self-image encourages them to help in other situations.

131. (p. 663) One more point is that norms of _____ encourage us to help others who have helped us. For all these reasons, helping others not only assists them directly, it encourages others to help too.

132. (p. 664) By the year 2000 about _____-_____ of the population in the United States will be African American, Latino, Asian American, and Native American. In some large cities "minority" groups are already the majority.

133. (p. 665) Psychologists believe that we must learn to respect and appreciate cultural differences. _____, as this is called, gives equal status to different ethnic, racial, and cultural groups. It is a recognition and acceptance of human diversity.

134. (p. 665) There are still lingering biases. Recent surveys show that white Americans are more supportive than ever of efforts to improve racial integration. Yet, many continue to hold _____ images of blacks, Latinos, Asians and other racial and ethnic minorities.

135. (p. 665) Patricia Devine has shown that a decision to forsake prejudice does not immediately eliminate prejudiced _____ and _____.

136. (p. 665) Non-prejudiced people may continue to respond emotionally to members of other racial or ethnic groups. Quite likely this reflects lingering stereotypes and prejudices learned in _____.

137. (p. 665) For many people the process of prejudice reduction begins with sincerely accepting values of _____ and _____. Such persons feel pangs of guilt, conscience, or self-criticism when they have intolerant thoughts or feelings which motivate them to try to alter their own biased reactions.

138. (p. 665) _____ make the social world more manageable. But placing people in categories almost always causes them to appear more similar than they really are.

139. (p. 665) Both prejudiced and non-prejudiced persons are equally aware of stereotypes. Non-prejudiced persons, however, work hard to actively inhibit stereotyped thoughts and to emphasize _____ and _____.

140. (p. 665) We are most tempted to apply stereotypes when we only have minimal _____ about a person. Stereotypes allow us to make inferences about what a person is like and how he or she will act. Unfortunately, these inferences are usually _____.

141. (p. 665) One of the best antidotes for stereotypes is _____ _____. Anything that helps you see a person as an individual, rather than as a member of a group or a particular social category tends to negate stereotyped thinking.

142. (p. 665) The effects of individuating information is shown in a Canadian study of English-speaking students in a French language program. Students who were "immersed" became more _____ toward French Canadians. They were _____ likely to say they had come to appreciate and like French Canadians; they were _____ willing to meet and interact with them; and they saw themselves as _____ different from French Canadians.

143. (p. 665) You may believe that the world is sufficiently just so that people generally get what they deserve. Such just-world beliefs can directly increase _____ thinking. They can lead us to assume that minority groups wouldn't be in lower socio-economic positions in relatively high numbers if they weren't _____ in some way.

144. (p. 666) If you hold strong stereotypes about members of various groups, a vicious cycle can be set up. You may treat such people in a way that is consistent with your stereotypes. If the other person is influenced by your behavior, he or she may act in ways that seem to match your stereotype. This creates a _____-_____ _____ and reinforces your belief in the stereotype.

145. (p. 666) Some conflicts between groups cannot be avoided. What can be avoided is unnecessary _____ _____. This concept refers to the fact that some individuals seek to enhance their self-esteem by identifying with a group. This works only if the group can be seen as superior to others.

146. (p. 666) Because of social competition, groups tend to view themselves as _____ than their rivals. In a recent survey, every major ethnic group in the United States rated itself as _____ than any other group.

147. (p. 666) A person who has high _____-_____ does not need to treat others as inferior in order to feel good about himself or herself. Also, it is not necessary to _____ other groups in order to feel positive about one's own group identity.

148. (p. 666) We live in a society that puts a premium on _____ and individual effort. But being placed in competition with others fosters desires to demean, defeat, and vanquish them. When we _____ with others we tend to share their joys and suffer when they are in distress.

149. (p. 666) The importance of cultural awareness often lies in subtleties and details. For example, lack of cultural awareness on both sides helped trigger an African-American boycott of _____ grocers in New York City in 1991.

150. (p. 667) Sociobiologists such as Edward Wilson believe that competition, war, territoriality, aggression, sibling rivalry, conformity, male-female differences, fear of strangers, altruism, and many other behaviors are "in our _____."

151. (p. 667) The core idea in _____ is that social behavior evolves in ways that maximize the fitness of a species for survival. For instance, animals that compete successfully for food, territory, mates, and so forth are more likely to survive and reproduce. Thus, competitiveness gradually becomes a trait of following generations.

152. (p. 667) Sociobiologists explain altruistic actions like the selfless heroism of a soldier by pointing out that such actions help improve chances that an individual's _____ will survive.

153. (p. 668) Sociobiology seems to say that genes manipulate our behavior to ensure their survival. It's major strength is that it helps relate human _____ to _____. Its major weakness is that it probably overstates its case. The degree of _____ _____ assumed by sociobiologists is so extreme that even most biologists question it.

154. (p. 668) The danger inherent in sociobiology is that it can be used to support the social _____ _____. By defining human nature as relatively fixed and unchanging, sociobiology discourages attempts to change current cultural practices.

SELF-TEST

1.   (p. 645) A(n) _____ is a mixture of belief and emotion that predisposes a person to respond to other people, objects, or institutions in a positive or negative way.
     a.   role   c.   belief
     b.   attitude   d.   emotion

2.   (p. 645) Of the following, which is *not* a component of attitudes?
     a.   emotional   c.   belief
     b.   residual   d.   action

3.   (p. 645) Of the following, which is *not* a factor that influences attitude formation?
     a.   group membership   c.   chance happenings
     b.   order of birth   d.   child rearing

4. (p. 646) Which of the following is *not* true of mass media such as television as they relate to attitude formation?
    a.   Images of male and female roles, and racial or ethnic minorities are fairly and accurately represented.
    b.   Heavy doses of violence may lead viewers to develop a "mean" world view.
    c.   Heavy viewers are less likely to feel that most people can be trusted.
    d.   Frequent viewers overestimate their chances of being involved in a violent accident.

5. (p. 647) Which of the following is a reason why some attitudes are acted upon and others are not?
    a.   immediate consequences   c.   evaluation by others
    b.   habits   d.   all of the above

6. (p. 647) Of the following, which is a method for measuring attitudes?
    a.   open-ended interviews   c.   attitude scales
    b.   social distance scales   d.   all of the above

7. (p. 647) True-False. Reference groups are control groups used in social psychology experiments.

8. (p. 648) Which of the following would *not* be expected to encourage attitude change through persuasion?
    a.   The communicator is dissimilar to the audience.
    b.   The persuader appears to have nothing to gain if the audience accepts the message.
    c.   The message is repeated as frequently as possible.
    d.   The message appeals to emotions, particularly anxiety and fear.

9. (p. 648) True-False. Role playing can be an effective technique for bringing about attitude changes.

10. (p. 649) Which of the following defines the position of cognitive dissonance theory?
    a.   Tensions between groups in conflict can be reduced through cognitive mediation.
    b.   Cognitive attitudes can best be understood by understanding dissonance between the communicator, message, and audience.
    c.   If behavior is inconsistent with attitudes it will produce discomfort that may change thoughts to bring them into agreement with actions.
    d.   Frustration produces increased arousal which may result in heightened tendencies toward aggression.

11. (p. 649) True-False. Cognitive dissonance theory holds that people tend to seek out new information that contradicts ideas they already possess.

12. (p. 649) True-False. Cognitive dissonance theory states that the amount of reward or justification for acting contrary to one's beliefs determines the amount of dissonance created.

13. (p. 651) Which of the following is *not* a brainwashing technique identified by McConnell?
    a.   The indoctrinating agent is in a position to reward the "target" for changes in attitudes or behavior.
    b.   The "target" person is isolated from other people who would support his or her original attitudes.
    c.   The "target" is made completely dependent on his or her captors for satisfaction of needs.
    d.   The captors try to reason with the "target" rather than using psychology or physical abuse.

14. (p. 651) True-False. One of the most frightening aspects of brainwashing is that it is often permanent because of the intensity of indoctrination.

15. (p. 651) In her work with cult members, Margaret Singer found that most converts joined
    a. when they were suffering marked psychological distress
    b. because they enjoyed the initiation process
    c. when they were undergoing a period of mild depression, indecision, or alienation from family and friends
    d. because they were kidnapped and literally forced to join

16. (p. 651) True-False. Love bombing is a brainwashing technique often used by various cults.

17. (p. 651) True-False. Previous cult members most often mention guilt and fear as the main reasons for remaining with the group.

18. (p. 652) Which of the following is *not* true of the authoritarian personality?
    a. Authoritarians were usually severely punished as children and learned to fear and covet authority.
    b. Authoritarians tend to focus their rejection on only one group rather than on all out-groups.
    c. Authoritarians tend to be very ethnocentric.
    d. It can be described as a collection of personal attitudes and values marked by rigidity, inhibition, and oversimplification.

19. (p. 652) The "F" scale is used to measure
    a. qualities of the authoritarian personality
    b. susceptibility to brainwashing
    c. social status
    d. aggression

20. (p. 654) Which of the following is *not* true of social stereotypes and the individuals who hold them?
    a. Social stereotypes are oversimplified images of people who fall into a particular category.
    b. Stereotypes are always negative.
    c. Stereotypes held by the prejudiced tend to be unusually irrational.
    d. Pleasant or likeable members of a rejected group are seen as "an exception to the rule," not a disconfirmation of the stereotype.

21. (p. 655) Jane Elliot's experiment with blue-and brown-eyed children showed the importance of _____ in the development of prejudice.
    a. status inequalities   c. racism
    b. social stereotypes   d. insubordinate goals

22. (p. 656) True-False. Research on racism indicates that more frequent equal-status interaction between groups in conflict helps reduce stereotypes and prejudice.

23. (p. 656) True-False. One technique for minimizing hostilities between conflicting groups is to create superordinate goals for the groups to work on together.

24. (p. 657) Which of the following is *not* true of "jigsaw" classrooms developed by Aronson?
    a. They facilitate individual effort and independence.
    b. They involve giving students individual pieces of information they must teach to other students.
    c. Children in such classrooms are less prejudiced and like their classmates more than in traditional classrooms.
    d. Students in such classrooms do not have to compete against each other for attention and grades in the same way they do in traditional classrooms.

25. (p. 658) True-False. Some ethologists, such as Konrad Lorenz, feel that human aggression is an innate predisposition.

26. (p. 658) True-False. When frustration encourages aggression it probably does so by raising overall arousal levels so that we become more sensitive to cues for aggression.

27. (p. 659) The idea that aggression is learned is an explanation offered by
    a. the frustration-aggression hypothesis
    b. cognitive dissonance theory
    c. social learning theory
    d. Lorenz's ethological theory

28. (p. 660) True-False. Most recent evidence suggests that viewing aggressive pornography has no major adverse effects.

29. (p. 660) The key to anger control is
    a. the principle of fairness—if you keep your temper so will the other person
    b. the fact that people who respond calmly to upsetting situations tend to see them as problems to be solved
    c. letting hostilities out all at once so that less-control is necessary for day-to-day frustrations
    d. suppressing anger until it is appropriate to release it in safe or nonviolent situations

30. (p. 661) True-False. According to Latane and Darley, one reason for bystander apathy is that bystanders are inhibited from taking action by the presence of others.

31. (p. 662) Which of the following is *not* a "decision point" individuals must pass through before giving help?
    a. They must define the event as an emergency.
    b. They must notice that something is happening.
    c. They must diffuse responsibility for action.
    d. They must select a course of action.

32. (p. 662) True-False. Groups are often less likely than individuals to offer help in an emergency due to the problem of diffusion of responsibility.

33. (p. 667) Which of the following is *not* true of sociobiology?
    a. It states that social behavior evolves in ways that maximize the fitness of a species for survival.
    b. Its danger lies in the fact that it can be used to support the social status quo.
    c. Its major strength is that it takes a strong position of biological determinism.
    d. It postulates that altruistic actions occur because this helps improve chances that an organism's kin will survive.

APPLYING YOUR KNOWLEDGE

1. Next time you're in a lively conversation about some issue that most people seem to agree on, try taking a directly opposite point of view. Do you find that the other participants react to you in ways similar to those observed in Schachter's experiment on group forces that operate to bring about conformity?

2. Public images of "the enemy" tend to depict our national rivals as evil or less than human. For example, media images of the Soviets have long depicted them as inhumane, vicious torturers who enjoy murder and inflicting pain. Do a research project to assess how the Iraqis were depicted during the recent Middle East crisis. Do such images relate to psychological studies of prejudice, racism, or stereotypes?

3.   Multiculturalism gives equal status to different ethnic, racial, and cultural groups. To learn more about various cultures in your area, contact some of the social and political groups that represent minorities. What are some of the important local issues facing such groups? Are there things you can do to help?

ANSWERS—PROGRAMMED REVIEW

1.   attitude
2.   misdirected letter
3.   belief, emotional, action
4.   direct contact; interaction
5.   child rearing; 2
6.   all
7.   excluded; rejected
8.   mass media
9.   overestimate; less
10. chance conditioning
11. rock music videos
12. less; lower
13. classical conditioning
14. immediate consequences
15. evaluate
16. habits
17. conviction
18. personal behavior
19. open-ended interview
20. social distance scale
21. attitude scales
22. reference groups
23. liberal
24. reference
25. Persuasion
26. communicator; message; audience
27. fear, anxiety; conclusions; both; gain
28. role playing
29. reduced; little
30. cognitive dissonance
31. avoid; reject
32. reward; justification
33. pleasant, interesting
34. cause
35. 16
36. captive
37. isolated; dependent; reward
38. unfreeze; Change; refreeze
39. temporary
40. cult
41. isolation; fear

42. depression, alienation
43. belonging
44. independent
45. love bombing
46. isolation; disciplines, rituals
47. cognitive dissonance
48. reference; isolated
49. fear, guilt
50. Prejudice
51. racism, sexism, ageism
52. discrimination
53. 33
54. scapegoating
55. lower
56. direct experiences
57. Personal prejudice
58. group norms
59. authoritarian personality
60. out-groups
61. ethnocentric
62. F
63. punished; authority
64. dogmatism
65. more willing
66. stereotyped
67. positive, negative
68. decrease; increased
69. reversals
70. symbolic prejudice
71. irrational; conflicting
72. nonexistent
73. exception to the rule
74. dehumanizing
75. sinister; positive
76. status inequalities
77. belief
78. equal-status
79. favorable; more
80. equal
81. positive
82. Muzafer Sherif
83. superordinate goals
84. nuclear winter
85. integrating
86. not
87. interdependent

88. jigsaw
89. less; more; more; grades
90. worse; better
91. 58
92. murder; abuse
93. 25
94. killer instinct
95. biologically; inhibit
96. hypoglycemia; allergy; brain
97. threshold
98. murders; violent
99. capable; inevitable
100. frustration-aggression
101. stereotyped; absence
102. aversive
103. aggression cues
104. stronger
105. weapons effect
106. social learning
107. violent
108. violent; firearms; 70; 18
109. aggressive
110. increase
111. increase; drain off
112. more
113. anger control
114. precisely; list; Rank
115. number
116. lower
117. notice; define; responsibility; action
118. few; most
119. no one
120. diffusion of responsibility
121. third
122. more
123. arousal
124. decrease
125. empathic
126. sympathy, compassion
127. connected
128. empathy-helping
129. more likely
130. helpful

131. fairness
132. one-third
133. Multiculturalism
134. negative
135. thoughts, feelings
136. childhood
137. tolerance, equity
138. Stereotypes
139. fairness, equality

140. information; wrong
141. individuating information
142. positive; more; more; less
143. prejudiced; inferior
144. self-fulfilling prophecy
145. social competition
146. better; better

147. self-esteem; degrade
148. competition; cooperate
149. Korean
150. genes
151. sociobiology
152. kin
153. behavior; biology; biological determinism
154. status quo

ANSWERS—SELF-TEST

1.	b	7.	False	13.	d	19.	a	25.	True	31.	c
2.	b	8.	a	14.	False	20.	b	26.	True	32.	True
3.	b	9.	True	15.	c	21.	a	27.	c	33.	c
4.	a	10.	c	16.	True	22.	True	28.	False		
5.	d	11.	False	17.	True	23.	True	29.	b		
6.	d	12.	True	18.	b	24.	a	30.	True		

ACROSS

3. a negative attitude held toward members of various "out-groups"
4. viewpoint that social behaviors have roots in heredity
8. cognitive _____ means clashing thoughts
12. _____ goals restored relations between "Rattlers" and "Eagles"
13. this is strongly connected to frustration
14. Reverend Jim Jones was leader of one of these

DOWN

1. these classrooms emphasize cooperation rather than competition
2. she studied and helped cult members
3. deliberate attempt to change attitudes by imparting information
5. she was murdered in Queens, N.Y.
6. form of forced attitude change dependent on control of target person's environment
7. first step in brainwashing technique
9. _____ behavior is helping behavior
10. final step in brainwashing technique
11. the _____ learning theory holds we learn to be aggressive via observing others' aggressive acts

CHAPTER 25

Sexuality and Gender

CONTENTS

The Development of Sex Differences
Sexual Behavior
Human Sexual Response
Attitudes and Sexual Behavior
Sexual Problems
Touching—Does It Always Have Sexual Implications?

TERMS AND CONCEPTS

primary sexual characteristics
secondary sexual characteristics
menarche
ovulation
menopause
sex hormones
gonads
estrogens
androgens
testes
ovaries
adrenal glands
testosterone
hermaphroditism
progestin
androgenital syndrome
biological biasing effect
gender identity
sex role socialization
sex roles
instrumental behaviors
expressive behaviors
sexual scripts
erogenous zones
nocturnal emissions
castration
sterilization

masturbation
homosexuality
lesbianism
ego-dystonic homosexuality
homophobia
sexual response phases
    excitement
    plateau
    orgasm
    resolution
ejaculation
refractory period
acquaintance (date) rape
sexually transmitted disease (STD)
acquired immune deficiency syndrome (AIDS)
human immunodeficiency virus (HIV)
erectile dysfunction
primary impotence
secondary impotence
sensate focus
premature ejaculation
squeeze technique
retarded ejaculation
general sexual dysfunction (frigidity)
orgasmic dysfunction
vaginismus

IMPORTANT INDIVIDUALS

John Money
Ethel Albert
Margaret Mead
Alfred Kinsey
John Gagnon

Morton Hunt
William Masters
Virginia Johnson
Shere Hite
Helen Kaplan

Bryan Strong
Christine DeVault
Sidney Jourard

PROGRAMMED REVIEW

1. (p. 672) _____ _____ characteristics refer to the sexual and reproductive organs themselves: the penis; _____, and _____ in males; and the ovaries, _____, and _____ in females.

2. (p. 673) _____ _____ characteristics appear at puberty in response to hormonal signals from the pituitary gland.

3. (p. 673) In females, they include development of the _____, the broadening of the _____, and other changes in body shape; for males, they include development of facial and body _____, and deepening of the _____.

4. (p. 673) These changes signal physical readiness for reproduction. This maturity is especially evident in the female _____ (the onset of menstruation).

5. (p. 673) Soon after menarche, monthly _____ begins. This refers to the release of ova (eggs) from the ovaries. From this time until _____ (the end of regular monthly fertility cycles), women can bear children.

6. (p. 673) Both primary and secondary sexual characteristics are closely related to the action of _____ _____ (chemical substances secreted by glands of the endocrine system).

7. (p. 673) The _____, or sex glands, affect sexual development by secreting female hormones called _____ and male hormones called _____.

8. (p. 673) The gonads in the male are the _____, and in the female, the _____.

9. (p. 673) The _____ glands, located above the kidneys, also supply sex hormones in both males and females and add to the development of secondary sexual characteristics at puberty.

10. (p. 673) All individuals normally produce both estrogens and androgens, the proportion of which influences sexual differences. The development of male or female anatomy is largely due to the presence or absence—before birth—of _____, one of the androgens.

11. (p. 674) _____ _____ is determined at the instant of conception: two X chromosomes initiate development of a female; an X chromosome plus a Y chromosome produces a male.

12. (p. 674) For the first _____ weeks of prenatal development, there is no difference between genetically male and female embryos. However, if a Y chromosome is present, testes develop and supply testosterone, stimulating male development.

13. (p. 674) In the absence of testosterone, the embryo will develop female reproductive organs and genitals, regardless of _____ _____. Nature's primary impulse, then, is to make a female.

14. (p. 674) A genetic male will fail to develop male _____ if too little testosterone is formed during prenatal growth.

15. (p. 674) Even if testosterone is present, an inherited _____ _____ may exist, again resulting in female development.

16. (p. 674) Hormonal problems before birth may result in _____ where dual or ambiguous sexual anatomy occurs.

17. (p. 674) For instance, a developing female may be masculinized by _____ (a drug given to prevent miscarriage).

18. (p. 674) Masculinization can also result when normal amounts of estrogen are produced, but a genetic abnormality causes the adrenal glands to release too much androgen. This condition is called the _____ _____ and can produce a female child with male genitals.

19. (p. 675) Some of these children are reared as male. Usually, however, the condition is detected and corrected by _____. If necessary, extra estrogen may be given after birth.

20. (p. 675) In addition to determining genital development, the interplay of sex hormones before birth may also permanently "sex-type" the _____ which is thought to alter later chances of developing masculine or feminine characteristics.

21. (p. 675) Although hormonal action is important in human sexual development, evidence suggests that most sex-linked behavior is _____.

22. (p. 675) Still, some researchers feel that prenatal exposure to androgens or estrogens exerts a biological _____ _____ on later psychosexual development in humans.

23. (p. 675) Support for this comes from the work of John Money who has shown that women exposed to androgens before birth are typically "_____" during childhood. However, after adolescence, the girls evidence traditional interests in marriage and motherhood.

24. (p. 675) Some researchers feel that biology underlies male-female differences in thinking abilities. They claim that women are more often "_____-brained" and thus are better at _____ skills and rote learning, while men are more "_____-brained" and thus do better on _____ tasks.

25. (p. 675) Others strongly reject this theory. To them, such claims are based on shaky evidence and sexist thinking. After all, they point out, men (as a group) do only _____ better on spatial tasks and women are only _____ better at language skills.

26. (p. 675) The most telling recent evidence may be the fact that differences between male and female scores on the _____ _____ Test are rapidly declining. This is probably best explained by the growing similarity of male and female interests, experiences, and educational goals.

27. (p. 676) The one thing that is certain in the gender debate is that males and females are _____ more than they are _____. There is no biological basis for the unequal treatment women have often faced at work, school, and elsewhere.

28. (p. 676) One's personal, private sense of maleness or femaleness is referred to as _____ _____. This term can be distinguished from _____ _____ which are observable traits, mannerisms, interests, and behaviors defined by one's culture as "male" or "female."

29. (p. 676) Gender identity appears to be a _____ self-perception. Cases of hermaphroditism emphasize this point. Those individuals raised as boys will act like and consider themselves boys; those raised as girls will act like and consider themselves girls.

30. (p. 676) Gender identity is essentially formed by _____ or _____ years of age and few problems occur with hermaphroditic individuals as long as a final decision concerning their sex is made by the age of _____ months.

31. (p. 676) Gender identity begins with male-female labels and is then influenced by _____ _____ _____, that is, by subtle pressure exerted by parents, peers, and cultural forces that urge boys to "act like boys" and girls to "act like girls."

32. (p. 676) In determining adult sexual behavior and sex-linked personality traits, _____ _____ are probably as important as chromosomal, genital or hormonal sex. This term refers to the favored pattern of behavior expected of individuals on the basis of their gender.

33. (p. 676) All cultures define sex roles. This often leads to over-simplified assumptions about the nature of men and women. Such sex role _____ treat learned sex roles as if they were real gender differences.

34. (p. 677) Sex role stereotypes are a major obstacle where _____ for women in the U.S. is concerned. Unequal pay for comparable work and experience still persists. Even on college campuses, female faculty members lag behind males in pay and promotions.

35. (p. 677) For many jobs your chances of being hired could be _____ by your gender, be it male or female.

36. (p. 677) The naturalness of sex roles is certainly questionable based on cross-cultural observations. For example, Ethel Albert has identified numerous cultures in which women do the heavy work because men are considered too _____ for it.

37. (p. 677) Also, in the Soviet Union, roughly _____ percent of the medical doctors and a large proportion of the work force are women.

38. (p. 677) Margaret Mead's observations of the _____ people of New Guinea offer another good example. She found that sex roles in that culture are a nearly perfect _____ of the American stereotypes. That is, women do the fishing and manufacturing, are expected to control the power and economic life of the community, and take the initiative in courting and sexual relations. Men are expected to be dependent, flirtatious, and concerned with their appearance.

39. (p. 677) A side effect of sex role socialization is the imprint left on activities having nothing to do with gender. For example, there is also evidence that boys are more _____ than girls, and that girls have more emotional _____ than boys.

40. (p. 677) Learning sex roles begins immediately after birth. Infant girls are held more _____ and treated more _____ than boys. Both parents play more _____ with their sons than with their daughters.

41. (p. 677) Later, _____ are allowed to roam over a wider area without special permission and are expected to run errands earlier.

42. (p. 678) Daughters are told that they are _____ and that "nice girls don't fight." Boys are told to be _____ and that "boys don't cry." Sons are more often urged to control _____, while parents tolerate aggression toward other children more in _____ than _____.

43. (p. 678) _____, especially, tend to encourage their children to play with "appropriate" sex-typed toys: dolls for girls; trucks and guns for boys.

44. (p. 678) The work force in America is still highly segregated by sex, and children learn from what they observe. Stereotyped sex roles are even the norm in children's _____ _____.

45. (p. 678) Overall, parents tend to encourage their sons to engage in _____ (goal-directed) behaviors, to control their emotions, and to prepare for the world of work. Daughters are encouraged in _____ (emotion-oriented) behaviors, and to a lesser degree, are socialized for the maternal role.

46. (p. 678) When told that they respond differently to boys and girls, parents often explain that it is because there are "_____" differences between the sexes. But what comes first, such differences or the expectations that create them?

47. (p. 678) It appears that in our culture, male seems to be defined by many people as "_____ _____." There is a vague fear of expressive and emotional behavior in male children, because it seems to imply _____.

48. (p. 679) A capacity for sexual arousal is apparent at _____ or soon after. This fact has been verified by sexual researcher Alfred Kinsey who found instances of _____ (sexual climax) in boys as young as five months old and in girls as young as four months.

49. (p. 679) Kinsey also found that children aged _____ to _____ years spontaneously engage in manipulation and exhibition of their genitals.

50. (p. 679) Fifty percent of males and twenty-five percent of females report having engaged in preadolescent _____ _____.

51. (p. 679) Sexual arousal is a complex phenomenon. It may be produced by direct stimulation of the body's _____ _____: genitals, mouth, breasts, ears, anus, and to a lesser degree the surface of the body in general.

52. (p. 679) John Gagnon believes that we learn a variety of _____ _____ that determine when and where we are likely to express sexual feelings, and with whom.

53. (p. 679) When two people follow markedly different scripts, misunderstandings are almost sure to occur. In such cases considerable "_____" of scripts is often needed for sexual compatibility.

54. (p. 679) To study gender differences in sexual arousal, one study used medical recording devices to measure sexual arousal in males and females as they listened to erotic tape recordings. The material was _____ arousing for both sexes.

55. (p. 679) This and similar findings suggest that women are no less physically aroused by erotic stimuli than are men. However, compared with men, women more often have a negative _____ response to explicit pictures of sex. That is, women more often report feeling upset and disgusted by these stimuli.

56. (p. 679) If capacity for sexual arousal is measured by frequency of orgasm (brought about by masturbation or intercourse), the peak of male sexual activity is at age _____.

57. (p. 679) Kinsey's studies (done in the early 1950s) placed the peak of female sexual activity at about _____ years of age.

58. (p. 679) However, in recent years women have participated more fully in sexual activities, and at an earlier age. The peak rate of female sexual activity is still _____ than that of males but is becoming more comparable.

59. (p. 679) In males, the strength of the sex drive is related to the amount of _____ secreted by the testes. When it dramatically increases at puberty, so does the sex drive.

60. (p. 680) In addition to estrogen, androgens may also be important to the female sex drive. One study found that frequency of intercourse for married women was _____ when their androgen levels were at a peak.

61. (p. 680) Furthermore, when women are given androgens for medical reasons, some report _____ sexual desire.

62. (p. 680) Some women also report variations in arousal at various times during their monthly cycle. If such a relationship does exist, its effects are probably _____, since women may engage in sexual activity at any time during their monthly cycles (including during menstruation).

63. (p. 680) According to Kinsey, about 85 percent of males and 35 percent of females have had sexual _____ that resulted in orgasm. These experiences typically begin during adolescence and may continue throughout adulthood.

64. (p. 680) Kinsey found some _____ in the number of men who have nocturnal orgasm after marriage, but _____ _____ among women.

65. (p. 680) Alcohol is a _____. As such, it may, in small doses, stimulate erotic desire by lowering inhibitions. However, in larger doses alcohol suppresses _____ in women and _____ in men.

66. (p. 680) In lower animals, _____ (surgical removal of the testicles) or removal of the ovaries usually completely abolishes sexual activity in _____ animals. However, sexually _____ animals (particularly higher animals) may show little immediate change in sexual behavior.

67. (p. 680) In humans, the effects of castration _____; initially, some individuals show a sex drive decline, others do not. However, after several years have passed almost all subjects report a _____ in sex drive.

68. (p. 680) _____ (surgically based birth control such as a vasectomy or a tubal ligation) has nothing do with castration. Men and women who undergo this procedure experience no loss of sex drive. If anything, they may become more sexually active when pregnancy is no longer a concern.

69. (p. 681) Aging does not unavoidably end sexual activity. The crucial factor appears to be _____ and opportunity. Individuals who fairly regularly engage in intercourse after age _____ to _____ have little difficulty in later years.

70. (p. 681) _____ may be defined as deliberate self-stimulation which causes sexual pleasure or orgasm. Rhythmic self-stimulation has been observed in infants under one year of age.

71. (p. 681) Masturbation in the male usually takes the form of _____ or other manipulation of the penis. Female masturbation most often centers on stimulation of the _____ or the areas immediately surrounding it.

72. (p. 681) Kinsey reports that _____ percent of the women he surveyed had masturbated at some time, and _____ percent of the males reported having masturbated.

73. (p. 681) Morton Hunt's more recent survey showed almost identical rates. But he believes that a liberalization of attitudes toward masturbation has taken place as reflected in the fact that _____ now begin masturbation earlier.

74. (p. 681) Through masturbation people discover what is pleasing sexually and what their natural rhythms and preferences are. It is therefore an important part of the _____ development of most adolescents.

75. (p. 681) Among other things, it provides a healthy _____ for sexual intercourse during a period when sexual activity is discouraged and young people are maturing emotionally.

76. (p. 681) Morton Hunt found that a sizable number of married people masturbate at least occasionally— approximately _____ percent.

77. (p. 681) "Self-abuse," as masturbation was once called, has enjoyed a long and unfortunate history of religious and medical condemnation. For example, 50 years ago a child might be told that masturbation would cause _____, _____, sterility, or other such nonsense.

78. (p. 681) The contemporary view is that masturbation is a normal and acceptable sexual outlet. There is no harm caused by masturbation itself. Typically, the only negative effects of masturbation are the _____, _____, or _____ that occur when an individual has learned negative attitudes toward it.

79. (p. 681) Based on a recent national survey, it is estimated that about _____ percent of all American adults are having, or have had, homosexual or bisexual relationships.

80. (p. 681) At any given time, approximately _____ percent of all American adults have same-sex partners. This indicates that roughly 1 person out of every 63 in the U.S. is bisexual or homosexual.

81. (p. 681) A major survey of 76 cultures found that almost _____-_____ accept some form of homosexuality.

82. (p. 681) Many people mistakenly believe that homosexuality is caused by a _____ imbalance. However, this is highly unlikely since measured levels for most gay men and lesbians are within the normal range.

83. (p. 681) Research suggests that a combination of _____, biological, and social and _____ influences combine to produce one's sexual orientation.

84. (p. 681) Testing consistently shows no difference in _____ or adjustment between heterosexuals and homosexuals.

85. (p. 681) Emotional adjustment, then, appears to be independent of sexual preference. Therefore, homosexuality cannot be considered a sexual _____.

86. (p. 682) Psychologically, homosexuality is regarded as a problem only if a person feels lasting guilt, self-hate, or similar negative emotions. This condition is referred to as _____-_____ homosexuality.

87. (p. 682) This problem is probably rare because the majority of adult homosexuals display _____ patterns and _____ histories similar to those of heterosexuals.

88. (p. 682) The problems faced by homosexuals are more often related to rejection by family, discrimination in employment and housing, and to the undercurrent of _____ (referring to prejudice, fear, and dislike aimed at homosexuals) in American society.

89. (p. 682) _____-_____ percent of gay males and _____ percent of lesbian women have at one time or another suffered verbal abuse because of their sexual orientation. Much of this rejection is based on false stereotypes.

90. (p. 682) In a series of experiments, interviews, and controlled observations, William Masters and Virginia Johnson directly studied sexual intercourse and masterbation in nearly 700 males and females. They have classified sexual response in both males and females into four phases: _____, _____, _____, and _____.

91. (p. 682) Sexual arousal in the male is signaled by _____ of the _____ during the excitement phase.

92. (p. 682) There is also a rise in _____ rate, increased _____ flow to the genitals, enlargement of the _____, erection of the _____, and numerous other bodily changes.

93. (p. 682) If sexual stimulation ends, the excitement phase will gradually subside. Continued stimulation moves the individual into the _____ phase, in which physical changes and subjective feelings of arousal become more intense.

94. (p. 682) If stimulation ends during this phase, sexual arousal will subside more slowly and may produce considerable _____. Further stimulation during the plateau phase brings about a reflex release of tension resulting in sexual climax, or _____.

95. (p. 682) In the mature male, orgasm is usually accompanied by _____ (release of seminal fluid) and is followed by a short _____ period during which a second orgasm is impossible.

96. (p. 683) Only rarely is the male refractory period immediately followed by a second orgasm. Orgasm is usually followed by _____, a return to lower levels of sexual tension and arousal.

97. (p. 683) Although the timing and intensity of the phases vary for individual women, the basic pattern of response is the same as that for men. During the excitement phase, a complex pattern of changes prepares the vagina for intercourse. Also, the _____ become erect, _____ rate rises, and the skin may become _____.

98. (p. 683) During orgasm, from _____ to _____ muscular contractions of the vagina, uterus, and related structures serve to discharge accumulated sexual tension. No form of _____ accompanies female orgasm.

99. (p. 683) Both _____ and _____ in the female usually last longer than they do in the male. After orgasm, about _____ percent of all women return to the plateau phase, after which orgasm may occur again.

100. (p. 684) Masters and Johnson exploded the Freudian myth that clitoral orgasm is an immature form of female response. They showed there is no difference in _____ _____ no matter what form of stimulation produces orgasm.

101. (p. 684) As a matter of fact, the _____ is quite lacking in nerve endings for touch. Most sensations during intercourse, therefore, come from stimulation of the clitoris and other external tissues.

102. (p. 684) Women in one study said they would rather not choose between vaginal or clitoral stimulation, but if forced, _____-_____ preferred clitoral sensations.

103. (p. 684) Also, Shere Hite found that, among 3000 women surveyed, only _____ percent regularly achieved orgasm during intercourse without separate massaging of the clitoris.

104. (p. 684) During lovemaking, _____ to _____ minutes are usually required for a woman to go from excitement to orgasm. Males may experience all four stages in as little as _____ minutes.

105. (p. 684) In a study of 1000 married women, _____ percent reached orgasm if intercourse lasted 1 to 11 minutes, and _____ percent climaxed if intercourse lasted 15 minutes or more. _____-_____ percent said that orgasm occurred within 1 minute of the start of intercourse.

106. (p. 684) At one time the concept of _____ _____ was considered the goal of lovemaking. More recently, this notion has been rejected as an artificial concern that may reduce enjoyment.

107. (p. 684) During _____, 70 percent of females reach orgasm in four minutes or less. Slower female response during intercourse probably occurs because stimulation to the _____ is less direct.

108. (p. 684) Masters and Johnson found that for women, subjective feelings of pleasure and intensity of orgasm are not related to penis _____. Also, while individual differences exist in flacid penis size, there is much less variation in size during _____.

109. (p. 684) It is true that about 1 woman in _____ does not experience orgasm during the first year of marriage, and only about _____ percent regularly reach orgasm through intercourse alone.

110. (p. 684) However, this does not imply lack of physical responsiveness, since approximately _____ of all women reach orgasm when masturbating.

111. (p. 684) Only about _____ percent of the male population is capable of multiple orgasm (and then only after an unavoidable refractory period). Most males are limited to a second orgasm at best.

112. (p. 684) Most women who regularly experience orgasm are capable of multiple orgasm, although only about _____ percent do. A woman should not assume that something is wrong if she isn't orgasmic or multiorgasmic. Undoubtedly, many women have satisfying sexual experiences even when orgasm is not involved.

113. (p. 685) Compared with earlier decades, the gap between sexual values and actual behavior has narrowed. For example, traditional morality called for female virginity before marriage. Yet, in the 1940s and 50s, as many as _____ percent of women who married had engaged in premarital sexual relations.

114. (p. 685) Changing attitudes toward sex are illustrated by the result of national polls concerning the acceptability of premarital intercourse. In a 1959 poll _____ percent thought it was wrong; in 1969 only _____ percent rejected it; while by 1973 only _____ percent felt likewise.

115. (p. 685) In a more recent survey, only _____ percent of those between ages 18 and 29 believed that premarital sex is unacceptable. Similar changes have been observed in attitudes toward extramarital sex, homosexuality, sex education, and a variety of related issues.

116. (p. 685) Changes in sexual attitudes are still larger than changes in actual behavior. Largely, there is greater tolerance for sexual behavior, especially that engaged in by others. For example, a poll of *Psychology Today* readers found that _____ percent accepted extramarital sex under some circumstances. But in practice only _____ percent of its married readers had actually had extramarital sexual experience.

117. (p. 685) A recent Redbook magazine survey showed about the same results: _____ percent of respondents of all ages had engaged in at least one extramarital affair. These percentages have not changed greatly in the last 40 years.

118. (p. 685) Faithfulness in marriage is a widely shared norm. About _____-_____ of Americans consider marital infidelity always wrong.

119. (p. 685) In any given year only _____ percent of married people have sex partners other than their spouse.

120. (p. 685) Premarital intercourse rates have traditionally been considered a good indication of overall sexual activity. The social upheaval that began in the 1960s led to an especially sharp rise in sexual activity among _____. This increase has continued into the 1980s, although it has _____ recently.

121. (p. 685) In the early 1950s, Kinsey found that _____ percent of males and _____ percent of females had engaged in premarital intercourse by age 25. In the 1970s, Hunt obtained _____ percent for males and about _____ percent for females.

122. (p. 685) Another study found that _____ percent of women married after 1973 had engaged in premarital relations. A variety of additional studies support the idea that premarital intercourse rates have increased.

123. (p. 685) To some extent these changes are related to a tendency to postpone marriage. In the U.S. alone, _____ million unmarried couples are living together.

124. (p. 685) Another major element of the "sexual revolution" is earlier participation in sexual behavior by both sexes. A Louis Harris poll conducted in 1986 found that _____ percent of the nation's 17-year-olds were sexually experienced.

125. (p. 685) For 16-year-olds, the figure was _____ percent, for 15-year-olds it was _____ percent, and for 14-year-olds, _____ percent.

126. (p. 685) This particular aspect of increased sexual behavior remains troubling. Today, the U.S. has one of the highest teenage _____ rates among all industrialized nations.

127. (p. 685) Talk of a sexual revolution has quieted somewhat in recent years, and a conservative counter-movement has been visible. Some of the reaction may reflect concern about sexually transmitted _____.

128. (p. 686) Although sexual intercourse by unmarried couples is more common today, most couples emphasize mutual commitment and a loving relationship. Most women have only _____ premarital sexual partner(s) whom they eventually marry, while men typically have about _____ premarital partners.

129. (p. 686) The association between sexuality and love or affection remains strong for the _____ of the population. Both premarital sex and cohabitation are still widely viewed as preludes to marriage or as temporary substitutes for it.

130. (p. 686) A good summary of the changes that have occurred in sexual behavior is found in the phrase, "the slow death of the _____ _____." The gap between male and female sexual patterns has continued to close.

131. (p. 686) Some individuals feel pressured into sexual behavior because it is "expected." However, pressures such as these probably come as much from the individual as from others. If a greater acceptance of human sexuality is to be constructive, it must be perceived as a general increase in _____ _____.

132. (p. 686) About _____ percent of adult Americans are sexually abstinent during any given year.

133. (p. 686) The importance of respecting the right to say no is underscored by the recent dramatic increase in cases of acquaintance (or date) rape. One recent study found that _____ percent of all female college students had been raped. Roughly _____-_____ of these rapes were by first dates, casual dates, or romantic acquaintances.

134. (p. 686) Men who commit date rape often believe they have done nothing _____. But the effects of acquaintance rape are no less devastating than rape committed by a stranger.

135. (p. 686) The incidence of _____ _____ diseases (abbreviated _____) has been rising in the U.S. for the last 20 years. Today, sexually active individuals run an elevated risk of getting chlamydia, gonorrhea, hepatitis B, herpes, syphilis, and the like.

136. (p. 686) For many people, _____ _____ _____ _____ (AIDS) has added a new fear. Whereas most other STDs are treatable, AIDS is almost always fatal.

137. (p. 686) AIDS is caused by the _____ _____ virus (abbreviated _____) which disables the immune system. This allows various other "opportunistic" diseases to invade the body without resistance and most victims eventually die, usually of multiple infections.

138. (p. 687) The first symptoms of AIDS may show up as little as _____ months after infection, or they may not appear for up to _____ years. Because of this long incubation period, infected persons often pass AIDS on to others without knowing it.

139. (p. 687) Medical testing can detect the presence of an HIV infection. However, for at least the first _____ months after becoming infected, a person can test negative while carrying the disease.

140. (p. 687) HIV infections are spread by direct contact with _____ _____—especially blood, semen, and vaginal secretions. The AIDS virus cannot be transmitted by casual contact— shaking hands, social kissing, sharing drinking glasses, etc.

141. (p. 687) AIDS has been called the "_____ _____" because male homosexuals were its first highly visible victims. However, this label is in error, because AIDS can be spread by all forms of sexual intercourse and has affected persons of all sexual orientations.

142. (p. 687) Those who are at greatest risk include men who have had sex with other men, people who have shared _____, blood transfusion recipients (between 1977 and spring 1985), _____ (who require frequent blood transfusions), sexual partners of people in the above groups, and _____ with a history of multiple partners.

143. (p. 687) The vast majority of people are not at high risk of HIV infection. Still, 1 in _____ men and 1 in _____ women in the U.S. are now infected with HIV.

144. (p. 687) AIDS is having a strong impact on sexual behavior in some groups. Among gay men there has been a sharp _____ in monogamous relationships and in abstention from sex. Gay men have also significantly _____ participation in high-risk sexual behaviors.

145. (p. 687) Other groups are not showing much change in sexual behaviors. Two recent studies of college students show that the AIDS epidemic has thus far had little impact on their willingness to engage in risky behavior (casual sex) or to use _____. this is especially true for _____.

146. (p. 687) Apparently, heterosexual people still don't feel that they are truly at risk. However, worldwide _____ percent of people with the AIDS virus were infected through heterosexual sex.

147. (p. 687) In Europe and North America, only _____ percent of men and _____ of women contracted AIDS virus from a person of the opposite sex.

148. (p. 687) Over the next 20 to 30 years, _____ transmission is expected to become the primary means of spreading HIV infection in most industrialized countries.

149. (p. 687) A special concern is the fact that approximately _____ of all AIDS victims are teenagers. Also, the incidence of other STDs has risen dramatically among adolescents. Health officials predict that HIV infections will follow the same trend.

150. (p. 689) Impotence (also known as _____ _____) is the inability to maintain an erection for sexual intercourse. It may be an occasional or a continuous problem.

151. (p. 689) Males suffering from _____ impotence have never been able to produce or maintain an erection. Those who have previously performed successfully, but then have become impotent, are said to suffer from secondary impotence.

152. (p. 689) Sex therapists Masters and Johnson feel that a problem of impotence exists when failure occurs on _____ percent or more of a man's lovemaking attempts and should therefore be distinguished from an occasional inability. True impotence typically persists for months or years.

153. (p. 689) Repeated impotence should be distinguished from occasional erectile problems. Fatigue, _____, _____, and excessive consumption of _____ can cause temporary impotence in healthy males.

154. (p. 689) Occasional impotence is _____. Overreaction to it may generate fears and doubts that can contribute to further impotence. At such times, it is particularly important for the man's partner to practice patient reassurance to help prevent the establishment of a vicious cycle.

155. (p. 689) It is now recognized that roughly _____ percent of impotence cases are organic, or physically caused. Even then, it is almost always made worse by anxiety and other emotional reactions.

156. (p. 689) If a man can have an erection at times other than lovemaking (during sleep, for instance), the problem probably is not physical but rather _____ (a result of emotional factors).

157. (p. 689) Organic impotence may result from alcohol or drug abuse, diabetes, _____ disease, _____ and urological disorders, neurological problems, and reactions to _____ for high blood pressure, heart disease, or stomach ulcers.

158. (p. 689) Erectile problems are also a normal part of _____. As men grow older they typically experience a _____ in sexual desire and arousal and an _____ in sexual dysfunction.

159. (p. 689) According to Masters and Johnson, primary psychogenic impotence is often related to harsh _____ training, early sexual experience with a seductive _____, sexual molestation in childhood, or other experiences leading to guilt, fear, and sexual inhibition.

160. (p. 690) Secondary psychogenic impotence may be related to anxiety about _____ in general, _____ because of an extramarital affair, resentment or hostility toward a sexual partner, _____ of inability to perform, and similar emotions and conflicts.

161. (p. 690) Often impotence starts with repeated sexual failures caused by drinking too much _____ or by the presence of _____ _____. Initial doubts soon become severe fears of failure, which further inhibit sexual response.

162. (p. 690) Medical treatment for organic impotence may employ _____ or _____. Treatment for both organic and psychogenic impotence also usually includes _____ to remove fears and psychological blocks.

163. (p. 690) In _____ _____, a technique used in treating impotence and other sexual disorders, the couple is initially told to take turns stroking various parts of each other's bodies. Genital contact is avoided at first, with emphasis placed on giving pleasure and on signaling what is most gratifying.

164. (p. 690) Masters and Johnson define the problem of _____ _____ as one in which a man is unable to delay sexual climax long enough to satisfy his partner in at least one-half of their lovemaking attempts.

165. (p. 690) Helen Kaplan says that prematurity exists when ejaculation occurs _____ or when there is an inability to tolerate high levels of excitement at the plateau stage of arousal.

166. (p. 690) Theories advanced to explain this common problem in male sexual adjustment have ranged from the idea that it may represent _____ toward the man's sexual partner to the suggestion that most early male sexual experiences tend to encourage rapid _____.

167. (p. 690) Kaplan adds that excessive _____ and _____ over performance are usually present, and that some men simply engage in techniques that maximize sensation and make rapid orgasm inevitable.

168. (p. 690) The most common treatment for premature ejaculation is the _____ _____. Here the man's sexual partner stimulates him manually until he signals that ejaculation is about to occur. The man's partner then firmly squeezes the tip of the penis to inhibit orgasm. When the man feels he has control, stimulation is repeated.

169. (p. 690) Among males, _____ _____ (an inability to reach orgasm) was once considered a rare problem. But milder forms of this dysfunction have recently accounted for increasing numbers of clients seeking therapy.

170. (p. 690) Typical background factors are strict _____ training, fear of _____, lack of interest in the sexual partner, symbolic inability to give of oneself, unacknowledged homosexuality, or the recent occurrence of _____ life events.

171. (p. 690) Treatment for retarded ejaculation consists of sensate focus, _____ _____ by the man's partner, and stimulation to the point of orgasm followed by immediate intercourse and ejaculation. Work also focuses on resolving personal _____ and _____ difficulties.

172. (p. 690) Women who show little or no physical arousal to sexual stimulation and persistently derive no pleasure from sexual stimulation suffer from _____ _____ _____ commonly referred to as _____.

173. (p. 690) Frigidity appears to correspond directly to male impotence. The causes can often be traced to frightening childhood experiences, such as molestations (often by older relatives), incestuous relations that produced lasting guilt, a harshly religious background in which sex was considered evil, or to _____, _____ childhood relationships.

174. (p. 690) Also common is the need to maintain control over _____, deep-seated _____ over being female, and extreme distrust of others, especially males.

175. (p. 690) Treatment of frigidity includes sensate focus, genital stimulation by the woman's partner, and "_____" intercourse controlled by the woman.

176. (p. 690) The most prevalent sexual complaint among women is _____ _____, an inability to reach orgasm during intercourse.

177. (p. 690) Often it is clear in such cases that the woman is not completely unresponsive; rather, she is unresponsive in the context of a _____.

178. (p. 691) While sex therapists try to avoid placing blame, some instances of "orgasmic dysfunction" can be traced to inadequate _____ or faulty _____ on the part of the woman's partner. The male partner must be sexually adequate and must have a commitment to ensuring gratification of the woman.

179. (p. 691) If we focus only on the woman, the most common source of orgasmic difficulties is _____ of sexual response.

180. (p. 691) Female orgasm requires a degree of abandonment to erotic feelings that may be inhibited by ambivalence or hostility toward the relationship, by _____, by fears of expressing _____ _____, and by tendencies to control and intellectualize erotic feelings.

181. (p. 691) In Kaplan's treatment program, anorgasmic women are first trained to focus on their sexual responsiveness through _____ or vigorous stimulation by a partner. As the woman becomes consistently _____ in these circumstances, her responsiveness is gradually transferred to intercourse.

182. (p. 691) In the condition known as _____, muscle spasms make intercourse impossible. It is often accompanied by obvious fears of intercourse or at least high levels of anxiety.

183. (p. 691) The causes of vaginismus include experiences of _____ intercourse, rape and/or brutal and frightening sexual encounters, fear of _____, misinformation about sex (belief that it is injurious), fear of _____, and fear of the specific male partner.

184. (p. 691) Treatment of vaginismus is similar to what might be done for a non-sexual phobia. It includes _____ of conditioned muscle spasms by progressive relaxation of the vagina, _____ of fears of intercourse, and masturbation or manual stimulation to associate pleasure with sexual approach by the woman's partner.

185. (p. 691) _____ has also been used successfully in some cases of vaginismus.

186. (p. 692) It is best to view sexual adjustment within the broader context of a _____. It is a form of communication. Couples with strong and caring relationships can probably survive most sexual problems. A couple with a satisfactory sex life but a poor relationship _____ lasts.

187. (p. 692) Masters and Johnson believe that when there are disagreements about sex, the rule should be "each partner must accept the other as the final authority on his or her own feelings." Partners are urged to give feedback by following the "_____ and _____" rule.

188. (p. 692) When problems do arise, partners are urged to be responsive to each other's needs at an _____ level and to recognize that all sexual problems are _____. It is particularly important to avoid the "numbers game."

189. (p. 692) In a study that compared happily married couples with unhappily married couples, Navran found that in almost every regard the happily married couples showed superior _____ skills.

190. (p. 692) Several guidelines can be suggested to help facilitate communication. One of them is to avoid "_____," that is saving up feelings and complaints.

191. (p. 692) Another suggestion is to be open about _____. Happy couples not only talk more, they convey more personal feelings and show greater sensitivity to their partner's feelings.

192. (p. 692) Don't attack the other person's _____. Expressions of negative feelings should be given as statements of one's own feelings, not as statements of _____.

193. (p. 692) Don't try to _____ a fight; instead, try to resolve the differences without focusing on who is right or wrong.

194. (p. 692) Recognize that _____ is appropriate. However, constructive fights require that couples fight fair by sticking to the real issues and not "hitting below the belt."

195. (p. 692) Try to see things through your partner's _____. Marital harmony is closely related to the ability to put yourself in another person's place.

196. (p. 693) Don't be a "_____-_____." Assuming that you know what your partner is thinking or feeling can muddle or block communication.

197. (p. 693) Bryan Strong and Christine DeVault suggest that if you really want to mess up a relationship, follow "Ten Ways to Avoid Intimacy." One of these ways is "Don't talk about anything meaningful, especially about _____." You should be familiar with the others.

198. (p. 694) Sidney Jourard has conducted some intriguing studies in human touching, not only in our country, but cross-culturally. He discovered that, in American society, most regions of a young adult's body remain untouched unless one has a close friend of the _____ _____, and even that depends upon their relationship. This was not the case in such countries as France or Puerto Rico.

199. (p. 694) Jourard also found interesting sex differences. Daughters are touched more right into their twenties. Mothers are allowed to touch a girl's hair frequently. One-half the parents get to touch their daughter's _____, and one-half manage a literal pat on the _____. Sons, on the other hand, receive considerably less touching. Also, parents stop touching boys much earlier.

200. (p. 694) However, taboos do exist. Only _____ percent of the girls studied received a paternal pat on the bottom and _____ were touched by their fathers in the genital areas. The same restrictions did not necessarily hold true with male students and their mothers.

SELF-TEST

1. (p. 673) The penis, testes, and scrotum in the male and the ovaries, uterus, and vagina in females are
    a. gonads
    b. secondary sexual characteristics
    c. erogenous zones
    d. primary sexual characteristics

2. (p. 673) True-False. Secondary sexual characteristics refer to the lesser physical differences between males and females such as the position of sexual and reproductive organs.

3. (p. 673) True-False. Menarche marks the end of a female's ability to reproduce.

4. (p. 673) Female hormones, _____, and male hormones, _____, secreted by the gonads affect sexual development and behaviors.
    a. estrogens, androgens
    b. androgens, estrogens
    c. testosterones, progesterones
    d. adrenalins, noradrenalins

5. (p. 673) The gonad(s) in the male is (are) the
   a. penis
   b. scrotum
   c. testes
   d. prostate

6. (p. 673) The gonad(s) in the female is (are) the
   a. ovaries
   b. clitoris
   c. vagina
   d. uterus

7. (p. 673) Development of male or female anatomy is largely due to _____ before birth.
   a. genetic sex
   b. the presence or absence of testosterone
   c. secondary sexual characteristics
   d. gonadal sex

8. (p. 674) Which of the following is *not* associated with sexual abnormalities in prenatal development?
   a. androgen insensitivity among genetic males
   b. exposure to progestin among genetic females
   c. the XY chromosome combination where testosterone is produced
   d. the androgenital syndrome

9. (p. 674) When a genetic abnormality causes the adrenal glands to secrete excess amounts of androgen, it can produce a condition known as _____ where a female child has male genitals.
   a. gender misidentity
   b. androgenital syndrome
   c. vaginismus
   d. impotence

10. (p. 675) Some researchers feel that prenatal exposure to androgens or estrogens exerts a biological biasing effect on later psychosexual development. Which of the following suggests this idea?
    a. The fact that transsexuals such as Dr. Renee Richards become genetically different following hormonal treatments.
    b. Research conducted by John Money demonstrating that women exposed to androgens before birth were typically "tomboys" during childhood.
    c. The fact that women are more often "right-brained" and thus better at math and visual-spatial skills.
    d. The fact that men are more often "right-brained" and thus better at language skills.

11. (p. 676) A learned self-perception of one's maleness or femaleness is referred to as
    a. expressive behavior
    b. instrumental behavior
    c. sex role socialization
    d. gender identity

12. (p. 676) Which of the following is of primary importance in the acquisition of gender identity?
    a. primary sexual expression
    b. erogenous zones
    c. sex role socialization
    d. gender instrumentation development

13. (p. 677) The _____ reported by Mead have a nearly perfect reversal of American sex role stereotypes.
    a. Zulu culture
    b. Tchambuli people
    c. people of the Soviet Union
    d. Tsari society

14. (p. 678) Overall, parents tend to encourage their sons to engage in _____ _____, while daughters are encouraged in _____ _____.
    a. expressive behaviors, non-expressive behaviors
    b. sex roles, orgasmic functioning
    c. gender identity, instrumental responsiveness
    d. instrumental behaviors, expressive behaviors

15. (p. 679) Which of the following is *not* true of early sexual behavior?
    a. Kinsey found that females are more likely to be sexually aroused during infancy than males.
    b. Kinsey has verified instances of orgasm in boys as young as 5 months old and in girls as young as 4 months.
    c. Fifty percent of males and 25 percent of females report having engaged in preadolescent sex play.
    d. Children aged 2 to 5 spontaneously engage in manipulation and exhibition of their genitals.

16. (p. 679) True-False. Women are more inclined, when measured physiologically, to respond negatively to explicit pictures of sex than men.

17. (p. 679) In males, the strength of the sex drive is related to
    a. various times of the month in male cycles
    b. the degree of sperm available
    c. the amount of androgens secreted by the testes
    d. only cognitive factors, since males are physically always prepared for intercourse

18. (p. 680) Which of the following is *not* true of erotic dreams accompanied by orgasm?
    a. They typically begin in adolescence.
    b. According to Kinsey, about 85 percent of males and 35 percent of females have experienced them.
    c. They are an indication of possible sexual disorder if they occur beyond the late 20s.
    d. They are also known as noctural emissions.

19. (p. 680) True-False. In humans, the effects of male and female castration include increased sex drive related to freedom from anxieties regarding pregnancy.

20. (p. 681) True-False. A critical factor for an extended sex life appears to be regularity of sexual activity.

21. (p. 681) Which of the following is *not* true of masturbation?
    a. Approximately 90 percent of all women reach orgasm when masturbating.
    b. Hunt found that approximately 70 percent of married men and women masturbate at least occasionally.
    c. Adolescents now begin masturbation at a later age because intercourse occurs earlier.
    d. Hunt found that 94 percent of males and 63 percent of females have masturbated.

22. (p. 682) Which of the following is *not* true of male sexual response?
    a. Only 50 percent of males are capable of multiple orgasms.
    b. Males may experience all four sexual stages in as little as 4 minutes.
    c. Sexual arousal is signaled by erection of the penis and other bodily changes.
    d. In the mature male, orgasm is accompanied by ejaculation.

23. (p. 683) All of the following statements about female sexual response are true *except*
    a. no form of ejaculation accompanies female orgasm
    b. both orgasm and resolution last longer in females than they do in males
    c. there is no relationship between penis size and level of female sexual gratification
    d. vaginal orgasms are more intense than clitoral orgasms

24. (p. 684) True-False. Simultaneous male and female orgasm should be the ultimate goal of sexual intercourse.

25. (p. 684) True-False. Slower female sexual response during intercourse probably occurs because stimulation of the clitoris is less direct. During masturbation, 70 percent of females reach orgasm in 4 minutes or less.

26. (p. 685) Which of the following is *not* true of the "sexual revolution"?
     a. Generally attitudes about sexual behavior have changed more radically than actual sexual behavior.
     b. Comparing Kinsey's and Hunt's results, it seems that there has been a significant increase in the extent of extramarital sex.
     c. Results from several surveys support the idea that premarital intercourse rates have definitely increased in the last 20 years.
     d. Currently, most women have only one premarital sex partner while men have about six.

27. (p. 685) True-False. Recent surveys of sexual behavior indicate that a major element of the "sexual revolution" is a marked increase in sexual expression among females.

28. (p. 689) True-False. Secondary impotence refers to frigidity in females.

29. (p. 690) A major sexual adjustment technique which involves nongenital physical contact is
     a. sensate focus   c. sex role socialization
     b. squeeze technique   d. orgasmic relearning

30. (p. 690) The technique most often used in treating premature ejaculation is
     a. sensate focus   c. sex role socialization
     b. the squeeze technique   d. orgasmic relearning

31. (p. 690) Retarded ejaculation refers to an inability to
     a. sustain erection   c. achieve orgasm
     b. feel physical pleasure   d. achieve erection promptly

32. (p. 690) Which of the following is *not* true of female general sexual dysfunction?
     a. It is usually defined as a persistent inability to derive pleasure from sexual stimulation.
     b. As in male impotence, it may be primary or secondary.
     c. The causes bear general similarity to those seen in male impotence.
     d. Treatment usually includes the "squeeze technique."

33. (p. 691) True-False. The most prevalent sexual complaint among women is orgasmic dysfunction.

34. (p. 691) A condition in which muscle spasms make intercourse impossible for the female is known as
     a. frigidity   c. orgasmic dysfunction
     b. androgenital syndrome   d. vaginismus

35. (p. 692) Which of the following is *not* a useful guideline in improving and maintaining a healthy emotional relationship?
     a. recognize that anger is inappropriate
     b. avoid gunnysacking
     c. don't try to win a fight
     d. be open with feelings

36. (p. 694) True-False. Compared with countries such as France and Puerto Rico, there is very little touching between individuals in our culture.

37.   (p. 694) Which of the following is *not* true of familial contact as reported by Jourard?
    a.   Girls are touched by both parents much more frequently than boys.
    b.   Touching of boys ends much earlier than for girls.
    c.   Most fathers pat their daughters on the bottom.
    d.   One-half the parents touch their daughters on the lips, and half manage a pat on the back.

ANSWERS—PROGRAMMED REVIEW

1. Primary sexual; testes, scrotum; uterus, vagina	40. gently; tenderly; roughly	78. fear, guilt, anxiety
2. Secondary sexual	41. boys	79. 5.5
3. breasts; hips; hair; voice	42. pretty; strong; emotions; boys; girls	80. 1.6
4. menarche	43. Fathers	81. two-thirds
5. ovulation; menopause	44. picture books	82. hormone
6. sex hormones	45. instrumental; expressive	83. hereditary; psychological
7. gonads; estrogens; androgens	46. natural	84. personality
8. testes; ovaries	47. not female; effeminancy	85. disorder
9. adrenal	48. birth; orgasm	86. ego-dystonic
10. testosterone	49. 2; 5	87. adjustment; occupational
11. Genetic sex	50. sex play	88. homophobia
12. 6	51. erogenous zones	89. Ninety-two; 81
13. genetic sex	52. sexual scripts	90. excitement; plateau; orgasm; resolution
14. genitals	53. rewriting	91. erection; penis
15. androgen insensitivity	54. equally	92. heart; blood; testicles; nipples
16. hermaphroditism	55. emotional	93. plateau
17. progestin	56. 18	94. frustration; orgasm
18. androgenital syndrome	57. 30	95. ejaculation; refractory
19. surgery	58. later	96. resolution
20. brain	59. androgens	97. nipples; pulse; flushed
21. learned	60. highest	98. 3; 10; ejaculation
22. biasing effect	61. increased	99. orgasm, resolution; 15
23. tomboys	62. small	100. physical response
24. left; language; right; spatial	63. dreams	101. vagina
25. slightly; slightly	64. reduction; no change	102. two-thirds
26. Scholastic Aptitude	65. depressant; orgasm; erection	103. 26
27. alike; different	66. castration; inexperienced; experienced	104. 10; 20; 4
28. gender identity; sex roles	67. vary; decrease	105. 50; 66; Twenty-five
29. learned	68. Sterilization	106. simultaneous orgasm
30. 3; 4; 18	69. regularity; 45; 50	107. masturbation; clitoris
31. sex role socialization	70. Masturbation	108. size; erection
32. sex roles	71. stroking; clitoris	109. 3; 30
33. stereotypes	72. 60; 95	110. 90
34. employment	73. adolescents	111. 5
35. reduced	74. psychosexual	112. 15
36. weak	75. substitute	113. 75
37. 75	76. 70	114. 88; 68; 48
38. Tchambuli; reversal	77. insanity; acne	115. 22
39. aggressive; empathy		116. 80; 30
		117. 26

118. three-fourths
119. 1.5
120. teenagers; slowed
121. 70; 33; 97; 70
122. 93
123. 2.3
124. 57
125. 46; 29; 19
126. pregnancy
127. diseases
128. one; six
129. majority
130. double standard
131. personal freedom
132. 22
133. 15; one-half
134. wrong
135. sexually transmitted; STD
136. acquired immune deficiency syndrome
137. human immunodeficiency virus; HIV
138. 2; 7
139. 6
140. body fluids
141. gay plague
142. needles; hemophiliacs; heterosexuals
143. 75; 100
144. increase; reduced

145. condoms; men
146. 75
147. 3; 34
148. heterosexual
149. 20
150. erectile dysfunction
151. primary; secondary
152. 25
153. anger, anxiety; alcohol
154. normal
155. 40
156. psychogenic
157. vascular; prostate; medication
158. aging; decline; increase
159. religious; mother
160. sex; guilt; fear
161. alcohol; premature ejaculation
162. drugs; surgery; counseling
163. sensate focus
164. premature ejaculation
165. reflexively
166. hostility; climax
167. arousal; anxiety
168. squeeze technique
169. retarded ejaculation
170. religious; impregnating; traumatic
171. manual stimulation; conflicts; marital

172. general sexual dysfunction; frigidity
173. cold, unloving
174. emotions; conflicts
175. nondemanding
176. orgasmic dysfunction
177. relationship
178. stimulation; technique
179. overcontrol
180. guilt; sexual needs
181. masturbation; orgasmic
182. vaginismus
183. painful; men; pregnancy
184. extinction; desensitization
185. Hypnosis
186. relaionship; rarely
187. touch and ask
188. emotional; mutual
189. communication
190. gunnysacking
191. feelings
192. character; blame
193. win
194. anger
195. eyes
196. mind-reader
197. feelings
198. opposite sex
199. lips; back
200. 13; none

ANSWERS—SELF-TEST

1.	d	8.	c	15.	a	22.	a	29.	a
2.	False	9.	b	16.	False	23.	d	30.	b
3.	False	10.	b	17.	c	24.	False	31.	c
4.	a	11.	d	18.	c	25.	True	32.	d
5.	c	12.	c	19.	False	26.	b	33.	True
6.	a	13.	b	20.	True	27.	True	34.	d
7.	b	14.	d	21.	c	28.	False	35.	a

36. True
37. c

ACROSS

6. male hormones
7. gynecologist who studied human sexual response
11. Masters' research partner
12. inability to produce or maintain an erection
14. female may be masculinized by this drug
15. facial and body hair in males are examples of _____ sexual characteristics
16. among males an inability to reach orgasm is a condition known as _____ ejaculation

DOWN

1. spasm of muscles at entrance of vagina
2. prejudice, fear, and dislike aimed at homosexuals
3. one's private sense of maleness or femaleness is one's _____ identity
4. defects in sexual development resulting in dual or ambiguous sexual anatomy causes this condition
5. _____ sexual characteristics are the sexual and reproductive organs themselves
8. these _____ zones are productive of pleasure or erotic desire
9. gender _____ is essentially formed by 3 or 4 years of age
10. the squeeze technique is used to treat _____ ejaculation
13. sex glands

CHAPTER 26

Applied Psychology

CONTENTS

Introduction to Applied Psychology
Industrial/Organizational Psychology—Psychology at Work
Environmental Psychology—Life in the Big City
A Panorama of Applied Psychology
Improving Communication at Work
Space Psychology—Life on the High Frontier

TERMS AND CONCEPTS

applied psychology
community psychology
industrial/organizational psychology
personnel psychology
flexitime
engineering psychologist (human factors engineer)
natural design
feedback
job analysis
critical incidents
biodata
personal interview
vocational interest tests
aptitude tests
assessment center
scientific management (Theory X)
Theory Y
work efficiency
psychological efficiency
participative management
management by objectives
quality circles
job satisfaction
job enrichment
environmental psychology

physical environments
social environments
behavioral settings
territoriality
territorial markers
crowding
density
attentional overload
environmental assessment
architectural psychology
educational psychology
teaching strategy
direct instruction
open teaching
consumer psychology
consumer behavior
marketing research
brand images
consumerism
mock juries
demographic information
community survey
sports psychology
task analysis
peak performance (flow)

IMPORTANT INDIVIDUALS

Jack Keating
Elizabeth Loftus
Donald Norman

Robert Baron
Frederick Taylor
Douglas McGregor

Robert Levine
John Calhoun
Chris Kleinke

PROGRAMMED REVIEW

1. (p. 699) _____ psychology refers to the use of psychological principles and research methods to solve practical problems. Increasingly psychology is being used to enhance the quality of life and to improve human performance.

2. (p. 700) Applied psychology can make a life-or-death difference. For example, psychologists Jack Keating and Elizabeth Loftus created a life-saving "_____ _____" that tells people exactly what to do.

3. (p. 700) This unusual voice alarm has a simple message that contains three key elements: (1) Research has shown that switching from a female to a male voice (or the reverse) is very _____ _____. (2) During emergencies, people like to feel that some _____ is in control. (3) The crucial reminder to avoid the _____ is repeated, so it will be remembered.

4. (p. 700) The largest areas of applied psychology are _____ and counseling psychology. A closely related speciality is _____ psychology which treats whole neighborhoods or communities as "clients."

5. (p. 700) Community psychologists typically emphasize _____, _____, and _____. Often, they target drug abuse, child _____, unemployment, prejudice, and similar problems for solution.

6. (p. 700) From the 1920s until the present, _____/organizational psychologists have studied the problems people face at work. Their efforts will likely affect how you are selected for a job and how you are tested, trained, and evaluated for promotions. They may even help design your work environment or the machines you use at work.

7. (p. 700) I/O psychologists are employed mostly by government, industry, and business. Typically, they work in: _____ and _____ (personnel psychology), human _____ at work, and industrial _____ (the design of machines and work environments).

8. (p. 701) To improve worker morale, industrial psychologists have proposed the use of flexible working hours or _____. The basic idea is that starting and quitting times are made flexible, as long as employees are present during a core work period.

9. (p. 701) Studies of two groups of clerical workers suggest that flexitime did improve morale. A switch to this schedule brought a number of benefits, including more job _____, better work-group _____, better relations with supervisors, and less _____.

10. (p. 701) To adapt machines for human use, the engineering psychologist (or _____ engineer) must make them compatible with our sensory and motor capacities. For example, displays must be easy to perceive, controls easy to use, and the tendency to make errors must be minimized.

11. (p. 701) Donald Norman refers to effective human factors engineering as _____. Effective design makes use of signals that are naturally understood by people without any need to learn them.

12. (p. 701) Another major point that Norman emphasizes is that effective design supplies clear _____. In good design each control produces an immediate and obvious effect.

13. (p. 701) Since employed adults spend an average of over _____ hours a year at their jobs, and since the odds are _____ out of 10 that you are, or will be, employed in business or industry, there is value in knowing how selection for hiring and promotion is done.

14. (p. 702) Personnel selection begins with a _____ _____ to find out exactly what workers do and what skills or knowledge they need for success in a job.

15. (p. 702) A job analysis may be done by interviewing workers or supervisors, by giving them questionnaires, by observing work, or by identifying _____ _____— situations that an employee must be able to cope with if he or she is going to succeed in a particular job.

16. (p. 702) After desirable skills and characteristics are identified, the next step is to learn which job applicants possess them. Currently, the methods most often used for evaluating job candidates include the collection of _____, _____, standardized _____ tests, and the _____ center approach.

17. (p. 702) The idea behind biodata (detailed biographical information) is that past behavior is a good predictor of future behavior. Some of the most useful items are: past _____ interest, _____ achievement, _____ interest, extracurricular activities, _____ activities, social popularity, friction with brothers and sisters, attitudes toward school, and parents' socioeconomic status.

18. (p. 702) The traditional personal interview is still one of the most popular ways of selecting candidates for jobs or promotions. However, interviews are subject to the _____ effect and similar problems. For this reason, psychologists continue to investigate factors that affect interviews.

19. (p. 703) One "problem" with interviews is that physically _____ individuals are often given more positive evaluations even on traits that have no connection to appearance. Robert Baron tested whether this effect might even extend to the effects of wearing a pleasant perfume or cologne.

20. (p. 703) Baron found that _____ interviewers did, in fact, give higher ratings to job applicants who wore pleasant scents. But _____ gave lower ratings to persons who wore perfume or cologne. He speculates that the lowered ratings were due to greater awareness of the scents by the interviewers and resentment of the implied attempt to influence ratings.

21. (p. 703) In general, _____ efforts to make a positive impression, such as emphasizing your positive traits and past successes, appear to be most effective.

22. (p. 703) In addition to general intelligence and personality tests, personnel psychologists often use _____ _____ tests, such as the Kuder Occupational Interest Survey and the Strong-Campbell Interest Inventory.

23. (p. 703) If you take an interest test and your choices match those of people who are _____ in a given occupation, it is assumed that you, too, would be comfortable doing the work they do.

24. (p. 703) _____ tests are another mainstay of personnel psychology. Such tests rate a person's potential to learn tasks or skills used in various occupations. As an example, clerical tests emphasize the capacity to do rapid, precise, and accurate office work.

25. (p. 704) _____ _____ programs are set up by many large organizations to do in-depth evaluations of job candidates. They are used primarily to fill management and executive positions.

26. (p. 704) After applicants have been tested and interviewed at an assessment center, they are placed in simulated work situations for observation and evaluation. For example, in the _____-_____ test, the applicant is asked to quickly read a basket full of memos, requests, and problems typical of those faced by executives, and take appropriate action.

27. (p. 704) In another, more stressful test, applicants take part in a _____ _____ discussion in which they try to solve a realistic business problem. By observing applicants, it is possible to evaluate leadership skills and, especially, how job candidates cope with stress.

28. (p. 704) Assessment centers have had success in predicting performance in a variety of jobs. For instance, one recent study of women found that assessment center predictions of management potential were strongly related to career progress _____ years later.

29. (p. 704) On the basis of long-range studies, it appears that future success is most clearly predicted by _____ _____ skills, leadership, energy, _____ to stress, tolerance for _____, need for advancement, and planning skills.

30. (p. 704) One of the earliest attempts to improve worker efficiency was made in 1923 by Frederick _____. He standardized work procedures and emphasized careful planning, control, and orderliness.

31. (p. 704) Modern versions of Taylor's approach are called _____ _____ (also known as Theory X). Emphasis is placed on time-and-motion studies, task analysis, job specialization, assembly lines, pay schedules, and increased productivity.

32. (p. 704) Managers who follow Theory X tend to assume that workers must be goaded or guided into being productive. The term Theory X was coined by Douglas McGregor as a way to distinguish scientific management from a style that emphasizes human relations at work— _____ _____.

33. (p. 704) Many psychologists working in business are concerned with improving _____ efficiency —maximum output at lowest cost. As a result, they alter conditions they believe will affect workers (time schedules, work quotas, bonuses, etc.).

34. (p. 705) However, _____ efficiency is just as important as work efficiency. Businesses must be able to retain workers, minimize absenteeism, sustain good morale and labor relations, etc., if they are to prosper.

35. (p. 705) McGregor's Theory Y approach focuses on the human element. Theory Y managers assume that workers enjoy _____ and are willing to accept _____. They assume that worker needs and goals can be meshed with the company's, and that people are not naturally passive or lazy.

36. (p. 705) Theory Y assumes that people are industrious, creative, and rewarded by challenging _____. Given the proper conditions of freedom and responsibility, people will work hard to gain competence and to use their talents fully.

37. (p. 705) Many features of Theory Y are illustrated by the Honda plant at Marysville, Ohio. Two elements that stand out as effective methods are _____ management and management by _____.

38. (p. 705) In participative management, employees at all levels are included in decision making. Such employees come to see work as a cooperative effort. Resulting benefits include greater _____, greater job satisfaction, and less job-related _____.

39. (p. 705) In management by objectives, workers are given specific _____ to meet (for instance, reaching a certain sales figure, making a certain number of items, etc.) so they can tell if they are doing a good job.

40. (p. 706) Workers are free to choose (within limits) how they will achieve their goals. As a result they experience a greater sense of _____ and personal meaning in their work.

41. (p. 706) One popular answer as to how workers below management level can be involved more in their work is the use of _____ _____. These are voluntary discussion groups that meet regularly, with or without supervision, to try to find ways to solve business problems or improve efficiency.

42. (p. 706) Quality circles and similar worker involvement programs have many limitations. Usually such groups do not have the _____ to put their suggestions into practice directly. Nevertheless, studies verify that greater involvement can have a _____ impact on organizations and employees.

43. (p. 706) Applying Theory X methods to work without taking worker needs into account can produce an immediate rise in productivity while job _____ declines. When job _____ is low, morale falls, absenteeism skyrockets, and there is a high rate of employee turnover leading to high training costs and inefficiency.

44. (p. 706) Job satisfaction comes from a good fit between a person's interests, abilities, needs, and expectations, and his or her work. Eight of the most important aspects of work are: (1) _____ work; (2) enough help and equipment to get the job done; (3) enough _____ to get the job done; (4) enough _____ to get the job done; (5) good pay; (6) opportunity to develop special abilities; (7) job _____; (8) seeing the results of one's work.

45. (p. 706) A second survey done in the U.S. in the early 1980s again found that satisfying, rewarding work ranked first in worker preference. High _____ rose to second place.

46. (p. 706) These findings trouble some observers who worry that a swing toward greater _____ has occurred in the last 10 to 15 years. Even so, intrinsically interesting work still tops the list.

47. (p. 706) To summarize much research, we can say that job satisfaction is highest when workers are: (1) allowed ordinary _____ contacts with others; (2) allowed to use their own _____ and intelligence; (3) recognized for doing well; (4) given a chance to apply their skills; (5) given relative freedom from close _____; and (6) given opportunities for promotion and advancement

48. (p. 706) There is now ample evidence that incentives such as bonuses, earned time off, and profit sharing can _____ productivity. However, in recent years far too many jobs have become routine, _____, _____, and unfulfilling.

49. (p. 706) To combat the discontent this can breed, many psychologists recommend a strategy called _____ _____. This usually involves removing some of the controls and restrictions on employees and giving them greater responsibility, freedom, choice, and authority.

50. (p. 706) Also, instead of performing an _____ part of a larger process, employees may switch to doing a complete _____ of work or completing an entire item or project.

51. (p. 706) Whenever possible, workers are given _____ about their work or progress. This _____ comes to them directly instead of to a supervisor. Workers are encouraged to learn new and more difficult tasks and to learn a broad range of skills.

52. (p. 706) Job enrichment has been used with great success by large corporations. It usually leads to lower production _____, increased job _____, reduced _____, and less _____.

53. (p. 707) Robert Levine has studied the overall tempo of 36 American cities. He looked at four indicators: walking speed, _____ speed, _____ speed, and the percentage of men and women wearing _____.

54. (p. 707) The three fastest cities were _____, _____, and New York. The three slowest cities were Shreveport, _____, and Los Angeles.

55. (p. 707) Levine also found that there is a correlation between the pace of life and _____ disease. Just as there are Type A personalities, there also seem to be Type A cities.

56. (p. 707) Environmental psychologists are interested both in _____ environments (natural or constructed) and in _____ environments (such as a dance, business meeting, or party). They also give special attention to _____ settings (for example, an office, locker room, church, casino, or classroom).

57. (p. 708) As we move farther from the body, it becomes apparent that personal space also extends to adjacent areas that we claim as our "territory." For example, in the library _____ _____ might include protecting your space with a book, coat, notebook, or other personal belonging.

58. (p. 708) Researchers have found that the more attached you are to an area, the more likely you are to signal your "ownership" with obvious _____ _____, such as decorations, plants, photographs, posters, etc.

59. (p. 708) A major finding of environmental research is that much of our behavior is controlled, in part, by the environment. For example, psychologists have found that a variety of factors influence the amount of _____ that occurs in public places.

60. (p. 708) Many architects now "harden" and "de-opportunize" public settings to discourage vandalism and graffiti. Some such efforts _____ opportunities (doorless toilet stalls, tiled walls). Others _____ the lure of potential targets (a raised flower bed around signs helps protect them).

61.   (p. 708) Urban stress involves many factors in our country today; one of them is overcrowding. The world's population is now well over _____ billion, and it will more than double in the next 39 years.

62.   (p. 709) One way to assess the effect crowding has on people is to study the effects of overcrowding among animals. As one example, consider the work of John Calhoun. He let a group of laboratory rats breed without limit in a confined space. At its peak, the colony numbered _____ rats, yet was housed in a cage designed to comfortably hold about 50.

63.   (p. 709) Overcrowding was further exaggerated, since the two dominant males staked out private territory leaving the remaining space to the rest of the colony. Overcrowding resulted in a high incidence of pathological behavior. For example, females abandoned _____ _____ and _____ for their young. Pregnancies _____ and infant _____ ran extremely high.

64.   (p. 709) Many of the animals became indiscriminately _____ and went on rampaging attacks against others.

65.   (p. 709) Also, abnormal sexual behavior was rampant, with some animals displaying _____, _____, _____, or total sexual _____.

66.   (p. 709) Many of the animals died, apparently from _____-_____ diseases. The link between these problems and overcrowding is unmistakable.

67.   (p. 709) While many of these behaviors can be observed in crowded inner-city ghettos, factors such as _____, _____, _____, and health care disadvantages may also be to blame.

68.   (p. 709) In fact, most laboratory studies of crowding in humans have failed to show any serious ill effects. This result may occur because crowding is a _____ condition that is separate from _____ (the number of people in a given space).

69.   (p. 709) Crowding refers to subjective feelings of being _____ by social inputs or by a loss of _____.

70.   (p. 709) Crowding may interact with the type of situation in which it occurs to intensify existing stresses or pleasures. For example, Garvin McCain has reported that there are substantial increases in _____ _____ among prison inmates and mental hospital patients living in crowded conditions.

71.   (p. 710) One result of high densities and crowding is a condition psychologist Stanley Milgram called attentional _____, stress induced by continuous sensory stimulation, information, and contact with others.

72.   (p. 710) A recent study of the effects of daily exposure to noise showed that children attending schools near Los Angeles International Airport had higher _____ _____ than those from quieter schools.

73.   (p. 710) Children attending the noisy schools were more likely to give up attempts to solve a difficult puzzle and they were poorer at proofreading a printed paragraph. These effects may resemble a state of "learned _____."

74. (p. 710) Milgram believes city dwellers learn to prevent overload by engaging in only brief, superficial
     _____ _____, by ignoring _____ events and
     by adopting _____ and _____ expressions.

75. (p. 710) Support for this hypothesis comes from recent studies in several large and smaller nearby
     towns. Of persons approached in _____ _____ by a child asking for help, about 72
     ˙percent obliged, while in _____ they offered help only about 46 percent of the time. In
     some cities (Boston and Philadelphia) only about _____-_____ were willing to help.

76. (p. 710) A more recent analysis of _____ studies confirmed that "country people are more likely to help
     than city people." Thus, a blunting of sensitivity to the needs of others may be one of the more
     serious costs of urban stresses and crowding.

77. (p. 710) The way people think about the environment greatly affects behavior. Mental "maps" of various
     areas often guide actions and alter decisions. For instance, in a study recently done in
     Philadelphia researchers found that an existing school bus route contributed to
     _____, because many of its stops were at corners where children were afraid of
     being attacked and beaten.

78. (p. 711) This problem was approached by first doing an _____
     _____ through which psychologists could develop a picture of environments
     as they are perceived by people using them.

79. (p. 711) An assessment often includes such things as charting areas of _____ use in
     buildings, using _____ scales to measure reactions to various environments, and
     even having people draw a version of their "cognitive map" of a building, campus, or city.

80. (p. 711) In the Philadelphia experiment, residents of the neighborhood were asked to rate how much
     stress they felt when walking in various areas. The result was a _____ map that
     showed the areas of highest perceived stress. School buses could then be rerouted to "low
     pressure" areas.

81. (p. 711) In one well-known experiment, Baum and Valins found that students housed in long, narrow,
     corridor-designed dormitories often feel _____ and _____. Such
     students tended to withdraw from other residents and even made more trips to the same campus
     health center than did those living in other buildings.

82. (p. 711) By studying the effects of existing buildings, psychologists specializing in
     _____ psychology are often able to suggest design changes that solve
     or avoid problems.

83. (p. 711) Baum and Valins found that residents living in rooms clustered in threes, with each suite
     sharing a small bathroom, were more satisfied than those living in dorms with a long corridor
     and one central bathroom. The latter students made fewer _____ in their dorm and
     showed greater signs of _____ from social contact.

84. (p. 711) Baum and Davis also compared students living in a long-corridor dorm to those living in a
     long-corridor dorm where the hallway was divided into half with unlocked doors and the three
     center bedrooms converted into a lounge area. Residents of the latter building reported less
     stress from _____, formed more _____, and were more open to
     social contacts.

85. (p. 711) A major problem in the conservation of energy on a personal level is that _____ concerning energy use (the monthly bill) arrives long after the temptation to consume energy. Psychologists have shown that moderately lower energy bills result from simply giving families daily _____ about their use of gas or electricity.

86. (p. 712) Even more effective are programs that give _____ rewards for energy conservation. This is especially true for _____-_____ apartment complexes where families do not receive individual bills for their utilities.

87. (p. 712) In such apartments, families have no reason to save gas and electricity. Often, they consume about _____ percent more energy than they would in an individually metered apartment.

88. (p. 712) _____ psychology seeks to understand how people learn and how teachers instruct. Specialists in this field design aptitude and achievement tests, evaluate educational programs, and help train teachers at colleges and universities.

89. (p. 712) One good way to become more effective in sharing your knowledge with others is to use a specific _____ _____. One example involves using the following steps: (1) learner preparation, (2) stimulus presentation, (3) learner response, (4) reinforcement, (5) evaluation, and (6) spaced review.

90. (p. 713) There is little doubt that teaching styles can greatly affect student interest, motivation, and creativity. Two of the most basic types are _____ _____ and _____ _____.

91. (p. 713) In direct instruction, factual information is presented by _____, demonstration, and _____ practice. In open teaching, active teacher-student _____ is emphasized. Both have advantages.

92. (p. 713) Students of direct instruction do slightly better on _____ tests than do those in open classrooms. However, students of open teaching do somewhat better on tests of _____ thinking, creativity, and problem solving. They also tend to be more _____, curious, and _____ in their attitudes toward school.

93. (p. 713) _____ psychology is an applied field that focuses on why consumers act as they do.

94. (p. 713) Actually, _____ _____ can be separated into several steps. These include: deciding to spend, selecting a brand, shopping, making the purchase, and evaluating the product in use.

95. (p. 714) At each step, advertising, packaging, and a host of other factors affect our behavior. To pinpoint such factors, a type of public opinion polling called _____ _____ is often done.

96. (p. 714) In marketing research, people in a representative sample are asked to give their personal impressions of products, services, and advertising. In this way researchers have learned, among other things, that powerful, widely held _____ _____ often develop. This helps us understand why many people purchase products for their labels as much as for their performance.

97. (p. 714) In addition to marketing research, consumer psychologists do _____ testing of products; they try to match products to consumer _____; they test public acceptance of new products, brand names, and packaging; and they devise strategies to change buying _____.

98. (p. 714) Image-conscious advertising campaigns do affect our beliefs about products even when wrong. For example, in one recent test, three nationally advertised brands of beer were compared. When taste was the only cue available, there was _____ evidence of any noticeable difference in brands.

99. (p. 714) Not all consumer psychology is profit oriented. For instance, principles of consumer behavior may be used to encourage the _____ of water or fuels. Also, many consumer psychologists are interested in protecting and enhancing consumer _____ by persuading people to act in their own best interest.

100. (p. 714) It was consumer psychologists who documented the large number of commercials on "_____." Each year the average child sees over _____ commercials, most of which are for highly sugared cereals and overpriced toys.

101. (p. 714) Related research showed that children under age _____ are easily victimized because they often cannot distinguish commercials from the program itself.

102. (p. 714) Such findings have helped advance the cause of _____—attempts to enhance consumer knowledge, rights, and welfare for both children and adults.

103. (p. 715) Psychologists use _____ _____ made up of volunteers to probe how jurors reach decisions about the guilt or innocence of defendants. Some are simply given written evidence and arguments to read while others are shown videotaped trials staged by actors.

104. (p. 715) Studies show that jurors are rarely able to put aside their biases, attitudes, and values while making a decision. For example, jurors are less likely to find _____ defendants guilty (on the basis of the same evidence) than _____ defendants.

105. (p. 715) It appears, however, that if being attractive helped a person _____ a crime, it can work _____ her or him in court. An example would be a handsome man on trial for swindling money from an unmarried middle-aged woman.

106. (p. 715) A second major problem is that jurors are not very good at separating _____ from other information, such as their perceptions of the defendant, attorneys, witnesses, and what they think the judge wants. Jurors find it hard to _____ information that slips out in court.

107. (p. 715) A related problem occurs when jurors take into account the severity of the _____ a defendant faces. Jurors are not supposed to let this affect their verdict, but many do.

108. (p. 715) A third area of difficulty arises because jurors usually cannot _____ _____ until all the evidence is in. Typically, jurors form an opinion _____ in the trial, making it hard for them to fairly judge later evidence that contradicts what they think.

109. (p. 715) Problems like these are troubling in our legal system. However, each of these factors has much less effect as a crime becomes more _____ or the evidence becomes more _____-_____.

110. (p. 716) Before a trial begins, opposing attorneys are allowed to disqualify a limited number of potential jurors who may be biased. Psychologists help identify people who will favor or harm an attorney's efforts using several techniques. As a first step, _____ _____ (e.g., age, sex, race, occupation, etc.) is frequently collected for each juror.

111. (p. 716) To supplement demographic information, a _____ _____ may be done to find out how local citizens feel about the case. The assumption is that jurors probably have attitudes similar to people with backgrounds like their own.

112. (p. 716) Although talking with potential jurors outside the courtroom is _____ _____, other information networks are available. If possible, a psychologist may interview _____, acquaintances, _____, and co-workers of potential jurors.

113. (p. 716) Psychologists often watch for _____ personality traits in potential jurors. Such individuals tend to believe that punishment is effective, and they are more likely to vote for conviction.

114. (p. 716) At the same time, the psychologist typically observes potential jurors' _____ behavior. The idea is to try to learn from body language which side the person favors.

115. (p. 716) Cases where wealthy clients have the advantage of psychological jury selection raise ethical questions. But since both sides help select jurors, the net effect in most instances is a more _____ jury.

116. (p. 716) _____ psychologists seek to understand and improve sports performance and to enhance the benefits of sports participation.

117. (p. 716) Some sports psychologists might teach an athlete how to _____, ignore distractions, or cope with emotions. They might also provide personal counseling for performance-lowering _____ and _____. Others are interested in studying factors that affect athletic _____, such as skill learning, the personality profiles of champion athletes, the effects of spectators, etc.

118. (p. 716) Before the advent of sports psychology, it was debatable whether "homespun" coaching methods helped or hurt. For example, in early studies of volleyball and gymnastics, it became clear that people teaching these sports had very little _____ of crucial, underlying _____.

119. (p. 716) A major contribution by psychologists in this field has been their ability to do detailed studies of complex skills. In such a _____ _____, sports skills are broken into subparts, so that key elements can be identified and taught.

120. (p. 716) Sports psychologists have found that top marksmen consistently squeeze the trigger _____ heartbeats. As a result of careful study leading to this finding, competitors have begun to use various techniques to steady and control their heartbeat.

121. (p. 717) Sports often provide valuable information on human behavior in general. For example, a recent study found that children's _____-_____ improved significantly after a season of Little League baseball.

122. (p. 717) Such benefits are most likely to occur when competition, rejection, criticism, and the "one-winner mentality" are minimized. Psychologists emphasize _____ play, _____ rewards, _____-_____ of emotions, independence, and self-reliance.

123. (p. 717) Adults also benefit from sports. For instance, researchers have reported that distance running is associated with lower levels of _____, _____, fatigue, and _____than are found in the non-running population.

124. (p. 717) Many athletes report episodes during which they experience intense concentration, detachment from surroundings, a lack of fatigue and pain, a subjective slowing of time, and feelings of unusual power and control. This phenomenon is called _____ _____ and is when "personal bests" tend to occur.

125. (p. 717) This experience has also been called "_____" because the athlete feels as if he or she were in a trance. They become one with performance and flow with it.

126. (p. 717) A curious aspect of flow is that it cannot be _____ to happen. In fact, if a person stops to think about it, the flow state goes away.

127. (p. 719) Effective communication is crucial in many work settings. To improve communication skills, or to keep them sharp, several points are important. For one, you should state your ideas _____ and _____. Be precise about the "who, what, when, where, how, and why" of events.

128. (p. 719) Don't overuse big words. Overuse of obscure vocabulary is often a sign of _____. Big words may make you sound important, but they can also blur your message. Trendy, overused "_____ words" or phrases should also be avoided.

129. (p. 720) Avoid excessive use of _____ or _____. Technical lingo should be avoided unless you are sure that others are familiar with it. Terms that exclude people from a conversation make them feel belittled.

130. (p. 720) Avoid _____ words—those that have strong emotional meanings. Calling something a *dumb* idea brands anyone who agrees with the idea as foolish. Good decision making and problems solving require an atmosphere in which people feel that their ideas are _____, even when they disagree.

131. (p. 720) Use people's _____. An impersonal request is not likely to promote future cooperation.

132. (p. 720) Be _____ and respectful. True politeness puts others at ease. Phony politeness makes people feel that they are being made fun of, or manipulated, or that you are faking it to win approval.

133. (p. 720) Psychologist Chris Kleinke has noted several speech cues that communicate self-confidence and add credibility to your message. For one, use an _____ tone of voice. Speaking energetically, with good voice inflection, typically adds to one's credibility.

134. (p. 720) Speak _____. Get right to the point. Stammering, repeating yourself, frequent pauses, and overuse of "ahs" and "uhms" implies incompetence or nervousness.

135. (p. 720) Speak _____. A brisk rate of speech tends to be persuasive because it implies knowledge, competence, enthusiasm, and confidence. It also helps hold your listener's attention.

136. (p. 720) Make use of _____-_____ cues. Facial expression and hand gestures can help accentuate your message and structure it for listeners.

137. (p. 720) In Western cultures, making _____ _____ while speaking is a particularly important non-verbal cue. Doing so with each person in a group lets each feel included and aware that your message is meant for her or him. This also lets you watch for feedback from listeners, whose reactions can guide your communication efforts.

138. (p. 720) Be aware that your behavior sends _____, too. For example, being late for a meeting tells others that they are not very important to you. Likewise, your manner of dress, personal grooming, even the way you decorate your personal work space all send _____.

139. (p. 720) Effective communication requires expressing yourself clearly, but you must also be a good listener. Several points apply to work settings. For example, make an honest effort to _____ _____. Stop what you are doing and resist distractions. Communicate your interest by posture, body position, and eye contact.

140. (p. 721) Try to identify the speaker's _____. Listen for main themes rather than isolated facts. As you listen, pretend that you will have to summarize the speaker's message for someone else.

141. (p. 721) Suspend _____. Avoid hasty judging, disagreeing, rejecting, or criticizing. Keep an open mind until after you have heard an entire message.

142. (p. 721) Check your _____. Acknowledge and confirm what the speaker is saying. Restart important parts of the message in your own words. Ask questions and clarify points you don't understand. Don't let doubts or ambiguities go unresolved.

143. (p. 721) Pay attention to _____-_____ messages. Be aware of the information provided by gestures, facial expressions, voice qualities, etc.

144. (p. 721) Accept _____ for effective communication. It is up to you to actively search for meaning and value in what is said.

145. (p. 722) Long-term space inhabitants will face confinement and other trying conditions, including: _____ movement, _____ from loved ones, _____ monotony, noise, and many other stresses.

146. (p. 722) The Skylab-3 "space _____" was brief, but showed how important the human element will be in space. Psychologists have focused on understanding expected problems and possible solutions.

147. (p. 722) Space habitats must be designed with human behavior in mind. To begin, the _____ environment, or "micro-society," on a space station will need to operate as smoothly as possible.

148. (p. 722) For this reason many problems may be avoided by carefully _____ and _____ future space residents before they go aloft.

149. (p. 722) Design of a space station as a living environment must take many human factors into account. For instance, researchers have learned that astronauts prefer rooms with clearly defined "_____" and "_____"—even in the weightlessness of space.

150. (p. 722) Provisions must be made for regular exercise. Also full-body _____ are necessary since a lack of this provision was a major complaint among subjects in earlier confinement experiments.

151. (p. 723) Behavior patterns will change over time within a space station, and control of one's environment can help lower stress. At the same time people need stability. Eating at least one meal together each day can help keep a crew working as a _____ unit.

152. (p. 723) _____ _____ will need to be carefully controlled in space to avoid disrupting bodily rhythms. At best, a space station will be at least as noisy as the typical office. Researchers are experimenting with various earmuffs, eye shades, and sleeping arrangements to alleviate such difficulties.

153. (p. 723) Privacy in the first permanent space stations will have to be based mainly on temporarily blocking out _____ and _____ contact with others; there will be too little room for separate quarters.

154. (p. 723) Forced togetherness is stressful mainly because temporary retreat from contact with the group is difficult or impossible. Thus, control over the _____ of contact one has with others is more important than having a _____ room.

155. (p. 723) Space habitat designers recognize the need to define private _____. It will be important to identify small areas that can be personalized and "owned" by each individual.

156. (p. 723) _____ monotony will be a problem in space. Researchers are developing stimulus environments that will use music, videotapes, and other diversions to combat monotony and boredom.

157. (p. 723) Most people in restricted environments find that they prefer _____-_____ pastimes such as reading, listening to music (with individual earphones), looking out windows, writing, and watching films or television. This preference may show again the need for privacy and psychological withdrawal from the group.

158. (p. 724) Separation from family, friends, and one's home community is a major stressor. Abundant opportunities to communicate with associates and loved ones on earth will be the best antidote for _____ _____. Some psychologists also believe that there should be a psychological support group on earth with whom a space station crew would talk to prevent emotional problems.

159. (p. 724) Many studies of long-term isolation show steady declines in _____. Most inhabitants intend to use their free time for creative pursuits. But in reality they end up marking time and many become apathetic.

160. (p. 724) As many as _____ percent of space inhabitants may experience some psychological disturbance. Most often the problem has been _____. However, in rare instances people could become paranoid, psychotic, etc. It will be important to teach crew members basic counseling skills.

SELF-TEST

1. (p. 700) The largest area of applied psychology is
   a. industrial/organizational psychology
   b. behavioral medicine
   c. clinical/counseling psychology
   d. engineering psychology

2. (p. 701) Which of the following types of psychologist would be most likely to be involved in developing user-friendly computers, push-button telephones, and easy to perceive traffic signals?
   a. sports psychologist   c. consumer psychologist
   b. environmental psychologist   d. human factors engineer

3. (p. 701) The development of flexitime at a particular business would most likely be instituted with the help of a
   a. personnel psychologist   c. human factors engineer
   b. architectural pychologist   d. vocational counselor

4. (p. 702) Critical incidents are
   a. situations that an employee must be able to cope with if he or she is going to succeed in a particular job
   b. simulated test situations used by assessment centers to gauge the leadership qualities of potential executives
   c. potential dangerous situations caused by design flaws as determined by an industrial psychologist
   d. industrial accidents caused by conflicts between Theory X and Theory Y management styles

5. (p. 702) Which of the following would *not* be used by a personnel psychologist in making employee selections?
   a. biodata   c. standardized psychological tests
   b. biomedical data d. job analysis

6. (p. 703) True-False. Two examples of vocational interest tests include the Kuder Occupational Interest Survey and the Strong-Campbell Interest Inventory.

7. (p. 703) _____ tests are used to rate a person's potential to learn tasks or skills used in various occupations.
   a. Job analysis   c. Vocational interest
   b. Standardized   d. Aptitude

8. (p. 704) Which of the following is *not* true of the assessment center approach to personnel selection?
    a. It is used primarily to fill management and executive positions.
    b. Exercises such as the "in-basket test" and the "leaderless group" are typical of the type of situations used to monitor candidates' abilities.
    c. One recent study found that assessment center predictions of management potential among a group of women were only weakly related to career progress 7 years later.
    d. Assessment centers have had success in predicting performance in a variety of jobs, careers, and advanced positions in the military.

9. (p. 704) Which of the following is *not* true of Theory X?
    a. It is also known as scientific management.
    b. The term was coined by Douglas McGregor.
    c. It uses time-and-motion studies, task analysis, job specialization, assembly lines, pay schedules, etc. to increase productivity.
    d. It assumes that workers enjoy independence and are willing to accept responsibility.

10. (p. 705) Which of the following are elements that make Theory Y methods effective?
    a. management by objectives   c. work efficiency scheduling
    b. coercive management   d. psychological efficiency minimalization

11. (p. 706) True-False. While interesting work, adequate help, information, and authority are important features of any job, good pay is the main determinant of job satisfaction among workers.

12. (p. 707) Environmental psychologists are interested in each of the following *except*
    a. behavioral settings   c. physical environments
    b. social environments   d. interactive settings

13. (p. 708) Topics such as territoriality, vandalism, behavioral settings, architectural design, natural environment, pollution, etc. would be of special interest to
    a. environmental psychologists   c. human factors engineers
    b. educational psychologists   d. health psychologists

14. (p. 709) The term _____ refers to the number of people in a given space.
    a. crowding   c. overload
    b. discrimination   d. density

15. (p. 710) True-False. Attentional overload refers to subjective feelings of being overstimulated by social inputs or by a loss of privacy.

16. (p. 710) True-False. The greater tendency of children from noisy schools to give up or become distracted is a serious handicap. It may even indicate a state of "learned helplessness."

17. (p. 710) Milgram believes city dwellers learn to prevent overload by engaging in all of the following, *except*
    a. adopting cold and unfriendly expressions
    b. disregarding nonessential events
    c. engaging in only brief, superficial interpersonal contacts
    d. being more willing than people who live in small towns to help people in distress

18. (p. 711) An environmental assessment might be expected to include any of the following *except*
    a. having people draw a version of their "cognitive map" of a certain environment
    b. measuring all of the job-related components that define success within a certain business environment
    c. using attitude scales to measure reactions of schools, businesses, parks, etc.
    d. charting areas of highest or lowest use in buildings

19. (p. 712) True-False. Environmental psychologists have shown that programs which give monetary rewards for energy conservation are very effective, especially in master-metered apartment complexes.

20. (p. 713) Which of the following is true of teaching styles as studied by educational psychologists?
    a. In open teaching, factual information is presented by lecture, demonstration, and rote practice.
    b. Students of direct instruction do slightly better on achievement tests than do those in open classrooms.
    c. In direct instruction, active teacher-student discussion is emphasized.
    d. Students of open teaching do slightly poorer on tests of abstract thinking, creativity, and problem solving than do those receiving direct instruction.

21. (p. 714) Special interest topics such as brand loyalty, effects of advertising, package design, and shopping behavior would be of particular concern to which applied field?
    a. behavioral medicine   c. consumer psychology
    b. marketing psychology   d. human factors engineering

22. (p. 714) True-False. Not all consumer psychology is profit oriented. Principles of consumer behavior may be used to encourage the conservation of gasoline, water, or electricity.

23. (p. 715) Which of the following is *not* an area which might be investigated by psychologists interested in law?
    a. expert testimony   c. jury selection
    b. bail setting   d. peak performance

24. (p. 716) In a psychological task analysis
    a. sports skills are broken into subparts so that key elements can be identified and taught
    b. the individual components of a particular industrial job are identified for later integration with human factor considerations
    c. candidates for executive positions are given ambiguous roles to play to assess their ability to empathize
    d. athletes are required to perform at peak level in order to analyze those factors of greatest importance to the individual sportsman

25. (p. 717) Which of the following is a research finding that has been reported by sports psychologists?
    a. Distance running is associated with lower levels of tension, anxiety, fatigue, and depression.
    b. Children's self-esteem decreases following a losing season of play, especially when the "one-winner mentality" is minimized.
    c. During "flow" athletes experience reduced concentration, but heightened awareness of surroundings.
    d. Top marksmen consistently squeeze the trigger during heartbeats.

26. (p. 719) Which of the following is *not* an important point in effective communication?
    a. Avoid excessive use of jargon, slang, or technical language if you're not sure that others are familiar with such terms.
    b. State your ideas clearly and decisively.
    c. Use "buzz" words frequently, since these are short-hand terms that others can quickly understand.
    d. Avoid loaded words since these can have unintended effects on listeners.

27. (p. 720) True-False. Research shows that using people's names is less likely to put people at ease and promote future cooperation because people often feel "on the spot." For effective communication, try to use titles, or polite expressions such as sir or madame whenever possible.

28. (p. 720) Which of the following is *not* an important speech cue that adds credibility to your message?
    a. Speaking with an expressive, animated tone of voice.
    b. Using non-verbal cues, such as facial expressions and hand gestures that accentuate your message.
    c. Speaking fluently so that you get right to the point.
    d. Speaking slowly so that people have more time to consider the important points of your message.

29. (p. 721) Effective communication requires that you must be a good listener. Which of the following is *not* a good listening habit?
    a. Make an honest effort to pay attention and communicate your interest.
    b. Allow the speaker to accept responsibility for effective communication. Be an effectively passive listener.
    c. Suspend evaluation until you have heard the entire message.
    d. Pay attention to non-verbal messages. Good listeners are also good observers.

30. (p. 722) True-False. Researchers studying psychological adjustment to long-term space travel have found that astronauts prefer rooms with clearly defined "up" and "down"—even in the weightlessness of space.

31. (p. 723) Which of the following would *not* be a pastime frequently used by space crews?
    a. watching films or television   c. competitive contact sports
    b. reading   d. listening to music

32. (p. 724) True-False. Many studies of long-term isolation show steady increases in motivation. As recreational pastimes become more routine, workers focus more effort and energy into mission tasks.

APPLYING YOUR KNOWLEDGE

1. As you've learned from this chapter there are many different fields of psychology that use psychological principles and research methods to solve practical problems. Contact an "Applied" psychologist in your area and interview them about their background, interests, and current work. What types of approaches, techniques, and principles do they use in their jobs?

2. Survey a number of buildings, public areas, and facilities in your area. Do you find evidence that an architectural psychologist may have been at work in helping with design features? Give examples of your findings.

3.   Many different areas of psychology will contribute to the development of a continuously inhabited space station. What are some of the major research areas you can identify? What is already being done in these areas and what are some of the significant questions yet to be resolved?

Answers—Programmed Review

1.   Applied
2.   fire alarm
3.   attention getting; authority; elevators
4.   clinical; community
5.   prevention; education; consultation; neglect
6.   industrial
7.   testing, placement; relations; engineering
8.   flexitime
9.   satisfaction; relations; absenteeism
10. human factors
11. natural design
12. feedback
13. 2000; 9
14. job analysis
15. critical incidents
16. biodata; interviewing; standardized; assessment
17. athletic; academic; scientific; religious
18. halo
19. attractive
20. female; males
21. direct
22. vocational interest
23. successful
24. Aptitude
25. Assessment center
26. in-basket
27. leaderless group
28. 7
29. oral communication; resistance; uncertainty
30. Taylor
31. scientific management
32. Theory Y
33. work
34. psychological
35. independence; responsibility
36. work
37. participative; objectives
38. productivity; stress

39. goals
40. independence
41. quality circles
42. power; positive
43. satisfaction; satisfaction
44. interesting; information; authority; security
45. income
46. materialism
47. social; judgment; supervision
48. increase; repetitive; boring
49. job enrichment
50. isolated; cycle
51. feedback; feedback
52. costs; satisfaction; boredom; absenteeism
53. working; talking; watches
54. Boston, Buffalo; Sacramento
55. heart
56. physical; social; behavioral
57. territorial behavior
58. territorial markers
59. vandalism
60. limit
61. 5
62. 80
63. nest building; caring; decreased; mortality
64. aggressive
65. hypersexuality, bisexuality, homosexuality; passivity
66. stress-caused
67. nutrition; education; income
68. psychological; density
69. overstimulated; privacy
70. death rates
71. overload
72. blood pressure
73. helplessness

74. social contacts; nonessential; cold, unfriendly
75. small towns; cities; one-third
76. 65
77. truancy
78. environmental assessment
79. highest; attitude
80. contour
81. crowded, stressed
82. architectural
83. friends; withdrawing
84. crowding; friendships
85. feedback; feedback
86. monetary; master-metered
87. 25
88. Educational
89. teaching strategy
90. direct instruction, open teaching
91. lecture; rote; discussion
92. achievement; abstract; independent; positive
93. Consumer
94. consumer behavior
95. marketing research
96. brand images
97. laboratory; needs; habits
98. no
99. conservation; welfare
100. kid vid; 20,000
101. 6
102. consumerism
103. mock juries
104. attractive; unattractive
105. commit; against
106. evidence; ignore
107. punishment
108. suspend judgment; early
109. severe; clear-cut
110. demographic information
111. community survey

112. not permitted; relatives; neighbors
113. authoritarian
114. nonverbal
115. balanced
116. Sports
117. relax; stresses, conflicts; achievement
118. knowledge; skills
119. task analysis
120. between
121. self-esteem
122. fair; intrinsic; self-control
123. tension, anxiety, depression
124. peak performance
125. flow
126. forced
127. clearly; decisively
128. insecurity; buzz
129. jargon; slang
130. loaded; respected
131. names
132. polite
133. expressive
134. fluently
135. quickly
136. non-verbal
137. eye contact
138. messages
139. pay attention
140. purpose
141. evaluation
142. understanding
143. non-verbal
144. responsibility
145. restricted; separation; sensory
146. strike
147. social
148. selecting; training
149. up, down
150. showers
151. social
152. Sleep cycles
153. visual, auditory
154. amount; private
155. territories
156. Sensory
157. non-interactive
158. social isolation
159. motivation
160. 5; depression

ANSWERS—SELF-TEST

1.	c	7.	d	13.	a	19.	True	25.	a	31.	c
2.	d	8.	c	14.	d	20.	b	26.	c	32.	False
3.	a	9.	d	15.	True	21.	c	27.	False		
4.	a	10.	a	16.	True	22.	True	28.	d		
5.	b	11.	False	17.	d	23.	d	29.	b		
6.	True	12.	d	18.	b	24.	a	30.	True		

ACROSS

6. detailed biographical information
8. area of psychology concerned with design of machines and work environments for human use
11. work _____ (maximum output at lowest cost)
12. industrial/organizational (abbr.) psychologist
13. specialty of psychology concerned with territorial behavior and personal space

DOWN

1. _____ tests rate one's potential to learn
2. these psychologists work with athletes
3. he described attentional overload
4. this management procedure allows employees at all levels to help make decisions
5. area of psychology focusing on how and why consumers act as they do
7. the number of people in a given space
9. these psychologists seek to understand how people learn and teachers instruct
10. flexible working hours
14. it can be very distracting

Careers in Psychology

CONTENTS

PROGRAMMED REVIEW

1. (p. A-1) The majority of students studying introductory psychology are not psychology _____.

2. (p. A-1) About half of all undergraduate psychology majors do not plan to work as _____. Nearly 50 percent of all psychology majors seek full-time jobs immediately after they graduate.

3. (p. A-1) If you think you would like to major in psychology, but you are not interested in graduate training, here are some points to consider:
    1) _____ workers hold one job forever, or even remain in a single line of work for life.
    2) The nature of work is likely to _____ greatly in your lifetime, and adaptability will be important.
    3) A _____ education that develops many skills makes a person more vocationally adaptable.
    4) It is a major myth that every job requires a precise set of _____.
    5) Specific undergraduate programs do not exist for many mental health professions, making psychology a good undergraduate major leading to later specialized training.
    6) Job recruiters look primarily for general competence in verbal and written communication, plus social skills and facility in meeting the public.

4. (p. A-1) A brief list of "marketable" abilities provided by a psychology degree includes the following: clear, analytic _____; objectivity and keen observation; an ability to handle _____; recognize _____, and draw conclusions; ability to plan and organize complex activities; ability to _____ clearly, both verbally and in writing; the capacity to comprehend abstract principles and the subtleties of human behavior; ability to critically evaluate evidence; interpersonal skills; and _____ knowledge relevant to success in many settings.

5. (p. A-1) Training in psychology at the _____ degree level tends to yield fewer choices than those available to graduates with bachelor's degrees or more advanced training. People with this degree in psychology are qualified to do interviewing, to give and score specific psychological tests, and to communicate the needs of clients to psychologists and other professionals.

6. (p. A-2) In general, a person with an associate degree can expect to work directly with clients, but under the _____ of more highly trained professionals.

7. (p. A-2)   Some specific training programs exist where a year or two of training can lead directly to a job in a local mental health facility. Provisions have been made for "_____-_____" trainees to combine classroom study with on-the-job training.

8. (p. A-2)   A bachelor's degree in psychology can be considered preparation for a _____ of jobs or occupations. It is also a good prelude to _____ training in several related professions. Furthermore, it is a first step toward a master's or doctoral degree in psychology.

9. (p. A-2)   Some jobs for which an individual with a bachelor's degree in psychology might wish to apply require _____ training (becoming a high school teacher, for example).

10. (p. A-2)   Also, you may be more competitive for some types of positions if you were to _____ a psychology major with a minor in another area, such as business.

11. (p. A-2)   In other cases it would be better to make psychology your _____, in combination with a major in a related area (law enforcement and nursing are examples).

12. (p. A-2)   A _____ degree in psychology usually requires from 1 to 2 years of graduate-level training beyond the bachelor's degree. It usually requires completion of a research thesis and/or a certain number of hours of supervised practical experience in an applied setting.

13. (p. A-2)   At present the most popular master's-level specialty is _____ psychology— undoubtedly because this is one of the most direct routes to a career as a mental health professional.

14. (p. A-2)   Those with a master's degree in counseling psychology may further specialize in _____ and _____ counseling, vocational or educational counseling, _____ counseling, or _____ counseling.

15. (p. A-2)   Many counselors are _____-_____, but some work for human service agencies, at mental health clinics, and occasionally for the military or large businesses.

16. (p. A-2)   Recently, employment opportunities have become more limited for new master's-level psychologists. When positions open in noncounseling areas, they are often filled by _____-_____ psychologists.

17. (p. A-3)   On the other hand, a master's degree could make you more competitive for jobs at the bachelor's level. It might also help you qualify for higher _____.

18. (p. A-3)   It usually takes at least 3 years of education beyond a bachelor's degree to attain a _____ (Ph.D., Psy.D., or Ed.D.). More often, it takes 4 or more years to complete, and some specialties require at least 1 more year of _____.

19. (p. A-3)   If you want to become a psychologist, a Ph.D. is a _____ degree. It requires completion of a dissertation (an original research contribution to the field).

20. (p. A-3)   Psychologists who primarily want to work as therapists now earn a _____ degree (Doctor of Psychology). This newly created degree allows students to gain practical experience as a psychotherapist rather than doing a dissertation.

21. (p. A-3)   The _____ (Doctor of Education) is also typically more applied in orientation than the Ph.D. Course-work for this degree focuses on the psychology of learning and education.

22. (p. A-3) In most states a doctoral degree alone does not automatically allow a person to practice psychology. To be legally _____ or _____ as a psychologisät, a person usually must have a doctorate in psychology, plus at least 1 year of internship, as well as having passed written and oral state licensing exams.

23. (p. A-3) If you wish to pursue a doctorate in psychology, you should begin planning now. Getting admitted to a doctoral program in psychology is as difficult as getting into _____ _____.

24. (p. A-3) To learn more about applying for graduate school, consult the book *Graduate Study in Psychology* published by the American Psychological Association. Appendix _____ in the book gives practical, step-by-step information on how to get accepted to graduate school.

25. (p. A-3) There is value in deciding early if you intend to seek employment or to enter graduate school. Businesspeople and faculty members differ in what _____ they believe is most important when considering students for employment or admission.

26. (p. A-3) _____ and ability to present oneself effectively is highly valued in the business world. Courses taken, grades, recommendations, writing ability, and other academic performance factors are much more important when considering graduate training.

27. (p. A-4) Jobs for people with psychology degrees are expected to grow _____ than average in coming years. However, professional-level jobs (master's and doctorate) will account for a relatively small percentage of total new positions.

28. (p. A-4) With projections for a decline in college enrollments, _____ positions will be in especially short supply. Even in industrial, clinical, and other applied areas there will be much competition for positions.

29. (p. A-4) To make yourself highly employable, you should:
    1) attend an _____ accredited graduate school.
    2) gain work experience while in school (by working as a research assistant, or even as a volunteer).
    3) specialize in additional skills that are in demand.

30. (p. A-4) _____ areas of psychology are probably the best bet for employment in the near future. _____-related jobs also look good, especially anything associated with senior citizens.

31. (p. A-4) Two of the fastest growing jobs for the next decade are projected to be _____ _____ and _____ _____. Both positions are open to bachelor's and master's degree holders.

If you are interested in further study in psychology or in pursuing psychology as a career, you should be familiar with the references provided in the main text. Note that all of the resources listed are available through the American Psychological Association. Many of them are probably available through your college library or career center.

SELF-TEST

1. (p. A-1)   Which of the following is a true statement?
   a. Learning psychology can provide a general knowledge of behavior that aids success in various occupations.
   b. Most undergraduate psychology majors will go on to pursue graduate studies in psychology.
   c. The majority of students studying introductory psychology are psychology majors.
   d. The majority of undergraduate psychology majors plan to work as psychologists.

2. (p. A-1)   Which of the following is *not* a "marketable" ability provided by a psychology degree?
   a. ability to critically evaluate evidence
   b. ability to handle data, recognize patterns, and draw conclusions
   c. subjectivity and ability to read other people's personalities
   d. clear, analytic thinking

3. (p. A-2)   Which of the following is probably *not* a job that would be open to an individual with an A.A. degree?
   a. youth supervisor   c. self-employed marriage counselor
   b. nursing home attendant   d. public survey worker

4. (p. A-2)   If you are interested in becoming a job analyst, drug counselor, child welfare agent, college admissions representative, biofeedback technician, or family services worker you should have, as a minimum, which of the following degrees?
   a. A.A.   c. M.A.
   b. Ph.D.   d. B.A.

5. (p. A-2)   True-False. The most popular master's-level specialty is counseling psychology.

6. (p. A-2)   Which of the following is *not* true of psychologists with a master's degree?
   a. They are almost entirely self-employed individuals.
   b. They have begun to move into areas such as hospices, child abuse clinics, rape counseling centers, stress clinics, etc.
   c. Recently, employment opportunities have become more limited for new master's-level psychologists.
   d. Those with a degree in counseling psychology may further specialize in marriage and family counseling, vocational or educational counseling, or child counseling to name a few.

7. (p. A-3)   True-False. It usually takes at least 3 years or more of education beyond a bachelor's degree to attain a doctorate and some applied specialities may require at least 1 more year of internship.

8. (p. A-3)   Which of the following is *not* a correct statement?
   a. The Ed.D. is applied in orientation and focuses on the psychology of learning and education.
   b. A Ph.D. is a research degree.
   c. A Psy.D. allows students in clinical psychology to gain practical experience as a psychotherapist rather than doing a dissertation.
   d. Psychologists holding Psy.D. degrees are active in all areas of psychology.

9. (p. A-3)   True-False. In most states a doctoral degree alone can automatically allow a person to practice psychology.

10. (p. A-3) True-False. Getting admitted to a doctoral program in psychology is as difficult as getting into medical school.

11. (p. A-4) If you plan to pursue a doctoral-level career in psychology it is wise to follow all of the following suggestions *except*
    a. specialize in additional skills that are in demand
    b. seek the Psy.D. or Ed.D. degree rather than the Ph.D.
    c. attend an APA-accredited graduate school
    d. gain work experience while in school

12. (p. A-4) Which of the following is *not* an area of psychology with especially good job prospects for the immediate future?
    a. animal learning   c. clinical
    b. industrial/organizational   d. health

13. (p. A-4) True-False. Two of the fastest growing jobs for the next decade are projected to be employment interviewers and occupational therapists.

14. (p. A-4) Which of the following can help you in deciding upon a major or career in psychology?
    a. your psychology teacher   c. the American Psychological Association
    b. the campus career center   d. all of the above

ANSWERS—PROGRAMMED REVIEW

1. majors
2. psychologists
3. Few; change; broad; skills
4. thinking; data; patterns; communicate; general
5. associate
6. supervision
7. psych-tech
8. variety; advanced
9. additional
10. combine

11. minor
12. master's
13. counseling
14. marriage; family; child; rehabilitation
15. self-employed
16. doctoral-level
17. pay
18. doctorate; internship
19. research
20. Psy.D.
21. Ed.D.

22. licensed, certified
23. medical school
24. D
25. greatly
26. Personality
27. faster
28. academic
29. APA
30. Applied; Health
31. employment interviewers, occupational therapists

ANSWERS—SELF-TEST

1. a
2. c
3. c
4. d
5. True
6. a
7. True
8. d
9. False
10. True
11. b
12. a
13. True
14. d

Statistics

CONTENTS

TERMS AND CONCEPTS

descriptive statistics	standard deviation
inferential statistics	z-score
graphical statistics	normal curve
frequency distribution	population
histogram	sample
abscissa	tests of statistical significance
ordinate	correlation
frequency polygon	scatter diagram
measures of central tendency	positive correlation
mean	zero correlation
median	negative correlation
mode	Pearson r
measures of variability	percent of variance
range	

IMPORTANT FORMULAS

$$Mean = \frac{\Sigma X}{N}$$

$$SD = \sqrt{\frac{sum\ of\ d^2}{n}}$$

$$Z = \frac{X - \bar{X}}{SD}$$

$$r = \frac{\Sigma XY - \frac{(\Sigma X)(\Sigma Y)}{N}}{\sqrt{\left(\Sigma X^2 - \frac{(\Sigma X)^2}{N}(\Sigma Y^2) - \frac{(\Sigma Y)^2}{N}\right)}}$$

PROGRAMMED REVIEW

1. (p. A-5) One of the two major divisions of statistical methods is _____ _____. They are used to summarize numbers so they become more meaningful and more easily communicated to others.

2. (p. A-5) The second type of statistics, known as _____ statistics, is used for decision-making, for generalizing from small samples, and for drawing conclusions.

3. (p. A-5) A _____ _____ is made by breaking down the entire range of possible scores into classes of equal size and then recording the number of scores falling into each class.

4. (p. A-5) Frequency distributions can be used to demonstrate _____ statistics (a basic type of descriptive statistics that presents data in a "visual" format).

5. (p. A-6) Frequency distributions are often shown graphically using _____ where the height of the bars drawn for each class interval indicates the number of scores in that class.

6. (p. A-6) Histograms are made by labeling class intervals on the _____ (horizontal line) and frequencies (the number of scores in each class) on the _____ (vertical line).

7. (p. A-6) Next, _____ are drawn for each class interval. The height of each _____ is determined by the number of scores in each class.

8. (p. A-6) An alternative way of graphing a distribution of scores is the more familiar _____ _____. Here, points are placed at the center of each class interval to indicate the number of scores. Then, the dots are connected by straight lines.

9. (p. A-6) A second category of descriptive statistic includes measures of _____ _____. Such measures are simply numbers describing a "middle score" around which other scores fall.

10. (p. A-6) One type of "average" is the _____, computed by adding all the scores for each group and dividing by the number of scores in the group.

11. (p. A-6) The mean is sensitive to extremely _____ or _____ scores in a distribution and, consequently, is not always the best measure of central tendency.

12. (p. A-6) In such cases, the "middle score" in a group of scores, called the _____, is used instead.

13. (p. A-6) The median is found by _____ scores from the highest to the lowest and selecting the score that falls in the middle.

14. (p. A-6) If there is no "middle score" (which occurs when there is an even number of scores), the two scores which share the middle position are _____ to get a single score.

15. (p. A-6) A final measure of central tendency is the _____. It simply represents the most frequently occurring score in a group of scores.

16. (p. A-6) Although the mode is easy to obtain, it can be an _____ measure, especially in a small group of scores.

17. (p. A-6) The advantage of the mode is that it gives the score actually obtained by the _____ number of people.

18. (p. A-6) When we want to know if scores are grouped closely together or scattered widely, we use measures of _____ to attach a numerical value to the "spread" of scores.

19. (p. A-7) The simplest way to describe variability is to use the _____, which is the difference between the highest and lowest scores.

20. (p. A-8) The better measure of variability is the _____ _____.

21. (p. A-8) SD is obtained by computing the _____ (or difference) of each score from the mean and then _____ it (multiplying it by itself). These squared deviations are then added and averaged (the total is divided by the number of deviations). Taking the square root of this average yields the standard deviation.

22. (p. A-8) A particular advantage of the standard deviation is that it can be used to "standardize" scores in a way that gives them greater meaning. This process is done using the _____-_____.

23. (p. A-8) To convert original scores to z-scores, the mean is subtracted from the score and the resulting number is divided by the _____ _____ for the group of scores from which the original score came.

24. (p. A-9) When chance events are recorded and graphed, they typically resemble what is called a _____ _____. Measures of psychological variables tend to roughly match this.

25. (p. A-9) For example, _____, memory-span, and _____ are all known to be distributed approximately along a normal curve.

26. (p. A-10) Much is known about the normal curve. One valuable property concerns the relationship between the standard deviation and the normal curve. Specifically, the SD measures off set _____ of the curve above and below the mean.

27. (p. A-10) As an example of this principle, notice that roughly _____ percent of all cases fall between one standard deviation above and below the mean and _____ of all cases fall between $\pm$ 2 SD. Between $\pm$ 3 SD from the mean, _____ percent of all cases can be found.

28. (p. A-10) Relationships between the standard deviation (or z-scores) and the normal curve do not change. This makes it possible to _____ various tests or groups of scores if they come from distributions that are approximately normal.

29. (p. A-10) _____ _____, the other major division of statistical methods, includes techniques that allow us to generalize from the behavior of small groups of subjects to that of the larger groups they represent.

30. (p. A-10) In any scientific investigation, we would like to observe the entire set, or _____, of subjects, objects, or events being studied. However, this prospect is usually impossible or impractical.

31. (p. A-10) Instead, _____ or smaller cross sections of a population are selected, and used to draw conclusions about the entire population.

32. (p. A-10) For any sample to be meaningful, it must be _____. It must truly reflect the membership and characteristics of the larger population.

33. (p. A-10) A very important aspect of representative samples is that their members are chosen at _____. In other words, each member of the population must have an equal chance of being included in the sample.

34. (p. A-10) When we compare results from different groups, we wish to know if they might have simply occurred by chance or if they represent a real difference. Tests of _____ _____ provide an estimate of how often experimental results could have occurred by chance alone.

35. (p. A-10) The results of a test of statistical significance are stated as a probability giving the odds that the observed difference was due to chance. In psychology, any experimental condition attributable to chance _____ times or less out of 100 is considered significant.

36. (p. A-10) If we know, in an experiment where a drug increased memory, that the _____ is .025 (p = .025) that this effect was due to chance, we can conclude with reasonable certainty that the drug really did affect memory.

37. (p. A-11) Many of the statements that psychologists make about behavior do not result from the use of experimental methods and are usually not analyzed using tests of statistical significance. Instead, they deal with the fact that two variables are _____-_____ (varying together in some orderly fashion).

38. (p. A-11) The simplest way of visualizing a correlation is to construct a _____ _____ where one measure is indicated by the X axis and the second by the Y axis. The intersection of each pair of measurements is plotted as a single point.

39. (p. A-11) Scatter diagrams are useful in demonstrating the three basic kinds of relationships between variables or measures. When there is a _____ relationship, increases in scores for one variable are associated with increases in scores for the other.

40. (p. A-11) A _____ correlation occurs when there is no relationship between two variables.

41. (p. A-11) With a _____ correlation, increases in the scores of one variable are associated with decreases in the other.

42. (p. A-11) Correlations can also be expressed as a _____ of correlation, a number falling between +1.00 and -1.00.

43. (p. A-11) If the correlation is +1.00 a _____ _____ relationship exists; if it is-1.00 a _____ _____ relationship has been discovered.

44. (p. A-11) The most commonly used correlation coefficient is called the _____ _____. Be sure you know how to calculate this value.

45. (p. A-12) Correlations in psychology are rarely perfect. Most fall somewhere between _____ and plus or minus one. Still, they help us to identify relationships that are worth knowing.

46. (p. A-12) Correlations are particularly valuable for making _____. If we know two measures are correlated, and we know a person's score on one measure, then we can predict the person's score on the other.

47. (p. A-12) For example, most colleges use some combination of high school GPA, teacher ratings, SAT scores, etc., in making admission selections. Although no single predictor is perfectly correlated with success in college, together they correlate _____ and provide a useful screening technique.

48. (p. A-13) If you square the correlation coefficient (multiply r by itself) you get a number telling the percent of _____ accounted for by the correlation.

49. (p. A-13) For example, if the correlation between IQ scores and college GPA is 0.5, _____ percent of the variation in college grades is accounted for by knowing IQ scores.

50. (p. A-13) It is important to recognize that the existence of a correlation between two measures does not mean that one causes the other. This fact is expressed by the phrase, "_____ does not demonstrate _____." Often two correlated variables are related through the influence of a third variable.

SELF-TEST

1. (p. A-5) _____ statistics summarize data so they become more easily communicated.
   a. Inferential
   b. Cognitive
   c. Deviation
   d. Descriptive

2. (p. A-6) The graphical display of frequency distributions which uses bars to indicate the frequency of scores within class intervals is the
   a. frequency polygon
   b. histographic planing
   c. histogram
   d. scatter diagram

3. (p. A-6) Graphical display of a frequency distribution using straight lines connecting dots representing the number of cases for each class interval is called a
   a. scatter diagram
   b. normal line
   c. histogram
   d. frequency polygon

4. (p. A-6) True-False. When we speak of the middle score in a distribution of scores, we are automatically referring to the mean.

5. (p. A-6) The measure of central tendency which ranks scores from the highest to the lowest and selects the middle score is the
   a. mode
   b. mean
   c. standard deviation
   d. median

6. (p. A-6) The measure of central tendency which expresses the most frequently occurring score in a distribution is the
   a. mode
   b. mean
   c. standard deviation
   d. median

7. (p. A-7) A statistical range refers to
   a. a type of averaging
   b. a measure of variability
   c. a test of statistical significance
   d. one of the axes of a graph

8. (p. A-8) Which of the following is a measure of variability?
   a. Pearson r
   b. mode
   c. standard deviation
   d. correlation

9. (p. A-10) True-False. In a normal curve exactly 68 percent of all cases fall between 3 SD above and below the mean.

10. (p. A-10) True-False. The two major divisions of statistical methods are descriptive statistics and preferential statistics.

11. (p. A-10) All members of a set compose the _____, while a smaller part of that set is called a _____.
    a. norm, element
    b. group, deviation
    c. population, sample
    d. population, representative

12. (p. A-10) True-False. The major requirement for any sample is that it be representative.

13. (p. A-10) Differences in experimental results are considered significant when it is demonstrated that they could only have occurred _____ or fewer times out of 100 by chance alone.
    a. 5
    b. 10
    c. 20
    d. 50

14. (p. A-11) The simplest way of visualizing a correlation is to construct a
    a. normal curve
    b. scatter diagram
    c. frequency polygon
    d. histogram

15. (p. A-11) When two variables are not related, we speak of
    a. positive correlation
    b. zero correlation
    c. negative correlation
    d. statistical significance

16. (p. A-11) A negative correlation exists when _____ in the value of one score are associated with _____ in the value of an associated score.
    a. increases, increases
    b. decreases, decreases
    c. increases, decreases
    d. changes, changes

17. (p. A-11) The number +1.00 could represent all of the following *except*
    a. a coefficient of correlation
    b. the result of calculating Pearson's *r*
    c. a perfect positive relationship
    d. a perfect negative relationship

18. (p. A-12) Correlations are particularly valuable for
    a. expressing central tendency
    b. expressing variability
    c. estimating a population
    d. making a prediction

19. (p. A-13) If the correlation between two factors is .70, the number 49 represents _____ accounted for by the correlation.
    a. the standard deviation
    b. the z-score
    c. the percent of variance
    d. the range

20. (p. A-13) True-False. Correlation proves causation.

ANSWERS—PROGRAMMED REVIEW

1. descriptive statistics
2. inferential
3. frequency distribution
4. graphical
5. histograms
6. abscissa; ordinate
7. bars; bar
8. frequency polygon
9. central tendency
10. mean
11. high, low
12. median
13. arranging
14. averaged
15. mode
16. unreliable
17. greatest
18. variability
19. range
20. standard deviation
21. deviation; squaring
22. z-score
23. standard deviation
24. normal curve
25. height, intelligence
26. proportions
27. 68; 95; 99
28. compare
29. Inferential statistics
30. population
31. samples
32. representative
33. random
34. statistical significance
35. 5
36. probability
37. co-relating
38. scatter diagram
39. positive
40. zero
41. negative
42. coefficient
43. perfect positive; perfect negative
44. Pearson *r*

45. zero
46. predictions

47. highly
48. variance

49. 25
50. Correlation; causation

ANSWERS—SELF-TEST

1. d
2. c
3. d
4. False

5. d
6. a
7. b
8. c

9. False
10. False
11. c

12. True
13. a
14. b

15. b
16. c
17. d

18. d
19. c
20. False

PUZZLE KEY

CHAPTER 1

CHAPTER 2

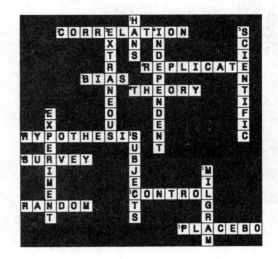

CHAPTER 3

CHAPTER 4

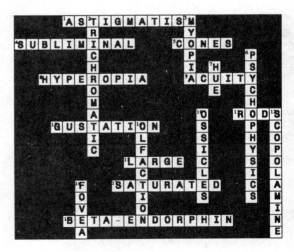

CHAPTER 5

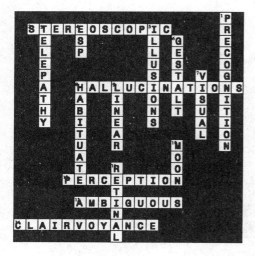

CHAPTER 6

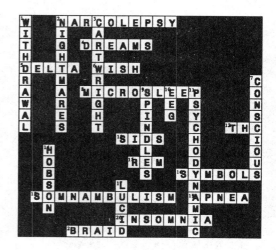

CHAPTER 7

CHAPTER 8

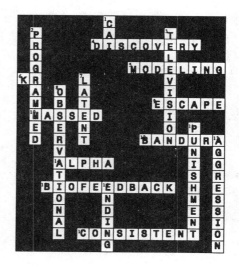

CHAPTER 9

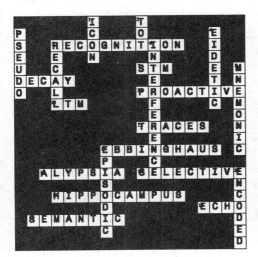

CHAPTER 10

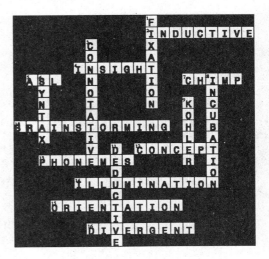

CHAPTER 11

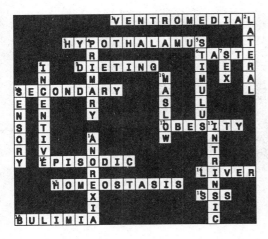

CHAPTER 12

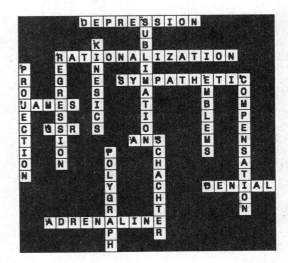

CHAPTER 13

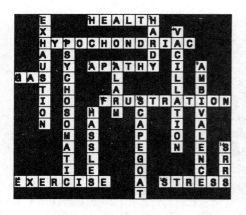

CHAPTER 14

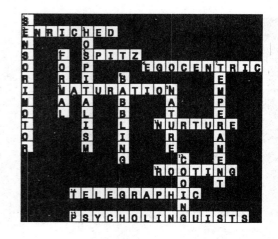

CHAPTER 15

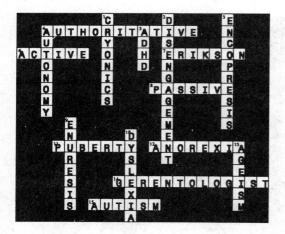

CHAPTER 16

CHAPTER 17

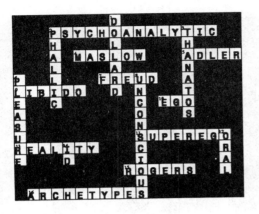

CHAPTER 18

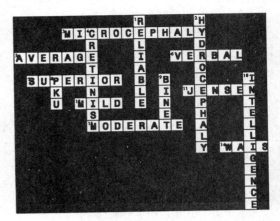

CHAPTER 19

CHAPTER 20

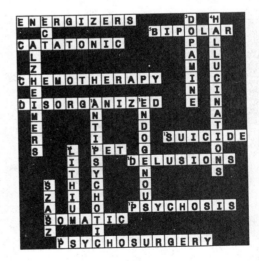

CHAPTER 21

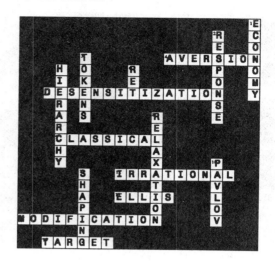

CHAPTER 22

CHAPTER 23

CHAPTER 24

CHAPTER 25

CHAPTER 26

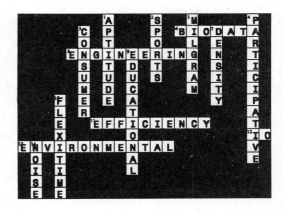